Lecture Notes in Computer Science 5153

Commenced Publication in 1973
Founding and Former Series Editors:
Gerhard Goos, Juris Hartmanis, and Jan van Leeuwen

Editorial Board

Andreas Rausch
Ralf Reussner
Raffaela Mirandola
František Plášil (Eds.)

The Common Component Modeling Example

Comparing Software Component Models

 Springer

Volume Editors

Andreas Rausch
TU Clausthal, Institut für Informatik
Julius-Albert-Str. 4, 38678 Clausthal-Zellerfeld, Germany
E-mail: andreas.rausch@tu-clausthal.de

Ralf Reussner
Universität Karlsruhe (TH)
Institute for Program Structures and Data Organization
Am Fasanengarten 5, 76131 Karlsruhe, Germany
E-mail: reussner@ipd.uka.de

Raffaela Mirandola
Politecnico di Milano, Dip. di Elettronica e Informazione
via Ponzio 34/5, 20133 Milano, Italy
E-mail: mirandola@elet.polimi.it

František Plášil
Charles University Prague, Faculty of Mathematics and Physics
School of Informatics, Dept. of Software Engineering
Malostranske nam. 25, 118 00 Prague, Czech Republic
E-mail: plasil@dsrg.mff.cuni.cz

Library of Congress Control Number: Applied for

CR Subject Classification (1998): D.2.4, D.4.8, D.2, C.4

LNCS Sublibrary: SL 2 – Programming and Software Engineering

ISSN   0302-9743
ISBN-10   3-540-85288-3 Springer Berlin Heidelberg New York
ISBN-13   978-3-540-85288-9 Springer Berlin Heidelberg New York

Springer is a part of Springer Science+Business Media

springer.com

© Springer-Verlag Berlin Heidelberg 2008
Printed in Germany

Typesetting: Camera-ready by author, data conversion by Scientific Publishing Services, Chennai, India
Printed on acid-free paper   SPIN: 12455034   06/3180   5 4 3 2 1 0

Preface

Several conference and workshop series are dedicated to formal component models and their use in verification and quality prediction, such as FMCO, CBSE, FESCA, FACS and QoSA. There are a plethora of component models published, all with specific merits and benefits. However, most often these models are not used for comparison, as each research group concentrates on different aspects of formal component modelling and quality prediction. Like the famous production cell approach[1] of the FZI, Karlsruhe, which has served since 1995 as a common example for different embedded systems safety verification, in this volume we define a common example for modelling approaches of component-based systems. This Common Component Modelling Example enables the comparability of different approaches, the validation of existing models, a better focus of research to tackle aspects less frequently dealt within the classification of existing models and approaches, an eased interchange of research ideas, as well as a simplified and increased coordination and research collaborations to join complementary models and approaches. In this volume we define the Common Component Modelling Example and present the models in current modelling and analysis approaches. The book concludes with comments on each modelling approach by an international jury.

August 2007

Andreas Rausch
Ralf Reussner
Raffaela Mirandola
František Plášil

---

[1] Springer LNCS vol. 891.

Organization

The Dagstuhl research seminar for CoCoME (Common Component Modelling Example) modelling contest is part of a series of seminars organized with support by the German Computer Science Society (*Gesellschaft für Informatik*, GI). It was held during August 1–3, 2007 at Schloss Dagstuhl, Germany, as event number 07312.

Organizers

Andreas Rausch	Clausthal University of Technology, Germany
Ralf Reussner	University of Karlsruhe, Germany
Raffaela Mirandola	Politecnico di Milano, Italy
František Plášil	Charles University, Prague, Czech Republic

Participants

Manfred Broy	Jan Kofroň	Anders P. Ravn
Antonio Cansado	Klaus Krogmann	Ralf Reussner
Constanze Deiters	Ingolf Krüger	Jan Schäfer
Vincenzo Grassi	Raffaela Mirandola	Johannes Siedersleben
Rolf Hennicker	Dirk Niebuhr	Volker Stolz
Sebastian Herold	Joseph Okika	Clemens Szyperski
Florian Hölzl	František Plášil	Petr Tůma
Oliver Hummel	Tomáš Poch	Pavlína Vařeková
Monika Juhasz	Arnd Poetzsch-Heffter	Barbora Zimmerova
Holger Klus	Enrico Randazzo	
Alexander Knapp	Andreas Rausch	

Table of Contents

1 Introduction

Andreas Rausch[1], Ralf Reussner[2], Raffaela Mirandola[3], and František Plášil[4]

[1] TU Clausthal
[2] Univ. Karlsruhe (TH) / FZI
[3] Politecnico Milano
[4] Charles University, Prague

Although the idea of a software component stems back to the end of the sixties, the component-based software engineering established itself to an dedicated research area during the end nineties. Nowadays, in particular the research in component models which is motivated by the verification and quality prediction of component-based systems forms such a large body of research with a plethora of specific and creative ideas that it is hard to keep the overview. Several conference and workshop series are dedicated to formal component models and their use in verification and quality prediction, such as FMCO, CBSE, FESCA, FACS and QoSA. The organisers of CoCoME came independently to the finding, that these component models are hard to compare, as each research group concentrate on different aspects of formal component modelling and quality prediction. For example, formal component models differ in

- Their ability of component composition
- Their treatment of communication (asynchronous or synchronous, blocking or non-blocking)
- Concurrency (on a inner-component-level as well as on a system-wide level)
- The treatment of component deployment (including the various aspects of deployment configuration)
- White-box packaging of components

Similarly, nowadays prediction approaches for quality attribute of a component based software architecture differ in

- The assumptions made on component specification
- The role and consideration of the underlying middleware
- Modelling of concurrency
- Modelling of resource congestion

During the Workshop of Component Oriented Programming (WCOP) at ECOOP 2005 in Glasgow, this issue was discussed and the idea was born to define a common example, which is modelled by different component modelling approaches. Like the famous production cell approach[1] of the FZI, Karlsruhe, which serves since 1995 as a common example for different embedded systems safety verification, such a common example for modelling approaches of component based systems will allow

---

[1] Springer LNCS vol. 891.

A. Rausch et al. (Eds.): Common Component Modeling Example, LNCS 5153, pp. 1–3, 2008.

1. The comparability of different approaches
2. The validation of existing models. Insights will lead to a better understanding of what are appropriate abstractions when modelling component based systems.
3. A better focus of research to tackle aspects less frequently dealt with
4. The classification of existing models and approaches
5. An eased interchange of research ideas
6. A simplified and increased coordination and research collaborations to join complementary models and approaches.

It should also be made explicit, what CoCoME is not: CoCoME is not a challenge in architecting systems. As a prescribed architecture is given, the challenge lies in using a specific formalism for modelling and analysing the CoCoME *according* to a given architecture. However, a different (but nevertheless very useful and interesting) project would be to ask participants to architect a system given the requirements documentation. We intentionally did *not* include this in CoCoME, as the resulting system descriptions would also differ in componensation etc., which lowers their comparability and thus freedom in the design would counter the intentions of the CoCoME project.

After a successful grant proposal for a Dagstuhl-Research-Seminar at the German Computer Science Society (G.I.), the project "Common Component Modelling Example" (CoCoME) was born. Via the newly created website (`http://www.cocome.org/`) nineteen teams registered from all over the world. A first meeting was held in November 2006 at the FZI, Karlsruhe, on historic ground: the home and origin of our role model, the production cell. During this meeting we agreed on the properties of a common example system. On the one hand, it had to include properties of real world systems, on the other hand, its size should be still limited so that academic groups are able to model the example with reasonable effort. Also the example should contain embedded elements but also parts of enterprise software and should come from a domain where most researchers have an intuitive understanding to avoid the creation and need to master a comprehensive and heavy-weighted requirements specification of the system. After several reviews, in January 2007 the organisers where able to publish the CoCoME specification (now in Chapter 3 in this volume). Luckily, outstanding researchers, equally at home in academia and industry, agreed to form a board (informally named "the jury") to give feedback on the submitted CoCoME models. Finally, thirteen models of CoCoME were submitted and underwent a peer-review process, before we met in Dagstuhl in August 2007. A short characterisation of the approaches presented during this meeting are listed in Chapter 2 while each approach and its model of CoCoME is presented in detail in Chapters 4 – 16.

After the finalisation of this volume, the CoCoME project has not ended, yet much more, we see this volume as the beginning where CoCoME is used as a shared example of the whole component commnity to validate and compare their approaches. Therefore, all relevant documents to start using CoCoME are online on our website (`http://www.cocome.org/`).

Beyond this future use of CoCoME, during our work on CoCoME and the discussions with our Jury, further areas of continued research have been identified which are presented in Chapter 17.

The success of such a large and complex project like CoCoME was made possible by several researchers who supported the organisers and kept things going. In particular we have to thank Holger Klus, Klaus Krogmann, and Sebastian Herold.

2   CoCoTA – Common Component Task*

Raffaela Mirandola[1] and František Plášil[2,3]

[1] Politecnico di Milano, Piazza Leonardo Da Vinci, 32, 20133 Milano, Italy
mirandola@elet.polimi.it
[2] Charles University in Prague, Faculty of Mathematics and Physics Department of
Software Engineering Malostranske namesti 25, 118 00 Prague 1, Czech Republic
plasil@dsrg.mff.cuni.cz
[3] Academy of Sciences of the Czech Republic Institute of Computer Science
plasil@cs.cas.cz

Abstract. This chapter overviews the scope, goals and timeline of the
modeling contest CoCoME. It also describes the input the competing
teams received and, furthermore, explains how the peer reviewing process
went ahead, and how the evaluation criteria were set with the aim to
balance the inherently heterogeneous modeling and expressive power of
different component models.

2.1   Introduction

Component-based software development (CBSD) has changed the current
paradigm of software development. Systems are no longer developed from
scratch, but composed of existing components as well as components to be developed. Nowadays, as systems become more and more complex, CBSD is to a
greater extent applied in industry. In order to leverage CBSD to build correct
and dependable component-based systems with predictable quality attributes,
research has developed various formal and semi-formal component models, like
for instance *-Calculus, DisCComp, Fractal, Focus, KOALA, Palladio, SOFA,
UML Extensions just to mention some of them. Common to these models is that
components are provided with specifications of their relevant functional and non-
functional properties to precisely describe their behavior and quality attributes.
Based on these specifications, methods and tools have been developed to analyze
and verify the functional correctness as well as to predict the dependability and
the quality attributes of the resulting component-based software architecture.

However, the different approaches concentrate on different yet related aspects
of component modeling, like for instance communication issues or performance
aspects. Due to this heterogeneity of modeling views and emphasis, it is hard
to compare these formal and semi-formal component models. This hinders their
validation for practical usage. The main goal of the CoCoME contest is to evaluate and compare the practical appliance of the existing component models and

---

* This work was partially supported by the Czech Academy of Sciences project
1ET400300504.

A. Rausch et al. (Eds.): Common Component Modeling Example, LNCS 5153, pp. 4–15, 2008.

the corresponding specification techniques. The key idea is that each registered team models a non-trivial common example using their own specific component model and its specific modeling techniques to show the models expressive power and potentially reveal not only its strengths but also its weaknesses.

2.2   Timeline, Input to the Teams and Expected Output

The key CoCoME related activities and milestones are listed below in the chronological order.

- June (2006): Formulation of the Call for Contribution and Participation Publishing the CfCP on the CoCoME -website http://www.cocome.org
- August, November: Joint searching for an appropriate example
- November 2-3 Workshop in Karlsruhe to discuss requirements for the common modeling example with the teams.
- November 24 Meeting in Kaiserslautern discussing and finalizing the common modeling example and organizational issues.
- November, December: Implementing and documenting the first version of the common modeling example ("assignment").
- January 6, (2007) First version of the assignment implementation was distributed.
- February 18 Distribution of the final version of the assignment
- May 2 Participating teams delivered the beta version of their modeling of the common component modeling example.
- May 30 Participating teams performed peer-review of the beta versions of their modeling of the common component modeling example (in the form of a LNCS chapter).
- June 6 Participating teams delivered their final modeling of the common component modeling example (in the form of a LNCS chapter).
- August 1-3 Participating teams present their final results in a joint GI-Dagstuhl Research Seminar, Schloss Dagstuhl, Germany. An international jury evaluated the results of the participating teams.

As input ("assignment" mentioned in the above timeline), every participating team received the following:

- A textual description of the example, which included eight textual use cases, along with UML diagrams of the key components and UML sequence diagrams illustrating how the use cases are reflected in component communication. Another part of the description was also a textual specification of extra-functional properties related to the use cases (in terms of timing, reliability and usage profile information.
- A Java implementation of all the components (source code), based on the following Java technologies: JMS (implementation of software buses), RMI (support of distribution), Hibernate (object persistence), Derby (Database).

The expected output of CoCoME was twofold. On one hand, the definition of the common example represents a common ground basing on which it would be possible to compare different approaches, to validate existing models, to focus on research aspects less frequently dealt with, and to classify existing models and approaches. On the other hand, the CoCoME aim was to set-up a multi-disciplinary community bringing together different competences to encourage communication, increased coordination and research collaborations to join complementary models and approaches for the design of component-based systems.

2.3   Participating Teams

Originally, nineteen teems responded to CfP and attended the November workshop in Karlsruhe. Of those, the following thirteen met the challenge fully and delivered their results in the required form. In the list below, we overview the basic characteristic of the teams and the key features of their component models.

KobrA-Team
   Affiliation: University Mannheim, Germany
   Team Leader: Colin Atkinson, atkinson@informatik.uni-mannheim.de
   Team Members: Colin Atkinson, Philipp Bostan, Daniel Brenner, Giovanni Falcone, Matthias Gutheil, Oliver Hummel, Monika Juhasz, Dietmar Stoll

Component Model
KobrA supports a model-driven, UML-based representation of components and component based systems. Two basic notions of composition are used to this end: a dynamic (i.e. run-time) one and a static (i.e. development time) one. The run-time one captures the core idea of a hierarchically structured system which forwards requests to one or more black-box components. These may be internal components (i.e. parts) of the system or external peers (i.e. servers). The development time concept of composition captures the idea of "definitional containment" similar to that provided by packages. In other words, it allows the design of a component or the system (which is regarded as a component) to be broken down into multiple, independent parts. KobrA's dynamic form of composition essentially corresponds to that used in the UML's component model, while the static form resembles that supported in the UML's traditional notion of subsystems. These two forms of composition should be "aligned" [1].

Rich Services Team
   Affiliation: University of California, San Diego, USA
   Team Leader: Ingolf Krüger
   Team Members: Barry Demchak, Vina Ermagan, Emilia Farcas, To-ju Huang, Ingolf Krüger, Massimiliano Menarini

Component Model

A service describes an interaction pattern among a set of logical entities (roles) required to provide functionality that realizes a use case. The interaction patterns are specified using a dialect of message sequence charts (MSCs) that contains various operators for service composition. The Rich Service architectural framework builds upon this service notion and organizes systems-of-systems into a hierarchically decomposed structure. The main entities of a composite Rich Service are: the Service/Data Connector, the communication infrastructure, and the set of sub-services, which can be further decomposed according to the same Rich Service pattern. We distinguish between Rich Application Services, which provide core application functionality and Rich Infrastructure Services, which address crosscutting concerns such as encryption, failure management, authentication, and policy enforcement. The Rich Services of the same hierarchical level communicate by connecting, via Service/Data Connectors, to a message-based communication infrastructure that provides message transmission, interception, and routing. We associate both a structural and a behavioral view with the interface of a Rich Service. Rich Services can easily map to an implementation architecture based on ESBs, threaded execution, or a range of other solutions. ESBs, in particular, provide message routing amongst well-defined, loosely coupled, coarsely granular services similar to our notion of Rich Services. Thus, Rich Services can be used both as a logical and deployment architecture model [2].

rCOS-Team

Affiliation: UNU-IIST Macao, China and Aalborg University, Denmark

Team Leader: Zhiming Liu, lzm@iist.unu.edu

Team Members: Zhenbang Chen, Abdel Hakim Hannousse, Dang Van Hung, Istvan Knoll, Xiaoshan Li, Zhiming Liu, Yang Liu, Qu Nan, Joseph C. Okika, Anders P. Ravn, Volker Stolz ,Lu Yang, Naijun Zhan

Component Model

rCOS, a relational Calculus for Object and component Systems, is an extended theory of Hoare and He's Unifying Theories of Programming (UTP) for object-oriented and component-based programming. A component is an aggregation of objects and processes with interfaces. Each interface has a contract, that specifies what is needed for the component to be used in building and maintaining a software without the need to know its design and implementation. A contract only specifies the functional behavior in terms of pre and post conditions and a protocol defining the permissible traces of method invocations. Components can be composed hierarchically by plugging, renaming, hiding and feedback. Application aspects are dealt with in a use-case driven Requirements Modelling phase. Each use case is specified as a contract of the provided interface of a component, in which the interaction protocol is specified by a set of traces and illustrated by a UML sequence diagram. The functionalities of the provided interface methods are given by the their pre and post conditions the dynamic behavior is given by guarded design and depicted by a UML state diagram. The data and class structure are specified by class declarations and depicted by a class diagram [3].

Component-Interaction Automata Team

Affiliation: Masaryk University, Brno, Czech Republic

Team Leader: Ivana Cerna

Team Members: Barbora Zimmerova, Pavlina Varekova, Nikola Benes, Ivana Cerna, Lubos Brim, Jiri Sochor

Component Model

Component-interaction automata are a language for modeling component interaction in hierarchical component-based software systems. The language builds on a simple, yet very powerful, composition operator that is able to reflect hierarchical assembly of the system and various communication strategies among components. Thanks to this operator, the language can be used for modelling the behaviour of components designed for or implemented in various component frameworks and models. The primary focus of our approach is on the automatic verification of communication behaviour modelled with Component-interaction automata. The verification is supported by a parallel model-checker DiVinE, which is able to handle very large, hence more realistic, models of component-based systems. Verified properties, like consequences of events or fairness of communication, are expressed in an extended version of the linear temporal logic LTL[4].

Focus/AutoFocus-Team

Affiliation: Technische Universität München, Germany

Team Leader: Michael Meisinger

Team Members: Jorge Fox, Florian Hölzl, Dagmar Koss, Marco Kuhrmann, Michael Meisinger, Birgit Penzenstadler, Sabine Rittmann, Bernhard Schätz, Mario Spichkova, Doris Wild

Component Model

The Focus/AutoFocus approach uses the formalism of timed infinite streams to specify component behavior. A system is formed of components that are connected via directed typed channels. Component behavior is specified by giving relations of input and output streams. Component-based software architectures are formed by connecting components in a hierarchical way with each other and the environment using channels. AutoFocus is a case tool that uses a simplified Focus semantics, which uses globally time synchronous component state machines to specify component behavior. Recent extensions to Focus and AutoFocus allow for service-based software design [5].

Java/A Team

Affiliation: Ludwig-Maximilians-Universität München; University of Edinburgh; Danmarks Tekniske Universitet, Lyngby

Team Leader Alexander Knapp

Team Members: Alexander Knapp, Stephan Janisch, Rolf Hennicker, Allan Clark, Stephen Gilmore, Florian Hacklinger, Hubert Baumeister, Martin Wirsing

Component Model

In the Java/A component model, components are strongly encapsulated behaviours. Only the exchange of messages with their environment according to provided and required operation interfaces can be observed. The component interfaces are bound to ports which regulate the message exchange by port behaviour and ports can be linked by connectors establishing a communication channel between their owning components. Components can be hierarchical containing again components and connections. The semantics of the Java/A component model uses the interface automata approach to I/O-transition systems for describing the observable behaviour and the states-as-algebras approach for representing the internals of components. The Java/A component model and its underlying semantical framework is used as a formal underpinning for the architectural programming language Java/A [6].

Cowch-Team

Affiliation: TU Kaiserslautern, Germany

Team Leader: Arnd Poetzsch-Heffter, poetzsch@informatik.uni-kl.de

Team Members: Jan Schäfer, Jean-Marie Gaillourdet, Markus Reitz, Arnd Poetzsch-Heffter

Component Model

The Cowch approach provides a precise model to describe the relation and consistency of system architectures and component-based implementations. The approach is based on a hierarchical component model for object-oriented programming, called the Box Model. A box is a runtime entity with state and a semantics-based encapsulation boundary. The implementation of a box consists of a number of classes and interfaces. A box is created by instantiating one distinguished class of the implementation. A box can encapsulate other boxes, so-called inner boxes. The result is a hierarchy of boxes at runtime. To hierarchically structure the communication between boxes, directed ports and channels are used. Ports are named interfaces and can be incoming or outgoing. All box boundary crossing references must be modeled by using ports. The concurrency model of Cowch is based on the Join Calculus and features asynchronous methods and join patterns. To graphically describe systems modeled in our executable modeling language, we contribute a graphical description language which provides a concise view to the runtime architecture of a system. The Cowch framework and its tools are still under development [7].

DisCComp-Team

Affiliation: Clausthal University of Technology, Software Systems Engineering Group

Team Leader: Sebastian Herold, sebastian.herold@tu-clausthal.de

Team Members: André Appel, Sebastian Herold, Holger Klus, Andreas Rausch

Component Model

DisCComp - A Formal Model for Distributed Concurrent Components - is based on set-theoretic formalizations of distributed concurrent systems. It allows modeling of dynamically changing structures, a shared global state and asynchronous message communication as well as synchronous and concurrent message calls. DisCComp provides a sound semantic model for concurrently executed components which is realistic enough to serve as formal foundation for current component technologies in use. Additionally, a description technique based on UML and OCL is provided which uses the semantic model to form executable specifications. The approach is supported by tools for code generation as well as simulation and execution of such specifications for testing purposes [8].

Palladio-Team

Affiliation: Universität Karlsruhe (TH), Germany

Team Leader: Ralf Reussner, reussner@ipd.uka.de

Team Members: Steffen Becker, Thomas Goldschmidt, Henning Groenda, Jens Happe, Heiko Koziolek, Klaus Krogmann, Michael Kuperberg, Anne Martens, Ralf Reussner, Johannes Stammel

Component Model

The Palladio Component Model (PCM) is a metamodel for a domain specific language to describe systems built using components. It is designed to support a component-based software development process including division of work. Its special capabilities allow the system designer to do early design-time predictions of performance attributes. The PCM supports explicit component parameterization over context dependencies: Usage profile, component assembly, and execution environment. Performance analysis is based on queuing network-based simulations, analytical solving of stochastic regular expressions, or mixed simulation-analytical solutions operating on stochastic process algebra. Performance descriptions support arbitrary distribution functions, not just mean values. The PCM is implemented using the Eclipse Modeling Framework (EMF). A closed tool chain ranging from modeling to interpretation of analysis results supports the approach [9].

KLAPER-Team

Affiliation: Politecnico di Milano, Italy

Team Leader: Raffaela Mirandola, mirandola@elet.polimi.it

Team Members: Vincenzo Grassi, Enrico Randazzo: Universitá Roma TorVergata; Raffaela Mkirandola: Politecnico di Milano,Antonino Sabetta: ISTI-CNR, Pisa.

Component Model

KLAPER is a modeling language aiming to capture the relevant information for the analysis of non-functional attributes of component-based systems, with a focus on performance and reliability. KLAPER is not actually a "component model", but it is rather meant as an intermediate model to be used in a transformation path from design-oriented models to analysis-oriented models. For this purpose, its goal is to help in distilling relevant information for analysis purposes from the original design-oriented model. The idea underlying KLAPER is to provide support for the modeling of a system as an assembly of interacting resources, where a resource denotes an entity that may offer services (and possibly requires others). Each offered service is characterized by a list of formal parameters that can be instantiated with actual values by other resources requiring that service. The formal parameters and their corresponding actual parameters are meant to represent a suitable analysis-oriented abstraction of the "real" service parameters. To support performance or reliability analysis, each KLAPER service provides information about its execution time or failure characteristics. A service behavior is characterized by a set of used services and consists of a set of execution steps. Steps can model either an internal activity, i.e. an activity performed by the same resource offering the service, or a set of service calls, i.e. a set of requests for services offered by external resources [10].

Fractal-Team

Affiliation: Charles University in Prague, Czech Republic
Team Leader: František Plášil
Team Members: Lubomír Bulej, Tomáš Bureš, Thierry Coupaye, Martin Děcký, Pavel Ježek, Pavel Parízek, František Plášil, Tomáš Poch, Nicolas Rivierre, Ondřej Šerý, Petr Tůma

Component Model
The Fractal is a modular and extensible hierarchical component model supporting dynamic reconfiguration of its architecture. The architecture of an application can be described by ADL (Architecture Description Language), while behavior is modeled using Behavior Protocols. There are two kinds of components: (i) primitive component directly implemented in a programming language, and (ii) composite ones, composed of other components. Each component consists of a membrane and a content, the membrane contains queue aggregating incoming method requests while content processes these requests. Besides business interfaces, each component features also control interfaces that are used for managing the component lifecycle, i.e., starting/stopping the component, settings attributes, etc. There are several implementations of the Fractal component model, e.g. Julia, AOKell, and Fractive [11].

SOFA-Team

Affiliation: Charles University in Prague, Czech Republic
Team Leader: František Plášil
Team Members: Tomáš Bureš, Martin Děcký, Petr Hnětynka, Jan Kofroň, Pavel Parízek, František Plášil, Tomáš Poch, Ondřej Šerý, Petr Tůma

Component Model
SOFA 2.0 is a component platform which uses a hierarchical component model formally defined using a meta-model. Primitive components in the SOFA 2.0 component model are directly implemented in a programming language (Java), while composite components are composed of other (either primitive or composite) components. The components are connected using automatically generated software connectors, which implement several communication styles and allow for distribution of applications among several computational nodes. Behavior of each component is modeled using Extended Behavior Protocols - a specification language describing component behavior as sequences of events (method call requests and responses and value changes of selected component local variables). Also, a limited dynamic reconfiguration of application architecture is possible via the factory pattern [12].

Grid Component Model Team
   Affiliation: INRIA Sophia Antipolis, Université de Nice-Sophia Antipolis, CNRS, France
   Team Leader: Eric Madelaine, eric.madelaine@sophia.inria.fr
   Team Members: Antonio Cansado, Denis Caromel, Eric Madelaine, Ludovic Henrio, Marcela Rivera, Emil Salageanu

Component Model
The Grid Component Model is a hierarchical, distributed, component model for computational grids, defined in the CoreGrid European NoE. This is a component model inspired and extended from a distributed implementation of the Fractal component model using the ProActive library. The team stresses on specification and validation of behavioural models of the components, based on a model called Parameterized Networks of Labelled Transition Systems. The Java Distributed Component specification language (JDC) is a Java-based language integrating architectural and behavioural aspects of component systems; a subset of this language can be represented also as UML diagrams. Model-generation methods are defined reflecting normal behaviour of systems but also deployment and reconfiguration phases. A set of supporting tools, for checking safety properties of components and validating their correct composition is available. This work at the formal model level is backed-up by the ProActive implementation of the component model, that is a wide-spread technology for developing component-based applications [13].

2.4   Reviewing and Evaluation Process

The reviewing process followed a two-steps procedure.
   As a first step, once a team had delivered a beta version of their modeling of the common modeling example, their submission was distributed by the organizers to another team for a peer review. Based on the reviews, the teams deliver their final, camera-ready versions.

As a second step, the results were presented by each of the teams at the joint GI-Dagstuhl Research Seminar, where an international jury was present, having the task to evaluate the teams' submissions and presentations and provide a valuable feedback. The jury, composed of well recognized researchers in the field (Manfred Broy,TU München, Germany; Ian Gorton, Empirical Software Engineering Research Group, National ICT, Australia; Johannes Siedersleben, T-Systems International, Germany; Clemens Szyperski, Microsoft Research, USA) asked to the teams to answer the questions below, and then evaluated the teams' results:

1. Questions to the General Claims of the Approach XXX

* What concept of a component do you use?
* What concept of a composition do you use and how to do specify ist semantics ?
* Does your approach support divide and conquer via interface specs?
* Do you have a clear separation of the application aspects and the technical aspects?
* Can you verify the component architecture independent of the implementation?
* Does your approach support hierarchical composition?
* What kind of properties can you specify/model formally?
* What kind of properties can you verify/analyse?
* Can you describe the deployment separately from the logical behaviour?
* Is there a formalized relation between your component model and the code and how do verify/check it?

2. Questions on How XXX Dealt with the CoCoME Example

* Which aspects did you treat?
* Which aspects did you not treat?
* Which aspects can not be treated in your approach?
* What are the strong parts of your treatment?
* What are the weak parts of your treatment?
* To what extent did you try to model the exact architecture of the CoCoME implementation (and if not - why not)?
* What did you verify (including test)?
* What kind of tool support did you use?
* How simple/easy is your approach to be used by someone else?

3. Questions on the Task Execution of Approach XXX

* How much effort went into your treatment of CoCoME (person months)?
* How much effort would you need to treat CoCoME as completely as possible?
* What did you learn by the exercise?
* What can be improved if we repeat the exercise?

2.5   Conclusions

This chapter presented the goals and the overall process underlying the modeling contest CoCoME, starting from the input the competing teams received, describing the reviewing process until the last step of discussion and evaluation carried out at the GI-Dagstuhl Research Seminar. As a result of the Dagstuhl presentations and discussions, the authors are asked to revise their chapter so to answer to the Jury questions. The final aim of this revision is to present an improved version of the approach whit special emphasis on the goal and scope of the proposed component model, on the benefits deriving from the modeling and finally, on the effort dedicated to this work and on the overall the lessons learned.

Acknowledgements

The authors would like to thank to Ralf Reussner, Andreas Rausch and Holger Klus for their effort, valuable comments and suggestions.

References

1. Atkinson, C., Bostan, P., Brenner, D., Falcone, G., Gutheil, M., Hummel, O., Juhasz, M., Stoll, D.: Modeling Components and Component-Based Systems in KobrA. In: Rausch, A., et al. (eds.) Common Component Modeling Example. LNCS, vol. 5153, pp. 54–84. Springer, Heidelberg (2008)
2. Demchak, B., Ermagan, V., Farcas, E., ju Huang, T., Krueger, I., Menarini, M.: A Rich Services Approach to CoCoME. In: Rausch, A., et al. (eds.) Common Component Modeling Example. LNCS, vol. 5153, pp. 85–115. Springer, Heidelberg (2008)
3. Chen, Z., Hannousse, A.H., Dang Van Hung, I.K., Xiaoshan Li, Z.L., Liu, Y., Nan, Q., Okika, J.C., Ravn, A.P., Stolz, V., Yang, L., Zhan, N.: Modelling with Relational Calculus of Object and Component Systems - rCOS. In: Rausch, A., et al. (eds.) Common Component Modeling Example. LNCS, vol. 5153, pp. 116–145. Springer, Heidelberg (2008)
4. Zimmerova, B., Varekova, P., Benes, N., Cerna, I., Brim, L., Socho, J.: Component-Interaction Automata Approach (CoIn). In: Rausch, A., et al. (eds.) Common Component Modeling Example. LNCS, vol. 5153, pp. 146–176. Springer, Heidelberg (2008)
5. Fox, J., Hölzl, F., Koss, D., Kuhrmann, M., Meisinger, M., Penzenstadler, B., Rittmann, S., Schtz, B., Spichkova, M., Wild, D.: Service-Oriented Modeling of CoCoME with Focus and AutoFocus. In: Rausch, A., et al. (eds.) Common Component Modeling Example. LNCS, vol. 5153, pp. 177–206. Springer, Heidelberg (2008)
6. Knapp, A., Janisch, S., Hennicker, R., Clark, A., Gilmore, S., Hacklinger, F., Baumeister, H., Wirsing, M.: Modelling the CoCoME with the Java/A Component Model. In: Rausch, A., et al. (eds.) Common Component Modeling Example. LNCS, vol. 5153, pp. 207–237. Springer, Heidelberg (2008)
7. Schäfer, J., Gaillourdet, J.M., Reitz, M., Poetzsch-Heffter, A.: Linking Programs to Architectures: An Object-Oriented Hierarchical Software Model based on Boxes. In: Rausch, A., et al. (eds.) Common Component Modeling Example. LNCS, vol. 5153, pp. 238–266. Springer, Heidelberg (2008)

8. Appel, A., Herold, S., Klus, H., Rausch, A.: Modelling the CoCoME with DisC-Comp. In: Rausch, A., et al. (eds.) Common Component Modeling Example. LNCS, vol. 5153, pp. 267–296. Springer, Heidelberg (2008)
9. Becker, S., Goldschmidt, T., Groenda, H., Happe, J., Koziolek, H., Krogmann, K., Kuperberg, M., Martens, A., Reussner, R., Stammel, J.: Palladio – Prediction of Performance Properties. In: Rausch, A., et al. (eds.) Common Component Modeling Example. LNCS, vol. 5153, pp. 297–326. Springer, Heidelberg (2008)
10. Grassi, V., Mirandola, R., Randazzo, E., Sabetta, A.: KLAPER: an Intermediate Language for Model-Driven Predictive Analysis of Performance and Reliability. In: Rausch, A., et al. (eds.) Common Component Modeling Example. LNCS, vol. 5153, pp. 327–356. Springer, Heidelberg (2008)
11. Bulej, L., Bureš, T., Coupaye, T., Děcký, M., Ježek, P., Parízek, P., Plášil, F., Poch, T., Rivierre, N., Šerý, O., Tůma, P.: CoCoME in Fractal. In: Rausch, A., et al. (eds.) Common Component Modeling Example. LNCS, vol. 5153, pp. 357–387. Springer, Heidelberg (2008)
12. Bureš, T., Děcký, M., Petr Hnětynka, J.K., Parízek, P., Plášil, F., Poch, T., Šerý, O., Tůma, P.: CoCoME in SOFA. In: Rausch, A., et al. (eds.) Common Component Modeling Example. LNCS, vol. 5153, pp. 388–417. Springer, Heidelberg (2008)
13. Cansado, A., Caromel, D., Madelaine, E., Henri, L., Rivera, M., Salageanu, E.: A Specification Language for Distributed Components implemented in GCM/ProActive. In: Rausch, A., et al. (eds.) Common Component Modeling Example. LNCS, vol. 5153, pp. 418–448. Springer, Heidelberg (2008)

3   CoCoME - The Common Component Modeling Example

Sebastian Herold[1], Holger Klus[1], Yannick Welsch[1], Constanze Deiters[1],
Andreas Rausch[1], Ralf Reussner[2], Klaus Krogmann[2], Heiko Koziolek[2],
Raffaela Mirandola[3], Benjamin Hummel[4], Michael Meisinger[4],
and Christian Pfaller[4]

[1] TU Clausthal, Germany
[2] Universität Karlsruhe, Germany
[3] Politecnico di Milano, Italy
[4] Technische Universität München, Germany

3.1   Introduction and System Overview

The example of use which was chosen as the Common Component Modeling
Example (CoCoME) and on which the several methods presented in this book
should be applied was designed according to the example described by Larman
in [1]. The description of this example and its use cases in the current chapter
shall be considered under the assumption that this information was delivered
by a business company as it could be in the reality. Therefore the specified
requirements are potentially incomplete or imprecise.

The mentioned example describes a *Trading System* as it can be
observed in a supermarket handling sales. This includes the processes at a single
Cash Desk like scanning products using a *Bar Code Scanner* or paying by credit
card or cash as well as administrative tasks like ordering of running out products or generating reports. The following section gives a brief overview of such
a Trading System and its hardware parts. Its required use cases and software
architecture are described later in this chapter.

The Cash Desk is the place where the *Cashier* scans the goods the *Customer*
wants to buy and where the paying (either by credit card or cash) is executed.
Furthermore it is possible to switch into an express checkout mode which allows
only Costumer with a few goods and also only cash payment to speed up the
clearing. To manage the processes at a Cash Desk a lot of hardware devices are
necessary (compare figure 1).

Using the *Cash Box* which is available at each Cash Desk a sale is started
and finished. Also the cash payment is handled by the Cash Box. To manage
payments by credit card a *Card Reader* is used. In order to identify all goods
the Customer wants to buy the Cashier uses the *Bar Code Scanner*. At the
end of the paying process a bill is produced using a *Printer*. Each Cash Desk
is also equipped with a *Light Display* to let the Costumer know if this Cash
Desk is in the express checkout mode or not. The central unit of each Cash Desk
is the *Cash Desk PC* which wires all other components with each other. Also the

A. Rausch et al. (Eds.): Common Component Modeling Example, LNCS 5153, pp. 16–53, 2008.
© Springer-Verlag Berlin Heidelberg 2008

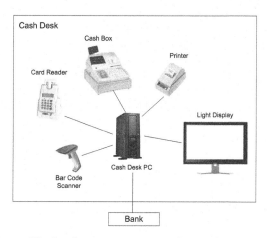

Fig. 1. The hardware components of a single Cash Desk

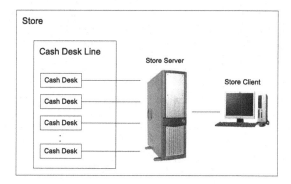

Fig. 2. An overview of entities in a store which are relevant for the Trading System

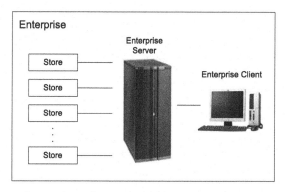

Fig. 3. The enterprise consists of several stores, an enterprise server and an enterprise client

software which is responsible for handling the sale process and amongst others for the communication with the *Bank* is running on that machine.

A *Store* itself contains of several Cash Desks whereas the set of Cash Desks is called *Cash Desk Line* here. The Cash Desk Line is connected to a *Store Server* which itself is also connected to a *Store Client* (compare figure 2). The Store Client can be used by the manager of the Store to view reports, order products or to chance the sales prices of goods. The Store Server also holds the *Inventory* of the corresponding Store.

A set of Stores is organized in an *Enterprise* where an *Enterprise Server* exists to which all Stores are connected (compare figure 3). With the assistance of an *Enterprise Client* the Enterprise Manager is able to generate several kinds of reports.

3.2   Functional Requirements and Use Case Analysis

In this section the considered use cases of the Trading System are introduced which are depicted in figure 4 with the involved actors. Each use case is described using a uniform template which includes a brief description of the use case itself, the standard process flow and its alternatives. Moreover, information like preconditions, postconditions and the trigger of the use cases are given. In the description of the use cases the codes in the squared brackets refer to extra-functional properties in section 3.3.

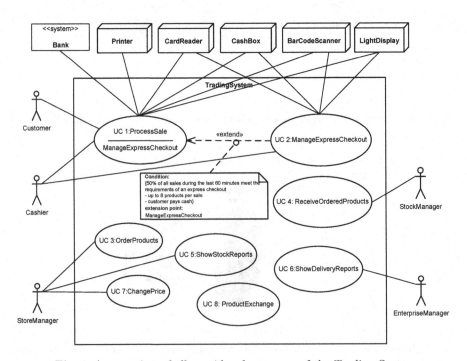

Fig. 4. An overview of all considered use cases of the Trading System

UC 1 - Process Sale

Brief Description. At the Cash Desk the products a Customer wants to buy are detected and the payment - either by credit card or cash - is performed.

Involved Actors. Customer, Cashier, Bank, Printer, Card Reader, Cash Box, Bar Code Scanner, Light Display.

Precondition. The Cash Desk and the Cashier are ready to start a new sale.

Trigger. Coming to the Cash Desk a Costumer wants to pay his chosen product items.

Postcondition. The Customer has paid, has received the bill and the sale is registered in the Inventory.

Standard Process

1. The Customer arrives at the Cash Desk with goods to purchase. [arr1]
2. The Cashier starts a new sale by pressing the button *Start New Sale* at the Cash Box. [t12-1]
3. The Cashier enters the item identifier. This can be done manually by using the keyboard of the Cash Box [p13-1, t13-1] or by using the Bar Code Scanner [p13-2, t13-2].
4. Using the item identifier the System presents the corresponding product description, price, and running total. [t14-1]
   The steps 3-4 are repeated until all items are registered. [n11-2]
5. Denoting the end of entering items the Cashier presses the button *Sale Finished* at the Cash Box. [t15-1]
   (a) To initiate cash payment the Cashier presses the button *Cash Payment* at the Cash Box. [p15-1,t15a-1]
      i. The Customer hands over the money for payment. [t15a1-1]
      ii. The Cashier enters the received cash using the Cash Box and confirms this by pressing Enter. [t15a2-1]
      iii. The Cash Box opens. [t15a3-1]
      iv. The received money and the change amount are displayed [t15a4-1], and the Cashier hands over the change. [t15a4-2]
      v. The Cashier closes the Cash Box. [t15a5-1]
   (b) In order to initiate card payment the Cashier presses the button *Card Payment* at the Cash Box. [p15-2, t15b-1]
      i. The Cashier receives the credit card from the Customer [t15b1-1] and pulls it through the Card Reader. [t15b1-2]
      ii. The Customer enters his PIN using the keyboard of the card reader and waits for validation. [t15b2-1]
         The step 5.b.ii is repeated until a successful validation or the Cashier presses the button for cash payment. [t15b2-2, n15b2-1]
6. Completed sales are logged by the Trading System and sale information are sent to the Inventory in order to update the stock. [t16-1]
7. The Printer writes the receipt and the Cashier hands it out to the Costumer. [t17-1]
8. The Customer leaves the Cash Desk with receipt and goods.

Alternative or Exceptional Processes

- *In step 3: Invalid item identifier if the system cannot find it in the Inventory.* [p13-4]
  1. The System signals error and rejects this entry. [t13-3]
  2. The Cashier can respond to the error as follows:
     (a) It exists a human-readable item identifier: [p13-5]
         i. The Cashier manually enters the item identifier. [t13-4]
         ii. The System displays the description and price. [t14-1]
     (b) Otherwise the product item is rejected. [p13-6]
- *In step 5.b: Card validation fails.* [p15b2-2]
  1. The Cashier and the Customer try again and again.
  2. Otherwise the Cashier requires the Customer to pay cash.
- *In step 6: Inventory not available.* [p16-1]
  The System caches each sale and writes them into the Inventory as soon as it is available again. [t161-1]

UC 2 - Manage Express Checkout

Brief Description. If some conditions are fulfilled a Cash Desk automatically switches into an express mode. The Cashier is able to switch back into normal mode by pressing a button at his Cash Desk. To indicate the mode the Light Display shows different colors.

Involved Actors. Cashier, Cash Box, Light Display, Card Reader.

Precondition. The Cash Desk is either in normal mode and the latest sale was finished (case 1) or the Cash Desk is in express mode (case 2).

Trigger. This use case is triggered by the system itself.

Postcondition. The Cash Desk has been switched into express mode or normal mode. The Light Display has changed its color accordingly.

Standard Process

1. The considered Cash Desk is in normal mode [p2-1] and just finished a sale which matches the condition of an express checkout sale. Now 50% of all sales during the last 60 minutes fulfill the condition for an express checkout.
   (a) This Cash Desk, which has caused the achievement of the condition, is switched into express mode. [t21a-1]
   (b) Furthermore the corresponding Light Display is switched from black into green to indicate the Cash Desk's express mode. [t21b-1]
   (c) Paying by credit card is not possible anymore. [t21c-1]
   (d) The maximum of items per sale is reduced to 8 and only paying by cash is allowed. [t21d-1]
2. The Cash Desk is in express mode [p2-2] and the Cashier decides to change back into normal mode.
   (a) The Cashier presses the button *Disable Express Mode*. [t22a-1]
   (b) The color of the Light Display is changed from green into black color. [t22b-1]

(c) Cash and also card payment is allowed and the Costumer is allowed to buy as much goods as he likes. [t22c-1]

UC 3 - Order Products

Brief Description. The Trading System provide the opportunity to order product items.

Involved Actors. Store Manager.

Precondition. An Overview over the Inventory is available and the Store Client was started.

Trigger. The Store Manager decided to buy new product items for his store.

Postcondition. The order was placed and a generated order identifier was presented to the Store Manager.

Standard Process

1. A list with all products [n3-1] and a list with products running out of stock are shown. [n3-2, p3-1, t31-1]
2. The Store Manager chooses the product items to order and enters the corresponding amount. [t32-1]
3. The Store Manager presses the button *Order* at the Store Client's GUI. [t33-1]
4. The appropriate suppliers are chosen and orders for each supplier are placed. An order identifier is generated for each order and is shown to the Store Manager. [t34-1, t34-2, t34-3]

UC 4 - Receive Ordered Products

Brief Description. Ordered products which arrive at the Store have to be checked for correctness and inventoried.

Involved Actors. Stock Manager.

Precondition. The Store Client was started and the part Inventory of the Trading System is available.

Trigger. The ordered products arrive at the Store.

Postcondition. The Inventory is updated with the ordered products.

Standard Process

1. Ordered products arrive at the stock attached by an order identifier which has been assigned during the ordering process. [n4-1]
2. The Stock Manager checks the delivery for completeness and correctness. [p4-1, t42-1]
3. In the case of correctness, the Stock Manager enters the order identifier and presses the button *Roll in received order*. [t43-1]
4. The Trading System updates the Inventory. [t44-1]

Alternative or Exceptional Processes

- *In step 2: Delivery not complete or not correct.* [p4-2]
  The products are sent back to the supplier and the Stock Manager has to wait until a correct and complete delivery has arrived. This action does not recognized by the System.

UC 5 - Show Stock Reports

Brief Description. The opportunity to generate stock-related reports is provided by the Trading System.

Involved Actors. Store Manager.

Precondition. The reporting GUI at the Store Client has been started.

Trigger. The Store Manager wants to see statistics about his store.

Postcondition. The report for the Store has been generated and is displayed on the reporting GUI.

Standard Process

1. The Store Manager enters the store identifier and presses the button *Create Report.* [t51-1]
2. A report including all available stock items in the store is displayed. [t52-1]

UC 6 - Show Delivery Reports

Brief Description. The Trading System provides the opportunity to calculate the mean times a delivery from each supplier to an considered enterprise takes.

Involved Actors. Enterprise Manager

Precondition. The reporting GUI at the Store Client has been started.

Trigger. The Enterprise Manager wants to see statistics about the enterprise.

Postcondition. The report for the Enterprise has been generated and is displayed to the Enterprise Manager.

Standard Process

1. The Enterprise Manager enters the enterprise identifier and presses the button *Create Report.* [t61-1]
2. A report which informs about the mean times is generated. [t62-1]

UC 7 - Change Price

Brief Description. The System provides the opportunity to change the sales price for a product.

Involved Actors. Store Manager.

Precondition. The store GUI at the Store Client has been started.

Trigger. The Store Manager wants to change the sales price of a product for his store.

Postcondition. The price for the considered product has been changed and it will be sold with the new price now.

Standard Process

1. The System presents an overview over all available products in the store. [t71-1]
2. The Store Manager selects a product item [t72-1] and changes its sales price. [t72-2]
3. The Store Manager commits the change by pressing ENTER. [t73-1]

UC 8 - Product Exchange (on Low Stock) among Stores

Brief Description. If a store runs out of a certain product (or a set of products; "required good"), it is possible to start a query to check whether those products are available at other Stores of the Enterprise ("providing Stores"). Therefore the Enterprise Server and the Store Servers need to synchronize their data on demand (one scheduled update per day or per hour is not sufficient). After a successful query the critical product can be shipped from one to other Stores. But it has to be decided (using heuristics to compute the future selling frequency), whether the transportation is meaningful. For example, if the product is propably sold out at all Stores within the same day, a transportation does not make sense.

Expressed in a more technical way one Store Server is able to start a query at the Enterprise Server. The Enterprise Server in turn starts a query for products available at other Stores. As the Enterprise Server does not have the current global data for Stores at any time (due to a write caching latency at the Store Servers) the Enterprise Server has to trigger all Store Servers to push their local data to the Enterprise Server.

Involved Actors. This use case is not an end-user use case. Only servers are involved.

Precondition. The Store Server with the shortage product is able to connect to the Enterprise Server.

Trigger. This use case is triggered by the system itself.

Postcondition. The products to deliver are marked as incoming or unavailable, respectively, in the according Stores.

Standard Process

1. A certain product of the Store runs out.
2. The Store Server recognizes low stock of the product. [t82-1]
3. The Store Server sends a request to the Enterprise Server (including an identification of the shortage products, and a Store id) [t83-1]
4. The Enterprise Server triggers all Stores that are "near by" (e. g. ¡300 km) the requiring store, to flush their local write caches. So the Enterprise Server database gets updated by the Store Server. [t84-1, t84-1]

5. The Enterprise Server does a database look-up for the required products to get a list of products (including amounts) that are available at providing Stores. [t85-1]
6. The Enterprise Server applies the "optimization criterion" (specified above) to decide, whether it is meaningful to transport the shortage product from one store to another (heuristics might be applied to minimize the total costs of transportation). This results in a list of products (including amounts) per providing store that have to be delivered to the requiring Store. [t86-1]
7. The Store Server, initially sending the recognition of the shortage product, is provided with the decision of the Enterprise Server. [t87-1]
   (a) The required product is marked as incoming. [t87-2]
8. The Store Server of a near by Store is provided with information that it has to deliver the product. [t88-1]
   (a) The required product is marked as unavailable in the Store. [t88-2]

Alternative or Exceptional Processes

- The Enterprise Server is not available: The request is queued until the Enterprise Server is available and then is send again.
- One or more Store Servers are not available: The Enterprise Server queues the requests for the Store Servers until they are available and then resend them. If a Store Server is not available for more than 15 minutes the request for this Server is canceled. It is assumed, that finally unavailable Store Servers do not have the required product.

Extension on Use Case 8 - Remove Incoming Status

Brief Description. If the first part of use case 8 (as described above) has passed, for moved products an amount marked as incoming remains at the Inventory of the Store receiving the products. An extension allows to change that incoming mark via a user interface at the Store Client if the moved products arrive at a Store.

Precondition. The Inventory is available and the Store Client has been started.

Trigger. The moved products (according to UC8) arrive at the Store.

Postcondition. For the amount of incoming products the status "incoming" is removed in the Inventory.

Standard Process

1. The products arrive at the stock of the Store.
2. For all arriving products the Stock Manager counts the incoming amount.
3. For every arriving product the Stock Manager enters the identifier and its amount into the Store Client.
4. The system updates the Inventory.

Alternative or Exceptional Processes

- If the entered amount of an incoming product is larger than the amount accounted in the Inventory, the input is rejected. The incoming amount has to be re-entered.

3.3   Extra-Functional Properties

The following table includes CoCoME's extra-functional properties in terms of timing, reliability, and usage profile related information. They can be seen as guiding values when conducting QoS-analysis with CoCoME. The results from different methods can be compared more adequately if they are based on the same extra-functional properties.

Table 1. CoCoME - Extra-functional Properties

CoCoME Overall
n0-1: Number of stores
200
n0-2: Cash desks per store
8
UC1 - Process Sale
arr1: Customer arrival rate per store
PAopenLoad.PAoccurrence = ('unbounded', ('exponential', 320.0, 'hr'))
n11-1: Number of open cash desks per store
('assm', 'dist', ('histogram', 0, 0.1, 2, 0.2, 4, 0.4, 6, 0.3, 8, '#Open Cash Desks'))
n11-2: Number of goods per customer
('assm', 'dist', ('histogram', 1, 0.3, 8, 0.1, 15, 0.15, 25, 0.15, 50, 0.2, 75, 0.1, 100, '#Goods per Customer'))
t12-1: Time for pressing button "Start New Sale"
PAdemand = ('assm', 'mean', (1.0, 's'))
t13-1: Time for scanning an item
PAdemand = ('assm', 'dist', ('histogram', 0.0, 0.9, 0.3, 0.05, 1.0, 0.04, 2.0, 0.01, 5.0, 's'))
t13-2: Time for manual entry
PAdemand = ('assm', 'mean', (5.0, 's'))
t13-3: Time for signaling error and rejecting an ID
PAdemand = ('req', 'mean', (10, 'ms'))
t13-4: Time for manually entering the item identifier after error
PAdemand = ('assm', 'mean', (5.0, 's'))
p13-1: Probability of using the bar code scanner per item
0.99
p13-2: Probability of manual entry per item
0.01
p13-3: Probability of valid item ID
0.999
p13-4: Probability of invalid item ID
0.001
p13-5: Probability of human-readable item ID
0.9

Table 1. (*continued*)

p13-6: Probability of rejecting an item 0.1
t14-1: Time for showing the product description, price, and running total PAdemand = ('req', 'mean', (10, 'ms'))
t15-1: Time for pressing button "Sale Finished" PAdemand = ('assm', 'mean', (1.0, 's'))
t15a-1: Time for pressing button "Cash Payment" PAdemand = ('assm', 'mean', (1.0, 's'))
t15a1-1: Time for handing over the money PAdemand = ('assm', 'dist', ('histogram', 2.0, 0.3, 5.0, 0.5, 8.0, 0.2, 10.0, 's'))
t15a2-1: Time for entering the cash received and confirming PAdemand = ('assm', 'mean', (2.0, 's'))
p15-1: Probability of cash payment 0.5
p15-2: Probability of credit card payment 0.5
n15b2-1: Number of times a customer has to enter the PIN ('assm', 'dist', ('histogram', 1, 0.9, 2, 0.09, 3, 0.01, 4, 'times entering PIN'))
p15b2-1: Probability of valid CC id 0.99
p15b2-2: Probability of invalid CC id 0.01
t15a3-1: Time for opening the cash box PAdemand = ('assm', 'mean', (1.0, 's'))
t15a4-1: Time until displaying received money and change amount PAdemand = ('req', 'mean', (10, 'ms'))
t15a4-2: Time for handing over the change PAdemand = ('assm', 'dist', ('histogram', 2.0, 0.2, 3.0, 0.6, 4.0, 0.2, 5.0, 's'))
t15a5-1: Time for closing the cash box PAdemand = ('assm', 'mean', (1.0, 's'))
t15b-1: Time for pressing button "Card Payment" PAdemand = ('assm', 'mean', (1.0, 's'))
t15b1-1: Time for receiving the credit card PAdemand = ('assm', 'dist', ('histogram', 3.0, 0.6, 4.0, 0.4, 5.0, 's'))
t15b1-2: Time for pulling the credit card through the reader PAdemand = ('assm', 'mean', (2.0, 's'))
t15b2-1: Time for entering the PIN PAdemand = ('assm', 'dist', ('uniform', 1.0, 5.0, 's'))
t15b2-2: Time waiting for validation PAdemand = ('assm', 'dist', ('histogram', 4.0, 0.9, 5.0, 0.1, 20.0, 's'))
t16-1: Time for sending sale information and updating stock PAdemand = ('req', 'mean', (100, 'ms'))

Table 1. (*continued*)

t161-1: Time for writing cached sales logs after inventory is back up PAdemand = ('req', 'mean', (2, 's'))
p16-1: Probability of Failure on Demand of Inventory System 0.001
t17-1: Time for printing the receipt and handing it out PAdemand = ('assm', 'mean', (3.0, 's'))
UC2 - Manage Express Checkout
arr-2: Manage Express Checkout arrival rate PAopenLoad.PAoccurrence = ('unbounded', ('exponential', 1, 'hr'))
p2-1: Probability of being in normal mode 0.8
p2-2: Probability of being in express mode 0.2
t21a-1: Time for switching to express mode PAdemand = ('req', 'mean', (10, 'ms'))
t21b-1: Time for switching light display PAdemand = ('req', 'mean', (10, 'ms'))
t21c-1: Time for deactivating credit card payment PAdemand = ('req', 'mean', (10, 'ms'))
t21d-1: Time for setting the maximum number of items PAdemand = ('req', 'mean', (10, 'ms'))
t22a-1: Time for pressing button "Disable Express Mode" PAdemand = ('assm', 'mean', (1.0, 's'))
t22b-1: Time for switching light display PAdemand = ('req', 'mean', (10, 'ms'))
t22c-1: Time for reactivating credit card payment PAdemand = ('req', 'mean', (10, 'ms'))
UC3 - OrderProducts
arr-3: Order arrival rate PAopenLoad.PAoccurrence = ('unbounded', ('exponential', 1, 'days'))
n3-1: Number of all products 5000
n3-2: Number of products running out of stock ('assm', 'dist', ('histogram', 100, 0.25, 200, 0.25, 300, 0.25, 400, 0.25, 500 '#Goods out of stock'))
p3-1: Percentage of out of stock products being reordered 0.98
t31-1: Time until showing the lists of all products and missing products PAdemand = ('req', 'mean', (10, 'ms'))
t32-1: Time for choosing the products to order and entering the amount PAdemand = ('assm', 'mean', (10, 's'))

Table 1. (*continued*)

t33-1: Time for pressing button "Order"   PAdemand = ('assm', 'mean', (1, 's'))
t34-1: Time for querying the inventory data store   PAdemand = ('req', 'mean', (20, 'ms'))
t34-2: Time for creating a new order entry   PAdemand = ('req', 'mean', (10, 'ms'))
t34-3: Time for creating a new product order   PAdemand = ('req', 'mean', (10, 'ms'))
UC4 - Receive Ordered Products
arr-4: Order arrival rate   PAopenLoad.PAoccurrence = ('unbounded', ('exponential', 1, 'days'))
n-4: Number of products arriving   ('assm', 'dist', ('histogram', 100, 0.25, 200, 0.25, 300, 0.25, 400, 0.25, 500   '#Goods arriving'))
p4-1: Probability of complete and correct order   0.99
p4-2: Probability of incomplete or incorrect order   0.01
t42-1: Time for checking completeness of order   PAdemand = ('assm', 'mean', (30, 'min'))
t43-1: Time for pressing button "Roll in received order"   PAdemand = ('assm', 'mean', (1, 's'))
t44-1: Time for updating the inventory   PAdemand = ('assm', 'mean', (100, 'ms'))
UC5 - Show Stock Reports
arr-5: Show Stock Reports arrival rate   PAopenLoad.PAoccurrence = ('unbounded', ('exponential', 3, 'hr'))
t51-1: Time for entering store id and pressing button "Create Report"   PAdemand = ('assm', 'mean', (1, 's'))
t52-1: Time for generating the report   PAdemand = ('req', 'mean', (0.5, 's'))
UC6 - Show Delivery Reports
arr-6: Show Delivery Reports arrival rate   PAopenLoad.PAoccurrence = ('unbounded', ('exponential', 1, 'days'))
t61-1: Time for entering store id and pressing button "Create Report"   PAdemand = ('assm', 'mean', (1, 's'))
t62-1: Time for generating the report   PAdemand = ('req', 'mean', (0.5, 's'))

Table 1. (*continued*)

UC7 - Change Price
arr-7: Change Price arrival rate PAopenLoad.PAoccurrence = ('unbounded', ('exponential', 3, 'hr'))
t71-1: Time for generating the overview PAdemand = ('req', 'mean', (10, 'ms'))
t72-1: Time for selecting a product item PAdemand = ('assm', 'mean', (5, 's'))
t72-2: Time for changing the sales price PAdemand = ('assm', 'mean', (5, 's'))
t73-1: Time for pressing button "Enter" PAdemand = ('assm', 'mean', (1, 's'))

UC8 - Product Exchange
arr-8: Show Stock Reports arrival rate PAopenLoad.PAoccurrence = ('unbounded', ('exponential', 1, 'days'))
n8-1: Number of stores nearby for a store server ('assm', 'dist', ('histogram', 10, 0.7, 20, 0.3, 30 '#Shops nearby'))
p8-1: Probability of failure on demand (enterprise server) 0.0001
p8-2: Probability of failure on demand (store server) 0.001
t82-1: Time for store server to detect low stock PAdemand = ('req', 'mean', (10, 'ms'))
t83-1: Time for store server to query enterprise server PAdemand = ('assm', 'dist', ('histogram', 0.0, 0.5, 0.5, 0.5, 1.0, 's'))
t84-1: Time for enterprise server to query one store server PAdemand = ('assm', 'dist', ('histogram', 0.0, 0.5, 0.5, 0.5, 1.0, 's'))
t84-2: Time for flushing the cache of one store server and returning the result PAdemand = ('assm', 'dist', ('histogram', 0.0, 0.5, 0.5, 0.5, 1.0, 's'))
t85-1: Time for database lookup at enterprise server PAdemand = ('req', 'mean', (10, 'ms'))
t86-1: Time for determining which store to deliver from PAdemand = ('req', 'mean', (1, 's'))
t87-1: Time for returning the result to the store server PAdemand = ('assm', 'dist', ('histogram', 0.0, 0.5, 0.5, 0.5, 1.0, 's'))
t87-2: Time for marking goods as incoming at store server PAdemand = ('req', 'mean', (10, 'ms'))
t88-1: Time for sending delivery request to store server PAdemand = ('assm', 'dist', ('histogram', 0.0, 0.5, 0.5, 0.5, 1.0, 's'))
t88-2: Time for marking good as unavailable PAdemand = ('req', 'mean', (10, 'ms'))

The extra-functional properties map to certain steps in the use cases and have labels to illustrate the relationship (e.g., t12-3 stands for "use case 1 step 2, time no. 3"). As a notation for the values, we have used the tagged value language from the OMG UML Profile for Schedulability, Performance, and Time [2]. We have used the tags `PAperfValue` [2, p.7-21] for timing values and `RTarrivalPattern` [2, p.4-35] for customer arrival rates, as they allow a fine-grained specification of probability distributions. Note for histogram specifications: "The histogram distribution has an ordered collection of one or more pairs that identify the start of an interval and the probability that applies within that interval (starting from the leftmost interval) and one end-interval value for the upper boundary of the last interval" [2, p.4-34].

The values in the table are either *assumed* ('assm') by us or *required* ('req') from the system as part of the specification. We estimated most of the values based on statistics for typical German super markets, and our own experience. The values should be understood as guiding values and should not restrict Co-CoME modelers from using their own extra-functional properties for CoCoME.

3.4   Architectural Component Model

In this section, the architecture of the *Trading System* is described in more detail using UML 2.0 ([2]) with additional own notations like multiplicities at ports. After an overview of the structure of the system which introduces single parts, like interfaces and connections between them, an overview of the behavior is given. To show the structure the single components beginning with the topmost, namely the component Trading System, and going on with the inner, more detailed components are beheld. For every use case the behavior of the system is visualized by sequence diagrams. Additional, a prototype of the system was implemented. As far as the real subject is meant, the name of it is written separately. The names of software components are written in one word.

Structural View on the Trading System. The structure of the Trading System is designed to integrate an embedded system based on a bus-architecture and an information system based on a layered architecture. Figure 5 shows the super-component Trading System and the two components *Inventory* and *CashDeskLine* Trading System consists of.

The information system is represented by the component Inventory, while the component CashDeskLine represents the embedded system. For each instance of Trading System exists respectively one instance of Inventory and CashDeskLine which is indicated by the number in the upper left of the components. Also visible is the fact that the communication between the components CashDeskLine and Inventory is handled by the interfaces *CashDeskConnectorIf* and *SaleRegistere-dEvent*. The interface CashDeskConnectorIf defines a method for getting product information like description and price using the product bar code. Events like starting a new sale are registered at an asynchronous event channel. To handle these events the event SaleRegisteredEvent is used. Furthermore, CashDeskLine is connected to the bank via an interface *BankIf* in order to handle the card payment.

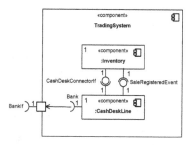

Fig. 5. Trading System and its two components Inventory and CashDeskLine

Structural View on the Component Inventory. As already mentioned, the component Inventory represents the information system and is organized as a layered architecture. As shown in figure 6, these layers are *GUI*, *Application* and *Data* which are completed by a component *Database*.

For each instance of Inventory exists only one instance of the component Database where all data is stored. Because of the case having only one instance of Inventory in TradingSystem there in all exists only one instance of Database per instance of TradingSystem. The component Data representing the data layer of a classical three-layer-architecture hides details of the database and provides data access to the application layer represented by the component Application. The communication between the components Database and Data is managed by JDBC ([3]) in connection with Hibernate ([4]), an implementation of the Java Persistence API ([5]).

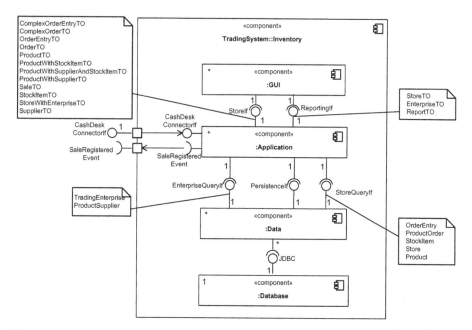

Fig. 6. The inner structure of the component Inventory. The notes show the data types which are relevant for the corresponding interface.

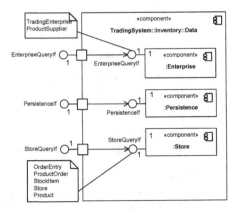

Fig. 7. The inner structure of the data layer of the component Inventory

The component Data provides the three interfaces *EnterpriseQueryIf, Store-QueryIf* and *PersistenceIf*. To get a persistence context the interface PersistenceIf offers an appropriate method. The interface EnterpriseQueryIf contains queries like the mean time to delivery by taking all stores of an enterprise into account. StoreQueryIf defines methods required at a Store like changing the sales price of a product or managing the Inventory.

The component Application contains the application logic. It uses the interfaces defined by the component Data in order to send queries or changes to the database and provides the interfaces *StoreIf* and *ReportingIf* to deliver results of database queries to the component GUI. Between the components Application and Data object-oriented interfaces and between Application and GUI services-oriented interfaces are used (EnterpriseQueryIf and StoreQueryIf respectively StoreIf and ReportingIf). As it is determined as a property of a service-oriented interfaces via the interfaces between Application and GUI no references are passed. Instead, so called *Transfer Objects (TO)* are defined which are used for the data transfer. The component Application itself has references on data objects located in the component Data in order to receive required data.

Data Layer. Figure 7 shows an overview of the component Data with its three subcomponents *Enterprise, Store* and *Persistence*. These components implement the similar named interfaces EnterpriseQueryIf, PersistenceIf and StoreQueryIf. In figure 7 the various data types the interfaces deal with are shown as notes whereas figure 8 gives a more detailed overview of the data model with attributes and possible navigation paths.

Application Layer. The component Application representing the application layer consists of the three components *Reporting, Store* and *ProductDispatcher* as shown in figure 9. The component Reporting implements the interface ReportingIf whereas the component Store implements the interfaces CashDeskConnectorIf and StoreIf. It also requires the interfaces SaleRegisteredEvent and ProductDispatcherIf. The latter defines a method for the Enterprise Server to search for a product at another Store.

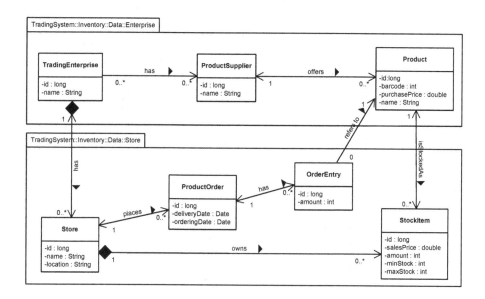

Fig. 8. The data model of the TradingSystem

While the communication between Data and Application is realized by passing references of persistent objects to the Application, the Application uses PoJOs (Plain old Java Objects) or Transfer Objects (TO) to pass information to the GUI and to the CashDeskLine. An overview of all Transfer Objects and their relation between each other is shown in figure 10.

GUI Layer. As shown in figure 11 the component GUI has the two subcomponents *Reporting* and *store.* The component Reporting implements the visualization of various kinds of reports using the interface ReportingIf to get the data. Whereas the component Store offers the user interface for the Store Manager in order to do managing tasks like ordering products or changing the sale prices.

Structural View on the Component CashDeskLine. The component *Cash DeskLine* represents the embedded part. It is responsible for managing all Cash Desks, their hardware, and the interaction between Cash Desks and between the devices connected with each Cash Desk. The main communication is done using events which are sent through event channels.

Figure 12 gives an overview of the structure of the component CashDeskLine. It is shown that CashDeskLine consists of several instances of CashDesk and a component *EventBus* which manages two instances of *EventChannel*, namely *cash DeskChannel* and *extCommChannel* which are shared by all instances of CashDesk. The channel cashDeskChannel is used by the CashDesk to enable communication between all device controllers which are connected to a CashDesk, like *CashDesk Application, LightDisplayController* or *CashDeskGUI.* Each controller itself is connected to the according hardware device and so builds the bridge between the

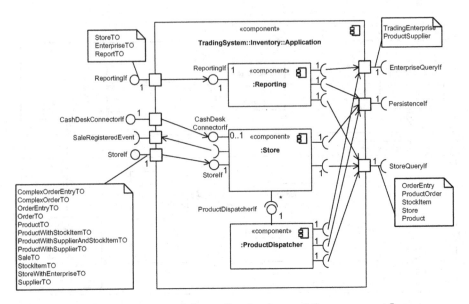

Fig. 9. The inner structure of the application layer of the component Inventory

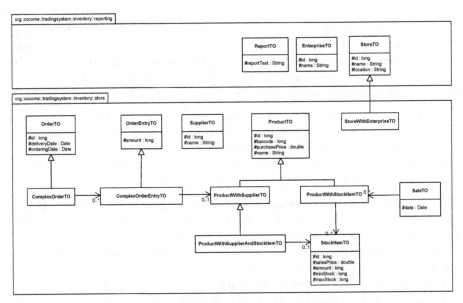

Fig. 10. The transfer objects used for data exchange between the application layer and the GUI layer

hardware and the middleware. The channel extCommChannel is used by the component CashDeskApplication to write the information about completed sales into the Inventory. Additionally, this channel is used for the communication between the components *Coordinator* and CashDesk. The Coordinator itself is responsible for dealing with managing express checkouts, whereas its task is to decide if a Cash Desk has to be switched into express mode (see use case 2).

As shown in figure 12, the component CashDeskApplication requires the interface *CashDeskConnectorIf*. This interface is provided by the component Inventory and is used to get the product description and sales price by transferring the bar code of a product. These information are required during the scanning of product items the customer wants to buy (see use case 1).

Figure 13 shows again the components CashDesk consists of and, in addition, the events each component sends and for which types of events each component is registered at the channel. The semicircles indicate events the component can handle while the circles indicate events which are sent by the component. For example, the controller *CardReaderController* handles the event *ExpressModeEnabledEvent* while sending the events *CreditCardScannedEvent* and *PINEnteredEvent*.

Deployment View on the Trading System

The deployment view of the Trading System zooms in on which devices are considered and where the different components are instantiated. Each Cash Desk is linked to an own Cash Desk PC. This Cash Desk PC is connected to several devices like Bar Code Scanner or Card Reader. The controllers of these devices run on the component *CashDeskPC* as well as all other subcomponents of the component CashDesk shown in figure 14. Furthermore, on each CashDeskPC an event channel is established which is used for the communication between the peripheral devices.

In each Store exists one Store Server to which all Cash Desk PCs in this Store are connected. At the component StoreServer the four components Coordinator, extCommChannel, Application and Data and their subcomponents are located. The first two components were presented in the section before and are responsible for managing the express checkout respectively for the communication. The component Data representing the data layer is connected via JDBC to the component Database which is placed at the component EnterpriseServer. Representing the application layer the component Application is communicating with the component Inventory::GUI deployed at the component *StoreClient*. In addition to the component Database, the component Data and the component Reporting

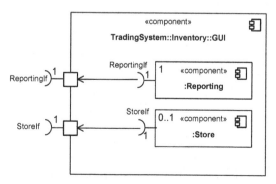

Fig. 11. The inner structure of the GUI layer of the component Inventory

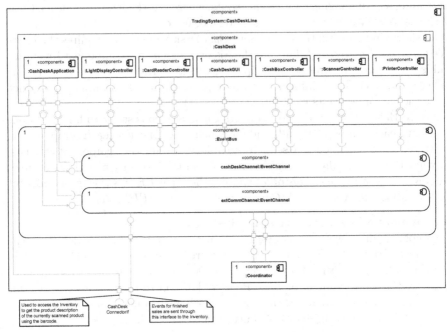

Fig. 12. The inner structure of the component CashDeskLine

are deployed at EnterpriseServer. The component Data is also connected to the component Database.

Behavioral View on the Trading System

This section provides a more detailed view of the realization of each use case introduced before by using UML 2.0 sequence diagrams which show the interaction between actors and components. First an important notation aspect is pointed out because of changes in the notation for sequence diagrams in UML 2.0. This

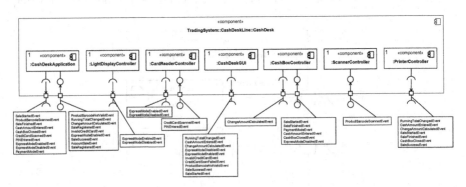

Fig. 13. A more detailed view on the component CashDesk and its published and subscribed events

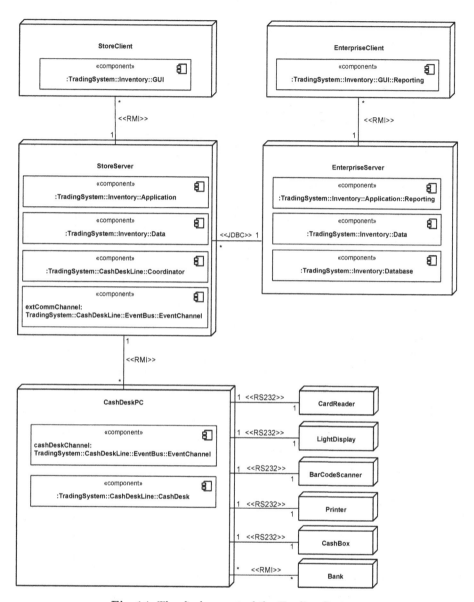

Fig. 14. The deployment of the Trading System

considers the notation for synchronous and asynchronous method calls where synchronous method calls are depicted using filled arrowheads, compared to asynchronous method calls which are depicted using unfilled arrowheads.

Behavioral View on UC 1 - Process Sale. The sequence diagrams in figures 15, 16 and 17 show the sale process including the communication between the various involved components. The sale process starts when the Cashier presses the

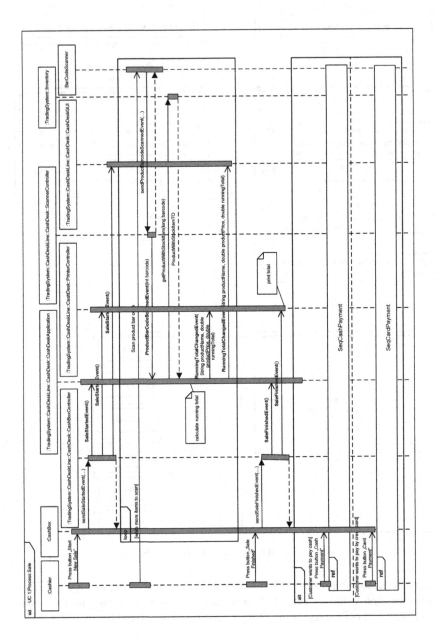

Fig. 15. Sequence diagram of the main sale process (UC 1)

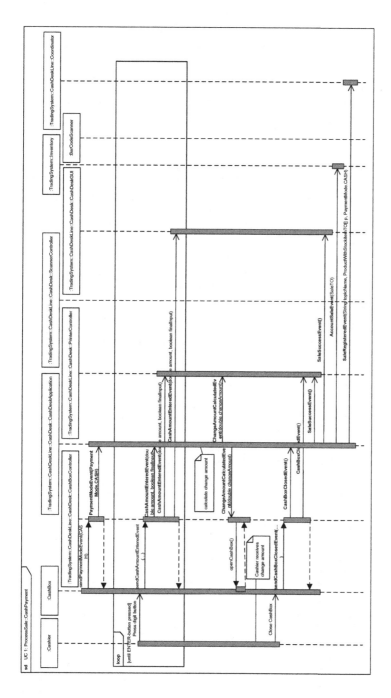

Fig. 16. Sequence diagram of the process of cash payment (UC 1)

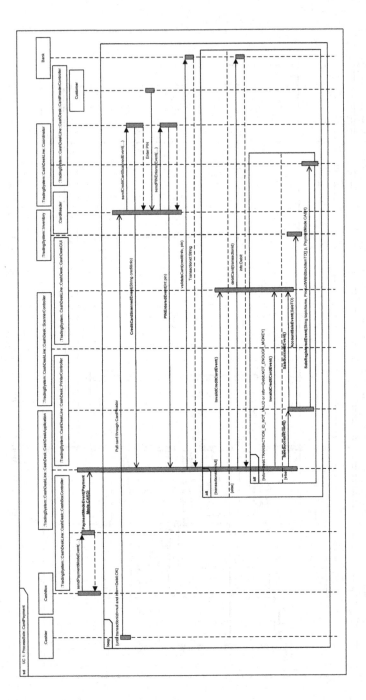

Fig. 17. Sequence diagram of the process of card payment (UC 1)

button *Start Sale* at his Cash Box. Then the corresponding software component CashBox calls a method at the component CashBoxController which publishes the *SaleStartedEvent* using the *cashDesk Channel* (compare figure 12). The three components CashDeskApplication, PrinterController and CashDeskGUI react to events of the kind SaleStartedEvent. In order to receive these they have to register themselves at the channel cashDesk Channel for these events and implement the according event handlers. These event handlers are called by the messaging middleware which JMS ([6]) is in the implementation of the prototype. At the Cash Desk the Printer starts printing the header of the receipt initiated by the component PrinterController and initiated by the component CashDeskGUI a text at the Cash Desk indicates the start of a new sale. Some components connected with the channel cashDeskChannel implement a finite state machine, like CashDesk Application or PrinterController in order to react appropriately on further incoming events. In the next phase of the selling process the desired products are identified using the Bar Code Scanner which submitts the data to the corresponding controller *ScannerController* which in turn publishes the event *ProductBarCode ScannedEvent*. The component CashDeskApplication gets the product description from the Inventory and calculates the running total and announces it on the channel. After finishing the scanning process, the Cashier presses the button *Sale Finished* at the Cash Box. Now the Cashier can choose the payment method based on the decision of the costumer by pressing the button *Cash Payment* or *Card Payment* at his Cash Desk.

Figure 16 and 17 illustrate the sequences for each payment method which shall not described in detail here.

Behavioral View on UC 2 - Manage Express Checkout. The basic idea behind the process of managing express checkouts is to hold a statistic about sales using the component *Coordinator*. If the condition for an express checkout is fulfilled, the Coordinator releases the event *ExpressModeEnabledEvent and due* to this a Cash Desk will change into express mode. The Cashier is allowed to decide to switch back into normal mode by simply pressing the button *Disable Express Mode* at his Cash Desk. This causes the event *ExpressModeDisabledEvent* which forces the devices to switch back into normal mode. The sequence diagram in figure 18 shows the described process in more detail.

Behavioral View on UC 3 - Order Products. This use case deals with ordering products from a supplier if they are running out of stock at a store. To initiate an order, the Store Manager can select the products which have to be ordered in the desired amount and then presses the button *Order* at the Store-GUI. As result of this use case the Store Manager gets a set of order identifiers. Not only one identifier is returned, because one order can be split and placed at different suppliers. These identifiers are used by the Stock Manager in use case 4 while receiving and accounting the products. Figure 19 shows the sequence diagram of this process with more details.

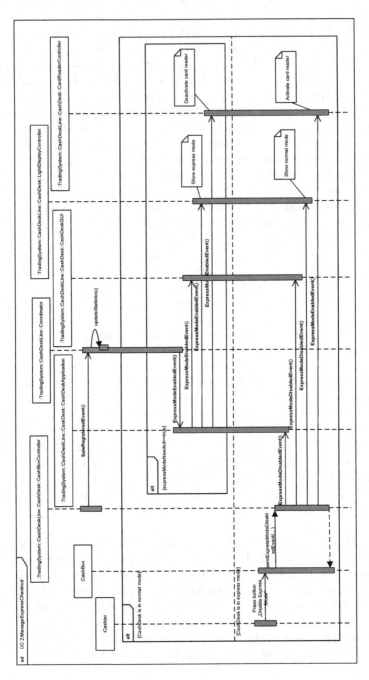

Fig. 18. Sequence diagram of managing the express checkout functionality (UC 2)

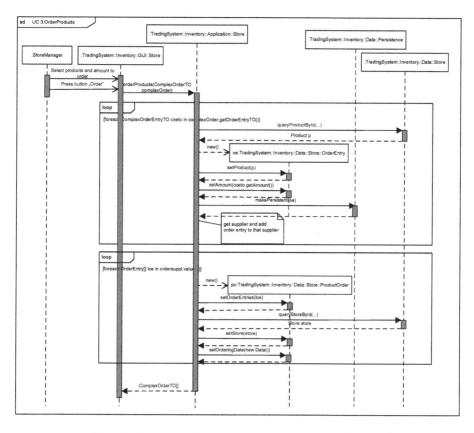

Fig. 19. Sequence diagram of ordering products (UC 3)

Behavioral View on UC 4 - Receive Ordered Products. If the Stock Manager has ordered products, they will arrive at the Store. To roll in the product items the StockManager enters the order identifier assigned during ordering and presses the button *Roll in received order*. This results in system actions like setting the order's delivery date and rising the amount of the stored products as it can be tracked in the sequence diagram in figure 20.

Behavioral View on UC 5 - Show Stock Reports. If the Store Manager wants to see if products are running out of stock in his store, he can get the according information using the component *GUI::Reporting*. The Store Manager therefore simply enters the store identifier and presses the button *Create Report*. Then the method *getStockReport()* is called at the component *Application::Reporting* which itself accesses the data layer component *Data::Store* in order to get the required information and to create the report as depicted in figure 21. The result is a object *ReportTO* which is then sent to the component GUI::Reporting and shown to the Store Manager at the GUI.

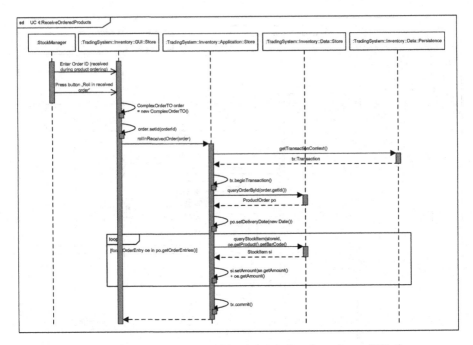

Fig. 20. Sequence diagram of receiving ordered products (UC 4)

Behavioral View on UC 6 - Show Delivery Reports. This use case is very similar to use case 5 but in this case the Enterprise Manager wants to know the mean time to the delivery of certain products. The Enterprise Manager therefore enters an enterprise identifier and presses the button *Create Report*. As depicted in figure 22 this report is created using the data layer component *Data::Enterprise* to get the required information.

Behavioral View on UC 7 - Change Price. The Store Manager is able to change the sales price using the Store GUI at the Enterprise Client. Therefor the Store Manager simply selects the desired product and changes the price in the shown table. After pressing *Enter*, the new price will persistently be written into the database as described in figure 23.

Behavioral View on UC 8 - Product Exchange among Stores. The main aspect of use case 8 is a more complex interaction of distributed components and servers. If the stock of a certain product or a number of products of a Store runs low, the application Inventory of the Store Server can start a request for that product. The component ProductDispatcher of the application running on the Enterprise Server initiates a cache flush of all Store Servers to update the central database at the Enterprise Server with the latest stock data of all Stores. The component ProductDispatcher is also responsible for calculating an optimal solution for transporting the required products from a number of Stores to the

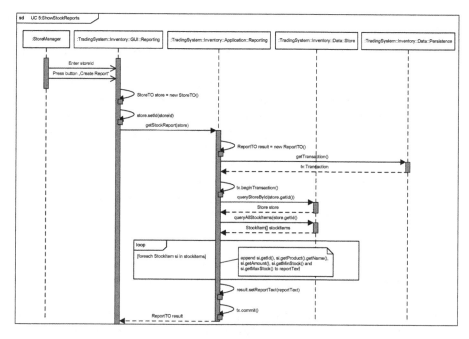

Fig. 21. Sequence diagram of getting stock reports (UC 5)

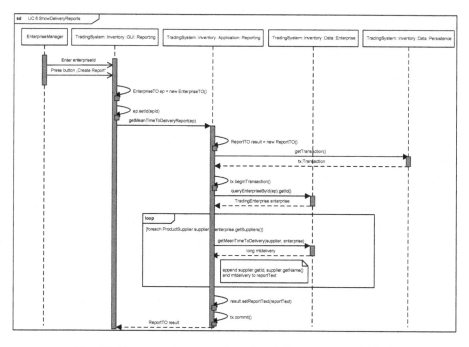

Fig. 22. Sequence diagram of getting delivery reports (UC 6)

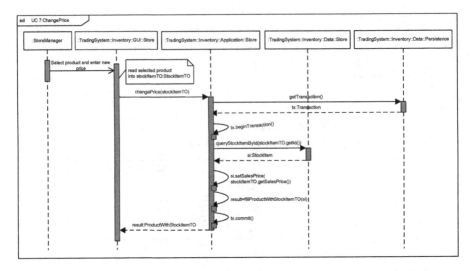

Fig. 23. Sequence diagram of changing the sales price of a product (UC 7)

requesting Store. To determine the optimal solution only the stocks of Stores are searched which are chosen by a heuristic for effort and costs. If a cost-effective solution is found, the transportation of the required goods is initiated and the requesting Store is informed about the results of its query. The sequence diagram in Figure 24 gives an overview on the dynamics in use case 8.

3.5 Implementation

In this section some important implementation aspects are briefly introduced. This includes the code design and structure as well as some hints for how to start the prototype of the Trading System.

Design

The code follows a specific structure in order to identify software components easily. A component is mapped to a Java package. The interfaces a component supports is located in that package. The implementation classes of the interfaces are located in a subpackage called *impl*. In that way the diagrams presented in this chapter can be mapped to their corresponding code in the implementation of the Trading System.

How to Start the Trading System?

The prototype can be started using Ant ([7]). The required targets are located in a file named build.xml. Furthermore a configuration file tradingsystem.properties exists where, for example, the number of Stores or Clients can be maintained. Further and detailed information can be found in the file readme.txt and in the code comments.

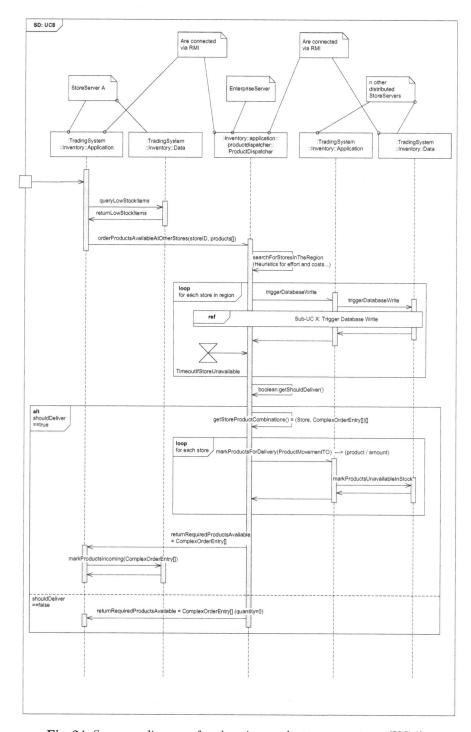

Fig. 24. Sequence diagram of exchanging products among stores (UC 8)

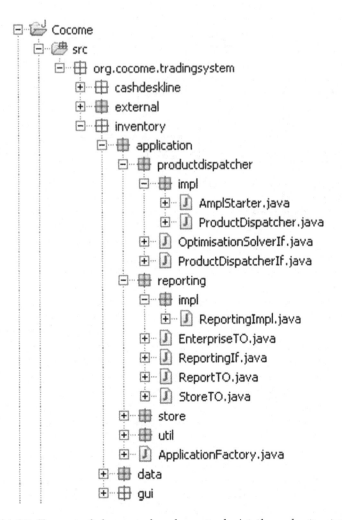

Fig. 25. Excerpt of classes and packages to depict the code structure

3.6   System Tests

In this section an overview of the system testing framework for the Trading System is given. The system tests are intended to be used in two ways: First to further detail certain aspects of the system and second to allow the different modeling teams to test their resulting implementation with a common set of (preferably automated) tests.

Test Architecture and Organisation

For a precise specification of the test scenarios and an easy way for automation of test execution it was decided to write the test cases using the *Java* programming

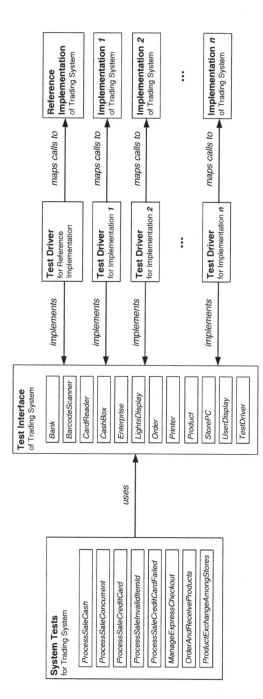

Fig. 26. Architecture of the system testing framework

language and the *JUnit* ([8]) testing framework as far as possible. Even when specifying the test scenarios in Java these were specified using self-explanatory identifiers and method names thus the test scenarios are also easily human readably and understandable.

Not for all of the before described use cases it was considered useful to specify a precise test scenario. Where the test conditions are not described detailed enough to judge the outcome of a test programmatically, an informal textual test script is provided instead.

The provided testing framework consists of different layers as shown in figure 26. The system tests use a common testing interface. This interface is implemented by test drivers for each implementation. The test drivers map the calls from the tests to the respective implementation.

To enable reusing the tests for several implementations of the same system, the test scenarios are implemented only against a set of interfaces describing the interactions of the Trading System with its environment. For example there is an Interface for the *Bar Code Scanner* defining a `scanBarcode` method, which is used for simulating the scanning of a product's bar code, while the interface for the *user display* provides a `isPriceShown` method which is used to check if the correct price is actually presented to the customer.

The link to the system's implementation is built by an implementation-specific test driver implementing these interfaces and mapping all interface calls to corresponding system actions. This configuration allows the tests to work with unknown realizations of the system, as the knowledge about the actual implementation (which messages to send and how to identify the current state) is encapsulated in the test driver, which in turn needs to be adapted to the used implementation. Thus if the resulting implementation of a participating team should be tested, only an appropriate test driver is required, *i.e.*, a suitable implementation of the test interfaces. The specified test scenarios will remain unchanged and may potentially be executed against any trading system implementation.

As a proof-of-concept a test driver for the reference implementation of the trading system is provided. Further details on the testing system and how to write a specific test driver may be found in the corresponding source code and the *JavaDoc* documentation which comes with the source code.

Test Scenarios

The single test scenarios are based on the description of the use cases of the trading system. It was not intended to fulfill any coverage criteria or completeness in testing but rather to give examples of how such tests could look like and to provide a formalization of the use cases.

Basically there are two kinds of test scenarios: Formally described test cases written as executable Java test classes and informal descriptions of tests. The choice of the representation of a test case depends on the kind of use case.

The use cases consisting of a sequence of executions steps with a defined result are given as Java test classes using the test interfaces. These test cases could be executed automatically (by means of *JUnit*) for a specific implementation. However, the source code of these tests can also be interpreted as a formalized test plan which could be followed manually. The remaining use cases which were not explicit enough but mainly set up a requirement for an entire piece of functionality (such as use case 5) were treated by describing the test case informally. Test cases of this form are intended to be checked manually. In table 2 the pass and fail conditions for these tests are specified.

Table 2 describes the single test cases. It states from which use case the test is derived and labels each test case with an identifier (this refers to the respective Java class of the test). For the test cases specified in Java a short description of the scenario is given. For details the reader may consult the source code of the test scenarios. For the informal stated test cases the pass and fail criteria are given instead.

Table 2. Test Scenarios for Trading System

Use Case	Test Case Id	Type	Description
1	ProcessSaleCash	Java	Purchase of some goods and cash payment, no exceptions.
1	ProcessSale Concurrent	Java	Concurrent purchase of some goods at n different cash desks, no exceptions.
1	ProcessSale CreditCard	Java	Purchase of some goods and credit card payment, no exceptions.
1	ProcessSale InvalidItemId	Java	Invalid item id read, manual entry of item id. (Exception in step 3 of use case 1)
1	ProcessSale CreditCardFailed	Java	Wrong PIN entry for credit card; card validation fails. (Exception in step 5.2 of use case 1)
2	ManageExpress Checkout	Java	System switches to express mode. Express mode is shown at cash desk, credit card payment not possible.

Table 2. (*continued*)

Use Case	Test Case Id	Type	Description
3	ShowProducts ForOrdering	infor- mal	Store shall provide functionality to generate a report about products which are low on stock. **Test:** Check if System offers functionality for reporting products low on stock. **PASS:** Generation of report with products low on stock possible **FAIL:** Generation of report with products low on stock NOT possible
3, 4	OrderAnd ReceiveProducts	Java	Products low on stock will be ordered and correct delivery will be recorded in the inventory.
5	ShowStockReports	infor- mal	System shall provide functionality to present a report including all available stock items in store or a report of cumulated available product items of a specified enterprise. **Test:** Check if System offers functionality for generation of stock reports **PASS:** Generation of stock reports possible **FAIL:** Generation of stock reports NOT possible
6	ShowDeliveryRe- ports	infor- mal	System shall provide functionality to present a report showing mean time to delivery for each supplier of a specific enterprise. **Test:** Check if System offers functionality for generation of a delivery report **PASS:** Generation of delivery report possible **FAIL:** Generation of delivery report NOT possible

Table 2. (*continued*)

Use Case	Test Case Id	Type	Description
7	ChangePrice	infor-mal	System shall provide functionality to change sales price of a product. **Test:** Check if System offers functionality for change sales price of a product **PASS:** Change of sales price for product item possible **FAIL:** Change of sales price for product item NOT possible
8	ProductExchange AmongStores	Java	After a sale which leads to a product being low on stock of the store, product exchange between stores should take place.

References

1. Larman, C.: Applying UML and Patterns: An Introduction to Object-Oriented Analysis and Design and Iterative Development, 3rd edn. Prentice-Hall, Englewood Cliffs (2004)
2. OMG, Object Management Group: UML Profile for Schedulability, Performance and Time (2005), http://www.omg.org/cgi-bin/doc?formal/2005-01-02
3. SUN Microsystems: The Java Database Connectivity (JDBC), http://java.sun.com/javase/technologies/database/index.jsp
4. JBoss (Red Hat Middleware): Hibernate, http://www.hibernate.org
5. SUN Microsystems: Java Persistence API, http://java.sun.com/javaee/technologies/persistence.jsp
6. SUN Microsystems: Java Message Service, http://java.sun.com/products/jms/
7. Apache: The Apache Ant Project, http://ant.apache.org
8. JUnit: JUnit, http://www.junit.org

4 Modeling Components and Component-Based Systems in KobrA

Colin Atkinson, Philipp Bostan, Daniel Brenner, Giovanni Falcone,
Matthias Gutheil, Oliver Hummel, Monika Juhasz, and Dietmar Stoll

University of Mannheim, Germany

4.1 Introduction

In this chapter we present a version of the Trading System case study modeled
according to the KobrA approach. KobrA is a UML-based method for describing
components and component-based systems developed at the Fraunhofer Institute for Experimental Software Engineering at the beginning of the decade. The
acronym stands for the term "Komponenten basierte Anwendungsentwicklung" –
German for "Component-based Application Development". KobrA has been successfully used by a number of companies in industrial settings and has given rise
to numerous specializations and offshoots (e.g. MARMOT [1] and MORABIT
[2]). The original version of the method [3] was developed for the UML 1.x flavor of the UML, but in this chapter we introduce an updated version optimized
for use with the 2.x versions of the UML [4] and its related standards such as
OCL [5]. KobrA also provides support for other advanced software engineering
approaches such as product-lines, but these are beyond the scope of this chapter.
Here we focus on the component-modeling aspects of the method.

4.1.1 Goals and Scope of the Component Model

KobrA's approach to component modeling is based on the recognition that (a)
components are fundamentally systems in their own right and thus can be described using the full spectrum of UML features and diagram types, and that
(b) component-based systems are essentially hierarchic and should ideally be
described in a way that brings out and reinforces their inherent hierarchical
composition. In KobrA, therefore, any "behavior rich" object that offers a well-
defined set of services (i.e. operations) can be regarded as a component. By
"behavior rich" we mean objects whose behavior is complex enough to warrant
"design" in the traditional sense of software engineering. Thus, large objects
such as systems and subsystems are natural KobrA components, but smaller
objects such as repositories and complex data structure can also be viewed as
components if they are complex enough to need a design. Simple data structures or information records are not usually viewed as components since their
implementation as classes or database schemata is usually straightforward.

The basic goal of KobrA is to allow the design of a complex system (i.e.
a component) to be split into separate parts (i.e. components) which can be

A. Rausch et al. (Eds.): Common Component Modeling Example, LNCS 5153, pp. 54–84, 2008.
© Springer-Verlag Berlin Heidelberg 2008

tackled separately. Two basic notions of composition are used to this end – a dynamic (i.e. run-time) one and a static (i.e. development time) one. The run-time one captures the core idea of a hierarchically structured system which forwards requests to one or more black-box components. These may be internal components (i.e. parts) of the system or external peers. The development time concept of composition captures the idea of definitional containment (similar to packages). In other words, it allows the design of a component (e.g. the system) to be broken down into the design of multiple parts. KobrA's dynamic form of composition essentially corresponds to that used in the UML's component model, while the static form resembles that supported in the UML's traditional view of subsystems. These two forms of composition are clearly related, and in KobrA the intention is that they should be "aligned".

KobrA was originally devised as a way of "dividing" the effort of designing a large system into smaller parts that could be "conquered" separately, and where necessary by further dividing these into smaller parts and conquering them separately in a recursive way. As a consequence, it separates the description of a component into a specification – which describes what a component does – and a realization – which describes how it does it in terms of interactions with other components. In a general sense, the specification of a component represents its interface (or the service that it offers) and the realization represents its design. The UML is the language used to describe the specification and realization of components since this is the language most commonly used to model requirements and designs in mainstream development. However, this is just a pragmatic choice. Other languages can be used instead if preferred. Moreover, it is possible to apply the UML and its associated languages to varying levels of precision. If the goal is simply to create a visual design of components, the UML can be used informally. However, if the goal is to reason and prove properties about the system, the UML can be used in a more formal style by capturing some of the models (e.g. functional models) in OCL and by augmenting other models with OCL constraints. Since some of the diagrams in the new version of the UML [4] now have precise semantics (e.g. state diagrams), and OCL can be used to remove any remaining ambiguity, KobrA models can provide the foundation for several forms of automated verification. KobrA also has a concrete set of consistency rule which can be used to check that component specifications and realizations are well formed, although the automated verification of consistency and system properties has not traditionally been a focus of the approach.

KobrA focuses on describing the architecture of components and component-based systems at the design level. In modern MDA (Model Driven Architecture) [6] terminology, this means that KobrA captures components at the level of a Platform Independent Model (PIM). It does this by modeling the interface (or services) supported by components (specifications) and how they are realized through interactions with other components (realizations). The mapping of component models to executable code and the deployment of physical components to nodes in a network are inherently separated from the description of application logic, but they are not dealt with explicitly in KobrA. Neither is the mapping of the design models to executable code. However, since it applies UML as a design language, KobrA allows the automatic implementation capabilities of mainstream UML tools to be used in the usual way. With the greater precision now available in most UML diagrams and the possibility of augmenting them with OCL constraints, KobrA also provides the foundation for more formal mappings between component models and implementations.

4.1.2   Modeled Cutout of CoCoME

Since KobrA is not a formal language, but rather a set of principles for using mainstream modeling language to describe and break down the design of a complex system in a component-based way, it is not possible to concretely state what KobrA can and cannot handle. There is a certain degree of flexibility in the way that the KobrA principles can be applied, and anything that conforms to these principles can in practice be accommodated within the method. In other words, because KobrA is built on mainstream modeling languages and principles, anything that is not explicitly handled in the official KobrA documentation, such as how to map components to code or how to deploy them, can be performed using mainstream tools and practices.

The aspects of the CoCoME which KobrA handles well are the PIM-level (i.e. design level) modeling of a component-based system's properties, architecture and components. The KobrA incarnation of the CoCoME therefore focuses on describing the logical properties of the components in the case study from three fundamental viewpoints (functional, structural and behavioral). The KobrA version of the CoCoME faithfully represented the externally (i.e. user) visible properties of the system, but does not adopt the original decomposition of the system where this does not fit with KobrA's principles. As a result, many of the smaller components in the KobrA version are the same as in the original design, but some of the intermediate scale components have been omitted. None of the issues related to quality of service, implementation, testing or deployment are addressed in the KobrA version.

By far the biggest practice obstacle to the use of KobrA at the present time is that lack of a dedicated tool that "understands" KobrA and is able to ensure that the UML is applied in a KobrA-compliant way. As a result, the generation of all the different viewpoints required in KobrA currently has to be performed by hand, which is a tedious process. However, we hope to provide tool support for KobrA in the near future.

4.1.3   Benefit of the Modeling

Because KobrA is a design method, the benefits derived from KobrA are the same as those derived from any platform independent design activity. These include the ability to experiment with potential designs before committing to concrete implementations, the availability of easy-to-read descriptions (e.g. system specification) that can be understood by (and discussed with) customers and users, the availability of common designs to facilitate joint understanding amongst the members of the development team, and the creation of a platform independent record of the system structure and project design decisions.

The advantages of applying the UML in the style of KobrA rather than another method are threefold. Firstly, KobrA encourages the benefits of "divide and conquer" at the design level by breaking the overall system into parts (components) and allowing the design of larger components (and the whole system) to ignore the designs of their sub-components. Secondly, KobrA greatly reduces the complexity of individual diagrams by dividing the full description of a component's specification or realization into several separate, but well-defined, views. In other words, the method provides a natural mechanism for breaking down the "description" of a complex system, not just its logical structure, into separate, manageable views. Thirdly, KobrA is highly prescriptive in its use of the UML. The KobrA method actually embodies many of the principles of agile modeling as documented by Ambler [7]. However, in contrast with agile modeling and other methods, KobrA provides concrete guidelines about how to apply these principles – that is, it explains what models should be created, what should go into the models and how they should be related.

The benefits of using UML/OCL to model components in the style of KobrA over the use of another more formal language are also twofold. First, UML is a mainstream notation which can be used with any established development practice where appropriate. Second, when supported by a method like KobrA, the UML offers a customizable level of formality (or precision). It can be used in the informal style supported by most development methods. However, when supported by OCL, it can be used in a more formal style to create precise and unambiguous representations of components. When used in thus way, the creation of executable, platform specific images of the components can be automated, and rather than being "just a design", the models become the primary representations of components.

4.1.4   Effort and Lessons Learned

Modeling the CoCoME reinforced the fact that applying KobrA without a tool is highly tedious and error prone. The creation of the KobrA CoCoME models and associated documentation took up about 3 person months of effort. Completely implementing and testing the components using normal development practices would probably take another 1 to 1.5 person months.

The CoCoME modelling effort was beneficial because it highlighted aspects of the KobrA method which would most benefit from enhancement and concretization. This includes the specification of the non-functional and "quality of services" aspects of components, and the provision of clear guidelines on how to use KobrA in a more formal style and thus attain the benefits of automated verification and translation. The project also provided good evidence for the need for a new form of component within KobrA – the so called "virtual component". The need for virtual components was recognized in the original version of the method but was never explicitly documented. The CoCoME modelling exercise helped clarify the precise properties and role of virtual components, and they are used in several places in the KobrA solution.

4.2   Component Model

4.2.1   Separation of Development Dimensions

Engineers use a small number of mental tools to help manage the complexity of large systems and artifacts. These include **abstraction** – which filters out information that is not needed at a particular place or point of time – **composition** – which describes how a large complex artifact is made up from smaller and simpler parts – and **genericity** – which captures information across families of similar artifacts. These are found in all engineering disciplines, but in software engineering they are usually intertwined in an ad hoc and tangled manner. In particular, few software engineering methods make it clear whether different views of an artifact are related to each other through differences in abstraction, differences in location within a composition hierarchy or differences in levels of genericity, or some combination of these. Moreover, when a software engineer performs a step in a development process, it is rarely clear what changes he/she should be attempting to make with respect to these concerns.

KobrA addresses these problems by strictly separating concerns for abstraction, composition, and genericity into different development dimensions. These dimensions, illustrated in figure 1, are one of the bases for defining viewpoints and the goals of development activities.

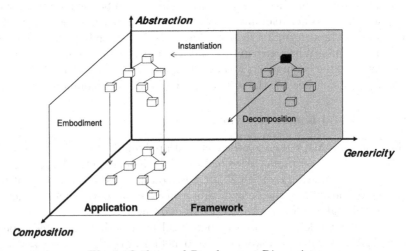

Fig. 1. Orthogonal Development Dimensions

In fact these are not the only possible development dimensions. In section 4.5 an example of another possible dimension is given.

4.2.2   Separation of Projections

The notion of documenting engineering artifacts from different viewpoints has taken hold in software engineering over recent years. However, the viewpoints and the contents of the views are generally defined in an ad hoc and unsystematic way. Their definition is also typically tangled with the other development dimensions identified above (i.e. composition, abstraction, and genericity). Thus, for example, the views used to visualize a *system* (which often constitute the root of the composition hierarchy) are usually quite different from those used to visualize simple components (at a low level in the composition hierarchy, e.g. a stack). Similarly, many more views are usually available at high levels of abstraction (e.g. in the form of UML diagrams) than at lower levels of abstraction (e.g. in the form of source code artifacts).

KobrA addresses this problem by defining and strictly separating three fundamental information projections – structural, functional, and behavioral. As illustrated in figure 2, these are orthogonal to one another, and are applied uniformly across all three development dimensions identified in the previous subsection.

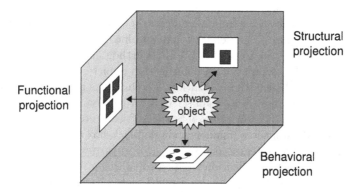

Fig. 2. Information Projections

KobrA defines various "localized" views on the system based on its principles of locality and parsimony, i.e. a view contains only the current component under consideration – the so-called subject – and its immediate environment. The properties of the subject are then described from the perspective of these three projections. In figure 2, the cloud represents the underlying component that is the current subject of development and the surfaces at right angles represent the three different projections.

The structural projection of a component describes the classes and relationships which the subject of the view is involved in and (depending on the abstraction level) its structural composition. The functional view describes the functions (i.e. operations) that the subject of a view possesses and (depending on the abstraction level) any functional decomposition that these functions participate in. The behavioral view describes the timing and algorithmic properties of the subject of the view and (depending on the abstraction level) any behavioral composition that the subject participates in.

4.2.3 Separation of Specifications and Realizations

One of the oldest "separations of concerns" principles in software engineering is
the principle of separating the description of "what" something does from the
description of "how" it does it. This should apply to components just as it does
to any other software object. KobrA refers to the former as the specification of
the component and the latter as the realization. UML 2.0 also now recognizes
the difference between the "specification level" and "realization level" representations of a component. The realization describes its internal architecture – what
it is composed of, how it makes use of other components and what internal data
structures and algorithms it uses. The specification contains the subset of the information in the realization which is intended to be externally visible to clients.
In other words, the specification defines the overall interface to the component.
It defines the interface(s) of the component in terms of the possible messages
that it can support (i.e. the lists of operation signatures that it supports), but
also contains additional behavioral, functional, and structural information. The
specification also defines the component's contracts with each of its clients.

As illustrated in figure 3, the separation of specification from realization is applied across all projections uniformly (i.e. it is orthogonal to them). In figure 3
the inner, slightly darker area of each projection depicts the specification part
while the outer area depicts the realization. The intent is to show that the specification should be thought of as a subset of, or a window onto, the realization.

The cloud in figure 3 again represents the software object under consideration. When viewed from the outside as a single black-box abstraction the entity
is regarded as a single integrated object – a **component**. In terms of UML
concepts, therefore, the specification treats a software entity as a component. In
other words, the specification provides a multi-view way of capturing the UML
notion of component. When viewed from the inside as a white box, however,
the structure of the entity, including its composition in terms of other lower
level components, is described. In terms of UML concepts, therefore, the realization treats a software entity as a **composite system**. In effect, therefore, a

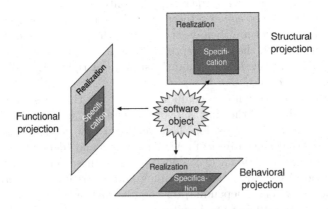

Fig. 3. Separation of Specification and Realization

specification provides a "component" view of a system or a subsystem while a realization provides a "composite system" view of them.

4.2.4   Separation of Process and Product

The fourth fundamental separation of concerns in KobrA is the separation of product issues – the question of "what" should be built – from process issues – the question of "how" and "when" these things should be built. This is achieved by defining the artifacts making up a KobrA representation of a system separately from the activities and guidelines used to create and maintain them. In other words, the arrangement of KobrA views and their relationship are defined completely independently of the notion of time. In effect, the different projections of a component depicted in figure 2 represent a snapshot of the component at a particular point in the development process.

The advantage of defining the views of the system independently of process concerns is that they are completely agnostic to the process used to develop them. In other word, KobrA allows the information in each of the fundamental dimensions defined above (abstraction, composition, and genericity) to be elaborated in any order. Thus, in the composition dimension it is possible to develop composition information in a top-down way or a bottom-up way. In the abstraction dimension it is possible to develop abstraction levels in a forward engineering or a backward engineering way, and in the genericity dimension it is possible to develop specialization levels by specializing from the general, or generalizing from the specific. Of course, in practice, a combination of the extreme approaches is usually used.

In line with the goals of this book, in this chapter we focus on the "product" aspects of KobrA – that is how components and component-based systems are represented rather than how the information that goes into the representation is generated. We also focus on the composition dimension since the topic of the book is components and component-based development. The genericity dimension is not of direct interest as it focuses on Product Line Engineering (e.g. [8], [9]) which is not addressed by the example.

A key principle in KobrA is that the system and all components of the system should be treated alike (i.e. viewed in the same way) and that the composition hierarchy should be made explicit. As illustrated in figure 4, therefore, in general the complete description of a system is composed of a nested hierarchy of components, each of which can be viewed using the same projections outlined above. Of course, there are strict consistency constraints between the views of composite components and their subcomponents and client components and their server. The properties of a subcomponent as represented in its specification have to match the usage of the component as defined in the realizations of its clients and the component it is contained within. As can be seen from figure 4, in UML terms, a KobrA representation of a component-based system can be thought of as a nested tree of component views (i.e. specifications) and composite system views (i.e. realizations).

Most approaches to component-based development ignore the issue of how to nest components within one another, even if they theoretically allow it, because

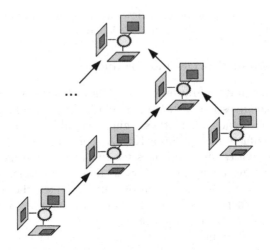

Fig. 4. Hierarchic System Architecture – Component Composition

it is a non-trivial topic. In KobrA, the optimal nesting of components is chosen by alignment with the visibility requirements of component instances and by application of the principle of information hiding. However, a more detailed discussion of this issue is beyond the scope of this paper.

Each of the core development dimensions discussed in section 4.2.1 has its own associated paradigm, conventions, and set of best practices. In the genericity dimension there is the notion of instantiating specific applications from the generic framework by resolving decisions about what features a particular system should provide. In the abstraction dimension, there is the notion of generating platform specific artifacts (i.e. views) from more platform independent ones, and gradually moving towards an executable incarnation of the components. In the composition dimension there is the issue of whether to develop components from scratch or whether to try to reuse them, and the question of how agile to make the architecture structuring process in terms of the levels of desirable re-factoring steps. In general, none of these paradigms or development processes has dominance over the others, and they can be combined in arbitrary ways. For the purposes of this chapter, however, we assume that the MDA [6] development process is the overarching process and present the KobrA component modeling approach in the context of the overall process advocated in MDA. Thus, in the next section we will present the artifacts (i.e. diagrams) that form part of the Computation Independent Model (CIM), in the section that follows we present the artifacts that form part of the PIM and in the section after that we present those that form part of a Platform Specific Model (PSM).

4.3   Modelling the CoCoME

It is not the goal of this chapter to show how every element of the CoCoME would appear in KobrA or to capture every conceivable piece of information. Rather, the goal is to try to give the reader the flavor of how the Trading System would be modelled in KobrA and to present its strengths and weaknesses. The information from CoCoME that is shown in the KobrA form is included as faithfully as possible so as to facilitate comparison with the other approaches. Where the CoCoME lacked information that we needed to optimally demonstrate a feature of KobrA we have extended the example in the way that seemed to us to be the most natural. Many of the differences between the KobrA models and the original CoCoME models stem from our attempt to show how KobrA can be used to support MDA by capturing the different CIM, PIM and PSM levels of abstraction.

4.3.1   Computation Independent Model

The MDA paradigm envisages the creation of a high-level model of the "problem" that the system under construction is intended to help solve, without concern for the fact that the system is a computer-based entity. In KobrA, the CIM is described by three different views (diagrams) representing the three core projections described above (see section 4.2.2). The Enterprise Concept Diagram represents the structural projection, the Enterprise Process Diagram represents the functional projection, and the Enterprise Workflow Diagram represents the behavioral projection.

4.3.1.1   Enterprise Concept Diagram

The Enterprise Concept Diagram (ECD) represents the structural projection of the problem space and describes the basic concepts of concern in the problem domain (similar to the domain model in classic OOAD [10]; in other words it can be understood as a computation-independent domain model). As can be seen in figure 5 the ECD shows the Store as simply one of a community of actors and relevant object types (conceptual classes). The actors are marked with the stereotype <<role>> and the object types with the stereotypes <<entity>>.

4.3.1.2   Enterprise Process Diagram

The Enterprise Process Diagram (EPD) represents the functional projection of the problem space and describes the basic functions (processes) that occur in the problem domain and how they are related to one another. It is similar to the structural models applied in the structured development techniques that used to be popular in the 1970s and 1980s (e.g. [11]). As can be seen in figure 6, it groups the processes (functions) in the domain into a hierarchy. In the trading system case study we have chosen to view the predefined use cases as subprocesses of three major processes: the *Store Management* process, the *Customer Interaction* process and the *Third Party Interaction* process. The customer interaction group is decomposed into the processes *UC1 – Process Sale* and *UC2 – Manage Express Checkout* – each representing a use case. The store management group is decomposed into the process *UC6 – Show Delivery Reports* and the subgroups *Inventory Management* and *Personnel Administration*. Other groupings are imaginable but are not shown in the diagram since the modeling of the

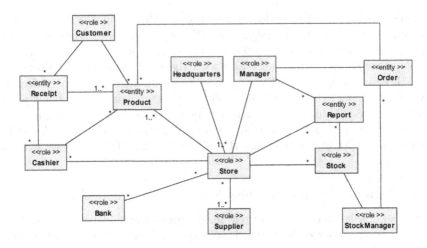

Fig. 5. Enterprise Concept Diagram of the Store

enterprise processes is restricted to those regarded as use cases. In KobrA, these are represented at the leaf nodes of the enterprise process tree. We added the node *Personnel Administration* to highlight the absence of some additional use cases describing the activities of staff management that are supported by the store system. Note the *UC8 – Product Exchange (on low stock) Among Stores* is a part of more than one parent group. This kind of situation is common in complex systems.

4.3.1.3   Enterprise Workflow Diagram
The Enterprise Workflow Diagram (EWD) represents the behavioral projection of the problem space and describes the control and data flows that occur in the domain. It takes the form of a workflow-style diagram such as supported in BPMN [12] or Scheer [13], or activity diagrams in the UML. The EWD complements the EPD by describing the relationship between the processes and the UCs respectively. To enhance legibility, it can be split up into several subparts as illustrated in figure 7. The workflow of the `Supplier` is not complete since it does not have a direct bearing on the store.

4.3.2   Platform Independent Model

The Computation Independent Model describes the problem that needs to be solved at a high level of abstraction without regard for the fact that IT technology will be used to realize a solution. The "system", if it appears at all, is simply viewed as one of the many actors involved in the domain. The next major level of abstraction in MDA is the Platform Independent Model which describes the IT solution without referring to the idiosyncrasies of a particular execution platform. This is the level of abstraction that KobrA primarily focuses on. In KobrA, the properties of the system and the various components making up the system are described in a platform independent way using UML views. However,

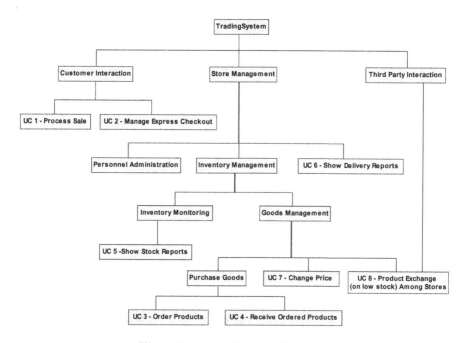

Fig. 6. Enterprise Process Diagram

in contrast with most other methods, KobrA treats every component separately and uniformly, and organizes the platform independent views of the components in a way that corresponds to, and highlights, the composition hierarchy.

4.3.2.1   Context Realization
At the top of KobrA's component modeling hierarchy is the context realization. This describes in detail how the system interacts with its environment (i.e. its context) and what types the system manipulates. The term "realization" reflects the fact that the design of a system's interaction with its environment constitutes a solution to the high-level problem defined in the CIM, and usually involves a redesign of existing practices. Also, as will be highlighted later, the context realization uses the same views as the realizations inside the system. In UML terminology, the context realization is a composite system, and is described using the standard "composite system" views advocated in KobrA.

Structural View
The structural view of the context realization describes the information and structural aspects of the environment of the system. It takes the form of a UML class diagram and shows the agents that the system interacts with, the types that the system shares with its environment (e.g. parameter types) and the operations that the various actors and the system expose to one another. The context realization explicitly focuses on those entities which will be implemented as part of the system. Therefore, the concept named **Store** in the ECD is renamed to

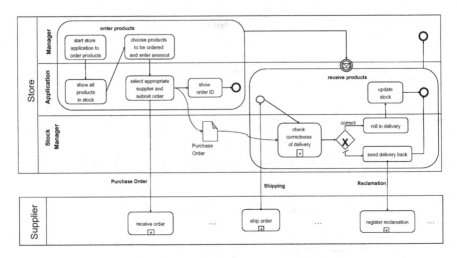

Fig. 7. Purchase Goods Enterprise Workflow Diagram

TradingSystem to make it clear that we are no longer considering the real world notion of "store", but are describing the entity to be developed as a computer based system. Figure 8 describes the structural model of the trading system based on the previously described enterprise environment, the use case have become responsibilities of the TradingSystem there.

Note that in the structural view of the context realization only those components are included that occur in the abstract interaction models at this level. Roles and types in the CIM that do not have a direct bearing on the operation of the system are not included.

Functional View

The functional view shows the functional responsibilities assigned to the system and to the actors/components in the environment of the system, and shows how these make use of each others functionality by sending messages. It takes the form of a set of interaction diagrams – one for each use case to be supported by the system.

As illustrated in figure 9, by convention in the context realization the functional view is shown in the form of sequence diagrams. This reflects the tradition of using sequence diagrams (rather than other forms of interaction diagrams) for showing interactions with the system when viewed as a black-box. In further refinement steps, when lower level components are modeled, communication diagrams are used instead.

Behavioral View

The behavioral view shows the workflows/algorithms that are used to realize the use cases that the system needs to support. It complements the functional view by showing the algorithms (i.e. control flows and data flows) used to invoke the operations involved in realizing the use case. It takes the form of a set of UML

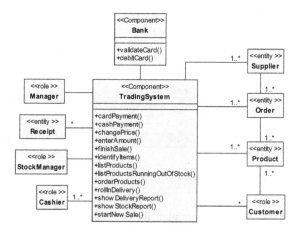

Fig. 8. Context Realization Structural View showing the responsibilities of TradingSystem

activity diagrams – one for each use case to be supported by the system. Figure 10 gives an example.

4.3.2.2   TradingSystem Specification

The focus of the context realization is the system's relationship to its environment. As mentioned above, the context realization represents a "composite system" view of the community of actors which interact to realize the goals and/or business processes of concern. The system specification, in contrast, takes a "component" view of the system and provides a complete "context independent" description of the externally visible properties of the system. By "context independent" we mean that the external actors that invoke the operations of the

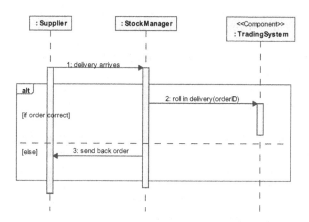

Fig. 9. Context Realization Functional View – Receive Ordered Products Use Case

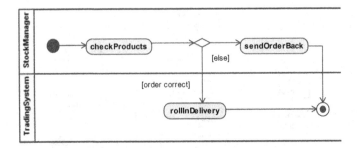

Fig. 10. Context Realization Behavioral View – Receive Ordered Products Use Case

system are only represented if their identity is essential to the functioning of the system. If the identity of users is not important, as is usually the case, they are not included in the specification.

Structural View
KobrA's principles of locality and parsimony require that the specification of a component only contains those components and actors that are directly needed by the component. In other words, the specification of a component should only contain the other components and actors that are called by the component under consideration. The subject of the specification is identified by the stereotype <<subject>> in the structural view. Actors that are only callers from a component's point of view are of minor importance, as these could be replaced by any other actor calling the same functionality without losing any information. In the TradingSystem, the Manager is a good example of this since it only calls the TradingSystem. As illustrated in figure 11, the structural view of the TradingSystem specification contains the components which are acquired and the major entities that are necessary for the interaction/information exchange between the components. The structural view can be complemented by OCL constraints, e.g. invariants as shown in figure 11.

Note that at this stage of refinement no distinction is made between the product type added to the inventory and the product type sold in the real existing store, as defined in the description of CoCoME. Both represent the same real world object and refinements are not needed here because the attributes are of no interest at this stage.

In general, components have two roles in a system – one role is as a container which encapsulates and provides an identity for a logically coherent group of components (i.e. a composite system in the UML) and the other role is as a contributor of its own functionality to the overall functionality of the system. Some components, however, may only fill one role or the other. Some components only serve to encapsulate a group of lower level components, and have no direct functionality of their own. Others only contribute functionality to the overall system and do not have any subcomponents. The latter represent the leaves of the composition hierarchy, since by definition they do not contain subcomponents,

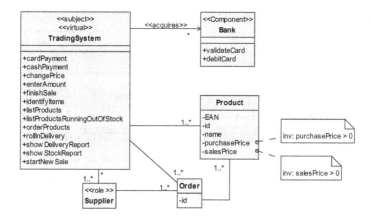

Fig. 11. Trading System Specification Structural View

and the former, known as "virtual" components in KobrA 2.0, occupy higher position in the composition hierarchy and by definition cannot be leaves because they must have subcomponents. The term "virtual" emphasizes the contrast to physical components with their own functionality.

The `TradingSystem` is an example of such a virtual component – that is, a component which has no direct functionality of its own, but simply serves as logical container that acts as a facade for a composite system. In UML terminology, `TradingSystem` is an example of a component which has no "behavior" of its own, but delegates the responsibility for realizing its functionality to its subcomponents. The stereotype `<<virtual>>` is used to indicate that a component is virtual. In addition, note that the structural view of the specification does not contain brackets after the operation names. The reason is that we regard the functionality of a component as a responsibility the component has been assigned rather than as an operation in normal sense. This is consistent with the virtual concept, as a virtual component cannot have normal operations of its own.

Functional View

The functional view of the `TradingSystem` specification describes the effects of each of its responsibilities. They are documented in the form of operation specifications whose general form is shown in the template in table 1.

Each entry in this template needs only to be included in an operation specification if it carries useful information for that operation. Moreover, the information can be represented formally in OCL or in the semiformal style popularized by the Fusion method [14]. In general there is one operation specification for each responsibility, but for space reasons we only show the specification of the `changePrice` operation in table 2 below. This uses the semi-formal Fusion style combined with OCL constraints.

Behavioral View

The behavioral view shows the externally visible states of the component and the meaningful sequences of operation invocations. Since the trading system serves

Table 1. Operation Specification Template

Name	name of the operation
Description	identifies the purpose and provides a short informal description of the normal and exceptional executions
Constraints	properties that constrain the realization and implementation of the component
Receives	information passed to the operation by the invoker (analogous to the arguments of an operation in a programming language)
Returns	information returned to the invoker by the operation (analogous to the return value of an operation in a programming language)
Sends	messages sent to acquired component instances, can be events or operation invocations
Reads	identifies externally visible information that is read but not changed by the operation
Changes	lists externally visible information that is changed by the operation
Rules	rules governing the computation of the result
Assumes	weakest precondition on the externally visible properties of the component and on the inputs (see receives clause) that must be true for the component to guarantee the post-condition (result clause)
Results	strongest post-condition on the externally visible properties of the component and the returned information (returns clause) that becomes true after execution of the operation with true assumes clause

multiple users simultaneously it has no externally visible states. Each operation can be invoked at any time.

4.3.2.3   TradingSystem Realization

The realization of a component describes its design as if it were a "composite system" in the UML sense. The information in the specification structural view is still valid, but is augmented by the additional design information used to realize the component's services – that is, by a description of how the properties exposed in the specification are supported in terms of internal algorithms and interactions with other components and data structures.

Structural View

Based on the original design of the system (see Chapter 3, Figure 5) the TradingSystem is composed of three types of subcomponents – Inventory, CashDesk, and Coordinator which coordinates interaction with the available CashDesk instances (see figure 12). From a UML perspective, the class diagram representing the realization structural projection can be regarded as a refinement of the class diagram representing the specification structural view. This means that all the information contained in the specification structural view is also present in the realization view, but additional design information has been added.

An interesting issue in deciding the internal make up of the trading system is the usefulness of the CashDeskLine component used in the original solution (see Chapter 3, Figure 5). Although this does not appear in the use case diagram, the sequence diagram (see Chapter 3, Figure 18) provides a clear description of how the express checkout is triggered by a Coordinator within the CashDeskLine. The CashDeskLine itself is actually a virtual component of the kind discussed above since it essentially serves to encapsulate the set of CashDesk instances

Table 2. TradingSystem Specification Functional View – changePrice Operation

Name	changePrice
Description	This method changes the salesPrice of a product.
Receives	productID : String – the identifier of the product price : Real – the new salesPrice of the product
Returns	success : Boolean – true, if the salesPrice is changed – false, otherwise.
Changes	The salesPrice of the product.
Assumes	-- exactly one Product exists with the ID = productID pre: Product.select(id = productID).size() = 1 pre: price > 0
Result	post: Product.select(id = productID).first().salesPrice = price

within the system, and provides no direct functionality of its own. However, since the TradingSystem is already a virtual component, and there is little to be gained from nesting virtual components directly within one another, we decided to omit CashDeskLine from our design.

An interesting aspect of the decomposition of the TradingSystem into the three subcomponents Coordinator, CashDesk and Inventory, is that we can now see a difference between the real world products added to the inventory and those passed through the cash desk, since those added to the inventory represent StockItems, with the additional information that the inventory should have a minimum or a maximum amount of this product. To stay as faithful as possible to the CoCoME we decided to model them as two separate classes – StockItem which represents products in the Inventory and SalesProduct which represents products associated with the CashDesk. To show that they are conceptually related they are both defined as specializations of Product.

Functional View

Each responsibility described in the specification of the TradingSystem component is refined and added to the realization of the component. In the case of a virtual component such as TradingSystem the responsibilities are divided into subresponsibilities and are distributed amongst the subcomponents. The functional view of an operation's realization is captured in terms of interaction diagrams. These take the form of communication diagrams and clearly illustrate which additional components are used. Only those that are called from or created by the component under consideration have a representation in the structural model.

Figure 13 shows the functional view of the realization of the rollInDelivery operation. Due to lack of space the other operations of TradingSystem are not shown here.

Behavioral View

The behavioral view shows the algorithms used to realize the component's operations in terms of activity diagrams – one for each operation. Again, for space reasons, we consider only one operation here, rollInDelivery (see figure 14). The small fork-like symbol in the activity indicates that it is further refined at the next level of decomposition (anchor notation).

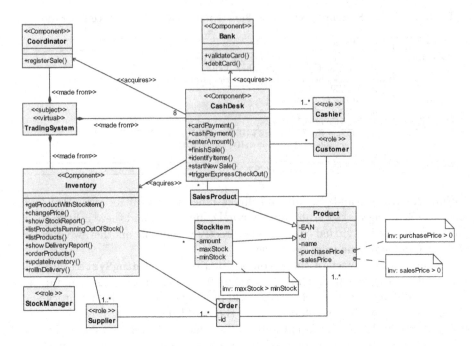

Fig. 12. TradingSystem Realization Structural View

4.3.2.4   CashDesk Specification

A fundamental principle of the KobrA approach is that all components should be described in the same way regardless of their location in the composition hierarchy. As long as a component is sufficiently complex it can be further decomposed into additional subcomponents. Due to the shortage of space we concentrate on the CashDesk component in this section since the Inventory and the Coordinator are treated in the same manner.

Structural View

All components have a specification and a realization which are viewed from the same perspectives as before. Like the TradingSystem component, CashDesk is a virtual component which means its responsibilities are implemented by delegation to operations of its subcomponents. Figure 15 shows the structural view of the CashDesk component.

Functional View

As before, the functional view of the components shows the effects of each operation in terms of declarative operation specifications. In table 3 we show the specification of the cardPayment responsibility.

Behavioral View

The behavioral view shows how the CashDesk component responds to external stimuli, and when the operations of the component may be sensibly executed.

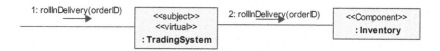

Fig. 13. TradingSystem Realization Functional View – rollInDelivery Operation

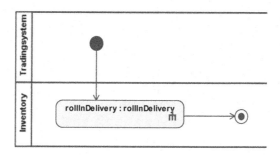

Fig. 14. TradingSystem Realization Behavioral View – rollInDelivery Operation

Figure 16 shows that there are two major operational states of the CashDesk, normalMode and expressMode. The latter is triggered from outside the CashDesk under certain conditions. It further shows the operations which can be executed within the states and the events leading to the state transitions.

4.3.2.5 CashDesk Realization

As usual, the realization of the CashDesk describes how the properties described in its specification (i.e its contract with other components) are realized in terms of internal algorithms and interactions with other components and data structures.

Structural View

Since the CashDesk is also a virtual component and therefore has no direct functionality of its own, none of the responsibilities of the component are shown in the structural view as shown in figure 17. This reinforces the idea that the component doesn't have any operations of its own, but fulfills its responsibilities by delegation.

Functional View

Figure 18 shows how the cardPayment responsibility of CashDesk is realized. In addition to the components involved in the cashPayment, paying by credit card also involves the components CardReader and Bank. The Customer also has to enter his PIN into the CardReader.

Behavioral View

At the level of the CashDesk realization the responsibility identifyItems has to be refined into lower level activities. Figure 19 shows the algorithm used to realize

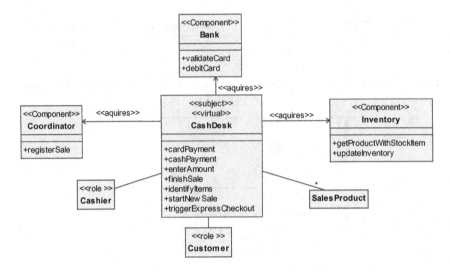

Fig. 15. CashDesk Specification Structural View

Table 3. CashDesk Specification Functional View – cardPayment Operation

Name	cardPayment
Description	This method realizes the card payment.
Constraints	For the payment the connection to the bank has to be established.
Receives	sum : Real – the sum to pay
Returns	success : Boolean – true, if the payment was successfull – false, if the customer cannot pay via card.
Sends	Bank:validateCard(cardInformation, pin) Bank::debitCard(transactionID)
Changes	The card of the customer is debited.
Rules	Bank::debitCard(transactionID) can only be called, if the card is valid. To validate the card the customer has to enter his PIN. The cardInformation is read from the credit card of the customer.
Assumes	pre: sum > 0
Result	The card of the customer is debited with sum.

identifyItems. Each `SalesProduct` is identified via the `BarCodeScanner`. If a `SalesProduct` is not recognized by the scanner it is possible either to add its identifier by hand (`enterEANByHand`) or to completely reject the `Product`. `Inventory` (not shown here) is also a virtual component whose functionality is delegated to its subcomponents.

4.3.2.6 CashDeskApplication Specification
Since the components of `CashDesk` are still relatively complex they are further decomposed into subcomponents using the same basic process. Here we focus on the `CashDeskApplication` subcomponent which was given in the CoCoME. As usual, we first describe the `CashDeskApplication`'s specification level. However, in this case, the component is a concrete one with concrete operations of its own (see table 4).

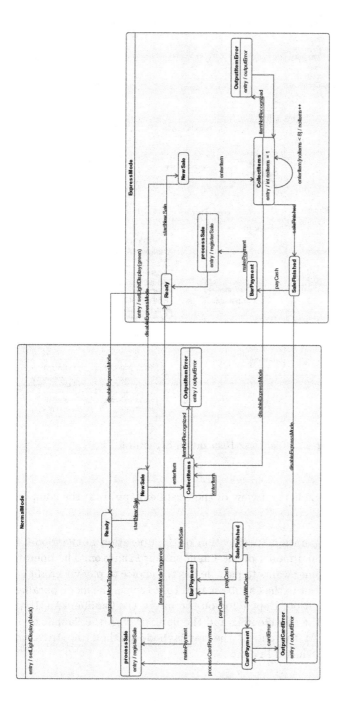

Fig. 16. CashDesk Specification Behavioral View

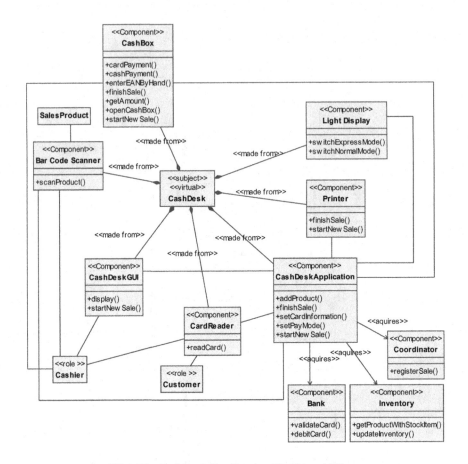

Fig. 17. CashDesk Realization Structural View

Structural View
Figure 20 shows the structural view of the CashDeskApplication component.

Functional View
Table 4 shows the operation specification of the operation setPayMode, which is part of the functional model of the CashDeskApplication. The operation is called when the customer wants to pay. He has the choice to pay via credit card or cash. His decision is sent to the CashDeskApplication via the mode parameter of the setPayMode operation. Depending on the mode, the CashDeskApplication communicates with the CardReader and the Bank or with the CashBox to complete the payment. At the end of the setPayMode method the Inventory is updated with the purchased Products.

Behavioral View
The behavioral view of CashDeskApplication in figure 21 shows the different externally visible states of the component.

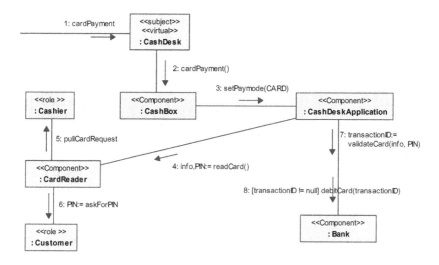

Fig. 18. CashDesk Realization Functional View – cardPayment Operation

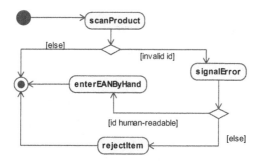

Fig. 19. CashDesk Realization Behavioral View – identifyItems Operation

This process of decomposition can be continued but due to the lack of space we do not show any further components here. Hopefully it should by now be clear how the KobrA approach is based on the hierarchical organization and description of components in the system.

4.3.3   Platform Specific Model

The platform independent description of the CoCoME example developed in section 4.3.2 describes the system at a level of abstraction which is independent of specific platform idiosyncrasies. The models focus on elaborating the component structure of the system by describing how the larger components are composed of smaller components which in turn are composed of smaller components until a level of granularity is reached where further decomposition is unnecessary. Each component is described in the same way whatever its location in the composition hierarchy is.

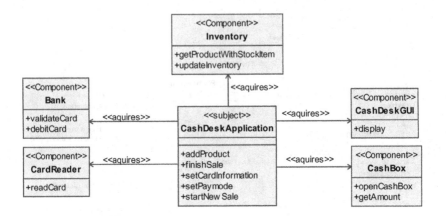

Fig. 20. CashDeskApplication Specification Structural View

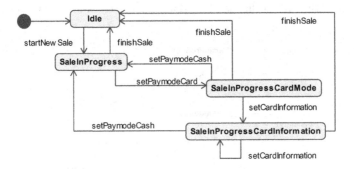

Fig. 21. CashDeskApplication Specification Behavioral View

The next step in the MDA process is to develop one or more platform specific models in which one or more of these abstract (or logical) component representations are mapped into a more platform specific form, with the eventual goal of creating executable incarnations of the components. KobrA does not prescribe how this is done or in what form the "platform specific" forms of components should be represented. This obviously varies in accordance with the nature of the platform. However, in order to illustrate what form the platform specific models of components might take, in this section we briefly show some examples.

Figure 12 in Chapter 3 shows how the `CashDeskLine` component is implemented with the help of the components of a middleware based platform. As we explained above, we chose to omit `CashDeskLine` in our model, but instead we can show how `CashDesk` might be realized using a similar approach. This is illustrated in figure 22.

Similarly, we can also show how specific instances of our overall architecture are deployed to specific nodes of the network. This is illustrated in figure 23.

4.4   Analysis

As explained in section 4.1, KobrA is intended to be a component-oriented way of performing system design using the UML. As with most uses of the UML for design, therefore, the analyzing, checking and/or prediction of system properties is not the main focus of the modeling effort. The main value of the models is as an easy-to-read communication vehicle to facilitate discussions and joint under-standing between members of the development team and between the develop-ment team and customers/users. The design models also serve as the starting point for the creation of the implementation.

Although most UML tools today provide assistance in creating of implemen-tations from models, no tool to date is able to provide a comprehensive mapping of all UML features to code. In mainstream development, therefore, some part of the implementation has to be written by hand. As a result, it is impossible to "prove" that an implementation so created will deliver the modeled prop-erties because it is impossible to rule out human error. However, by creating a consistent and precise design of a system, which describes the properties of the system from multiple, focused viewpoints, the chances of creating a correct implementation with the desired properties is greatly increased.

Table 4. CashDeskApplication Specification Functional View – setPayMode operation

Name	setPayMode
Description	The customer wants to pay via card or cash.
Constraints	For card payment the network connection to the bank has to be established.
Receives	mode:String – the paymode, could be "CASH" or "CARD"
Returns	Boolean: true for success, false for failure e.g. when card payment returns a false value, the Cashier could try bar payment.
Sends	Inventory::getProductWithStockItem(barcode) CardReader::readCard() – for card payment Bank:validateCard(cardInformation, pin) Bank::debitCard(transactionID) CashBox::getAmount() CashBox::openCashBox() – to open the CashBox CashDeskGUI::display() – to display the sum or the amount of change Inventory::updateInventory(shoppingCart) – to update the Inventory when the payment was successful
Reads	Inventory::getProductWithStockItem(barcode)
Changes	The Inventory is updated and in the case of card payment, the card of the customer is debited.
Rules	The amount which the customer has to pay is the sum of the items in shopping cart plus some taxes.
Assumes	pre: CashBox.getAmount() > 0
Result	The Inventory is updated. The card of the customer is debited with the amount of the shopping cart or the customer paid cash.

Since many UML diagrams are now inherently precise and unambiguous (be-cause of the well defined semantics of the applied UML features) or can be made precise by the addition of OCL constraints, KobrA can be used to create precise and unambiguous descriptions of components and their designs. Moreover, be-cause of the expressiveness of UML and OCL almost all kinds of system proper-ties can be specified, especially if additional UML profiles are used, such as the

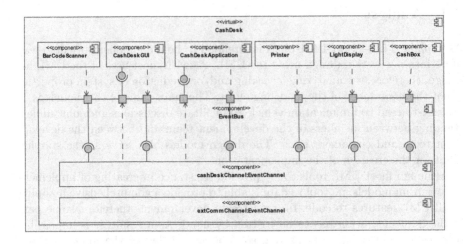

Fig. 22. CashDesk Platform Specific Realization Structural View

Real Time [15] and Quality of Service profiles [16]. The essential prerequisite for a sound set of models is that they are internally well-formed and mutually consistent. At present we have no tool for checking this, although we have defined many well-formedness and consistency rules. In principle the usual well-formedness and consistency checking techniques used with other formalisms can be used with KobrA models. As well as checking inter-model consistency, this includes

1. Verification of state machines (e.g. reachability, dead-ends) on the specification behavioral views,
2. Checks of pre and post condition compatibility and logical consistency on the specification functional views,
3. Formal verification of algorithms on the realization functional and behavioral views.

4.5   Tools

As can be seen from the numerous diagrams, at its core KobrA is a view-based method which prescribes what content the different views of a component should contain and how they should be organized. Although there is no strict requirement to use tools when applying KobrA, developing all these views by hand and keeping them all consistent with one another is impractical without tool support. In this section we therefore give a brief overview of the tool support that we are developing at the Lehrstuhl für Softwaretechnik at the University of Mannheim to address this need.

The tool was designed with three main goals in mind

– to provide a systematic and user friendly conceptual model and framework for defining and navigating around different views of a component and/or component based system

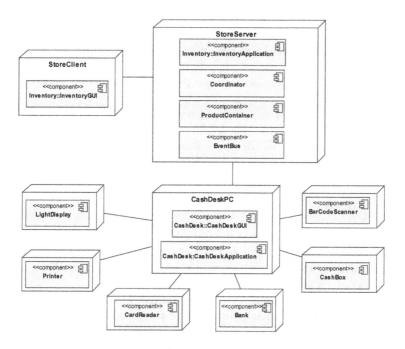

Fig. 23. TradingSystem Deployment Diagram

– to provide a flexible infrastructure which allows consistency checking and view-generation tools to be easily and systematically defined and added
– to use a unifying meta-model which allows all views to be generated automatically from a single underlying representation of a component

To make the complexity tractable for developers, the user interface is based on the metaphor of a multidimensional cube consisting of multiple cells. An example of a cell would be the structural view of the specification of the TradingSystem. A cell of the cube is determined by choosing a value for each dimension. The preconfigured dimensions for KobrA component development are "component", "abstraction", and "projection". The component dimension specifies the (sub-) component which is being worked on at a particular point in time. The abstraction dimension determines the level of abstraction, with the default values being specification, realization, and implementation. The projection dimension identifies the structural, functional or behavioral viewpoint from which the component is being viewed. A cell can have one or more perspectives (e.g. a UML class diagram) on which the developer works with his favorite editor.

The navigation, management and consistent maintenance of artifacts become increasingly difficult as their number increases. An ideal solution would be to have every editor working directly on a common model of the component and have changes synchronized with the model so that consistency among different views is ensured. This is the long term goal of the tool. As a pragmatic intermediate approach, multiple formats are supported and are synchronized by specially written "consistency checking" plugins. The environment is easily extendable, so that new editors or consistency checkers can be added at any time.

It is possible to add an element to an existing dimension or to add a whole new dimension. For example, to support versioning, one could add a version dimension with each dimension element representing different versions of the component.

In summary, our tool serves as a framework for integrating professional CASE tools as well as self-made editors and offers a unified navigation paradigm and a single underlying metamodel. Artifacts from the employed tools, such as UML diagrams from MagicDraw, can of course be used outside our tool at any time.

4.6   Summary

In this chapter we have presented the CoCoME example as it might be modeled using the KobrA approach. The underlying nature of the components and system architecture is much the same as in the other approaches. What differs is KobrA's way of visualizing and presenting components and composite systems. As mentioned at the beginning, KobrA encourages a uniform representation of components regardless of their granularity or their location in the composition hierarchy. This means that the same views and principles are used to model smaller components near the leaf of the tree (e.g. `CashDeskApplication`) as are used to model larger component at the root of the tree (e.g. `TradingSystem`). In addition, KobrA requires all components in the tree to be described at the same level of abstraction (i.e. at the same level of platform independence). Thus, `CashDeskApplication` has the same level of platform independence as `TradingSystem`. Changes in platform specificity are clearly visible and are separated out into a different set of models (i.e. one or more platform specific models).

An important aspect of all software specification approaches is the ability to define extra functional properties and requirements. In KobrA the difference between extra functional *requirements* and extra functional *properties* is that the former are associated with specifications and the latter with realizations. An extra functional "statement" in a specification is a promise that the component makes to its clients. It is part of its contract with them and thus is something that the builder of the component must fulfill – it is a requirement. In contrast, an extra functional "statement" in the realization of a component is a description of some fact that is true about the chosen design – it is a property.

Extra functional requirements and properties can be added to KobrA models in one of two ways. They can either be added to the existing views in the form of constraints or annotations or they can be defined in an additional "extra functional properties/requirements" view, or both. At the specification level, extra functional requirements that apply to a single method can easily be added to the operation specification of that method by adding specialized clauses (rows). Extra functional requirements that span methods (i.e. invariants) are best defined in a separate view, however.

At first sight, KobrA's strategy of creating "localized" views of each component may seem to involve a great deal more redundancy and verbosity than is necessary. To a certain extent this is true. However, provided that suitable tool support is available, we believe the advantages of separating concerns, treating all components uniformly, and fully elaborating their properties from a number of orthogonal viewpoints, greatly outweigh the costs. They not only simplify and clarify the initial development process, they make the resulting components and component-based systems much more maintainable and reusable.

Acknowledgements

The presented work was partially supported by the ECOMODIS project funded by the "Förderprogramm Informationstechnik Baden-Württemberg (BW-FIT)" (http://www.ecomodis.de).

References

1. Fraunhofer Institute for Experimental Software Engineering: The MAR-MOT Project - Component-based Development of Embedded Systems (2003), http://www.marmot-project.de/de/home/index.html
2. Brenner, D., Atkinson, C., Paech, B., Malaka, R., Merdes, M., Suliman, D.: Reducing Verification Effort in Component-Based Software Engineering through Built-In Testing. In: Proceedings of the International IEEE Enterprise Computing Conference (EDOC 2006), 16th-20th October, Hong Kong (2006)
3. Atkinson, C., Bayer, J., Bunse, C., Kamsties, E., Laitenberger, O., Laqua, R., Muthig, D., Paech, B., Wüst, J., Zettel, J.: Component-Based Product Line Engineering with UML, 1st edn. Addison Wesley, Reading (2001)
4. OMG: UML 2.0 Superstructure Specification (2003), http://www.omg.org/docs/ptc/03-08-02.pdf
5. Warmer, J., Kleppe, A.: The Object Constraint Language: Precise Modeling with UML. Addison-Wesley Longman Publishing Co., Inc., Boston (1998)
6. OMG: MDA Guide Version 1.0.1 (2003), http://www.omg.org/docs/omg/03-06-01.pdf
7. Ambler, S.W.: Agile Modeling (2006), http://www.agilemodeling.com
8. Clements, P., Northrop, L.: Software Product Lines. Addison-Wesley, Boston (2002)
9. Bayer, J., Flege, O., Knauber, P., Laqua, R., Muthig, D., Schmid, K., Widen, T., Debaud, J.M.: PuLSE. A Methodology to Develop Software Product Lines. In: Proceedings of the Symposium on Software Reuse (SSR 1999) (1999)
10. Larman, C.: Applying UML and Patterns: An Introduction to Object-Oriented Analysis and Design, 3rd edn. Prentice-Hall, Englewood Cliffs (2005)
11. Coad, P., Mayfield, M.: Coad, Yourdon, and Nicola: OOA, OOD, & OOP. Wiley-QED Publishing, Somerset (1994)
12. OMG: Business Process Modeling Notation Specification - version 1.0. Final Adopted BPMN 1-0 Spec 06-02-01.pdf (2006), http://www.bpmn.org/Documents/OMG

13. Scheer, A.W.: ARIS - Modellierungsmethoden, Metamodelle, Anwendungen. Springer, Heidelberg (2001)
14. Coleman, D., Arnold, P., Bodoff, S., Dollin, C., Gilchrist, H., Hayes, F., Jeremaes, P.: Object-Oriented Development. The Fusion Method. Prentice-Hall, Englewood Cliffs (1994)
15. OMG: UML Profile for Schedulability, Performance and Time (2005), http://www.omg.org/cgi-bin/doc?formal/2005-01-02
16. OMG: UML Profile for Modeling QoS and Fault Tolerance Characteristics and Mechanisms (2006), http://www.omg.org/cgi-bin/doc?formal/06-05-02

5   A Rich Services Approach to CoCoME

Barry Demchak, Vina Ermagan, Emilia Farcas, To-ju Huang, Ingolf H. Krüger, and Massimiliano Menarini

University of California, San Diego – Calit2

5.1   Introduction

Systems-of-systems integration projects present exquisite challenges for software and systems engineering researchers and practitioners. Traditional integration approaches involve time-consuming rework bearing major financial and technical risk. Service-Oriented Architectures (SOAs) have emerged as a widely accepted solution to this challenge because they use standards-based infrastructure to forge large-scale systems out of loosely-coupled, interoperable services. SOAs can create systems-of-systems by mapping existing systems into services, then orchestrating communication between the services. New functionality can be created by either adding new services or modifying communication among existing services. Because of these features, SOA projects are particularly amenable to agile development processes. Consequently, well executed SOAs can drive down financial and technical risk by improving flexibility and reducing time to market.

Unleashing the full potential of the service-oriented approach, however, requires going beyond the prevalent tendency to equate SOAs with the currently predominant Web services implementation infrastructure. Undoubtedly, the move toward Web services has helped to solve many challenges of prior attempts at implementing integration middleware. This was accomplished by disentangling the technical integration concerns such as transport mechanisms, data marshalling and unmarshalling, service publishing, discovery and binding, security, and reliability – to name just a few – into separate, openly accessible standards.

At the same time, the major concerns of system integration have not gone away. On the contrary, most integration projects combine a variety of concerns, ranging from business drivers and policies to technical infrastructure requirements. Physical and logical distribution of resources induces a corresponding distribution of these concerns across an integrated system. To address this challenge, we created the Rich Service architecture and associated development process. Because CoCoME can be viewed as a system-of-systems with similar integration concerns, the Rich Services approach fits well to this case study.

5.1.1   Goals and Scope of the Component Model

The Rich Service architecture is a type of SOA that maintains the lightweight integration approach of traditional SOAs while introducing (a) a mechanism for dealing with the crosscutting concerns of a set of services within the same logical or physical domain (horizontal integration) and (b) a mechanism for structural

A. Rausch et al. (Eds.): Common Component Modeling Example, LNCS 5153, pp. 85–115, 2008.
© Springer-Verlag Berlin Heidelberg 2008

decomposition of services to address scalability and encapsulation of concerns (vertical integration). We achieve horizontal integration by connecting the relevant set of services to a communication infrastructure, which can intercept and coordinate interactions among the services. This allows management of crosscutting concerns at the level of service orchestration. Typical examples of crosscutting concerns are security, policies, QoS properties, and failure management. We achieve vertical integration by allowing every service to be decomposed according to the same architectural blueprint. Of course, this requires introduction of meaningful service interfaces – another feature of Rich Services.

To achieve hierarchical composition, Rich Services leverage channels for communication according to point-to-point or publish-subscribe models. Modeling the communication channels enables the independent implementation of each component. We use a dialect of message sequence charts (MSCs) to capture interactions over channels, which allows us to formally verify our models against temporal properties and to verify that the implementation fulfills the required communication interface. Furthermore, Rich Services can be easily deployed using Enterprise Service Bus (ESB) middleware, thus reducing development time. The associated iterative development process covers all phases from early requirements gathering to architecture design and deployment.

5.1.2 Modeled Cutout of CoCoME

The CoCoME case study is an excellent example: a combination of legacy and emergent systems with heterogeneous computational capabilities, data formats, and user interface characteristics that exist in a variety of locales. Each locale has its own set of requirements, and we identified different policies for managing crosscutting concerns. We decided to modify the CoCoME architecture according to the Rich Services architectural blueprint, which provides decoupling between the various concerns and allows a direct mapping to ESB middleware.

In this chapter, we show how we leveraged the Rich Services architecture and process to model the CoCoME case study as a system-of-systems integration project. Thus, we focused on the integration architecture instead of the implementation. We modeled the logical architecture (static and behavioral views), crosscutting concerns (encryption, logging, QoS, and failure management), and various deployment mappings. Because Rich Services is a new framework, our tool chain for services is not fully carried over to Rich Services yet. Thus, we did not formally verify our models, but we identified underspecified requirements via model inspection, which was facilitated by our development process.

5.1.3 Benefit of the Modeling

Rich Services provide a flexible architectural framework that reconciles the notion of service with hierarchy. The benefit of using Rich Services is that we can treat extra-functional requirements, policies, and system integration up front at the modeling level, while providing an architecture scalable to complex systems. Furthermore, the flexible adaptation to communication paradigms and the short distance to deployment allows discharging of requirements to properties of the infrastructure. For example, ESBs often have builtin store-and-forward mechanisms that support disconnected operation and transient clients, thereby eliminating the need to develop these mechanisms separately.

The Rich Service approach fits well as a consistent architectural blueprint with support for extra-functional properties such as policy management. Rich Services provide the ability to analyze, design, and decompose the system according to various major concerns in isolation, and they provide a direct means of addressing crosscutting concerns. In CoCoME, vertical decomposition allows us to create models for the logical architecture that follow CoCoME's major management layers. Horizontal integration allows us to address concerns such as security and failure management both within a management domain and, together with vertical integration, across management domains. Rich Services provide flexible handling of both horizontal and vertical integration concerns, and can be used both as a logical and deployment architecture model.

5.1.4   Effort and Lessons Learned

Because our goal was to create a robust and flexible enterprise architecture, we invested five person-months in our treatment of CoCoME. To achieve the Rich Services architecture we had to deeply change the architecture provided in the CoCoME example. We estimate that a prototype implementation could be done in one person-month by leveraging ESB middleware. ESBs reduce development time due to builtin services and intercepting mechanisms, and a close mapping between the architecture and deployment.

CoCoME helped us refine our development process and the interface specification techniques for Rich Services. We also learned that hierarchy in the logical architecture is very useful, but can lead to the creation of artificial "proxies" that export entities across hierarchical levels. One approach to reduce the number of explicit "proxies" is to use multi-view models at the logical level. We plan to experiment with these in future work.

5.2   Component Model

The Trading System can be viewed as an interaction between a number of complex component systems. Some components, such as the Bank and Suppliers, already exist. Other components, such as the Store and the Cash Desk, are emergent, and can themselves be decomposed into subcomponents. Thus, the Trading System can be viewed as a system-of-systems – a hierarchy of component systems, with some components interacting with peers, and others interacting with components at other levels. At each level of the hierarchy, crosscutting concerns such as auditing, failure management, and security must be enforced.

To model the Trading System, we use a Rich Service architecture pattern [1], which manages the complexity of a system-of-systems by decomposing it into primary and crosscutting concerns, thus providing flexible encapsulation for these concerns and generating a model that can easily be leveraged into a deployment. The following sections describe the Rich Service pattern in detail, a development process tailored to the Rich Service pattern, and our use of supporting methodologies such as Message Sequence Charts.

5.2.1 Rich Services Logical Model

In our interpretation, a service describes an interaction pattern of domain objects [2] that provide a functionality to the system for the realization of a use case. Because system requirements often span multiple components captured by different architectural entities, our definition of services allows us to capture the required complex interaction dependencies and map them to implementation components. Therefore, services describe interaction scenarios; each service "orchestrates" interactions among system entities to achieve a specific goal [3]. For this reason, a service does not completely mandate the behavior of a component, but specifies only its behavior during a particular interaction with the rest of the system. Thus, services are partial specifications of the system behavior [2].

The Rich Service architectural pattern builds upon our service notion and organizes systems-of-systems into a hierarchically decomposed structure that supports both "horizontal" and "vertical" service integration. Horizontal service integration refers to the interplay of application services and the corresponding crosscutting concerns at the same hierarchical level. Vertical service integration refers to the hierarchical decomposition of one application service (and the crosscutting concerns pertaining to this service) into a set of sub-services. Their communication with the rest of the system is mediated by connectors and is shielded from the structural and behavioral complexity of their composition.

Figure 1 depicts our logical Rich Services architecture, inspired by ESB architectures and implementations, such as Mule [4] and Cape Clear. The main entities of the architecture are (a) the Service/Data Connector, which serves as the sole mechanism for interaction between the Rich Service and its environment, (b) the Messenger and the Router/Interceptor, which together form the communication infrastructure, and (c) the Rich Services connected to Messenger and Router/Interceptor, which encapsulate various application and infrastructure functionalities. In the following, we elaborate on each of these main entities and their role in the system.

To address the horizontal integration challenge, the logical architecture is organized around a message-based communication infrastructure having two main layers. The Messenger layer is responsible for message transmission between endpoints. By providing the means for asynchronous messaging, the Messenger supports decoupling of Rich Services. The Router/Interceptor layer is in charge of intercepting messages placed on the Messenger, then routing them. The routing policies of the communication infrastructure are the heart of the Router/Interceptor layer. Leveraging the Interceptor pattern readily facilitates dynamic behavior injection based on the interactions among Rich Services. This is useful for the injection of policies governing the integration of a set of horizontally decomposed services.

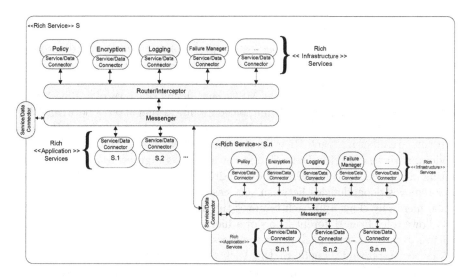

Fig. 1. Rich Services Architecture

The main entity of the architecture is the notion of Rich Service. A Rich Service could be a simple functionality block such as a COTS or Web service, or it could be hierarchically decomposed. We distinguish between Rich Application Services (RASs) and Rich Infrastructure Services (RISs). RASs provide core application functionality; they mandate some communication to be initiated by some party in the business workflow, including how the interaction is to be carried out. RISs address crosscutting concerns and do not initiate any communication by themselves. RISs can modify interactions defined by RASs by rerouting, filtering, or modifying in other ways the messages exchanged.

Policy enforcement, encryption, failure management, and authentication are typical examples of RISs, which are mainly intermediary services. The purpose of an encryption service, for instance, is to ensure that all messages transmitted over the communication medium are encrypted. A traditional service approach would require modifications to every service in the system in order to integrate the encryption mechanism, leading to scattered functionality. On the other hand, the Rich Service architecture introduces encryption as an infrastructure service that can inform the Router/Interceptor layer to modify the message routing tables to ensure that every message sent to the external network must first be processed by the encryption service. Only the communication infrastructure needs to be aware of the encryption service.

A Service/Data Connector is the means by which Rich Services are connected to the communication infrastructure. It encapsulates and hides the internal structure of the connected Rich Service, and exports only the description and interfaces that the connected Rich Service intends to provide and make visible externally. This helps tackle the vertical integration challenge introduced by systems-of-systems. The Service/Data Connector is an instance of a behavior interface. In the tradition of [5,6], we associate both a structural and a behavioral view with the interface of a Rich Service. In particular, the interaction interface between two Rich Services is defined as the protocol required to coordinate the roles played by these services according to the MSCs we identify for the business processes and use cases in our development process. Consequently, we associate with every Rich Service interface the MSCs that define this interplay. The MSCs in the Service/Data Connectors define the communication patterns between roles outside the Rich Service (*Imported Roles*) and roles inside it (*Exported Roles*).

In this architecture, each Rich Service can be decomposed into further Rich Services, with the Service/Data Connector acting as a gateway responsible for routing messages between layers. Additionally, the use of the Router/Interceptor layer removes dependencies between services and their relative locations in the logical hierarchy. This approach removes the direct connection between entities and allows roles from different levels of a hierarchy, possibly subject to different policies, to interact with each other seamlessly.

Another important benefit of the Rich Services architecture is the ability to analyze, design, and decompose the system according to various major concerns (e.g., security, policies, and governance) in isolation. Each major concern can be designed separately, and then made available to the entire Rich Service via the Router/Interceptor layer. This feature greatly contributes to the design of systems-of-systems where multiple authorities are involved, as would likely be the case for the Trading System. As an example, from the security viewpoint, multiple security-related services can be designed and connected to the system at different levels in the Rich Service hierarchy to address the authentication, access control permissions, and privileges across multiple authority domains.

5.2.2   Rich Services Deployment Model

Rich Services can easily map to an implementation architecture based on ESBs, threaded execution, or a range of other solutions. ESBs, in particular, provide message routing amongst well-defined, loosely coupled, coarsely granular services similar to our notion of Rich Services. They achieve cost efficiency and flexibility through the integration and reuse of services and service-based applications. Additionally, ESBs may employ many routing strategies (e.g., static routing, content-based rules, and itinerary) to achieve architectural goals such as distributed execution, load balancing, flow throttling, auditing, redundancy, failover, online maintenance, provisioning, and minimal service interdependence. This makes them particularly attractive as deployment architectures.

Thus, the instantiation of the architecture leverages existing technologies such as the Mule ESB framework [4]. In this case, the Mule transport layer corresponding to the Messenger element of the logical architecture can be leveraged to connect both components local to Mule and generic external components. COTS can be connected to the Mule framework using the Mule-supported transport technologies. For instance, they could be implemented as Web services and connected through the Mule SOAP transport provider.

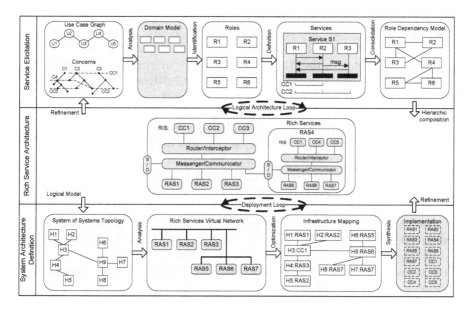

Fig. 2. Rich Service Development Process

The close alignment of the logical architecture for the Rich Services and the ESB deployment architecture yields a direct logical-to-deployment concept mapping, though other deployment architectures would work, too.

5.2.3   Rich Services Development Process

The Rich Service architecture can be leveraged into an end-to-end software engineering process that ranges from use case elicitation to system deployment. In this section, we present our service-oriented development process [7] that cleanly separates the system's logical model and its implementation.

To model a system using our Rich Service architecture we employ an iterative development process with three phases, each with one or more stages (see Figure 2). Each phase (and also the entire sequence of phases) can be iterated several times to refine the system architecture and obtain an implementation that satisfies the requirements of the system. This is a key feature because crosscutting concerns can be identified both early *and* late in the development process.

The first phase, Service Elicitation, captures the system requirements in a domain model and a service repository integrated with crosscutting system concerns such as governance, security, fault tolerance, confidentiality, encryption, error handling, tracing, and transactions. For each concern, we can leverage existing techniques of requirements gathering [8,9].

We begin by capturing the general functional requirements of the system as use cases and incorporating additional stakeholder concerns. The resulting use case graph also stores the dependencies between use cases. Note that we perform requirements gathering in all stages of the development process. Thus, we can operate with partial specifications for crosscutting concerns that are identified at the use case stage and are passed to the other stages where we detail them and identify new concerns. In CoCoME, the use cases were given and we could not directly interact with the stakeholders. Instead, we employed brainstorming sessions to reason about the business model and identify stakeholder concerns.

From the use cases we construct a domain model of the system, including all logical entities, data structures, or other knowledge representations. From the domain model, we identify roles as unique, abstract entities interacting in each use case; we define services as interaction patterns between roles. Crosscutting concerns may apply to the entire interaction pattern or only to a fragment of it. The complete set of interactions defined at this stage constitutes the service repository. Next, we obtain the role dependency model through a consolidation of the dependencies between roles participating in the identified services. Within a service, roles exchange messages, thereby switching from one state to another. A role's full behavior is the complete set of states and state transitions involving the role, obtained from all services in which the role participates.

The second phase, Rich Services Architecture, defines a hierarchic set of Rich Services as a logical model of the system. It chooses a main concern and decomposes the interactions in the service repository according to it. The concerns are based on stakeholder values such as manageability, architecture comprehensibility, performance, and organization domains. In the process of mapping roles and services to Rich Services, we decide what to publish through the Service/Data Connectors. Crosscutting concerns map to RISs. For instance, for run-time monitoring of QoS properties, we can add a QoS monitor as a separate infrastructure service. At run-time, each interaction is observed by these monitors, offering the possibility of assessing the correctness and quality of the services. Because the logic needed to orchestrate the message flow is captured by MSCs, we can leverage our work on state machine generation to synthesize it [2]; another option is to describe the orchestration logic by means of WS-BPEL.

Each of these steps feed back into the definition of the use cases; hence, we can refine the model without worrying about the deployment architecture. Newly identified use cases translate at the next iteration into individual Rich Services, and the relationships between the use cases translate into corresponding relationships between Rich Services.

The third phase, System Architecture Definition, establishes a relationship between the Rich Service model of the system and its implementation. Because the target of our approach is system-of-systems integration, we first analyze the system topology in terms of computational and storage nodes (i.e., hosts), and available networks. When such systems are not yet available, the logical model from the second phase can provide hints for building and configuring an adequate topology. In the case of the Trading System, much of the computational and storage node structure is already defined.

In the second stage, we create an idealized network of the identified Rich Services, where each RAS is represented as a virtual host connected to a common bus. This stage focuses on logical connections between RASs. Afterward, we

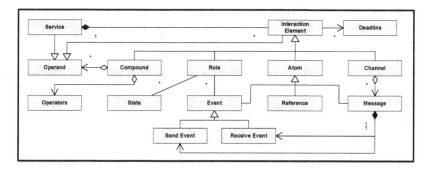

Fig. 3. Message Sequence Chart Service Model

perform a mapping of the Rich Services virtual network to the middleware running on the physical hosts of the systems. Several optimizations for performance,
security, and other crosscutting concerns are possible at this stage. For example,
the logical Rich Service architecture can be mapped 1:1 to an ESB deployment
architecture. Depending on the system requirements and the available resources,
some levels in the hierarchy can be flattened.

In the final stage of the development process, we proceed to the actual implementation of both RASs and RISs. Depending on the middleware infrastructure,
COTS software components can be used to implement some functionality of the
Rich Services. Moreover, some services shared across multiple applications can
be mapped to the same component.

5.2.4   Message Sequence Charts

In this section, we briefly discuss our interaction model for Services. A more
elaborate explanation of this model can be found in [10].

Services are crosscutting; therefore, the best way to define them is based on
interactions. We use Message Sequence Charts (MSCs) [5] in order to specify
interactions. Figure 3 captures the model for MSCs. A Service provides a specified functionality, as defined by the interaction of its Roles. Hence, a Service is
captured as a composite Interaction Element. An Interaction Element can be a
Role, a Channel, an Atom, or a Compound.

In an interaction, a Role represents the participation of a system entity in
an interaction pattern. We can put a star (*) next to the role name to capture
broadcast communication to multiple instances of that role. The semantics of
this notation is that a message sent to such a role is broadcast to all instances of
it. An arrow from such a role, on the other hand, represents a set of messages,
one for each instance. The receiving role has to wait to receive messages. An
Atom can be a Message, an Event, or a Reference to another Service. An Event
is either a Send Event or a Receive Event.

Compound interaction elements consist of a number of Interaction Elements
composed by Operators. This leads to a hierarchy of Services. Instances of Operators are Sequence, Loop, Alternative, Parallel and Join, representing sequential

composition, repetition, choice, parallel and join composition, respectively. The join of two interaction specifications synchronizes its operands on shared interactions while interleaving all others. As we have described in [11], join supports the composition of overlapping system functions.

Note that this interaction model abstracts away from concrete notations. In this text, we used MSCs based on this interaction model to specify the services of the Trading System. The interaction model can also be easily married with the UML2 Sequence Diagram and state machine model [12].

5.3   Modeling the CoCoME

In this section, we present how we applied our Rich Service methodology to the modeling of the Trading System. The Rich Service approach allows us to decompose the system according to different concerns. Following the development process described in the previous section, the first step is capturing functional requirements and additional stakeholders' concerns in the form of use cases. As use cases were already provided as part of the specification, we analyzed them, identified a list of system concerns, and established priorities from the perspective of the Enterprise. This step needs to be done in direct discussions with the stakeholders, but this was not possible in the case study. Therefore, we estimated the priorities as following: manageability (in direct correlation with business operations), governance, workflow performance, reliability, security, and logging. We created the Domain Model for the Trading System, including all participating entities and their relationships. The Domain Model provides us with enough information to extract the participating roles in each use case. Using the extracted roles and the use cases, we modeled each use case with one or more Services by capturing the appropriate interaction patterns in the form of MSCs, and we added each Service to the Service Repository.

After we created the Service Repository, we created the Rich Service Architecture. We defined the logical model for Rich Services by performing a decomposition according to the most important concern, manageability. This led us to an alignment of the Rich Services with the structure of the Enterprise. We then rearranged the Services in the Service Repository to match the Rich Service model, and provided the corresponding mapping between the two. Finally, we identified a possible deployment model.

In the following, we first present the Domain Model for the system's logical roles and data entities. Next, we introduce each Rich Service from a structural and a behavioral viewpoint, including the mapped Services. Due to space considerations, we cannot revisit all models in this chapter. Instead, we present the interactions associated with the use cases for processing a sale and exchanging products between stores. In the end, we provide a deployment mapping from the logical architecture to the infrastructure identified in the CoCoME specification.

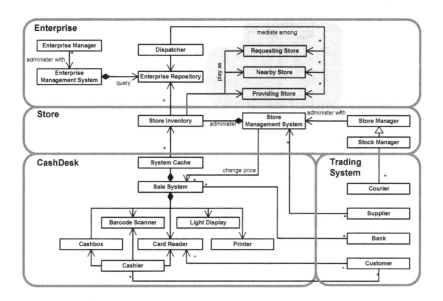

Fig. 4. Domain model for the Trading System: roles

5.3.1 Domain Model

Based on the use cases provided to us, we can identify the major participating entities and generate the domain model. Then, we capture the interaction patterns between entities as services and define *roles* as the contribution of an entity to a service. We describe the subset of the domain model formed by role entities and the communication channels between them as the Role Domain Model.

An entity can participate in different interactions so to achieve various functionalities – by referring to an entity as different roles depending on the functionalities it contributes to, we can achieve better separation of concerns. For example, the grayed area of the domain model in Figure 4 demonstrates the three different roles Stores can play in the product exchange functionality. By defining these roles, we can decouple the action of *providing product* from that of *requesting product exchange*, as well as precisely express the entire interaction involved in the product exchange use case. In addition to the communication channels, a domain model should also convey information on the messages that go on these channels. Figure 5 supplements the domain model for CoCoME by detailing the internal structure of compound messages.

To take full advantage of Rich Services, we must recognize the stakeholders' highest priority, then decompose the domain model based on it. Among the various candidate concerns we chose "business manageability", a core concern of most enterprises, as the main criterion of decomposition. Using the role domain model, we can clearly set out the decomposition boundaries (the grey lines in Figure 4), and we can see the interactions that can occur along or inside the boundaries.

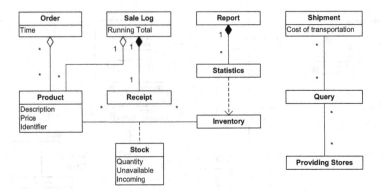

Fig. 5. Domain model for the Trading System: data

5.3.2   Trading System Rich Service

In our ranking of concerns, *business manageability* was the most important, and we decomposed according to management domain. The highest level Rich Service (presented in Figure 6) is the *Trading System*. It comprises the entities that participate in the workflow of the CoCoME case study and are managed by different entities. Elements of the Rich Service include the *Customer*, the *Courier*, the *Bank*, the *Supplier*, and the *Enterprise*.

A Rich Service has *Interactions*, expressed as MSCs, that define how its entities interact. The interface for each *Rich Application Service* (RAS) is given in the Service/Data Connector. If the service is decomposed, the connector can export roles and interactions that define how the service can participate in interactions at a higher level. If, on the other hand, the service is not decomposed and the Service/Data Connector interface is not given explicitly, the RAS can play only one role – the one identified by its name. In this case, all of its interactions are defined by the MSCs in the containing Rich Service.

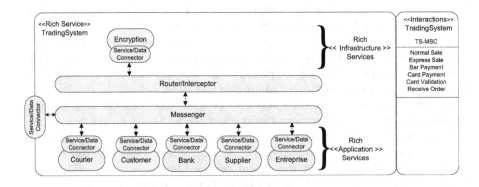

Fig. 6. Trading System Rich Service

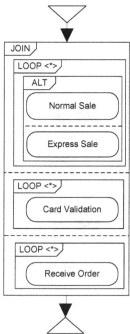

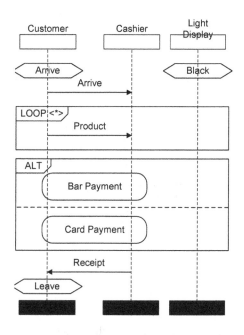

Fig. 7. Main MSC for the Trading System Rich Service

Fig. 8. Interaction for Normal Sale service in the Trading System Rich Service

We also defined a *Rich Infrastructure Service* (RIS) named *Encryption*. It is responsible for decrypting every message from the Enterprise to the Bank and encrypting messages from the Bank to the Enterprise. Inside the Enterprise, other Encryption plugins are responsible for enforcing encryption/decryption in the components that communicate with the Bank. The *Encryption* concern is addressed in our model by two different plugins at different levels of the hierarchy. The Encryption RIS from the Trading System Rich Service specifies that the Bank must decrypt messages received by the Enterprise before consuming them and must encrypt messages before sending them to the Enterprise. The encryption/decryption inside the Enterprise is specified by an Encryption RIS in the Cash Desk Rich Service. The *Encryption* concern has been decomposed into two RISs to allow for end-to-end encryption. In fact, we want the data to be encrypted in the Cash Desk, then to be decrypted in the Bank, and then to travel in encrypted form through the rest of the hierarchy. The need to address this concern in different parts of the system arises from the decomposition choice we made; we further discuss the issues arising form decomposition choices in Section 5.4.

Trading System MSCs. The *Trading System* Rich Service has various interactions expressed as MSCs. The main MSC used to compose all other MSCs in

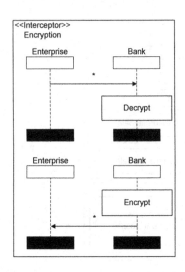

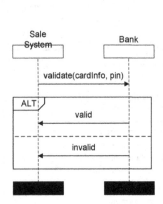

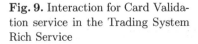

Fig. 9. Interaction for Card Validation service in the Trading System
Rich Service

Fig. 10. Interaction for the Encryption Infrastructure Rich Service in the Trading
System Rich Service

the Rich Service is TS-MSC, as shown in Figure 7. It joins the other services together, meaning that each service runs in parallel, and the common messages are
synchronized. The loop and alternative diagrams containing the Normal and Express Sales show that an infinite number of clients can arrive and make purchases.
The other loops also enable unbounded repetition of the remaining interactions.
Figure 7 defines the interaction behavior of the Trading System Rich Service; all
other MSCs that participate in this behavior must be directly or indirectly referenced through it. Furthermore, the behavior defined by TS-MSC is implicitly
joined with the behaviors defined in all RASs contained in the Trading System
Rich Service.

Figure 8 represents the interaction between a Customer and a Store involved
in a Normal purchase. We expose all roles that the Customer and the Bank must
interact with during a purchase via the Enterprise Service/Data Connector. The
advantage of carrying out the purchase via the connector is that we can enforce
company policies at all levels of management we have defined. For example, only
encrypted messages are allowed between the Bank and the Enterprise.

Figure 9 represents the interaction between the Sale System and the Bank
for card validation. The Sale System is a role exported by the Enterprise, and
it goes down several levels in the hierarchy to the Cash Desk. A complete card
payment interaction requires that the customer provides the credit card and enters a PIN, and that the Bank is contacted by the Sale System and approves
the transaction. However, from the customer's point of view, the interaction
occurs with the Cash Desk in the Store, and from the Bank's point of view, it
occurs with the Sale System. Therefore, from the original interaction, we remove

the roles and the interactions we do not want to expose to the external level. We also break the original interaction into two pieces: the one performed by the client (Card Payment), and the one between the Bank and the Sale System (Card Validation). The benefit of this approach is the encapsulation of information and behavior, thereby allowing us to concentrate on the high level policies and to ignore many details. For example, we can concentrate on the encryption policy for communication between the Bank and Sale System, disregarding the fact that it happens during a Card Payment.

Figure 10 captures the definition of a RIS. It does not define an interaction per se, but associates with interactions defined in RASs. In this case, it mandates the execution of an encryption local action before a message is sent to the Sale System, and the execution of a decryption action when a message is received from the Sale System. It is important to note that this definition addresses a crosscutting concern (privacy) that is not the one we use for the main hierarchical decomposition. Therefore, another RIS addressing encryption is deployed in the Cash Desk service. Another approach to this problem would have been to perform the main decomposition according to privacy domains, thereby encapsulating this information in only one Rich Service.

5.3.3 Enterprise Rich Service

Figure 11 presents the *Enterprise* Rich Service, which provides services such as product exchange among stores and delivery reports. The entities that participate in the enterprise-level workflow are the *Enterprise Manager*, all *Stores*, the *Enterprise Repository*, the *Dispatcher*, and the *Enterprise Management System*. The latter three entities represent logical roles for the enterprise application.

The *Store* Rich Service is further decomposed, and thus its connector provides an interface for the services within the *Enterprise*. A *Store* can play several roles within the *Enterprise*, as we show later in this section.

The *Enterprise* also has RISs for QoS policies and Failure Management. The *QoS Monitor* supervises interactions and verifies that runtime performance matches the specification.

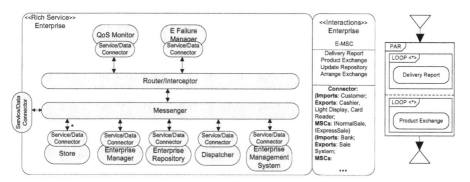

Fig. 11. Enterprise Rich Service

Fig. 12. E-MSC

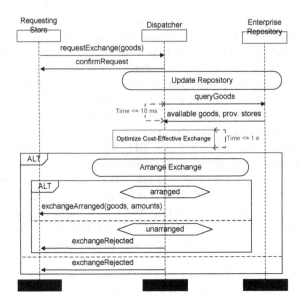

Fig. 13. Interaction for Product Exchange service in the Enterprise Rich Service

Enterprise MSCs. Figure 5.3.3 presents the main MSC, which composes all interactions within the *Enterprise* Rich Service. Because Delivery Report and Exchange Product are independent services that run in parallel, their MSCs are composed with the par operator. We do not show the MSC for the Delivery Report service, as it is fairly simple: the Enterprise Manager interacts with the Enterprise Management System, which queries the Enterprise Repository to generate a report with the mean time to delivery for each supplier.

Figure 13 presents the interactions between Stores, the Dispatcher, and Enterprise Repository as they coordinate the exchange of low-running goods between stores. The interactions are augmented with deadline requirements according to the extra-functional specifications of CoCoME – these messages are intercepted by the QoS Monitor RIS. If the exchange of goods is cost effective, the Dispatcher coordinates the delivery between the Requesting Store and the Providing Stores. The Dispatchers reject the request from the Requesting Store if the exchange is found not to be cost effective, or if no providing store confirms that the exchange is arranged.

Figure 14 shows the interactions between the Dispatcher and the Nearby Stores, resulting in updates to the Enterprise Repository. The Dispatcher invokes a local action to bind actual stores to the Nearby Stores roles, and it changes the routing of messages between these *Stores* and the *Enterprise*. As there may be several Nearby Stores, we express this in the MSC by appending * to the role name. The requestFlush message is *broadcast* to all Nearby Stores, and the stores respond in parallel in a nondeterministic order. The Dispatcher collects the confirmation messages from all stores. The E-Failure Manager Rich Infrastructure Service detects if a store does not confirm in time, and notifies the

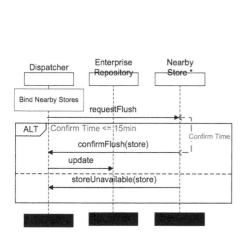

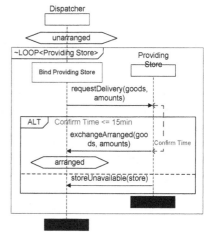

Fig. 14. Interaction for Update Repository service in the Enterprise Rich Service

Fig. 15. Interaction for Arrange Exchange service in the Enterprise Rich Service

Dispatcher that the store is unavailable by sending the storeUnavailable message on behalf of the store.

Figure 15 presents arranging the exchange of goods as interactions between the Dispatcher and the *Providing Store* instances. Note that several different stores could be assigned Providing Store roles. As each store might be requested to deliver different goods, we cannot use broadcast communication to multiple instances of a role* as in Figure 14. Instead, we use a loop operator, where Providing Store is a variable that iterates over the set Providing Stores, which is constructed by the Dispatcher in the previous step in Figure 13. We use the notation ∼LOOP for executing all loop bodies in parallel. The Dispatcher invokes a local action to bind the Providing Store role with the actual Store instance. The requestDelivery message is sent independently to each *Providing Store*, each message having different parameters. The UC8 use case does not mention what should be done if the providing stores do not confirm the exchange. We decided that the exchange is deemed to be arranged if at least one Providing Store sends a confirmation within 15 minutes, the same confirmation time as for Nearby Stores to confirm the flush. The Dispatcher collects the confirmation messages exchangeArranged from all Providing Stores that answer within the deadline.

5.3.4 Store Rich Service

The Store Rich Service includes all entities that are part of a store, each being represented by a different RAS, as shown in Figure 16. Additionally, the Store Rich Service serves as a service relay point between the Cash Desk Rich Service and the Enterprise Rich Service. Therefore, it exports Cash Desk interfaces and imports Enterprise interfaces. (The Trading System Rich Service also exports interfaces that the Enterprise Rich Service imports and passes on.)

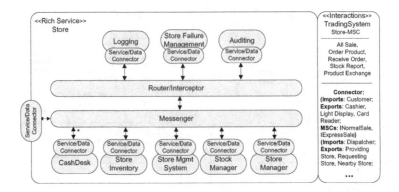

Fig. 16. Store Rich Service

Store MSCs. A sale is illustrated in the MSC in Figure 17. While a sale is somewhat complicated at the Cash Desk Rich Service level, the store participates in the transaction only at the end. Therefore, the MSC shows only the interaction between the Cash Desk's System Cache role and the Store's Store Inventory role. Note that the Cash Desk's System Cash role transmits the Sale Log to the Store Inventory either immediately upon completion of a purchase, or immediately upon resumption of a connection outage. Either way, the interaction with the Store is the same.

The Store Rich Service contains MSCs for the Order Product, Receive Order, and Stock Report interactions. These MSCs track closely with their uses cases, and do not expose any novel concerns. Therefore, in the interest of brevity, they are not presented here.

A Product Exchange Request is illustrated in Figure 18. Most of the complexity of a product exchange occurs in the Enterprise Rich Service, with the Stores participating at the edges of the exchange. An individual store can play the role of either the requestor of goods, a store nearby the requestor store, or a provider of goods to the requestor store. A given product exchange is initiated by the *Requesting Store*, and the Enterprise Rich Service determines which other stores are *Nearby Stores*, and of those, which are also *Providing Stores*.

The Enterprise Rich Service is represented by the Dispatcher role, and the exchange is triggered by an interaction from the System Cache in the Requesting

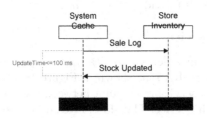

Fig. 17. Store All Sale MSC

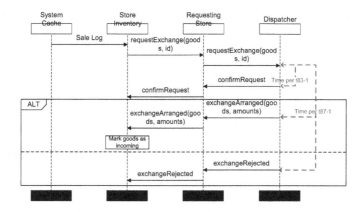

Fig. 18. Store Product Exchange Request MSC

Store's Cash Desk. From the point of view of the requesting store, the Dispatcher returns a confirmation and then a list of goods it has determined can be exchanged. The requesting store then adds these goods into its own inventory and marks them as *incoming*. If no goods can be transferred, the Dispatcher sends a reject message to the requesting store.

The *Requesting Store* role in the MSC of Figure 18 acts as a proxy for the *Store Inventory* to participate with that role in the interactions at the upper level. It is therefore exposed through the connector. Other MSCs capture the behavior of the *Store Inventory* when playing the other roles (*Nearby Store* and *Providing Store*) in the interactions at the upper level.

5.3.5   Cash Desk Rich Service

The Cash Desk Rich Service shown in Figure 19 includes all the entities that are part of the cash desk as Rich Application Services. It includes two Rich Infrastructure Services, namely the Failure Management and the Logging. Figure 19 also shows the exported and imported roles along with the name of their interfaces. A high level MSC for the Cash Desk Rich Service includes the alternative of Normal Sale and Express Sale, joined with a number of other MSCs such as Enter/Exit Express and Update Cached Sales. Due to lack of space, we only describe the Normal Sale in this section.

The Rich Infrastructure Service *Encryption* is the counterpart of the one from the Trading System. As discussed in Section 5.3.2, this plugin allows for end-to-end encryption of the communication between the Cash Desk and the Bank.

Cash Desk MSCs. Figure 20 illustrates the Normal Sale MSC. It is triggered by arrival of the Customer. Note that the Customer role is imported from the higher level and hence is visible to the specific Cash Desk internal Rich Services that are part of the defined import interface, namely the Cashier and the Card Reader. Normal Sale references Sale AddItem MSC for adding each item to

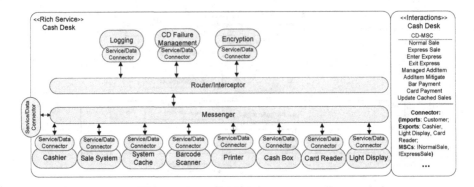

Fig. 19. Cash Desk Rich Service

the shopping list. Then it either proceeds with the Card Payment or the Bar Payment. After completing the payment, the system sends the Sale information to the System Cache. The Cache then periodically updates the sale logs into the Store Inventory to update the stock. The Inventory should confirm the update within 100 ms as declared in the extrafunctional requirements. The receipt is then printed and handed to the Customer.

Sale Add Item is the join of Managed Add Item and Rejected Item MSCs. The Managed AddItem service is shown in Figure 21. Managed AddItem captures adding an item either via Barcode Scanner or by manually entering the item ID. The Item ID is then sent to Store Inventory, which provides the Item Description. If the item is not recognized, the Store Inventory rejects the item by responding with an Item Not Found message. The Rejected Item MSC, which was joined with this Managed AddItem MSC is triggered by the Item Not Found message and captures the Cashier's response – the Cashier either rejects the item and lets the Customer know that the item is rejected, or he enters the human readable item ID and the system identifies the item information. We do not show the Rejected Item MSC, as it is trivial based on the requirements. However, based on the extra-functional requirements, there is a requirement regarding the deadline for the item to be either identified or rejected. In order to capture this requirement, we use a CD-Failure Management Rich Infrastructure Service as shown in Figure 22. The DET operator captures that CD-Failure Management acts as an interceptor and monitors the interaction specified in the first part of this operator. If the deadline for identifying an item, namely the ID Time is not met, then CD-Failure Management signals an error and reject the item by sending the Item Not Found message on behalf of the Store Inventory. The Item Not Found message then again activates the Reject Item MSC.

When the sale is finished (See Figure 20), the Sale System caches the Sale Log. System Cache is responsible for updating the sale into the Store Inventory. As stated in the requirements, the Inventory might be unavailable when the Sale System is trying to update it. Therefore, the Normal Sale is joined with the Update Cached Sales in the main MSC for the Cash Desk. The System Cache periodically tries to update the Inventory if the cache is not empty. If the

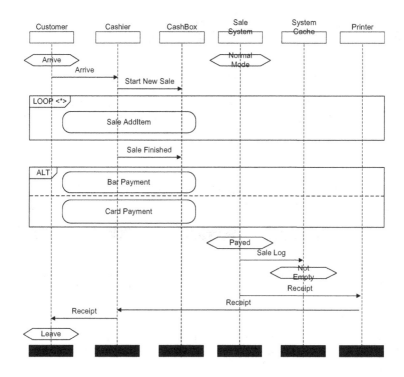

Fig. 20. Normal Sale MSC capturing Use Case 1

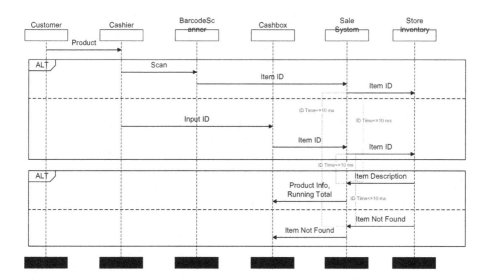

Fig. 21. Managed AddItem MSC capturing adding an Item to shop list

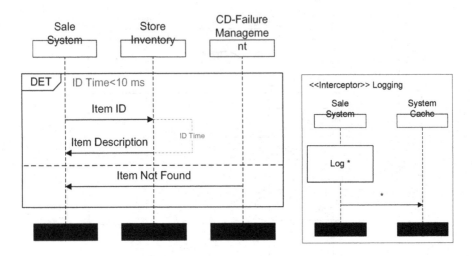

Fig. 22. AddItem Failure Management MSC   **Fig. 23.** Logging MSC capturing logging each Sale

Deadline for updating the Inventory is met, meaning that the Inventory responds to the Sale Log message within 100 ms, then the cache changes its state to empty. If the Inventory is not available, the System Cache tries to update the Inventory after waiting one minute.

Note that based on the requirements, each Sale must be logged before it is sent to the Inventory for updating the stock. This requirement is addressed by using a Logging Rich Infrastructure Service. The Logging service intercepts each message sent by the Sale system to the System Cache and logs it before being sent. This way, all the Sale information is logged before updating the Inventory. This intercepting interaction is illustrated in Figure 23.

5.3.6   Deployment of Rich Services

Because the concept of Rich Service was inspired by ESBs, elements of the Rich Service pattern have conceptually equivalent counterparts in the ESB pattern. This close alignment makes ESB platforms good targets for the physical deployment of Rich Services. Given a specific ESB implementation, such as Mule, we show in this section how a Rich Services model can be deployed.

A Rich Service can be *composite* or *basic*, depending on whether it is further decomposed into other Rich Services. A basic RAS is deployed as a Mule Universal Message Object (UMO). A composite RAS can be deployed as a Mule ESB instance, where the Mule transport layer serves as the Messenger and transmits messages among constituent RASs. A composite RAS enclosed in a higher-level Rich Service can be deployed as a Mule ESB instance plugged into a higher-level Mule ESB instance using any of the Mule-supported transport technologies. A Mule router can receive messages from one channel and republish them according to arbitrary routing rules. This machinery, along with the Mule transport layer, can form the Service/Data Connector as in Figure 24. Mule interceptors can be used to implement RISs and address crosscutting concerns by modifying the collaboration among constituent RASs.

Although creating an ESB instance for each composite Rich Service is straight-forward, in practice we can flatten the Mule hierarchy and achieve better per-formance while still keeping the logical architecture conceptually clean. For example, a composite Rich Service can be deployed as a set of UMOs instead of instantiating a complete ESB for it. Also, if different Rich Services share the same Java Virtual Machine (JVM), connections between Rich Services can be implemented using simple intra-VM method calls, significantly decreasing the communication overhead.

Figure 25 shows one possible deployment layout that aligns with the Rich Ser-vice hierarchy. Composite RASs – *TradingSystem*, *Enterprise*, *Store*, and *Cash Desk* – are deployed as Mule ESB instances. Basic RASs, such as Cash Desk devices, are wrapped as UMOs. RISs are encapsulated as interception/routing rules. In addition to these Rich Services, there are entities beyond the system boundary. For example, the *Bank* communicates with the Enterprise in the log-ical domain, but physically it talks to the Cash Desk directly. However, the policies defined for this communication in the Trading System, Enterprise, and Store Rich Services must still be applied.

The solution to the mismatch between conceptual and physical link is two-fold: recovering the physical link in the deployment layout, and at the same time keep-ing the logical link by message duplication and rerouting. The first can be done by consulting the Domain Model to identify mismatched links. The second can be done by duplicating messages that go through that link, then rerouting them to the encompassing Rich Services. Neither step alters the logical architecture, and both can be executed automatically with tool support. By reconciling the mis-match, we get a physically-aligned deployment layout as in Figure 25.

Besides the hierarchical deployment, it is possible to have a flattened deploy-ment layout (see Figure 26) in which all Rich Services are deployed into a single ESB. The process of flattening a Rich Service hierarchy is the same as the steps

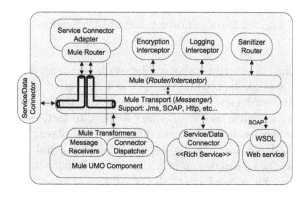

Fig. 24. Deployment of Rich Service using Mule ESB

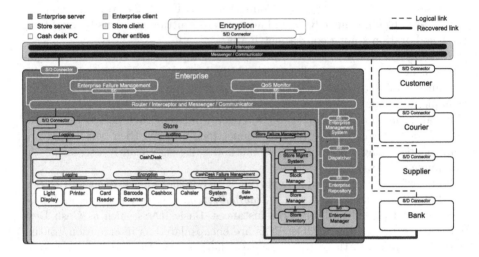

Fig. 25. Deployment of Trading System

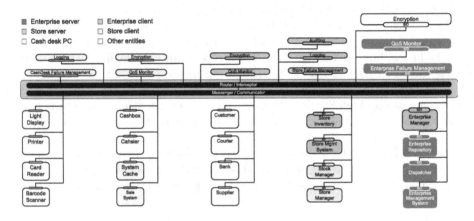

Fig. 26. Flattened deployment of Rich Services

of mismatch resolution described above. The result is a deployment layout that physically aligns a single bus, while the logical links between Rich Service are unaltered. The flattened view of deployment can lead to the deeper discussion of system composition presented in the next section. In fact, we can deploy the same logical Rich Service architecture in different ways, observing various physical constraints and requirements by applying mismatch link resolution. This demonstrates that the logical design of Rich Services is independent of the physical deployment, which is one form of the separation of concerns we claimed in previous sections.

5.4   Discussion and Analysis

In this section, we examine the various decisions we made during the creation of the CoCoME architecture, and we analyze their impact on the resulting system. We modeled a subset of the extra-functional requirements described in the case study to demonstrate the ability of Rich Services to deal gracefully with cross-cutting requirements aspects. In this chapter, we included only a subset of the models we produced. Many refinements are possible, including adding more of the extra-functional timing requirements and defining error recovery behaviors when the timing constraints are not met.

Decomposition. The first important decision we made was how to decompose the system. In section 5.3, we presented the list of concerns we considered. Assuming that *business manageability* is the chief concern, we presented a corresponding decomposition of the system into a hierarchy of Rich Services. Because we performed decomposition along only one dimension, the architecture we presented is subject to the common problem known as "tyranny of the dominant decomposition" [13]: when one decomposition dimension is chosen, many trade-offs are determined by that decision.

In our Rich Service hierarchy, for example, the *Bank* at the *Trading System* level must communicate with the *Cash Desk* three levels below. This has consequences for the architecture: communication must be allowed explicitly through three different *Connectors*, and end-to-end encryption requires that an encryption RIS be deployed in several Rich Services. Choosing another decomposition strategy, such as by privacy concerns, would have yielded a different hierarchy where *Bank* and *Sale System* would be in the same Rich Service. In this decomposition, only one encryption RIS would be required for end-to-end encryption. However, by decomposing along business manageability concerns, we can easily deal with policies imposed at different business tiers. If, for example, it is necessary to create a new enterprise policy that limits orders from stores to only certain suppliers, an RIS could easily be inserted into the Enterprise Rich Service – it would filter the communication from stores to suppliers.

The benefit of our Rich Service approach is that each Rich Service is just a partial specification of the behavior. Thus, it is possible to decompose the system according to more than one concern, providing different views, each capturing a different decomposition of the Rich Services. The drawback of this multi-view approach, as in most multi-perspective specifications [14], is that ensuring consistency of the different models is more challenging. We are actively working on the model consistency problem to make the multi-view approach more appealing. In this case study, in order to avoid the consistency issues that arise from decomposing according to multiple concerns, we chose to present only one decomposition – according to the concern ranked highest in our analysis.

Deployment. Another important discussion point is the choice of deployment. In section 5.3.6, we provided two views of deployment. A flattened view represented the logical ESB architecture, where each connector and policy infrastructure service is represented by one block. All communication is routed through the various plugins to enforce all policies defined by the Rich Service view. This view is useful for presenting all policy blocks and the order in which each is applied. Interestingly enough, in our physical deployment we had different instances of each policy block in the deployment hierarchy, which closely resembles the Rich Service hierarchy. The use of replication for policy blocks allows for optimization of communications. However, the choice makes updating such policy blocks more challenging because consistency must be assured over different instances across the entire system.

The flattened deployment view allows us to interpret all the constraints defined in the connectors of the various Rich Services and in the infrastructure services such that they are independent of the original hierarchy. Those are the elements we can compose to create a system out of different Rich Service views, capturing decompositions according to different concerns. Our future research aims to leverage flexible routing policies between the blocks in the flattened implementation view to obtain implementations from multi-perspective Rich Services models.

In our physical model view, we deployed an ESB infrastructure in each PC and implemented all application and infrastructure Rich Services as middleware plugins. This choice, even if convenient and natural, is not mandated by the Rich Service approach. For example, the Cash Desk PC could be replaced by an embedded system where the code is written in C without using any middleware. The communication with the Store PC could be performed with an ad-hoc protocol, and from there the same ESB-based application could take over. However, using an ESB framework has several advantages. First, its flexible communication infrastructure enables communication between different platforms without the need to create any new code. Moreover, the creation of each computation block is independent of the communication protocol used to interact with other blocks. This enables seamless reuse of components in different parts of the system, allowing for replication of policy plugins without the need to change code. Another benefit of using ESB middleware is that it enables the definition of routing policies and method interceptors without changing code. This closely resembles the semantics of our infrastructure services and connectors in the logical deployment view. It is easy to develop the system based on that view and deploy it in different physical configurations by simply configuring the ESB infrastructure, greatly increasing code reuse for product line development.

An ESB can discharge many common requirements of a system. In the Co-CoME case study, we needed to allow the Cash Desk to work in isolation if the Store PC is not online, and then to synchronize with the Store PC once it is back online. This requirement has led us to introduce cache roles in the model. Most ESBs can leverage messaging platforms that can guarantee delivery automatically. Therefore, by simply using the ESB's messaging infrastructure to send the update message from the Cash Desk PC to the Store PC, we can achieve the offline caching and resynchronization, thus discharging the disconnected operation requirement. Because there exists many ESBs that provide common services such as authentication, encryption, logging, and auditing, we can often discharge many requirements by using COTS components [15].

Crosscutting concerns. Finally, when analyzing the implementation strategy for infrastructure Rich Services, we recognize that the goal of such services is to address crosscutting issues in a centralized way. We capture the crosscutting requirements in a single block and apply the needed policy. We have already explained that infrastructure services can leverage an ESB to modify interactions without explicit code modifications. In fact, there are two possible mechanisms in an ESB that enable easy implementation of infrastructure services. The first approach is to use interceptors. This technique can be used to intercept method calls in the implementation of application services, then run alternative or additional code from infrastructure services. This technique can, for example, be used to implement the infrastructure service of Figure 10. Here, the use of local actions enforces end-to-end encryption. It mandates that the decryption code is executed before processing any received message, and the encryption code is executed before sending any message. Using interceptors, the code is executed before and after the local action that sends or receives the message. Another implementation strategy uses routing to insert a processing filter into the communication pattern. The same encryption/decryption service could have been implemented by having the messages between Bank and Sale System routed through an encryption/decryption plugin. The benefit of such technique is that the computation can easily be delegated to a different PC because the routing of the communication channels can be seamlessly adapted to forward the message to different machines. Our end-to-end privacy requirement, however, does not allow the message to be sent unencrypted to any other machine. We can model the second implementation strategy by using an additional role in the infrastructure service that receives the message and does the processing.

Failure management is an example of a crosscutting concern that can be expressed using infrastructure services. By its very nature, because the hardware on which some application Rich Services run can fail, failure management often requires the service being implemented in a different process or on a different hardware platform. The infrastructure Rich Service definition that uses an external role is therefore very valuable for detecting or mitigating a failure in some application Rich Service.

5.5   Tool Support

We have built a complete tool chain to support a traditional service-oriented software development process, and it can be extended to support Rich Services. Because Rich Services are a derivative of traditional services, a natural path exists to the creation of an integrated Rich Service development tool chain. We briefly introduce the tool chain and explain how it fits with the Rich Service notion.

The existing tool chain consists of a number of tools supporting interaction-based and service-oriented development. Fig. 27 gives an overview of some of our

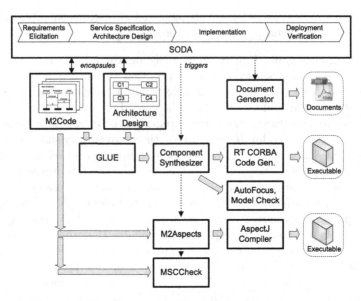

Fig. 27. Service-Oriented Tool-chain

tools and their dependencies. We divide the tool chain roughly by stages in the overall development cycle: *Requirements Elicitation*, *Service Specification and Architecture Design*, *Implementation*, as well as *Deployment and Verification*.

The overall dependencies are as follows: The *SODA tool* tracks requirements of service-oriented systems and generates requirements and architecture documentation. *M2Code* provides facilities for intuitive graphical service modeling with MSCs. M2Code also contains a *Component Synthesizer* that generates state machines for all components participating in the modeled services. The GLUE tool maps the component state machines to more complicated target architectures, for instance, replicated component instances. The component state machines are the basis for code generation of executable prototypes (using RT CORBA CodeGen and M2Aspects) and verification by model checking (using S2Promela, ServiceDebug, and MSCCheck).

The tools we currently have available allow us to convert interaction specifications (described by MSCs) to automata suitable for automated verification. We are in particular able to convert MSCs specifications to the Promela language and verify their properties using the SPIN model checker. We can leverage these verification tools in the context of Rich Service development toward two ends. First, we can verify the consistency of Rich Service interfaces with the internal interaction behavior specified by MSCs. Second, we can verify properties of the communication patterns defined in each Rich Service.

ESBs are new to our tool chain. In the previous sections, we discussed the benefits of leveraging an ESB to implement Rich Service models. The benefit of configuring an ESB infrastructure from available components is that it allows us to quickly configure and easily augment services.

ESBs can be configured with myriad infrastructure choices. We have experimented with some choices in multiple technologies [16]: Authentication protocols (such as Acegi), encryption standards (SSL, HTTPS), persistence providers (MySQL, Postgresql, Apache Derby), transaction support (XA, JOTM, JTA), messaging (ActiveMQ, JBOSS Messaging, WebsphereMQ, SonicMQ), and object broker middleware (Xbean, Spring, Mule).

An ESB can, for example, be configured to support integration through web services. It can either use stand alone services, or create complex, distributed composite applications spanning multiple transport and message formats. The messaging backbone configured in an ESB supports both Publish/Subscribe and point-to-point messaging paradigms. It can support durable, fault tolerant, and highly available connections.

In summary, enhancing the existing tool chain by introducing ESB support to facilitate Rich Service development is a promising direction.

5.6   Summary

The Rich Services architecture and process we used to model the CoCoME case study leverages and goes beyond the state of the art in current SOA – and, more specifically, Web services – development by providing a flexible and comprehensive architectural framework that can be used as a basis for a methodological approach to complex systems of systems integration projects.

Rich Services address two major integration concerns.

First, they support the managed orchestration of a set of services that is connected to a common communication infrastructure. Management is achieved by providing a mechanism for the infrastructure to monitor and intercept service conversations, followed by targeted re-routing of these conversations to enforce policies among the set of services. This can easily be exploited to introduce a common set of security policies, or, as we demonstrated in the case study, a comprehensive failure management approach. In general, this mechanism allows us to address crosscutting concerns among the services under consideration.

Second, Rich Services reconcile the notion of hierarchy with the otherwise typically flat service notion – this is of fundamental importance in ultra-large scale system-of-systems integration projects. Here, typically we have to deal with different domains of governance and policy, as was demonstrated in the case study in terms of the levels of Enterprise to Store to CashBox. This is prototypical also of large enterprise architectures, which often grow beyond national boundaries, with different laws, standards and policies in every locale. The ability to localize the management of policies, while guaranteeing the adherence also to architecture-wide policies, is vital for an architecture-based enterprise integration strategy. Purely centralized solutions are seldom sustainable in this scenario.

Rich Services provide a model for both logical and deployment/ implementation architectures. At the logical level, the architectural blueprint allows the designer to bring forward crosscutting architectural concerns while disentangling them from purely application-based concerns. We model this with our distinction between Rich Infrastructure and Rich Application Services. Because the Rich Services blueprint was inspired by the emerging Enterprise Service Bus (ESB) and existing Web services technologies, there is minimum distance between a logical Rich Service architecture and its corresponding ESB/Web service deployment. On the other hand, the logical decomposition into communication infrastructure, router/interceptor, and RAS/RIS is independent of concrete deployment technologies. In fact, with little overhead, the blueprint can be mapped, for instance, into a Java VM.

The models we created for CoCoME support the observations above. Our logical architecture follows the decomposition of the system along the various domains of management. At the same time, we are able to model the conversations between all entities at all levels of the hierarchy by means of an import/export mechanism for structure and behavior at the level of service interface/gateways. In particular, we are able to model crosscutting policy and failure management concerns at all architectural levels. The deployment mapping, on the other hand, follows the physical distribution of IT systems across the various organizational layers while keeping the properties specified at the logical architecture level intact.

Clearly, there is ample opportunity for refinement of both the models we created and the Rich Service architecture framework and process, including the integration of dedicated refactoring techniques to simplify the integration of legacy systems into the Rich Services framework. We believe that the flexibility of the Rich Services architecture framework, in particular, supports rapid changes at the architectural level while maintaining overall architectural integrity of the integration solution.

References

1. Arrott, M., Demchak, B., Ermagan, V., Farcas, C., Farcas, E., Krüger, I.H., Menarini, M.: Rich Services: The integration piece of the SOA puzzle. In: Proceedings of the IEEE International Conference on Web Services (ICWS) (July 2007)
2. Krüger, I.H., Mathew, R.: Component synthesis from service specifications. In: Leue, S., Systä, T.J. (eds.) Scenarios: Models, Transformations and Tools. LNCS, vol. 3466, pp. 255–277. Springer, Berlin (2005)
3. Evans, E.: Domain Driven Design. Addison-Wesley, Reading (2003)
4. MuleSource Inc.: Mule Open Source ESB and Integration Platform (2007), http://mule.mulesource.org/wiki/display/MULE/Home
5. Krüger, I.: Distributed System Design with Message Sequence Charts. PhD thesis, Technische Universität München (2000)
6. Broy, M., Krüger, I.: Interaction interfaces - towards a scientific foundation of a methodological usage of Message Sequence Charts. In: Staples, J., Hinchey, M.G., Liu, S. (eds.) Formal Engineering Methods (ICFEM), IEEE Computer Society Press, Los Alamitos (1998)

7. Demchak, B., Farcas, C., Farcas, E., Krüger, I.H.: The treasure map for Rich Services. In: Proceedings of the 2007 IEEE International Conference on Information Reuse and Integration (IRI), IEEE, Los Alamitos (2007)
8. National Information Assurance Partnership: The Common Criteria Evaluation and Validation Scheme (2007), `http://niap.nist.gov/cc-scheme/`
9. Prasad, K.V., Giuli, T., Watson, D.: The case for modeling security, privacy, usability and reliability (SPUR) in automotive software. In: Automotive Software Workshop, San Diego, CA (2006)
10. Ermagan, V., Krueger, I., Menarini, M., Mizutani, J.I., Oguchi, K., Weir, D.: Towards model-based failure-management for automotive software. In: Proceedings of the ICSE Fourth International Workshop on Software Engineering for Automotive Systems (SEAS), p. 8. IEEE Computer Society Press, Los Alamitos (2007)
11. Krüger, I.H.: Capturing overlapping, triggered, and preemptive collaborations using MSCs. In: Pezzé, M. (ed.) FASE 2003. LNCS, vol. 2621, pp. 387–402. Springer, Heidelberg (2003)
12. OMG: UML 2.1.1 Superstructure Specification Number formal/07-02-03 (2007)
13. Tarr, P., Ossher, H., Harrison, W., Sutton, S.J.: N degrees of separation: multidimensional separation of concerns. In: Proceedings of the International Conference on Software Engineering, pp. 107–119. IEEE Computer Society Press, Los Alamitos (1999)
14. Finkelstein, A., Gabbay, D., Hunter, A., Kramer, J., Nuseibeh, B.: Inconsistency handling in multiperspective specifications. IEEE Transactions on Software Engineering 20(8), 569–578 (1994)
15. Ermagan, V., Farcas, C., Farcas, E., Krüger, I.H., Menarini, M.: A service-oriented blueprint for COTS integration: the hidden part of the iceberg. In: Proceedings of the ICSE Second International Workshop on Incorporating COTS Software into Software Systems: Tools and Techniques (IWICSS). IEEE Computer Society Press, Los Alamitos (2007)
16. Krüger, I.H., Meisinger, M., Menarini, M., Pasco, S.: Rapid systems of systems integration - combining an architecture-centric approach with Enterprise Service Bus infrastructure. In: Proceedings of IEEE 2006 International Conference on Information Reuse and Integration, pp. 51–56. EEE Systems, Man, and Cybernetics Society, Piscataway (2006)

6 Modelling with Relational Calculus of Object and Component Systems - rCOS

Zhenbang Chen[1,5], Abdel Hakim Hannousse[1], Dang Van Hung[1], Istvan Knoll[3],
Xiaoshan Li[2], Zhiming Liu[1,*], Yang Liu[1], Qu Nan[4], Joseph C. Okika[1,3],
Anders P. Ravn[3], Volker Stolz[1], Lu Yang[1], and Naijun Zhan[1,4]

[1] International Institute for Software Technology –
United Nations University, Macao
Z.Liu@iist.unu.edu
[2] Faculty of Science and Technology, The University of Macau
[3] Department of Computer Science, Aalborg University, Denmark
[4] Lab. of Computer Science, Institute of Software, CAS, China
[5] National Laboratory for Parallel and Distributed Processing, China

Abstract. This chapter presents a formalization of functional and behavioural requirements, and a refinement of requirements to a design for CoCoME using the *Relational Calculus of Object and Component Systems* (rCOS). We give a model of requirements based on an abstraction of the use cases described in Chapter 3.2. Then the refinement calculus of rCOS is used to derive design models corresponding to the top level designs of Chapter 3.4. We demonstrate how rCOS supports modelling different views and their relationships of the system and the separation of concerns in the development.

Keywords: Requirements Modelling, Design, Refinement, Transformation.

6.1 Introduction

The complexity of modern software applications ranging from enterprise to embedded systems is growing. In the development of a system like the CoCoME system, in addition to the design of the application functionality, design of the interactions among the GUI, the controllers of the hardware devices and the application software components is a demanding task. A most effective means to handle complexity is *separation of concerns*, and assurance of correctness is enhanced by *formal modelling* and *formal analysis*.

Separation of concerns. Separation of concerns is to divide and conquer. At any stage of the development of a system, the system is divided into a number

---

* Team Leader and corresponding author, UNU-IIST, P.O.Box 3058, Macao. This work is supported by the projects HighQSoftD and HTTS funded by Macao Science and Technology Development Fund; Nordunet3; the 973 Project of China 2005CB321802; the 863 Project of China 2006AA01Z165; and the NSFC Projects 60573081, 60573085, and 90612009.

A. Rausch et al. (Eds.): Common Component Modeling Example, LNCS 5153, pp. 116–145, 2008.

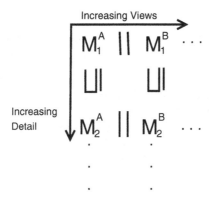

Fig. 1. rCOS approach with views and refinements

of views or aspects: the static structural view, the interaction view, the dynamic view and their timing aspects. These views can be modeled separately and their integration forms a model of the whole system. Different concerns require different models and different techniques; state-based static specifications of functionality and their refinement is good for specification and design of the functionality, while event-based techniques are the simplest for designing and analyzing interactions among different components including application software components, GUI components and controllers of hardware devices.

Formalization. In recent UML-based development, the static structural view is modeled by packages of *class diagrams* and/or *component diagrams*, dynamic behavior by state diagrams, and *interactions* by sequence diagrams. However, UML has a formal syntax only, and its semantics is not formally definable without imposing strong restrictions.

To assure correctness, we need to incorporate semantic reasoning through specification, refinement, verification and analysis into the development process.

To provide formal support to multi-view and multi-level modelling and analysis in a model-driven development process, a desirable method should

1. Allow to model different views of the system at different levels of abstraction,
2. Provide analysis and verification techniques and tools that assist in showing that the models have the desired properties,
3. Give precise definitions of correctness preserving model transformations, and provide effective rules and tool support for these transformations.

Based on these considerations, we have recently developed a refinement calculus, named rCOS, for design of object and component oriented software systems [9,14,10,5]. It provides a two dimensional refinement framework, that is, *consistent increments* to the models for the multiple parallel ($\|$) views in the horizontal dimension, and *refinement*, a relation ($\sqsubseteq$) between models at different levels of abstraction in the vertical dimension.

6.1.1   Goals and Scope of the Component Model

rCOS is an extended theory of Hoare and He's Unifying Theories of Programming (UTP) for object-oriented and component-based programming. The key concepts in the rCOS approach are:

- A component is an aggregation of objects and processes with interfaces. Each interface has a contract, that specifies what is needed for the component to be *used* in building and maintaining a software *without the need to know its design and implementation*. A contract only specifies the functional behavior in terms of pre and post conditions and a protocol defining the permissible traces of method invocations.
- Components can be composed hierarchically by plugging, renaming, hiding and feedback. These operators are defined by a relational semantics for object-oriented programs. Procedural programs are special cases of object-oriented programs in rCOS.
- Composition is supported by required and provided interfaces.
- The refinements are verifiable through rCOS laws. The compatibility of the compositions in the concrete example have been checked for the protocols using the FDR tool, and some of the functionality specifications have been checked using JML.
- Application aspects are dealt with in a use-case driven Requirements Modelling phase. Each use case is specified as a contract of the provided interface of a component, in which the interaction protocol is specified by a set of traces and illustrated by a UML sequence diagram. The functionalities of the provided interface methods are given by the their pre and post conditions, the dynamic behavior is given by guarded design and depicted by a UML state diagram. The data and class structure are specified by class declarations and depicted by a class diagram. The consistency conditions of the requirements include the consistency between the interaction protocol and the dynamic behavior for each use case, and system invariants that relate all use cases.
- The use cases are then designed by using object-oriented refinements, including functionality delegation (via the *expert pattern*), class decomposition and data encapsulation. Such a model of object-oriented design describes how the interface methods (i.e. methods of the use cases) are realized via interaction of internal domain objects of the class diagram. This model is then transformed into a component-based architecture, called a *model of logical design*, by wrapping related objects into components and identifying the interfaces among them from interactions between objects in different components.
- The logical design is refined and refactored to a specific component architecture suitable for a given technical platform, and each component can be further refined to a model which is ready for coding (or code generation).
- The approach does not address deployment but can include code to the extent that the implementation language is given an rCOS semantics.

6.1.2   Modelled Cutout of CoCoME

For the example, we have covered the following:

- The aspects of Requirements Modelling, Logical Design and Component Architecture Design are illustrated. Testing can be done using JML, although translation of an rCOS functionality specification of a class to its JML counterpart is carried out manually. Deployment has not been done.
- The rCOS approach is not currently able to handle dynamic composition.
- The strong parts of the treatment are formal component specifications, refinement and multi-view consistency checks.
- The weak parts are extra-functional properties and missing tool support.
- We did not model the exact architecture of the CoCoME because we focused on the systematic refinements step from requirements to a component architecture very similar to the one of CoCoME implementation.
- The protocol and multi-view consistency were verified for the logical design using FDR and JML respectively.

6.1.3   Benefit of the Modelling

In a model driven development process, the rCOS approach offers:

- A formal specification and analysis of different views including static structure, interactions and functionalities.
- High-level refinement rules for adding details in moving from one level of design to another.
- How different tools for verification and analysis may be incorporated.

6.1.4   Effort and Lessons Learned

Getting acquainted with rCOS requires three months with reasonable background in formal methods in general. In the context of the CoCoME experiment, the current treatment took experienced rCOS people about 2 work months (about 5 people over 1.5 calendar month). We estimate that a complete treatment of the example to the level of a component architecture design would require about 12 work months.

In more detail, one experienced formal rCOS expert spent one day working out the specification of **UC 1**, and the other six use cases took a 4-person week of PhD students, supervised by the experienced person. The OO design of **UC 1** took the rCOS expert less than one hour with writing, but the design of the other use cases took another 4-student week. A lot of effort had to be spent on ensuring model consistency manually. Just from the presented design we have derived around 65 Java classes with over 4000 lines including comments and blank lines. The packages of the *classes* for the resulting component-based model are shown in Appendix B.

Among the important lessons from the exercise are that after developing the functional specifications, the other tasks follow almost mechanically. However, there is still much room in both design and implementation for an efficient solution, taking into account for example, knowledge about the uniqueness of keys in lookups resulting from existential quantification.

6.1.5   Overview

In the next section the fundamental concepts and ideas of the rCOS Component Model are introduced. Section 6.3 shows an rCOS formalization of the requirements for the common example including specifications of classes with local protocols and functional specification. Based on the functional specifications, an object-oriented design is generated. This is refined to components that are fitted into the prescribed architecture of the exercise. In Section 6.4, we discuss Extra-functional properties and related Tool Support. Finally, Section 6.5 concludes and discusses the perspectives and limitations of the solution. In particular we comment on how extra-functional properties can be included through observables, and likely approaches to extensive tool support.

6.2   Component Model

We introduce the basic syntax of rCOS that we will use in the case study, with their informal semantics. We will keep the introduction mostly informal and minimal that is enough for the understanding of the rCOS models of CoCoME. For detailed study, we refer the reader to our work in [9,14,10,5].

The *Relational Calculus of Object and Component Systems* (rCOS) has its roots in the *Unified Theory of Programming* (UTP) [11].

UTP - The background of rCOS. UTP is the completion of many years of effort in the formalization of programming language concepts and reasoning techniques for programs by Tony Hoare and He Jifeng. It combines the reasoning power of ordinary predicate calculus with the structuring power of relational algebra. All programs are seen as binary relations on a state space which is a valuation of a set X of program variables or other observables. An example of an observable is a variable ok', which is true exactly when a program terminates. In all generality, the partial relation for a sequential program P is specified by a pair of predicates over the state variables, denoted by $pre(x) \vdash post(x, x')$ and called a *design*, where x represents the values of the variables before the execution of the program and x' denotes the new values for the variables after the execution, $pre(x)$ is the *precondition* defining the domain of the relation, and $post(x, x')$ is the *postcondition* defining the relation itself.

The meaning of the design $pre(x) \vdash post(x, x')$ is defined by the predicate: $pre(x) \wedge ok \Rightarrow ok' \wedge post(x, x')$, asserting that if the program is activated from a well-defined state (i.e. its preceding program terminated) that satisfies the precondition $pre(x)$ then the execution of the program will *terminate* (i.e. $ok' = true$) in a state such that the new values in this state are related with the old values before the execution by *post*. For example, an assignment $x := x + y$ is defined as $true \vdash x' = x + y$.

In UTP, it is known that designs are closed under all the standard programming constructs like sequential composition, choice, and iteration. For example, $D_1; D_2$ is defined to be the relational composition $\exists x_0 : (D_1(x_0/x') \land D_2(x_0/x))$. For concurrency with communicating processes, additional observables record communication traces; communication readiness can be expressed by *guard* predicates. A major virtue of using a relational calculus is that *refinement* between programs is easily defined as relation inclusion or logical implication.

It is clear that UTP needs adaptation to specific programming paradigms, and rCOS has emerged from the work of He Jifeng and Zhiming Liu to formalize the concepts of object oriented programming: classes, object references, method invocation, subtyping and polymorphism [9]. They have continued to include concepts of component-based and model-driven development: interfaces, protocols, components, connectors, and coordination [10,5]. Thus rCOS is a solid semantic foundation for component-based design. Also, its refinement calculus has been further developed such that it offers a systematic approach to deriving component based software from specifications of requirements.

With a programming language like Java, OO and component-based refinement can effectively ensure correctness. Most refinement rules have corresponding design patterns and thus Java implementations. This takes refinement from programming in the small to programming in the large.

6.2.1   Object Modelling in rCOS

Just as in Java, an OO program in rCOS has *class declarations* and a *main program* [9]. A class can be public or private and declares its attributes and methods, they can be public, private or protected. The main program is given as a *main class*. Its attributes are the global variables of program and it has a main method *main()*, that implements the application processes. Unlike Java, the definition of a method allows specification statements which use the notion of design *pre ⊢ post*. Notice that the use of the variables *ok* and *ok'* implies that rCOS is a total correctness model, that is if the precondition holds the execution terminates correctly.

Types and Notations. Another difference of rCOS from an OO programming language is that we distinguish data from objects and thus a datum, such as an integer or a boolean value does not have a reference. For the CoCoME case study, we assume the following data types:

$$V ::= long \mid double \mid char \mid string \mid bool$$

Assuming an infinite set CN of symbols, called class names, we define the following type system, where C ranges over CN

$$T ::= V \mid C \mid array[1..n](T) \mid set(T) \mid bag(T)$$

where $array[1 : n](T)$ the type of arrays of type T, and $set(T)$ is the type of sets of type T. We assume the operations $add(T\ a)$, $contains(T\ a)$, $delete(T\ a)$ and $sum()$ on a set and a bag with their standard semantics. For a variable s of type $set(T)$, the specification statement $s.add(a)$ equals $s' = s \cup \{a\}$, $s.sum()$ is the sum of all elements of s, which is assumed to a set of numbers. We use curly brackets $\{e_1, \ldots, e_n\}$ and the square brackets $[[e_1, \ldots, e_m]]$ to define a set and a bag. For set s such that each element has an identifier, $s.find(id)$ denotes the function that returns the element whose identifier equals id if there is one, it returns *null* otherwise. Java provides the implementations of these types via the *Collection* interface. Thus these operations in specifications can be directly coded in Java.

In specifications, $C\,o$ means that object o has type C, and $o \neq null$ means that o is in the object heap if the type of o is a class, and that o is defined if its type is a data type. The shorthand $o \in C$ denotes that $o \neq null$ and its type is C.

In rCOS, evaluation of expressions does not change the state of the system, and thus the Java expression **new** $C()$ is not a rCOS expression. Instead, we take $C.New(C\,x)$ as a command that creates an object of C and assigns it to variable x. The attributes of this object are assigned with the initial values or objects declared in C. If no initial value is declared it will be *null*. However, in the specification of CoCoME, we use $x' = C.New()$ to denote $C.New(x)$, and $x' = C.New[v_1/a_1, \ldots, a_k/v_k]$ to denote the predicate $C.New[v_1/a_1, \ldots, a_k/v_k](x)$ that a new object of class C is created with the attributes a_1 initialized with v_i for $i = 1, \ldots, k$, and this objects is assigned to variable x.

A *design pre* $\vdash$ *post* for a method in rCOS is here written separately as **Pre** *pre* and **Post** *post*. For the sake of systematic refinement, we write the specification of static functionality of a use case handler class in the following format:

> **class** C [**extends** D] {
> **attributes** $T\,x = d, \ldots, T_k\,x = d$
> **methods** $m(T\ in;\ V\ return)$ {
>   pre: $c \vee \ldots \vee c$
>   post: $\wedge\ (R; \ldots; R) \vee \ldots \vee (R; \ldots; R)$
> $\wedge \ldots \ldots$
> $\wedge\ (R; \ldots; R) \vee \ldots \vee (R; \ldots; R)$ }
> $\ldots \ldots$
> $m(T\ in;\ V\ return)$ { $\ldots \ldots$ }
> **invariant**   *Inv*
>   }

where

- The list of class declarations can be represented as a UML class diagram.
- The initial value of an attribute is optional.
- Each c in the precondition, is a conjunction of primitive predicates.
- Each relation R in the postcondition is of the form $c \wedge (le' = e)$, where c is a boolean condition and le an *assignable expression* and e is an expression. An assignable le is either a primitive variable x, or an attribute name, a, or $le.a$ for an attribute name a. We use **if** c **then** $le' = e_1$ **else** $le' = e_2$ for $c \wedge (le' = e_1) \vee \neg c \wedge (le' = e_2)$ and **if** c **then** $le' = e$ for $c \wedge (le' = e) \vee \neg c \wedge$ **skip**. Notice here that the expression e does not have to be an executable expression. Instead, e is a logically specified expression, such as the greatest common divisor of two given integers.

We allow the use of *indexed conjunction* $\forall i \in I : R(i)$ and *indexed disjunctions* $\exists i \in I : R(i)$ for a finite set I. These would be the quantifications if the index set is infinite.

The above format has been influenced by TLA$^+$ [12], UNITY [4] and Java. We also need a notation for traces; in this setting, they are given by UML sequence diagrams and the UML state diagrams.

6.2.2 Refinement

In rCOS, we provide three levels of refinement:

1. Refinement of a whole object program. This may involve the change of anything as long as the visible behavior of the main method is preserved. It is an extension to the notion of data refinement in imperative programming, with a semantic model dealing with object references. In such a refinement, all non-public attributes of objects are treated as local (or internal) variables [9].
2. Refinement of the class declaration section $Classes_1$ is a refinement of $Classes$ if $Classes_1 \bullet main$ refines $Classes \bullet main$ for all $main$. This means that $Classes_1$ supports at least as many functional services as $Classes$.
3. Refinement of a method of a class. This extends the theory of refinement in imperative programming, with a semantic model dealing with object references. Obviously, $Class_1$ refines $Class$ if the public class names in $Classes$ are all in $Classes_1$ and for each public method of each public class in $Classes$ there is a refined method in the corresponding class of $Classes_1$.

An rCOS design has mainly three kinds of refinement: *Delegation of functionality* (or *responsibility*), *attribute encapsulation*, and *class decomposition*. Interesting results on completeness of the refinement calculus are available in [14].

Delegation of functionality. Assume that C and C_1 are classes in $Classes$, $C_1\ o$ is an attribute of C and $T\ x$ is an attribute of C_1. Let $m()\{c(o.x', o.x)\}$ be a method of C that directly accesses and/or modifies attribute x of C_1. Then, if all other variables in command c are accessible in C_1, we have that $Classes$ is refined by $Classes_1$, where $Classes_1$ is obtained from $Classes$ by changing $m()\{c(o.x', o.x)\}$ to $m()\{o.n()\}$ in class C and adding a fresh method $n()\{c[x'/o.x', x/o.x]\}$. This is also called the *expert pattern of responsibility assignment*.

Encapsulation. When we write the specifications of the methods of a class C before designing the interactions between objects, we often need to directly refer to attributes of the classes that are associated with C. Therefore, those attributes are required to be public. After designing the interactions by application of the expert pattern for functionality assignments, the attributes that were directly referred are now only referred locally in their classes. These attributes can then be encapsulated by changing them to protected or private.

The *encapsulation rule* says that if an attribute of a class C is only referred directly in the specification (or code) of methods in C, this attribute can be made a *private attribute*; and it can be made *protected* if it is only directly referred in specifications of methods of C and its subclasses.

Class decomposition. During an OO design, we often need to decompose a class into a number of classes. For example, consider classes $C_1 :: D\ a_1$, $C_2 :: D\ a_2$, and $D :: T_1\ x$, $T_2\ y$. If methods of C_1 only call a method $D :: m()\{...\}$ that only involves x, and methods of C_2 only call a method $D :: n()\{...\}$ that only involves y, we can decompose D into $D_1 :: T_1\ x; m()\{...\}$ and $D_2 :: T_2\ y; n()\{...\}$, and change the type of a_1 in C_1 to D_1 and the type of a_2 in C_2 to D_2. There are other rules for class decomposition [9,14].

With these and other refinement rules in rCOS, we can prove a big-step refinement rule, such as the following **expert pattern**, that will be repeatedly used in the design of CoCoME.

Theorem 1 (Expert Pattern)
Given a class declarations section Classes and its navigation paths $r_1.....r_f.x$, (denoted by le as an assignable expression), $\{a_{11}.....a_{1k_1}.x_1, \ldots, a_{\ell 1}.....a_{\ell k_\ell}.x_\ell\}$, and $\{b_{11}.....b_{1j_1}.y_1, \ldots, b_{t1}.....a_{tj_t}.y_t\}$ starting from class C, let $m()$ be a method of C specified as

$$C :: m()\{\quad c(a_{11}.....a_{1k_1}.x_1, \ldots, a_{\ell 1}.....a_{\ell k_\ell}.x_\ell)$$
$$\wedge\ le' = e(b_{11}.....b_{1s_1}.y_1, \ldots, b_{ts1}.....b_{ts_t}.y_t)\ \}$$

then Classes can be refined by redefining $m()$ in C and defining the following fresh methods in the corresponding classes:

$$
\begin{aligned}
C :: \quad & check()\{return'=c(a_{11}.get_{\pi_{a_{11}}x_1}(), \ldots, a_{\ell 1}.get_{\pi_{a_{\ell 1}}x_\ell}())\} \\
& m()\{\textbf{if } check()\ \textbf{then } r_1.do\text{-}m_{\pi_{r_1}}(b_{11}.get_{\pi_{b_{11}}y_1}(), \\
& \qquad \ldots, b_{s1}.get_{\pi_{b_{s1}}y_s}())\} \\
T(a_{ij}) :: \quad & get_{\pi_{a_{ij}}x_i}()\{return'=a_{ij+1}.get_{\pi_{a_{ij+1}}x_i}()\}\ (i:1..\ell, j:1..k_i-1) \\
T(a_{ik_i}) :: \quad & get_{\pi_{a_{ik_i}}x_i}()\{return'=x_i\}\ (i:1..\ell) \\
T(r_i) :: \quad & do\text{-}m_{\pi_{r_i}}(d_{11}, \ldots, d_{s1})\{r_{i+1}.do\text{-}m_{\pi_{r_{i+1}}}(d_{11}, \ldots, d_{s1})\} \\
& for\ i:1..f-1 \\
T(r_f) :: \quad & do\text{-}m_{\pi_{r_f}}(d_{11}, \ldots, d_{s1})\{x'=e(d_{11}, \ldots, d_{s1})\} \\
T(b_{ij}) :: \quad & get_{\pi_{b_{ij}}y_i}()\{return'=b_{ij+1}.get_{\pi_{b_{ij+1}}y_i}()\}\ (i:1..t, j:1..s_i-1) \\
T(b_{is_i}) :: \quad & get_{\pi_{b_{is_i}}y_i}()\{return'=y_i\}\ (i:1..t)
\end{aligned}
$$

where $T(a)$ is the type name of attribute a and π_{v_i} denotes the remainder of the corresponding navigation path v starting at position j.

If the paths $\{a_{11}.....a_{1k_1}.x_1, \ldots, a_{\ell 1}.....a_{\ell k_\ell}.x_\ell\}$ have a common prefix up to a_{1j}, then class C can directly delegate the responsibility of getting the x-attributes and checking the condition to $T(a_{ij})$ via the path $a_{11}...., a_{ij}$ and then follow the above rule from $T(a_{ij})$. The same rule can be applied to the b-navigation paths.

The expert pattern is the most often used refinement rule in OO design. One feature of this rule is that it does not introduce more couplings by associations between classes into the class structure. It also ensures that functional responsibilities are allocated to the appropriate objects that *know* the data needed for the responsibilities assigned to them.

An important point to make here is that the expert pattern and the rule of encapsulation can be implemented by automated model transformations. In general, transformations for structure refinement can be aided by transformations in which changes are made on the structure model, such as the class diagram, with a diagram editing tool and then automatic transformations can be derived for the change in the specification of the functionality and object interactions [14].

6.2.3   Component Modelling in rCOS

There are two kinds of components in rCOS, *service components* (simply called *components*) and *process components* (also simply called *processes*).

Like a service component, a *process component* has an interface declaring its own local state variables and methods, and its behavior is specified by a process contract. Unlike a service component that is passively waiting for a client to call its provided services, a process is active and has its own control on when to call out to required services or to wait for a call to its provided services. For such an active process, we cannot have separate contracts for its provided interface and required interface, because we cannot have separate specifications of outgoing calls and incoming calls. So a process only has an interface and its associated contract (or code).

Compositions for *disjoint union* of components and *plugging* components together, for *gluing components* by processes are defined in rCOS, and their closure properties and the algebraic properties of these compositions are studied [5]. Note that an interface can be the union of a number of interfaces. Therefore, in a specification we can write the interfaces separately.

The contracts in rCOS also define the unified semantic model of implementations of interfaces in different programming languages, and thus clearly support interoperability of components and analysis of the correctness of a component with respect to its interface contract. The theory of refinements of contracts and components in rCOS characterizes component substitutivity, as well as it supports independent development of components.

6.2.4   Related Work

The work on rCOS takes place within a large body of work [15] on modelling and analysis techniques for object-oriented and component based software. Some of these works we would like to acknowledge.

Eiffel [17] first introduced the idea of design by contract into object-oriented programming. The notion of designs for methods in the object-oriented rCOS is similar to the use of assertions in Eiffel, and thus also supports similar techniques for static analysis and testing. JML [13] has recently become a popular language for modelling and analysis of object-oriented designs. It shares similar ideas of using assertions and refinement as behavioral subtype in Eiffel. The strong point of JML is that it is well integrated with Java and comes with parsers and tools for UML like modelling.

In Fractal [20], behavior protocols are used to specify interaction behavior of a component. rCOS also uses traces of method invocations and returns to model the interaction protocol of a component with its environment. However, the protocol does not have to be a regular language, although that suffices for the examples in this chapter. Also, for components rCOS separates the protocol of the provided interface methods from that of the required interface methods. This allows better pluggability among components. On the other hand, the behavior protocols of components in Fractal are the same for the protocols of coordinators and glue units that are modeled as processes in rCOS. In addition to interaction protocols, rCOS also supports state-based modelling with guards and pre-post conditions. This allows us to carry out stepwise functionality refinement.

We share many ideas with work done in Oldenburg by the group of Olderog on linking CSP-OZ with UML [18] in that a multi-notational modelling language is used for encompassing different views of a system. However, rCOS has taken UTP as its single point of departure and thus avoids some of the complexities of merging existing notations. Yet, their framework has the virtue of well-developed underlying frameworks and tools.

6.3   The Example

The requirements capture starts with identifying *business processes* described as *use cases*. The use case specification includes four views. One view is the *interactions* between the external environment, modeled as *actors*, and the system. The interaction is described as a protocol in which an actor is allowed to invoke *methods* (also called *use case operations*) provided by the system. In rCOS, we specify such a protocol as a set of *traces* of method invocations, and depict it by a UML *sequence diagram* (cf. Fig. 2), called a *use case sequence diagram*.

In the real use of the system the actors interact with the system via the GUI and hardware devices. However, in the early stage of the design, we abstract from the GUI and the concrete input and output technologies and focus on specifying what the system should produce for output after the input data or signals are received. The design of the GUI and the controllers of the input and output devices is a concern when the application interfaces are clear after the design of the application software. Also, a use case sequence diagram does not show the interactions among the domain objects of the system, as the interactions among those internal objects can only be designed after the specification of what the use case operations do when being invoked. There are many different ways in which the internal objects can interact to realize the same use case.

The interaction trace of a use case is a constraint on the flow of control of the main application program or processes. The flow of control can be modeled by a *guarded state transition system*, that can be depicted by a UML state diagram (cf. Fig. 4). While a sequence diagram focuses on the interactions between the actors and the system, the state diagram is an operational model of the *dynamic behavior* of the use case. They must be trace equivalent. This model may be used for verification of deadlock and livelock freedom by model checking state reachability.

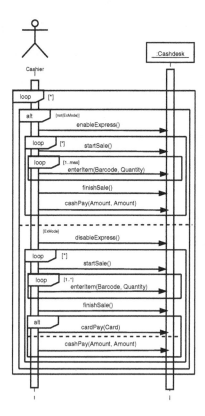

Fig. 2. Use case sequence diagram for **UC 1 & 2**

Another important view is the static *functionality view* of the system. The requirements should precisely specify what each use case operation should do when invoked. That is, what state change it should make in terms of what new objects are to be created, what old objects should be destroyed, what links between which objects are established, and what data attributes of which objects are modified, and the precondition for carrying out these changes. For the purpose of *compositional* and *incremental* specification, we introduce a designated *use case controller class* for each use case, and we specify each method of the use case as a method of this controller class. A method is specified by its signature and its design in the form *pre ⊢ post*. The signatures of the methods must be consistent with those used in the interaction and dynamic views. During specification of the static functionality of the use case operations, all types and classes (together with their attributes) required in the specification must be defined.

The type and class definitions in the specification of functionality of the methods of the use case controls form the *structure view* of the system. It can be depicted by a class diagram or packages of class diagrams (cf. Fig. 3). The consistency and integrated semantics of the different views are studied in [6].

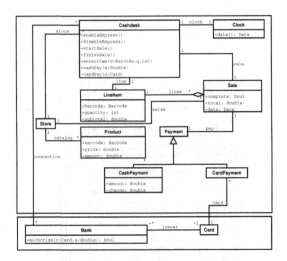

Fig. 3. Use case class diagram for **UC 1 & 2**

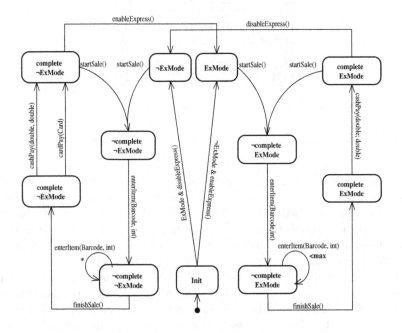

Fig. 4. State diagram for **UC 1 and 2**

UC 1 & UC 2: Process Sale. As both the first and the second use case relate to a single sale, we handle them in a single section. It would be possible to keep the mode change in a separate use case, but the combination saves space.

We first model the interaction protocol that the system offers the actor, i.e. Cashier. This is given in a *use case sequence diagram* in Fig. 2. As a simplification, we assume that the Cashier controls switching between normal and express mode; in the end it makes no difference who does it. In this sequence diagram, *max* denotes the maximum number of items that the current sale can process.

The protocol that the sequence diagram defines is specified by the set of traces represented by the following regular expression:

$tr(SD_{uc1}) =$
((*enableExpress* (*startSale enterItem*$^{(max)}$ *finishSale cashPay*)*)
  + (*disableExpress* (*startSale enterItem** *finishSale* (*cashPay* + *cardPay*))*))*

These traces are accepted by the state diagram given in Fig. 4 (note that labels of states only serve as documentation and are not UML compliant). We assume that the *ExMode* guard is initialized non-deterministically in the *Init* state.

Functionality Specification. We now start to analyze the functionality of each of the operations in the use case. An informal understanding of the functionality is to identify the classes, their properties, and to construct an initial class diagram, see Fig. 3. For the specification of the operations we assume:

1. There exists a *Store* object, *store : Store*.
2. The object *store* owns a set of *Product* objects with their barcode, amount, and price, denoted by *store.catalog*. It accesses the attribute *catalog : set(Product)* (we omit properties not relevant to modelling, like product descriptions).
3. The *Cashdesk* object accesses the store via an association *store*.
4. There exists a *Clock* object associated with the *desk* via the association *clock*.
5. There is a *Bank* class with a method *authorize(Card c,double a;bool returns)*, which checks a credit card transaction with amount a and returns whether it is valid.

We now specify the functionality of the methods in *Cashdesk*.

Use Case	UC 1: Process Sale
Class	*Cashdesk*
Method	*enableExpress()*
	pre: *true*
	post: *ExMode'* = *true*
Method	*disableExpress()*
	pre: *true*
	post: *ExMode'* = *false*
Method	*startSale()*
	pre: *true*
	post: /* a new *sale* is created, and its *line items* initialized to empty, and the date correctly recorded */
	sale' = *Sale.New(false/complete, empty/lines, clock.date()/date)*
Method	*enterItem(Barcode c, int q)*
	pre: /* there exists a product with the input barcode c */
	store.catalog.find(c) $\neq$ *null*
	post: /* a new *line* is created with its *barcode c* and *quantity q* */
	line' = *LineItem.New(c/barcode,q/quantity)*
	; *line.subtotal'* = *store.catalog*.find(c).price $\times$ q
	; *sale.lines*.add(*line*)

Method   *finishSale()*
          pre: *true*
          post: $sale.complete' = true$
              $\wedge\ sale.total' = sum[[l.subtotal \mid l \in sale.lines]]$
Method   *cashPay(double a; double c)*
          pre: $a \geq sale.total$
          post: $sale.pay' = CashPayment.New(a/amount,\ a\text{-}sale.total/change)$
              /* the completed *sale* is logged in *store*, and */
              ; *store.sales*.add(*sale*); /* the inventory is updated */
              $\forall l \in sale.lines,\ p \in store.catalog \bullet$ (**if** $p.barcode = l.barcode$ **then**
                  $p.amount' = p.amount - l.quantity$)
              ; *store.sales*.add(*sale*);
              $\forall l \in sale.lines,\ p \in store.catalog \bullet$ (**if** $p.barcode = l.barcode$ **then**
                  $p.amount' = p.amount - l.quantity$)

Invariants. A *class invariant* is established on initialization of an instance, i.e. through the constructor. It must hold after each subsequent method call to that class. We specify correct initialization of the cash desk as a *class invariant*:

Class Invariant *Cashdesk* : $store \neq null \wedge store.catalog \neq null$
                    $\wedge\ clock \neq null \wedge bank \neq null$

Static and Dynamic Consistency. When we have the constituents of the specification document: *class diagram, state diagram, sequence diagram* and the *functional specification*, we need to make sure that they are consistent [6]. The *static consistency* of the requirement model is ensured by checking that

1. All types used in the specification are given in the class diagram,
2. All data attributes of any class used in the specification are correctly given in the class diagram,
3. All properties are correctly given as attributes or associations in the class diagram, and the multiplicities are determined according to whether the type of the property is *set(C)* or *bag(C)* for some class C,
4. Each method given in the functional specification is used in the other diagrams according to its signature, that is, the arguments (and return values) and their types match,
5. Expressions occurring as guards are (type) consistent with their functional specifications, i.e., of right type, initialised before first use, etc.

Dynamic Consistency. means that the dynamic flow of control and the interaction protocol are consistent:

1. If the actors follow the interaction protocol when interacting with the use case controller, the state diagram should ensure that the interaction is not blocked by guards. Formally speaking, the traces of method calls defined by the sequence diagram should be accepted by the state machine.
2. On the other hand, the traces that are accepted by the state diagram should be allowable interactions in the protocol defined by the sequence diagram.

The above two conditions are formalised and checked as trace equivalence between the sequence diagram and the state diagram in FDR [23,21]. We point the interested reader to [22] and [19] for more detailed applications of CSP to different flavours of state diagrams. However, we note that the reasons for having a sequence diagram and a state diagram are different:

- The denotational trace semantics for the sequence diagram is easy to use as the specification of the protocol in terms of temporal order of the events,
- The state diagram has an operational semantics which is easier to use for verification of both safety and liveness properties.

The event-based sequence diagrams and state diagrams abstract the data functionality away and thus make checking practically feasible—i.e., naive model-checking of an OO program would require considering all possible values for attributes and arguments of methods.

6.3.1 Detailed Design

At this point, we illustrate the refinement rules of rCOS (see Sec. 6.2.2) to the operations that were specified for the use cases in the previous section. We take each operation of each use case and decompose it, assigning functionalities to use cases according to attributes of classes. This happens mainly through application of the refinement rule for functional decomposition, called the *expert pattern*.

Navigation in the functional specification will be translated to setters and getters for attributes, and direct access for associations.

Occasionally, refinement will not directly introduce a concrete implementation, but may also lead to refinement on the functionality specification level. For an example, observe how the handling of sets in the following examples evolves first through further refinement before being eventually modeled in code.

Refinement of UC 1 & 2

We successively handle the previously specified operations. The refinement of the mode handling to code is trivial. We remind the reader that according to the problem description changing the physical light will be handled by a separate component.

$$\textbf{class } \textit{Cashdesk}:: \textit{ enableExpress() } \{ \textit{ exmode } := \textit{ true } \}$$
$$\textit{disableExpress() } \{ \textit{ exmode } := \textit{ false } \}$$

The *startSale()* operation is refined by making the *Cashdesk* instance invoke the constructor of the *Sale* class. As the *Clock* is an entity located in the *Cashdesk*, we have to pass the current *Date* as an argument. This follows the *expert pattern*:

```
class Cashdesk:: startSale() { sale:=Sale.New(clock.date()) }
class Sale::      Sale(Date d)
                  { date := d; complete := false; total := 0; lines := empty }
```

In Java, sets are implemented as a class that *implements* the *interface Collection*. The constructor of the set class initializes the instance as an empty set. The formal treatment of set operations like *find()*, *add()*, and constructors in general is given in the existing rCOS literature. Thus, the constructor *Sale()* can be further refined to the following code:

```
class Sale:: Sale(Date d)
        { date := d; complete := false; total := 0; lines := set(LineItem).New() }
```

However, when design of a significant algorithm is required, such as calculating the greatest common divisor of two integer attributes or finding the shortest path in a directed graph object, the specification of the algorithm instead of code can be first designed in the refinement. For operation *enterItem()*, the pre-condition is checked by finding the product in the catalog that matches the input bar code. From the refinement rule for the *expert pattern*, the *navigation path* store.catalog.find() indicates the need for a method *find()* in the use case handler, that calls a method *find()* which in turn calls the method *find()* of the set *catalog*. Thus, we need to design the following methods in the relevant classes:

```
class Cashdesk::     find(Barcode code; Product returns) { store.find(code; returns) }
class Store::        find(Barcode code; Product returns) { catalog.find(code; returns) }
Class set(Product):: Method find(Barcode code; Product returns)
             Pre  ∃p : Product • (p.barcode = code ∧ contains(p))
             Post returns.barcode' = code
```

Applying the expert pattern to the navigation paths *line.subtotal*, *store.catalog*.find() and *sale.lines*.add(), we can refine the specification of *enterItem()* to:

```
class Cashdesk:: enterItem(Barcode code, int qty) {
             if find(code) ≠ null then {
             line:=LineItem.New(code, qty);
             line.setSubtotal(find(code).price × qty);
             sale.addLine(line)
             } else { throw exception e() }   }
class Sale::      addLine(LineItem l) { lines.add(l) }
class LineItem:: setSubtotal(double a) { subtotal:=a }
```

Note that we use exception handling to signal that the precondition is violated. This allows us to introduce more graceful error handling later through refinement. This is different to translating the condition into an **assert** statement which would terminate the application, as that would preclude refinement.

We now refine method *finishSale()* using the expert pattern and define a method *setComplete()* and a method *setTotal()* in class *Sale*. These methods then will be called by the use case handler class.

```
class Cashdesk:: finishSale()   { sale.setComplete(); sale.setTotal(); }
class Sale::     setComplete() { complete:=true }
                 setTotal()    { total:=lines.sum() }
```

For *cashPay()*, we need the total of the sale to check the precondition, accordingly we define *getTotal()* in class *Sale*. To create a payment, we define a method *makeCashPay()* called by the cash desk, and creates an object of type *CashPayment*. For logging the sale, we define a method *addSale()* in class *Store* that is called by the cash desk, that will use the method *add()* of the set of sales.

For updating the inventory, the universal quantification will be implemented by a loop, so we defer the implementation to a helper method:

```
class Cashdesk:: cashPay(double amount; double return) {
                 if (amount ≥ sale.getTotal()) then  {
                 sale.makeCashPay(amount; return);
                 store.addSale(sale);
                 updateInventory() /* defined separately */
                 } else { throw exception e(amount ≥ sale.getTotal())}   }
class Sale::      getTotal(; double returns) { returns := total }
                 makeCashPay(double amount; double returns)
                    { payment:=CashPay.New(amount); returns:=getChange() }
                 getChange(; double returns) { returns := amount - total }
class Store::     addSale(Sale s) { sales.add(s) }
```

Recall the functional specification corresponding to *updateInventory()*:

Class *Cashdesk*::
$\forall l \in sale.lines, \ p \in store.catalog \bullet ($ **if** $p.barcode = l.barcode$ **then**
$$p.amount' = p.amount - l.quantity)$$

It involves universal quantification over elements of a set. Such a specification is usually covered by some *design pattern*. The solutions always require loop statements, which, in an object-oriented setting, are for example covered by (Java) *iterators*, or they might be implemented in a database.

A design pattern is to first define a method for changing the variables, i.e., to update the amount of the product in the catalog. This implies a method *update(int qty)* in class *Product*, and then a method *update(Barcode code, int qty)* in *catalog* whose type is *set(Product)* and which implements the loop for the quantification on p (we consider the iteration over *sale.lines* in the next step):

```
class Product::       update(int qty) { amount := amount-qty }
class set(Product):: update(Barcode code, int qty) {
                     Iterator i := iterator();
                     while (i.hasNext()) {
                       Product p := i.next();
                       if p.barcode=code then p.update(qty);
                     } }
class Store::         update(Barcode code, int qty) { catalog.update(code,qty) }
```

The quantification on *sale.lines* is then designed as another loop in the class of the method that contains the formula in its specification:

```
class Cashdesk:: updateInventory() {
                 Iterator j := sale.lines.iterator();
                 while (j.hasNext()) {
                   LineItem l := j.next();
                   store.update(l.barcode,quantity)
                 } }
```

Now we can also give an equivalent, more direct encoding of the two quantifications, where the inner loop is for the objects whose state is being modified by the specification.

```
class Cashdesk:: updateInventory() {
            Iterator j := sale.lines.iterator();
            while (j.hasNext()) {
            LineItem l := (j.next();
            /* inlined store.update()/catalog.update() call: */
            Iterator i := store.catalog.iterator();
            while  (i.hasNext()) {
            Product p := i.next();
            if p.barcode=l.barcode then p.update(l.quantity)
            } } }
```

In *cardPay()*, the precondition invokes the function *authorize(Card, double)* of the *Bank*. We reuse *addSale(sale)* and *updateInventory()* unchanged from the refinement for *cashPay()*. At this stage, where the *Bank* is an external class we do not need to specify the *authorize(Card, double)* method.

```
class Cashdesk:: cardPay(Card c) {
            if (Bank.authorize(c,sale.total)) then  {
            payment:=CardPay.New(c);
            store.addSale(sale);
            updateInventory()
            } else { throw exception e(c)}   }
```

The other use cases expand in a similar way. The refinement of specifications involving universal and existential quantifications over a collection of objects/-data to Java implementation of the *Collection interface* show that formal methods should now take the advantages of the libraries of the modern programming languages such as Java. This can significantly reduce the burden on (or the amount of) verification.

6.3.2   Component-Based Architecture

The component architecture is designed from the object-oriented models in the previous sections. In contrast to the component layout in Chapter 3, where already deployment has been taken into account for the component mapping, we will first map the object-oriented model to logical components, and then discuss how they are affected by deployment. Also, we have some *a priori* components, like the hardware devices and the *Bank*.

The adaptation of the object-oriented model to a component-based model *reduces system coupling*, such that less related functionalities are performed by different components. This is done according to use cases and users (i.e. actors).

Logical Model of the Component-Based Architecture. The primary use case **UC 1** is performed by the the *SalesHandler* component, while the composition of the handler with the components for the peripherals yields the *CashDesk*. A *Store* component aggregates several *CashDesks* and an *Inventory*.

For the other use cases, we obtain a similar structure with a controller and supporting classes (not shown in detail): Ordering stock (**UC 3**), handling deliveries (**UC 4**), stock report (**UC 5**), and changing prices (**UC 7**) are components within a *Store*.

Delivery reports (**UC 6**) are generated inside the *Enterprise* component, while product exchange between stores (**UC 8**) is managed in the *Exchange* component, which resides within *Enterprise*.

The model is called a *logical component-based architecture* because

1. It is the model of the design for the application components,
2. The interfaces are object-oriented interfaces, that is interactions are only through local object method invocations.

However, it is important to note that the object-oriented functional refinement are needed for the identification of the components and their interfaces.

We take some liberties with the design of Chapter 3: we do not model a *CashDeskLine* (see Chapter 3, Fig. 12), but only a single cash desk that accesses the inventory. Also, we omit the *CashBox* as it does not contribute to the presentation. Note that in the following, only the *SalesHandler* is actually derived from the requirements (as would be the *Clock*, the *Bank*, and the *Inventory*).

The *SalesHandler* component will be the "work horse" of our cash desk. It implements the actual *Sale* use case protocol and also provides the necessary API for accessing the ongoing sale from the GUI. As a simplification, we assume that they can happen atomically at anytime, that is, the **pure** keyword indicates that the methods calls can be interleaved with those from the protocol. The provided protocol corresponds to the trace given in the Functional Description of the **UC 1**. The method invocations on the required side are derived (manually) from the refinement of the functional specification. The multiple **update** call-outs stem from the iteration when a sale is logged and the inventory updated.

```
component SalesHandler
required interface ClockIf { date() }
required interface BankIf { authorize(..) }
required interface StoreIf { update(..), find (..), addSale(..) }
provided pure interface CashdeskIf { getItem(..), getSubTotal(..), getTotal (..), getPayment() }
provided interface SaleIf
protocol { ( [ [ ?enableExpress ( ?startSale date! (?enterItem find!)^{(max)} ?finishSale
                                  ?cardPay authorize! addSale!)*
             | ?disableExpress ( ?startSale date! (?enterItem find!)* ?finishSale
                                  [ ?cardPay authorize! addSale! update!*
                                  | ?cashPay addSale! update!* ] )* ] )* }
class Cashdesk implements SaleIf, CashdeskIf
```

Design of the Concrete Interaction Mechanisms. After obtaining the model of the logical component-based architecture, we can replace the object-oriented interfaces by different interaction protocols according to the requirement descriptions and the physical locations of the components.

There are more than one *CashDesk* component instance, each having its own clock and sharing one *Inventory* instance per store. The interaction between them can then be implemented asynchronously using an event channel. RMI or CORBA can be used for interactions between a *Store* component and the *Enterprise* component.

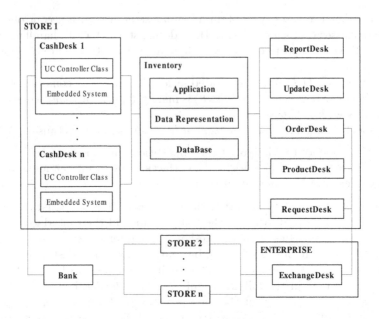

Fig. 5. Overall component view of the system

If we decompose the *Inventory* into sub-components (the three layer architecture): the *application layer*, the *data representation layer* and the *database*, we can

- Keep the OO interface between the application and data representation layer,
- Implement interaction between the data representation and the database in JDBC.

Most of these interactions mechanisms are international standards and the change from an OO interface to any of them has been a routine practice. We believe that there is no need for providing their formal models and analysis, though a formal method like rCOS is able to do this with some effort. Fig. 5 gives the overall view of the system. In the following, we discuss the detailed decomposition of the peripherals of a cash desk.

Hardware Components. The peripheral device components are modelled in rCOS only at the *contract* level, that is, with regard to the protocols. We do not give their functional description or implementation here and assume they implement their behaviour correctly. The required protocols (call-outs with trailing exclamation mark; see [8]) have been derived from the functional specifications/refinement.

The input devices are modelled as (active) rCOS processes that call provided methods of another component on input. For manual input, we model the cash desk terminal as a *black box* (we dispense with the implementing class) with buttons for starting/ending a sale, and manual input of an item and its quantity. Remember from Sec. 6.3 that we designed the controller class to handle both express mode changes. Nonetheless, here we stick to the original problem description and allow the cashier to disable it only. Thus, the protocol is still a subset of the one induced by the use case (we omit method signatures for conciseness of the presentation):

```
// define short−hand for methods
define SaleIf { enableExpress(), disableExpress(), startSale (), enterItem (..),
               finishSale (), cardPay (..), cashPay(..) }
```

```
component Terminal
required interface SaleIf
protocol { ([disableExpress!] startSale! enterItem!* finishSale! [cardPay! | cashPay!])* }
```

Furthermore, we assume that the bar code scanner has the same interface (although it will in practice only ever invoke the *enterItem()* method). To connect both devices to the cash desk application, we have to introduce a *controller* which merges input from both devices. For later composition, we introduce unique names to the two provided interfaces of the same type and specify the class which handles the call-ins (implementation not shown). Here, we give the *combined* required/provided protocol of call-ins (methods prefixed by ?)/call-outs (suffixed by !). rCOS also permits separate protocols for a component interface, which does not reveal any dependencies on method calls.

```
component InputController
required interface SaleIf
provided interface SaleIf at PortA, PortB // interleaving
protocol { ( [?disableExpress disableExpress!] ?startSale startSale! // relay messages
            // fan in from both devices:
            (?enterItem enterItem!)*
            ?finishSale finishSale! [ ?cardPay cardPay! | ?cashPay cashPay!])* }
class Merge implements SaleIf
```

The cash desk display provides a way of updating the display with the current sale. For each event, the display controller queries the cash desk's current sale via getter-methods and updates the screen. The interface will be provided by the *SaleHandler* component. Also, we handle displaying the mode here. Note that the GUI has a more general protocol as we do not need to take mode changes into account for an individual sale.

```
component CashDeskGUI
required interface LightIf { lightExpress(), lightNormal() }
required interface CashdeskIf { getItem(..), getSubTotal(..), getTotal (..), getPayment() }
required interface ClockIf { date }
provided interface GUIIf { enterItem(..), startSale(), finishSale (), cardPay (..),
                          cashPay (..), enableExpress(), disableExpress() }
protocol { ( [?enableExpress lightExpress!| ?disableExpress lightNormal!] ?startSale date!
            (?enterItem getItem! getSubTotal!)* ?endSale getTotal!
            [?cardPay | ?cashPay] getPayment! )* }
class GUI implements GUIIf
```

The *Printer* component shall employ the same design, providing PRINTER. PRINTERIF.

As the system should use a bus architecture, updates have to be done in an event-based fashion, i.e., we need a *BusController* component that proxies between all devices and acts as a fan-out when an event has multiple subscribers. Contrary to the design document, we do not employ a broadcast architecture: for example, the controller makes sure that the business logic processes an **enterItem** event *first*, and only *then* notifies the display. Likewise, it drives the printer.

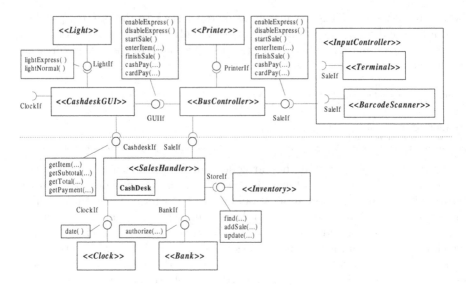

Fig. 6. Deployed components for a single Cashdesk

```
component BusController
provided interface SaleIf // to InputController
required interface CashDeskGUI.GUIIf // elided, see above
required interface Printer.PrinterIf // ditto
required interface SaleIf // from business logic
protocol { /* fan−out for each call−in elided */ }
class Bus implements SaleIf
```

We concede that this component design means that the *BusController* must be modified each time a new subscriber is added to the system.

We plumb the *BarcodeScanner* and *Terminal* component into the *InputController*, which we connect to the *BusController*. That is in turn connected to the *SalesHandler*. We omit detailed discussion of the other interfaces; dependent components mentioned in **with**-clauses are deployed automatically as long as there are no ambiguities with regard to interfaces:

```
component Cashdesk
  deploy CashDeskGUI with Clock, Light
  deploy InputController with Barcode at PortA, Terminal at PortB
  deploy BusController with InputController, CashDeskGUI, Printer
  deploy SalesHandler with Clock,Bank,Inventory,CashDeskGUI,BusController
```

Assuming availability of the required components of the *SalesHandler*, the resulting component is *closed*, as all required interfaces are provided. For the resulting component diagram, see Fig. 6; the upper half indicates the peripherals, the lower half the components derived from the use case.

With regard to formal rCOS (see e.g. [5,10]), we note that only components whose traces start with a call-in are *rCOS-components*. Those that have a call-out at the start of their trace, are actually *rCOS-processes*. For **UC 1**, only the input devices used by the actor are processes.

Modelling Deployment. For a consistent rCOS model, this means we must modify the existing model to take into account the *deployment boundaries*, *middle-ware* and their effect on communication object references.

We also note that the different failure modes of remote communication must be taken into account and may require to revisit the Design, as for example, suddenly functions (in the mathematical sense) may *fail* when they are invoked on remote hosts. This is a field of ongoing investigation.

6.4   Analyses

This section outlines how to add the specification and analysis of the extra functionalities given in the description document. It then continues with a description of the actual analyses of the functional and behavioural properties that have been carried out with tool support.

Extra-Functional Properties

We specify extra functionality of a method as a property for the time interval for the execution of the method. We use temporal variables whose values depend on the reference time interval for the execution of methods for our specification. Those variables could be ET_m which is the duration of the execution of method m in the worst case, or $N\_Customers$ which is the number of customers in the referenced observation time interval. From the intended meaning, the variable ET_m is rigid, its value does not depend on the reference interval. For a formula f on the rigid and temporal variables, for a probability p, $[f]_p$ is a formula saying that f is satisfied with the probability p. As it is well-known in the interval logic, the formulas $\phi; \psi$, which corresponds to the sequential composition of formulas ϕ and ψ, holds for an interval $[a, b]$ iff there is $m \in a..b$ such that ϕ holds for interval $[a, m]$ and ψ holds for interval $[m, b]$. Let ℓ be a temporal variable denoting the length of the interval it applied to. Intuitively, the formula

$$[0 \leq ET\_ScanItem < 5]_{0.9} \wedge [0 \leq ET\_ScanItem < 1.0]_{0.05}$$

says that the execution time for the operation *ScanItem* is within 5 seconds with probability 0.9, and it is less than 1 second with probability 0.05.

Since the arrival and leaving rates are the same: 320/3600 arrivals per second, and constant, with an exponential distribution, we can derive that $[N\_Customers = \frac{2}{45}\ell]_1$ holds for all intervals. As another example, by estimating the average waiting time for customers here we show how to include QoS analysis in our framework. Let $ET\_Service$ stand for the average service time for customers. It is easy to calculate the possibility of $ET\_Service$ from the above specification, i.e. $ET\_Service = 32.075$. Therefore, the rate of service is $\mu = 1/ET\_Service = 1/32.075 = 0.0311$. Also, we have that the rate of customers arriving is $\lambda = N\_Customers/\ell = 4/45$.

6.4.1   Verification, Analysis and Tool Support

Various verifications and analyses are carried out on different models. For the requirement model, the trace equivalence between the sequence diagram and its state diagram has been experimentally checked with FDR. We manually checked the consistency between the class declarations (i.e. the class diagrams) and the functionality specification to ensure that all classes and attributes are declared in the class declarations. This is obviously a syntactic and static semantic check that can be automated in a tool. We can further ensure the consistency by translating the rCOS functionality specification into a JML specification and then carry out runtime checking and testing. Also, some of the development steps involving recurrent patterns can be automated.

Runtime Checking and Testing in JML. We have not checked the correctness of the design against the requirement specification for removing possible mistakes made when manually applying the rules. However, we have translated some of the design into JML [13] and carried out runtime testing of specifications and the validity of an implementation.

We translate each rCOS class C into two JML files, one is $C.jml$ that contains the specification translated from the rCOS specification, and the other is a Java source file $C.java$ containing a code that implements the specification. During the translation, the variables used in the rCOS specification are taken as specification-only variables in $C.jml$, that are mapped to program variables in $C.java$. The translated JML files can be compiled by the JML Runtime Assertion Checker Compiler ($jmlc$). Then, test cases can be executed to check the satisfaction of the specification by the implementation. The automatic unit testing tool of JML ($jmlunit$) can be used to generate unit testing code, and the testing process can be executed with *JUnit*.

For example, a JML code snippet of the *enterItem*() design in Section 6.3 is shown on the left of Fig. 7. Notice that the code in the dotted rectangle gives the specification of the exception that was left unspecified in Section 6.3.

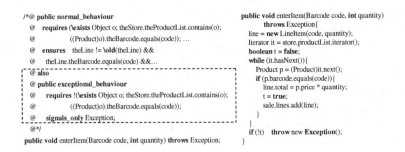

Fig. 7. JML Specification and Implementation

The final code implementing the *enterItem*() specification is shown on the right of Fig. 7. Before getting the final code, we encountered two runtime errors reported by the testing process. One error resulted from the implementation which did not handle an input that falsifies the precondition. The reason for the other error is that one invariant is false after method execution. Testing is not sufficient for correctness. Therefore, it is also desirable to carry out static analysis, for instance with ESC/Java [3].

QVT Transformation Support. Our long term goal is to implement correctness preserving transformations that support a full model driven development process. The problems we are concerned with are the consistency among models on the same level, and the correctness relation between models in different levels. The meaning of consistency among models on the same level is that the models of various views need to be syntactically and semantically compatible with each other. The meaning of correctness relation between models on different levels is that a model must be semantically consistent with its refinements [16].

We plan to use QVT [7], a model transformation language standard by OMG, to implement these model transformations. We have already defined the required rCOS metamodels for object diagrams, object sequence diagrams, component diagrams, component interaction diagrams and state machines. Pre- and post-conditions can also be translated into the respective clauses of a QVT program.

The refinement of the use cases on the object level through the expert pattern is done manually now, but it can be implemented using QVT, and automated. The correctness of the expert pattern is proved by rCOS. We have already explored correctness preserving transformations in a object-oriented design in [24].

Then we can apply architectural design to decompose the object model into a component model by allocating use cases, classes, associations and services to components. The component model should be a refinement of the application requirement model. This step can also be implemented as a QVT transformation. The correctness of the transformation from object model to component model should be proved in rCOS.

Verifying Interaction Protocols. Composition of components not only requires that the interfaces and their types match. Also, the interaction protocols must be compatible; if two interfaces are composed, the corresponding traces must match, i.e., the sequences of call-ins/call-outs must align: unexpected call-ins are ignored by the callee and will deadlock the caller.

We automatically check protocol consistency by generating CSP processes for each interface. Interface composition is then modelled through pairwise parallel composition. As a composed interface is uniquely defined in the specification, we can successively check each composition for deadlock freedom and incrementally add successive interfaces. Model checking with FDR would indicate a deadlock if an operation call required by some component is not provided by any of its partner components at some moment in time.

In an application, these can also be implemented as runtime checks using extensions for aspect-oriented programming that capture temporal behaviour like Tracematches [1] or Tracechecks [2].

6.5   Summary

We have presented our modelling of the Common Component Example in rCOS, the Relational Calculus of Object and Component Systems. Based on the problem description, we have developed a set of interrelated models for each use case which separately models the different concerns of control and data. The rigorous approach ensures that we can be of *high confidence* that the resulting *program* implements the desired behaviour *correctly* without having to prove this on the generated code, which usually is very difficult or even impossible. As the problem description is not always amenable to modelling in rCOS, we occasionally had to simplify the model.

For each use case, a state diagram, a sequence diagram, its trace and the functional specification of its operations with pre- and postconditions are provided. These different aspects shall help all participants involved in the development process (designers, programmers) to share the same overall understanding of the system. Consistency of models is checked through processes that can be automated, e.g. by type checking of OO methods and model checking of traces.

The functional specifications in rCOS are then refined to a detailed design very close to Java code through *correct* rules for patterns like the Expert Pattern or translation of quantification. The generated code can be enriched with JML annotations derived from the functional specification and invariants. The annotations can then be used for runtime checking or static analysis.

From the OO model, we then derive a more convenient component model using Class Decomposition and grouping classes into components. The rCOS component model allows us to reason about component interaction, defined by the traces from the specifications, ruling out "bad" behaviour like deadlocks. We discuss issues of (distributed) deployment and necessary middle-ware.

For extra-functional analysis, we applied the Probabilistic Interval Temporal Logic to specify extra-functional properties given in the problem description. Then, we conducted the estimation of the average waiting time for customers.

Apart from concrete tool support, we also point out ongoing work and research on automating the different parts of the development process.

The generated code and additional information is available from the project web page at `http://www.iist.unu.edu/cocome/`.

Acknowledgements. The authors thank Wang Xu and Siraj Shaikh at UNU-IIST for helpful suggestion on CSP and FDR, and the careful reviewers.

References

1. Allan, C., Avgustinov, P., Simon, A.S., Hendren, L., Kuzins, S., Lhoták, O., de Moor, O., Sereni, D., Sittamplan, G., Tibble, J.: Adding Trace Matching with Free Variables to Aspect J. In: OOPSLA 2005 (2005)
2. Bodden, E., Stolz, V.: Tracechecks: Defining semantic interfaces with temporal logic. In: Löwe, W., Südholt, M. (eds.) SC 2006. LNCS, vol. 4089, Springer, Heidelberg (2006)
3. Chalin, P., Kiniry, J.R., Leavens, G.T., Poll, E.: Beyond assertions: Advanced specification and verification with JML and ESC/Java2. In: de Boer, F.S., Bonsangue, M.M., Graf, S., de Roever, W.-P. (eds.) FMCO 2005. LNCS, vol. 4111, pp. 342–363. Springer, Heidelberg (2006)

4. Chandy, K.M., Misra, J.: Parallel Program Design: a Foundation. Addison-Wesley, Reading (1988)
5. Chen, X., He, J., Liu, Z., Zhan, N.: A model of component-based programming. Technical Report 350, UNU-IIST, P.O. Box 3058, Macao SAR, China, Accepted by FSEN 2007 (2006), http://www.iist.unu.edu
6. Chen, X., Liu, Z., Mencl, V.: Separation of concerns and consistent integration in requirements modelling. In: van Leeuwen, J., Italiano, G.F., van der Hoek, W., Meinel, C., Sack, H., Plášil, F. (eds.) SOFSEM 2007. LNCS, vol. 4362, Springer, Heidelberg (2007)
7. Object Management Group. MOF QVT final adopted specification, ptc/05-11-01 (2005), http://www.omg.org/docs/ptc/05-11-01.pdf
8. He, J., Li, X., Liu, Z.: Component-based software engineering. In: Van Hung, D., Wirsing, M. (eds.) ICTAC 2005. LNCS, vol. 3722, Springer, Heidelberg (2005)
9. He, J., Li, X., Liu, Z.: rCOS: A refinement calculus for object systems. Theoretical Computer Science 365(1-2), 109–142 (2006)
10. He, J., Li, X., Liu, Z.: A theory of reactive components. In: Liu, Z., Barbosa, L. (eds.) Intl. Workshop on Formal Aspects of Component Software (FACS 2005). ENTCS, vol. 160, pp. 173–195. Elsevier, Amsterdam (2006)
11. Hoare, C.A.R., He, J.: Unifying Theories of Programming. Prentice-Hall, Englewood Cliffs (1998)
12. Lamport, L.: Specifying Systems: The TLA+ Language and Tools for Hardware and Software Engineers. Addison-Wesley, Reading (2002)
13. Leavens, J.L.: JML's rich, inherited specification for behavioural subtypes. In: Liu, Z., He, J. (eds.) ICFEM 2006. LNCS, vol. 4260, Springer, Heidelberg (2006)
14. Liu, X., Liu, Z., Zhao, L.: Object-oriented structure refinement - a graph transformational approach. Technical Report 340, UNU-IIST, P.O. Box 3058, Macao SAR, China (2006), http://www.iist.unu.edu; In: Proc. Intl. Workshop on Refinement, ENTCS (Extended version accepted for journal publication)
15. Liu, Z., He, J. (eds.): Mathematical Frameworks for Component software: Models for Analysis and Synthesis, Series on Component-Based Software Development, vol. 2. World Scientific, Singapore (2006)
16. Liu, Z., Mencl, V., Ravn, A.P., Yang, L.: Harnessing theories for tool support. International Symposium on Leveraging Applications of Formal Methods, Verification and Validation (ISoLA06), Full version as UNU-IIST Technical Report 343 (2006), http://www.iist.unu.edu
17. Meyer, B.: Object-oriented software construction, 2nd edn. Prentice-Hall, Englewood Cliffs (1997)
18. Möller, M., Olderog, E.-R., Rasch, H., Wehrheim, H.: Linking CSP-OZ with UML and Java: A case study. In: Boiten, E.A., Derrick, J., Smith, G.P. (eds.) IFM 2004. LNCS, vol. 2999, Springer, Heidelberg (2004)
19. Ng, M.Y., Butler, M.: Towards formalizing UML state diagrams in CSP. In: 1st Intl. Conf. on Software Engineering and Formal Methods (SEFM 2003), IEEE Computer Society Press, Los Alamitos (2003)
20. Plasil, F., Visnosky, S.: Behavior protocols for software components. IEEE Trans. Software Eng. 28(11), 1056–1070 (2002)
21. Roscoe, A.W.: The Theory and Practice of Concurrency. Prentice-Hall, Englewood Cliffs (1998)
22. Roscoe, A.W., Wu, Z.: Verifying Statemate statecharts using CSP and FDR. In: Liu, Z., He, J. (eds.) ICFEM 2006. LNCS, vol. 4260, Springer, Heidelberg (2006)

23. Schneider, S.: Concurrent and Real-time Systems. Wiley, Chichester (2000)
24. Yang, L., Mencl, V., Stolz, V., Liu, Z.: Automating correctness preserving model-to-model transformation in MDA. In: Proc. of Asian Working Conference on Verified Software, UNU-IIST Technical Report 348 (2006), http://www.iist.unu.edu

A   Full CSP/FDR Listing for Consistency

```
-- Define events:
channel enableExpress, disableExpress, startSale , enterItem, finishSale , cashPay, cardPay

-- Define the process corresponding to the regular expression:
Trace = (TraceExMode [] TraceNormalMode) ; Trace
TraceNormalMode = disableExpress -> TraceNormalSale
TraceNormalSale = startSale -> enterItem -> TraceEnterItemLoopStar
                ; finishSale  -> ((TraceCashPay [] TraceCardPay)
                ; (SKIP [] TraceNormalSale))
TraceEnterItemLoopStar = SKIP [] (enterItem -> TraceEnterItemLoopStar)
TraceCashPay = cashPay -> SKIP
TraceCardPay = cardPay -> SKIP

TraceExMode = enableExpress -> TraceESale
TraceESale = startSale -> enterItem -> TraceEMode(7)
           ; ( finishSale  -> (TraceCashPay ; (SKIP [] TraceESale)))
TraceEMode(c) = if c == 0 then SKIP
                     else (SKIP [] (enterItem -> TraceEMode(c-1)))

-- State Diagram:
datatype Mode = on | off
State = Init(on) [] Init (off)
-- Resolve outgoing branches non-deterministically:
Init (mode) = (if mode == on then disableExpress -> StateNormalMode(off)
                     else STOP)
          [] ( if mode == off then enableExpress -> StateExpressMode(on)
                     else STOP)
StateNormalMode(mode) = (startSale -> enterItem -> StateEnterItemLoopStar)
                      ; finishSale  -> ((StateCashPay [] StateCardPay)
                      ; ((enableExpress -> StateExpressMode(on))
                          [] StateNormalMode(mode)))

StateEnterItemLoopStar = SKIP [] (enterItem -> StateEnterItemLoopStar)
StateCashPay = cashPay -> SKIP
StateCardPay = cardPay -> SKIP

StateEMode(c) = if c == 0 then SKIP
                     else (SKIP [] (enterItem -> StateEMode(c-1)))

StateExpressMode(mode) = startSale -> enterItem -> StateEMode(7)
                       ; finishSale  -> (StateCashPay
                       ; ((disableExpress -> StateNormalMode(off))
                           [] StateExpressMode(mode)))

-- Check trace equivalence:
assert State [T= Trace
--^ does not hold as trace abstracts from the guard,
-- permits: enableExpress -> ... -> enableExpress
assert Trace [T= State

-- Make sure both mechanisms can't deadlock:
assert Trace :[deadlock free [F]]
assert State :[deadlock free [F]]
```

B   Packages

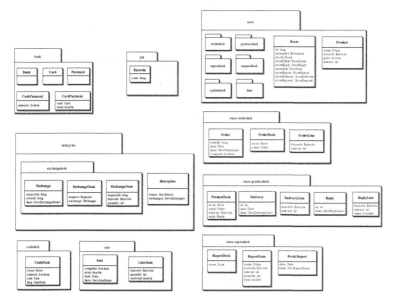

Fig. 8. Packages

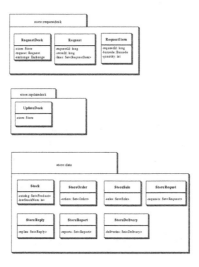

Fig. 9. Packages

7 Component-Interaction Automata Approach (CoIn)

Barbora Zimmerova*, Pavlína Vařeková**, Nikola Beneš**,
Ivana Černá***, Luboš Brim†, and Jiří Sochor**

Masaryk University, Brno, Czech Republic

7.1 Introduction

The aim of the *CoIn approach (Component-Interaction Automata approach)* is
to create a framework for formal analysis of behavioural aspects of large scale
component-based systems. For the modelling purpose, we use the *Component-
interaction automata* language [1]. For the verification, we employ a parallel
model-checker DiVinE [2], which is able to handle very large, hence more realistic, models of component-based systems. Verified properties, like consequences of
service calls or fairness of communication, are expressed in an extended version
of the Linear Temporal Logic CI-LTL.

7.1.1 Goals and Scope of the Component Model

The *Component-interaction automata* model behaviour of each component (both
basic and composite) as a labelled transition system. The language builds on
a simple, yet very powerful, composition operator that is able to reflect hierarchical assembly of the system and various communication strategies among
components. Thanks to this operator, the language can be used for modelling
the behaviour of components designed for or implemented in various component
frameworks and models.

7.1.2 Modeled Cutout of CoCoME

While modelling the CoCoME, we have focused on the aspect of communicational behaviour of components. Hence we did not treat aspects like non-
functional properties or data manipulation. However in terms of component
interaction, we have modelled the CoCoME completely in fine detail, based on
the provided Java implementation of the system. We modelled also parts like
GUI, Event Channels, or the Product Dispatcher component. The final model
was verified using the DiVinE verification tool. We have checked the compliance
of the model to the Use Cases from Chapter 3, we have verified the Test Cases,
and various other CI-LTL properties.

---

  * Supported by the Czech Science Foundation within the project No. 102/05/H050.
  ** The authors have been supported by the grant No. 1ET400300504.
  *** The author has been supported by the grant No. GACR 201/06/1338.
  † The author has been supported by the grant No. 1ET408050503.

A. Rausch et al. (Eds.): Common Component Modeling Example, LNCS 5153, pp. 146–176, 2008.
© Springer-Verlag Berlin Heidelberg 2008

7.1.3   Benefit of the Modeling

One of our main benefits is that we use a general formal modelling language that is, thanks to its flexible composition operator, able to capture behaviour of various kinds of component-based systems. The created model is in fact a labelled transition system, which is a format that can be directly verified using a large variety of existing methods.

7.1.4   Effort and Lessons Learned

For the full modelling of the CoCoME, we needed two person months. The verification was then performed automatically using the DiVinE tool. This exercise helped us to discover the limits and capabilities of our modelling language and verification methods. In particular, we have found general solutions to various modelling issues, like creation and destruction of instances, modelling of global shared state, or exception handling. In terms of verification, we have examined the efficiency of our verification methods on a large model of a real system.

7.2   Component Model

Our framework is represented by the *Component-interaction automata* language [1,3]. It should be emphasized that Component-interaction automata are not meant to support implementation of component-based systems. They are intended as a modelling language that can be used to create detailed models of behaviour of component-based systems to support their formal analysis.

The language is very general, which follows from two things. First, the Component-interaction automata language does not explicitly associate *action names* used in the labels of automata with interfaces/services/events/etc., which allows the designers to make the association themselves. The association must only respect that if the same action name is used in two components, in one as an input and in the other one as an output, it marks a point on which the components may communicate. Second, the language defines one flexible *composition operator* that can be parametrized to simulate several communication strategies used in various component models. In this manner, Component-interaction automata can be instantiated to a particular component model by fixing the *composition operator* and *semantics of actions*.

7.2.1   Definition of a Component-Interaction Automaton

Component-interaction automata capture each component as a labelled transition system with structured labels (to remember components which communicated on an action) and a hierarchy of component names (which represents the architectural structure of the component).

A *hierarchy of component names* is a tuple $H = (H_1, \ldots, H_n)$, $n \in \mathbb{N}$, of one of the following forms, S_H denotes the set of component names corresponding to H. The first case is that $H_1, \ldots, H_n$ are pairwise different natural numbers; then

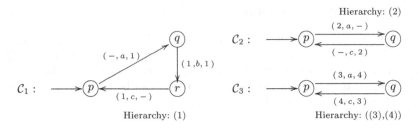

Fig. 1. Examples of CI automata

$S_H = \bigcup_{i=1}^{n}\{H_i\}$. The second case is that $H_1, \ldots, H_n$ are hierarchies of component names where $S_{H_1}, \ldots, S_{H_n}$ are pairwise disjoint; then $S_H = \bigcup_{i=1}^{n} S_{H_i}$.

A *component-interaction automaton* (or a *CI automaton* for short) is a 5-tuple $\mathcal{C} = (Q, Act, \delta, I, H)$ where Q is a finite set of states, Act is a finite set of *actions*, $\Sigma = ((S_H \cup \{-\}) \times Act \times (S_H \cup \{-\})) \setminus (\{-\} \times Act \times \{-\})$ is a set of *labels*, $\delta \subseteq Q \times \Sigma \times Q$ is a finite set of *labelled transitions*, $I \subseteq Q$ is a nonempty set of *initial states*, and H is a hierarchy of component names.

The labels have semantics of input, output, or internal, based on their structure. In the triple, the middle item represents an action name, the first item represents a name of the component that outputs the action, and the third item represents a name of the component that inputs the action. Examples of three CI automata are in figure 1. Here $(-, a, 1)$ in $\mathcal{C}_1$ signifies that a component with a numerical name 1 inputs an action a, $(1, c, -)$ in $\mathcal{C}_1$ signifies that a component 1 outputs an action c, $(4, c, 3)$ in $\mathcal{C}_3$ represents an internal communication of components 4 (sender) and 3 (receiver) on c, and $(1, b, 1)$ in $\mathcal{C}_1$ an internal communication on b inside the component 1 (it abstracts from the names of the sub-components of 1 that participated in the communication).

7.2.2   Composition of Component-Interaction Automata

CI automata (a set of them) can be composed to form a composite CI automaton. The language of Component-interaction automata allows us to compose any finite set of CI automata (not necessarily two of them as usual in related languages) that have disjoint sets of component names. This guarantees that each primitive component in the model of the system has a unique name, which we use to identify the component in the model.

Informal description of the composition follows. For formal definitions see [1]. You can consult the description with a composite automaton of $\{\mathcal{C}_1, \mathcal{C}_2\}$ in fig. 2; the automata $\mathcal{C}_1, \mathcal{C}_2$ are in fig. 1. The *states* of the composite automaton are items of the Cartesian product of states of given automata. Among the states, the syntactically possible transitions (we call the set of them a *complete transition space*) are all transitions capturing that either (1) one of the automata follows its original transition or (2) two automata synchronize on a complementary transition (input of the first one, output of the second one, both with the same action). Finally, we decide which of these transitions we really want to be part of the composite automaton, and remove the rest. The inscription $\mathcal{C} = \otimes_T \{\mathcal{C}_1, \mathcal{C}_2\}$,

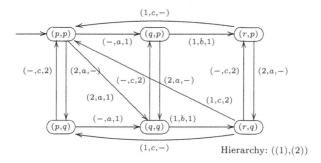

Fig. 2. A possible composition of the set $\{\mathcal{C}_1, \mathcal{C}_2\}$

where T is a set of transitions, means that $\mathcal{C}$ is a composite automaton created by composition of $\mathcal{C}_1, \mathcal{C}_2$ and it consists of only those transitions from the complete transition space, that are included in T.

The automaton in fig. 2 is $\otimes_T\{\mathcal{C}_1, \mathcal{C}_2\}$ where T contains all transitions from the complete transition space. We write this as $\otimes\{\mathcal{C}_1, \mathcal{C}_2\}$. In addition to $\otimes$, along the text we use the following shortcuts for various types of $\otimes_T$. Denote Δ the complete transition space (set of all syntactically possible transitions) for the set of automata that enters the composition. Then

- $\otimes_{\bar{T}}$ is equivalent to $\otimes_{\Delta \setminus T}$
  The parameter T in this case specifies the *forbidden transitions*.
- $\otimes^{\mathcal{F}}$ is equivalent to $\otimes_T$ where $T = \{(q, x, q') \in \Delta \mid x \in \mathcal{F}\}$
  The parameter $\mathcal{F}$ specifies *allowed labels* – only the transitions with these labels may remain.
- $\otimes^{\bar{\mathcal{F}}}$ is equivalent to $\otimes_T$ where $T = \{(q, x, q') \in \Delta \mid x \notin \mathcal{F}\}$
  The parameter $\mathcal{F}$ specifies *forbidden labels* – no transition with any of these labels can remain in the composition.

Remember that the labels and transitions represent *items of behaviour* of the component-based system. Each internal label represents communication between two components, and each external label a demand for such communication. A transition signifies a specific communication (represented by the label) that takes place in the context given by the respective states.

7.2.3 Textual Notation

For linear transcription of CI automata, we have defined the following textual notation, which was used for writing the CoCoME models. To introduce the notation, we rewrite some of the automata from the text above into the notation. The fig. 3 a) presents the automaton $\mathcal{C}_1$ from fig. 1. The keyword `automaton` states that we are going to define a new automaton by describing its state space. This is followed by the name of the automaton and the hierarchy of component names the automaton represents. The keyword `state` is followed by a list of states, `init` by a list of initial states, and `trans` by a list of transitions.

```
automaton C1 (1) {        |    composite C {       |    composite C {
  state p, q, r;          |      C1, C2;           |      C1, C2;
  init p;                 |    }                   |      restrictL
  trans                   |                        |        (-,a,1), (2,a,-),
    p -> q (-,a,1),       |                        |        (1,c,-), (-,c,2);
    q -> r (1,b,1),       |                        |    }
    r -> p (1,c,-);       |                        |
}                         |                        |
```

Fig. 3. a) Automaton $\mathcal{C}_1$ (left); **b)** Composition $\mathcal{C} = \otimes\{\mathcal{C}_1, \mathcal{C}_2\}$ (center); **c)** Composition $\mathcal{C} = \otimes^{\mathcal{F}}\{\mathcal{C}_1, \mathcal{C}_2\}$ where $\mathcal{F} = \{(-, a, 1), (2, a, -), (1, c, -), (-, c, 2)\}$ (right)

The composite automaton $\mathcal{C} = \otimes\{\mathcal{C}_1, \mathcal{C}_2\}$ from fig. 2 is rewritten in fig. 3 b). No parameter T needs to be given here. For restricted composition we include a keyword representing the type of composition and the list of transitions or labels (see 7.2.2). Example of such composite is in fig. 3 c). For $\otimes_T$ the keyword is `onlyT` (only the **T**ransitions given), for $\otimes_{\bar{T}}$ the keyword is `restrictT`, for $\otimes^{\mathcal{F}}$ the keyword is `onlyL` (only the **L**abels given), for $\otimes^{\bar{\mathcal{F}}}$ the keyword is `restrictL`.

7.3 Modelling the CoCoME

In this section, we present our modelling approach on the CoCoME system, the *Trading System*, which we have modelled completely in fine detail (models available in [4]). First, we describe the input and output of the modelling process.

Input. The CoIn modelling process has two inputs: specification of the behaviour of primitive components and description of the static structure of the system (assembly and interconnection of components). The *specification of behaviour of primitive components* can be given e.g. as an informal description (used in preliminary design phase for estimating/predicting the future behaviour of the system) or as the implementation of the system (used for verification or formal analysis of an existing system). In our approach we use the implementation to derive CI automata of primitive components. The *static structure of the system* reveals the hierarchy of components, their interfaces and interconnections between them. This can be given in any syntactic form that allows a modeller to extract the information about the actions that can be communicated among the components and the restrictions on the communication, if any. The structural description is used to arrange the automata of primitive components into a hierarchy, and to parameterize the composition operator for each level of the hierarchy.

Output. The output of the modelling process is basically a CI automaton that represents the whole system (composition of the components that make up the system). In the CoIn approach, this automaton is used as an input of verification methods that will be discussed in section 7.5.

7.3.1 Static View

In our approach, the model of the static structure is an input (not an output) of the modelling process. In the case of this modelling example, we derive the basic information about the components, their interconnection, and system's hierarchy from the UML component diagrams presented in Chapter 3. The information about the actions that can be communicated among components is extracted from the Java implementation, namely from the interfaces of the classes. Fig. 4 reprints the hierarchical structure of the components and assigns each primitive component a unique numerical name that will be used to identify it. This diagram, in addition to the provided ones, includes the *ProductDispatcher* component that is also part of the implementation, and excludes the *Database* because we do not model it as a component. We decided to abstract from the Database, because the logic of data manipulation is already part of the *Data* component that we do model.

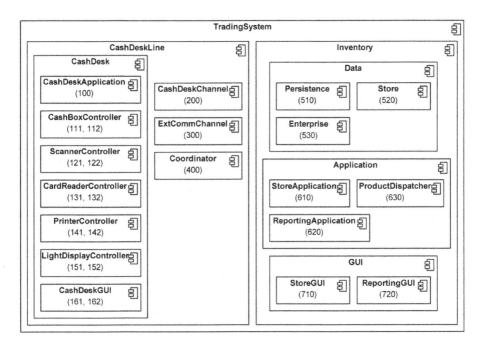

Fig. 4. Trading System overview

7.3.2   Behavioural View

For the behavioural view modelling, which is of our main interest, we use the *Component-interaction automata* language discussed in section 7.2. We decided to use the Java implementation as the main source for the modelling because it allows us to present a complex and interesting model of the system that is suitable for automatic analysis. Before we proceed to the models of the components, we present general modelling decision we did with respect to the implementation.

Initial Decisions. The components of the static view can be easily identified in the implementation as packages/classes. However we do not consider all packages and classes to be components. We omit modelling of classes that have no interesting interaction behaviour and act rather as data types than interaction entities. These include classes for different kinds of events, transfer objects and database entries. The same applies to Java library classes and supportive classes of the *Trading System*, like *DataIfFactory* or *ApplicationFactory*. Interfaces of the components and their parts can be identified as Java interfaces, resp. the sets of public methods constituting the parts.

We do not model the start of the system – the process of initial creation of all components and execution of their `main()` methods. We model the system from the point where everything is ready to be used. However we do model creation and destruction of the components that may be initialised during the run of the system, because in such case it is a part of system's behaviour.

Modelling Components as CI Automata. The main idea for creating the automaton of a component is that we first capture component's behaviour on each service as a separate automaton, and then compose the automata for all the services into the model of the component. The services of components are represented by methods of the classes that implement the components. Therefore we will use the term *method* when referring to the implementation of a service that we model.

An automaton for a method. We assign each method, say `doIt()`, a tuple of actions where the first one represents the *call* of the method (we write it as `doIt`) and the second one the *return* (we write it as `doIt'`). These two determine the start and the end of the method's execution. Each method is modelled as a loop, which means that each of its behaviours starts and finishes in the same state, the initial one. Fig. 5 shows automata for two simple methods. The automaton $\mathcal{C}_1$ models a method `doA()` that does not call other methods to compute the result, the automaton $\mathcal{C}_2$ models a method `doB()` that calls the method `doA()` and when `doA()` returns, `doB()` also returns. More interesting examples follow in the text, see fig. 18 for an automaton of a complex method `changePrice()`.

An automaton for a primitive (basic) component. Having automata for all the methods of a component, we can use the composition operator $\otimes_T$ to automatically create the automaton for the whole component. The composition operator allows us to compose the methods in various ways. When we apply $\otimes$, the resulting automaton simulates a component that can serve its methods (services) concurrently (modelled by interleaving of method parts). For example see $\mathcal{C}_3 = \otimes\{\mathcal{C}_1, \mathcal{C}_2\}$ in fig. 6 (*doA, doB, computeA, computeB* are shortened to

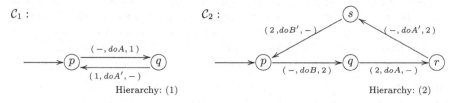

Fig. 5. Automata for simple methods

dA, dB, cA, cB respectively). As the component constitutes of two methods, its state space is in fact a two-dimensional grid. In case of three methods, it would be three-dimensional, and so forth. For this reason, we sometimes refer to this interleaving-like notion of composition as a *cube-like composition*.

Note, that the component $\mathcal{C}_3$ in fig. 6 may handle the methods doA() and doB() concurrently, but cannot accept a new call to a method that is currently executed. If we would like to model concurrent execution of several copies of one method, we would need to include the corresponding number of the automaton copies in the composition.

Another notion of composition that is common for composing models of methods, is the *star-like composition*, which reflects that from the initial state, the component may start executing any of its methods, but cannot start a new one before the previous method is finished. This can be found in GUI components where the calls on their (GUI-based) methods are serialized by the *event dispatching thread*. For example see $\mathcal{C}_4 = \otimes_{\bar{T}}\{\mathcal{C}_1, \mathcal{C}_2\}$ in fig. 6. The star-like notion of composition can be realized by the $\otimes_{\bar{T}}$ where T consists of the transitions that represent start of a method-call from other than the initial state.

In a similar way, the composition gives us possibility to design other compositional strategies that would e.g. permit only specific ordering of services. For modelling of the CoCoME *Trading System* we use the cube-like and star-like compositions most of the time to create the models of basic components by composing automata of their methods or other parts.

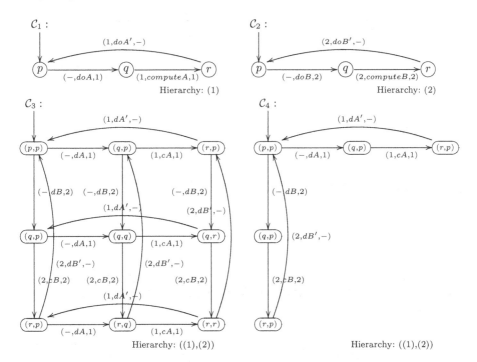

Fig. 6. Examples of the cube-like $\mathcal{C}_3$ and the star-like $\mathcal{C}_4$ composition of $\{\mathcal{C}_1, \mathcal{C}_2\}$

An automaton for a composite component. The situation is different for models of composite components. These are composed from the automata that usually interact with each other. Here, the most common notion of composition is the *handshake-like composition* which proceeds with a principle that anytime a component inside the composite is ready to perform an action that has its counterpart at one of the other components, it waits for this component to synchronize on the action. This kind of composition can be realized by $\otimes^{\mathcal{F}}$ where $\mathcal{F}$ consists of (1) all internal labels of components that enter the composition, (2) all new internal labels that may emerge from the composition, and (3) all external labels that have no counterpart at any other component. In the CoCoME modelling process, we use a modified version of this kind of composition where we manually, for each composite component, create $\mathcal{F}$ as a set consisting of (1) all internal labels of components that enter the composition, (2) only the new internal labels emerging from the composition *that are supported by a binding between the components* in the static view, and (3) all external labels *that represent methods provided/required on interfaces of the composite component* we are creating the model for, no matter if they synchronized inside the component or not.

Example. Imagine a *ComponentC* consisting of a *ComponentA* and *ComponentB* as in fig. 7. Suppose that the automaton of ComponentA has a set of labels $\mathcal{L}_A = \{ (-, serviceA, 1), (1, serviceA', -), (-, serviceC, 1), (1, serviceC', -), (1, serviceB, -), (-, serviceB', 1), (1, internalA, 1) \}$ and the ComponentB $\mathcal{L}_B = \{ (-, serviceB, 2), (2, serviceB', -), (2, serviceD, -), (-, serviceD', 2), (2, internalB, 2) \}$. Such sets of labels can be intuitively guessed from the figure. Then the automaton representing behaviour of ComponentC can be constructed as *AutomatonC* $= \otimes^{\mathcal{F}} \{ AutomatonA, AutomatonB \}$ where $\mathcal{F} = \{ (1, internalA, 1), (2, internalB, 2), (1, serviceB, 2), (2, serviceB', 1), (-, serviceC, 1), (1, serviceC', -), (2, serviceD, -), (-, serviceD', 2) \}$.

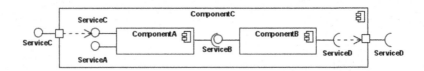

Fig. 7. A composite component

The static view given in fig. 7 is important here. Note that if the interfaces of ComponentA and ComponentB on `serviceB()` were not connected, the labels $(1, serviceB, 2), (2, serviceB', 1)$ would not represent feasible interactions and could not be part of $\mathcal{F}$. Analogically, the labels $(-, serviceA, 1), (1, serviceA', -)$ cannot be part of $\mathcal{F}$ because `serviceA()` is not provided on the interface of ComponentC.

In the rest of this section, we demonstrate the capabilities of Component-interaction automata to model various kinds of interaction scenarios that we have faced when creating the model of the *Trading System*. We start with the models of primitive components (see fig. 4) and then present the composition anytime we have described all components needed for the composition. For space reasons, we do not describe all components completely. We just emphasize our solutions to interesting modelling issues when used for the first time. After reading this section, we believe that the reader would able to understand the whole CI automata model of the *Trading System*, even if some parts are not discussed here. The complete model of the *Trading System* is available in [4].

7.3.3   Specification of the CashDeskApplication (Level 3)

The *CashDeskApplication* (component id *100*) is the main sub-component of the *CashDesk* composite component (see fig. 4). It is subscribed to receive events from two event channels, handles the events, and publishes new ones to control cash-desk devices. We start with the automata representing behaviour of its services, represented by the methods of the *ApplicationEventHandlerImpl* class. We have modelled all methods with only two exceptions. First, we omit the onMessage() method because it only delegates messages from event channels to onEvent() methods, which we decided to model as direct calls. Second, we skip the constructor ApplicationEventHandlerImpl() which is called only once when the system is started (and never during system's execution).

```
private void makeSale(PaymentMode mode) throws JMSException {
  SaleTO saleTO = new SaleTO();
  saleTO.setProductTOs(products);
  appPublisher.publish(topicSession
      .createObjectMessage(new SaleSuccessEvent()));
  externalPublisher.publish(topicSession
      .createObjectMessage(new AccountSaleEvent(saleTO)));
  externalPublisher.publish(topicSession
      .createObjectMessage(new SaleRegisteredEvent(
          topicName, saleTO.getProductTOs().size(), mode)));
}
```

Fig. 8. Java source of the makeSale() method

The Component as a Publisher. The makeSale() (fig. 8, numerical name 2) is one of the methods that demonstrate the capability of the CashDeskApplication to publish events to event channels, the *CashDeskChannel (200)* and the *ExtCommChannel (300)* in particular. Each publication of an event (underlined in fig. 8) is identified by the event channel and the type of the event. We reflect both in the action names that we associate with each publish(). For instance the first publish() in fig. 8 is referred to as publishSaleSuccessEvent whereas the second one as publishExtAccountSaleEvent.

CI automata model of the method is in fig. 9. For short, *makeSale* is written as *mS*, *publishSaleSuccessEvent* as *pSSE*, *publishExtAccountSaleEvent* as *pEASE*, and *publishExtSaleRegisteredEvent* as *pESRE*.

First consider only the states $00 - 07$ and transitions among them. They represent three subsequent calls of publish() methods as one may expect from the

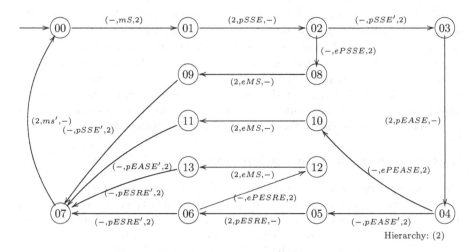

Fig. 9. CI automaton of the `makeSale()` method

Java code. The rest of the model captures that each of the `publish()` methods may throw an exception which is not caught by `makeSale()`. Consider the first publication. If an exception is thrown when `publishSaleSuccessEvent` is executed[1] (state 02), `makeSale()` synchronizes with it $(-, exception Publish-SaleSuccessEvent, 2)$, written as $(-, ePSSE, 2)$, and moves to the state 08 where it forwards the exception $(2, exception MakeSale, -)$, finishes the publication and returns. We model `makeSale()` to forward the exception via catch and throw because it enables it to change its state and return when the exception occurs. Additionally, the exception is renamed because it makes it easier in the models of other methods to catch the exceptions of `makeSale()`.

The Component as a Subscriber. The CashDeskApplication implements a variety of `onEvent()` methods, which handle the events the component is subscribed to. We assign each of them a unique tuple of action names reflecting the type of their argument to distinguish them. For instance the `onEvent(Cash-AmountEnteredEvent)` method (fig. 10) is referred `onEventCashAmountEntered`.

In fig. 10, the interesting behaviour is again underlined. It shows that the behaviour of the method differs significantly based on its argument. For this reason we decided to split this method into two, which can be done in our approach. We get `onEventCashAmountEntered`, which is called whenever a digit button is pressed, and `onEventCashAmountEntered_Enter`, which is called only when the Enter button is used. See fig. 11 for the automata of both of them. In the model, the $onEventCashAmountEntered$ is shortened to $oECAE$, $onEvent-CashAmountEntered\_Enter$ to $oECAEE$, $publishChangeAmountCalculatedEvent$ to $pCACE$, and $exceptionPublishChangeAmountCalculatedEvent$ to $ePCACE$. If

---

[1] The automaton of the event channel performs $(200, exceptionPublishSaleSuccess-Event, -)$ when serving `publishSaleSuccessEvent`.

```
public void onEvent(CashAmountEnteredEvent cashAmountEnteredEvent) {
  ...
  if (currState.equals(PAYING_BY_CASH)) {
    switch (cashAmountEnteredEvent.getKeyStroke()) {
    case ONE: total = total.append("1"); break;
    case TWO: total = total.append("2"); break;
    ...
    case ENTER:
      try {
        appPublisher.publish(topicSession
          .createObjectMessage(new ChangeAmountCalculatedEvent(changeamount)));
        ...
        currState = PAID;
        ...
      } catch (JMSException e) {
        ...
      }
      break;
} } }
```

Fig. 10. Java source of the onEvent(CashAmountEnteredEvent) method

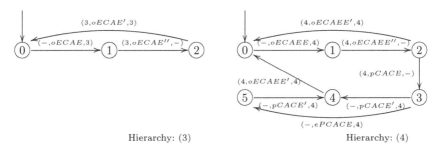

Hierarchy: (3)   Hierarchy: (4)

Fig. 11. CI automata of the onEvent(CashAmountEnteredEvent) method parts

we did not want to split the method into two, we would finish with one model that non-deterministically allows for both behaviours.

The onEvent() methods are called asynchronously with a notification (represented by the action $onEventCashAmountEntered''$, or $oECAE''$ in the figure). Asynchronous methods start with getting the request as the synchronous ones $(-, onEventCashAmountEntered, 3)$, but returns internally because the caller is not interested in their response $(3, onEventCashAmountEntered', 3)$.

Exception Handling. The onEvent(CashAmountEnteredEvent) method (fig. 10) calls the publish() method inside a try block, which means that if the method throws an exception, onEvent(CashAmountEnteredEvent) catches it and moves to an appropriate catch block that handles the exception.

This principle is realized in the automaton of onEventCashAmountEntered_Enter (fig. 11 on the right). Here the execution after calling publishChangeAmountCalculatedEvent moves to the state 3 where it waits for publish() to return $(-, publishChangeAmountCalculatedEvent', 4)$ to get to the state 4. If an exception arrives before the return does $(-, exceptionPublishChangeAmountCalculatedEvent, 4)$, the execution moves to the state 5, confirms the return of the publication, and possibly continues with the exception handling provided by the catch block, which is empty in this case. Then this exceptional branch joins the normal execution flow in state 4. The execution between this join and the end of the method is again empty here.

For more complex example of exception handling see the description of the changePrice() method in section 7.3.11.

Full Model of a Method Provided on the Interface. Using the approach discussed above, we have created models of all methods constituting the CashDeskApplication. However, not all the methods are finally provided on the interface, some methods have only supportive character. One of the provided methods is the onEvent(CashBoxClosedEvent), fig. 12, which uses two private methods – makeSale(), fig. 9, and reset(), which has the same structure as C_1 in fig. 5 and a hierarchy (1).

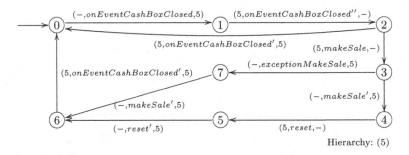

Fig. 12. CI automaton of the onEvent(CashBoxClosedEvent) method

The complete model of onEvent(CashBoxClosedEvent) is simply the composition of the automaton in fig. 12 with the automata of makeSale() and reset(). The composition is the *handshake-like* composition described in section 7.3.2. The composite automaton for onEvent(CashBoxClosedEvent) is in fig. 13. The actions are again shortened in the usual way.

Full Model of the CashDeskApplication. When we create the full models of all the methods available on the CashDeskApplication's interface (which are exactly all the onEvent() methods), we compose them into the automaton representing the model of the CashDeskApplication. In this case, we must use the *star-like* composition because the access to the onEvent() methods is controlled by a *Java session* that serializes them.

Note that the resulting model is a composite automaton where the basic units (represented by the component names in labels) are its methods. However, we are not interested in the interaction of methods, we want to model the interaction of primitive components, where the CashDeskApplication is one of them. Hence we transforms the automaton into a primitive one. This only means, that we rename all the component names used in the labels and transitions to a new numerical name 100 representing the CashDeskApplication, and change the hierarchy of

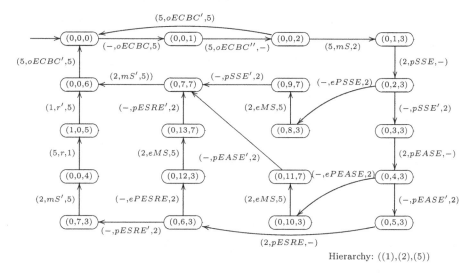

Fig. 13. Full model of the onEvent(CashBoxClosedEvent) method

component names to (100). See [1] for the definition of a primitive automaton and the relation of being primitive to a composite automaton. From now on, we suppose this final step of making the automaton primitive as implicit, and when presenting models of component parts, we use directly the numerical name of the resulting component in the labels.

Remember that by making an automaton primitive, we do not lose any information about its behaviours, we only lose the information about the names of component parts that participated in the behaviour.

Internal State of a Component. In this modelling example, we decided to determine the state of a component only with the interactions that the component is ready to perform. We do not take its internal state[2] into account. When a component decides, based on its state, whether it performs one interaction or another one, we model this basically as a non-deterministic choice. However this is just a modelling decision for the CoCoME. We are able to regard the internal state of a component (in case the number of internal states is finite). The basic idea of our approach follows.

Suppose that the internal state of the CashDeskApplication is represented only by the states defined as *CashDeskStates* (see the implementation for details), which are: INITIALIZED, SALE_STARTED, SALE_FINISHED, PAYING_BY_CREDITCARD, CREDIT_CARD_SCANNED, PAYING_BY_CASH, PAID. Possible transitions between the states are depicted in fig. 14. Now consider for instance the onEvent (CashAmount- EnteredEvent) method and its onEventCashAmountEntered_Enter model in particular (fig. 11 on the right). In its behaviour in between

---

[2] We understand the internal state of a component as a current assignment of values to its attributes.

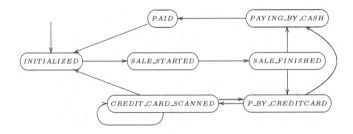

Fig. 14. Internal states of the CashDeskApplication

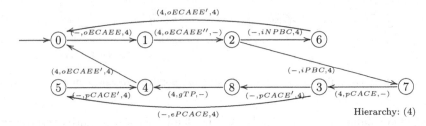

Fig. 15. Modified model of the onEventCashAmountEntered_Enter

receive of the call and return, it either performs nothing, or tries to publish a *ChangeAmountCalculatedEvent*. The choice is non-deterministic here. However in reality, the choice is determined by the state of the component which can be seen in fig. 10. If we wanted to reflect the state, we would remodel onEventCashAmountEntered_Enter as in fig. 15.

The automaton first asks if the state equals to PAYING_BY_CASH – represented by $(-, isPAYING\_BY\_CASH, 4)$ and $(-, isNotPAYING\_BY\_CASH, 4)$ (in fig. 15 $(-, iPBC, 4)$ and $(-, iNPBC, 4)$) – and then follows the corresponding way. The automaton may also change the internal state of the component by asking it to do so via $(4, goToPAID, -)$, in the figure $(4, gTP, -)$. Last, the information about the component's state is added to the model of the CashDeskApplication itself. We do it by the *handshake-like* composition of the model of the CashDeskApplication with an additional automaton representing its states. The additional automaton is basically the automaton in fig. 14, where each transition is labeled with $(-, goToX, 1000)$, where X is the name of the state the transition is going to, and each state is additionally equipped with a self-transition with label $(1000, isX, -)$, where X is again the name of the state, and self-transitions with $(1000, isNotY, -)$ for all states Y different from X.

7.3.4   Specification of the CashBoxControllerComposite (Level 3)

The *CashBoxController* component from fig. 4 is in fact a composite component that consists of two primitive components, the *CashBox (111)* and the

CashBoxController (112). Hence we refer to the composite as the *CashBoxController Composite* to avoid confusion. The *CashBox* component represents the user interface to the cash box device while the *CashBoxController* handles the communication of the CashBox with the rest of the system. We have assigned a different number to each of them, because they are distinguished also in the Use Cases presented in Chapter 3.

CashBox (111). The CashBox consists of two kind of methods, the GUI-based methods that represent response to pressing a button by the Cashier, and regular methods that can be called by the rest of the system. These are openCashBox() and closeCashBox(). Methods of both kinds are modelled in a usual way. The difference between these two is that while openCashBox() and closeCashBox() can be called concurrently with other methods, the calls on the GUI-based methods are serialized by the event dispatching thread and hence no two GUI-based methods may execute at the same time.

In CI automata, we are able to respect this restriction when creating the composite automaton for the CashBox. We first create an auxiliary automaton CashBoxGUI with the star-like composition of GUI-based methods, and then compose this with the rest of the methods using the cube-like composition. This gives us exactly the result we want to have.

CashBoxController (112). The same applies to the *CashBoxController* model. Here, again two types of methods can be identified. The onEvent() methods, that are accessed serially, and the others that may be accessed in parallel. However in this case, there is only one onEvent() method, so we can apply the cube-like composition directly.

CashBoxControllerComposite. For the composition of the *CashBox* and *CashBoxController*, we use the handshake-like composition with synchronization on the sendX() methods. This composition results in the model of the *CashBoxControllerComposite* with only 555 states in total, even if the automaton of the *CashBoxController* has more than 390.000 states. This means that a composite component has nearly 1000-times less states than one of its sub-components. This is caused by the synchronization on common actions, which the handshake-like composition necessitates. In effect, the sendX() methods of the *CashBoxController* (modelled as callable in parallel) are serialized by the calls from the GUI-based methods of the *CashBox*, which are callable only in a serial order. Hence, all the states that represent concurrent execution of several sendX() methods disappear from the composition.

Models of the remaining CashDesk components, namely the *ScannerControllerComposite (121, 122)*, *CardReaderControllerComposite (131, 132)*, *PrinterControllerComposite (141, 142)*, *LightDisplayControllerComposite (151, 152)*, and *CashDeskGUIComposite (161, 162)* were created using the principles already discussed above. Therefore we decided to not to include their description here. The complete models of all of them can be found in [4].

7.3.5   Specification of the CashDesk (Level 2)

The *CashDesk* component is a composite component that consists of all the components discussed above. Its model is a cube-like composition (with no restriction on transitions) because the components do not communicate with each other directly. They communicate via the *CashDeskChannel*, which is outside the CashDesk component. As there is exactly one CashDeskChannel for each CashDesk, it would be better design decision to move the CashDeskChannel inside the CashDesk, which would make the CashDesk component more coherent while not influencing the model of the whole system. Only the hierarchy of component names would be different.

We decided to do it. We have created the model of the CashDesk using the handshake-like composition of the components discussed above with the CashDeskChannel (discussed below) with synchronization on the publish() and onEvent() methods that involve the CashDeskChannel, which can now happen only internally.

7.3.6   Specification of the CashDeskChannel (Level 2)

The purpose of the *CashDeskChannel (200)* is in general to broadcast events that it receives from publishers to all subscribers that are interested in the events. The publication of an event is initiated by a publisher via calling publish(). The publish() method returns whenever the event is received by the channel. The channel then broadcasts the event to all subscribers that are interested in the event. We model this broadcast as a set of asynchronous calls to the onEvent() methods of the subscribers. These calls must be asynchronous to permit concurrent execution of the onEvent() methods. Based on this notes, the automaton for handling one event, namely the *SaleStartedEvent* (written as *SSEvent* for short) with three subscribers interested in it, is in fig. 16.

The delivery of the event consists of two parts, the channel first initiates an onEvent() method of a subscriber $(200, onEventSaleStarted, -)$ and then waits for the notification from it $(-, onEventSaleStarted'', 200)$. The reason for this notification is only auxiliary. It guarantees that none of the subscribers acquires the event twice because it must first wait for the channel to take the notification

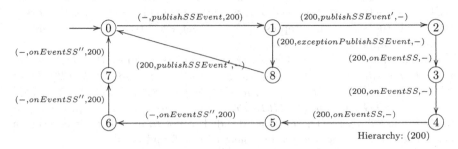

Fig. 16. CI automaton for SaleStartedEvent

from it. And the channel starts accepting the notifications after all the copies of the event are delivered. See fig. 11 for a model of an onEvent() method.

The drawback of this solution is that the channel needs to know the number of the subscribers in advance. If it was not possible to know the number in advance, we could model the transitions with $(200, onEventSaleStarted, -)$ and $(-, onEventSaleStarted'', 200)$ as two subsequent loops. However in such case we could not guarantee that all the subscribers really get the event, because of not having the information of the actual number of them.

In the same way, we create an automaton for every event that can be handled by the channel, and compose them together using the cube-like composition.

The *ExtCommChannel (300)* is modelled in exactly the same way as the CashDeskChannel, therefore we do not discuss its model here.

7.3.7   Specification of the Coordinator (Level 2)

The *Coordinator (400)* component is used for managing express checkouts. For this purpose, it keeps a list of sales that were done during last 60 minutes, which helps it to decide whether an express cash desk is needed. The component consists of two classes, the *CoordinatorEventHandler (410)* and the *Sale (420)*. Anytime a new sale arrives, the CoordinatorEventHandler creates a new instance of the Sale class to represent it in the list. Whenever the sale represented by an instance expires, the CoordinatorEventHandler removes the instance from the list which causes its destruction. We use this example to demonstrate, how we can model the dynamic creation and destruction of instances.

Before we explain our approach, remember that CI automata are finite state. This means, that we will never be able to model a system with unlimited number of instances. However this does not mean that we cannot verify such systems. In [5] we have proposed a verification approach addressing this issue. The solution there is based on getting the value k, dependent on the system and the property we want to verify, such that it guarantees that if we verify the system with $0, 1, 2, \ldots, k$ instances, we can conclude that the property holds on the system no matter how many instance are in use.

Now we come back to the modelling of the Coordinator component with a bounded number of Sale instances. For example let us set the maximum number of active instances to 10. First, we create the models of the Sale and the CoordinatorEventHandler in a usual way. In the model of the CoordinatorEventHandler we also model actions that cause the creation and destruction of Sale instances. In the case of creation, the code new Sale(numberofitems, paymentmode, new Date()) is represented by the sequence $(410, Sale, -), (-, Sale', 410)$, in the case of destruction, the code i.remove() is represented by the sequence $(410, SaleD, -)$, $(-, SaleD', 410)$.

Second, we create a model of an *instance* of the Sale. It is an extension of the model of the Sale we have (fig. 17 on the left) with an initial activation part (fig. 17 on the right). The path $p \rightarrow q \rightarrow 0$ represents a call of the constructor of the component, and the way back $0 \rightarrow r \rightarrow p$ represents the destruction, which could start also from other states than 0. However it should not be possible for

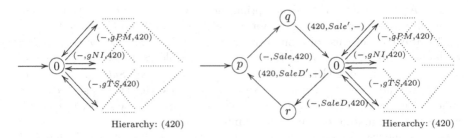

Fig. 17. CI automata of the *Sale class* and the *Sale instance*

it to start in states p or q to guarantee that the system can destruct only the instances that have been created before.

The model of the Coordinator is a handshake-like composition of the set consisting of the model of the CoordinatorEventHandler and 10 copies of the automaton for the Sale instance. In the composite, all the Sale-instance automata start in the state p, which means that they are inactive at the beginning – the CoordinatorEventHandler cannot access their behaviour which starts to be available in state 0. However, when the CoordinatorEventHandler calls a constructor of the Sale $(410, Sale, -), (-, Sale', 410)$, one of the instances synchronizes with it and moves to the state that makes its functionality available. When the CoordinatorEventHandler removes the Sale from its list $(410, SaleD, -), (-, SaleD', 410)$, it returns back to the state p and waits for another call of its constructor. Note that if the Sale performed some calls inside its constructor or destructor, these calls could be included in the paths $p \rightarrow q \rightarrow 0$ and $0 \rightarrow r \rightarrow p$ as one may intuitively think.

We have experimented with different numbers of Sale instances in the system and realized that no matter how many of them we allow, the external behaviour of the Coordinator component remains the same. For this reason, we finally decided to regard the Sale class as something internal to the Coordinator and not to include it in the final model of the Coordinator.

7.3.8   Specification of the CashDeskLine (Level 1)

The model of the *CashDeskLine* component is a composition of the CashDesk, ExtCommChannel and Coordinator components using the handshake-like composition.

7.3.9   Specification of the Persistence (Level 3)

The *Persistence (510)* is the first component belonging to the *Inventory* part of the *Trading System*. It consists of three parts, that we interpret as subcomponents. That are *PersistenceImpl, PersistenceContextImpl* and *TransactionContextImpl*.

Both PersistenceContextImpl and TransactionContextImpl are modelled with the initial activation part, because they may be created and destructed. Their creation is managed by `getPersistenceContext()` (in the PersistenceImpl) and `getTransactionContext()` (in the PersistenceContextImpl) methods that call the constructors in their bodies. However their destruction is not managed inside the Persistence component. We will discuss the destruction when describing the *StoreApplication*, which uses these components.

The PersistenceContextImpl and TransactionContextImpl are used in the way that at any time, only one instance of each is needed to be active. Therefore we create the model of the Persistence as a composition of the PersistenceImpl, one instance of the PersistenceContextImpl and one instance of the TransactionContextImpl. In section 7.5 you may see how we can verify that one instance of each is really sufficient.

The *Store (520)* and the *Enterprise (530)* components are created in a usual way. Hence we do not discuss them here.

7.3.10   Specification of the Data (Level 2)

The *Data* component is a composition of the Persistence, Store and Enterprise components. However, there are not only one of each. The Data component is used by the *StoreApplication*, *ReportingApplication* and *ProductDispatcher* where each of them requires its own Persistence, Store and Enterprise according to the Java implementation. Hence also in the model, we include three copies of the Persistence (511, 512, 513), Store (521, 522, 523), and Enterprise (531, 532, 533). The copies differ only in the name of the automata and the component name that identifies them. Currently, the copies are created via *copy-paste*, however we aim to support the *type-instance* treatment in future.

During the composition, we need to take care of the communication among these. For instance, the Store component calls the `getEntityManager()` method of the Persistence. And we want the first Store (521) to call just the first Persistence (511), event if it is syntactically possible to call also the second (512) and the third one (513). Our composition is able to respect such restrictions. We only state that the labels $(521, getEntityManager, 512), (512, getEntityManager', 521)$, $(521, getEntityManager, 513), (513, getEntityManager', 521)$ do not represent feasible behaviour of the composite system and hence all transitions with such labels must be removed during the composition.

7.3.11   Specification of the StoreApplication (Level 3)

For the *StoreApplication (610)*, we present a model of one method to illustrate, what structure these methods have. It is the `changePrice()` method (automaton in fig. 18, implementation in fig. 19).

The automaton of the method (fig. 18) has 35 states. The states 00 – 17 form the main execution flow (if no exception occurs), which is typeset in bold-face. The execution starts with asking for a new instance of the PersistenceContextImpl by calling `getPersistenceContext()`, and analogically for a new instance of the TransactionContextImpl via `getTransactionContext()`. The `changePrice()`, which owns the only reference to these instances, loses the reference when its execution finishes. And so the instances get destructed eventually.

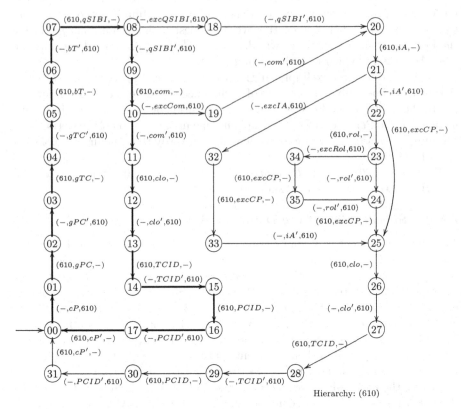

Fig. 18. CI automaton of the `changePrice()` method

ACTION NAME	ABBREVIATION
changePrice	*cP*
exceptionChangePrice	*excCP*
getPersistenceContext	*gPC*
getTransactionContext	*gTC*
beginTransaction	*bT*
queryStockItemById	*qSIBI*
exceptionQueryStockItemById	*excQSIBI*
commit	*com*
exceptionCommit	*excCom*
close	*clo*
TransactionContextImplD	*TCID*
PersistenceContextImplD	*PCID*
isActive	*iA*
exceptionIsActive	*excIA*
rollback	*rol*
exceptionRollback	*excRol*

```
public ProductWithStockItemTO changePrice(StockItemTO stockItemTO) {
  ProductWithStockItemTO result = new ProductWithStockItemTO();
  PersistenceContext pctx = persistmanager.getPersistenceContext();
  TransactionContext tx = null;
  try {
    tx = pctx.getTransactionContext();
    tx.beginTransaction();
    StockItem si = storequery.queryStockItemById(stockItemTO.getId(), pctx);
    si.setSalesPrice(stockItemTO.getSalesPrice());
    result = FillTransferObjects.fillProductWithStockItemTO(si);
    tx.commit();
  } catch (RuntimeException e) {
    if (tx != null && tx.isActive())
      tx.rollback();
    e.printStackTrace();
    throw e; // or display error message
  } finally {
    pctx.close();
  }
  return result;
}
```

Fig. 19. Java source of the `changePrice()` method

We model this by calling `PersistenceContextImplD` and `TransactionContext-ImplD` at the end of each possible execution flow of the method.

The path between states 03 – 11 corresponds to a try block in the code. If an exception occurs in any of these states (which may happen in 08 and 10), the execution of the methods that thrown the exception is finished and the flow goes to the state 20 where the exception handling starts. The execution between states 20 – 25 corresponds to the catch block in the code. Along this way two methods are called, `isActive()` and `rollback()`. Both of them may throw an exception. In such a case, the exception is not caught, it is propagated higher up. We model this as an output of a new exception that is caused by input of the existing one. If any of these paths finished correctly (without throwing an exception), the flow would continue to the finally block, which is represented by the states 11 – 13. However all paths resulting from the catch block do throw an exception, therefore all lead to an exceptional finally block (after which the method is finished immediately, whereas after the normal finally block the execution may continue). This is represented by the states 25 – 27.

The model of the *ReportingApplication (620)* component is similar to the one of the StoreApplication, therefore we do not discuss it here.

7.3.12   Specification of the ProductDispatcher (Level 3)

The *ProductDispatcher (630)* component manages the exchange of low running goods among stores. It uses an *AmplStarter* sub-component that computes optimizations, and itself implements a variety of methods to support the only method it provides on its interface, the `orderProductsAvailableAtOtherStores()`.

We comment only on the `markProductsAvailableInStockPD()` method, which calls a `markProductsAvailableAInStock()` method on selected Stores to mark the products that are a subject of product exchange. In the model, we are naturally not able to find out, what Stores should be addressed at

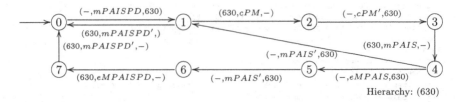

Fig. 20. CI automaton of the `markProductsAvailableAInStockPD()` method

the time the method is called. The Stores are selected by a complicated algorithm. For this reason, we model the call of Stores in a loop (see fig. 20), which may synchronize with any subset of the Stores that are currently active in the model. This is a simple solution that does not assure that the Product-Dispatcher calls each Store at most once, but we decided to accept this over-approximation. In fig. 20 the *markProductsAvailableInStockPD* is shortened to *mPAISPD*, *computeProductMovements* to *cPM*, and *markProductsAvailableInStock* to *mPAIS*.

The models of the *Application*, *GUI* and finally also *Inventory* composite components are created in a usual way.

7.3.13   Specification of the TradingSystem (Level 0)

The last thing to do is to compose the CashDeskLine component and the Inventory component into the *TradingSystem* which is done using the handshake-like composition. The resulting model of the TradingSystem is not closed (containing internal transitions only). It has a lot of external transitions representing receive of input on the GUI of both CashDeskLine and Inventory. And it has a few external transitions representing communication with the Bank. We can decide if we want to analyse the TradingSystem as it is (no restriction on the usage profile), or create automata of the Cashier, Manager, and Bank and compose them with the TradingSystem into a closed model with internal transitions only. It is up to the designer to choose one of these strategies.

7.4   Transformations

In the context of the CoCoME, there are two types of transformations that can be helpful during the process. The first one is the *transformation of a composite automaton into a primitive one*. See the end of the section 7.3.3 for its description. This transformation is used as a final step of modelling of any primitive component that is created as a composition of its parts.

The second one is the *reduction of the model with respect to an equivalence that overlooks unimportant labels*. In [6] we have defined various kinds of such relations for CI automata. The relations are designed to indicate situations where a substitution of components preserves properties of the whole model. At the same time, they can be exploited to minimize the model by substituting a component by a smaller yet equivalent one. In the CoCoME project, we have not used this transformation because our tool was able to analyse the whole model. However if the model was larger, we would use it to reduce the models of primitive components, which consist of a significant number of transitions representing inner interaction with private methods, which is not very important in the context of the whole system.

7.5   Analysis

Each modelling process is driven by the purpose the model is used for. In the case of our approach, the purpose is the automatic verification of temporal properties of component-based system. Verification can be used in the design phase to predict the behaviour of the system that we are going to assemble, or after it when we want to analyse properties of an existing system.

Moreover, verification techniques may help also in the modelling process to find modelling errors, or to evaluate whether the simplifications that were done during modelling do not introduce unexpected behaviours, like deadlocks. In the project, we found this very helpful when evaluating various modelling decisions.

In this section, we demonstrate the capability of the formal verification on analysis of the model created in the previous section. First, we focus on checking general temporal properties and on searching deadlock situations in the model. Next, we discuss how the use cases and test cases presented in Chapter 3 can be evaluated on the model.

7.5.1   Temporal-Logic Properties

For verification of temporal properties, we use the model checking technique [7]. The input of the technique is the model of the system (a CI automaton in our case) and a temporal property we want to check. For properties specification, we use an extended version of the linear temporal logic LTL [8] which we refer to as *CI-LTL* along the text. CI-LTL is designed to be able to express properties about component interaction (i.e. labels in automata), but also about possible interaction (i.e. label enableness). Therefore, it is both state-based and action-based. CI-LTL uses all standard LTL operators, namely the next-step $\mathcal{X}$, and the until $\mathcal{U}$ operator, as well as the standard boolean operators. It has, however, no atomic propositions as their role is played by two operators, $\mathcal{E}(l)$ and $\mathcal{P}(l)$, where l is a label. Their meaning is informally given as follows.

- $\mathcal{E}(l)$ means "Label l is **E**nabled" and is true in all states of the system such that the interaction represented by label l can possibly happen.
- $\mathcal{P}(l)$ means "Label l is **P**roceeding" and is true whenever the interaction represented by label l is actually happening.

Syntax. Formally, for a given set of labels, formulas of CI-LTL are defined as

1. $\mathcal{P}(l)$ and $\mathcal{E}(l)$ are formulas, where l is a label.
2. If Φ and Ψ are formulas, then also $\Phi \wedge \Psi, \neg \Phi, \mathcal{X} \Phi$ and $\Phi \, \mathcal{U} \, \Psi$ are formulas.
3. Every formula can be obtained by a finite number of applications of steps (1) and (2).

Other operators can be defined as shortcuts: $\Phi \vee \Psi \equiv \neg (\neg \Phi \wedge \neg \Psi)$, $\Phi \Rightarrow \Psi \equiv \neg (\Phi \wedge \neg \Psi)$, $\mathcal{F} \Phi \equiv \text{true} \, \mathcal{U} \, \Phi$, $\mathcal{G} \Phi \equiv \neg \mathcal{F} \neg \Phi$, where $\mathcal{F}$ is the *future* and $\mathcal{G}$ the *globally* operator.

Semantics. Let $\mathcal{C} = (Q, Act, \delta, I, H)$ be a CI automaton. We define a *run* of $\mathcal{C}$ as an infinite sequence $\sigma = q_0, l_0, q_1, l_1, q_2, \ldots$ where $q_i \in Q$, and $\forall i \, . \, (q_i, l_i, q_{i+1}) \in \delta$. We further define:

- $\sigma(i) = q_i$ (*i*-th state of σ)
- $\sigma^i = q_i, l_i, q_{i+1}, l_{i+1}, q_{i+2}, \ldots$ (*i*-th sub-run of σ)
- $\mathcal{L}(\sigma, i) = l_i$ (*i*-th label of σ)

CI formulas are interpreted over runs where the satisfaction relation $\models$ is defined inductively as

$$
\begin{aligned}
\sigma &\models \mathcal{E}(l) & &\Longleftrightarrow \exists q \, . \, \sigma(0) \xrightarrow{l} q \\
\sigma &\models \mathcal{P}(l) & &\Longleftrightarrow \mathcal{L}(\sigma, 0) = l \\
\sigma &\models \Phi \wedge \Psi & &\Longleftrightarrow \sigma \models \Phi \text{ and } \sigma \models \Psi \\
\sigma &\models \neg \Phi & &\Longleftrightarrow \sigma \not\models \Phi \\
\sigma &\models \mathcal{X} \Phi & &\Longleftrightarrow \sigma^1 \models \Phi \\
\sigma &\models \Phi \, \mathcal{U} \, \Psi & &\Longleftrightarrow \exists j \in \mathbb{N}_0 \, . \, \sigma^j \models \Psi \text{ and } \forall k \in \mathbb{N}_0, k < j \, . \, \sigma^k \models \Phi
\end{aligned}
$$

Properties Expressed in CI-LTL. The logic enables us to specify many interesting properties about component-based systems. Let us consider the model resulting from the composition of the *Trading System* with a *Manager* who performs some operations on the Inventory. Here are some properties of the model we may want to check.

1. Whenever the *StoreApplication (610)* calls *getTransactionContext()* on the *Persistence (511)*, it gets a response at some point in the future. This can be used to check that a new instance of the *TransactionContextImpl* can be activated when demanded.

$$\mathcal{G} \, (\mathcal{P}(610, \text{getTransactionContext}, 511)$$
$$\Rightarrow \mathcal{F} \, \mathcal{P}(511, \text{getTransactionContext}', 610))$$

2. If the *Persistence (511)* receives a call from the *Store (521)*, it returns a result to it. And before it does so, it is not able to deliver the result to someone else - to *Store (522)*.

$$\mathcal{G} \, (\mathcal{P}(521, \text{getEntityManager}, 511)$$
$$\Rightarrow \mathcal{X} \, (\neg \, \mathcal{E}(511, \text{getEntityManager}', 522) \, \mathcal{U} \, \mathcal{P}(511, \text{getEntityManager}', 521)))$$

3. If the *StoreApplication (610)* starts a transaction with the *Persistence (511)*, it correctly closes the transaction before it is able to start another one.

$$\mathcal{G}\ (\mathcal{P}(610, \text{beginTransaction}, 511)$$
$$\Rightarrow \mathcal{X}\ (\neg\ \mathcal{E}(610, \text{beginTransaction}, 511)\ \mathcal{U}\ \mathcal{P}(610, \text{close}, 511)))$$

Another type of interesting properties are deadlock situations. Deadlocks are the states from which in the model it is not possible to perform any step further. On the level of the system, they do not necessarily need to represent halting of the system. They may also reflect other kinds of failures, like breakdown, infinite cycling, or just return of a warning message. In the context of component-based systems, it is useful to check the model for *local* deadlocks, which we define as deadlocks of a single component. A deadlock of a component in the model may be very difficult to find, because even if a component cannot move, the system may continue its execution because other components are running. CI-LTL allows us to capture local deadlocks in the following way.

4. It cannot happen that the *StoreApplication (610)* is ready to call queryStock-ItemById() but never can do so because its counterpart is never ready to receive the call.

$$\mathcal{G}\ (\mathcal{E}(610, \text{queryStockItemById}, -)$$
$$\Rightarrow \mathcal{F}\ \mathcal{E}(610, \text{queryStockItemById}, 521))$$

5. It cannot happen that the *StoreApplication (610)* wants to begin a transaction, but the *Persistence (511)* is not *right in the current state* ready to serve it (stricter version of local deadlock).

$$\mathcal{G}\ \neg\ \big(\mathcal{E}(610, \text{beginTransaction}, -)\ \wedge\ \neg\ \mathcal{E}(610, \text{beginTransaction}, 511)\big)$$

For the above mentioned model all the properties were automatically verified with the help of the verification tool DiVinE (see section 7.6). The verification confirmed that the model has all listed properties.

7.5.2   Use Cases

Chapter 3 presents a set of sequence diagrams showing the behavioural scenarios of the *Trading System* in terms of component interaction. However, we have created our model independently on these scenarios. Now we show how we can check that the model complies to them.

Each scenario is in fact a sequence of execution steps driven by the user-given inputs. If we describe the scenarios as sequences of CI-automata labels, the model-checking method enables us to automatically explore the model and find out whether the behaviours are present in it. We demonstrate the process on the **UC 1: ProcessSale :: CashPayment**. For all other use cases it can be done analogically.

First, we define the model that will be checked. It is a composition of the *Trading System* with the automaton representing the usage profile determined by

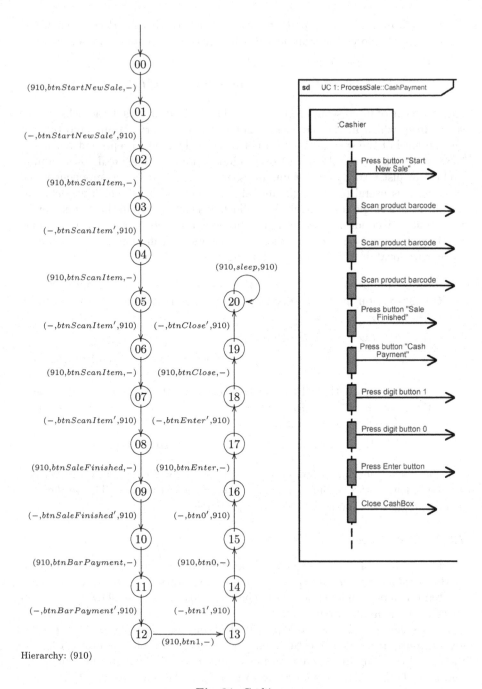

Hierarchy: (910)

Fig. 21. Cashier

Table 1. UC 1: ProcessSale :: CashPayment scenario

No.	SENDER	ACTION	RECEIVER
1.	**Cashier (910)**	**btnStartNewSale**	CashBox (111)
2.	CashBox (111)	sendSaleStartedEvent	CashBoxController (112)
3.	CashBoxController (112)	publishSaleStartedEvent	CashDeskChannel (200)
4.	CashDeskChannel (200)	onEventSaleStarted	CashDeskApplication (100)
5.	CashDeskChannel (200)	onEventSaleStarted	PrinterController (142)
6.	CashDeskChannel (200)	onEventSaleStarted	CashDeskGUI (162)
7.	CashBoxController (112)	sendSaleStartedEvent'	CashBox (111)
8.	**Cashier (910)**	**btnScanItem**	Scanner (121)
9.	Scanner (121)	sendProductBarcodeScannedEvent	ScannerController (122)
10.	ScannerController (122)	publishProductBarcodeScannedEvent	CashDeskChannel (200)
...	...	...	...
75.	**Cashier (910)**	**btnClose**	CashBox (111)
76.	CashBox (111)	sendCashBoxClosedEvent	CashBoxController (112)
77.	CashBoxController (112)	publishCashBoxClosedEvent	CashDeskChannel (200)
78.	CashDeskChannel (200)	onEventCashBoxClosed	CashDeskApplication (100)
79.	CashDeskChannel (200)	onEventCashBoxClosed	PrinterController (142)
80.	CashBoxController (112)	sendCashBoxClosedEvent'	CashBox (111)
81.	CashDeskApplication (100)	publishSaleSuccessEvent	CashDeskChannel (200)
82.	CashDeskChannel (200)	onEventSaleSuccess	PrinterController (142)
83.	CashDeskChannel (200)	onEventSaleSuccess	CashDeskGUI (162)
84.	CashDeskApplication (100)	publishExtAccountSaleEvent	ExtCommChannel (300)
85.	ExtCommChannel (300)	onEventExtAccountSale	StoreApplication (610)
86.	CashDeskApplication (100)	publishExtSaleRegisteredEvent	ExtCommChannel (300)
87.	ExtCommChannel (300)	onEventExtSaleRegistered	Coordinator (400)

the Cashier (fig. 21). We model a finite behaviour of the cashier as an infinite one (with a loop in the end) not to introduce deadlock states into the composition.

Second, we capture the use case scenario of **UC 1: ProcessSale :: Cash-Payment** (Chapter 3, Figure 15 and 16) as a sequence of labels and check that such a behaviour is really present in the model. Part of the scenario is rewritten in table 1, where each line corresponds to a label in the sequence, e.g. the first line to the label $(910, btnStartNewSale, 111)$.

Last, we automatically verify that there is such a sequence present in the model, possibly interleaved with other labels (execution of other components or fine-grained interaction which is not captured on the sequence diagram). In case it is, the verification process reports a run which shows this. From the run, one can get the full interaction scenario which can be used later on to improve the sequence diagram of the use case.

7.5.3   Test Cases

Besides the use cases, Chapter 3 provides formalization of use case behaviour by way of test scenarios, which can be also evaluated on the model. The scenarios are of two types: the *informal* ones that prospect for the existence of a *good* behaviour, and the formal ones, given as Java test classes, that check that all behaviours of the system are *good* in some sense. For both of them, we formulate a corresponding CI-LTL formula that can be verified on the model.

Informal Scenarios. The informal scenarios are verified in a negative way. The formula states that all the behaviours are *bad*, and we want to prove it false – there is a behaviour that is not *bad*. We present this on the *ShowProductsForOrdering* scenario, which states that: *Store shall provide functionality to generate a report about products which are low on stock*.

This functionality is represented by the `getProductsWithLowStock()` method of the *StoreApplication (610)* component. So the formula is

$$\neg \, \mathcal{F} \, \mathcal{E}(610, \text{getProductsWithLowStock}', -)$$

and it states that from the initial state of the model we cannot reach a transition that represents successful return of the `getProductsWithLowStock()` method. The verification reported a run that does not satisfy this and hence represents the *good* behaviour we have searched for.

Formal Scenarios. The Java test cases are specified by sequences of method calls that should be correctly processed by the system. This can be interpreted in two ways: the test passes if (1) the sequence of methods always finishes (possibly by throwing an exception), or (2) it always finishes *correctly* (with no exceptions). For both alternatives we present the formula that expresses it and verify it on the model. Consider the test case *ProcessSaleCase*, which is represented by the following sequence of methods:

```
initializeCashDesk(0,0); startNewSale(); enterAllRemainingProducts();
finishSale(); handleCashPayment(); updateInventory();
```

Alternative (1). We say that the test passes if each *fair* run in the model, corresponding to the scenario given by the test case, comes to the end (is finite). This can be expressed by the formula

$$\psi_{PSC} \Rightarrow (\psi_{INF} \Rightarrow \neg \psi_{FAIR})$$

where
- ψ_{PSC} is satisfied iff the usage profile of the system corresponds to the sequence given by the *ProcessSaleCase*.
- $\psi_{INF} = \mathcal{G} \Big(\bigvee_{(n, \text{act}, m) \in SYST} \mathcal{P}(n, \text{act}, m) \Big)$
  is satisfied on all runs on which all steps correspond to the steps of the system ($SYST$). Those runs model exactly the infinite runs of the system.
- $\psi_{FAIR} = \bigwedge_{(n, \text{act}, m) \in \mathcal{L}} \mathcal{G} \Big((\mathcal{G} \, \mathcal{E}(n, \text{act}, m)) \Rightarrow (\mathcal{F} \bigvee_{\text{act}', m'} \mathcal{P}(n, \text{act}', m')) \Big)$
  is satisfied on all fair runs. We say that a run is not fair iff in any of its states one of the components is able to send an action, but never does anything, because it is preempted by others.

Alternative (2). The test passes if it finishes in the sense of the alternative (1) and *no exception occurs* during the execution. This can be expressed by the formula

$$\psi_{PSC} \Rightarrow \Big(\neg \psi_{EXC} \wedge (\psi_{INF} \Rightarrow \neg \psi_{FAIR}) \Big)$$

where

- $\psi_{EXC} = \mathcal{F}\left(\bigvee_{(n,exc,m)\in E} \mathcal{P}(n, \mathrm{exc}, m)\right)$

  is satisfied on all runs where an exception occurs, E represents the labels for all exceptions.

The verification of the properties showed that the test alternative (2) fails, because exceptions may occur during the scenario, but (1) passes successfully.

7.6   Tools

To accomplish automated verification we use the DiVinE tool [2] (`http://anna.fi.muni.cz/divine/`) which implements distributed-memory LTL model-checking and state-space analysis. Our language (described in subsection 7.2.3, referred as the CoIn language) is however slightly different from the standard input language of DiVinE, therefore we actually use a modified version of DiVinE, with added support for CoIn models. This is not a part of the official release at this moment, but will be included in the coming release.

The input to the tool consists of two parts. The first is a text file with the model of the system. The file contains the specification of all basic components and the composition operations. The second part of the input is the property to be verified. It can be given either as a formula of CI-LTL (which is to be preprocessed into a property automaton and added to the input file) or a hand-written property automaton. The tool automatically verifies the model against the given property and reports its validity. If the property is not valid, the tool returns a run of the model that violates the property. The verification process itself is performed in parallel on a cluster of processors and hence the tool is capable of verifying even extremely large models.

7.7   Summary

The text discusses the capabilities of Component-interaction automata for creation of a detailed model of component-based system behaviour, which can be later on used for formal analysis and verification. Component-interaction automata are very general and can be used for modelling of various kinds of component-based systems.

In the CoCoME project, we have applied it to the modelling of a component-based system given as Java implementation. For this type of systems, we have defined the mapping of Java methods and events to the actions in the model, and we have identified three basic types of composition (the cube-like, star-like, and handshake-like) that we have realized by the parameterizable composition operator the language provides.

During the modelling process, we have faced many modelling issues. These include exception handling, dynamic creation and destruction of instances, reflection of the internal state of a component, and simulation of the publish-subscriber communicational model. We have realized that thanks to the generality of the Component-interaction automata language, we are able to handle all of these in an elegant way.

For the analysis of the model, we have employed the parallel model checking tool DiVinE (see section 7.6), which is able to automatically verify system models, namely the communicational behaviour and interactions of individual components. The tool can be used both for checking the properties of the system and compliance of the model with the specification. The tool support for the analysis has shown to be very capable. However we currently miss tool support for the modelling phase. The models are written directly in the textual notation. In future, we aim to support the modelling with a user-friendly interface, or some automatization in form of transformation from other formalisms, which would allow other approaches to take advantage of our verification methods.

References

1. Černá, I., Vařeková, P., Zimmerova, B.: Component-interaction automata modelling language. Technical Report FIMU-RS-2006-08, Masaryk University, Faculty of Informatics, Brno, Czech Republic (2006)
2. Barnat, J., Brim, L., Černá, I., Moravec, P., Ročkai, P., Šimecek, P.: Divine – a tool for distributed verification. In: Ball, T., Jones, R.B. (eds.) CAV 2006. LNCS, vol. 4144, pp. 278–281. Springer, Heidelberg (2006)
3. Brim, L., Černá, I., Vařeková, P., Zimmerova, B.: Component-Interaction automata as a verification-oriented component-based system specification. In: Proceedings of the ESEC/FSE Workshop on Specification and Verification of Component-Based Systems (SAVCBS 2005), Lisbon, Portugal, September 2005, pp. 31–38. Iowa State University, USA (2005)
4. The CoIn Team: The complete CoIn model of the Trading System (2007), http://anna.fi.muni.cz/coin/cocome/
5. Vařeková, P., Moravec, P., Černá, I., Zimmerova, B.: Effective verification of systems with a dynamic number of components. In: Proceedings of the ESEC/FSE Conference on Specification and Verification of Component-Based Systems (SAVCBS 2007), Dubrovnik, Croatia, September 2007, pp. 3–13. ACM Press, USA (2007)
6. Černá, I., Vařeková, P., Zimmerova, B.: Component substitutability via equivalencies of component-interaction automata. In: Proceedings of the Workshop on Formal Aspects of Component Software (FACS 2006), Prague, Czech Republic. ENTCS, pp. 39–55. Elsevier, Amsterdam (2006)
7. Clarke, E., Grumberg, O., Peled, D.: Model Checking. MIT Press, USA (2000)
8. Pnueli, A.: The temporal logic of programs. In: Proceedings of the 18th IEEE Symposium on the Foundations of Computer Science, pp. 46–57. IEEE Computer Society Press, Los Alamitos (1977)

8 Service-Oriented Modeling of CoCoME with Focus and AutoFocus

Manfred Broy, Jorge Fox, Florian Hölzl, Dagmar Koss, Marco Kuhrmann,
Michael Meisinger, Birgit Penzenstadler, Sabine Rittmann, Bernhard Schätz,
Maria Spichkova, and Doris Wild

Institut für Informatik
Technische Universität München
Boltzmannstr. 3
85748 Garching, Germany

8.1 Introduction

Reactive distributed systems, including business information systems and embedded control systems, require systematic software engineering approaches that can manage the complexity of the system and the development. This helps to ensure resulting implementations of high quality within reasonable cost and time frames. The CoCoME POS system (see Chapter 3) is a telling example that combines elements of both system classes.

In this chapter, we present a systematic model-based approach of the engineering of distributed systems. It is based on experiences from numerous projects in research and application out of various domains over more than two decades. Using an expressive but simple mathematical formalism of streams as foundation, we have elaborated a model-based process supporting systematic iterative development of distributed reactive systems. Due to its modular nature it enables the use of tailored and domain-specific methods suitable for different application domains.

8.1.1 Goals and Scope of the Component Model

We see strengths of our approach in providing a development process based upon a formally founded, unified model. This process supports the systematic description of a system at different levels of abstraction. We define precisely the intent and interpretation of each abstraction level (cf. for instance [1]). Higher, more abstract levels hide details and provide manageable views on the different system aspects and parts thereof. Lower, more concrete abstraction levels add additional concerns that remain consistent with the higher levels.

Precisely defined interfaces and transitions between these levels form the frame of an integrated development process. At each level, we can choose from a collection of methods and notations that integrate modularly into the generic framework. Development constraints and application domain determine the specific choice of a method or notation, leading to a tailored development process.

A. Rausch et al. (Eds.): Common Component Modeling Example, LNCS 5153, pp. 177–206, 2008.

In general, we distinguish the following abstraction levels in a system and software design process: *Informal Requirements Level, Formal Specification Level, Functional/Service Architecture Level, Logical Architecture Level, Deployment Level,* and *Implementation Level* (see Fig. 1).

On the *Informal Requirements Level,* requirements are collected in informal descriptions using natural language. Commonly applied are use cases and application scenarios, possibly in form of structured textual descriptions enriched with diagrams. Due to their informal character, these requirements are often ambiguous and inconsistent.

Optionally, analysis and formalization of the requirements can result in formal specifications at the *Formal Specification Level,* for instance using formalisms such as temporal logics and process algebras, promoting inambiguity and consistency. A formal specification can be omitted if formal verification is not required or desired.

Functionality and functional structure of a system are described on the *Functional/Service Architecture Level.* We emphasize modular, implementation independent descriptions of functional units, also called services. Such services are used as building blocks of more complex functionality and as variation options for instance in product line development. Functional properties expressed on this level can be verified against the formal specification.

The *Logical Architecture Level* contains descriptions of the logical structure of a system in form of communicating components and their communication links. Components are described by their syntactic and semantic interfaces, characterizing their full functionality. Components can be structurally decomposed into connected subcomponents with a compatible interface; they can also be implemented by a refined specification that fulfills the interface of the component. This interface assumption/guarantee principle is the foundation of compositionality: proven properties on a component specification level will remain true for the refinement, both for substructure and for implementation. Any properties expressed on this level, can be verified against the formal specification as well.

The *Deployment Level* captures details about the actual deployment, network, communication infrastructure, and component execution environment. Here, we need to define executable instances of components (i.e. the technical architecture) and connect them using an appropriate execution environment (i.e. the operational architecture, also referred to as middleware).

On the *Implementation Level,* we find the actual implementation, for instance as source code that can be built and deployed. In case of complete and detailed models and specifications, implementations can be generated, for instance used as prototypes.

8.1.2 Benefits of the Modeling: A Tailored Approach for the CoCoME Example

We model the CoCoME example following the mentioned methodological framework and abstraction levels, using approaches described in [2,3,4,5]. We combine techniques and notations covering multiple levels of abstraction. Fig. 1 depicts

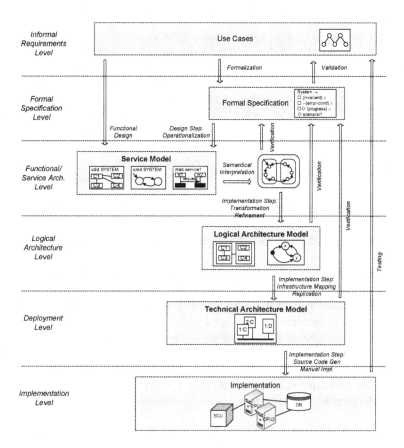

Fig. 1. Abstraction Levels Underlying our Model-Based Development Approach

the abstraction levels and the main artifacts of these approaches together with their dependencies.

The CoCoME requirements, as part of the *Informal Requirements Level* are given in Chapter 3 of this volume as use cases and accompanying textual descriptions, for instance for extra-functional requirements and architectural constraints. Since we do not focus on formal verification, we skip a formalization of the requirements on the *Formal Specification Level*.

On the *Functional/Service Architecture Level*, we apply a service-oriented architecture development approach. It is based on joint work with the group of Krueger et al. described in [4], which roots back to ideas described in [6]. All these approaches are founded on formal models from [3,5]. We use a hierarchical functional architecture model and interaction scenarios as service-oriented behavior descriptions. Their semantical interpretation as state machines applies ideas of the synthesis algorithm described in [6].

Our component model is represented on the *Logical Architecture Level*. We specify components in FOCUS [2] by providing their syntactical and semantical interfaces, completely characterizing their behavior. FOCUS offers structural views on the architecture and provides multiple ways to describe the behavior of the components, which we use depending on our needs: A denotational, logical expression based style for black-box behavior specifications, and a state-machine oriented representation as directly operationalizable description. We obtain the component descriptions by refining and transforming the service descriptions. We call the externally visible behavior of a component *black-box behavior*; the view consisting of black-box behavior and internal constraints is called *glass-box view*.

On the *Deployment Level*, we provide models describing an execution environment for FOCUS specified distributed components that communicate via asynchronous message passing. This is realized by transmission of explicit NoVal messages in the operational architecture, which in fact uses synchronous message exchange. We use our CASE tool AutoFOCUS2 [7,8] to model the CoCoME deployment, and use code generators targeting the CoCoME execution environment on the *Implementation Level*. Thereby, we can automatically generate executable implementations for our FOCUS component specifications. These generated threads can be arbitrarily distributed to Java Virtual Machines.

We have selected the above approaches for the following reasons: CoCoME is a multi-functional distributed and embedded system with limited information system aspects. A service-oriented approach based on the precise specification of independent functions is well suited to describe such a system. Models of this kind seamlessly translate into FOCUS models. We use FOCUS, as our core approach and center of interest. The target deployment and model-based code generation for distributed Java RMI middleware fits the architectural constraints given in Chapter 3.

Alternative Approaches on the Abstraction Levels. Our approach distinguishes different well-defined levels of abstraction as described. Besides the approaches selected in the previous section for the example discussed in this volume, we have further choices, out of which we mention a few here. We present alternative approaches for the Functional/Service Architecture Level, the Logical Architecture Level and the Deployment Level. We use the FOCUS theory [2] as formal basis for all our approaches. For modeling CoCoME, we chose those alternative approaches which we deemed most appropriate for the POS system type. AutoFOCUS2 [7] provides tool support.

Functional/Service Architecture Level: We have developed and analyzed alternative approaches for functional modeling; for instance our functional architecture modeling approach [9] provides mode and service diagrams that enable structuring an architecture functionally. The *mobilSoft* approach provides a service dependency model based on a logical expression based matrix [9]. *MEwaDis* relies on modeling service dependencies [10,11] and targets the automotive domain.

Logical Architecture Level: To support descriptions of the logical architecture of embedded control applications, we have integrated mode-based data-flow oriented descriptions, using mode and block diagrams. These notations – described in [12] – including specific consistency checks and deployment support have been implemented into AutoFocus2. In [13] we introduce a composition model for security aspects based on logical components.

Deployment Level: On the technical level, we have a number of alternatives for modeling as well as implementation. Possible modeling approaches are Entity-Relationship-Modeling, development with the Eclipse Modeling Framework, development using Microsoft .NET or System Definition Model, or even designing an own Domain Specific Language, but all these possibilities were less suited for the example than the chosen solution.

For the implementation, alternative approaches include a Java code generator, RT CORBA code generator or OSGI service deployment.

8.1.3   Modeled Cutout of CoCoME

The CoCoME description and requirements provide a multitude of features of the actual POS system that need to be addressed when implementing or reverse engineering it completely. Requirements cover many topics: use cases, exceptional scenarios, probabilistic availability assumptions, timing constraints, data model constraints, transactional aspects, architectural constraints etc. to address and challenge many different component modeling approaches.

Our service-oriented approach using Focus as component model targets in particular functional modeling, architecture design, partial and total specifications of structure and behavior, and model-based development of distributed embedded systems. In order to demonstrate its core ideas, we mainly focus on the functional and architectural requirements, mostly covering the higher level system development models within the first phases of the development process; additionally, we also show how to deploy and execute our component specifications.

In particular, we do not address questions of non-availability, dynamic architectures (adding and removing nodes while the system is in operation), probabilistic assumptions, transactional processing, and particular component execution and communication environments. We also do not attempt to model exactly the reference implementation in all detail. We apply a systematic top-down development process based on the given requirements (use cases and architectural constraints) and consider the reference implementation and any UML models describing it only as reference in case of uncertainty.

8.1.4   Effort and Lessons Learned

Effort. Focusing on the specification of the system across the different abstraction layers and on building a mock-up prototype, we invested roughly six person months.

Correctness is the key concern of our approach. We show the correct specification and implementation of a single store system. A complete system, which includes the enterprise level of scale, must be extended to support more than one store and more than one cashdesk in each store. We assume another six person months to accomplish this, since the basic components, like cashdesk or inventory, are already known and the system only needs to be scaled up. Extensive sytem testing and verification activities should be manageable with another six person months.

The non-functional requirements need to be addressed more thoroughly. Here, concepts and methodologies are still to be developed. Thus we cannot give a reliable estimation of the effort needed.

Lessons Learned. The problem stated by the CoCoME example is feasible with our approach. We succeeded in applying our rigorous development process onto the development of a real world example. We combined several independently developed approaches into one procedure, which worked well.

We also learned that our tool support lacks several modeling options for implementing aspects conceptually specified in the logical architecture. Since system structure is fixed from the logical level onwards, we also ran into trouble building large systems using AutoFocus2.

These lessons learned are valueable contributions to the development of the next generation of AutoFocus.

8.1.5 Outline

The further parts of our contribution are organized as follows: In Sect. 8.2 we introduce as our component model and foundational basis of our approach the stream-based system theory Focus. In Sect. 8.3 we describe our model-based development process and apply it to the CoCoME example. We show how the POS functionality is modeled on each abstraction level. Sect. 8.4 analyzes the advantages and limitations of our approach. In Sect. 8.5 we briefly refer to tool support for our approach. A summary and evaluation is given in Sect. 8.6.

8.2 Component Model: FOCUS

In the introduction, we have sketched our systematic development approach across abstraction levels, leading from requirements through functional service-oriented design to a logical component model and from there to an executable implementation. At the core of our model-based development approach is our component model, Focus. In the following, we will explain the foundations and application of Focus, first as a mathematical formalism and later as a specification technique for distributed reactive systems.

Focus [2] is a framework for the formal specification and development of distributed interactive systems. A distributed system is represented by components connected by communication links or *channels*. Components are described in terms of their input/output behavior which is total. The components can interact or work independently from one another.

The channels in this specification framework are *asynchronous communication links* without delays. They are *directed*, *reliable*, and *order preserving*. Via these channels components exchange information in terms of typed *messages*. Messages are passed along the channels one after the other and delivered in exactly the same order in which they were sent.

A specification is characterized through the relation between *communication histories* for the external *input* and *output channels*. *External* considering the distinction between component interface and component internal specification (which might also have internal channels). The formal meaning of a specification is exactly this external *input/output relation*. Specifications can be structured into a number of formulas each characterizing a different kind of property.

The main concept in FOCUS is the *stream*. Streams represent the communication histories of *directed channels*. Streams in FOCUS are functions mapping the indexes in their domains to their messages. For any set of messages M, M^ω denotes the set of all streams, M^∞ and M^* denote the sets of all infinite and all finite streams respectively. $M^{\underline{\omega}}$ denotes the set of all timed streams, $M^{\underline{\infty}}$ and $M^{\underline{*}}$ denote the sets of all infinite and all finite timed streams respectively. A *timed stream* is represented by a sequence of messages and *time ticks* (represented by $\sqrt{\ }$), the messages are also listed in their order of transmission. The ticks represent a discrete notion of time.

The streams mentioned above can be defined as follows:

$$M^\omega \stackrel{\text{def}}{=} M^* \cup M^\infty \qquad\qquad M^{\underline{\omega}} = M^{\underline{*}} \cup M^{\underline{\infty}}$$

$$M^* \stackrel{\text{def}}{=} \cup_{n\in\mathbb{N}}([1..n] \to M) \qquad M^{\underline{*}} \stackrel{\text{def}}{=} \cup_{n\in\mathbb{N}}([1..n] \to M \cup \{\sqrt{\ }\})$$

$$M^\infty \stackrel{\text{def}}{=} \mathbb{N}_+ \to M \qquad\qquad M^{\underline{\infty}} \stackrel{\text{def}}{=} \mathbb{N}_+ \to M \cup \{\sqrt{\ }\}$$

An empty stream is represented by $\langle\rangle$, while $\langle x\rangle$ denotes an one-element stream. The following operators will be used in the remainder of this chapter:

- $\#x$ denotes the length of the stream x;
- $x.j$ denotes the jth element of the stream x;
- The predicate $\mathsf{disjoint}(s_1, \ldots, s_n)$ is true, if all streams $s_1, \ldots, s_n$ are disjoint, i.e. in every time unit only one of these streams contains a message;
- To simplify the specification of the real-time systems we introduce the operator $\mathsf{ti}(s, n)$ that yields the list of messages that are in the timed stream s between the ticks n and $n+1$ (at the nth time unit)
- The operator $\mathsf{msg}_n(s)$ holds a timed stream s, if the stream contains at most n messages in every time unit;

In this framework we can have both *elementary* and *composite* specifications. Elementary specifications are the building blocks for system representation In this case we distinguish among three frames: the *untimed*, the *timed* and the *time-synchronous frame*. These frames correspond to the stream types in the specification.

An elementary specification, regardless of the type of frame, has the following syntax:

Name (Parameter_Declarations)	Frame_Labels
in *Input_Declarations*	
out *Output_Declarations*	
Body	

Where *Name* is the name of the specification; *Frame_Labels* lists the type of frame, e.g. *untimed, timed* or *time-synchronous*, that corresponds to the stream types in the specification; *Parameter_Declarations* lists a number of parameters (optional); *Input_Declarations* and *Output_Declarations* list the names and types of input and output channels, respectively. *Body* characterizes the relation between the input and output streams, and can be a number of formulas, a table, a diagram, or a combination thereof. The *Body* of an elementary FOCUS specification (*S*, for short) is represented by a number of logic formulas. Each formula represents some logic property and looks as follows[1]:

P_1

P_2

...

P_n

One special kind of specification is the *assumption/guarantee*[2] style, where the body consists of two parts: an assumption over the input declarations which must be met by the environment of the component (introduced by the asm keyword), and a guarantee (introduced by the gar keyword) which holds over the output declarations of the component[2]. The semantics of such a specification in FOCUS is a logical implication: the assumption part implies the guarantee part.

Having a timed specification we have always to deal with infinite timed streams by the definition of the *semantics of a timed frame*.

Definition 1. *The semantics of any elementary timed specification S (written $[\![S]\!]$) is defined[2] by the formula:*

$$i_S \in I_S^\infty \ \wedge \ o_S \in O_S^\infty \ \wedge \ B_S \tag{1}$$

where i_S and o_S denote lists of input and output channel identifiers, I_S and O_S denote their corresponding types, and B_S is a formula in predicate logic that describes the body of the specification S. □

Composite specifications are built hierarchically from elementary ones using constructors for composition and network description.

Definition 2. *For any composite specification S consisting of n sub-specifications $S_1, \ldots, S_n$, we define its semantics, written $[\![S]\!]$, to be the formula:*

$$[\![S]\!] \overset{def}{=} \exists l_S \in L_S^\infty : \bigwedge_{j=1}^{n} [\![S_j]\!] \tag{2}$$

where l_S denotes a list of local channel identifiers and L_S denotes their corresponding types. □

---

[1] The line breaks denote a conjunction in FOCUS.

[2] We use this kind of specification in Sect. 8.3.2.

Timed State Transition Diagrams. The behavior of a system can be described in a timed frame using *timed state transition diagrams* (TSTDs, see [14]). A specification of transitions between system states is based on time intervals. A node of a TSTD represents a control state. Here the following notation for TSTDs will be used:

- The argumentation is over time intervals, the "current" time interval number is t, $t \in \mathbb{N}$.
- For any stream x, its tth time interval, $\mathsf{ti}(x, t)$, will be denoted on the TSTD labels by x. To denote $\mathsf{ti}(x, t + k)$ the abbreviation x^k can be used. The same notation is used in $\mathsf{tiTables}$.
- For any **input** stream y (y belongs to the list of input channels used in the TSTD): if an expression of the form $\mathsf{ti}(y, t) = \textit{SomeTimeInterval}$ is omitted, the value of the tth time interval of the stream y can be arbitrary.
- For any **output** stream z (z belongs to the list of output channels used in the TSTD) all expression of the form $\mathsf{ti}(z, t) = \langle \rangle$ are omitted.
- For any local (or state) variable l all expression of the form $l' = l$ are omitted.

8.3   Modeling the CoCoME POS System

FOCUS is the component model and core of our model-based development approach, as introduced in the previous section. The described mathematical foundations, notations and operations of FOCUS provide the basis for the specification of and reasoning about distributed reactive systems. A systematic development process is required to put the individual pieces into context to form a seamless, integrated model-based development approach. In particular, further notations and methodology are required to obtain an elaborated FOCUS model.

In this section, we explain the systematic development process that we apply to obtain a complete and consistent FOCUS specification of CoCoME that can be executed subsequently in a suitable target environment. We discuss all three abstraction levels that we target, namely Functional/Service Architecture Level, Logical Architecture Level and Deployment Level. All levels provide particular notations and concepts.

We will describe process and artifacts for the considered abstraction levels in the following three sections, respectively. We will provide examples as excerpt out of our full CoCoME model [15]. We focus mainly on the "CashDesk" component with its internal control logic and show it on different levels of abstraction.

8.3.1   Functional/Service Architecture Level

Overview. On the functional and service architecture level, we model behavior and structure of the system on an abstract logical level. We abstract from component clustering, replication, timing and communication and provide a functional system model with a highly partial nature. As input, we take the requirements in form of use cases. Alternatively, we could base our system modeling on a formal system behavior specification, for instance expressed by temporal logics.

We apply a hierarchical approach for functional system modeling. First for the system as entirety and subsequently for each identified subcomponent, we perform the following steps *iteratively* (cf. also [4]). Not all steps need to be carried out for each component and their ordering may vary slightly. We call the entity, which we specify, component on all levels of decomposition.

1. Identify the external and internal services of the component by name and informal description.
2. Express the external interfaces of the component as interaction patterns in form of *Message Sequence Charts* (MSCs).
3. Identify and relate the modes of the component, by giving a *component mode diagram* (CMD), by analyzing requirements and component services.
4. Identify the logical subcomponents of the component and relate them with each other and external component interfaces based on their communication dependencies, by giving a *component decomposition diagram* (CDD).
5. Specify the services of the component as MSCs, giving interaction patterns involving subcomponents and external component interfaces. Arrange the MSCs in a systematical structure by using HMSCs and MSC references. Qualify services with component modes if services are enabled conditionally.
6. Refactor the component interfaces, modes and services, if necessary.
7. Apply the same process to all subcomponents, if necessary.

Application of the methodological steps to CoCoME.   In the following, we show the application of the process steps to CoCoME as a commented walk-through, covering both its full extent and its hierarchical applicability to subcomponents. Note that we explain process results not necessarily in the order as given above. Structural basis of the functional model is a hierarchical functional component architecture. Functional components are sometimes also called roles. We use component decomposition diagrams (cdd) to specify the inner structure of a functional component, any external interfaces and communication dependencies. The system itself can be seen as the top level functional component.

Fig. 2 shows a component decomposition diagram, as a result of performing step 4 of our process for the SYSTEM component. It shows how the system decomposes into a number of functional components – the boxes on the left side – and their communication relations – the connecting lines. External interfaces are given on the right side of the dashed line. At this level of specification we are only interested in the communicating entities and not in the detailed communication layout; i.e. multiple instances of components may occur or not.

In the following, we concentrate on the functional component "CashDesk". From the requirements we know that cash desks can either operate in normal mode or switch to an express mode when a certain condition is true. Our approach provides a notation to capture such distinct operation modes of a system, which we call *modes* in our approach (cf. [12]).

We use component mode diagrams (cmd) to capture these modes, in the form of unlabeled state transition graphs. Fig. 3 shows a component mode diagram

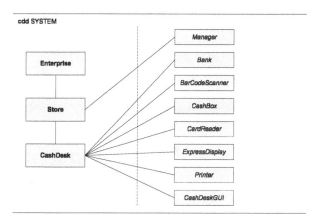

Fig. 2. Component Decomposition Diagram (ccd) of the POS System

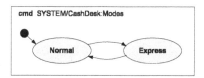

Fig. 3. Component Mode Diagram (cmd) of the Functional Component CashDesk

for the functional component "CashDesk", with the two modes "Normal" and "Express" and their relationships. The cmd is a result of performing process step 3 for "CashDesk".

We expect a cash desk to exhibit a certain behavior, as expressed in the requirements as use cases. Use cases are partial pieces of behavior, illustrating certain scenarios. Our modeling approach provides a similar concept called *service*. Services are independent, separate and thus partial pieces of functionality. We have chosen to use a dialect of Message Sequence Charts (MSCs) [16] for the precise specification of the services. We specify their behavior as interaction patterns (or sequences) of communication between disparate entities, our functional components. Note that the actual communication mechanism, be it message passing, method invocation, signal broadcasting, etc. is left unspecified.

We use diagrams labeled "msc" with an identifying name for service specifications. Two distinct forms of MSCs exist: High-level MSCs and Basic MSCs. Fig. 4 shows a high-level MSC (HMSC) with two services that are enabled in parallel: "ProcessSale" and "ManageExpressCheckout", modeling use cases 1 and 2 of the requirements. This is a result of process step 5. The two services in the figure are references to further, more detailed MSC specifications. Note that although a service structuring along the lines of the use cases is reasonable, the system designer not constrained to a certain service structuring.

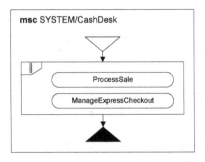

Fig. 4. High-Level MSC (HMSC) of Cash Desk describing the parallel execution of two services

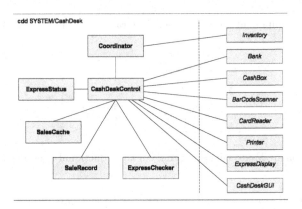

Fig. 5. Hierarchical Decomposition of CashDesk into Functional Subcomponents (Component Decomposition Diagram)

Fig. 5 shows the hierarchical decomposition of a cash desk into functional subcomponents. Performing step 4 again, we use a cdd to specify decomposition, external interfaces and communication relationships. The substructure of the cash desk is for one part design decision of the system designer and for the other part constrained by a given architecture. In our case, external devices such as a cash box, credit card reader and display exist and interact with a number of functional entities (controller, express status keeper). A consistency requirement for the cdd of Fig. 5 is that it needs to refine its parent component of Fig. 2, i. e. it can only access external interfaces that are specified for its parent.

Fig. 6 shows a component mode diagram (cmd) with the modes of the cash desk controller entity (process step 3). The modes model the logical steps associated with processing a sale (ready, scanning products, payment, finishing) with an additional canceling possibility.

The sale processing behavior of use case 1 and the specification of the service "ProcessSale" is given in Fig. 7. It is another HMSC showing a flow of subbehaviors that form a sale process. Note, that the flow is structured similar to the flow of modes

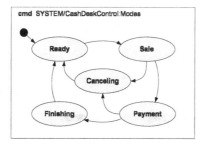

Fig. 6. Component Mode Diagram (cmd) for the CashDeskControl Entity

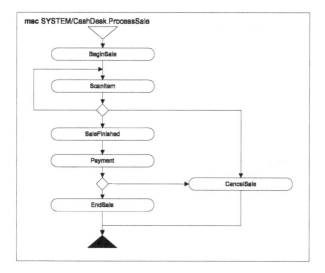

Fig. 7. High-level MSC (HMSC) of CashDesk Describing a Sale Process

in Fig. 6. Whenever a service is specified, it must adhere to the specifications given by the component decomposition and the modes.

Fig. 8 shows two basic MSCs with a actual interaction patterns specifying the behavior of scanning an individual product item as part of the entire scan process. Vertical axes represent functional components and horizontal arrows indicate message exchange. Operators, such as alternatives, loops, etc. are depicted as boxes. Operators can make an interaction specification very flexible and powerful (see [4]). Depicted as dashed hexagons at the beginning and end of the axes are mode labels, which indicate in which mode a functional component needs to be. The outlined hexagons specify conditions that need to be true at a certain point. When used in alternatives, they indicate which of the alternative behaviors applies.

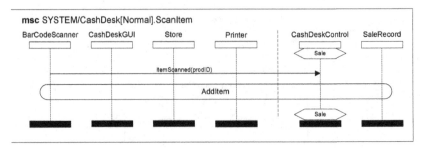

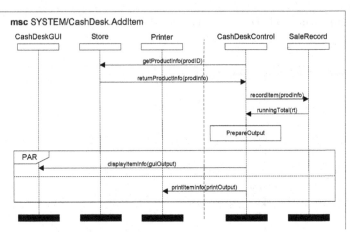

Fig. 8. MSC Describing the Process of Scanning and Adding an Item

The full functional specification of the POS example can be found in [15]. Fig. 9 shows the full decomposition of the POS system into functional components and subcomponents as a tree.

Functional components are separate entities for the purpose of specifying partial pieces of functionality distributed across a number of computational nodes. In practice, not the full distribution is necessary, and depending on replication requirements, coupling-coherence, criticality, complexity etc. more entities will be clustered into implementable components. In such cases, parts of the interactions are real distributed interactions while others will result in internal calls within a component.

Semantical Interpretation of Functional Specifications and Transformation Scheme into Behavioral Automata. We interpret the functional system specification by providing an automaton based semantics for it. Services specifying interaction patterns provide the behavioral requirements for all subcomponents involved. For each subcomponent and each applicable mode, the projection of all services to this subcomponent will result in a state transition diagram. In the following, we briefly explain the systematic automaton construction step-by-step.

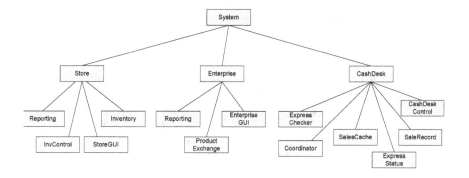

Fig. 9. Decomposition of the POS System into Functional Components and Subcomponents

For each subcomponent (axis appearing in the MSCs), we create an automaton. The identified system modi determine the basic structure (high-level structure) of the (hierarchical) automaton. The transitions between modes are captured in the High-level MSC specifications and by the modes within MSCs (depicted by the dashed hexagons at the beginning and the end of axes within MSCs).

For each mode, we create a sub-automaton according to the behavior specified in the MSCs and we introduce an initial state. The transitions are labeled with either (1) messages received, (2) messages sent, or (3) internal actions performed. We insert ϵ-transitions to "glue" states which might be interrupted by other behaviors. The functional specification enables the specification of parallel interactions by using the parallel operator (PAR). When constructing the automaton for such a specification, we provide alternative paths for all possible interleavings.

Fig. 10 shows the automaton of the "CashDeskControl" component for the normal mode and the sale sub mode. An exclamation mark (!) on the transition indicates that this is an output action/message, and a question mark (?) determines an input message/action. Because the messages "printItemInfo(prodInfo)" and "displayItemInfo(prodInfo)" are sent in parallel, we introduce two alternative paths to represent the interleaved sending of the messages. Fig. 8 shows two MSCs that were input for constructing the automaton of Fig. 10.

A functional specification is

- *Consistent*, if all mode transitions within the service specifications comply with the mode diagram, and if all interactions with external interfaces comply with the interface specifications of the component.
- *Complete*, if all external and internal component services have a service specification, a service definition exists for each mode of the component and if all mode transitions are provided by the service specifications.
- *Causal*, if there exists a set of state automatons representing the subcomponents that when combined produces exactly the same results as specified by the functional system specification.

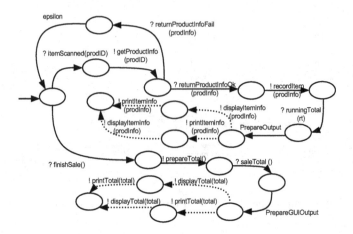

Fig. 10. The NSale Automata Generated from the Functional Model

When considering the interpretation of the automata on the logical architecture level, we apply a *closed world assumption*. We assume that the behavioral specification, comprised of the complete and consistent set of service specifications form the exact specification of the components' behavior. Assuming this provides the basis for constructing total state automata that can subsequently be minimized and optimized. Additionally any implicit parallelism in an automaton by alternative interleaving paths can be interpreted as parallel behavior and represented like this on the next lower level of abstraction.

8.3.2 Logical Level

Overview. In the logical level we model the system in the FOCUS specification language. First of all we cluster the entities of the functional level (roles) into the logical components and define the mapping from the messages of the functional level to the FOCUS channels and the corresponding FOCUS data types. After that we transform in a schematic way the automata, which were generated from the MSCs (see Section 8.3.1) to have the complete FOCUS specification based on the TSTDs (see Section 8.2).

Mapping Roles to Focus-Components. We group all the components of the service architecture into one logical component *CashDeskSystem*, which represents the system as a whole. We recall that there are three main subsystems (*CashDesk, Enterprise, and Store*) at the functional level (see Fig. 2). Each subsystem comprises a number of components and interfaces which we map to logical components (defined in Sect. 8.2).

An overall view of this layer's structure can be found in Fig. 11. The cash desk system consists of the components *Bank*, CashDeskCoord, Store and *n* copies of the components *Node* and *ExpressDisplay* (the notion of the specification

Table 1. Mapping CashDesk Roles to Focus Components

Role	Focus Component	Type
CashDesk.ExpressChecker	*ExpressChecker*	component logic (*CashDeskCoord*)
CashDesk.Coordinator	*Coordinator*	component logic (*CashDeskCoord*)
CashDesk.SalesCache	*Coordinator*	local variable
CashDesk.CashDeskControl	*CashDeskControl*	component logic
CashDesk.ExpressStatus	*CashDeskControl*	local variable
CashDesk.SaleRecord	*CashDeskControl*	local variable

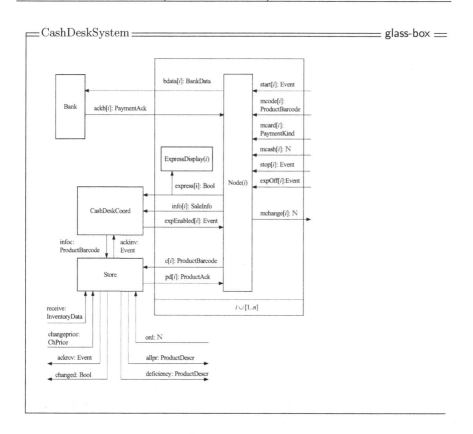

Fig. 11. Overall View of the Logical Architecture: Focus specification *CashDeskSystem*

replication and sheaves of channels is used here). With respect to the refinement from the functional to the logical level, the reader should note that this is not a one to one mapping, a number of refinement steps are design decisions. The behavior of certain elements at the functional level can better be represented by modeling them as a variable in a component (or as a subcomponent) at the logical level. We indicate the mapping of roles/components from the functional

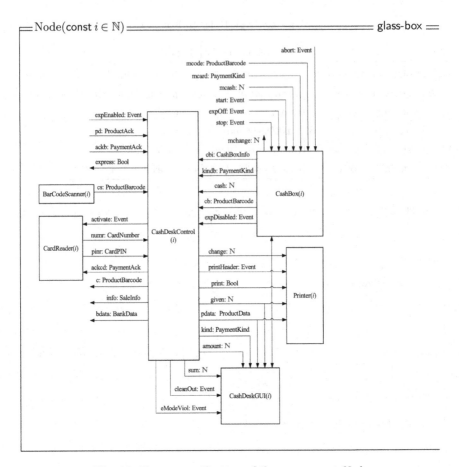

Fig. 12. Focus specification of the component *Node*

layer to components in the logical one in Table 1, particularly for the CashDesk system.

The distinction between *interface* and *component* made at the functional level is left apart. For instance, in case there is a minimal interaction between a candidate main component and another one, such as the *BarCodeScanner* which we included in the *CashDesk* component. The *BarCodeScanner* is comprised in the CashDesk Node as shown in Fig. 12.

For the sake of brevity, we will only present here the mapping of roles from the functional layer to components in the logical one only for the functional component *CashDesk* (see Table 1). The *CashDeskControl* role of the *CashDesk* will be represented by a Focus component with the same name.

The *SaleRecord* role of the *CashDesk* is just a buffer to save the data about product items, which are successfully scanned to sale. Therefore, in Focus it is more convenient to represent it as a local variable (let us name it l) of the component *CashDeskControl*.

Table 2. Mapping MSC Messages to Formal Data Types (*CashDeskControl*)

MSC Message	out	in	Data Type	Channels
startSale()	CashBox	CashDeskControl	CashBoxInfo	*cbi*
finishSale()	CashBox	CashDeskControl	CashBoxInfo	*cbi*
cashBoxClosed()	CashBox	CashDeskControls	CashBoxInfo	*cbi*
openCashBox()	CashBox	CashDeskControl	CashBoxInfo	*cbi*
cashPayment()	CashBox	CashDeskControl	PaymentKind	*kindb*
cardPayment()	CashBox	CashDeskControl	PaymentKind	*kindb*
itemScanned(...)	BarCodeScanner	CashDeskControl	ProductBarcode	*cs*
getProductInfo()	CashDesk	Inventory	ProductBarcode	*c*

Mapping MSC-Messages to Data Structures. An important step in the refinement from one level to another is the definition of data types and communication channels. For the sake of brevity, we present here the mapping of the MSC messages to the concrete FOCUS channels and the corresponding FOCUS data types exemplarily (see Table 2).[3]

Transformation Schema for the Behavior Automata. In order to describe the behavior for the logical model, the functional behavior automaton, which was derived from the MSCs (see Fig. 10), has to be schematic transformed into an equivalent FOCUS TSTD. The transformation schema consists of five steps, which are necessary to eliminate redundancy and refine the behavior to the timed representation.

We illustrate how the transformation process works on the example of the automaton for the *NSale*, shown in Fig. 10.

Step 1: Merge parallel output actions
The first step is to establish, which of output actions are performed in parallel (regardless of their ordering). The corresponding transitions of the automaton can be merged together into one transition. The resulting transition is labeled by all actions from labels of the merged transitions (see Fig. 13). This means, that these actions will have to take place at the same time unit (this is a refinement vs. the functional model).

In the automaton of the *NSale* process the following transitions can be merged: *!printItemInfo* and *!displayItemInfo*, *!printTotal* and *!displayTotal* (these pairs are marked as dotted lines on Fig. 7). The automata resulting from step 1 is illustrated in Fig. 14.

Step 2: Remove ε-transitions
Now all the ε-transitions (marked as dashed lines on Fig. 14) have to be removed. The resulting automaton for the *NSale* process is illustrated in Fig. 15.

---

[3] For reasons of space we also do not introduce here the definition of the data types.

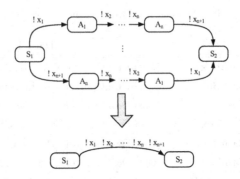

Fig. 13. Merging Actions Performed in Parallel

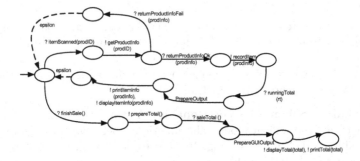

Fig. 14. NSale Automata: Parallel Actions are Merged

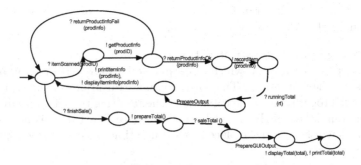

Fig. 15. NSale Automata: ε-Transitions are Removed

Step 3: Remove transitions I

The following step removes all transitions which actions belongs to the transformation of local variables of the logical components. The corresponding transformation constraints on the affected local variables must be added to the label of the prior transition. The transitions which represent a conversation between the

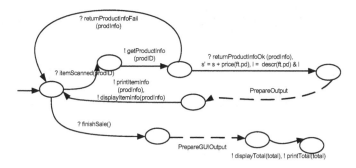

Fig. 16. NSale Automata: Local Variables Transformation are Taken into Account

functional components (roles) and are represented on the logical layer by a single component, are simply removed from the automaton.

In the case of the *NSale* process:

- The *!recordItem* and *?runningTotal* transitions (marked as dashed lines on Fig. 15) represent the updates of local variable l (the list of sale items) and s (the running total). We remove these transitions from the automaton and add two new constraints describing the local variables updates to the label of the prior transition.
- The *!prepareTotal()* and *saleTotal()* transitions (marked as dashed lines on Fig. 15) represent a conversation between the functional components (roles) which are represented on the logical layer by a single component with local variables. Thus, we can remove these transitions.

The result of these transformations can be seen in Fig. 16.

Step 4: Remove transitions II

At this step we remove all transitions which actions are some general computations. The corresponding transformation constraints must be added to the label of the prior transition, if the computation is non-primitive one.

For the *NSale* process: The *PrepareOutput* and *PrepareGUIOutput* (marked as dashed lines on Fig. 16) transitions are meant only for getting the results ready for presentation. In the logical model we do not need any extra preparation of the results ("primitive computation"). Thus, these transitions can be left out. The resulting automata can be found in Fig. 17.

Step 5: Final transformation into Focus messages

Finally, the syntax of the transition labels must be changed to the FOCUS syntax to get the equivalent TSTD. All the remaining MSC-Messages are replaced by the corresponding FOCUS messages according the mapping discussed in Section 8.3.2. More formally:

Let c_x denote the channel, which corresponds to the translation of the MSC-message x and let m_x denote the FOCUS message, which

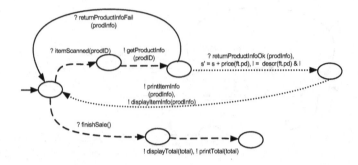

Fig. 17. NSale Automata: Computations are Taken into Account

corresponds to the MSC-message x.

Replace the transition pairs

$$s_1 \overset{?a}{\to} s_2 \overset{!b_1,\dots,!b_n}{\to} s_3$$

by the transformations

$$s_1 \overset{c_a=\langle m_a\rangle / c'_{b1}=\langle m_{b1}\rangle,\dots,c'_{b1}=\langle m_{bn}\rangle}{\to} s_3.$$

The messages $b_1,\dots,b_n$ will normally be output via different channels $c'_{b_1},\dots,c'_{b_n}$. If the messages $b_i,\dots,b_j$ must be output via the channel b_{ij}, the corresponding relation will be $c'_{b_{ij}} = \langle m_{b_i},\dots,m_{b_j}\rangle$.

Replace the labels on the rest of the transitions as following:

An input $?a$ hast to be replaced by $c_a = \langle m_a\rangle$, an output $!b$ has to be replaced by $c'_b = \langle m_b\rangle$.

In the case of the *NSale* process after the transformation according to the mapping from Section 8.3.2 we get a FOCUS TSTD presented in Fig. 18. We refer to

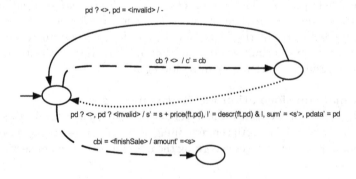

Fig. 18. MNSale Automata: The FOCUS TSTD

this TSTD in the Focus specification of the *CashDeskControl* component (see Section 8.3.2) by the name *CashDeskControlAutomat*.

Cash Desk Control Component. In the MSC specification of the *CashDeskControl* role we have two modes: *Normal* and *Express*. The most natural way to represent this notion in the current syntax of Focus is to use a local variable to save the current mode. Let us name this variable *mode*. Thus, the modes of the *CashDesk* unit correspond to the values of the local variable *mode* of the *CashDeskControl* component: Normal $\cong$ false, Express $\cong$ true.

CashDeskControl ═══════════════════════════════════ **timed** ═

in	$expEnabled, expDisabled : Event;$ $cbi : CashBoxInfo;$ $cash : \mathbb{N};$ $cb, cs : ProductBarcode;$ $pd : ProductAck;$ $ackb : PaymentAck;$ $numr : CardNumber;$ $pinr : CardPIN;$ $kindb : PaymentKind;$
out	$c : ProductBarcode;$ $info : SaleInfo;$ $bdata : BankData;$ $express : \mathbb{B}ool;$ $amount, sum, given, change : \mathbb{N};$ $ackcd : PaymentAck;$ $print : \mathbb{B}ool;$ $printHeader, activate, cleanOut, eModeViol : Event;$ $pdata : ProductData;$ $kind : PaymentKind;$

---

local	$st \in Status;$ $l \in ProductDescr\,^*;$ $cnum \in CardNumber;$ $mode, modecash \in \mathbb{B}ool;$ $s \in \mathbb{N}$
univ	$x, y : Event\,^*;$ $xcbi \in CashBoxInfo\,^*;$ $xk \in PaymentKind\,^*;$ $xcash \in \mathbb{N}\,^*;$ $xcb, xcs \in ProductBarcode\,^*;$ $xpd \in ProductAck\,^*;$ $xackb \in PaymentAck\,^*;$ $xnumr \in CardNumber\,^*;$ $xpinr \in CardPIN\,^*;$

- -

init	$st = init;$ $l = \langle\rangle;$ $mode = $ false$;$ $modecash = $ false$;$ $s = 0;$

- -

asm	disjoint(cb, cs) $\mathsf{msg}_1(cbi) \wedge \mathsf{msg}_1(kindb) \wedge \mathsf{msg}_1(cash) \wedge \mathsf{msg}_1(cb)$ $\mathsf{msg}_1(cs) \wedge \mathsf{msg}_1(pd) \wedge \mathsf{msg}_1(ackb) \wedge \mathsf{msg}_1(numr) \wedge \mathsf{msg}_1(pinr)$

- -

gar	$\mathsf{ti}(c,0) = \langle\rangle \wedge \mathsf{ti}(info,0) = \langle\rangle \wedge \mathsf{ti}(bdata,0) = \langle\rangle$ $\wedge\ \mathsf{ti}(cleanOut,t) = \langle\rangle \wedge \mathsf{ti}(eModeViol,t) = \langle\rangle$ $\wedge\ \mathsf{ti}(express,0) = \langle\rangle \wedge \mathsf{ti}(amount,0) = \langle\rangle \wedge \mathsf{ti}(sum,0) = \langle\rangle$ $\wedge \mathsf{ti}(given,0) = \langle\rangle$ $\wedge\ \mathsf{ti}(change,0) = \langle\rangle \wedge \mathsf{ti}(ackcd,0) = \langle\rangle \wedge \mathsf{ti}(print,0) = \langle\rangle$ $\wedge \mathsf{ti}(printHeader,0) = \langle\rangle$ $\wedge\ \mathsf{ti}(activate,0) = \langle\rangle \wedge \mathsf{ti}(kind,0) = \langle\rangle \wedge \mathsf{ti}(pdata,0) = \langle\rangle$ tiTable *ExpressCheckerTable* tiAutomat *CashDeskControlAutomat*

tiTable $ExpressCheckerTable$: $\forall\, t \in \mathbb{N}$

	$expressEnabled$	$ExpressDisabled$	$express^1$	$modecash'$	Assumptions
1	$\langle\rangle$	y	$\langle\rangle$	$modecash$	$modecash = \text{true}$
2	x	y	$\langle\text{false}\rangle$	false	$modecash = \text{true} \wedge y \neq \langle\rangle$
3	x	$\langle\rangle$	$\langle\rangle$	$modecash$	$modecash = \text{false}$
4	x	y	$\langle\text{true}\rangle$	true	$modecash = \text{false} \wedge x \neq \langle\rangle$

The command to change the mode can come from the *ExpressChecker* each time, but the mode can be changed only when the sale process is finished (not started). Thus, we need to use another variable to cash this command until the sale process is finished. Let us name this variable *modecash*. The corresponding behavior is described by the table *ExpressCheckerTable* (see above).

8.3.3   Deployment Level

Overview. Up to now our development method was concerned with system functions, system data models, system decomposition into components and their behavior specifications. Any consideration of the technical implementation has been left out. Now, we focus technical issues and explain the system's deployment into a Java-driven execution environment. An early outline related to our approach can be found in [17].

Deployment layers. The deployment level is split into two layers: the *technical* and the *operational* architecture. Since the technical architecture takes care of implementing logical components as executable objects, i.e. tasks, the operational architecture defines the execution environment and necessary operating system services, like task scheduling or communication facilities.

The technical and operational architecture should provide the capabilities to execute the logical components in parallel in a distributed environment. The most important property to be ensured is the strong causality, meaning all components are synchronized to a global logical time frame and message exchange is delayed exactly one logical time unit. Logical components exchange messages every time tick. If the component behavior does not specify a data value for transmission the special NoVal message is transmitted to represent the absence of a data value message. Since no real-time mechanisms like worst-case execution time checks are applied, the operational architecture provides synchronous communication to guarantee synchronous task execution. We assume that all necessary tasks run and communicate as expected. Appropriate error and failure handling is not addressed in this case study. For example, we have not included communication monitoring or task restart and recovery mechanism, which would increase system robustness, but also makes the operational architecture and the communication protocol more complex.

The implementation activity was carried out using modeling tools, automating most of the deployment steps. The tool, used here, is especially designed around

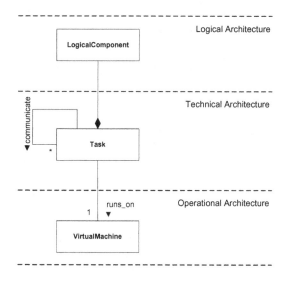

Fig. 19. Entity model of the architecture level

the Focus system theory: AutoFOCUS2. In the following we briefly describe the deployment relevant architectural elements, as outlined in Fig. 19, and look at the code generation facility. Our tool-supported method, used to implement the logical, technical and operational models, is then described in section 8.5. There, we also outline the steps used during the deployment phase.

Technical Architecture. In the technical architecture we obtain executable, reactive units, called *tasks*, from the (atomic) logical components of the system. Since these components are functional units, tasks are the deployable units of the distributed system. Tasks inherit the properties from the logical level, i.e. they work in parallel in a possibly distributed execution environment and are supposed to communicate with each other as defined by the communication links, i.e. channels. The execution environment and communication facilities are provided by the operational architecture as described below.

For reasons of simplicity, we concentrate on atomic components, each yielding a single task, that executes the specified behavior. It is also possible to obtain tasks from compositional, hierarchical components, but we do not address this here. Instead our overall system consists of a network of atomic components. Then the transition from the logical level to the technical architecture is a rather simple code generation activity.

For each atomic component we obtain a task including the code generated from its behavior specification. Each task provides an interface to write messages to input ports, execute a transition of the automaton and read result messages from the output ports. We also get generated code from the data model, which allows to instantiate messages passed between tasks.

As a matter of fact tasks are the counterparts of components, i.e. the technical architecture is in one-to-one correspondence with the atomic logical architecture. As mentioned above, a more sophisticated deployment is possible. Next, the task entities of the technical architecture will be embedded into entities of the operational architecture, which is described in the following.

Operational Architecture. The operational architecture delivers the execution environment and the communication infrastructure. Here, we rely on the Java virtual machine and Remote Method Invocation (RMI) facility. Tasks of the technical architecture are enclosed by Java threads. The obtained executable objects use a round-based execution protocol: input communication is followed by task computation, which is followed by output communication. The communication phases are realized by RMI, which provides synchronous communication between Java objects, independent of their distribution settings (local or remote). Note that the distribution of threads into Java Virtual Machines is arbitrary from the technical point of view, but must obey the real world distribution, e.g. the *CardReader* thread is located on the card reader device, while the *CashDesk* thread is located on the cash desk machine. Fig. 20 shows a simplified deployment view of this part of the model.

Synchronous communication is the basis of the communication protocol that guarantees synchronous execution of tasks with respect to the logical time frame. In a logical time synchronous system, as described by the logical architecture, no component is allowed to execute a second step before all neighboring components have completed their first step and transmitted their results. This overall system behavior, which corresponds to the strong causality property, has to be guaranteed by the operational architecture.

To achieve this goal, we use a simple protocol for each communication line, i.e. each channel of the logical architecture. For every channel, we implement a *producer-consumer* mechanism with a transmission buffer size of one item. This means that the receiving task has an input buffer for exactly one message and a boolean flag indicating who is next to access the buffer. These data items, provided for each channel, are used to implement the synchronous execution of the whole system.

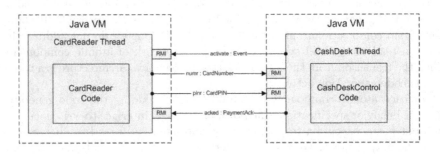

Fig. 20. Deployment example: partial model of CashDesk and CardReader

First, let us look at the *consumer role* of a task, i.e. the task receives messages before computing its next result. For every input channel (if the indicator flag is set) a task reads the buffered message, clears the indicator flag and notifies a possibly blocked sender (see below). If the indicator flag was not set, the task blocks and waits for notification by the sender. Thus a task waits for all incoming messages to be delivered (possibly being blocked multiple times, at most once for every input channel). After this consumption part, all input channels have been read, their indicators have been cleared and any blocked sender is notified. Now, the task is ready to compute its next result, since all neighbours have finished the current cycle.

After computing the next result, a task switches to the *producer role*. For every outgoing channel it makes a remote call and writes the result into the input buffer of the receiver. If the indicator flag is cleared, the remote call returns immediately after writing the buffer, setting the indicator flag and notifying the receiver task. If the indicator flag is set, meaning the input buffer has not been read by the receiver, the remote call and thus the sender (producer) is blocked until the receiver clears the input buffer and the indicator flag. This means that a sender task, in case of being one step ahead, is blocked until the receiving task catches up. Therefore a task waits for all outgoing messages to be transmitted (possibly being blocked multiple times, at most once for every output channel). After that the task switches back to the consumer role to start its next computation round.

This protocol guarantees the synchronous execution with a small addition: at system start-up (before the first computation round starts) input buffers are filled with initial values (provided as part of the logical architecture model). This means that every task can complete its first computation round without the need of a remotely produced message. With this addition the communication protocol yields a *dead-lock free* system execution.

Code Generation. As we will outline in section 8.5 our development and deployment method is supported by AutoFocus2, our research prototype tool for model-based development of reactive systems. From the point of view of the deployment level, the code generation facility is of primary concern. It provides the necessary generation functions for Java threads and RMI-interfaces. The following code entities are generated from the logical architecture model:

- For each atomic component, a singleton class is generated that provides the doStep() method. It executes a single transition of the automaton. The class also provides methods to write values of input ports and read results from output ports. Generated classes implement the task entities of the technical architecture.
- For each atomic component, a Java RMI interface is generated. It provides remote methods to send messages between components, i.e. task.
- For each task, a class is generated that provides the thread implementation. Here, the execution protocol (read input, compute result, write output) is implemented using the interfaces.
- For each environment output channel a uniquely named remote interface is generated. This interface has to be implemented by the environment,

e.g. some graphical user interface, and must also provide a synchronous be-havior. The environment can be seen as a special, atomic, logical component that forms the counterpart of the developed system. To allow maximum flex-ibility for the environment each channel yields a single interface with a single `send()` method.

8.4   Analysis

The advantage of the presented approach is that AutoFocus2 can be connected to common model checkers (with restriction that the we can have only a constant number of components in the model). Thus, properties of the model can be proved automatically. The main challenge here is dealing with the state space explosion problem. This problem occurs in systems with many components that can interact with each other or systems with data structures that can assume many different values.

Furthermore, the Focus model can be schematically translated into the proof assistant Isabelle (see [18]) in order to further verify the model semi-automatically, but without the restriction to a finite constant number of com-ponents in the model (see [14] for details).

8.5   Tools

Our method is supported by and can be carried out with our scientific research prototype AutoFocus2 [7], which is a tool implementation based on the Focus approach [2]. We used AutoFocus2 to build the model of the logical architecture and the component behavior. Afterwards the Java code generator was used to generate the components' and the deployment code.

Here, we give a brief overview of the tool-supported development activities and steps necessary to obtain the executable code starting with the modeling of the logical architecture:

1. Define the system data model using data type definitions.
2. Model the logical architecture in a top-down manner using the hierarchical system structure diagrams.
3. Add the behavior of every atomic component using the hierarchical state transition diagrams, thus specifying the components input/output relation.
4. Finally use the extended AutoFocus2 Java code generator to obtain exe-cutable and deployment code for each component. The former contains Java implementations of the state transition diagrams, while the latter comprises Java RMI remote interfaces and thread implementations.
5. The generated code provides the necessary interfaces and methods to plug-in graphical and/or textual user interfaces as hand-written extension code.

Apart from these steps, AutoFocus2 provides further support during the model-based development. For example, logical models can be validated and tested using the simulator function or even verified using model-checking methods.

8.6 Summary

In this chapter, we have presented and explained our group's systems engineering philosophy for distributed reactive systems. This philosophy has been distilled from numerous research and application projects over years. We propose a modular development approach based on a precisely defined mathematical model Focus. Our approach defines abstraction levels that each show particular views of the system in various degrees of detail. A systematic development process links the abstraction levels based on the overall foundation on the formalism Focus, infinite streams on distributed components.

The actual applied methodology and notations within an abstraction level can vary significantly depending on application domain and other needs. We have selected suitable notations tailored to CoCoME and have presented alternatives. All methods however follow the given scheme of abstraction levels, their interfaces and the underlying formalism for semantic interpretation. For CoCoME, we have chosen a service-oriented development approach that puts interactions of distributed components (here called roles) in the center of interest. From these service-oriented specifications, we derive the actual component specifications on a logical level that we can deploy on a suitable CoCoME target architecture and execution environment. We use our component model Focus for the component specifications and specify behavior both in state automaton syntax and in form of logical expressions. We provide tool support around the tool AutoFocus2, that enables us to execute our specified models in a distributed environment targeted to the CoCoME example.

We have limited the focus of the present work to a subset of the CoCoME requirements to show the core ideas of our component model. As future work remains to complete the model for all use cases and requirements.

References

1. Gruler, A., Harhurin, A., Hartmann, J.: Modeling the Functionality of Multi-Functional Software Systems. In: 14th Annual IEEE International Conference on the Engineering of Computer Based Systems (ECBS), pp. 349–358. IEEE Computer Society Press, Los Alamitos (2007)
2. Broy, M., Stølen, K.: Specification and Development of Interactive Systems: Focus on Streams, Interfaces and Refinement. Springer, New York (2001)
3. Broy, M.: Service-oriented Systems Engineering: Specification and Design of Services and Layered Architectures–The Janus-Approach. In: Broy, M., Grünbauer, J., Harel, D., Hoare, T. (eds.) Engineering Theories of Software Intensive Systems: Proceedings of the NATO Advanced Study Institute, pp. 47–82. Springer, Heidelberg (2005)
4. Krüger, I., Mathew, R., Meisinger, M.: Efficient Exploration of Service-Oriented Architectures using Aspects. In: Proceedings of the 28th International Conference on Software Engineering (ICSE) (2006)
5. Broy, M., Krüger, I., Meisinger, M.: A Formal Model of Services. ACM Transactions on Software Engineering and Methodology (TOSEM) 16(1) (2007)

6. Krüger, I.: Distributed System Design with Message Sequence Charts. PhD thesis, Technische Universität München (2000)
7. Technische Universität München: AutoFocus 2 (2007), http://www4.informatik.tu-muenchen.de/~af2
8. Huber, F., Schätz, B., Schmidt, A., Spies, K.: AutoFocus - A Tool for Distributed Systems Specification. In: Jonsson, B., Parrow, J. (eds.) FTRTFT 1996. LNCS, vol. 1135, pp. 467–470. Springer, Heidelberg (1996)
9. Hartmann, J., Rittmann, S., Scholz, P., Wild, D.: A Compositional Approach for Functional Requirement Specifications of Automotive Software Systems. In: Proceedings of the Workshop on Automotive Requirements Engineering (AuRE 2006) (2006)
10. Deubler, M., Grünbauer, J., Holzbach, A., Popp, G., Wimmel, G.: Kontextadaptivität in dienstbasierten Softwaresystemen. Technical Report TUM-I0511, Institut für Informatik, Technische Universität München TUM (2005)
11. Deubler, M., Grünbauer, J., Jürjens, J., Wimmel, G.: Sound development of secure service based systems. In: Proceedings of the 2nd International Conference on Service Oriented Computing (ICSOC) (2004)
12. Broy, M., Bauer, A., Romberg, J., Schätz, B., Braun, P., Freund, U., Mata, N., Sandner, R., Ziegenbein, D.: AutoMoDe – Notations, Methods, and Tools for Model-Based Development of Automotive Software. In: Proceedings of the SAE, Detroit (2005) SAE 05AE-268
13. Fox, J., Jürjens, J.: A Framework for Analyzing Composition of Security Aspects. In: Brinksma, E., Harel, D., Mader, A., Stevens, P., Wieringa, R., eds.: Methods for Modelling Software Systems (MMOSS). Number 06351 in Dagstuhl Seminar Proceedings, Internationales Begegnungs- und Forschungszentrum fuer Informatik (IBFI), Schloss Dagstuhl, Germany (2007)
14. Spichkova, M.: Specification and Seamless Verification of Embedded Real-Time Systems: FOCUS on Isabelle. PhD thesis, Technische Universität München (2007)
15. Technische Universität München, Institut für Informatik: CoCoME Full Model (2007), http://www4.in.tum.de/~af2/cocome.zip
16. ITU-TS: Recommendation Z.120: Message Sequence Chart (MSC), Geneva (1996)
17. Huber, F., Schätz, B.: Rapid Prototyping with AutoFocus. In: GI-FDT 1997 (1997)
18. Nipkow, T., Paulson, L.C., Wenzel, M.: Isabelle/HOL – A Proof Assistant for Higher-Order Logic. LNCS, vol. 2283. Springer, Heidelberg (2002)

9 Modelling the CoCoME with the JAVA/A Component Model*

Alexander Knapp[1], Stephan Janisch[1], Rolf Hennicker[1], Allan Clark[2],
Stephen Gilmore[2], Florian Hacklinger[1], Hubert Baumeister[3], and Martin Wirsing[1]

[1] Institut für Informatik, Ludwig-Maximilians-Universität München
{hacklinger, hennicker, janisch, knapp, wirsing}@ifi.lmu.de
[2] Laboratory for Foundations of Computer Science, University of Edinburgh
{a.d.clark, Stephen.Gilmore}@ed.ac.uk
[3] Informatik og Matematisk Modellering, Danmarks Tekniske Universitet, Lyngby
hub@imm.dtu.dk

9.1 Introduction

The JAVA/A approach aims at semantically well-founded and coherent modelling and programming concepts for components: based on sound theoretical foundations it enhances the widely used UML 2.0 component model by modular analysis and verification techniques and a Java-based architectural programming language.

9.1.1 Goals and Scope of the Component Model

The JAVA/A component model, formally characterised within the algebraic semantic framework of [1], is inspired by ideas from "Real-Time Object Oriented Modeling" (ROOM [2]): components are strongly encapsulated, instantiable behaviours and any interaction of components with their environment is regulated by ports. We took up the ROOM model in its version integrated into the "Unified Modeling Language 2.0" (UML 2.0 [3]), though in a simplified form which, however, keeps the main structuring mechanisms and focuses on strong encapsulation as well as hierarchical composition.

In contrast to interface-based component approaches (like COM, CORBA, Koala, KobrA, SOFA; see [4] for an overview), the primary distinguishing feature of ROOM, and hence of the JAVA/A component model, is the consistent use of ports as explicit architectural modelling elements. Ports allow designers to segment the communication interface of components and thus the representation of different "faces" to other components. Moreover, ports are equipped with behavioural protocols regulating message exchanges according to a particular viewpoint. Explicit modelling of port behaviours supports a divide-and-conquer approach to the design of component-based systems on the level of components and also on the level of particular views to a component.

---

* This research has been partially supported by the EC 6th Framework project SENSORIA "Software Engineering for Service-Oriented Overlay Computers" (IST 016004) and the GLOWA-Danube project (01LW0303A) sponsored by the German Federal Ministry of Education and Research.

A. Rausch et al. (Eds.): Common Component Modeling Example, LNCS 5153, pp. 207–237, 2008.

Furthermore, taking components to be strongly encapsulated behaviours communicating through ports fosters modular verification, which is one of the aims of the JAVA/A approach. Using our semantic foundations, we employ the model checking tools HUGO/RT and LTSA to verify that components comply to their ports and that connected ports can communicate successfully; by a compositionality theorem we can lift these properties to hierarchical, composite components. Starting with deadlock-free component and port behaviours, we verify the absence of deadlocks in composed behaviours. Since HUGO/RT and LTSA are general model checking tools we may also analyse arbitrary temporal logical formulae. For quantitative properties, we represent the component semantics, though rather abstractly, in the PEPA process algebra [5] and use continuous-time Markov chains for performance analysis with the IPC tool [6].

The second aim of the JAVA/A approach is the representation of software architecture entities in a programming language. For this purpose we introduced an "architectural programming" language, JAVA/A [7], which allows programmers to represent software architectures directly in the implementation language and thus helps to prevent "architectural erosion" [8]. We used the code generation engine HUGO/RT to translate the behaviour of components into Java code; the code generation is not formally verified but strictly adheres to the UML-semantics of the state machines. The usage of the same tool for verification and code generation helps in transferring design properties into the code. The generated Java code is then embedded into JAVA/A source code, which in turn is compiled and deployed to yield the executable system. The deployment is not described separately from the logical behaviour of the components.

9.1.2   Modelled Cutout of the CoCoME

We present selected parts of our model of the CoCoME trading system in Sect. 9.3 including the embedded system part with the CashDeskLine and the information system part with the Inventory. In particular we treated the structural aspects of CoCoME completely. The functional (behavioural) aspects were modelled also completely for the embedded system part of the CashDeskLine and partly for the information system part with the Inventory at its core. We touched only upon non-functional aspects by provision of an example in the context of express checkouts. We did not specify pure data-based specifications such as invariants and pre-/post-conditions but focused on the control flow behaviours of ports and components instead.

All deviations from the original architecture of the CoCoME are discussed in detail in Sect. 9.3.1. Our approach does not directly allow for n-ary connectors and broadcast messages between components. In both cases adaptor components need to be applied; as far as the modelling of the CoCoME is concerned we did not feel this to be a severe restriction. The full description of our model of the CoCoME as well as more details on the theoretical background for the functional analysis can be found on our web page [9].

9.1.3   Benefits of the Modelling

In Sect. 9.4 we show how the formal algebraic basis of our model allows one to thoroughly analyse and verify important qualitative and quantitative properties. In particular, we show that the composite component CashDeskLine is correct and deadlock free; as an example for performance analysis we study the use of express checkouts and show that their advantage is surprisingly small. In Sect. 9.5 we briefly present the model checking and architectural programming tools we used for the CoCoME.

9.1.4   Effort and Lessons Learned

We spent about two and a half person months on modelling, analysing and implementing the CoCoME with the JAVA/A component model and the JAVA/A architectural programming language. A completion of the modelling endeavour, including, in particular, data-based specifications would take about two more person months. However, an inclusion of all non-functional requirements would require some more work on the foundational aspects of the JAVA/A component model.

The CoCoME helped us on the one hand to consolidate the JAVA/A metamodel. On the other hand, we gained important insights into glass-box views for composite components and on the formulation of criteria for modular verification on the basis of a port based component model. We plan to extend our model with data-based specifications (invariants, pre-/post-conditions) to develop and study an approach to state/event-integration.

9.2   Component Model

In the JAVA/A component model, components are strongly encapsulated behaviours. Only the exchange of messages with their environment according to provided and required operation interfaces can be observed. The component interfaces are bound to ports which regulate the message exchange by port behaviour and ports can be linked by connectors establishing a communication channel between their owning components. Components can be hierarchical containing again components and connections.

In the following we briefly review JAVA/A's component metamodel, see Fig. 1. Although being based on corresponding concepts in the UML 2.0 and, in fact, easily mappable, we at least strive to give a more independent definition which only relies on well-known UML 2.0 concepts. In Fig. 1, UML concepts modified by the JAVA/A component model are shown with a white background while unmodified UML concepts are shown with grey background. We assume a working UML 2.0 knowledge [3] when explaining some of the specialities of our modelling notation and semantics. An algebraic semantics framework for the JAVA/A component model can be found in [1].

Port. A *port* (see Fig. 1(a)) describes a view on a component (like particular functionality or communication), the operations offered and needed in the context of this view and the mandatory sequencing of operation calls from the outside and from the inside. The operations offered by a port are summarised in its *provided interface*; the operations needed in its *required interface*. The sequencing of operations being called from and on a port is described in a *port behaviour*. Any auxiliary attributes and operations in order to properly define the port behaviour are added as internal features.

As an example, consider the port C-CD (showing stereotype «port») in Fig. 12 describing the coordinator's view on a cash desk: Its provided and required interfaces (attached to the port by using the ball and socket notation, respectively) declare only

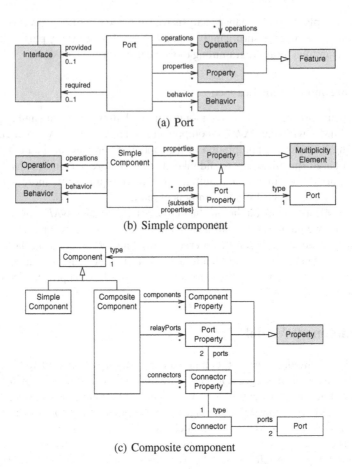

(a) Port

(b) Simple component

(c) Composite component

Fig. 1. JAVA/A component metamodel

asynchronous operations (i.e., on calling these operations the caller does not wait for the callee to handle the call; for succinctness we use a stereotype «async» to express that all operations of an interface are meant to be asynchronous); it also shows an internal attribute for storing the identity of a cash desk. The behaviour of port C-CD is described by the UML state machine in Fig. 12 (top right). Besides the UML state machine features we use, on the one hand, a special completion trigger «tau» for modelling internal choice (of the port's owning component) which is enabled on state completion but, in contrast to completion triggers (used for those transitions not showing a trigger), is not prioritised over other events. On the other hand, we assume all state machines to behave like UML 2.0's protocol state machines in the sense that it is an error if an event occurs in a state where it cannot be handled by one of the outgoing transitions.

Simple component. A *simple component* (see Fig. 1(b)) consists of port properties (sometimes referred to as port declarations), internal attributes and operations, and a behaviour linking and using these ingredients. Port properties (like all properties) are equipped with a *multiplicity*, setting lower and upper bounds on how many port instances of a particular type exist during runtime, permitting dynamic reconfiguration.

As an example, consider the simple component Coordinator (showing stereotype «component») in Fig. 12. Besides an internal attribute and two internal operations it declares a port property cds of type C-CD with unlimited multiplicity. The behaviour of Coordinator is laid down in the state machine of Fig. 12 (bottom right). In fact, as indicated by the stereotype «orthogonal» with tag { param = cd : cds }, this behaviour description abbreviates a composite orthogonal state with as many orthogonal regions (containing the given behaviour) as there are currently port instances in cds. Note also that the internal operation updateSaleHistory is declared to be { sequential }, that is, all calls to this operation are sequentialised.

Composite component. A *composite component* (see Fig. 1(c)) groups components, simple as well as composite, by declaring component properties, and connectors between ports of contained components, by declaring connector properties. A *connector* (which is always binary) describes the type of a connector property which links two port properties such that the ports of the connector match the ports of the port properties. Composite components do not show a behaviour of their own, their behaviour is determined by the interplay of the behaviours of their contained component instances and the connections, i.e., connector instances. The ports offered by a composite component are exclusively *relay ports*, i.e., the mirroring of ports from the contained components which must not be declared to be connected by some connector property.

As an example, consider the composite component CashDeskLine (showing stereotype «component») in Fig. 6. It declares, via the component properties cashDesks and coordinator, components CashDesk and Coordinator as sub-components where each instance of CashDeskLine must show at least one instance of CashDesk. Port property co of CashDesk is connected to port property cds of Coordinator meaning that at runtime each port instance in co of a cash desk in cashDesks is connected to a port instance in cds of coordinator. The port declarations i and b of CashDesk are relayed. However, as in fact there may be several cash desks but there is to be only a single port instance of CDA-Bank we would have to introduce an adapter component which declares a port with multiplicity 1 to be relayed to the outside of CashDeskLine and a port with multiplicity 1..* (matching the multiplicity of cashDesks) to be connected to the different b instances of the different cashDesks. We abbreviate this by using the

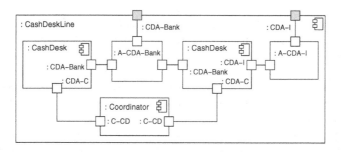

Fig. 2. Sample configuration of component CashDeskLine of Fig. 6

stereotype «adapter» on connector declarations; in particular, as indicated by the tagged value { kind = "seq" }, the adapter component sequentialises the different calls.

A sample runtime configuration of the composite component CashDeskLine is given in Fig. 2. This configuration shows two instances of component CashDesk and a single instance of component Coordinator. The CDA-C port instances of the cash desks are connected to two different instances of the C-CD coordinator port. The CDA-Bank port instances of the cash desks are adapted to one relay port instance of the cash desk line by the auxiliary adapter component A-CDA-Bank. Similarly, the CDA-I port instance of the cash desk to the right (the other cash desk does not show a CDA-I port instance, in accordance with the multiplicity of the port feature declaration i) is relayed.

9.3   Modelling the CoCoME

We started the design of the CoCoME from the use case descriptions and sequence diagrams as given in [10]. After and during static structure modelling for simple (non-composite) components we designed component and port behaviours hand in hand, in case of the embedded system part accompanied by formal analysis. Finally, the simple components were applied for the design of the composite components, yielding a first draft of the complete architecture. Within the next iterations, the alternative and exceptional processes of the use case descriptions were taken into account to extend and correct the initial design. In case of ambiguous or unclear requirements our design followed the prototype implementation of the CoCoME. Since we fully agree with the data model provided in [10], we omit specifications of data types, transfer objects for data exchange and enumerations.

Our specifications comprise UML 2.0 class and composite structure diagrams to specify the static structure of components, ports and interfaces; and UML 2.0 state machine diagrams to specify the behavioural view for ports and components. Familiarity with terms, notions and functional requirements of the trading system [10] is assumed. For lack of space we do not discuss the specifications of components and ports shown in grey in Figs. 3–7. Instead we restrict our attention on a detailed presentation of the embedded system part which is also the focus of our functional analysis. Additionally we provide a representative extract of our model for the information system part of the CoCoME. Specifications not discussed here can be found on our web page [9].

9.3.1   Architectural Deviations

Two of the essential features of our component model are, on the one hand, its strict use of ports as first-class citizen to encapsulate (parts of) component behaviour and, on the other hand, the distinction between component, port types respectively and their instantiation. These features enabled us to model some aspects of the trading system in a more convenient way. In the following we describe and justify structural deviations from the original modelling along Fig. 3. On the left-hand side the component hierarchy as described in [10] is shown. The right-hand side shows the corresponding modelling within our approach. From deviations with our static model almost naturally some deviations in behavioural aspects follow. We omit a detailed discussion here and refer to [9] for component-wise details on this issue.

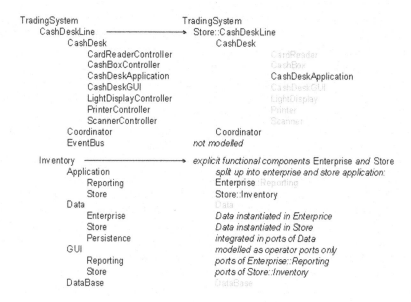

```
TradingSystem                    TradingSystem
   CashDeskLine   ────────────→    Store::CashDeskLine
      CashDesk                        CashDesk
         CardReaderController              CardReader
         CashBoxController                 CashBox
         CashDeskApplication           CashDeskApplication
         CashDeskGUI                       CashDeskGUI
         LightDisplayController            LightDisplay
         PrinterController                 Printer
         ScannerController                 Scanner
      Coordinator                      Coordinator
      EventBus                      not modelled

   Inventory     ────────────→    explicit functional components Enterprise and Store
      Application                     split up into enterprise and store application:
         Reporting                    Enterprise::Reporting
         Store                        Store::Inventory
      Data                               Data
         Enterprise                   Data instantiated in Enterprice
         Store                        Data instantiated in Store
         Persistence                  integrated in ports of Data
      GUI                             modelled as operator ports only
         Reporting                    ports of Enterprise::Reporting
         Store                        ports of Store::Inventory
      DataBase                           DataBase
```

Fig. 3. Component hierarchy of given (left) and modelled (right) architecture

As the most important deviation in the embedded system part we did not model the event bus component, which is used in the CoCoME for the communication between the subcomponents of the cash desk line on the one hand, and between those, the coordinator and external components on the other hand. Instead of a functional component, our approach provides explicit models of component communications and interactions using port and component behaviour specifications. We consider the integration of an event bus to be an implementation decision where the implementation should guarantee that the specified communication structure of the design model is respected.

Explicit modelling of the cash desk's internal interaction structure constitutes the internal topology of our composite component CashDesk (see Fig. 7) deviating from the cash desk's inner structure as shown in [10, Fig. 6]. During the modelling of the subcomponent's communication it soon became apparent that, in our approach, the most appropriate topology for the CashDesk is the one specified in Fig. 7. The central functionality of handling sales almost always requires the cash desk application to receive some signal or message respectively from an "input" component such as the cash box and to send a corresponding notification to an "output" component such as the cash desk GUI or the printer.

Furthermore we dropped the distinction of functional and controller components within the cash desk component of the CoCoME. In our approach, controller components such as the CashBoxController [10, e.g. Fig. 6, 6], linking the middleware and the hardware devices, could be modelled with ports.

The main structural deviation from the CoCoME requirements of the information system part concerns the layered approach to the modelling of the component Inventory on the left-hand side of Fig. 3. The layers Application, Data and GUI (represented by components) distinguish between an "enterprise part" and a "store part": within the component Data this distinction is manifested directly in the components Enterprise and Store. Within the components Application and GUI the distinction is between Reporting and Store. The former is, according to the deployment of Inventory::Application::Reporting on the EnterpriseServer (see [10, Fig. 6]), not only part of the enterprise context but also located at the store server (as part of Inventory::Application). However, according to the use case descriptions and sequence diagrams of [10], Reporting seems actually not to be used in the store context. In fact, the functionality of this component is exclusively to generate reports for the enterprise manager. Therefore we decided to model Store and Enterprise as functional components on their own. An enterprise may contain a number of stores comprising an inventory and a cash desk line. Reporting then is part of Enterprise but not of Store as this seems to model the application domain of the required trading system more naturally. The Data layer of the CoCoME is represented by the component Data with ports modelling the enterprise and the store related data aspects. Notice that, as required in the CoCoME, different instances of the Data component may share the same instance of a DataBase component. This issue depends on a concrete system configuration only. Last, the GUI layer is represented by the operator ports of the components Enterprise and Store.

Further structural deviations concern the original component Data::Persistence which is in our approach not modelled explicitly but integrated with the port modelling of the Data component instead. Also, the sequence diagram [10, Fig. 6] concerning the product exchange among stores of the same enterprise (Use Case 8) shows a component ProductDispatcher which is not mentioned in the structural view of the CoCoME. We modelled this component as part of the enterprise component.

9.3.2   Trading System — Stores and Enterprises

This section describes the specifications for the root component TradingSystem as well as the two fundamental components Stores and Enterprises, all of them being composed from further components.

TradingSystem.   The composite component TradingSystem in Fig. 4 provides flexible instantiation possibilities for different system configurations. As will be evident from the specifications of the composite components Enterprise and Store described hereafter, the former contains, among others, a number of stores and a Store in turn contains further components such as the CashDeskLine. In fact a system configuration following the hierarchy further down from one instance of Enterprise already suffices to meet the original CoCoME requirements for a trading system with an enterprise and a number of stores which belong to this enterprise. In this case the sets of simpleStores and simpleStoresDB would be empty as these are used only in case of extended system configurations with stores independent from any enterprise.

The bank component, required for card payment at the cash desks of a store, is considered external to the trading system. Therefore the component TradingSystem declares a relay port of type CDA-Bank to delegate incoming and outgoing communications between a bank and internal components, respectively. The port multiplicity with a lower bound of 1 of indicates that for a proper instantiation of TradingSystem it is strictly required to provide appropriate bank connections to the system.

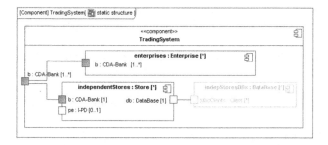

Fig. 4. Static structure of the component TradingSystem

Beyond, the component TradingSystem allows for several further system configurations. For example the system might be used with store components which are independent of any enterprise. On this account the TradingSystem contains a set of stores (simpleStores), each of them connected to its own instance of a data base (simpleStoresDB). Since the port feature pe:I-PD is required only for stores belonging to an enterprise, the port must not be connected in this case.

Enterprise. An enterprise is modelled by the composite component Enterprise in Fig. 5. It consists of a number of stores, of a component Reporting which provides means to create several reports from the enterprise manager's point of view, of a component Data as an intermediate layer between Reporting and the concrete DataBase which

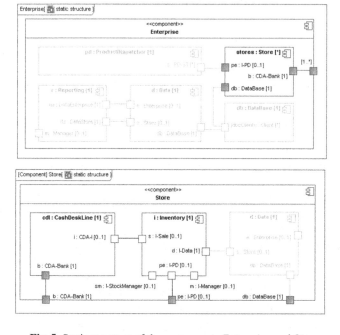

Fig. 5. Static structure of the components Enterprise and Store

is also instantiated as part of an Enterprise and shared between Data and the stores, and finally of a component ProductDispatcher to coordinate the product exchange among the stores of the enterprise.

In order to provide connections for the bank ports b of the contained stores, the component uses a relay port with multiplicity 1..* and instantiates one port for each store. Hence, in contrast to the cash desks as part of the CashDeskLine (Fig. 6) the different stores of an enterprise do not share the same bank connection.

Store. As depicted in Fig. 5 the component Store is a composition of a CashDeskLine (see Sect. 9.3.3), an Inventory (see Sect. 9.3.4) and an instance of the component Data. The inventory is connected to the Data instance hiding the concrete data base from the application as required in the CoCoME. In contrast to the enterprise context, the port e : Enterprise of Data is not used, when instantiating the component as part of a Store. The optional operator ports of Inventory remain unconnected, as we did not model explicit GUI components. These would be connected to the particular ports for testing purposes; in the deployed system we may also connect actual operator interfaces.

The component Store uses mandatory relay ports to connect to a bank component and a data base. Relaying the port I-PD of component Inventory is optional, in order to take into account the requirements of the exceptional processes in Use Case 8 (enterprise server may be temporally not available). Optionality is also required for system configurations with stores that are independent of any enterprise. In this case, there is definitely no other store to exchange products with.

9.3.3   Cash Desks — The Embedded System Part

Any store instantiated as part of the trading system comprises a cash desk line which in turn represents a set of cash desks, monitored by a coordinator. Each cash desk consists of several hardware devices managed by a cash desk PC. The specification of the cash desk line models the embedded system part of the CoCoME with characteristic features of reactive systems such as asynchronous message exchange or topologies with a distinguished controller component. The former is illustrated by the subsequent behaviour specifications for ports and components, the latter is exemplified directly in the static structure of the composite component CashDesk with the cash desk application playing the role of the controlling component at the centre (Fig. 7). Due to this topology, most of this section is devoted to the specification of the component CashDeskApplication.

CashDeskLine. A CashDeskLine (Fig. 6) consists of at least one cash desk connected to a coordinator which decides on the express mode status of the cash desks. The composite component CashDeskLine declares two relay ports delegating the communication between the cash desks, the inventory (i : CDA-I) and the bank (b : CDA-Bank).

The connector declarations in Fig. 6 are annotated with the stereotype adapter of kind seq, meaning that the communication between the ports of the cash desks and the relay ports i and b respectively, is implemented by a sequential adapter. In contrast, the communication between the cash desks and the coordinator does not need to be adapted, because each CashDesk instance is linked via its CDA-C port to its own instance of the coordinator port C-CD. To share the bank connection among the desks of a cash desk

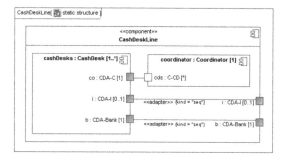

Fig. 6. Static structure of the component CashDeskLine

line follows the CoCoME requirement in [10, Fig. 6] which shows a multiplicity of 1 for the particular required Bank interface, port respectively.

CashDesk (CD). The CashDesk component specified in Fig. 7 is the most complex composite of the trading system. The component consists of six components modelling the hardware devices as described in the CoCoME and one component modelling the cash desk application. A cash desk has three relay ports to allow for the communication with a bank, inventory and coordinator component. The component and port multiplicities of the static structure in Fig. 7 reflect the requirements of the CoCoME. Since an exceptional process for Use Case 1 (Process Sale [10]) explicitly mentions that the inventory might not be available, the relay port i may sometimes not be connected. The optional ports of CashBox, Scanner and CardReader model the communication of an operator with the particular hardware device. In case of a cash desk actually deployed, these ports might be connected with some low-level interrupt handler.

CashDeskApplication (CDA). The cash desk application links all internal components of a cash desk and communicates with components external to the cash desk such as a

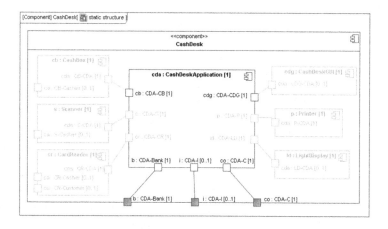

Fig. 7. Static structure of the component CashDesk

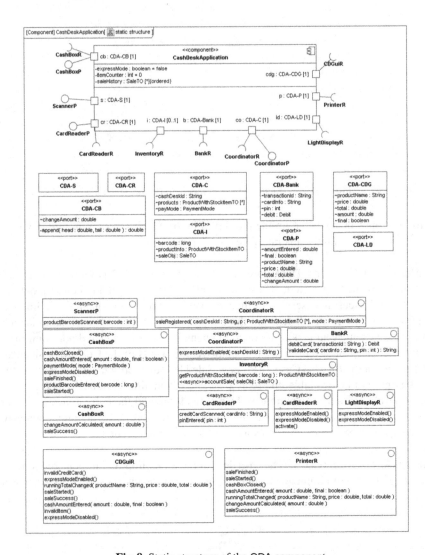

Fig. 8. Static structure of the CDA component

bank, the inventory or the coordinator. In order to facilitate the particular communication, CashDeskApplication declares one port for each. Figure 8 (top) shows an overview of the component with its private state as well as its ports and interfaces; the ports' state attributes and the interface details are given in the middle and lower region respectively. As a naming convention, we have used component abbreviations such as CDA-CB for the port types and the suffixes R (P) for interfaces required (provided) by a port.

In the following we briefly describe representative port behaviours of the CDA. Thereafter, we discuss the specification of the component behaviour which interrelates the constituent port behaviours within a single state machine.

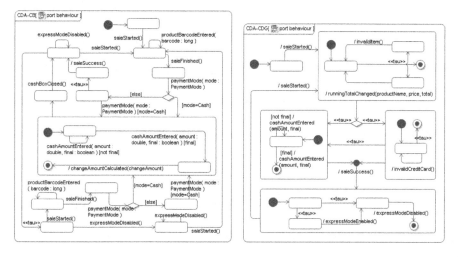

Fig. 9. Behaviour of the CDA ports CB and CDG

CDA Port Behaviour. The state machine CDA-CB in Fig. 9 specifies the communication between the cash desk application and the cash box (CB). In general, the state machine for a port receives events and signals named in the provided interface of that port and sends out signals and events named in the required interface of that port. After initially having received the signal saleStarted, defined in the port's provided interface CashBoxP in Fig. 8, the port may receive arbitrary many manually entered product bar codes before moving to the next state due to the reception of saleFinished; manually entered product bar codes are part of an exceptional process in Use Case 1 of the CoCoME. The next step within the sale process is the selection of card or cash payment as the payment procedure. If payment mode Cash was selected, the port waits for messages concerning the cash amount received from the customer. It sends back information concerning the change amount calculated (by sending changeAmountCalculated defined in CDA-CB's required interface CashBoxR in Fig. 8), assumes that the cash box is subsequently opened and finally waits for the cash box to be closed again. If payment mode CreditCard was chosen, the port changes to a state where the chosen mode may be cancelled by switching to cash payment and, additionally, a τ-transition may be triggered internally, whereupon the cash box should be prepared to receive a saleSuccess as a signal for the successful clearing of the sale process via card payment. In both cases the port waits afterwards for the next saleStarted and until then allows to disable the express mode the cash desk may have been switched into in the meantime.

In contrast to the behaviour at an "input" port, Fig. 9 also shows an example for an "output" port behaviour: the specification of CDA-CDG, which is intended to connect to the cash desk's GUI. In fact the behaviour is very similar to the specification of CDA-P, connecting to the printer (not shown here). Both ports signal the status of the sale process such as saleStarted or saleFinished and both show mostly internal choice transitions. The main difference is that only the GUI port signals problems with the credit card (invalidCreditCard). Also, besides the light display, it is the GUI which is notified in case of mode switches from or to express mode.

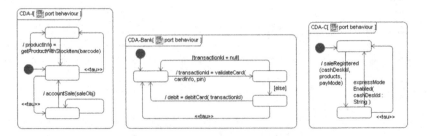

Fig. 10. Behaviour of the CDA ports I, C and Bank

The communication with components external to the cash desk is prescribed by the port behaviour specifications for CDA-I, CDA-Bank and CDA-C shown in Fig. 10. The port behaviours of CDA-I and CDA-Bank demonstrate our modelling of synchronous communication. The behaviour of CDA-C is used in Sect. 9.4.1 to illustrate our formal analysis of functional requirements.

For a discussion on the behaviour specifications of the remaining ports CDA-S, CDA-CR, CDA-P and CDA-LD not relayed to the environment, we refer to [9].

CDA Component Behaviour. Figure 11 specifies the component behaviour of the cash desk application. Using the port declarations of the static structure in Fig. 8 it shows the dependencies and inter-linkages between the different ports of the CDA. For example messages sent via ports p or cdg such as p.saleStarted and cdg.saleStarted are sequentially arranged after the message cb.saleStarted was received at port cb. Furthermore port attributes as well as component attributes such as itemCounter are assigned as an effect, and afterwards used as actual parameters in messages sent.

Since the specification of the cash desk application's behaviour is rather involved we used submachines to factor out the major steps of the entire sale process. For lack of space we refer to [9] for their detailed specification. However, a brief description may

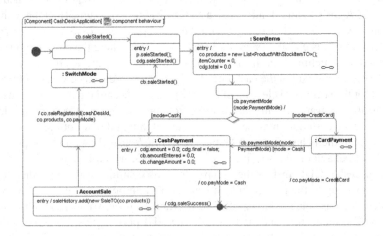

Fig. 11. Component behaviour of CashDeskApplication

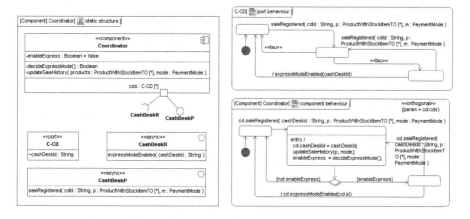

Fig. 12. Static structure and behaviour specifications of Coordinator

provide an intuitive understanding of the component's behaviour: after saleStarted was received at the cash box port cb, the submachine ScanItems repeatedly receives product bar codes and notifies the printer and the GUI about product details like name and price. Thereafter the payment mode must be chosen, resulting in a transition to the corresponding submachine. CardPayment may be left at any state by the reception of cb.paymentMode(Cash) modelling the cashier's ability to switch from card to cash payment, e.g., in case of problems with the credit card. Before the sale process is completed the component tries to account the sale at the inventory using port i within AccountSale. If the inventory is not available the sale information is stored locally and delivered during the next sale processes. Finally, in SwitchMode the component waits for a signal to switch into express mode, to disable a previous express mode, or to start a new sale.

Coordinator (C). The cash desk line (see Fig. 6) of a store consists of a number of cash desks and an instance of Coordinator, see Fig. 12, which decides on the mode of the cash desks (express or normal). The component declares its port of type C-CD with multiplicity * to allow to connect an arbitrary number of cash desks, which should be monitored by this coordinator. Note that even if the coordinator decided for express mode, the port may receive yet another sale registration from the same cash desk because the communication partners are executing concurrently. In this case the sale registration has precedence over the coordinator's decision: the port recomputes its internal decision.

The component behaviour shown alongside the port behaviour in Fig. 12 illustrates the modelling of internal actions of a component which are hidden by τ-transitions in the port behaviour specification. For each cash desk the component keeps track of the particular sale history and decides upon this history to eventually switch a cash desk into express mode. The update of the sale history is synchronised (annotation sequential) due to the concurrent execution of the port instances cd in cds.

9.3.4 Inventory — The Information System Part

The information system part is modelled with an inventory at the core. The inventory plays a crucial role in the Use Cases 3, 4, 7 and 8 (see [10, Figs. 6,6,6,6]), which

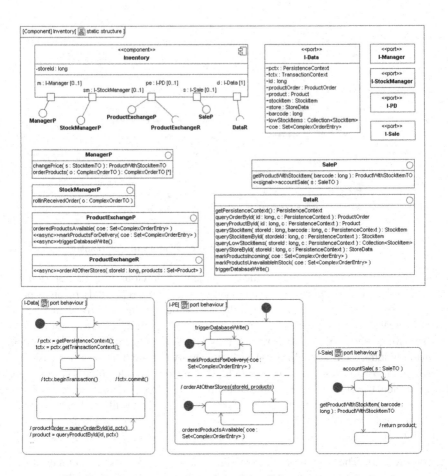

Fig. 13. Static structure and port behaviour of the component Inventory

describe how to order products, receive ordered products, change the price of a product and how products might be exchanged among the stores of a enterprise. The most prominent new modelling aspect with respect to the embedded system part in Sect. 9.3.3 is the specification of synchronous message call receptions. The specifications of Data, Reporting, ProductDispatcher and DataBase can be found on our web page [9].

Inventory (I). The component Inventory[1] is a model of the store's portion of the application layer of the CoCoME. As depicted in the static structure of Fig. 13, Inventory provides two optional ports m : I-Manager and sm : I-StockManager to allow for manager and stock manager requests. The behaviour specifications of these ports are trivial and omitted here. The ports may be used for instance to connect simulation components in order to test the developed system or, of course, to connect actual control interfaces in the deployed system.

---

[1] Note that our component Inventory models Inventory::Application::Store of [10], see Sect. 9.3.1.

The ports of type I-Data and I-Sale are used to connect to the data layer of a store component and to the cash desks of the store, respectively. As the port behaviour of I-Data in Fig. 13 exemplifies for two operations of the interface DataR, any operation call on the data layer is transactional, i.e., is framed by an explicit transaction start (tctx.beginTransaction) and end (tctx.commit); the remaining operations of DataR are applied analogously. Connections via I-Sale support the reception of messages required during the sale process at a cash desk.

The component declares a port pe : I-PE in order to cope with product exchange among stores as described in Use Case 8 of the CoCoME. The port behaviour specification in Fig. 13 uses an orthogonal state with two regions to model the two distinct roles of an inventory: the port may request to order some products at the other stores of the enterprise, i.e., play the active role of initiating product exchange; on the other hand, it provides a trigger for a data base update with possibly cached and not yet submitted data, as well as to mark products for delivery to other stores, i.e. playing the passive role of being asked for product exchange. Both messages are eventually received during a connection with the component ProductDispatcher (see Fig. 5) responsible to coordinate the product exchange among the stores (see [10, Fig. 6]).

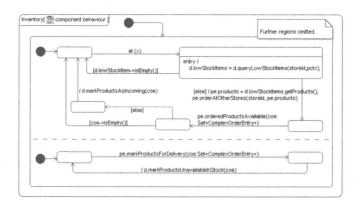

Fig. 14. Component behaviour of the Inventory (regions omitted)

The component behaviour specification of Inventory comprises of six orthogonal regions, essentially each of them modelling the interaction with one possible communication partner along the ports of the component. For a lack of space, Fig. 14 shows only two of them. Again, for more details we refer to [9]. The regions shown illustrate part of the interplay between the ports d and pe in the course of executing a product exchange among stores. The upper region specifies the component's behaviour with respect to the inventory's check if the stock is getting low for some products. The check occurs cyclical after some not further specified time period x. The lower region shows the direct forwarding of a product order actually to be executed. Note, that we do not show the message exchange related to the transactional data communication with port d. For this purpose the operation calls on d would simply be framed by begin and commit transitions analogously to the port behaviour of I-Data.

9.4 Analysis

9.4.1 Analysis of Functional Requirements

For the analysis of the functional requirements we focus on the semantical properties of our CoCoME model specified by the behaviour specifications of ports and components in Sect. 9.3. We consider the asynchronous part of our model for the CoCoME and we will check deadlock-freeness and component correctness. For the synchronous, information-oriented part we believe that the behavioural aspects of message exchange and parallel execution, which are in the centre of our interest here, are not so relevant.

The basic idea of our approach is to proceed hierarchically, starting from the analysis of (local) properties of simple components and their ports from which we can then derive, by a compositionality theorem, properties of composite components. Thus, following the hierarchical construction of components, we obtain results for the behaviour of the global system. Our analysis process consists of the following steps:

1. For each simple component we analyse
   - the behaviour specification of each of its ports,
   - the behaviour specification of the component itself, and
   - the relationships between the component behaviour and the behaviour specified for each of its ports.
2. For each composite component we analyse
   - the interaction behaviour of connected ports,
   - the behaviour of the composite component which can be inferred from the behaviours of its constituent parts, and
   - the relationships between the behaviour of the composite component and the behaviour of each of its relay ports.

The semantic basis of our study are the given UML state machines for the behaviour specifications of ports and components. In order to treat them in a formal way, we represent them by labelled I/O-transition systems which are automata with an initial state and with distinguished *input* (or *provided*), *output* (or *required*), and *internal* labels. Additionally, we assume that there is a special *invisible* (or *silent*) action τ.[2] Two I/O-transition systems A and B (over the same I/O-labelling) are *observationally equivalent*, denoted by $A \approx B$, if there exists a weak bisimulation relation between A and B, e.g. in the sense of [11], where all actions apart from τ are considered to be visible. We also use standard operators on I/O-transition systems like *relabelling*, *hiding* and the formation of *products*.[3] In some cases we will need a simple form of relabelling of an I/O-transition system A, denoted by $n.A$, where the labels of A are just prefixed by a given name n thus obtaining a copy of A. An I/O-transition system A is *deadlock-free* if for any reachable state there is an outgoing sequence of transitions $\tau^* a \tau^*$ with some label $a \neq \tau$ preceded and followed by arbitrary many τ actions. The observational equivalence relation is compatible with deadlock-freeness and, moreover, it

---

[2] Internal actions are not invisible; to construct particular component views, they can, however, be hidden.

[3] The product of two I/O-transition systems is used to model their parallel composition with synchronisation on corresponding input/output labels.

is preserved by the above mentioned operators on transition systems. For the precise technical definitions we refer to [9].

Let us first consider how behaviour specifications of ports are represented by I/O-transition systems. As pointed out in Sect. 9.2 a port has a provided and a required interface. For calls of operations of the provided interface we use input labels; for sending an operation request according to the required interface of a port we use output labels. In most cases the label is just the name of an interface operation where we have abstracted from operation parameters and results which is possible if the transitions in the original state machine do not depend on the arguments and results of the operation. In the other cases we must assume, for the purpose of model checking later on, that the impact of arguments and/or results and/or guards occurring on UML transitions can be resolved by a finitary case distinction which is encoded by appropriate labels. Note, that transitions with the invisible action τ can occur in the behaviour specification of a port in order to model a possible internal choice (of the port's owner component) which is not visible at the port but may have an impact on the future behaviour of the port.

As a concrete example we consider the component Coordinator and the behaviour specification of its port C-CD; see Fig. 12. The corresponding I/O-transition system, shown in Fig. 15, is directly inferred from the behaviour specification.[4] According to the given behaviour specification of the port, the silent action τ represents a non-visible choice whether an express mode should be enabled or not.

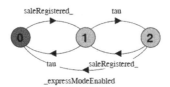

Fig. 15. I/O-transition system for port C-CD

Let us now look to the behaviour specifications of simple components and their representation by I/O-transition systems. A simple component contains a set of port declarations of the form $p : P[mult]$ where p is a port name, P its port type and $mult$ specifies the port multiplicity indicating how many instances of that port a component (instance) can have. Since a component can only communicate with its environment via its ports, any input label of a component has the form $p.i$ where p is a port name and i is an input label of the port. Similarly, the output labels of a component have the form $p.o$. For the definition of input and output labels of components we do not take into account here the multiplicities of ports. This is possible if we assume that actions of different port instances of the same port declaration are independent from each other which is indeed the case in our example. In the following we will always omit multiplicities in port declarations. In contrast to ports, components can have internal labels which are just given by some name representing an internal action of the component.

---

[4] For the representation of the transition systems we have used the LTSA tool (cf. Sect. 9.5) which does not support the symbol "/" used in UML state machines. In order to indicate that i is an input label we use i_- and, symmetrically, to indicate that o is an output label we use $_-o$.

Again, for the purpose of model checking, we assume that arguments, results and/or guards of internal operations are encoded into appropriate labels.

As an example we consider the behaviour specification of the Coordinator component (see Fig. 12). The behaviour specification uses an entry action and a pseudo-state for a guarded alternative which both have to be resolved in the corresponding transition system. For representing the entry action we introduce the (internal) label entry and for representing the two guarded alternatives we introduce two internal labels enableExpress, describing the decision that the express mode should be enabled, and notEnableExpress, expressing the converse case. Operation calls have now the prefix cds of the port on which the operation is received or sent. The whole transition system representing the behaviour of the Coordinator component is shown in Fig. 16.

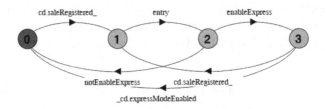

Fig. 16. I/O-transition system for component Coordinator

Analysis of Simple Components. In the first step of our model analysis we consider simple components which are the basic building blocks of our system model. For each simple component we check the deadlock-freeness of the behaviour specifications of each of its ports and of the component itself. Obviously, this condition is satisfied for all simple components and ports of our behavioural model for the CoCoME.

A more subtle point concerns the relationships between the behaviour of a component and the behaviour specified for each of its ports which must in some sense fit together. To consider this issue more closely, let C be a component with associated behaviour represented by the I/O-transition system A_C and let $p : P$ be a port declaration of C such that the behaviour specification associated to P is represented by the I/O-transition system A_P. Intuitively, the component C is correct w.r.t. its port declaration $p : P$ if the component behaviour supports the behaviour specified for that port. Apparently this is the case if the component's behaviour observable at port p is observationally equivalent to the behaviour specification of P (up to an appropriate relabelling).

Formally, the *observable behaviour of* C *at port* p, denoted by $obs_p(C)$, can be constructed by hiding all labels of A_C which do not refer to p. Using the hiding operator, $obs_p(C)$ is just $A_C \setminus H$ where the set H of hidden labels consists of the internal labels of A_C together with all input or output labels $q.op$ of A_C such that $q \neq p$. Since the transition system $obs_p(C)$ has no internal labels and, up to the prefix p, the same input and output labels as A_P we can now require that it is observationally equivalent to $p.A_P$, i.e., $obs_p(C) \approx p.A_P$ (where $p.A_P$ is the copy of A_P explained above). In this case we say that the component C is *correct w.r.t. its port declaration* $p : P$.

Let us illustrate how we can check the correctness of the component Coordinator w.r.t. to a port instance cd of type C-CD. First we consider the observable behaviour of the Coordinator at the port instance cd which is just the transition system shown in Fig. 16 where all labels which are not prefixed by cd are replaced by τ. If we minimise this transition system w.r.t. observational equivalence then we obtain (up to the prefix cd) the transition system in Fig. 15 which represents the behaviour of the port type C-CD. This shows the correctness of the Coordinator component. Indeed we have checked with the LTSA tool (cf. Sect. 9.5) that all simple components occurring in the CashDesk and CashDeskLine composite components (cf. Sect. 9.2) are correct.

The definition of the observable behaviour of a component at a particular port can be generalised in a straightforward way to arbitrary subsets of the port declarations of a component and, in particular, to the case where all ports of a component are simultaneously considered to be observable. For a component C, the latter is called the *(fully) observable behaviour* of C and denoted by $obs(C)$.

Obviously, the above definitions of correctness and observable behaviour apply not only to simple but also to composite components considered in the next step.

Analysis of composite components. The analysis of composite components is related to the task of a system architect who puts components together to build larger ones. Before we can analyse the behaviour of a composite component it is crucial to consider the connections that have been established between the ports of their subcomponents.

Analysis of connectors. For the analysis of connectors one has first to check whether the connections between the ports of components are syntactically well-defined. After that we can analyse the interaction behaviour of two connected ports.

In the following let us consider a connection between two port declarations $p_l : P_l$ and $p_r : P_r$ occurring in components C_l and C_r respectively. The connection is syntactically well-defined, if the operations of the required interface of P_l coincide with the operations of the provided interface of P_r and conversely.[5] To study the interaction behaviour of the two ports, let A_{P_l} and A_{P_r} be the I/O-transition systems representing the behaviour of P_l and P_r, respectively. Any communication between the connected ports is expressed by synchronising output labels of one port with the corresponding input labels of the other port. Hence, the interaction behaviour of A_{P_l} and A_{P_r} can be formally represented by the *port product* $A_{P_l} \otimes A_{P_r}$ of A_{P_l} and A_{P_r}; see [9] for the definition of products.

A first semantic condition which should be required for a port connection is that any two port instances can communicate with each other without the possibility to run into a deadlock which means that the port product is deadlock-free. In this case we say that the ports are *behaviourally compatible*.

Let us, for instance, consider the composite component CashDeskLine (cf. Fig. 6) which has one connector between the port CDA-C of the CashDesk component and the port C-CD of the Coordinator. The transition system representing the behaviour of the port CDA-C (cf. Fig. 10) is shown in Fig. 17 (top) and the transition system representing the behaviour of the port C-CD was shown in Fig. 15. Hence, the interaction behaviour of the two ports is represented by the transition system of their port product which is

---

[5] Our approach would also allow a more general condition where the required operations of one port are included in the provided operations of the other one which, however, is not needed for the current case study.

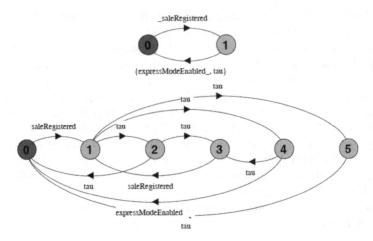

Fig. 17. Port product of CDA-C and C-CD

shown in Fig. 17 (bottom). Obviously, the port product has no deadlock and therefore the two ports are behaviourally compatible.

In general, the potential capabilities for interaction of a port will not be used when the port is connected to another port. In this case the behaviour specified for that port is restricted by the interaction with another port. It is, however, often the case that this restriction applies only to one side of a connection while the behaviour of the other port is not restricted and hence fully reflected by the interaction. Given two ports P_l and P_r with behaviours represented by I/O-transition systems A_{P_l}, A_{P_r} respectively, the interaction behaviour of P_l and P_r *reflects* the behaviour of P_l, if the port product is observationally equivalent to the behaviour of P_l, i.e. $A_{P_l} \approx (A_{P_l} \otimes A_{P_r})$. This property plays an essential role for the compositionality of component behaviours considered below. An obvious consequence of this definition is that if the interaction behaviour of P_l and P_r reflects the behaviour of P_l (P_r resp.) and if the behaviour of the port P_l (P_r resp.) is deadlock-free, then P_l and P_r are behaviourally compatible.

For instance, let us consider again the port product of CDA-C and C-CD in Fig. 17 (bottom). After minimisation of the transition system w.r.t. observational equivalence with the LTSA tool we obtain just the transition system of the port CDA-C; cf. Fig. 17 (top). Hence, the interaction behaviour of CDA-C and C-CD even reflects the behaviour of the port CDA-C.

Analysis of the behaviour of composite components. In contrast to simple components the behaviour of a composite component is not explicitly specified by the developer but can be derived from the behaviours of the single parts of the composite component. For that purpose we construct the product of the transition systems representing the observable behaviours of all subcomponents declared in a composite component whereby the single behaviours of the subcomponents observed at their ports are synchronised according to the shared labels determined by the connectors. Hence, we focus on the interactions between the subcomponents (via their connected ports) and on the actions

on the relay ports of the composite component while the internal behaviour of the subcomponents is not relevant; see [9] for the detailed definitions.

Of course, one may again construct the observable behaviour of a composite component which then could be used for further analysis but also for the construction of the
behaviour of another composite component on the next hierarchy level. When climbing
up the hierarchy of composite components one can always first perform a minimisation
of the observable behaviour of the subcomponents before the behaviour of the composite component on the next level is constructed. This technique can indeed be very
efficient to reduce the state space of nested components because, depending on the application, many (or even all) τ-transitions may be removed.[6] In fact, our experience
shows that in this way there is often not even an increment of the size of the state
space [12].

In the following we focus on checking the deadlock-freeness of the behaviour of a
composite component. It is well-known that, in general, the deadlock-freeness of subcomponents does not guarantee the deadlock-freeness of a global system (as nicely
illustrated by Dijkstra's philosophers example). Indeed this is unfortunately still the
case if all components are correct w.r.t. their ports (in the sense from above) and if
all ports are connected in a behaviourally compatible way, as soon as more than two
subcomponents are involved. Hence, we are looking for particular topologies of component structures where deadlock-freeness is preserved. An appropriate candidate are
(acyclic) star topologies as shown in Fig. 18 containing one central component C with
n ports such that each port is connected to the port of one of the components C_i for
$i = 1, \ldots, n$.

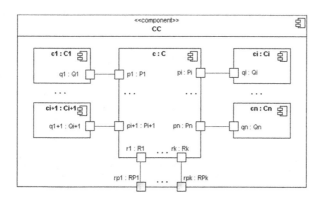

Fig. 18. Star topology of composite component

We assume that all single subcomponents, C and C_i, are correct w.r.t. their ports
and that their local behaviours are deadlock-free. Then, if all connected ports are behaviourally compatible, the composite component CC can only deadlock if at least
two ports $p_\alpha : P_\alpha$, $p_\beta : P_\beta$ of the central component C are connected to ports $q_\alpha : Q_\alpha$,
$q_\beta : Q_\beta$ of components C_α and C_β resp. such that the behaviours specified for both port

---

[6] Only τ-transitions occurring in an alternative may not be removable according to the well-
known fact that alternatives are i.g. not compatible with the observational equivalence.

types Q_α and Q_β properly restrict the behaviour of P_α *and* of P_β in an incompatible way.[7] This may happen, if C introduces a dependency between P_α and P_β that is incompatible with the simultaneous restrictions imposed by the connections with Q_α and Q_β on both sides of C. An example for such a situation is provided in [12]. If, however, at most the behaviour of one port of C is restricted by the connection and the interaction behaviours of all other connections reflect the behaviour of all other ports of C then deadlock-freeness is preserved by the component composition. This fact is expressed by the following theorem (for the proof see [12]) which shows that indeed for the global deadlock check it is enough if the subcomponents are locally checked for deadlock-freeness and correctness and if the architect of the composite component checks each single port connection on the basis of the interaction behaviour of the connected ports.

Theorem 1 (Deadlock-freeness of composite components). *Let* CC *be a composite component with component structure as shown in Fig. 18. Let the following hold:*

1. *The components* $C_1, \ldots, C_n$ *are correct w.r.t. their ports* $q_1 : Q_1, \ldots, q_n : Q_n$ *resp., and* C *is correct w.r.t. to each of its ports* $p_1 : P_1, \ldots, p_n : P_n$.
2. *All I/O-transition systems representing the behaviours of* $C_1, \ldots, C_n$ *and* C *are deadlock-free.*
3. *For all* $i \in \{1, \ldots, n-1\}$ *the interaction behaviour of* P_i *and* Q_i *reflects the behaviour of* P_i.
4. *The ports* P_n *and* Q_n *are behaviourally compatible.*

Then the I/O-transition system representing the behaviour of CC *is deadlock-free.*

This theorem is related to a result of Bernardo et al. [13] which is also motivated by the derivation of global properties from local ones, not using an explicit port concept, however. In [13] a significantly stronger condition is used requiring what we call "behaviour reflection" for all connections between components with no exception where behavioural compatibility is sufficient as in the above theorem. A further generalisation of the theorem to arbitrary many non behaviour reflecting but behavioural compatible connections is given in [12] which, however, needs further assumptions.

We can directly apply Thm. 1 to analyse the behaviour of the composite component CashDesk (cf. Fig. 7) where CashDeskApplication plays the role of the central component C. As pointed out above all subcomponents of CashDesk are correct w.r.t. their respective ports and their behaviour is deadlock-free. We also have analysed (with HUGO/RT and the LTSA tool, see Sect. 9.5.1) the given connectors between the ports of CashDeskApplication and the ports of the other subcomponents of CashDesk. It turns out that the port CDA-CB of CashDeskApplication is behaviourally compatible with the port CB-CDA of the CashBox component and that for all other connected ports the interaction behaviour even reflects the behaviour of the corresponding port of CashDeskApplication. Hence, Thm. 1 shows that the component CashDesk does not deadlock. We can also show (see [9]) that the CashDesk component is correct w.r.t. its relay ports.

---

[7] Note that it is sufficient to consider the behaviours of the *ports* of C_α and C_β instead of considering the observable behaviour of the components C_α and C_β since both components are assumed to be correct w.r.t. their respective ports.

Following our analysis method we now go one step up in the component hierarchy and consider the composite component CashDeskLine (cf. Fig. 6) which has connected subcomponents of type CashDesk and Coordinator. Obviously, the structure of CashDeskLine fits again to the component structure assumed in Thm. 1. Hence, we can directly apply Thm. 1 since we know that CashDesk is correct and deadlock-free, Coordinator is correct and deadlock-free (see paragraph on the analysis of simple components), and that the connection between the ports (of type) CDA-C and C-CD reflects the behaviour of CDA-C (see paragraph on the analysis of connectors). Thus component CashDeskLine does not deadlock and, according to the reflection of the appropriate port behaviour, it is also correct w.r.t. its relay ports.

Note again that we did not take into account here multiplicities of component declarations which means in this example, that we have disregarded the number of CashDesk instances that are connected to one Coordinator instance. This abstraction works because, first, the Coordinator instance has as many port instances of type C-CD as there are cash desks connected, and, more importantly, the interactions of the coordinator with the single cash desks are independent. More formally, this means that if there are n cash desks connected to the coordinator then arbitrary interleaving is allowed and thus deadlock-freeness of the cash desk line does not depend on n.

Let us now come back to the original proposal of the CashDeskLine structure which has used an event bus for communication [10]. We have refrained from using the event bus in the design model, as we believe that the introduction of an event bus is an implementation decision to be taken after the design model has been established and analysed. Indeed we could introduce right now an implementation model which implements the communication between the components of the CashDesk and CashDeskLine in terms of an event bus, provided that the bus follows the first-in first-out principle. Then, obviously, the order of communications between the single components specified in our design model would be preserved by the implementation model and hence the deadlock-freeness of the design model would also hold for the event bus based implementation.

This concludes the behavioural analysis of the asynchronous part of our model for the CoCoME which was in the centre of our interest. For the synchronous, information-oriented part we suggest to apply pre-/post-condition techniques which have been lifted to the level of components in our previous [14] and recent [15] work.

9.4.2 Non-functional Requirements

We perform quantitative analysis of the Process Sale Use Case 1 by modelling the example in the process algebra PEPA [5] and mapping it onto a Continuous-Time Markov Chain (CTMC) for performance analysis. The analysis shows that the advantage of express checkout is not as great as might be expected. Currently, however, this analysis has to be performed manually; a closer integration could be achieved by decorating UML state machines and sequence diagrams with rate information using the UML performance profile as in the Choreographer design platform [16], allowing a PEPA model to be extracted from the UML diagrams.

Model. Markovian models associate an exponentially distributed random variable with each transition from state to state. The random variable expresses quantitative information about the rate at which the transition can be performed. Formally, a random variable is said to have an exponential distribution with parameter λ (where $\lambda > 0$) if it has the probability distribution function F with $F(x) = 1 - e^{-\lambda x}$ if $x > 0$, and $F(x) = 0$ otherwise. The mean, μ, of this exponential distribution is $\mu = \int_0^\infty x\lambda e^{-\lambda x}dx = 1/\lambda$. Thus if we know the mean value of the duration associated with an activity then we can easily calculate from this the rate parameter of the exponential distribution: $\lambda = 1/\mu$.

In the case where we only know the mean value then the exponential distribution is the correct distribution to use because any other distribution would need to make additional assumptions about the shape of the expected distribution. However, for example in the case of waiting for credit card validation, the extra-functional properties state that we have a histogram representing the distribution over the expected durations stating that with probability 0.9 validation will take between 4 and 5 seconds and with probability 0.1 it will take between 5 and 20 seconds.

We encode distributions such as these in the process algebra PEPA as an immediate probabilistic choice followed by a validation occurring at expected rate (4.5 is mid-way between 4 and 5 and 12.5 is mid-way between 5 and 20 so we use these as our means).

$$(\tau, 0.9 : \mathbf{immediate}).(validate, 1/4.5) \ldots$$
$$+ (\tau, 0.1 : \mathbf{immediate}).(validate, 1/12.5) \ldots$$

Whichever branch is taken, the next activity is validation; the only difference is the rate at which the validation happens. In Fig. 19 we show how 700000 values from a uniformly-distributed interpretation of the histogram for credit card validation would differ from the exponentially-distributed interpretation.

In our experience, a distribution such as that shown in Fig. 19 (left) is unlikely to occur in practice. For example, it has the surprising property that delays of four seconds are very likely but delays of three seconds are impossible. Also, there is a very marked difference between the number of delays of five seconds and delays of six. In contrast, distributions as seen from our sample in Fig. 19 (right) occur frequently because they are a convolution of two heavy-tailed distributions. Other histogram-specified continuous distributions are treated similarly. We first make a weighted probabilistic choice and then delay for a exponentially-distributed time.

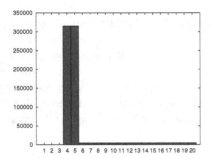 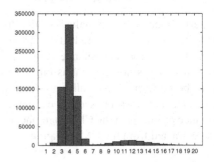

Fig. 19. Specified (left) and sampled (right) distributions for credit card validation

Analysis. From our process algebra model we obtain a finite-state continuous-time Markov chain represented as a matrix, Q, to be analysed to find the probability of being in each of the states of the model. At equilibrium the probability flow into every state is exactly balanced by the probability flow out so the equilibrium probability distribution can be found by solving the *global balance equation* $\pi Q = 0$ subject to the normalisation condition $\sum_i \pi(x_i) = 1$. From this probability distribution can be calculated performance measures of the system such as throughput and utilisation.

From this information we can assess a service-level agreement for the system. A service-level agreement typically incorporates a time bound and a probability bound on paths through the system behaviour. We considered the advantage to be gained by using the express checkout where customers in the queue have no more than 8 items to purchase. As would be expected, the sale is always likely to be completed more quickly at the express checkout but the advantage is not as great as might be expected. At the express checkout 50% of sales are completed within 40 seconds as opposed to the 44 seconds spent at a normal checkout (see Fig. 20 (right)). In our model we included the possibility of customers with 8 items or fewer choosing to go to a normal checkout instead of the express checkout, because we have seen this happening in practice. This goes some way to explaining why the difference in the results is not larger.

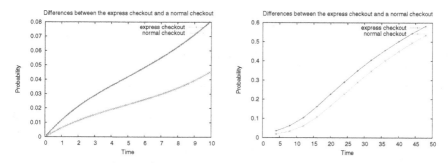

Fig. 20. Graphs showing how the advantage of using the express checkout (8 items or fewer) over using a normal checkout (100 items or fewer) varies over 10 (left) and 50 seconds (right)

9.5 Tools

9.5.1 Qualitative and Quantitative Analysis

HUGO/RT. HUGO/RT [17] is a UML model translator for model checking, theorem proving, and code generation: A UML model containing active classes with state machines, collaborations, interactions, and OCL constraints can be translated into the system languages of the real-time model checker UPPAAL, the on-the-fly model checker SPIN, the system language of the theorem prover KIV, and into Java and SystemC code. The input can either be directly be given as an XMI (1.0, 1.1) file or in a textual format called UTE (for an example see Fig. 22).

In the CoCoME, we use HUGO/RT for two purposes: On the one hand, we check the deadlock-freedom of connectors by translation into a model checker; however, as currently HUGO/RT's model checking support is limited to finite-state systems, abstraction has to be applied (manually) to infinite parameter domains. On the other hand, we use code generation into Java for component behaviours (see Sect. 9.5.2).

LTSA. For producing the graphs of the I/O-transition systems used in the behavioural analysis of our model and for the analysis of component correctness and behaviour reflection of ports we have used the Labelled Transition System Analyser (LTSA [11]). The LTSA tool supports the process algebra FSP [11] and, indeed, we have defined appropriate FSP processes for most of the transitions systems used in our model for the CoCoME. In this way we have expressed port products by parallel composition with synchronisation on shared labels and we have proved observational equivalence of transition systems by exploiting the minimisation procedure of LTSA. The concrete form of the used FSP processes is not shown here but can be examined in [9].

PEPA. PEPA (Performance Evaluation Process Algebra [5]) is a process algebra that allows for quantitative analysis of the CoCoME using Continuous-Time Markov Chains (CTMC). For the quantitative analysis of Sect. 9.4.2 we used the IPC tool [6].

9.5.2   Architectural Programming

JAVA/A [1,7] is a Java-based architectural programming language which features syntactical constructs to express JAVA/A component model elements (see Sect. 9.2) directly in source code. Thus, the implementation of a component-based system using JAVA/A is straightforward. Additionally, JAVA/A programs gain robustness with respect to architectural erosion: it is obvious to software maintainers which parts of the code belong to the architecture and therefore need special attention during maintenance.

We implemented a subset of the CoCoME, consisting of one component CashDesk including all of its sub-components and a simplified component Inventory to highlight JAVA/A as implementation language for component-based systems. Fig. 21 shows the source code of the top level composite component SimplifiedStore which contains the CashDesk and the Inventory. The assembly (l. 2–3) declares the sets of component and connector types which may be used in the configuration of the composite component. The initial configuration, consisting of one cash desk connected to one inventory, is established in the constructor of the composite component (l. 4–11). Components which are declared with the additional keyword `active` will be started after the

```
   composite component SimplifiedStore {
 2   assembly { components { Inventory, CashDesk }
                connectors { Inventory.Sale, CashDesk.CDAI; } }
 4   constructor Store() {
       initial configuration {
 6       active component Inventory inv = new Inventory();
         active component CashDesk cd = new CashDesk();
 8       connector Connector con = new Connector();
         con.connect(inv.Sale, cd.CDAI);
10     }
     }
12 }
```

Fig. 21. JAVA/A composite component SimplifiedStore

```
  simple component CashDeskApplication {
2   int itemCounter = 0; ...
    port CDACB {
4     provided { async saleStarted();
                 async productBarCodeEntered(int barcode);
6                async saleFinished();
                 async paymentModeCash(); ... }
8     required { void changeAmountCalculated(double amount);
                 void saleSuccess(); }
10    protocol <! behaviour {
        states { initial init;
12              simple a; simple b; simple e; ... simple h; }
        transitions { init -> a;
14                     a -> b { trigger saleStarted; }
                       b -> b { trigger productBarCodeEntered; }
16                     ...
                       e -> h { effect out.saleSuccess(); }
18                     h -> b { trigger saleStarted; }
                     } } !>
20  } ...
    void saleStarted() implements CDACB.saleStarted() {
22    Event event = Event.signal("send saleStarted", new Object[]{});
      this.eventQueue.insert(event);
24  } ...
    void processSaleStarted() {
26    try {
        CDAP.saleStarted();
28      CDACDG.saleStarted();
      }
30    catch (ConnectionException e) { e.printStackTrace(); }
    } ...
32 }
```

Fig. 22. The JAVA/A simple component CashDeskApplication

initialisation process (which basically consists of initialising and connecting the components).

In Fig. 22 we give a very brief overview of the JAVA/A implementation of the component CashDeskApplication.[8] In lines 3–20 the port CDACB is declared (see Fig. 9). Provided operations annotated with the keyword `async` instead of a return type are asynchronous. The port protocol (lines 10–19) is specified using the language UTE. In order to verify the absence of deadlocks of the connection of two ports, the JAVA/A compiler is closely integrated with HUGO/RT (see Sect. 9.5.1).[9]

The operations declared in a port's provided interface must have a realisation in the respective port's component. The implementation of the provided operation `saleStarted` of the port CDACB is shown in lines 21–24. In the body of the private helper method `processSaleStarted` (lines 25–31) required port operations are invoked. These invocations leave the component's boundaries and therefore the checked exception `ConnectionException` has to be handled.

We have used HUGO/RT to generate Java-based implementations of the state machines to realise the components' behaviour. Thus the components' behaviour adheres

---

[8] Of course, most of the component's body is omitted here. However, the complete implementation is available online [9].

[9] In contrast to Sect. 9.3, in the JAVA/A implementation port names are written without hyphens due to Java naming conventions.

strictly to the specifications given in the previous sections. However, to use the specified state machines for code generation, a few minor adoptions have been necessary: i.e., calls to required port operations are delegated to internal helper operations (e.g. `processSaleStarted` in Fig. 22, lines 25sqq.) and parameter values of incoming operation calls are stored in helper variables. The complete JAVA/A implementation of the simplified CoCoME is available online [9].

9.6   Summary

Our approach to modelling the CoCoME has been based on a practical component model with a strong focus on implementability and modular (component-wise) verification. In fact our UML based component model was originally introduced for the architectural programming language JAVA/A supporting encapsulation of components by ports. Based on the semantic foundations, we have that our strategy for modular verification of properties of hierarchically constructed components works for the architectural patterns used in the CoCoME. The semantic basis of our functional analysis was given in terms of I/O-transition systems to which we could apply standard operators, for instance for information hiding, thus focusing only on the observable behaviour of components on particular ports. Although the port-based approach alone does not suffice for guaranteeing full component substitutability, the analysis method can be used to ensure special properties, like deadlock-freedom, compositionally. These properties are transferred to the architectural programming language JAVA/A by code generation where deadlock-freedom corresponds to the ability of the components to communicate indefinitely. For non-functional properties, we used continuous-time Markov chains to quantify performance.

Currently we are developing support for modelling runtime reconfigurations of component networks. This will be necessary if the CoCoME requirements would be extended, e.g., to use cases for opening and closing cash desks. Also, the current component model does not directly integrate means for specifying non-functional properties. Our component model assumes that all connectors are binary which, due to the possibility to define ports with an arbitrary multiplicity, is no proper restriction. However, our analysis method actually supports multiplicities greater than one only if the actions of parallel executing instances of the same port or component declaration can be arbitrarily interleaved, which was indeed the case in the example. In the centre of our behavioural analysis was the interaction behaviour of components with asynchronous message exchange via their ports. For synchronous, data-oriented behaviours we still should add assertion-based techniques (e.g., in terms of pre- and post-conditions) whose integration in a concurrent environment, however, needs further investigation.

Acknowledgement. We would like to thank the organisers for the detailed preparation of the common component modelling example. We gratefully acknowledge many very useful and detailed comments made by the referees of a previous version of this study. We also would like to thank Mila Majster-Cederbaum for many fruitful discussions on the topic of interacting systems and their verification.

References

1. Baumeister, H., Hacklinger, F., Hennicker, R., Knapp, A., Wirsing, M.: A Component Model for Architectural Programming. In: Barbosa, L., Liu, Z. (eds.) Proc. 2nd Int. Wsh. Formal Aspects of Component Software (FACS 2005). Elect. Notes Theo. Comp. Sci, vol. 160, pp. 75–96 (2006)
2. Selic, B., Gullekson, G., Ward, P.T.: Real-Time Object-Oriented Modeling. John Wiley & Sons, New York (1994)
3. Object Management Group: Unified Modeling Language: Superstructure, Version 2.0. Technical report, OMG (2005)
4. Lau, K.K., Wang, Z.: A Survey of Software Component Models (Second Edition). Technical Report CSPP-38, School of Computer Science, The University of Manchester (2006)
5. Hillston, J.: A Compositional Approach to Performance Modelling. Cambridge University Press, Cambridge (1996)
6. Bradley, J., Clark, A., Gilmore, S.: User manual for ipc: The Imperial PEPA Compiler (05/02/07), http://www.doc.ic.ac.uk/ipc
7. Hacklinger, F.: JAVA/A – Taking Components into Java. In: Proc. 13th ISCA Int. Conf. Intelligent and Adaptive Systems and Software Engineering (IASSE 2004), ISCA, Cary, NC, pp. 163–169 (2004)
8. Perry, D.E., Wolf, A.L.: Foundations for the Study of Software Architecture. ACM SIGSOFT Softw. Eng. Notes 17(4), 40–52 (1992)
9. Baumeister, H., Clark, A., Gilmore, S., Hacklinger, F., Hennicker, R., Janisch, S., Knapp, A., Wirsing, M.: Modelling the CoCoME with the JAVA/A Component Model (05/02/07), http://www.pst.ifi.lmu.de/Research/current-projects/cocome/
10. Reussner, R., Krogmann, K., Koziolek, H., Rausch, A., Herold, S., Klus, H., Welsch, Y., Hummel, B., Meisinger, M., Pfaller, C., Mirandola, R.: CoCoME — The Common Component Modelling Example. In: The Common Component Modeling Example: Comparing Software Component Models, ch. 3 (2007)
11. Magee, J., Kramer, J.: Concurrency — State Models and Java Programs. John Wiley & Sons, Chichester (1999)
12. Hennicker, R., Janisch, S., Knapp, A.: On the Compositional Analysis of Hierarchical Components with Explicit Ports (submitted, 2007) (06/22/07), http://www.pst.ifi.lmu.de/Research/current-projects/cocome/
13. Bernardo, M., Ciancarini, P., Donatiello, L.: Architecting Families of Software Systems with Process Algebras. ACM Trans. Softw. Eng. Methodol. 11(4), 386–426 (2002)
14. Hennicker, R., Baumeister, H., Knapp, A., Wirsing, M.: Specifying Component Invariants with OCL. In: Bauknecht, K., Brauer, W., Mück, T. (eds.) Proc. GI/OCG-Jahrestagung, vol. 157/I of books@ocg.at., pp. 600–607. Austrian Computer Society (2001)
15. Bidoit, M., Hennicker, R.: A Model-theoretic Foundation for Contract-based Software Components (submitted, 2007), http://www.pst.ifi.lmu.de/people/staff/hennicker/
16. Buchholtz, M., Gilmore, S., Haenel, V., Montangero, C.: End-to-End Integrated Security and Performance Analysis on the DEGAS Choreographer Platform. In: Fitzgerald, J.S., Hayes, I.J., Tarlecki, A. (eds.) FM 2005. LNCS, vol. 3582, pp. 286–301. Springer, Berlin (2005)
17. Knapp, A.: Hugo/RT Web page (05/02/07), http://www.pst.ifi.lmu.de/projekte/hugo

10 Linking Programs to Architectures: An Object-Oriented Hierarchical Software Model Based on Boxes

Jan Schäfer, Markus Reitz, Jean-Marie Gaillourdet, and Arnd Poetzsch-Heffter

University of Kaiserslautern, Germany

10.1 Introduction

Modeling software systems has several purposes. The model provides a communication means between developers, a backbone to specify and check properties of the system, and a structure to organize, explain, and develop the implementation of the system. The focus of our approach is to address these purposes for hierarchically structured, object-oriented software systems. The hierarchical structure refers to the component instances at runtime: a *runtime component* may consist of a dynamically changing number of objects and other runtime components. Our modeling technique builds on and extends the concepts of class-based object-oriented languages. Runtime components are created by instantiating *box classes*. The modeling technique provides ports to tame object references and aliasing and to decouple components from their environment. It supports *dynamic linkage,* i.e. ports can be connected and disconnected at runtime. The used concurrency model is based on the join calculus.

Hierarchical software models allow to structure a system into components of different sizes where large components are recursively built from smaller ones. Dynamic linkage enables modeling of client–server behavior and open systems. For such systems, it is more difficult to separate the typical architectural level that deals with components and connectors and the realization level that describes the internals of components. The reasons are:

1. The architectural description on one layer of the hierarchy is the implementation of the component one layer up in the hierarchy.
2. Dynamic linkage is tighter intertwined with realization aspects.

Our approach to achieve a deeper integration of the architectural and component realization is by integrating them based on a common semantical framework supporting executable models. The development of our modeling technique is still in progress. CoCoME provided us with an interesting case study to evaluate our approach and to compare it to other techniques.

10.1.1 Goals and Scope of the Component Model

The goal of our approach is to fill the gap between high-level description techniques and the implementation of component-based systems. We use a two-layer

A. Rausch et al. (Eds.): Common Component Modeling Example, LNCS 5153, pp. 238–266, 2008.
© Springer-Verlag Berlin Heidelberg 2008

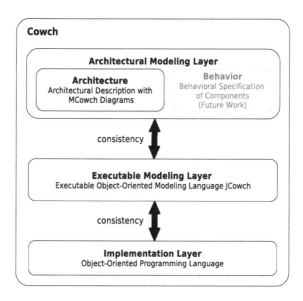

Fig. 1. The COWCH approach

approach with an executable modeling layer just above the implementation to describe the behavior of a system, and a graphical description language on top of that layer to describe the runtime architecture of the executable layer. Our component model is closely related to object-oriented programming languages allowing us to clearly identify components on the code-level. This is the cornerstone to achieve consistency between architectural descriptions and implementation.

10.1.2   Modeled Cutout of CoCoME

We used our graphical architectural description technique to give a hierarchical overview to the whole CoCoME system. Our focus are the structural aspects of the system at runtime. The behavior of the system can be fully described by our executable model. However, we only show this exemplarily in this paper, as our executable model is closely related to the implementation level it is straightforward to create that model for CoCoME. Although we are working on the behavioral specification of object-oriented components, we are not able to formulate functional properties yet. Non-functional properties are not in the focus of our approach, but could be integrated in principle.

10.1.3   Benefit of the Modeling

Our modeling technique has the benefit that it is close to the underlying implementation. This allows to identify components on the code-level, providing a link between high-level descriptions and implementation. This link makes it easier to ensure consistency between these layers, preventing erosion of architectures. As our model is hierarchical, it allows to concisely describe the architecture of an implementation in a top-down fashion. Our system describes the runtime structure of an object-oriented system, allowing to capture the aliasing of components, which is an important feature distinguishing our approach from others that only describe the class and package-level of systems. In addition, we provide a high-level concurrency mechanism based on the join calculus which allows to express concurrency in terms of asynchronous messages and synchronization by join patterns.

10.1.4   Effort and Lessons Learned

We needed one person month to understand any detail of the system to be modeled. This includes understanding the delivered reference documentation as well as the delivered reference implementation. As our executable model is close to the underlying implementation it was not difficult to find an executable model for CoCoME. Most time went into drawing the graphical architectural model, as we do not have productive tools for this task, yet. Altogether it took us approximately one person month for creating our models. An additional person month was needed to write this paper. So the CoCoME contest took us about three person months in total.

We have been able to successfully model the CoCoME system with the COWCH approach. The resulting MCOWCH diagrams provide high-level and concise views to the CoCoME system. The CoCoME contest gave us valuable feedback to improve our modeling technique.

Related Work. Architectural Description Languages (ADLs) [1] serve as high-level structuring techniques for software systems. Examples include Darwin [2], Wright [3], Rapide [4], and UniCon [5]. These languages allow the formal description of software architectures as well as the specification and verification of architectural and behavioral properties on the architectural level. However, ADLs are loosely coupled to implementation languages, making it difficult to check consistency of architectural description and the actual implementation. Without consistency, however, all guarantees on the architectural level are lost on the implementation level.

A different approach is to extend programming languages by architectural elements. Examples for these approaches are ArchJava [6], ComponentJ [7], and ACOEL [8]. The advantage of these approaches it that there is no gap between architecture and implementation. The disadvantage is that they do not provide high-level views on the structure of a system. In addition, these approaches do not introduce new concurrency constructs, making it difficult to apply them to distributed systems.

Our approach falls into both mentioned categories. We define an executable modeling language which is closely related to the underlying implementation language. This language contains architectural elements which define the runtime structure of programs within the programming language. In addition, we define a graphical description language to describe the architecture of a system. The semantics of that language is closely related to the executable modeling language so consistency checking is easier, when compared to implementation-independent ADLs.

Overview. The remainder of this paper is structured as follows. In the next section we give a general overview and introduction to our approach. Section 10.2.1 explains the executable modeling layer. The parts of the architectural model layer used in this paper are described in Section 10.2.2. Our model of the Co-CoME system is given in Section 10.3. We shortly discuss analysis techniques for our approach in Section 10.4. Current tool support is sketched in Section 10.5. Finally, we give a summary in Section 10.6.

10.2   Component Model

Our COWCH[1] provides three layers of abstraction: the implementation layer, the executable modeling layer, and the architectural modeling layer (cf. Figure 1). On the implementation layer, the system is described using ordinary programming languages. In our current setting, we use Java as the language of the implementation layer.

To describe executable models, we develop an object-oriented modeling language called JCOWCH. JCOWCH provides support for hierarchical heap structuring and encapsulation, ports to make component interfaces and component linkage more explicit, and a high-level concurrency mechanisms based on the join calculus [9]. The sequential core of JCOWCH is based on Java's statements and object-oriented features. An implementation is consistent with a JCOWCH model if it has the same behavior at the interfaces of runtime components (see [10] for a formal treatment of component behavior). In the future we plan to specify the behavior of components on the architectural layer. We also plan to develop (semi-)automatic methods to verify consistency between executable modeling and implementation layer. Another goal is to generate efficient and consistent implementations from executable models.

The architectural modeling layer provides a high-level view on the system which only consists of the hierarchy of component instances and their communication structure. This layer abstracts from the creation and linkage phase of components and describes dynamic restructuring behavior of a system only by underspecification (in the future this layer will as well support behavioral specification of component properties). The architectural model is consistent with an executable model if the structure and component connections of the system during runtime correspond to the structures and connections described by the architectural models. Again, consistency can be achieved by checking techniques and by generating the structural aspects of the executable model from the architectural model.

Software components have to support composition by providing contractually specified interfaces and explicit dependency descriptions [11, p. 41]. As a prerequisite for this, the COWCH approach provides the notion of runtime components

---

[1] Component-oriented Development with Channels.

with well-defined boundaries and ports as communication points to its surrounding environment. Ingoing ports represent functionality usable by other entities within the environment whereas outgoing ports define functionality needed for proper functioning of the component. Communication with other entities in a component's environment is routed through its ports. Components which create other runtime components are responsible for establishing the connections between them.

10.2.1   The Executable Modeling Layer

In this section we describe the executable modeling language JCowch. The sequential part of JCowch is based on Java's statements and object-oriented features. We do not explain these standard features here and refer to the Java language specification [12]. Here we explain the central constructs to structure the heap, to control component interfaces, and to handle concurrency. We first describe the core elements of the language, and then show convenience extensions.

JCowch: Core Language

Boxes. A runtime component or component instance in our approach is called a *box*. A box consists of an *owner object* and a set of other objects. A box is created together with its owner by instantiating the class of its owner. Boxes are tree-structured, that is, a box b can have *inner* boxes. We distinguish two kinds of classes, normal classes and box classes (annotated by the keyword box). The instantiation of a normal class creates an object in the *current box*, that is, in the box of the current this-object. The instantiation of a box class creates a new inner box of the current box together with its owner. For simplicity, we do not support the direct creation of objects outside the current box. Such nonlocal creations can only be done by using a method. Note that this is similar to a distributed setting with remote method invocation. Currently, we do not support the transfer of objects from one box to another one.

Our approach only uses structural aspects of ownership (similar to [13]). It uses the box boundary to distinguishes between local method calls and external calls, i.e. calls on ports or objects of other boxes. We use the term *component* for the pair consisting of a box class and its *code base* where the code base of a class is defined as the smallest set containing all classes and interfaces transitively used by the class.

Boxes allow to clearly separate objects into groups which semantically belong together. This clear separation can then be used to describe the behavior of such runtime components in a representation-independent way [10]. In Cowch, boxes are the foundation for interfaces and the architectural structure. Boxes are used to control object references crossing box boundaries. Only the box owner is allowed to be used directly from the outside. All other internal objects can only be accessed through ports. Currently, this restriction is not enforced by the type system of JCowch, so the programmer must manually ensure this discipline.

Work to incorporate ownership type systems into JCOWCH are under way (see [14] for first steps).

Channels and Ports. A formally well-understood way to structure communication is to use channels [15, 16]. A channel is a point-to-point connection between two partners. In our approach, these partners are ports or objects. Channels are *anonymous*, i.e. two partners connected via a channel communicate without "knowing" each other. This supports a loose-coupling of communication partners. It also allows transparent *exogenous coordination* [16], i.e. communication partners can be transparently changed at runtime. The anonymity of channels allows to specify component behavior in an abstract way. A channel is also *private*, as communication cannot accidentally or intentionally be interfered by third parties [16]. This also means that it is always clear which entities can communicate with each other by looking at the channel structure. This gives strong invariants which support system verification.

In JCOWCH we use channels to express box communication. *Peer* boxes, i.e. boxes with the same surrounding box, can only communicate via channels. In addition, the surrounding box is allowed to directly call methods on inner boxes by using the reference returned when an inner box was created. Communication links crossing more than one layer in the box hierarchy can only be established by forwarding. Thus the surrounding box controls all communication to and from inner boxes.

The notion of a port defines a component's relationship to its surrounding environment. *Ingoing ports* represent functionality usable by other entities within the environment whereas *outgoing ports* define functionality needed for proper functioning of the component.

Ingoing Ports. An ingoing port in JCOWCH is a member of a class and is declared by the keyword **inport**. A simple ingoing port declaration may look as follows:

```
box class A {
  inport J p {
    void m() { }
  }
}
```

Class A has a single ingoing port p of type J. J is an interface with a single method m(). The ingoing port in this example provides a trivial, empty implementation of interface J. An inport can be used by connecting it to another port (see below) or by direct use from the surrounding box. If a is variable of type A referencing an inner box, method m() of port p can be invoked by a.p.m(). It is also possible to treat ports similar to objects, to assign them to local variables, and to use them like ordinary object references, e.g. J b = a.p.

A class having an ingoing port p of a type J is responsible for providing an implementation for p. This implementation can be provided directly as part of the port declaration (see above) or indirectly by connecting the ingoing port to an inner object or port (connections are explained below). In that case the ingoing port is declared without a body.

Outgoing Ports. Outgoing ports are declared by the keyword **outport**. Like in-going ports they have a type and a name, but they do not provide an implementation. From a class's perspective, an outgoing port is an interaction point with the environment. The implementation of outgoing ports must be provided by the environment, which is complementary to ingoing ports. A simple declaration of an outgoing port may look as follows.

```
box class B {
  outport J q;
  void n() {
    q.m();
  }
}
```

Class B declares an outgoing port q of type J. Like ingoing ports, outgoing ports can be used like regular object references. The difference is that the actual implementation of an outgoing port is determined at runtime depending on the channels established by the environment.

Connect Statements. To provide an implementation for an outgoing port, the environment has to create a channel from that port to another port or object. A channel in JCOWCH is created by a **connect** statement with the following syntax:

```
connect <source> to <sink>
```

The source parameter has to be a reference to a port, the sink parameter can be either an object reference or a port reference. After the **connect** statement has been executed, all method invocations on the source are forwarded to the sink. As connect statements must not break type-safety, the type of the sink expression has to be a subtype of the source expression. Calling a method on an unconnected outgoing port results in a runtime exception being thrown.

The following example reuses the classes A and B. The outgoing port q of an instance of A is connected to the ingoing port q of an instance of B. As port b.q is connected to port a.p and method n invokes m on port q, the effect of b.n() is essentially the same as calling a.p.m() directly.

```
box class C {
  A a = new A();
  B b = new B();
  void k() {
    connect b.q to a.p;
    b.n();
    a.p.m(); // same effect
  }
}
```

Deleting a previously created channel is performed by the **disconnect** statement, having the following syntax:

```
disconnect <source> from <sink>
```

If no channel exists from the given source to the given sink, the statement has no effect.

Concurrency. Modern software systems need distributed and local concurrency. A modeling language has to be both flexible with respect to the concurrency patterns it supports and restrictive to achieve controlled concurrent behavior. To approach these goals, JCOWCH combines the concurrency model of the join calculus [9] with the structuring and interfacing techniques of boxes. Concurrency models based on the join calculus have already been integrated into OCaml (called JoCaml [17]), $C^{\#}$ (called C^{ω}[18]), and Java (called Join Java [19]). Similar to these realization, JCOWCH does not support the explicit creation of threads. Instead, it distinguishes between synchronous and asynchronous methods.

Synchronous methods are syntactically and semantically similar to methods in object-oriented programming languages like Java or $C^{\#}$. The caller waits until the called method terminates, receives its return value if any, and continues execution. Asynchronous methods are denoted by the keyword **async** in place of a return type. They have no return value. Calling an asynchronous method causes it to be executed concurrently to the caller without blocking the caller. Calls to asynchronous methods implicitly spawn a new thread. Synchronization of threads is expressed by *chords*.

Chords. Chords, or *join patterns*, provide a powerful and elegant synchronization mechanism which groups methods that wait for each other and share one method body. That is, chords can be considered as a generalized construct for method declaration. Syntactically, a chord is a method with multiple method signatures separated by &. In the body, the arguments of all method signatures are accessible. There may be at most one synchronous method per chord. The body of a chord is executed when all methods it includes have been called, i.e. calls to methods which are part of a chord are enqueued until the chord is executed.

A method header may appear in several chords. It is dynamically decided to which chord it contributes, depending on which chord is executable first. These unbounded method queues extend the state space of objects. Chords must not appear in interfaces, whereas the methods they consist of are declared in interfaces.

The code in Fig. 2 shows an unbounded asynchronous buffer for strings. An arbitrary number of calls of method *put* is stored in conjunction with the corresponding arguments and removed when appropriate *get* method calls arrive.

JCowch: Convenient Extensions to the Core

The language elements described so far are the core of JCOWCH. We now introduce some additional concepts which can be seen as convenience constructs to make the life easier for developers in practice.

Optional Ports. We said above that the environment has to provide an implementation for an outgoing port. Invoking a method on an unconnected outgoing

```
interface StringBuffer {
  async put(String s);
  String get();
}
class StringBufferImpl implements StringBuffer {
  String get() & put(String s) { return s; }
}
```

Fig. 2. An unbounded buffer

port results in a runtime exception. However, it is often the case that a component has outgoing ports which it does not require to work properly. For example, a logger port for debugging purposes is in general not needed by a component. It is just a port to inform the environment of some events happening inside the class. These kinds of messages are typically called *oneway messages* [20]. For this reason we introduce *optional* outgoing ports in contrast to *required* outgoing ports. Outgoing ports are by default required and can be declared to be optional by using the optional keyword. An unconnected optional port acts as a *Null Object* [21]. If a method is called on such a port, the method call is silently ignored. For simplicity, we only allow calls to **void** and **async** methods on optional ports.

Nested Ports. So far ports have been flat in the sense that they only contained methods. However, to be able to hierarchically structure interfaces of larger components, it is essential to have *nested ports*. To enable port nesting, interfaces have to be extended to allow the declaration of ports. A simple interface J with a single port declaration of type K may look as follows:

```
interface J {
  port K k;
}
```

The direction of a nested port is left open in the interface. Thus such interfaces can be used for ingoing as well as outgoing ports. The direction of the nested ports is always equal to the direction of its surrounding port. For example, a class can have a port of type J, which in turn has nested port K. If that port is an ingoing port, the class has to provide an implementation for the port itself and the nested port. Assuming an interface K containing a single method m(), this looks as follows.

```
class A {
  inport J p {
    inport K k {
      void m() { }
    }
  }
}
```

Method Channels. In many cases interface-based wiring of ports and objects is the right choice. However, there are at least three situations in which interface-based connections are inconvenient.

1. If two ports with different interfaces should be connected.
2. If only single methods, but not all methods of a port are of interest.
3. If a class only needs one or two outgoing methods with no fitting interface.

The first situation requires the creation of an adapter class that has a port of each interface and which forwards each method of the first interface to the appropriate method of the second interface. The second situation requires the implementation of methods with empty bodies. In the third case the introduction of an artificial interface is needed. Because of these reasons we allow the wiring of single methods.

Method Connections. To be able to connect single methods, we extend the **connect** statement to take method targets as sources and sinks. A method target consists of two parts, the first part is an expression which defines the target object or port of the method, and the second part defines the method which should be used. The second part can be either a simple method name or a full method signature. The latter is needed if the target method is overloaded.

To maintain type-safety the parameter and result types of the sink method must match the parameter and result types of the source method. The matching rules are equal to the overriding rules in regular Java, i.e. the parameter types can be contra-variant and the result types can be co-variant. However, method names are irrelevant when connecting methods, only the parameter and return types are important.

Outgoing methods. To avoid artificial interfaces when only single methods are of interest, we allow the declaration of single *outgoing methods* without ports. Outgoing methods are declared by the keyword **out** and have no body. They can be seen as anonymous ports with a single method. Like outgoing ports, outgoing methods can be declared to be optional by the optional keyword. A simple outgoing method declaration may look as follows.

```
class A {
  out void m();
}
```

A Larger Example

Figure 3 illustrates the use of the discussed concepts. Box class A's only functionality is to forward a call of p.m to q.m after having increased the passed integer parameter by one. Method m of box class B of port in is implemented by calling the outgoing printInt method with the passed integer value being used as parameter. The constructor of box class C creates two inner boxes, one of box class A and one of box class B, and forwards ingoing port in to port p of the inner box A using the **connect** statement. The q port of box A is connected to port in of box B by the **connect** statement. Finally, the outgoing method printInt of box B is forwarded to the print method of the printer port.

Box class C represents a composing entity which creates and wires instances of box class A and B. We defined a new box component with a distinguished behavior. A call of in.m results in increasing the passed integer value by one and then printing the new value to the output stream.

```
interface Print {                    box class B {
    void print(int i);                   inport J in {
    ...                                      void m(int i) { printInt(i); }
}                                        }
                                         out void printInt(int i);
interface J {                        }
    void m(int i);
}                                    box class C {
                                         private A a = new A();
box class A {                            private B b = new B();
    outport J q;                         outport Print printer;
    inport J p {                         inport J in;
        void m(int i) {                  C() {
            q.m(i+1)                         connect in to a.p;
        }                                    connect a.q to b.in;
    }                                        connect b.printInt(int) to printer.print(int);
}                                        }
                                     }
```

Fig. 3. Code example which shows the usage of port and connections

10.2.2 The Architectural Modeling Layer

The architectural modeling layer consists of a graphical language – MCOWCH – depicting the structure and communication topology of the modeled systems. A single MCOWCH diagram describes the internal structure and the communication endpoints of one component of the JCOWCH implementation. The described component is denoted in the upper left corner of the diagram with its full qualified package name. The boundary of a diagram must show all nonprivate methods and ports of the declared box class. Thus an MCOWCH diagram always shows the complete external interface of a component.

Beside this easily derivable information, the diagram shows a conservative view to the runtime structure of its described component, which is done by the following architectural elements.

Architectural Elements. Within MCowch diagrams the following architectural elements can appear.

Inner boxes are indicated by rectangles.

Ports are depicted by the symbols ▶ for outgoing ports and ▶ for ingoing ports. Ports that have interfaces which only consist of asynchronous methods are represented by the symbols ▶ and ▶.

Methods are depicted by the symbols ⊐ for ingoing methods and ⊃ for outgoing methods. Asynchronous methods are depicted by ⊲ and ⊠, respectively.

Channels are indicated by lines with arrows. Thick lines represent port channels, thin lines represent method channels.

Figure 4 shows an MCOWCH diagram which is consistent to the JCOWCH example in Figure 3 on Page 248. It contains most of the architectural elements. The semantics of MCOWCH diagrams is explained in the next section.

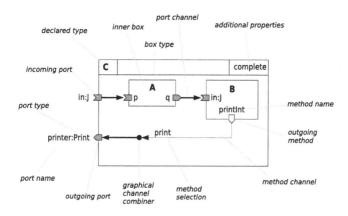

Fig. 4. Example of an MCowch diagram

Relation to the Executable Modeling Layer. An architectural model denotes the static aspects of a program in the executable modeling layer. The semantics of the model are described, rather than defined, by relating the architectural elements of the model to artefacts of the program.

Boxes. Every rectangle drawn in a MCOWCH diagram represents a box that is created by the defined component at runtime. The exact number is determined by the given multiplicity with a default of one. If the given multiplicity is constant it means that during the whole lifetime of the component instance the stated number of boxes exist. This means that these boxes have to be created in the constructor of the component. A plus (+) used as multiplicity denotes one or more boxes, i.e. at least one box must exist during the whole lifetime of the component. A star (*) indicates an arbitrary number of boxes (including zero) being created during the box lifetime. Boxes can be drawn by dashed lines denoting a multiplicity of zero or one.

To be consistent to the underlying implementation, the MCowch diagram must show *all* possibly created boxes. That is, if a diagram is consistent to the underlying implementation, the implementation cannot create boxes that do not appear in the diagram. In addition, all boxes appearing in a diagram can only communicate via the indicated channels.

Channels. The channels appearing in MCowch diagrams represent channels created by **connect** statements in the executable layer during runtime of the defined component. We distinguish *durable* channels and *optional* channels. A solid line indicates a durable channel and represents a channel that always exists at runtime when both connected boxes exist. Usually this means that the channel is directly created after both boxes are created, and it is never disconnected. A dotted line denotes an optional channel, expressing the fact that the channel *might exist* at runtime.

Connecting a line to a rectangle with a multiplicity greater than one implies that there exist a channel for each box of the box set. This allows to express 1 and N:1 connections. To express arbitrary N:M connections we use a special *unknown* connection indicated by a question mark which indicates that connections exist but leaves the exact wiring unspecified.

Helper Objects. An MCowch diagram only illustrates the inner box structure of a component, i.e. all instances of box classes and their connections. It does not show helper objects which are used by the component implementation, i.e. objects of regular non–box classes.

Complete Diagrams. An MCowch diagram can be specified to be *complete*. To be complete, the corresponding component implementation may not have any behavior other than specified by the diagram, it has a constant number of boxes and only durable channels. From a complete MCowch diagram it is always possible to generate its executable model.

Active and Reactive Components. An additional property of components is shown in MCowch diagrams which can be derived from the executable layer, namely whether a component is *active* or *reactive*. Reactive components are only able of reacting to incoming method invocations. This means that after the invoking thread has left the component, a reactive component cannot send any further messages on its outgoing methods or ports. On the other hand, an active component can send messages on its outgoing entities whether or not a method has been invoked on it. On the modeling layer, a component can be identified to be active if it either uses an active component or has an asynchronous method that appears in a chord without a synchronous method, as only these chords can create new threads. If a component has neither an outgoing method nor an outgoing port, the component is always reactive, as the environment cannot observe any activity.

MCowch diagrams of active components are declared to be active in the meta-bar, otherwise they are reactive. In addition, active boxes are drawn with a thicker border than reactive boxes when appearing as boxes in MCowch diagrams.

```
interface J {              box class B {              box class C {
  void m();                  inport J q;                inport J q;
  void n();                  outport J p;               // ...
}                            // ...                    }
                           }
```

Fig. 5. An interface and two box classes needed by the following examples

```
box class A {
  inport J q;
  B b; C c;
  A() {
    b = new B();
    c = new C();
    connect this.q to b.q;
    connect b.p to c.q;
  }
}
```

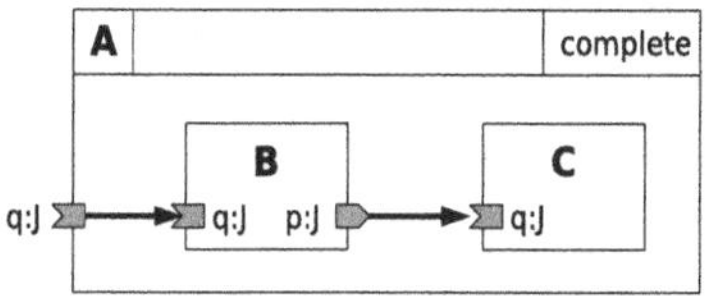

Fig. 6. An implementation of a box class and its corresponding MCOWCH diagram

```
box class D {
  inport J q;
  B b;
  D(boolean createB) {
    if (createB) {
      b = new B();
      connect b.p to c.q;
    }
  }
}
```

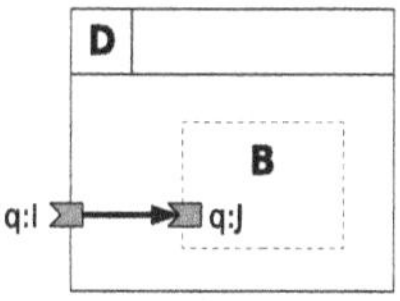

Fig. 7. An example of an optional inner box

Graphical Channel Combiner. To graphically express that a channel is only connected to a part of a port and not the whole port, we allow to explicitly name the connected part and write it next to the channel. This can be combined with the graphical channel combiner. For example in the MCOWCH diagram in Figure 4 the printInt method of the B box is connected to the print method of the printer port.

Examples. To better understand the relation between the modeling and the architectural layer we give some simple examples shown in Figures 6, 7, 8, and 9. On the left side we show the implementation in JCOWCH and on the right side we show an MCOWCH diagram which is consistent to that. We use the interface and the box classes shown in Figure 5 for this purpose.

```
box class E {
  C c;
  B[] b;
  E(int numB) {
    c = new C();
    b = new B[numB];
    for (int i=0; i <numB; i++) {
      b[i] = new B();
      connect b[i].p to c.q;
    }
  }
}
```

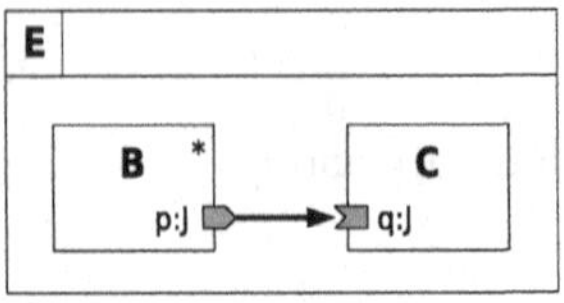

Fig. 8. An example of an arbitrary multiplicity

```
box class F {
  outport J q;
  B b;
  F(boolean createChannel) {
    b = new B();
    if (createChannel) {
      connect b.p to this.q;
    }
  }
}
```

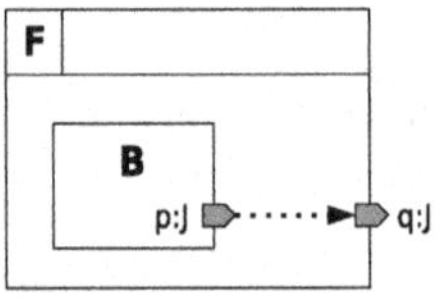

Fig. 9. An example of an optional channel

10.3 Modeling the CoCoME

We now present our model of the CoCoME system. Figure 10 shows a high-level view on the CoCoME system specified by an MCowch diagram. An instance of the CoCoME component consists of a TradingSystem box and a Bank box. In addition, the outgoing bank port (depicted by ▶) of the TradingSystem box is connected to the Bank box. Notice that the rectangle of the TradingSystem box is drawn with a thicker line than the Bank box rectangle, which indicates that the TradingSystem is active and the Bank is reactive. As the CoCoME component has no further functionality the diagram is specified to be complete.

10.3.1 The Bank Component

The Bank component is used to validate credit cards and to debit money from bank accounts. As it is an external component, not modeled by CoCoME, we only give its interface which consists of two ingoing methods (cf. Figure 11).

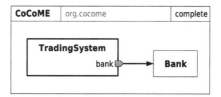

Fig. 10. The top level view on CoCoME

Fig. 11. The Bank component

10.3.2   The TradingSystem Component

To go deeper into the CoCoME system we take a look at the TradingSystem component (cf. Figure 12). The first difference to the CoCoME component is that the TradingSystem component has a port declaration. In this case the port has name bank and is of type Bank. The symbol ▶ indicates that it is an outgoing port. This port declaration is consistent to the port usage in the previous diagram, where the bank port is connected to a Bank instance. The TradingSystem component uses three different components, namely EnterpiseClient, StoreModel, and Database. The number of StoreModel and EnterpriseClient boxes is left unspecified, indicated by a star (*), but there exists exactly one Database box per TradingSystem box as this is the default multiplicity. No matter how many EnterpriseClient or StoreModel boxes exist, the diagram specifies that the db port of each of them is connected to the ingoing (▶) jdbc port of the Database box (the bullet (●) graphically summarizes these two parallel running lines). In addition, the bank port of each existing Store box is connected to the bank port of the TradingSystem box.

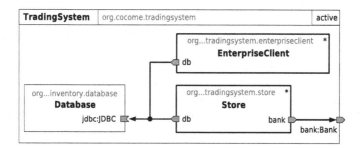

Fig. 12. The TradingSystem component

10.3.3   The EnterpriseClient Component

The EnterpriseClient component is shown in Figure 13. It offers the enterprise manager the possibility to look at the statistical data of the enterprise by using the graphical user interface of the Reporting box. To access the database the EnterpriseClient box uses Application and Data boxes and forwards the outgoing port of the Data box to its own outgoing db port of type JDBC.

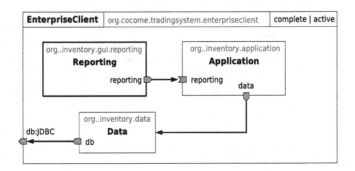

Fig. 13. The EnterpriseClient component

10.3.4   The TradingSystem::Store Component

Figure 14 shows the Store component, which represent a single store. Such a component does not exist in the reference description of CoCoME. We believe that such a component is useful and thus we give a model here. A Store box consists of a single CashDeskLine box, an Application and a Data box to abstract from the JDBC interface, and an unspecified number of Inventory::GUI boxes to allow the stock manager and the store manager to access the database. In the CoCoME reference implementation the CashDeskLine and the Application communicates via an event bus as well as via RMI. We model the bus communication by an asynchronous method channel, the RMI communication is modeled by synchronous port channels.

10.3.5   The CashDeskLine Component

The CashDeskLine component is shown in Figure 15. An instance of a CashDeskLine consists of several CashDesk boxes and a single Coordinator box. The Coordinator box manages the express checkout, wheras the CashDesk boxes represent the cash desks. Like before, we model the bus communication by asynchronous method channels. In addition, the outgoing bank and inventory ports, as well as the accountSale method of each CashDesk box are forwarded to the corresponding ports and method of the CashDeskLine component.

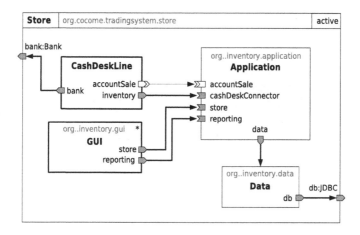

Fig. 14. The Store component

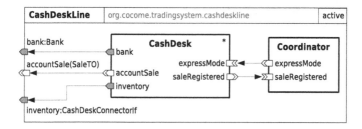

Fig. 15. The CashDeskLine component

10.3.6 The Coordinator Component

Figure 16 shows the Coordinator component, which is responsible for managing express checkouts. For this reason it has an inner SaleStatistics box which collects information about sales. When a call to the saleRegistered is made, it informs an inner SaleStatistics box about the new sale and asks it whether an express mode is needed. If this is the case the outgoing method expressMode is invoked with the previously passed cashdesk string. The MCOWCH diagram is shown in Figure 16. What might not be obvious is that the Coordinator component is active. To clearify this we give its JCOWCH model in Figure 17. As the Coordinator component must access the iternal SaleStatistics box in a sequential way, it has to sequentialize its incoming asynchronous saleRegistered messages. For this reason it has an internal loop which sequentially handles these messages, which is started by invoking the asynchronous waitForMessage method in the constructor. The loop sequentially calls the synchronous handleNextMessage method. As this method is in a chord together with the saleRegistered method, it is only executed when that method has been invoked. This realization ensures a sequential access

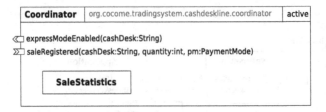

Fig. 16. The MCOWCH diagram of the Coordinator component

```
public box class Coordinator {
  private SaleStatistics saleStats;

  public out async expressModeEnabled(String cashDesk);
  public async saleRegistered(String cashDesk, int quantity, PaymentMode pm);

  public Coordinator() {
    saleStats = new SaleStatistics();
    allowAccess();
    waitForMessage();
  }

  private void handleNextMessage()
    & saleRegistered(String cashDesk, int quantity, PaymentMode pm);
  {
    saleStats.registerSale(quantity,pm);
    if (saleStats.isExpressModeNeeded()) {
      expressModeEnabled(cashDesk);
    }
  }

  private async waitForMessage() {
    while (true) {
      handleNextMessage();
    }
  }
}
```

Fig. 17. The JCOWCH model of the Coordinator component

to the internal SaleStatistics box. It also resembles the semantics of the event
bus system which is used by the CoCoME reference implementation.

10.3.7   The SaleStatistics Component

Figure 18 shows the SaleStatistics component. It calculates the express mode
necessity depending on the sale history. As it has no further inner boxes, the

Fig. 18. The SaleStatistics component

MCOWCH diagram only shows its external interface consisting of two ingoing methods.

10.3.8   The CashDesk Component

The CashDesk component is the most complex component in the CoCoME system. We decided not to directly model the event bus. Instead we present a

```
public interface ScannerEvents {
  async productBarcodeScanned(Barcode b);
}

public interface ApplicationEvents {
  async runningTotalChanged(String productName, double productPrice,
                            double runningTotal);
  async changeAmountCalculated(double changeAmount);
  async saleSuccess();
  async productBarcodeNotValid(long barcode);
  async invalidCreditCard();
}

public interface CashBoxEvents {
  async saleStarted();
  async saleFinished();
  async paymentMode(PaymentMode paymentMode);
  async cashAmountEntered(KeyStroke keyStroke);
  async cashBoxClosed();
}

public interface CardReaderEvents {
  async pinEntered(int pin);
  async creditCardScanned(String cardInfo);
}

public interface ExpressMode {
  async expressModeEnabled(String cashBox);
  async expressModeDisabled();
}
```

Fig. 19. The different interfaces summarizing bus events

conceptional view on the CashDesk component which is behavioral equivalent to the actual implementation. For this reason we structured the different events of the bus that semantically belong together into several new interfaces, which can be seen in Figure 19. Figure 20 shows the CashDesk component. This architectural view shows the exact communication structure of a single cash desk.

10.3.9   The CardReaderController Component

The CardReaderController component abstracts from the card reader hardware (cf. Figure 21). To be able to react to express mode changes, it has an ingoing expressMode port. To send card reader events it has an outgoing events port.

10.3.10   The ScannerController Component

The ScannerController component handles events from the barcode scanner and emits them on its outgoing events port by sending productBarcodeScanned events (Figure 22). As we do not model the scanner hardware, it has no further inner boxes.

10.3.11   The LightDisplayController Component

The LightDisplayController reacts on incoming expressMode messages and switches the light display on or off. It has no further inner boxes (Figure 23).

10.3.12   The CashDesk::Application Component

The CashDesk::Application component is shown in Figure 24. It can be seen as the control center of the CashDesk component. It contains the application logic of the CashDesk component, and it handles the external communication with the Bank, the Inventory and the Coordinator components. As it has no further inner boxes the MCOWCH diagram only shows its interface.

10.3.13   The CashBoxController Component

The CashBoxController component is shown in Figure 25. It represents the cash box which is operated by the cashier. It has an outgoing port events of type CashBoxEvents as well as an outgoing method expressModeDisabled(), which represent the different kinds of keys which may be pressed by the cashier. The only ingoing method cashAmountCalculated(**double**) opens the cash box.

10.3.14   PrinterController

The PrinterController component is shown in Figure 26. It reacts to certain events from the Application and the CashBox component and prints useful information for the customer on a receipt.

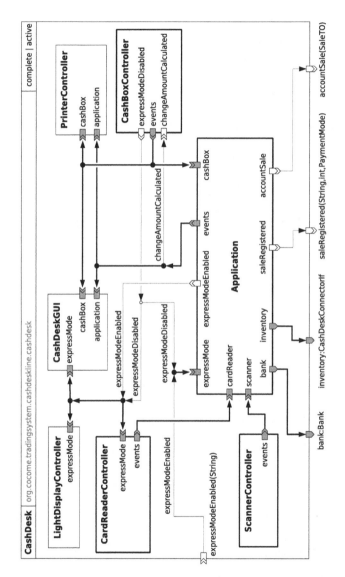

Fig. 20. The CashDesk component

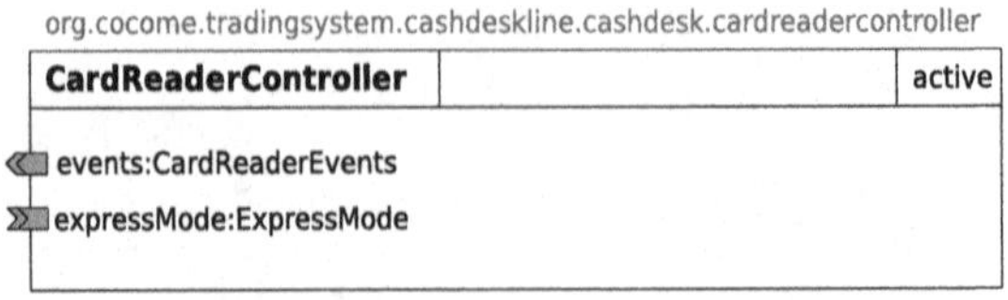

org.cocome.tradingsystem.cashdeskline.cashdesk.cardreadercontroller

CardReaderController		active

◁ events:CardReaderEvents
▷ expressMode:ExpressMode

Fig. 21. The CardReaderController component

org.cocome.tradingsystem.cashdeskline.cashdesk.scannercontroller

ScannerController		active

◁ events:ScannerEvents

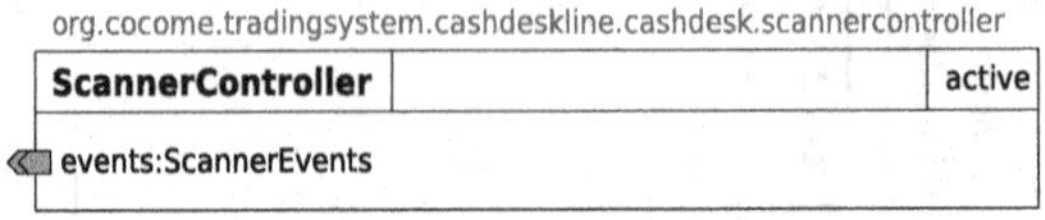

Fig. 22. The ScannerController component

org.cocome.tradingsystem.cashdeskline.cashdesk.lightdisplaycontroller

LightDisplayController	

▷ expressMode:ExpressMode

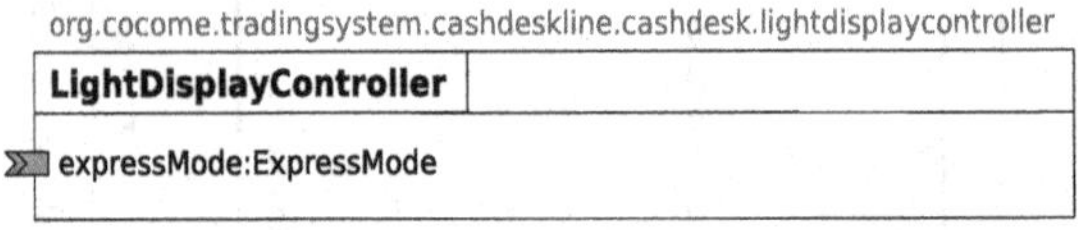

Fig. 23. The light display controller

org.cocome.tradingsystem.cashdeskline.cashdesk.Application

Application		active

◁ events:ApplicationEvents
◁ expressModeEnabled(name:String)
◁ saleRegistered(String, int, PaymentMode)
◁ accountSale(SaleTO)
◁ inventory:CashDeskConnectorIf
◁ bank:Bank
▷ cardReader:CardReaderEvents
▷ expressMode:ExpressMode
▷ cashBox:CashBoxEvents
▷ scanner:ScannerEvents

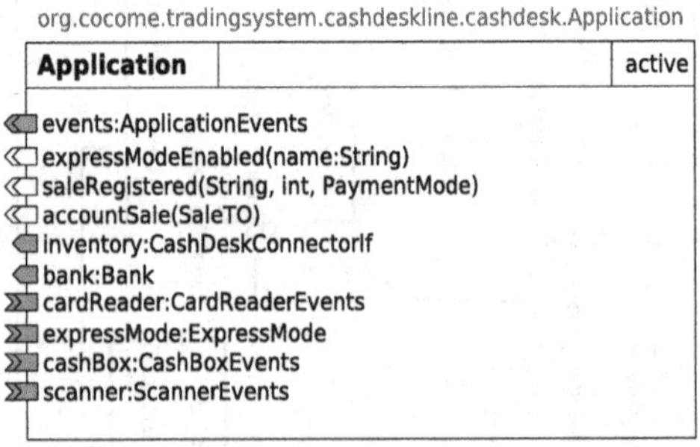

Fig. 24. The Application component

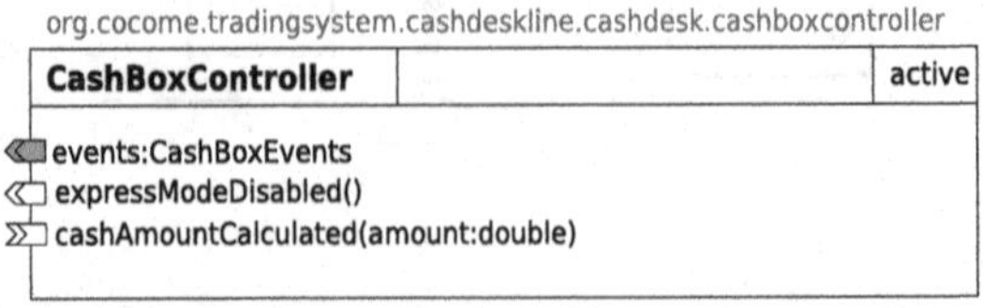

org.cocome.tradingsystem.cashdeskline.cashdesk.cashboxcontroller

CashBoxController		active

◁ events:CashBoxEvents
◁ expressModeDisabled()
▷ cashAmountCalculated(amount:double)

Fig. 25. The CashBoxController component

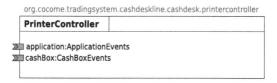

Fig. 26. The PrinterController component

10.3.15   CashDeskGUI

Figure 27 shows the CashDeskGUI component. Its purpose is to show useful information on a little display for the customer as well as the cashier. For this reason it has a set of ingoing ports for certain kinds of events.

Fig. 27. The CashDeskGUI component

10.3.16   Inventory::Application

The Inventory::Application component is responsible for abstracting from the direct access to the Inventory::Data component, as well as handling accountSale messages. The runtime structure of the component is shown in Figure 28. It internally consists of three inner boxes, namly a Reporting, a Store box, and a ProductDispatcher box. The ingoing ports are forwarded to the Reporting and the Store box, respectively. In addition, the Application component has an ingoing accountSale method, which is handled internally and not shown by the MCOWCH diagram. The Store box uses the ProductDispatcher box to realize the product exchange among different stores (Use Case 8). All three inner boxes need access to the DataIf interface which is done by forwarding their corresponding ports to the outgoing data port.

10.3.17   Inventory::Data

The reference implementation of the Inventory::Data component does not fit well into our model. We found two problems that make this task difficult. The Data component of the reference implementation provides three interfaces namely PersistenceIf, StoreQueryIf, and EnterpriseQueryIf. Instances of these interfaces can be created by the DataIf interface. In order to use the StoreQueryIf and the EnterpriseQueryIf, however, a client must first get an instance of the PersistenceIf and then obtain a PersistenceContext by calling the getPersistenceContext() method

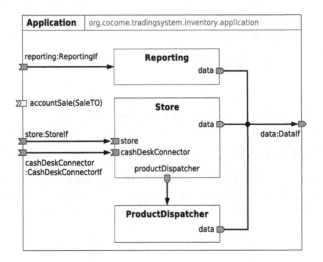

Fig. 28. The Inventory::Application component

on that interface. After that the client can use the other two interfaces, as all methods of these expect a PersistenceContext as an additional parameter.

This implementation does not follow an object-oriented programming style and thus does not fit well into our model. To give a more object-oriented model of the Data component, we changed the implementation in the following way. We removed the methods from the DataIf interface that allow to gain references to the EnterpriseQueryIf and the StoreQueryIf interfaces. We left PersistenceIf as it is, but we changed the PersistenceContext interface by adding two ports that allow access to the EnterpriseQueryIf and StoreQueryIf interfaces. We then could simplify the EnterpriseQueryIf and StoreQueryIf interfaces, as we were able to remove all PersistentContext parameters. The new interfaces are shown in Figure 29 The interesting aspect is that the COWCH approach led to a cleaner, more object-oriented design.

10.3.18 Missing Parts

Because of space reasons we did not present all parts of the CoCoME system. We left out the Inventory::GUI component as well as the architecture of the Inventory::Data component. We also mainly showed the architectural diagrams instead of the JCOWCH models, which we believe are more interesting.

10.4 Analysis

The COWCH approach provides a hierarchical structuring of runtime components and their communication structure. The runtime structure is the cornerstone to enable a modular specification of the behavior of components. Modularity

```
public interface DataIf {
  port PersistenceIf persistenceManager;
}

public interface PersistenceIf {
  PersistenceContext getPersistanceContext();
}

public interface PersistenceContext {
  port EnterpriseQueryIf enterpriseQuery;
  port StoreQueryIf storeQuery;
  port TransactionContext transactionContext;
  void makePersistent(Object o);
  void close();
}

public interface EnterpriseQueryIf {
  TradingEnterprise queryEnterpriseById(long enterpriseId);
  long getMeanTimeToDelivery(ProductSupplier supplier,
                             TradingEnterprise enterprise);
}

public interface StoreQueryIf {
  Store queryStoreById(long storeId);
  Collection<Product> queryProducts(long storeId);
  Collection<StockItem> queryLowStockItems(long storeId);
  Collection<StockItem> queryAllStockItems(long storeId);
  ProductOrder queryOrderById(long orderId);
  StockItem queryStockItem(long storeId, long productbarcode);
  StockItem queryStockItemById(long stockId);
  Product queryProductById(long productId);
  Collection<StockItem> getStockItems(long storeId, long[] productIds);
}
```

Fig. 29. The new interfaces of the Inventory::Data component

is a key-property for the scalability of any analysis technique. So we see our approach as a basis to enable scalable analysis for object-oriented programs. Our approach is still at the beginning. We plan to develop behavioral specifications of components to be able to specify and verify functional properties.

While (manually) applying the COWCH approach to the CoCoME system we discovered some design flaws as well as errors. The main design flaw we found was the realization of the Data component. The COWCH approach forced us to find a different design. The result is cleaner and more object-oriented than the original design. Other errors we found were mainly inconsistencies between the reference implementation and the documentation. We found one "real" error in the reference implementation. Due to the explicit communication structure of the MCOWCH models, we discovered that the reference implementation of the CardReaderController did not receive any messages. Thus the card reader was not disabled when the ExpressModeEnabledEnabled event was sent. Other errors have been posted to the CoCoME forum [22].

10.5   Tools

As our approach is still in an early phase, we cannot yet provide finished tools. However, we currently work on three different tools. First, we work on a library-based implementation of JCOWCH in Java called JCowchLib. It is based on Java's reflection mechanisms, thus it works with standard Java tools. Second, we work on a modification of the Eclipse Java Development Tools [23] called JCowchDT. This will lead to an integrated development environment for JCowch. And third, we work on a tool called CowchGM which is based on the Eclipse Modeling Framework [24]. The goal of this tool is to be able to create MCowch models. At a later stage we will merge CowchGM with JCowchDT to ensure the consistency of the architectural model and the underlying implementation. For certain kinds of models it will even be able to directly generate working code.

10.6   Summary

The COWCH approach is still at its beginning and under development. The Co-CoME modeling contest gave us the opportunity to evaluate our approach on a larger example system. During the modeling of the system we gained valuable insights which will influence the further development of our approach.

10.6.1   Limitations

With the architectural description language we are only able to show the structure of object-oriented systems. This includes the component structure as well as the communication structure. Currently, we are not able to specify functional and nonfunctional properties.

10.6.2   Future Work

In this paper we described our architectural description techniques and applied it to the CoCoME system. Consistency checking between architectural, executable, and implementation layer is currently done manually without tool support. In addition, the semantics of the executable layer is only partially formalized. We have a formal model of the Box Model semantics which we explain elsewhere [10]. As our concurrency model is based on the join calculus [9] we have a solid formal basis for this part as well. We are currently working on a formal description of the port and channel constructs which is the third part of our Java extension.

The architectural modeling is the basis to allow modular behavioral specifications of components. For the future we plan to develop behavioral specifications techniques to describe the behavior of concurrent object-oriented components and to be able to specify and verify functional properties.

10.6.3 Response to the Jury Comments

The main criticism of the Jury is that the approach only provides weak abstraction mechanisms and that the modeling technique is too close to the code level.

Our approach considers three layers (cf. Figure 1). To keep consistency between these layers manageable, we assume certain semantic similarities for the languages used on these layers. In principle, the approach is open to use less coupled languages as long as the consistency criteria is expressible.

It is true that the level of abstraction of our approach is not as high as compared to UML. However, both modeling layers in Cowch support well-defined and helpful abstractions. The executable modeling layer allows us to abstract from communication technologies and distribution and provides a more abstract notion of concurrency and synchronization. The architectural modeling layer allows to abstract from method implementations, from the process of creating and initializing components, and from dynamic system reconfigurations.

Acknowledgments

We thank the reviewers Antonio Cansado, Eric Madelaine, and Ludovic Henrio for their helpful comments on previous versions of this paper.

References

[1] Medvidovic, N., Taylor, R.N.: A classification and comparison framework for software architecture description languages. IEEE Trans. Softw. Eng. 26(1), 70–93 (2000)

[2] Magee, J., Dulay, N., Eisenbach, S., Kramer, J.: Specifying distributed software architectures. In: Schäfer, W., Botella, P. (eds.) ESEC 1995. LNCS, vol. 989, pp. 137–153. Springer, Heidelberg (1995)

[3] Allen, R., Garlan, D.: A formal basis for architectural connection. ACM Trans. Softw. Eng. Methodol. 6(3), 213–249 (1997)

[4] Luckham, D.C., Kenney, J.J., Augustin, L.M., Vera, J., Bryan, D., Mann, W.: Specification and analysis of system architecture using rapide. IEEE Trans. Softw. Eng. 21(4), 336–355 (1995)

[5] Shaw, M., DeLine, R., Klein, D.V., Ross, T.L., Young, D.M., Zelesnik, G.: Abstractions for software architecture and tools to support them. IEEE Trans. Softw. Eng. 21(4), 314–335 (1995)

[6] Aldrich, J., Chambers, C., Notkin, D.: ArchJava: connecting software architecture to implementation. In: ICSE 2002: Proceedings of the 24th International Conference on Software Engineering, pp. 187–197. ACM Press, New York (2002)

[7] Seco, J.C., Caires, L.: A basic model of typed components. In: Bertino, E. (ed.) ECOOP 2000. LNCS, vol. 1850, pp. 108–128. Springer, Heidelberg (2000)

[8] Sreedhar, V.C.: Mixin'up components. In: ICSE 2002: Proceedings of the 24th International Conference on Software Engineering, pp. 198–207. ACM Press, New York (2002)

[9] Fournet, C., Gonthier, G.: The reflexive CHAM and the join-calculus. In: Proceedings of the 23rd ACM SIGPLAN-SIGACT Symposium on Principles of Programming Languages (POPL 1996), pp. 372–385. ACM Press, New York (1996)

[10] Poetzsch-Heffter, A., Schäfer, J.: A representation-independent behavioral semantics for object-oriented components. In: Bonsangue, M.M., Johnsen, E.B. (eds.) FMOODS 2007. LNCS, vol. 4468. Springer, Heidelberg (2007)

[11] Szyperski, C.: Component Software - Beyond Object-Oriented Programming, 2nd edn. Addison-Wesley Publishing Company Inc, Reading (2002)

[12] Gosling, J., Joy, B., Steele, G., Bracha, G.: The Java^{TM} Language Specification, 2nd edn. Addison-Wesley, Reading (2000)

[13] Barnett, M., DeLine, R., Fähndrich, M., Leino, K.R.M., Schulte, W.: Verification of object-oriented programs with invariants. Journal of Object Technology 3(6) (2004)

[14] Poetzsch-Heffter, A., Geilmann, K., Schäfer, J.: Infering ownership types for encapsulated object-oriented program components. In: Program Analysis and Compilation, Theory and Practice: Essays Dedicated to Reinhard Wilhelm. Springer, Heidelberg (to appear, 2007)

[15] Milner, R.: Communicating and Mobile Systems: the Pi-Calculus. Cambridge University Press, Cambridge (1999)

[16] Scholten, J.G., Arbab, F., de Boer, F.S., Bonsangue, M.M.: Mobile channels, implementation within and outside component. Electronic Notes in Theoretical Computer Science 66(4) (2002)

[17] Institut National de Recherche en Informatique et en Automatique: JoCaml (2007), http://jocaml.inria.fr

[18] Benton, N., Cardelli, L., Fournet, C.: Modern concurrency abstractions for C#. In: Magnusson, B. (ed.) ECOOP 2002. LNCS, vol. 2374, pp. 415–440. Springer, Heidelberg (2002)

[19] von Itzstein, G.S.: Introduction of High Level Concurrency Semantics in Object Oriented Languages. PhD thesis, University of South Australia (2005)

[20] Lea, D.: Concurrent Programming in Java, 2nd edn. Addison-Wesley, Reading (2000)

[21] Woolf, B.: Null object. In: Martin, R.C., Riehle, D., Ruschman, F. (eds.) Pattern Languages of Program Design, vol. 3, pp. 5–18. Addison-Wesley, Reading (1998)

[22] The CoCoME forum (2007), http://naf.informatik.uni-kl.de/php/phpBB2/index.php

[23] The Eclipse Foundation: Eclipse Java Development Tools (JDT) (2007), http://www.eclipse.org/jdt/

[24] The Eclipse Foundation: Eclipse Modeling Framework Project (EMF) (2007), http://www.eclipse.org/modeling/emf/

11   Modelling the CoCoME with DisCComp

André Appel, Sebastian Herold, Holger Klus, and Andreas Rausch

Clausthal University of Technology
Department of Informatics - Software Systems Engineering
Julius-Albert-Str. 4
38678 Clausthal-Zellerfeld, Germany

11.1   Introduction

Most large-scaled software systems are logically structured in subsystems resp. components to cope with complexity. These components are deployed and executed within an distributed system infrastructure. Consequently, for many reasons, like for instance multi-user support or performance issues, the components are to some extent concurrently executed within an distributed environement. Note, this also holds for the *Common Component Modelling Example* (CoCoME).

11.1.1   Goals and Scope of the Component Model

The first main goal of DisCComp is to provide a *sound formal semantic component model* that is powerful enough to handle distributed concurrent components but also realistic enough to provide a foundation for component technologies actually in use, like for instance CORBA, J2EE, and .NET [1,2,3]. Thereby we claim to close the gap between formal component models and existing programming models (see Section 11.2.1). Hence the semantic component model of DisCComp contains all concepts well known from component programming models like for instance, dynamically changing structures, a shared global state and asynchronous message communication, as well as synchronous and concurrent message calls.

The second main goal of DisCComp is to provide proper *UML-based description techniques* to describe the structural and behavioural aspects of component-based systems (see Section 11.2.2). These description techniques have a clear semantics as they are mapped on the formal semantic component model of DisCComp. The formal component model of DisCComp contains an operational semantics for distributed concurrent component-based systems the UML-based descriptons of DisCComp can be directly executed resp. interpreted.

This leeds us to the third main goal of DisCComp: With DisCComp we claim to support system and component architects and designers in modelling component-based systems, simulate and execute these models, test and validate the functional correctness of those models, and finally generate the code for the finaly system out of the models. Therefore DisCComp provides a set of tools, like for instance plug-ins for modelling tools, simulation environments for DisCComp specifications, and code generators.

A. Rausch et al. (Eds.): Common Component Modeling Example, LNCS 5153, pp. 267–296, 2008.

11.1.2   Modeled Cutout of CoCoME

In the Secion 11.3 we present a cutout of the CoCoME modelled using our proposed description technique. In order to focus on specific aspects of our modelling approach and for the sake of brevity, we will illustrate the parts of the system which are relevant for the use case *Change Price* only.

11.1.3   Benefit of the Modeling

The DisCComp approach provides several benefits: As the DisCComp component model is close to existing programming models no paradigm gap exists between the DisCComp and the predominant programming approaches. Hence programmers, designers, and architects use the same paradigm and share a common understanding of the models. Thus software engineers can easily learn and apply the DisCComp approach as it is close to models they are familiar with.

As the description techniques of DisCComp have a clear semantics the resulting models and specifications are not ambiguous but precise. Thus, they can be directly simulated and executed. Hence the feedback loop and the iteration cycles are extremely shortened. Models and specifications can directly be tested and verified in advance without the need of coding them in the target component technique, which is more laborious and time-consuming due to the complex technologies programmers have to cope with.

11.1.4   Effort and Lessons Learned

To model our cutout of CoCoME with DisCComp an effort of 4 person month were used. During the contest we have learned the following lessons: The formal model of DisCComp is valid and fits well for real software systems like CoCoME. The provided specification techniques can be used to describe real software systems like CoCoME. However, the effort to elaborate these specifications is too high. The reason for this is, that currently our description techniques are too low-level. They are closer to the coding level than to a more abstract specification level. Hence we have to improve our approach and provide more abstract specification techniques.

11.2   Component Model

This section elaborates the basic concepts of the proposed formal model for distributed concurrent component-based software systems. Such a model incorporates two levels: The *instance level* and the *description level* [4]. The *description level* - described in Section 11.2.2 - contains a normalized abstract description of a subset of common instance level elements with similar properties. The *instance level* - described in the Section 11.2.1 - is the reliable semantic foundation of the description level. It provides an operational semantics for distributed concurrent components - it is an abstraction of existing programming models like CORBA,

J2EE, and .NET [1,2,3]. Thereby, it defines the universe of all possible software systems that may be specified at the description level and implemented using the mentioned programming models.

11.2.1   The DisCComp System Model

The instance level of our proposed formal model for distributed concurrent components must be powerful enough to handle the most difficult behavioural aspects:

- dynamically changing structures,
- shared global state,
- asynchronous message communication, and
- concurrent method calls.

Figure 1 summarizes these behavioural aspects of the formal model for distributed concurrent components at the instance level on an abstract level. Thereby, software systems consist of a set of disjoint instances during run-time: system, component, interface, attribute, connection, message, thread, and value. In order to uniquely address these basic elements of the instance level we introduce the infinite set INSTANCE of all instances:

INSTANCE $=_{def}$ { SYSTEM $\cup$ COMPONENT $\cup$ INTERFACE $\cup$ ATTRIBUTE $\cup$ CONNECTION $\cup$ MESSAGE $\cup$ THREAD $\cup$ VALUE }

The presented four behavioural aspects of distributed concurrent component-based systems are described in the following.

Structural Behaviour. A system may change its structure dynamically. Some instances may be created or deleted (ALIVE). New attributes resp. interfaces may be assigned to interfaces resp. components (ALLOCATION resp. ASSIGN-MENT). Interfaces and components may have a directed connection to interfaces (CONNECTS). Note, the target of a connection can only be an interface.:

ALIVE $=_{def}$ INSTANCE $\rightarrow$ BOOLEAN
ASSIGNMENT $=_{def}$ INTERFACE $\rightarrow$ COMPONENT
ALLOCATION $=_{def}$ ATTRIBUTE $\rightarrow$ INTERFACE
CONNECTS $=_{def}$ CONNECTION $\rightarrow$ {{ from, to } | from $\in$ COMPONENT $\cup$ INTERFACE, to $\in$ INTERFACE}

Valuation Behaviour. A system's state space is not only determined by its current structure but also by the values of the component's attributes. Mappings of attributes or parameters to values of appropriate type are covered by the following definition:

VALUATION $=_{def}$ ATTRIBUTE $\rightarrow$ VALUE

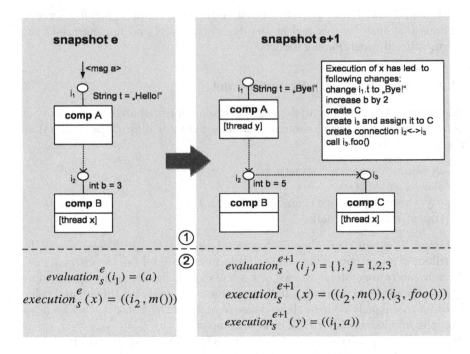

Fig. 1. Instance level of concurrent components

Communication Behaviour. Sequences of asynchronous messages represent the fundamental units of asynchronous communication. Therefore we distinguish the set MESSAGE in two non disjoint subsets: MESSAGE $=_{def}$ ASYNC_MESSAGE ∪ CALL_MESSAGE In order to model message-based asynchronous communication, we denote the set of arbitrary finite asynchronous message sequences with ASYNC_MESSAGE*. Within each observation point components process message sequences arriving at their interfaces and send message sequences to other interfaces:

EVALUATION $=_{def}$ INTERFACE → ASYNC_MESSAGE*

Execution Behaviour. Besides asynchronous communication, synchronous method calls (CALL_MESSAGE) performed by concurrent executed threads is the predominant execution mechanism in contemporary software systems. Each method is called at a certain interface (INTERFACE). Hence, to model a thread's call stack, we denote the set of arbitrary finite method call sequences with (INTERFACE × CALL_MESSAGE)* . Each thread has its own method call history - its call stack (EXECUTION). Note that threads may change the hosting component in case of a method call at an interface belonging to another component:

EXECUTION $=_{def}$ THREAD → (INTERFACE × CALL_MESSAGE)*

System Snapshot. Based on the former definitions, we are now able to characterize a snapshot of a software system. Such a snapshot captures the current structure, variable valuation, actual received messages, and current method calls. Let SNAPSHOT denote the type of all possible system snapshots:

$$\text{SNAPSHOT} =_{def} \text{ALIVE} \times \text{ASSIGNMENT} \times \text{ALLOCATION} \times \text{CONNECTS}$$
$$\times \text{VALUATION} \times \text{EVALUATION} \times \text{EXECUTION}$$

System Behaviour. In contrast to related approaches like [5], we do not focus on timed streams but on execution streams. We regard observation points as an infinite chain of execution intervals of various lengths. Whenever a thread's call stack changes - in case of a new method call or a method return - a new observation point is reached. We use the set of natural numbers N as an abstract axis of those observation points, and denote it by E for clarity.

Furthermore, we assume an observation synchronous model because of the resulting simplicity and generality. This means that there is a global order of all observation points and thereby of all method calls and returns. Note that this is not a critical constraint. Existing distributed component environments like CORBA, J2EE, and .NET control and manage all method calls and returns. Such a component environment may transparently force a global order of all method calls and returns.

We use execution streams, i.e. finite or infinite sequences of elements from a given domain, to represent histories of conceptual entities that change over observation points. An execution stream - more precisely, a stream with discrete execution interval - of elements from the set X is an element of the type

$$X^E =_{def} N^+ \rightarrow X, \text{ where } N^+ =_{def} N \setminus \{0\}$$

Thus, an execution stream maps each observation point to an element of X. The notation x^e is used to denote the element of the valuation $x \in X^E$ at the observation point $e \in E$ with $x^e = x(e)$.

Execution streams may be used to model the behaviour of software systems. Accordingly, SNAPSHOT^E is the type of all system snapshot histories or simply the type of the behaviour relation of all possible software systems:

$$\text{SNAPSHOT}^E =_{def} \text{ALIVE}^E \times \text{ASSIGNMENT}^E \times \text{ALLOCATION}^E \times \text{CONNECTS}^E$$
$$\times \text{VALUATION}^E \times \text{EVALUATION}^E \times \text{EXECUTION}^E$$

Let $\text{Snapshot}_s^E \subseteq \text{SNAPSHOT}^E$ be the behaviour relation of an arbitrary system $s \in \text{SYSTEM}$[1]. A given snapshot history $\text{snapshot}_s \in \text{Snapshot}_s^E$ is an execution stream of tuples that capture the changing snapshots snapshot_s^e over observation points $e \in \text{E}$.

Obviously, a couple of consistency conditions can be defined on a formal behaviour $\text{Snapshot}_s^E \subseteq \text{SNAPSHOT}^E$. For instance, it may be required that all

---

[1] In the remainder of this paper we will use this shortcut. Whenever we want to assign a relation X (element x) to a system $s \in \text{SYSTEM}$ we say $X_s(x_s)$.

attributes obtain the same activation state as the interface they belong to: $\forall a \in$ $\mathsf{Attribute}_s, i \in \mathsf{Interface}_s, e \in \mathsf{E}.\mathsf{allocation}_s^e(a) = i \Rightarrow \mathsf{alive}_s^e(a) = \mathsf{alive}_s^e(i)$ Or furthermore, instances that are deleted are not allowed to be reactivated: $\forall i \in$ $\mathsf{Instance}_s, e, n, m \in \mathsf{E}.\ e < n < m \wedge \mathsf{alive}_s^e(i) \wedge \neg\mathsf{alive}_s^n(i) \Rightarrow \neg\mathsf{alive}_s^m(i)$

We can imagine plenty of those consistency conditions. A full treatment is beyond the scope of this paper, as the resulting formulae are rather lengthy. A deeper discussion of this issue can be found in [6,7].

Thread Behaviour. A system's observable behaviour is a result of the composition of all thread behaviours. These threads are executed concurrently and are potentially distributed. To compute the system behaviour from the parallel executed threads, the thread's execution results have to be integrated taking possible inconsistencies due to parallelism into account.

To compose the system behaviour out of the results of the parallel executed threads DisCComp provides a simple but powerful abstraction. Therefore we introduce the notion of an *atomic unit of execution* of threads. In DisCComp this atomic unit of execution is given by the execution of method calls and returns. Whenever a thread executes a method call or a method return the current atomic unit of execution is finished and the next one starts. Hence the execution of method calls resp. method returns define the atomic execution results of threads, which have to be integrate by the run-time environment into the system-wide snapshot and thus composing the system's observable behaviour.

To describe these atomic units of execution of each thread we define a relation between a system-wide snapshot and the thread's wished changes on the system-wide snapshot after performing a method call or return. The run-time environment integrates these wished changes into the syste-wide snapshot and thereby it calculates the the system-wide successor snapshot:

$$\mathsf{BEHAVIOUR} =_{def} \mathsf{SNAPSHOT} \rightarrow \mathsf{SNAPSHOT}$$

Let $\mathsf{behaviour}_t \subseteq \mathsf{BEHAVIOUR}$ be the behaviour of a thread $t \in \mathsf{THREAD}_s$ in the system $s \in \mathsf{SYSTEM}$. The informal meaning of the thread behaviour is as follows: A thread executes the program code (and therefore has a program counter, which is given by its call stack $\mathsf{EXECUTION}$). Each transition relation $\mathsf{transition} \in \mathsf{behaviour}_t$ represents an atomic unit of execution. Intuitively it can be be seen as the execution result (second part of the transition relation) of the atomic unit of execution. Whereas the atomic unit of execution has started with the system-wide snapshot given by the first part of the transition relation.

Each thread performs a sequence of those atomic units of execution represented by transition relations. Each atomic unit of execution resp. transition relation $\mathsf{transition} \in \mathsf{behaviour}_t$ can intuitively be seen as the interpretation of an atomic piece of program code by the thread, which has the following schema:

1. The thread evaluates the system-wide snapshot given by the first snapshot of the tuple transition. If the relevant parts of the system-wide snapshot fits to the conditions contained in the atomic piece of program code to execute (e.g. conditions in if statements).

2. The thread requests the corresponding set of changes on the system-wide snapshot described in the atomic piece of program code like for instance changing the value of an attribute. These changes on the system-wide snapshot are described by the second snapshot of the tuple transition.
3. Finally, the thread – following the atomic piece of program code to execute – has to perform a new method call or return. Again this is given by a call-stack change described in the function $execution_t \subseteq$ EXECUTION, which is part of the second snapshot in the tuple transition.

Note that the behaviour relation of threads neither left-unique nor right-unique. Moreover the relation has not to be total. Hence, thread behaviour is not non-deterministic as it describes a concrete execution trace of a thread. However the thread behaviour is partial as a thread may not terminate. This is not a general restriction of the proposed approach it just reflects reality.

Behaviour Composition. Consequently, we need some specialized run-time system that asks all threads - one by one - if one wants to perform a new method call or return from a method call. Whenever a thread wants to perform a new method call or return, which means that its behaviour relation fires, the run-time system composes a new well-defined system-wide successor snapshot based on the thread's requested changes and the current system-wide snapshot.

Hence, such a run-time system is similar to a virtual machine. It observes and manages the execution of all threads. Again, this is not a critical constraint even in a concurrent and distributed environment. Existing distributed component environments like CORBA, J2EE, and .NET control and manage all executed components within the environment.

To sum up, the main task of such a run-time system is to determine the next system snapshot $snapshot_s^{e+1}$ from the current snapshot $snapshot_s^e \in$ Snapshot$_s^E$. In essence, we can provide formulae to calculate the system behaviour from the initial configuration $snapshot_s^0$, the behaviour relations $\{behaviour_{t_1}, ..., behaviour_{t_n}\}$ of all threads $t_1, ..., t_n \in$ THREAD$_s$, $n \in N$, and external stimulations via asynchronous messages and synchronous method calls at free interfaces. Note that free interfaces are interfaces that are not connected with other interfaces and thus can be stimulated from the environment.

Before we can come up with the final formulae to specify the run-time system, we need a new operator on relations. This operator takes a relation X and replaces all tuples of X with tuples of Y if the first element of both tuples is equal[2]:

$$X \triangleleft Y =_{def} \{a | a \in Y \vee (a \in X \wedge \pi_1(\{a\}) \cap \pi_1(Y) = \emptyset)\}$$

We are now able to provide the complete formulae to determine the next system snapshot $snapshot_s^{e+1}$:

---

[2] Note that the "standard" notation $\pi_{i_1,...,i_n}(R)$ denotes the set of n-tuples with $n \in N \wedge n \leq r$ as a result of the projection on the relation R. Whereas in each tuple in $\pi_{i_1,...,i_n}(R)$ contains the elements at the position $i_1, ..., i_n$ of the corresponding tuple from R with $1 \leq i_k \leq r$, with $k \in \{1, ..., n\} \subseteq N$.

next-snapshot: SNAPSHOT → SNAPSHOT

$$\text{next-snapshot}(\text{snapshot}_s^e) =_{def} \text{snapshot}_s^{e+1} =$$

$$= (\text{alive}_s^{e+1}, \text{assignment}_s^{e+1}, \text{allocation}_s^{e+1}, \text{connects}_s^{e+1}, \text{valuation}_s^{e+1}, \text{evaluation}_s^{e+1}, \text{execution}_s^{e+1}) :$$

$\text{alive}_s^{e+1} = \text{alive}_s^e \lhd \pi_1(\text{behaviour}_{next\_thread}(\text{snapshot}_s^e)) \lhd \pi_1(\text{message\_execution}(\text{snapshot}_s^e)) \wedge$

$\text{assignment}_s^{e+1} = \text{assignment}_s^e \lhd \pi_2(\text{behaviour}_{next\_thread}(\text{snapshot}_s^e)) \wedge$

$\text{allocation}_s^{e+1} = \text{allocation}_s^e \lhd \pi_3(\text{behaviour}_{next\_thread}(\text{snapshot}_s^e)) \wedge$

$\text{connects}_s^{e+1} = \text{connects}_s^e \lhd \pi_4(\text{behaviour}_{next\_thread}(\text{snapshot}_s^e)) \wedge$

$\text{valuation}_s^{e+1} = \text{valuation}_s^e \lhd \pi_5(\text{behaviour}_{next\_thread}(\text{snapshot}_s^e)) \wedge$

$\text{evaluation}_s^{e+1} = \pi_6(\text{behaviour}_{next\_thread}(\text{snapshot}_s^e)) \wedge$

$\text{execution}_s^{e+1} = \text{execution}_s^e \lhd \pi_7(\text{behaviour}_{next\_thread}(\text{snapshot}_s^e)) \lhd \pi_7(\text{message\_execution}(\text{snapshot}_s^e))$

Intuitively spoken, the next system snapshot snapshot_s^{e+1} is a tuple. Each element of this tuple, for instance $\text{assignment}_s^{e+1}$, is a function that is determined simply by merging the former function assignment_s^e and the 'delta-function' of $\pi_2(\text{behaviour}_{next\_thread}(\text{snapshot}_s^e))$. This 'delta-function' includes all 'wishes' of the next relevant thread determined by the function next_thread.

This intuitive understanding does not completely hold for alive_s^{e+1}, $\text{evaluation}_s^{e+1}$ and execution_s^{e+1}. In alive_s^{e+1} and execution_s^{e+1}, not only the wishes of thread next_thread have to be included. These wishes must contain the thread's actual method call or return. Additionally they may contain new parallel threads created by the current thread.

Moreover, alive_s^{e+1} and execution_s^{e+1} also contain the result of the application of the function $\text{message\_execution}(\text{snapshot}_s^e)$. This function includes new threads created to process the asynchronous messages. Thereby, for each asynchronous message - given by evaluation_s^e which is included in snapshot_s^e - a new thread is created in alive_s^{e+1} to execute the corresponding request in execution_s^{e+1}. message_execution is defined as follows:

message_execution: SNAPSHOT → SNAPSHOT

$\text{message\_execution}(\text{snapshot}_s^e) =_{def} \text{snapshot}' = (\text{alive}', \emptyset, \emptyset, \emptyset, \emptyset, \emptyset, \text{execution}').$

$\forall i \in \text{Interface}_s, m \in \text{Message}_s . m \in \text{evaluation}_s^e(i) \Leftrightarrow$

$\Leftrightarrow \exists t' \in \text{Thread}_s . \neg\text{alive}_s^e(t') \wedge \text{alive}'(t') \wedge \text{execution}'(t') = \{(i, m)\}$

Intuitively spoken for each asynchronous message a new thread is activated and the corresponding call stack is initialized. As all asynchronous messages are with each observation point transformed to corresponding concurrently executed threads, the new system snapshot has only to contain the new asynchronous messages, as denoted by $\text{evaluation}_s^{e+1} = \pi_6(\text{behaviour}_t(\text{snapshot}_s^e))$.

Note that thereby, the delivery of asynchronous message takes some time, exactly one observation point. To model network latency or network failure one would have to provide a more sophisticated function message_execution. Thus, not only delay and loss of asynchronous messages could be integrated but also network related failures in executing method calls.

Moreover note, the function next-snapshot currently does not include the case that a thread terminates as the last return statement has been executed by the thread (empty call stack). This trivial case could be straight forward added. As it would enlarge the formulae we have omitted this case in the paper.

To complete the formal model, the function next_thread has to be defined: next_thread : $\rightarrow$ THREAD

This function returns the next thread to be visited by the run-time system. To provide a simple but general model we propose a round-robin model. Therefore, a given strict order of all active system's threads is required. next_thread follows this given order and provides the next relevant thread to be visited and integrated into the system-wide snapshot by the run-time system.

Note that one can integrate additional features into the model providing other implementations of the function next_thread, like for instance non-determinism and priority-based thread scheduling. Non-determinism could be used to model an unsure execution order or to support under-specification.

Whenever concurrent threads or components are executed, inconsistency or deadlocks may occur. A deadlock concerning elements explicitly modeled in the semantics - like for instance two threads each locking an attribute and waiting to get the lock on the other's thread attribute - cannot occur in this model as all threads are visited one by one and each thread has to release all blocked resources after it has been visited. However, deadlocks on a higher level, like for instance one thread waits for a given condition to become true and another thread waits for this thread to make another condition true, can not be detected in advance.

The model does not suppress inconsistent situations but it helps to detect them. In order to ensure that the next system snapshot $\mathsf{snapshot}_s^{e+1}$ is well-defined, a single basic condition must be satisfied: all elements in the wished successor snapshot given by $\mathsf{behaviour}_{next\_thread}(\mathsf{snapshot}_s^e)$ that cause a change in the resulting next system snapshot must not be changed after the thread next_thread has made his last method call or method return.

For instance, assume that a thread performs a method call. The value of an attribute is 5 as the thread has started the method call execution and the thread wants to change the value to 7 as it returns from this method call. At the observation point where the thread returns from the method call the value of the attribute is already 6, as another thread has changed the value in the meantime. Hence, a possible inconsistency caused by concurrent thread execution occurs.

A run-time system implementing the function next_snapshot has to calculate the next system snapshot. Thereby it can observe this consistency predicate and verify whether such a possible inconsistency situation occurs or not. If the run-time system detects such a possible inconsistent situation it may stop the system execution for reliability reasons. Note that this formal consistency concept for concurrent threads is similar to optimistic locking techniques in databases.

11.2.2 The DisCComp Description Technique

In the previous section the instance level has been introduced. These instances are the semantic domain of the description level. In other words, the description level provides the notations and description techniques to describe the run-time instances in an uniform and precise manner.

Along with the initial DisCComp system model from [7], a description technique for components was developed which consists of a graphical, UML-based notation for the statical structure of systems and a textual description of their behaviours. Further extensions aimed at extending this description technique by specifying behavioural aspects by UML activity diagrams (s. [8]). The specification technique proposed here is essentially based upon that approach and extends it by following features:

- Consideration of system model extensions: The possibility of synchronous communication, which has been added on the system model in [9], has massive impact on the modularity of a component's specification. If a method of an interface which is assigned to a component A calls a method of an interface assigned to a component B, the behaviour of component A can only be fully specified if B's behaviour is known as well. The original DisC-Comp system model allows only asynchronous communication [7]. So called "island specifications" with explicit specifications for required interfaces are necessary to obtain modularity.
- Usability: The explicit specification of required interfaces as shown in [7] increases the effort of specifying the behaviour of interfaces because behaviour is additionally specified along with the component which assures that interface. In our approach, the behaviour of required interfaces is described in form of contracts [10], whereas an operational language is used to describe methods provided by assured interfaces. These descriptions can be analysed to check whether wiring two components is possible, meaning whether the provided interface is a refinement of the required interface.
- Application of UML 2.0 features: Since version 2.0 [11], UML as a broadly accepted modelling language provides some additional concepts for composite structures, which were not yet available for the original description technique. In contrast, we will focus on a textual specification language for behavioural aspects due to the maturity of graphical approach in the context of DisCComp.

Fig. 2 shows the structure of a component's specification which can be conceptually split into three parts.

The static structure part of a component's specification is described by a UML component diagram and an arbitrary number of class diagrams. The UML terms (components, interfaces, attributes, etc.) used in this context can be mapped one-to-one to the elements of the DisCComp system model. The component diagram gives an overview of the interfaces provided (or assured) and required by a component, whereas the class diagrams visualize the attributes and methods of interfaces as well as relationships between interfaces. These specify the structure and permitted connections between interface instances. The set of instances of a required interface that are assigned to a component is modelled as a *port* of the component. Since a port is a specialisation of the meta-model element *Feature*, it is a quantifiable part of a *Classifier* (see [11] and [12]). By this means, we

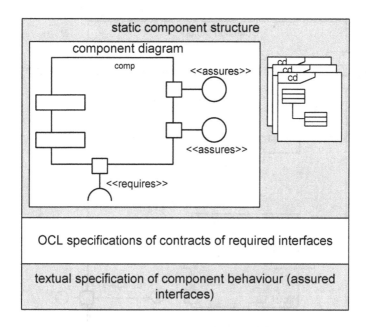

Fig. 2. Conceptual Structure of Component Specifications

are able to reflect the assignment of interface instances to components from the DisCComp system model. We also specify the set of instances of required interfaces by ports to refer to the set of provided interface instances of serving components.

The second part specifies the required interfaces' behaviours by terms of contracts ([10], [13]). We make use of OCL's means to specify pre- and post-conditions of methods and invariants that have to hold for required interfaces. When wiring components and building larger, more complex components, we map the required interfaces of a client component to provided interfaces of serving components, whereas the behaviour of provided interfaces has to "match" the required interfaces of the client component.

The third part consists of a set of textual behaviour specifications which describe the behaviour of interfaces assured by the component. Syntax and semantics are similar to the original approach in [7]. When wiring components, it will be checked by program analysis techniques whether the provided interface fulfills the contract specified by the client interface.

Static specification. The static specification of a component basically consists of an ordinary UML component diagram and additional class diagrams. The component diagram gives an overview of the interfaces that are provided by the component[3]. There are two levels which have to be considered when specifying

---

[3] We additionally define new stereotypes "requires" and "assures" to be conform to the usual DisCComp terms.

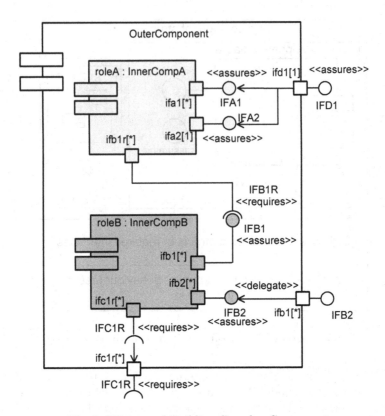

Fig. 3. Wiring and Building Complex Components

the interrelation between components and interfaces. First, on the type level, we define by dependencies with stereotypes <<requires>> or <<assures>> to specify interface types a component provides for use, and which interface types it requires for operation. Secondly, by assigning ports to components we define specifiers for the set of instances of an interface type which is assigned to the component.

Complex, hierarchical components are specified as a white box (see Fig. 3). Inner sub-components are used as black boxes which can only accessed by the interface types and ports they define. Only these specifiers and specifiers which are defined by the outer surrounding component itself can be used inside its specification. Beside this, we use the same means of UML component diagrams to specify hierarchical components as mentioned above.

The outer component can use assured interfaces of inner components to realize its own functionality which is modelled as a dependency between the corresponding ports in the component diagram, as between the interface IFD1 in Fig. 3 and the interfaces IFA1 and IFA2. This means semantically that interfaces instances of IFD1 can connect to instances of IFA1 and IFA2 to call methods and send messages. In contrast, dependencies with the stereotype <<delegate>>

indicate interfaces of inner components which are accessible from and connectable to clients of the specified hierarchical component (see IFB2 in Fig. 3). The instances are assigned to the inner component.

Interfaces labeled as required by inner components can similarly be specified as being required by the surrounding component (IFC1R in Fig. 3). The inner component, which requires such an interface, and interfaces assigned to it can connect to instances of an interface type which is mapped to the required interface.

After describing the specification of the static structure of components, we will illustrate how their behaviours and initialization are specified. That includes an abstract, contract-based specification of required interfaces and an operational description language for assured interfaces.

Abstract behaviour specification. We call the description of required interface behaviour *abstract behaviour specification* because it describes interfaces and their behaviours as abstract as possible, resulting in a specification of what "is needed at least". A component that provides an interface to another component has to specify a behaviour that is a valid refinement of the required behaviour - otherwise wiring the components would not be possible.

The textual description of abstract behaviours is formulated by contracts of the methods an interface is required to have, and by interface invariants. We use OCL [14] to specify such additional constraints which integrates seamlessly with the UML component and class diagrams of the static view. OCL supports pre- and post-conditions as well as invariants. By pre- and post-conditions, we specify which condition for the component's state is going to hold after the method's return if the pre-conditon holds before its invocation[4].

For syntactical details on OCL, please refer to [14]. If necessary, constructs will be introduced in the following component specifications.

Operational behaviour specification. The proposed behavioural specification language is a textual language based on [7]. It is similar to imperative programming languages but is syntactically and semantically designed to match the DisCComp system model. In this section, we will focus on language constructs that reflect the peculiarities of the system model and will omit syntax and semantics for well known constructs like control structures, assignments, etc., for the sake of brevity. The component specifications for the modelling example in the following sections will be explained in more detail.

A behavioural component description consists of an initialization block and a set of interface specifications which again consist of method specifications. The initialization block is executed when a component instance is created. It contains a specifier mapping to map the required interface types of sub-components to assured interfaces of other components. Furthermore, the initial wiring is done, specified by a set of instructions to create an initial set of interfaces and connections. These instructions define the initial port assignment and connection

---

[4] This is similar for asynchronous messages but the post-condition has to hold after sending, not processing the message.

among components and interfaces. We will see examples of initialization blocks in the following sections.

The DisCComp system model is able to realize asynchronous as well as synchronous communication. The signatures of messages, which can be processed asynchronously by an interface, and synchronous methods, which can be invoked at it, are specified in the UML class diagrams of the static specifications as mentioned above. Behavioural descriptions are described textually in MESSAGE or METHOD blocks respectively[5].

The most important possibility to change the structural state of the system inside methods is to create instances of interfaces and connections (see Table 1). Interfaces have to be connected to communicate with each other. For that reason, the creation of an interface instance can optionally be coupled with creating a connection to that instance for direct use.

Table 1. Creation of Instances

Syntax	Informal Semantics
ifInst : IfType = NEW INTERFACE IfType [CONNECT BY ConnType]	A new interface instance of type IfType is created. The instance is assigned to the same component as the calling interface. A new connection is optionally established between the newly created and the existing, calling interface. The connection type is a valid association name. IfType must be assured by the component.
connInst : ConnType = NEW CONNECTION ConnType TO ifInst	A new connection is established between the calling interface and the interface ifInst. ifInst must be of a type that is conform to the static specification of the according association and its ends.
connInst : ConnType = NEW CONNECTION ConnType BETWEEN ifInst1, ifInst2	Creates a connection of type ConnType between the interface instances ifInst1 and ifInst2. Only available in initialization blocks.
compInst : CompType = NEW COMPONENT CompType	A new component of type CompType is created.

However, this just allows us to create interface instances that are assigned to the same component as the calling interface. To connect to interfaces that are provided by different components, we have to call appropriate methods (or send appropriate messages) of those components which create instances and connect them to the calling or sending interfaces. This is comparable to passing return values of methods to the requesting client. Table 2 shows the according language constructs. The upper construct can be compared to returning a reference to an object which someone else (the serving component) is responsible for. The second

---

[5] For details regarding the execution of synchronous methods in DisCComp, please refer to [9].

Table 2. Returning Interface Instances

Syntax	Informal Semantics
CONNECT ifInst TO CALLER	ifInst is connected with the calling interface. Assignment of ifInst is not changed.
CONNECT ifInst TO CALLER AND REASSIGN	ifInst is connected with the calling interface and assigned to the same component.

statement is comparable to returning a copy of an object, but instead of actually copying the object, the object itself is separated from the creating component and assigned to the calling component.

After processing a message or method call, locally created instances are disposed.

The keywords and specification blocks will be used and explained in more detail in the example component specification in the following sections.

11.3   Modelling the CoCoME

In order to present our modelling techniques, we decided to take a certain cutout of the *Trading System*. The following sections will describe our approach to model the use case *ChangePrice* (UC 7). This use case requires us to specify many components on different layers, reaching from the GUI to the application layer and down to the data layer and is therefore representative for our modelling approach.

11.3.1   Static View

We decided to model the use case *ChangePrice*. Therefore, we first of all will have a look at the components which are relevant in order to implement the use case. In Fig. 4, the component diagram of the component :TradingSystem::Inventory is given. All components relevant for use case *ChangePrice* are subcomponents of :TradingSystem::Inventory.

The purpose of the use case is to let the manager change the price of a product. Therefore, the manager chooses a stock item from a list of available stock items in his store. The component :TradingSystem::Inventory::GUI is responsible for showing the dialog and forward the information to the application layer. The component therefore uses the interface StoreIf which defines among others a method for changing a price of a stock item. The component :TradingSystem::Inventory::Application implements the application layer of the classical three-layer-architecture (see [15], for example) and decouples the graphical user interface from the data access layer. The application layer communicates with the data layer, which is implemented by :TradingSystem::Inventory::Data, by using the interface StoreQueryIf.

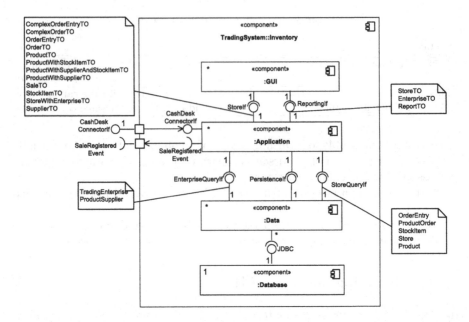

Fig. 4. Overview of the component :TradingSystem::Inventory

11.3.2 Behavioural View

To present the behavioural view on the use case we consider, we use a sequence diagram to visualize how the components presented before interact. In Fig. 5 you can see the Sequence Diagram which depicts how the components interact and how they are involved while realizing the use case.

After the manager has choosen a product item, a so called *transfer object* of type StockItemTO is created and sent to the component *:TradingSystem::Inventory::Application::Store*. After this component has established a new transaction, the price of the product item is changed by first querying the corresponding persistent object in the database and, secondly, change the price by calling *setSalesPrice()* at this object. The new price is then sent back to the GUI component in form of a new transfer object of type *ProductWithStockItemTO*. In the next sections we will show how we model these components and their behaviours using our modelling approach and description technique.

11.3.3 Component Specifications

Taking a closer look at the sequence diagram, you can see that we need to specify the components :GUI::Store, :Application::Store, :Data::Persistence and :Data::Store. Furthermore we need to describe the operational behaviour of interfaces like StockItemTO, StoreIf, etc. So we start with a static view of single components and then switch over to complex, hierarchical components. All these are described by ordinary UML component diagrams extended by "assures" and

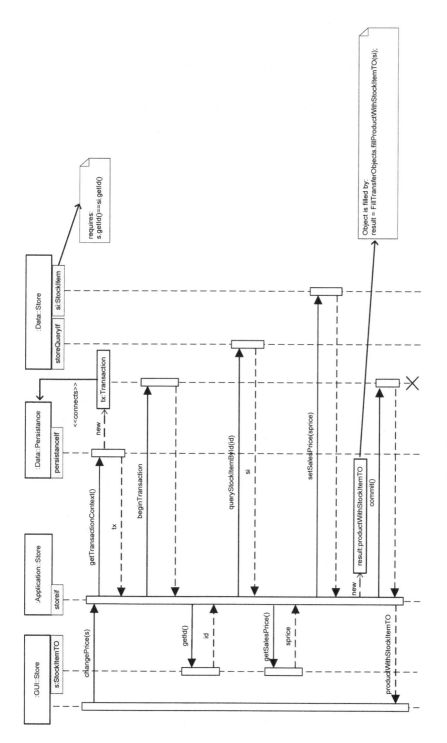

Fig. 5. Sequence Diagram for Use Case 7

"requires" at the according interfaces. An "assures" defines, that this component can provide these interfaces for other components which require it. On the other hand, "requires" provides the counterpart to "assures" and defines that this component needs the "required" interface from another component. The numbers at the port names show whether the corresponding interface is required more than once or whether it can be assured by the component more than once. Afterwards the operational behaviour for the assured interfaces of the component is specified by using a textual description according to the DisCComp system model. The operational behaviour for the required interfaces is specified by OCL code that is embedded into that textual description. It is structured into four consecutive sections:

1. *Specifier Mapping Section:* It defines the mapping between required and assured interfaces components inside the specified component.
2. *Initialization Section:* Here, the initial instantiation of interfaces is specified.
3. *Assured Interfaces Section:* This section contains the behavioural specification of assured interfaces.
4. *Required Interfaces Section:* This section contains the contracts of required interfaces.

We will illustrate this structure by the following components of the modelled cutout of the CoCoME.

11.3.4   Specification of Component Inventory::Application::Store

According to Fig. 6 this component assures the interfaces ProductWithStock-ItemTO and StoreIf. Furthermore it "requires" several interfaces to work correctly, namely PersistenceIfR, StoreQueryIfR, StockItemR, TransactionContextR and PersistenceContextR. Omitted multiplicities indicate single instances (multiplicity of one).

Since an atomic component is not wired in order to form some more complex and surrounding component, a specifier mapping section in its textual specification would be empty. As a consequence, we can omit the specifier mapping for this component. Listings 11.1 and 11.2 describe the remaining sections.

```
1  COMPONENT Inventory::Application::Store
2
3  INITIALIZATION
4     storeIf := NEW INTERFACE StoreIf;
5
6  ASSURES
7     INTERFACE StockItemTO
8        METHOD getId():long
9           RETURN VALUE OF self.id TO CALLER;
10       END METHOD
11       //... further methods omitted here
12    END INTERFACE
13
```

```
14   INTERFACE ProductWithStockItemTO
15      METHOD getId():long
16         RETURN VALUE OF self.id TO CALLER;
17      END METHOD
18
19      METHOD getSalesPrice(): double
20         RETURN VALUE OF self.salesPrice TO CALLER;
21      END METHOD
22      //... further methods omitted here
23   END INTERFACE
24
25   INTERFACE StoreIf
26      METHOD changePrice(StockItemTO stockItemTO):
            ProductWithStockItemTO
27         result: ProductWithStockItemTO := NEW INTERFACE
              ProductWithStockItemTO;
28         pctx: PersistenceContextR := persistenceIfR.
              getPersistenceContext();
29         tx: TransactionContextR := pctx.
              getTransactionContext();
30         tx.beginTransaction();
31         si: StockItemR := storequery.queryStockItemById(
              stockItemTO.getId())
32         IF (si != NULL) THEN
33            si.setSalesPrice(stockItemTO.getSalesPrice());
34            //copy data to result transfer object
35         ELSE
36            result := NULL;
37         ENDIF
38         tx.commit();
39         pctx.close();
40         CONNECT result TO CALLER AND REASSIGN;
41      END METHOD
42      //... further methods omitted here
43   END INTERFACE
44
45 END ASSURES
```

Listing 11.1. Operational Behaviour of Assured Interfaces of Inventory::Application:: Store

The section of assured interfaces starts with **ASSURES** and contains the interfaces being assured by the component. Single interface blocks start with **INTERFACE** ifName and end with **END INTERFACE** while each method provided by the interface starts with **METHOD** methodname (PARAMETERS):RETURNTYPE and ends with **END METHOD**. Then the **ASSURES** block is closed by **END ASSURES** (see Listing 11.1).

Identifiers from the component diagram can be used here as, for example, in changePrice(...) of the interface StoreIf. The instance persistenceIfR is used to get the persistence and transaction contexts. After that, the method queries

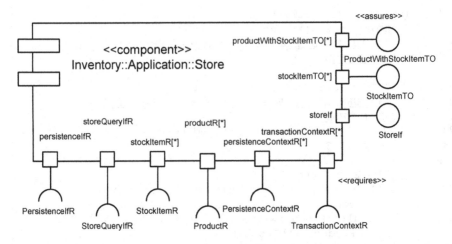

Fig. 6. Static View of Component Inventory::Application::Store

the data layer for the stock item and changes its price. The result is returned and reassigned. Thus, the according instance of ProductWithStockItemTO, which was created during the method call, will be passed to the calling component.

TheASSURESblockisfollowedbytheREQUIRESblockforthiscomponent(seeListing 11.2), which also encapsulates interface and method blocks. Instead of operational method bodies, the method blocks contain pre- and/or postconditions in OCL. For example, the postcondition for queryStockItemById(long) states that if there is a stock item with the given id, it will be returned, otherwise the result is null[6].

The initialization section specifies the creation of a single StoreIf instance during the creation of a component instance.

The end of the component description is declared by END COMPONENT.

In the following, for the sake of brevity, we will show incomplete specifications of the modelled components, interfaces, and methods that are nevertheless sufficient to cover UC 7.

```
47
48  REQUIRES
49
50      INTERFACE PersistenceIfR
51          METHOD getPersistenceContext():PersistenceContext
52              Post: result!=NULL
53          END METHOD
54      END INTERFACE
55
56      INTERFACE StockItemR
57          METHOD getId():long
58              Post: result = self.getId()@pre
```

---

[6] The postcondition assumes an invariant which states that the ID of a stock item is unique.

```
59     END METHOD
60
61     METHOD setSalesPriceR(real salesPrice):void
62       Pre: salesPrice >0
63       Post: self.getSalesPrice()=salesPrice
64     END METHOD
65   END INTERFACE
66
67   INTERFACE StoreQueryIfR
68     METHOD queryStockItemById(long sId): StockItem
69       Pre: sId >= 0
70       Post: let queriedItems : Set(StockItemR) =
                 stockItemR->select(s|s.getId()=sId) in
71         if queriedItems->notEmpty then
72         result = queriedItems->first();
73       else
74         result = NULL
75       endif
76     END METHOD
77   END INTERFACE
78
79   INTERFACE TransactionContextR
80     METHOD beginTransaction(): void
81       Post: // Transaction is started
82     END METHOD
83
84     METHOD commitTransaction(): void
85       Post: // Transaction is commited
86     END METHOD
87
88     METHOD rollback():void
89       Post: //Rollback executed
90     END METHOD
91   END INTERFACE
92
93   INTERFACE PersistenceContextR
94     METHOD getTransactionContext(): TransactionContext
95       Post: result != NULL
96     END METHOD
97
98     METHOD close():void
99       POST: //Close the Persistence context
100    END METHOD
101   END INTERFACE
102 END REQUIRES
103
104 END COMPONENT
```

Listing 11.2. Operational Behaviour of Required Interfaces of Inventory::Application::
Store

11.3.5   Specification of Component Inventory::Data::Persistence

The component Inventory::Data::Persistence provides services that deal with persisting and storing objects into a database as well as managing transactions. It assures a single instance interface PersistenceIf which provides methods for clients to get the persistence context. This interface again enables us to create transaction contexts which contains methods to create and commit transactions.

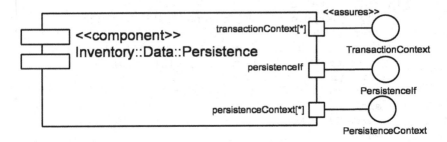

Fig. 7. Static View of Component Inventory::Data::Persistence

Since this component is a rather technical one and externally provided in larger parts, we were not able to model the behaviour properly by analyzing the CoCoME code. We simplify its behaviour by only specifying those methods that create instances of the corresponding context interface instances.

```
 1
 2  COMPONENT Inventory::Data::Persistence
 3
 4  INITIALIZATION
 5     persistenceRole.persistenceIf := NEW INTERFACE
           PersistenceIf;
 6
 7  ASSURES
 8
 9     INTERFACE TransactionContext
10       METHOD beginTransaction() : void
11         //external behaviour, no operational description here
12       END METHOD
13
14       METHOD commit() : void
15         //external behaviour, no operational description here
16       END METHOD
17
18       METHOD rollback() : void
19         //external behaviour, no operational description here
20       END METHOD
21
22       METHOD isActive() : Boolean
23         //external behaviour, no operational description here
```

```
24        END METHOD
25     END INTERFACE
26
27
28     INTERFACE PersistenceIf
29       METHOD getPersistenceContext(): PersistenceContext
30          result : PersistenceContext := NEW INTERFACE
                 PersistenceContext;
31          CONNECT result TO CALLER AND REASSIGN;
32       END METHOD
33     END INTERFACE
34
35     INTERFACE PersistenceContext
36       METHOD getTransactionContext():TransactionContext
37          result : TransactionContext := NEW INTERFACE
                 TransactionContext;
38          CONNECT result TO CALLER AND REASSIGN;
39       END METHOD
40
41          //further methods omitted here
42       END INTERFACE
43  END ASSURES
44
45  END COMPONENT
```

Listing 11.3. Operational behaviour of assured Interfaces of Inventory::Data:: Persistence

11.3.6 Specification of Component Inventory::Data::Store

The component Inventory::Data::Store provides the interfaces StoreQueryIf and StockItem (see fig. 8). The methods of StoreQueryIf encapsulate methods for querying persistent objects represented by interfaces like StockItem, Product, etc. These interfaces provide methods for retrieving and changing their attribute values. For this reason, it requires technical services like PersistenceIfR, TransitionContextR and PersistenceContextR.

```
1  COMPONENT Inventory::Data::Store
2
3  ASSURES
4
5     INTERFACE StoreQueryIf
6       METHOD queryStockItemById(long stockId): StockItem
7         StockItem result;
8         //calls to persistence framework which were not
               modelled explicitly
9         //the StockItem instance is retrieved from the
               database if it exists, otherwise result is set to
               NULL
```

```
10|        CONNECT result to CALLER;
11|      END METHOD
12|    END INTERFACE
13|
14|
15|    INTERFACE StockItem
16|      METHOD setSalesPrice(SalesPrice salesPrice): void
17|        self.salesPrice:=salesPrice;
18|      END METHOD
19|    END INTERFACE
20|
21| END ASSURES
22|
23|
24|
25| REQUIRES
26|
27|    INTERFACE PersistenceIfR
28|      METHOD getPersistenceContextR(): PersistenceContext
29|        Post: result != NULL
30|      END METHOD
31|    END INTERFACE
32|
33|    INTERFACE TransactionContextR
34|      METHOD beginTransaction(): void
35|        Post: //Transaction must be started!
36|      END METHOD
37|
38|      METHOD commit(): void
39|        Post: //Transaction committed
40|      END METHOD
41|    END INTERFACE
42|
43|    INTERFACE PersistenceContextR
44|      METHOD getTransactionContext():TransactionContext
45|        Post: result!=NULL
46|      END METHOD
47|    END INTERFACE
48|
49| END REQUIRES
50| END COMPONENT
```

Listing 11.4. Operational behaviour of assured and required Interfaces of Inventory::Data::Store

11.3.7   Specification View of Component Inventory::GUI::Store

We have not reconstructed the inner structure of the GUI from the code for reasons of simplification, thus Inventory::Gui::Store is quite trivial. It only requires a StoreIf to invoke the changePrice() method.

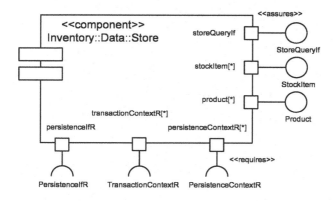

Fig. 8. Static View of Component Inventory::Data::Store

11.3.8   Specification of Component Inventory::Data

Inventory::Data represents the data layer (ref. to Fig. 10) of the inventory system. It consists of Inventory::Data::Persistence and Inventory::Data::Store. The required interfaces of the inner component Inventory::Data::Store are provided by Inventory::Data::Persistence. All assured interfaces are delegated to inner components to allow access from the environment, for example from the application layer of the inventory system.

The specifier mapping for this hierarchical component is described in Listing 11.5.

```
1  COMPONENT Inventory::Data
2
3  SPECIFIER MAPPING
4    persistenceRole::PersistenceIfR <-> storeRole::
         PersistenceIf
5    persistenceRole::TransactionContextR <-> storeRole::
         TransactionContext
6    persistenceRole::PersistenceContextR <-> storeRole::
         PersistenceContext
```

Listing 11.5. Operational behaviour of required Interfaces of Inventory::Data

The specifier mapping simply maps all required interfaces of one component to its assured pendants at another component, namely the interfaces which assure what the other one requires, e.g. `Data::Persistence::PersistenceIfR` will be assured by the interface `PersistenceIf` of the component `Data::Store`.

11.3.9   Specification of Component Inventory::Application

This hierarchical component (ref. to Fig. 11) consists of Inventory::Application:: Store and Inventory::Application::Reporting and thereby specifies the application

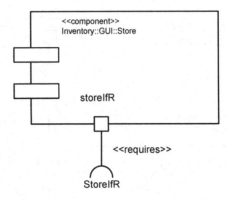

Fig. 9. Static View of Component Inventory::GUI::Store

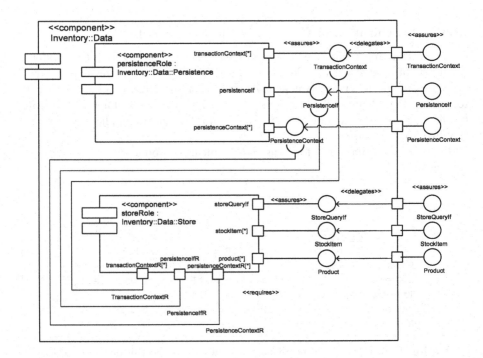

Fig. 10. Static View of Component Inventory::Data

layer. We have not modelled Application::Reporting since it is not required by UC7, so everything it assures or requires is left out.

Once again all assured interfaces of the outer component are delegated to interfaces of inner components, whereas the new required interfaces may not contradict or tighten the existing requirements.

11.3.10   Specification of Component Inventory

This is the hierarchical component which describes the whole system. We left out Inventory::GUI for graphical reasons, so the diagram in Fig. 12 shows only the two components Inventory::Application and Inventory::Data. The wiring between the layers basically reflects the wiring between the components of different

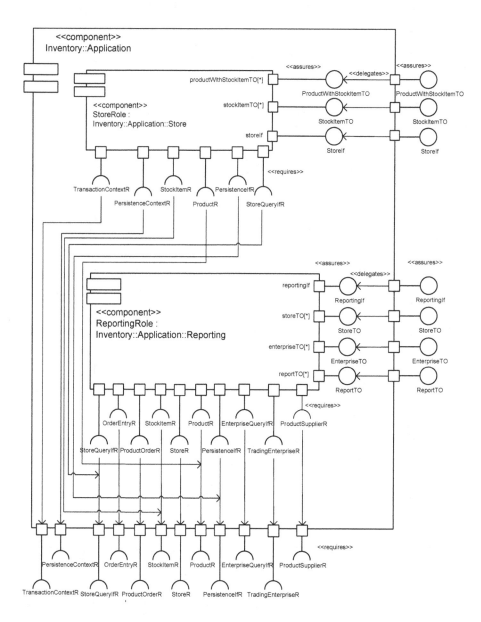

Fig. 11. Static View of Component Inventory::Application

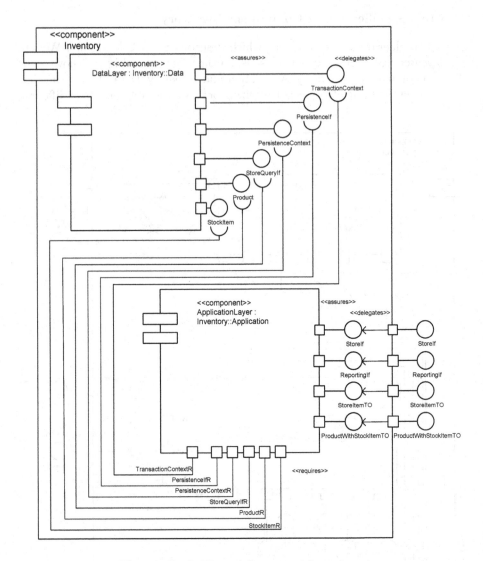

Fig. 12. Static View of Component Inventory

layers. For instance, the component Inventory::Application::Store requires interfaces of Inventory::Data::Store or Inventory::Data::Persistence (s. Fig. 6). Only the interfaces of the application layer are delegated to the environment, since the application layer will control access by different applications to the data layer.

```
1  COMPONENT Inventory
2
3  SPECIFIER MAPPING
4    Application::PersistenceIfR <-> Data::PersistenceIf
```

```
5  Application::TransactionContextR <-> Data::
        TransactionContext
6  Application::PersistenceContextR <-> Data::
        PersistenceContext
7  Application::StoreQueryIfR <-> Data::StoreQuery
8  Application::StockItemR <-> Data::StockItem
9  Application::ProductR <-> Data::Product
```

Listing 11.6. Specifier Mapping and Initialization of Inventory

11.4   Transformations

During research work regarding the DisCComp approach, the tool *DesignIt* was developed which includes a generator for generating executable code from XML-based representations of specifications as described in [7]. It is controlled by templates which enable it to generate code for different target languages. A detailed description of the code generator is included in [16] and [17]. Model-to-model transformations are not yet considered.

11.5   Analysis

As mentioned above, we aim at a modelling approach which allows us to specify components in a modular way. To compose components, we have to check whether the wiring of components is correct, meaning whether the specified contracts are fulfilled, at design time. For this purpose, the operational behaviour specifications of assured interfaces are analyzed and used to generate some representation which can be compared to the abstract behaviour specifications of the corresponding required interfaces. By using a more intuitive operational description technique and automatic generation, we hope to avoid the disadvantage of specifying the abstract contracts of the wired interfaces twice.

11.6   Tools

As mentioned above, the existing tool DesignIt is based upon the original specification technique of [7]. Tool support for that approach exists in the form of modelling tools, consistency checking, code generation, and runtime and testing environments. Most of this support has to be adapted to the specification techniques we have proposed here.

11.7   Summary

In this chapter we presented the DisCComp model for modelling distributed and concurrent component-based systems. It is separated into the system model and a description techniques which enables us to specify such systems. The proposed description technique differs greatly from the original proposals in the

DisCComp context (s. [7]). Although it is still young, we can summarize some lessons learned by applying it to the common modelling example.

First, the imperative specification of assured interfaces has reduced the effort of specifying both, assured and required interfaces. The imperative way of specifying them seems to be more intuitive. But secondly, it still causes some overhead in comparison to specifications without contracts which seems to be unavoidable to get modular specifications.

The overall approach still lacks of tool support which is part of the future work. Especially program analysis and the checking of component wirings will have to be theoretically founded and embedded into the approach and realized by tools.

References

1. Aleksy, M., Korthaus, A., Schader, M.: Implementing Distributed Systems with Java and CORBA. Springer, Heidelberg (2005)
2. Juric, M.B.: Professional J2EE EAI. Wrox Press (2002)
3. Beer, W., Birngruber, D., Mössenböck, H., Prähofer, H., Wöß, A.: Die .NET-Technologie. dpunkt.verlag (2006)
4. Harel, D., Rumpe, B.: What's the semantics of semantics. IEEE Computer 37(10), 64–72 (2004)
5. Broy, M., Len, K.S.: Specification and Development of Interactive Systems. Springer, Heidelberg (2001)
6. Bergner, K., Broy, M., Rausch, A., Sihling, M., Vilbig, A.: A formal model for componentware. In: Foundations of Component-Based Systems. Cambridge University Press, Cambridge (2000)
7. Rausch, A.: Componentware: Methodik des evolutionären Architekturentwurfs. PhD thesis, Technische Universität München (2001)
8. Seiler, M.: UML-basierte Spezifikation und Simulation verteilter komponentenbasierter Anwendungen. Master's thesis, Technische Universität Kaiserslautern (2005)
9. Rausch, A.: DisCComp - A Formal Model for Distributed Concurrent Components. In: Workshop Formal Foundations of Embedded Software and Component-Based Software Architectures (FESCA 2006) (2006)
10. Meyer, B.: Applying 'design by contract'. IEEE Computer 25(10) (1992)
11. Object Management Group (OMG): Unified Modeling Language (UML) 2.0 Superstructure Specification (2005), http://www.omg.org/docs/formal/05-07-04.pdf
12. Object Management Group (OMG): Meta Object Facility Core Specification Version 2.0 (2006), http://www.omg.org/docs/formal/06-01-01.pdf
13. Rausch, A.: Design by Contract + Componentware = Design by Signed Contract. Journal of Object Technology 1(3) (2002)
14. Object Management Group (OMG): Object Constraint Language (OCL) Specification (2006), http://www.omg.org/docs/formal/06-05-01.pdf
15. Buschmann, F., Meunier, R., Rohnert, H., Sommerlad, P.: Pattern-Oriented Software Architecture. A System of Patterns, vol. 1. John Wiley, Chichester (1996)
16. Kivlehan, D.: DesignIt: Code Generator based on XML and Code Templates. Master's thesis, The Queen's University of Belfast (2000)
17. Rausch, A.: A Proposal for a Code Generator based on XML and Code Templates. In: Proceedings of the Workshop of Generative Techniques for Product Lines, 23rd International Conference on Software Engineering (2001)

12 Palladio – Prediction of Performance Properties

Klaus Krogmann and Ralf Reussner

Universität Karlsruhe (TH), Germany

12.1 Introduction

Palladio[1] is a component modelling approach with a focus on performance (i.e. response time, throughput, resource utilisation) analysis to enable early design-time evaluation of software architectures. It targets modelling business information systems. The Palladio approach includes

- a *meta-model* called "Palladio Component Model" for structural views, component behaviour specifications, resource environment, component allocation and the modelling of system usage and
- multiple *analysis techniques* ranging from process algebra analysis to discrete event simulation.
- Additionally, the Palladio approach is aligned with a development process model tailored for component-based software systems.

Early design-time predictions avoid costly redesigns and reimplementation. Palladio enables software architects to analyse different architectural design alternatives supporting their design decisions with quantitative performance predictions, provided with the Palladio approach.

12.1.1 Goals and Scope of the Component Model

Component Concept. A component is a building block of software which can be deployed and composed without having to understand its internals (cf. [1]). For Palladio, a component is a *model* of a software component. For performance predictions, the performance relevant behaviour of a service is specified by a so-called "Service Effect Specification" (SEFF). Interfaces are first class entities that can be in provided or required relationship with a component.

Our component model supports various component type levels ranging from high-level "provided component types", specifying mainly provided interfaces, to detailed "implementation component types", including provided and required interfaces and the behavioural "Service Effect Specifications". These type levels allow rapid coarse-grained models or detailed specifications.

---

[1] Our approach is named after the Italian renaissance architect Andrea Palladio (1508–1580), who, in a certain way, tried to predict the aesthetic impact of his buildings in advance.

A. Rausch et al. (Eds.): Common Component Modeling Example, LNCS 5153, pp. 297–326, 2008.

Concept of Composition and its Semantics. Our model supports hierarchical composite components. A composite component is represented by its inner components and connectors specifying their interactions. Service Effect Specifications are composed from the SEFFs of their inner components. The semantics of a SEFF is given by a mapping into a stochastic process algebra.

Model coverage. The Palladio Component Model covers: Modelling usage profiles of a system, component behaviour with Service Effect Specifications, the composition/assembly structure, the deployment context, and the resource environment. For each of these models, we include only performance relevant aspects (delays, data abstractions, etc).

Analysis. Our analysis approaches and our component model support arbitrary stochastic distribution functions to provide feedback on response time, throughput, and resource utilisation. All analyses can be performed without an implementation, supporting early design time predictions.

12.1.2 Modeled Cutout of CoCoME

Focus. For CoCoME, we focused on the most complex use case 8. We modelled components, interfaces, resource environment, allocation, usage profile, and behavioural specifications of components with respect to non-functional properties. Our component specifications are context-independent and therefore parameterised over usage model, implementation, external dependencies, and underlying execution environment allowing the re-use of component specifications.

Not treated. The embedded system part was not covered by Palladio. For supporting the event channels of the embedded part, we need to translate them into a component. As our component model currently does not support runtime creation of components, we modelled one fixed instance of the *ProductDispatcher* component instead. We simplified the distribution of the store servers to just one instance of the store server and simulated the rest – which was sufficient for performance prediction.

12.1.3 Benefit of the Modeling

The Palladio approach allows early design time predictions of performance properties, including support for *sizing scenarios*: Estimating the performance, if for example the usage profile changes (implying more concurrent users and different user behaviour), and *relocation scenarios*: Existing components are reused within a different context.

By applying the Palladio approach, users get detailed performance predictions, represented by arbitrary distribution function instead of mean values. An extensive sensor frameworks allows user-defined measuring points to observe performance within a simulation, e.g. contention of a certain resource or response time of a component-internal service for finding bottlenecks.

12.1.4   Effort and Lessons Learned

Due to mature tool support, the selected cutout of CoCoME could be modeled within 0.2 person month. A complete treatment would probably take about 1 person month. A student experiment shows that it requires about 5x2 hours of lectures to train students for applying the Palladio approach (cf. [2]).

CoCoME turned out to be a good debugging and testing system for our approach. "Sub-systems", in addition to composite components, one-to-many connections and replication should be explicitly supported by the Palladio approach.

12.1.5   History

The Palladio project started in 2001 at the University of Oldenburg, Germany. The approach perpetuates the idea of parametric contracts [3], allowing to reason about the functionality a component can provide if not all of its required services are available, thus defining a relation between provided and required interfaces of a component. Palladio has evolved over the last six years to a comprehensive approach, with a detailed, hierarchical meta-model with about 200 entities. While the approach was focused on reliability and protocol checking in the beginning, it later grew to a broader approach including performance prediction and support for architectural design decisions. In 2006, the central Palladio Component Model was migrated from a hand-written implementation to a ECORE-based meta-model. This eased the use of recent model-driven transformation techniques.

12.1.6   Related Work

Component Models. A taxonomy of component models can be found in [4]. ROBOCOP [5] and PACC [6] allow performance predictions, but aim at embedded systems. Opposed to Palladio, Koala [7] aims at product lines in embedded systems, SOFA [8] allows protocol checking, and Fractal [9] allows runtime reconfigurations of architectures, without considering Quality of Service (QoS) attributes. UML 2 [10] has a limited component concept, leaving out details on component properties that are required for analysis methods. Other approaches like CCM, EJB, or COM+ do not support QoS analysis.

Performance Meta-Models. To describe the performance properties of software systems, several meta-models have been introduced (survey in [11]). The Software Performance Engineering (SPE) meta-model [12] is designed for object-oriented software systems but not for component-based systems. UML, enriched by information from the Schedulability, Performance, and Time Specification (SPT) profile [13], offers capabilities to extend UML models with performance properties. It is not suited for parametric dependencies (i.e. describing control and data flow parametrized over input values, execution environment, and external services), which are needed for component specifications to allow more precise reasoning on performance properties. CSM [14] is closely aligned with the UML-SPT approach and does not target component-based systems. KLAPER [15] is designed for component-based architectures and reduces modelling complexity by treating components and resources in a unified way.

External Dependencies. For accurate predictions, external dependencies have to be made explicit in component specifications. Opposed to other approaches, Palladio makes these factors affecting the perceived performance of a software component explicit. In [16,17] the influences by external services is not considered, [18,19,20] do not deal with changing resource environments, and [21] does not support different input parameters.

12.2   Component Model

The Palladio approach includes the so-called Palladio Component Model (PCM) [22] – a meta-model for component-based software architectures. Two key features of the PCM are the parameterised component QoS specifications and the developer role concept.

Parameterised component specification. The PCM is based on the component definition by Szyperski [1]: Software components are black-box entities with contractually specified interfaces; they encapsulate their contents and are a unit of independent deployment. Most importantly, components can be composed with other components via their interfaces. The PCM offers a special QoS-specification for software components, which is parameterised over environmental influences, which should be unknown to component developers during design and implementation. The PCM supports general distribution functions to specify possible usages of a software system (for example, the distribution of parameter values or user think time) as well as in prediction of QoS properties. Thus, results of predictions can be distribution functions for response time or throughput.

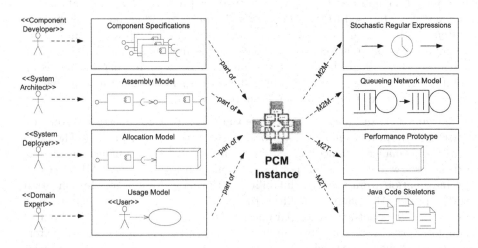

Fig. 1. Development roles and the corresponding models in the Palladio Component Model

Development roles. The PCM is aligned to different roles involved in component-based development (Figure 1). Component developers specify models of individual components, which are composed by software architects to architectures. Deployers model the environment of the architecture (hardware, middleware and operating systems), and domain experts supply a description of user behaviours. A QoS-driven development process supports the roles in combining their models.

To support each role, the PCM is split into several sub-models. Each role has a set of sub-models for its relevant part of a software system (for example, component developers deal with component repositories). These models can be considered as domain specific languages (DSL), which capture the information available to a specific developer role. So, large software systems can be better handled by division of labour. While, for example a component developer is changing the specification of a component, a deployer is already able to do the deployment independently. If a system contains many components, component developers can create their own repositories, without having resource conflicts.

The PCM reflects that a component can be used in different contexts: with respect to connected components (which component uses provided services; which components provide required services), allocation to resources (which CPU, memory etc. are available), or different usage scenarios (are users downloading files with a size of 1 GB or 1 KB). This is done by specifying context dependencies in a parametric way, meaning that context bindings are not fixed. Parametric dependencies allow deferring context decisions like assembly or allocation. The following section relates the views (cf. [23]), sub-models, and roles.

12.2.1   Views, Roles, and Sub-models

In the PCM, views and resulting sub-models are derived from roles (Figure 1). *Component developers* specify and implement components. The specification contains an abstract, parametric description of component behaviour. *System architects* assemble components to build applications. For the prediction of extra-functional properties, they retrieve component specifications, done by component developers, from a repository.

System deployers model the resource environment and afterwards the allocation of components from the assembly model to different resources of the resource environment. Business *domain experts*, who are familiar with users, provide models describing important usage scenarios as well as typical parameter values.

The complete system's model can be derived from the sub-models specified by each developer role and afterwards QoS properties can be predicted. Each role has a domain specific modelling language and only sees and alters the parts of the model in its responsibility. The introduced sub-models are aligned with the reuse of the software artefacts. Table 1 gives an overview on views, roles and sub-models. The examples Section 12.3 give more details on the PCM sub-models.

The three main views (structural, behavioural, and deployment) are supported by specific sub-meta-models. A complete PCM instance of the PCM consists of at least seven sub-models (cf. Table 1). They can be considered as viewpoints

Table 1. Views, roles, and sub-models

View	Role	Sub-Model
Structural	Component Developer	Repository
Structural	Component Assembler	System, Repository
Behavioural	Component Developer	Service Effect Specification
Behavioural	Domain Expert	Usage Model
Deployment	System Deployer	Allocation, Resource Environment, Resource Types

according to the IEEE Standard (cf. [23, p. 4]). Each sub-model is enriched with QoS-relevant information, as shown in the examples of Section 12.3.

The PCM allows multiple component developers to offer components via repositories. They are able to build composite components referencing components from other repositories. New composite component can again be offered via a repository. The same feature of independent sub-models applies to component assemblers and system deployers. They can use components from multiple repositories to build systems or deploy existing systems multiple times, respectively.

12.2.2   Repository Model

Component repositories contain a number of components and interfaces (both as first class entities). The PCM distinguishes: *basic components* representing atomic building blocks and *composite components* created from other components. Interfaces are characterised by a number of service signatures. A service signature has a name, a list of parameters, a return type and a list of exceptions (similar to the Corba Interface Definition Language, IDL, [24]). Furthermore, interfaces can include call protocols (e.g. using finite state machines). An interface serves as contract between a client requiring a service and a server providing the service. Components may provide and require multiple interfaces. The relation between components and interfaces is called "role".

To allow a systematic component development process, the PCM includes a hierarchy of component types (Figure 2). The *ProvidesComponentType* represents a component type where only provided interfaces are defined. A typical top-down development process of a component starts with the services a component is supposed to provide. Thus, a *ProvidesComponentType* contains only information on provided services. In the next step, the component developer specifies the external services required to provide the defined services. This is represented by the *CompleteComponentType*. Finally, the component developer specifies implementation details. This is reflected by the *ImplementationComponentType*. The *ImplementationComponentType* includes abstractions of component implementations, like the Service Effect Specification (Section 12.2.3). It can be realized either as a *BasicComponent* or a *CompositeComponent*.

The component type hierarchy supports both top-down and bottom-up development. To gain well-defined refinement and abstraction steps, the PCM defines

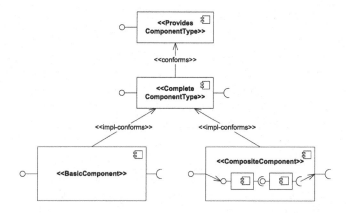

Fig. 2. Component type hierarchy

formal constraints to express the "conforms" / "impl-conforms" relations in the component type hierarchy. It is a derived attribute, whether two components are in such a relation. Lower levels are enriched by additional information, while upper levels abstract a component type.

12.2.3   Service Effect Specifications

Service Effect Specifications (SEFFs) provide a behavioural specification of components. The SEFF meta-model is a domain specific modelling language for component developers to specify performance related information of component services. SEFFs provide an abstraction of component internals, thus keeping the black-box principle of components by hiding implementation details.

To each provided service of a component, component developers can add a SEFF, describing which required services the component uses to provide its service. Calls for required services are bound to interfaces, not to concrete component instances; SEFFs are parametrised by calls for external component services. For performance analysis, the mere sequence of external calls is not sufficient. Therefore, component service implementations can be characterised by this abstraction of control- and data-flow. Besides the sequence of called required services, a SEFF contains resource usages, transition probabilities, loop iteration numbers, and parametric dependencies.

SEFFs are associated with components and thereby available from repositories. They include some of the key features of the PCM such as parameterised resource and variable usage or branching, required for exact QoS-predictions. We use a UML 2 activity diagram-like notation to depict SEFFs.

SEFFs are parametrised by:

– Required components (they reference signatures declared in required interfaces, but not components)
– Return values of required services

- Component usage: service input parameters
- Available resources (middleware, CPU, memory, etc.)

while representing an abstract model of a component implementation. For example, parameters of a service, described by SEFF, are reduced to only QoS-relevant parameters or parameter abstractions (like data bytesize, number of elements, (non-)ordered structure, the datatype, or the value itself).

Note, that our component specifications do not support persistent states. Only a static component configuration is supported. See Section 12.7.1 for further details.

Example. Figure 3 gives an example of a SEFF. The service described is doSomething(input1, input2, input3, input4). The basic structure of the SEFF is built from control flow statements (*AbstractAction*). In the example, there are a branch ("Diamond") and a loop. After the start node, there is an *ExternalCallAction*. *ExternalCallAction* is a call to the service "Call1()" declared in the component's required interface. The resource usage generated by executing a required service with an *ExternalCallAction* has to be specified in the SEFF of that required service. It is not part of the SEFF of the component requiring it.

Next in Figure 3, an *InternalAction* models component-internal computations of a service possibly combining a number of operations in a single model entity. The algorithms executed internally by the component are thus not visible in the SEFF to preserve the black-box principle. The *InternalAction* is annotated by a *ParametricResourceDemand*. The example declaration defines a use of "CPU-Units" depending on the bytesize of the input parameter "input1"

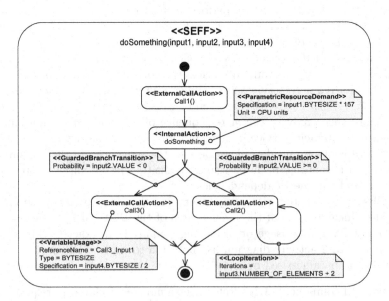

Fig. 3. Example: Service Effect Specification instance, including parametric dependencies

with a factor of 157 (e.g. an empirically evaluated value for the component implementation). Resource demands reference resource types like "CPU-Unit" from a *ResourceRepository* (see Section 12.2.5).

Next, a *BranchAction* follows. The control flow is split into two (non-concurrently executed) branches, each containing one external call action (note that this is an UML2 notation for branches). The external call action depicted at the right is executed in a loop. Finally, the control flow joins and immediately ends with a stop node.

A *BranchAction* consists of a number of *GuardedBranchTransitions* to define a parametric dependency: If the input parameter value of "input2" is less than "0" the left branch is taken, otherwise the right one. Any boolean expression is allowed. Alternative to a *GuardedBranchTransition*, *ProbabilisticBranchTransitions* can be used to express control flow branching. *ProbabilisticBranchTransitions* add *fixed* probabilities to branches.

For the *ExternalCallAction* in the left branch a *VariableUsage* is specified. This expresses a parameter that is passed to the called service. In the example the parameter abstraction bytesize is passed to the external service named "Call3()". The bytesize is computed from the bytesize of input parameter "input4".

In the right branch, there is a specification for the number of loop iterations. Such a *LoopAction* is attributed with the number of iterations. Control flow cycles always have to be modelled explicitly with *LoopActions*. A loop may not be specified with a probability of entering the loop and a probability of exiting the loop as it is done for example in Markov models. Loops in Markov models are restricted to a geometrically distributed number of iterations, whereas our evaluation model supports a generally distributed or fixed number of iterations, which allows analysing loops more realistically (for more details on loop modelling, see [jss 12]). The *ExternalCallAction* (Figure 3, bottom right) is executed for each element of input parameter "input3" plus a constant overhead of two times.

Figure 4 shows a special construct of the PCM to support the iteration of collection elements. For usual *LoopActions* multiple actions within the *LoopAction* are not granted to process the same element of a collection within one loop iteration. If, for example, the first action processes a 10 MB file, the second

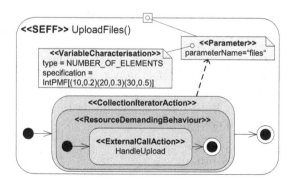

Fig. 4. Collection iterator action

action eventually processes a 3 MB file. To model iterations, where every action processes the *same* element, *CollectionIteratorActions* can be used.

The *VariableCharacterisation* from Figure 4 is discussed with the usage model (Section 12.2.8).

12.2.4   System Model

A system model, defined by component assemblers, combines components from one or a number of repositories. It specifies which services take the role of a system service and which services it requires. Though composite components and systems basically have the same structure, the provided system services can be accessed by users, opposed to services of a component which only can be directly accessed by other components.

Analyses and simulations (c.f. Section 12.5) include the parts belonging to a system, while the rest (system-external) is treated as environmental influence (see Figure 5). Consequently, *details* on required system services are not considered within the PCM: It is assumed that they have a fixed execution time.

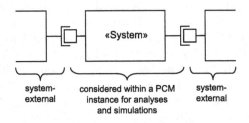

Fig. 5. System model: Defines system borders

12.2.5   Resource Types

Because the actual resources used by a component are not known during component specification, the component developer specifies resource demand for abstract *ResourceTypes* and not for concrete resource instances. Depending on the QoS-properties, which are going to be evaluated, resource types such as CPU, hard disk, or memory are defined in a separate model. These are abstract resources like "reference processors". This allows different roles (like component developer and system deployer) to communicate with each other. For example, a component developer defines a SEFF referencing a "myDefaultCPU". Later, in the *resource environment model* the system deployer expresses available resources using the same resource definitions to describe which servers communicate with each other. Both roles interact using the same resource types, expressing a common terminology.

12.2.6   Resource Environment

The PCM distinguishes three classes of resources: active resources, passive resources, and linking resources. Active resources process jobs (e.g., a CPU processing jobs or a hard disk processing read and write requests), while passive resources such as semaphores, threads, etc. do not. Instead, their possession is important as they are limited. For example, if there is only one database connection, it can only be used by one component and all other components needing it have to wait. Please note that the definition of middleware properties is part of the resource environment.

LinkingResources enable modelling of communication. They can be any kind of network connection but also some abstraction of it, like a RPC call. Active and passive resources are bundled in resource containers. A resource container is similar to a UML2 deployment node. Resource containers are connected through linking resources. System deployers specify resource environments.

12.2.7   Allocation Model

The allocation model maps system models and resource environments. Components from system models are mapped to resource containers from the resource environment like servers. For the prediction of QoS properties, the allocation model determines which hardware is used, allowing the predictions of timing values – only parameterised by run-time usage.

12.2.8   Usage Model

The usage model describes possible runtime use of a system, by the number of users, their behaviour in terms of requests to the system, and an abstract characterisation of the input parameters they use. It is a domain specific modelling language intended for business domain experts, who are able to describe the expected user behaviour. An usage model consists of several usage scenarios. They can contain open workloads, modelling users that enter with a given arrival rate and exit the system after they have executed their scenario. Or, they can contain closed workloads, modelling a fixed number of users (population), that enter the system, execute their scenario and then re-enter the system after a given think time. This resembles the common modelling of workloads used in performance models like queueing networks.

A usage scenario consists of a sequence of user actions. These can be control flow primitives (branches and loops) or system calls, which are calls to system interfaces directly accessible by users (on the entry level of the architecture), for example a sequence "login, select product, buy product, logout". Forks in the user control flow are not possible, as it is assumed that one user can only execute a single task at a time. System calls can be characterised by a number of *parameter usages*.

These *parameter usages* have been modelled especially for QoS analyses. Parameter usages of *primitive parameters* (such as int, float, char, boolean, etc.) can be characterised by their value, bytesize and type. *Collection parameters usages* (arrays, lists, sets, trees, hash maps, etc.) can additionally be characterised by the number of inner elements and their structure (e.g., sorted, unsorted etc.). They contain parameter usages to abstractly characterise their inner elements.

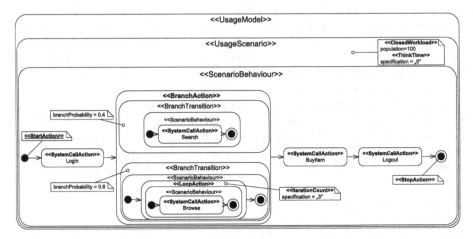

Fig. 6. Usage Model

In a *composite parameter* different primitive and collection parameters can be grouped together with an inner parameter usage for each of the grouped parameters. With this abstraction, more complex parameters (such as records, objects, etc.) can be modelled. The different attributes like value or bytesize can be specified as random variables, allowing for example to specify a distribution function for the bytesizes of inner elements of a collection.

Example. The structure of a usage model is comparable to the structure of a SEFF. In Figure 6 an example usage model is shown. A usage model always consists of a number of *UsageScenarios* – in the example just one. The *UsageScenario* might be either a *ClosedWorkload* or a *OpenWorkload*. For the first case a population of users ("100" in the example) returns into the *ScenarioBehaviour* after a specified think time ("5" sec). In the case of a *OpenWorkload* users enter the system, interact with the system, and leave the system. Therefore only the arrival rate is defined. Users execute a so-called *ScenarioBehaviours* specifying how they interact with the system (using *SystemInterfaces* via *SystemCallActions*). In the example users start with a login and then have two choices (*BranchAction*): Doing a single "search" or "browsing" in a loop. *BranchActions* and *LoopActions* are the same as in SEFFs. After having "searched" or "browsed", users buy an item ("BuyItem") and "logout" in the example .

Figure 4 shows a *VariableCharacterisation*, that has been left out in Section 12.2.3. It is a context dependent fragment from the usage model: If a whole system is specified using the PCM, including a usage model, concrete characterisations for parameters can be propagated through the architecture. Figure 4 shows such propagated values from the usage model that apply to the service "UploadFiles()". In the example, the parameter "files" is characterised by the number of elements. Therefore, an Integer Probabilty Mass Function "IntPMF" is used to describe a stochastic distribution.

12.2.9   Summary

In this section, we gave short descriptions of the PCM's sub-models. Finally, the different sub-models of the PCM are put together by the described process (cf. Section 12.2.1), referencing each other. The sub-models together make up a complete instance of the PCM describing a component-based software system.

To conclude the idea of several sub-models: Components are enabled to be re-used as a "unit of independent deployment", i.e., component specification and properties resulting from the context are strictly split. The same applies to systems, resource environments, and usage models. They can be re-used and are defined independent from a concrete context.

Though the PCM might seem to be a large and complex model, one should keep in mind that each role in the development process has just a limited view on the model. Each role has to learn only its domain specific language. For example, domain experts do not need to know about resources, and architects do not know about component internals (SEFFs) specified by the component developer.

12.2.10   Syntax and Semantics

The PCM is defined in the ECORE [25] meta-meta-model. Therefore, the *abstract syntax* of the PCM is precisely defined. Additionally, our tools (cf. Section 12.6) define a *concrete syntax*, which is similar to UML 2 [13] diagrams (cf. Section 12.2.1). We do not define a profile for UML 2, to restrict the model only to those constructs that can be handled by our evaluation methods and because we want to avoid ambiguities inherited from the UML 2 meta-model. For example, fork and join of UML activities are ambiguous: If there are multiple forks and joins, one cannot know which pairs belong together. Opposed to UML, the PCM includes advanced concepts like service effect specifications, a component type hierarchy, and an explicit context model.

In the Palladio approach stochastic expressions and distribution functions can be used to express parametric dependencies and details of the usage models. Those values are more expressive than mean values. Section 12.3 will give more details on them. For stochastic expressions and distribution functions a own grammar, respective syntax has been developed, including arithmetic operators ($*, /, +, -$; applicable to distribution functions) and boolean expressions (AND, OR). This grammar allows detailed specifications of components and usage models.

In addition to the ECORE meta-model, OCL [26] constraints define the *static semantic*, such as integrity conditions that cannot be expressed by the meta-model itself. Compared to a possible UML 2 profile, the amount of required constraints to restrict the meta-model is much smaller.

The *dynamic semantic* of the PCM is explained textually in a technical report [22]. More details on the service effect specification including parametrisation are given in [27]; [28] presents the concepts of parametrisation. The multi-layered context influence for components is discussed in [29].

12.3   Modelling the CoCoME

Presenting the entire PCM instance of CoCoME in this section would have exceeded the page limit[2]. Therefore, we present excerpts from CoCoME, combined with simplified model instances, to explain the PCM models and constructs more easily. As concrete syntax we use our GMF editor (cf. Section 12.6) notation.

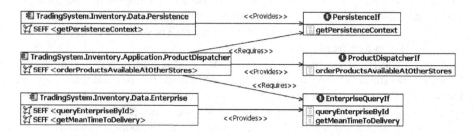

Fig. 7. Excerpt from the CoCoME repository model (editor screenshot)

12.3.1   Repository Model

The repository model (Figure 7 shows an excerpt from the repository) lists available components and interfaces. Additionally, provided and required interfaces are displayed as relations. In the example, three basic components from CoCoME are displayed. Each of them has a SEFF for every provided service, describing the effects of a service call. Interfaces can be seen from the example as entities with a list of service signatures. Optional protocol definitions for the interfaces are not present in the example (for details see [22]).

The final CoCoME repository holds ten basic components:

Each basic component has a SEFF for each provided service. Additionally, three composite components were modelled: TradingSystem.Inventory.Data,

Table 2. Basic Components

TradingSystem.Inventory.Data.Enterprise
TradingSystem.Inventory.Data.Persistence
TradingSystem.Inventory.Data.Store
TradingSystem.Inventory.GUI.Reporting
TradingSystem.Inventory.GUI.Store
TradingSystem.Inventory.Application.ProductDispatcher
TradingSystem.Inventory.Application.Reporting
TradingSystem.Inventory.Application.Store
including two façades for composite components:
TradingSystem.Inventory.Data.Facade
TradingSystem.Inventory.Application.Facade

---

[2] The full model is available from http://sdqweb.ipd.uka.de/wiki/CoCoME-PCM

TradingSystem.Inventory.GUI, TradingSystem.Inventory.Application, representing the main layers of CoCoME (see Section 12.3.3). The components available
from the repository basically have the same structure as indicated by the UML2
models of CoCoME.

12.3.2   Service Effect Specification

Figure 8 shows a simplified excerpt from the bookSale() SEFF of the Store
component. Time consumptions have been specified by fixed values according to
what has been defined in the "extra-functional properties" section of CoCoME.
Only significant *InternalActions* have time consumptions. ExternalCallActions
delegate to component external services and therefore consume no time. API-
calls are considered to be component internal. As API calls usually have no
dependency on other components, we assume that a API call can be modelled
by *InternalActions*, possibly being parameterised by input parameters. We go
through the most important steps of the SEFF for bookSale(), indicating the
relation to the CoCoME implementation.

The first action modelled (cf. Figure 8) is an *ExternalCallAction*, in this case
delegating to an instance of the persistence manager. The persistence manager
is considered as an external service, not implemented by the Store component
itself. Contrary to this, the initialisation of a transaction, operating on *PersistenceContext*, is considered as a component internal action. Consequently, the
following action is an *InternalAction* consuming time.

Next, the implementation of CoCoME iterates over a number of StockItems,
doing an external call for queryStockItemById() of StoreQueryIf for every Stock-
Item. This is explicitly modelled in the SEFF: For every element of the input parameter "saleTO" the body of the *LoopAction* is executed (specified as
"saleTO.NUMBER_OF_ELEMENTS" in the model). After the *LoopAction*, another *InternalAction* follows. It represents the commit statement of the transaction, having a fixed time consumption.

The rest of the SEFF is straight-forward: Every external action is modelled
explicitly, actions in between two external actions are merged to a single *InternalAction*. A SEFF is not concerned with the limits of a single class method,
as long no component external call is done, everything is treated as component
internal. For example, the SEFF for bookSale() includes executing checkFor-
LowRunningGoods() (itself containing further internal methods).

The next important construct is a *BranchAction*. The method checkFor-
LowRunningGoods() of the StoreIf implementation is included in the modelled
SEFF. The method's implementation includes a check whether products that
are going to be delivered are *null*. Depending on the selected branch a number
of component external queries using the StoreQueryIf are executed. Consequently,
the branch statement ("f") is modelled explicitly, to reflect the changing execution behaviour. The *BranchAction* contains two *GuardedBranchTransitions*: one,
representing the case "productList.NUMBER_OF_ELEMENTS > 0" (where pro-
ductList is a return value of the *ExternalAction* "orderProductsAvailableAtOther-
Stores"; right-hand side of Figure 8), the other representing the else case. According

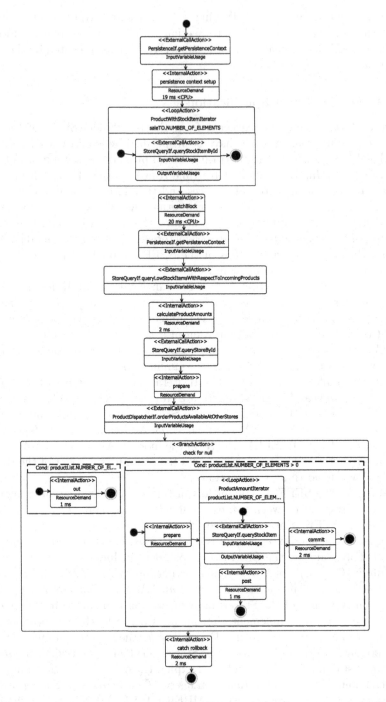

Fig. 8. Simplified SEFF of the bookSale() service of the Store component (editor screenshot)

to the evaluation of this guard, the statements specified in the chosen *Guarded-BranchTransitions* are executed.

The SEFF for bookSale() ends with another *InternalAction* and a stop node.

Discussion. As a SEFF is an abstraction of a real component's behaviour, there are several choices for modelling. For example, the branch transitions of the *BranchAction* are modelled with a *GuardedBranchTransitions*, as the exact branching condition could be easily identified. An alternative modelling might have used a *ProbabilisticBranchAction* to express a uncertain or complex condition for choosing a branch. In such a case one could specify that a branch is taken in *n* of 100 cases.

Due to the given specification of extra-functional properties in the CoCoME chapter, time consumptions were assumed to be static ("non-parametrised"). Alternatively to static time consumptions one could have specified parametric time consumptions.

12.3.3 System Model

Figure 9 shows the three layers (each one represented by a composite component) of the trading system inventory. For the PCM, the component TradingSystem::Inventory is modelled as the most outer component – called the "system". As we pointed out in Section 12.2.3, a system is not a usual component. The main implication of making a composite structure a "system" is a changed semantics: For CoCoME we express which parts are concerned for performance prediction; i.e. what the system borders are. The system environment is handled in a simplified way, for example using static timing values.

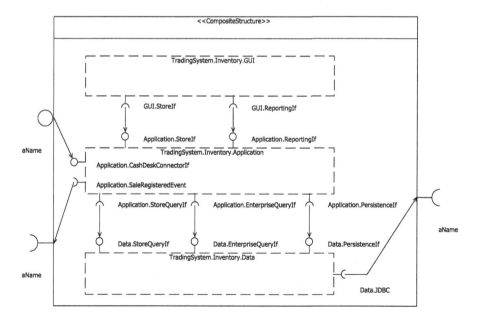

Fig. 9. CoCoME System model: Assembling components within a composite structure

Each of the three main layers of CoCoME Inventory is represented as a component assembled in the system. The CashDesk and the database are considered as system-external services, as PCM neither focuses on embedded systems (CashDesk) nor on modelling databases. The system interacts with them via its system interfaces (CashDeskConnectorIf is the provided interface, JDBC is a required interface, just as SaleRegisteredEvent). Components within a system are assembled like composite components. Assembly connectors make the association between the components. In the case of CoCoME all components inside the system are modelled as composite components.

12.3.4 Resource Types

For a first step, the resource types considered for CoCoME were kept simple. We consider only CPU (a *ProcessingResource*), and network connections (*CommunicationResource*). Passive resources like thread-pools, connection-pools, or semaphores are not present in the CoCoME implementation itself, they are encapsulated into the frameworks like Hibernate.

12.3.5 Resource Environment Model

The PCM resource environment model for CoCoME (cf. Figure 10) has been simplified, compared to what is depicted in Figure 14of the CoCoME Chapter 3: the set of deployment nodes (in the PCM called *ResourceContainer*) is reduced. As the whole CashDeskPC is considered to be system-external, it does not appear in the modelling. Each *ResourceContainer* has a resource specification, defining the concrete CPU, expressed in terms of the resource type specification. Additionally, the connections (*LinkingResources*) between *ResourceContainers* are annotated by its concrete properties (i.e. throughput and latency).

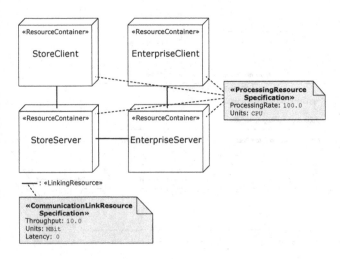

Fig. 10. Resource environment model of CoCoME

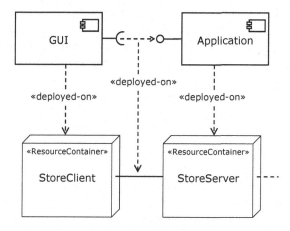

Fig. 11. Excerpt from the CoCoME allocation model

12.3.6 Allocation Model

The allocation model bridges the gap between resource environment and system model. Components from a system are allocated onto *ResourceContainers*. Figure 11 shows an excerpt from the CoCoME deployment (only for StoreServer and StoreClient with one component deployed on each *ResourceContainer*).

12.3.7 Usage Model

As explained in Section 12.3.3, the POS part of CoCoME was considered to be system-external. Therefore, users (the POS part of CoCoME) interact with StoreIf using the bookSale() service. Figure 12 shows the usage model for CoCoME. For CoCoME an *OpenWorkload* was modelled. Users enter the system with an inter arrival time of 11250 ms (according to extra-functional specifications of

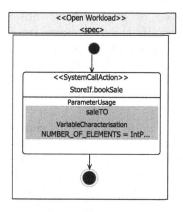

Fig. 12. CoCoME usage model

CoCoME: 320 customers per hour), execute the bookSale() service, and leave the system. For executing the bookSale() service a SaleTO is passed as parameter, representing the items a customer buys. Therefore, the usage model includes a characterisation for the number of elements of a SaleTO. We translated the extra-functional property "n11-2: Number of goods per customer" from the CoCoME specifications into a integer probability mass function.

12.4   Transformations

All analysis methods existing for the PCM transform instances of the PCM into input for analysis models. Details can be found in Section 12.5.

The effort spent on creating a model of a software architecture should be pre-served when implementing the system. For this, a model-to-text transformation based on the openArchitectureWare (oAW) framework generates code skeletons from PCM model instances. The implementation uses either Plain Old Java Ob-jects (POJOs) or Enterprise Java Beans (EJBs, cf. [30]) ready for deployment on a Java EE application server.

Another benefit of generated source code is increased specification compliance. The basic code structure is generated. Thus, implementers do not need to create class structures or the basic control flow to get an implementation of a PCM instance – we will give details in the following.

The transformation uses as much model information as possible for the gen-eration of artifacts. Repository models result in components, system assemblies in distributed method calls, the allocation is used to generate ant scripts to dis-tribute the components to their host environment and finally, the usage model results in test drivers.

A particular challenge is the mapping of concepts available in the PCM to objects used in Java or EJB. Consider for example the mapping of composite components to Java. As there is no direct support of composed structures in Java EE, a common solution to encapsulate functionality is the application of the session façade design pattern.

Another issue with classes as implementing entities for components is the missing capabilities to explicitly specify required interfaces of classes in object oriented languages. A solution for this is the application of the component con-text pattern by Völter et al. [31]. This pattern moves the references to required services into a context object. This object is injected into the component either by an explicit method call or by a dependency injection mechanism offered by the application server.

Our Code generation tools are not able to support the generation of full source code. The chosen representation of component implementation "SEFF" is hiding to much details on a component's realisation. The PCM tools support the generation of code skeletons leaving out implementation details. Opposite to that, QoS-prototypes (e.g. for simulation) can be generated from a PCM instance (sufficient information is available in the PCM). A QoS-prototype is a runnable instance of the PCM, having the modelled QoS behaviour. For example, time consumptions are simulated.

12.5 Analysis

The PCM provides two different approaches for performance evaluation, which both are still subject to research. The first approach directly transforms an instance of the PCM to a simulation, which can be executed to derive the required performance metrics (Section 12.5.1). This considers the full expressive power of the PCM for the prediction and does not require further assumptions. The second is a hybrid approach of analysis and simulation to provide an efficient and accurate way of performance evaluation (Section 12.5.2). To do so, PCM instances are transformed into expressions of the process algebra Capra. The analytical framework of Capra then simplifies the expressions and a simulation executes the results to determine the performance metrics of interest. An overview on both approaches follows in Section 12.5.1 and 12.5.2.

We evaluated the response time of the PCM model instance of CoCoME with our simulation approach. This instance was created based solely on the extra-functional properties section from the CoCoME chapter. Therefore, it contains constant time consumptions for actions and stochastic distributions of parameter values. For the evaluation, we chose the bookSale() method, provided by the Store component.

The Figure 13 shows the distribution of the response times of the service (x-axis) in ms and the y-axis depicts the probability for those response times. Figure 13(a) shows the use case with 20 store servers concurrently accessing the enterprise server, while Figure 13(b) shows how the response time changes if 50 store servers are concurrently accessing the enterprise server. For both cases the inter-arrival time of customers was fixed to 11.250 ms, according to the CoCoME specifications.

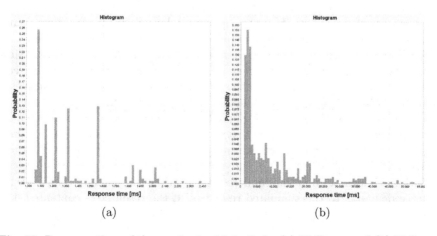

(a)   (b)

Fig. 13. Response time of the service bookSale() for (a) 20 Stores and (b) 50 Stores

For 20 store servers the response time is distributed in an interval from 1.050 to 2.400 ms, while the maximum response time for 50 store servers increases to about 53.000 ms, but the majority of response times was in a range from 1.050 to 20.000 ms. For 20 store servers, the enterprise server has a utilisation of about 45%, while for 50 store servers the enterprise server has a utilisation of 100%.

It becomes clear that the load produced by 50 store servers is already too high for the enterprise server. The enterprise server is not able to handle the load and its queues overflow. Based on the specification of extra-functional properties from the CoCoME chapter, we can state that the system will not support 200 concurrently accessing store servers as specified. Even for one store server, the response time already has a maximum of 1.800 ms with a probability of 7.5%.

Our complete prediction results will be published together with our models[3].

12.5.1   Queuing Network Simulation

Many performance analysis methods use queuing networks as underlying prediction models because of their capability to analyze concurrent system interactions. Queuing models contain a network of service centers with waiting queues which process jobs moving through the network. When applying queuing networks in performance predictions with the PCM, some of the commonly used assumptions need to be dropped. As the PCM uses arbitrary distribution functions for the random variables, generalized distributed service center service times, arrival rates, etc. occur in the model. Additionally, the requests travel through the queuing network according to the control flow specified in the SEFF. In contrast, common queuing networks assume probabilistic movement of the jobs in the network. As a result, only simulation approaches exist, which solve such models.

Hence, we use a model-to-text transformation to generate Java code realizing a custom queuing network simulation based on the simulation framework Desmo-J. The simulation generates service centers and their queues for each active resource. Passive resources are mapped on semaphores initialized with the resources capacity. The transformation generates Java classes for the components and their assembly. Service implementations reflect their respective SEFF.

For the usage model workload drivers for open or closed workloads simulating the behavior of users exist in the generated code. For any call issued to the simulated system, the simulation determines the parameter characterizations of the input parameters and passes them in a so called virtual stackframe to the called service. Originally, the concept of a stackframe comes from compiler construction where they are used to pass parameters to method calls. In the PCM simulation, stackframes pass the parameter characterizations instead.

With the information in the simulated stackframes, the simulated SEFF issues resource demands to the simulated resources. If the resource is contented, the waiting time increases the processing time of the demand.

---

[3] See http://sdqweb.ipd.uka.de/wiki/CoCoME-PCM

The simulation runs until simulation time reaches a predefined upper limit or until the width of the estimation for the confidence interval of the mean of any of the measured response times is smaller than a predefined width. After the end of a simulation run, the simulation result contains different performance indicators (response times, queue lengths, throughputs, ...) which the software architect can analyze to determine performance bottlenecks in the software architecture.

12.5.2   The Stochastic Process Algebra Capra

The stochastic process algebra Capra enhances the performance prediction of concurrent, component-based software architectures specified with the PCM. It employs a hybrid approach of analysis and simulation to increase the efficiency of the prediction. Furthermore, it allows the specification and analysis of current operating system schedulers to enhance prediction accuracy.

The PCM contains lot of information that can be analyzed, if the complete architecture of a software system has been specified. For example, parametric resource demands can be turned into actual values if the characterizations of the influencing parameters are known. Furthermore, multiple demands to the same resource can be combined into a single one if they are arranged in sequences, alternatives, or loops. Unfortunately, the requirements of generally distributed execution times, probabilistic behavior, and scheduled resources forbid a full analysis of architectures in general. However, the mentioned analytical computations offer a high potential for increasing the efficiency and accuracy of the simulation and are exploited in Capra.

In addition to its analytical capabilities, Capra models different scheduling strategies for resources. This includes classical scheduling strategies, such as round robin and first come first serve, known from the embedded systems domain as well as current operating system schedulers from Windows and Linux. Especially in the presence of multi-core and multi processor systems the latter schedulers can have a significant influence on response times and throughput of a software system.

To evaluate the performance of software architectures with Capra, PCM instances are transformed into Capra expressions. To do so, tools solve the parametric dependencies within the SEFFs. They use the parameter characterizations provided by the domain expert in the usage model to transform parametric resource demands to resource demands, guards on branches to probabilities, and parameter dependent loop iteration specifications into iteration numbers. Afterwards, the transformation into Capra is straightforward [27]. The remainder of this section gives a brief overview on Capra's syntax, semantics, and analytical capabilities.

The basic entities of a process are actions. In Capra, the set of actions Act is divided into a set of event actions $EAct$ and demand actions $DAct$. Event actions represent atomic, indivisible behavior which is mainly used for process communication. Demand actions on the other hand represent the usage of resources, like processors and hard disks, for a certain time span. During the execution of a demand action other activities might happen in the system. A random variable $D_{a,r}$ specifies the demand issued by a demand action a to a resource r. It is characterized by a probability density function (pdf) $f_{a,r}(t)$ with $t \in \mathbb{R}$. To create more complex behavioral structures, Capra offers a set of different operators for sequential and alternative composition as well as for the specification of recursive process behavior. The following describes the available operators.

Process $P \cdot Q$ denotes the sequential composition of two processes P and Q. It first executes P and then, after the successful termination of P, it executes Q.

The alternative composition models the execution of only one of the two processes P and Q. Capra distinguishes two types of alternative composition, depending on where the decision for the next activity is made. If the process itself decides on the next activity, the internal or probabilistic choice is used. Process $P \oplus_\pi Q$ selects process P with probability π and process Q with probability $1 - \pi$. On the other hand, the external or non-deterministic choice $P + Q$ models different possible behaviors. Here, the selection is determined by event actions issued by the process' environment, i.e. other processes running in parallel.

A process variable X can be used to define recursive processes. For example, $Do := a.Do$ specifies a process that executes an infinite number of a actions. In real systems, the number of recursive calls is usually bounded. In most cases, the limit is not fixed to a single value, but depends on the system's parameters. To approximate such behavior, Capra models the number of recursive calls as a discrete random variable specified by a probability mass function (pmf). Process $\langle P\ [I]\ Q \rangle$ describes the finite recursion of two processes P and Q. P represents the part before and Q the part after the recursive call. The random variable I characterized by a pmf $P(I = n)$ denotes the probability of executing the recursion n times.

Process $P \parallel_A Q$ denotes the parallel composition of two processes P and Q. The processes communicate (and synchronize) over the event actions in the set A. Both processes compete for the available resources what might delay their execution.

To reduce the complexity of the simulation, the total demand of some operations can be determined in advance. If two processes issue only demands to a single resource, their total demand can be computed for the operations sequential composition, probabilistic choice, and finite recursion. The following gives an impression on the possible analyses.

The total demand of a sequence of demand actions is the sum of the single demands. So, the random variable for the sequential demand is given by $D_{P \cdot Q, r} = D_{P,r} + D_{Q,r}$, where $D_{P,r}$ and $D_{Q,r}$ denote the accumulated demand of processes P and Q respectively. The sum of two random variables is the convolution of its pdfs. Thus, the pdf of $D_{P \cdot Q, r}$ is $f_{P \cdot Q, r}(t) = (f_{P,r} \circledast f_{Q,r})(t)$, where $\circledast$ denotes the convolution. For the probabilistic choice $P \oplus_\pi Q$, the demand is either $D_{P,r}$ with probability π or $D_{Q,r}$ with probability $1 - \pi$. Thus, the pdf of $D_{P \oplus_\pi Q, r}$ is the weighted sum of the probability density functions:

$$f_{P \oplus_\pi Q, r}(t) = \pi f_{P,r}(t) + (1 - \pi) f_{Q,r}(t).$$

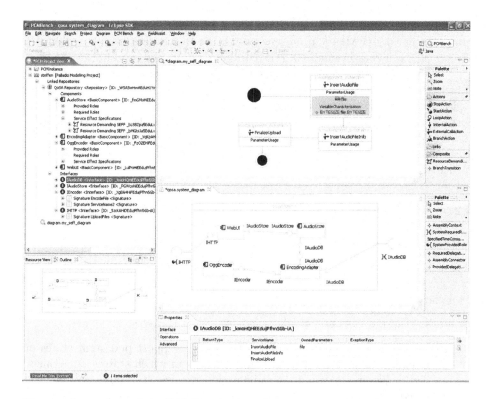

Fig. 14. Screenshot of the PCMBench: An editor suite for the Palladio Component Model

Finite recursion can be considered as large probabilistic choices over the n-time sequential composition of processes P and Q. The pmf $p_i(n) = P(I = n)$ defines the probabilities for the probabilistic choice. Thus, function

$$f_{\langle P \ [I] \ Q \rangle, r}(t) = \left(\sum_{i=0}^{N} p_I(i) \bigotimes_{j=1}^{i} (f_{P,r} \circledast f_{Q,r}) \right)(t)$$

computes the pdf for demand $D_{\langle P \ [I] \ Q \rangle, r}$.

The computations described here reduce the complexity of Capra expressions allowing a more efficient and more accurate simulation. In the special case, that all demands are issued to the same resource and no concurrency is used, the whole expression can be solved analytically. In this case, Capra is similar to stoachstic regular expressions [32].

12.6   Tools

For the PCM, a tool suite is freely available for download[4]. The so-called PCM-Bench combines different views on the PCM within an Eclipse Rich Client

---

[4] http://sdqweb.ipd.uka.de/wiki/Palladio_Component_Model

Platform [33]. While the model itself is implemented using the Eclipse Modelling Framework (EMF) [34], most views on the PCM are editors based on the Graphical Modeling Framework (GMF) [35]. Component repositories, SEFFs, systems, usage models, and resource environments can be edited graphically in a concrete syntax comparable to UML diagrams.

Figure 14 shows a screenshot of the PCMBench: The top view shows an instance of a SEFF, while the bottom view gives an example of a system model. The analysis approaches can be accessed from the PCMBench.

To extract PCM instances from given source code, tools exist [36] that reconstruct SEFFs.

12.7   Summary

12.7.1   Limitations

There are a few limitations that apply to the current version of the PCM. Some of them will be addressed in future work, other limitations are intrinsic with the Palladio approach.

Limitations of the current Palladio approach.

- The PCM and the analysis approaches do not support persistent states of components. Therefore, it is not differentiated in which state a component is – for every service call of the same provided service the same behaviour is expected. The only way to model a state is to use call parameters of a service. In this case a set of parameters is representing the state of a component. Support for component states is planned for the future, probably including support of special stateful entities like databases.
- Dynamic architectures (where component's bindings change at runtime) are not supported at the moment. The PCM supports static architectures, i.e. static bindings and contexts only, that do not change at run-time. Changes of component contexts at design time are supported.
- Connections have to be one to one connections in the PCM. If a component is requiring a service, this service can be provided only by one component at the same time. Especially redundancy or the choice among multiple routes is not supported. N to n connections are currently not supported because of ambiguities of semantics arising from the relaxation of the meta-model. To model such constructs one needs to model redundancy explicitly by a component. This component would delegate incoming calls to other components, keeping routing and redundancy explicit.

Shortcomings of the PCM when modelling CoCoME.

- The PCM is designed for business information systems, not for embedded systems. The point of sale (POS) part of CoCoME was left out for reasons of simplicity, because our analysis methods do not support embedded systems, and because the event-channel architecture would have lead to problems in modelling. One would have had to introduce an explicit own component to manage the control and data flow, represented by the event channel.

– Composite components in the PCM are pure logical entities. They are just bundling other entities, to support information hiding and composition. In the PCM they do not support a own business logic representation or SEFF, respectively. To model CoCoME adequate, we introduced facade components for two composite components that contained business logic: TradingSystem.Inventory.Data and TradingSystem.Inventory.Application.

– EnterpriseServer and StoreServer are in a 1:n relation at the deployment level. n StoreServers interact with one EnterpriseServer. The same applies to the GUI for Store and Enterprise Server. The PCM does not support 1:n relations between deployment nodes (*ResourceContainers*). If one requires those relations, they have to be modelled explicitly: for n StoreServers the model would contain n StoreServer instances. A simple multiplicity construct ("*") is not available. The example model instance of CoCoME does contain only four *ResourceContainers* for this reasons.

– Exceptions have not been modelled because it lacks support by analysis tools, although the PCM itself supports exception modelling.

– In the SEFF for the ProductDispatcher concurrency for the parallel database flush is not supported by the PCM. A loop was modelled instead with one iteration for each concurrent thread. Extensions of the PCM for concurrency are planned at an "architectural level", for example supporting patterns like rendezvous or replication. A component designer will be able to decide *whether* concurrency is used, but has no direct influence on the implemenation. Support of concurrency at an implementation level (`Thread.start()` or `Thread.join()`) is not planned for the future.

– The PCM allocates entities separately only if they are directly contained in a system. If for example Component A and B are included into Composite Component C, where C is part of the system model, only C can be directly deployed. This principle was introduced to keep the black-blox principle of components. It would be broken, if sub-components of composite components could be allocated white-box-like. The internals of composite components are hidden, while the internals of a system are visible for a component deployer. To support the distributed architecture of CoCoME, we had to "move" the system level: The composite component TODO was removed and the resulting structure was modelled explicitly in the system model.

– POS and the database were considered to be system-external services, as explained in Section 12.3.

12.7.2 Lessons Learned

An allocation, not only including components directly inside a system, was required for CoCoME. This challenges the PCM: either the modelling, given by the UML sources from CoCoME were not ideal for the PCM, or the allocation concept, maintaining the black-box principle for allocations, is not optimal.

12.7.3 Conclusion

In this chapter we presented the Palladio approach consisting of a comprehensive meta-model "Palladio Component Model", a number of analysis methods, and a component-based software development process, tied to the Palladio approach. Palladio focusses on software systems, especially business information system to support the prediction of QoS properties, namely performance (throughput, execution time).

The approach supports modelling of component repositories including behavioural component descriptions (SEFF) and protocol definitions, allows to take usage profiles into consideration, makes use of stochastic distributions and parametric dependencies, while keeping the approach simple via domain specific languages for multiple roles involved in the development process. Additionally, typical component claims are fulfilled: support of re-use, "unit of independent deployment", and contractually specified entity.

Analysis methods developed for the Palladio approach range from simulation based approaches to analysis methods, based on process algebras. Tool support for both, analysis and modelling, allows easy application.

We conclude the chapter on the Palladio approach with our primary targets for *future work*:

- We plan to introduce an additional abstraction level to support architectural patterns by an extended PCM. By using completions, we want to support high-level modelling: Users of the PCM use high-level constructs that are then automatically transformed into existing PCM constructs.

    For example, this are high-level concurrency modelling constructs: We plan to add special modelling constructs for concurrent control flow into the PCM. This shall relieve the burden from developers to specify concurrent behaviour with basic constructs, such as forks or semaphores for synchronisation. The concurrency modelling constructs shall be aligned with known concurrency patterns and be configurable via feature diagrams. Model-transformations shall transform the high-level modelling constructs to the performance domain of analytical and simulation models.

- Dynamic Architectures: The PCM is only targeted at static architectures, and does not allow the creation/deletion of components during runtime or changing links between components. With the advent of web services and systems with dynamic architectures changing during runtime, researchers pursuit methods to predict the dynamic performance properties of such systems.

- Resource Model: The PCM's resource model is still very limited and supports only a few types of abstract resource types on the hardware layer. QoS influencing factors from the middleware, the virtual machine, and operating system are still missing in the PCMs resource model. We plan to introduce a layered resource model, where different system levels (such as middleware, operating system, hardware) can be modelled independently and then composed vertically, just as software components are composed horizontally.

References

1. Szyperski, C., Gruntz, D., Murer, S.: Component Software: Beyond Object-Oriented Programming, 2nd edn. ACM Press, Addison-Wesley, New York (2002)
2. Martens, A.: Empirical Validation of the Model-driven Performance Prediction Approach Palladio. Master's thesis, Universität Oldenburg (2007)
3. Reussner, R.H.: Parametrisierte Verträge zur Protokolladaption bei Software-Komponenten. Logos Verlag, Berlin (2001)
4. Lau, K. K., Wang, Z.: A Taxonomy of Software Component Models. In: Proceedings of the 31st EUROMICRO Conference, pp. 88–95 (2005)
5. Bondarev, E., de With, P.H.N., Chaudron, M.: Predicting real-time properties of component-based applications. In: 10th International RTCSA Conference (2004)
6. Stafford, J.A., Wallnau, K.C.: Predicting feature interactions in component-based systems. In: Proceedings of the Workshop on Feature Interaction of Composed Systems (2001)
7. van Ommering, R., van der Linden, F., Kramer, J., Magee, J.: The Koala Component Model for Consumer Electronics Software. Computer 33(3), 78–85 (2000)
8. Plasil, F., Balek, D., Janecek, R.: SOFA/DCUP: Architecture for component trading and dynamic updating. In: ICCDS 1998, pp. 43–52. IEEE Press, Los Alamitos (1998)
9. Bruneton, E., Coupaye, T., Stefani, J.: The Fractal component model. Technical report specification v2, The ObjectWeb Consortium (2003)
10. (OMG), O.M.G.: Unified modeling language specification: Version 2, revised final adopted specification (ptc/05-07-04) (2005)
11. Cortellessa, V.: How far are we from the definition of a common software performance ontology? In: WOSP 2005: Proceedings of the 5th International Workshop on Software and Performance, Palma, Illes Balears, Spain, pp. 195–204 (2005)
12. Smith, C.U.: Performance Engineering of Software Systems (1990)
13. Object Management Group (OMG): UML Profile for Schedulability, Performance and Time (2005)
14. Petriu, D.B., Woodside, M.: A metamodel for generating performance models from UML designs. In: Baar, T., Strohmeier, A., Moreira, A., Mellor, S.J. (eds.) UML 2004. LNCS, vol. 3273, pp. 41–53. Springer, Heidelberg (2004)
15. Grassi, V., Mirandola, R., Sabetta, A.: Filling the gap between design and performance/reliability models of component-based systems: A model-driven approach. Journal on Systems and Software 80(4), 528–558 (2007)
16. Sitaraman, M., Kuczycki, G., Krone, J., Ogden, W.F., Reddy, A.L.N.: Performance Specification of Software Components. In: Proceedings of the 2001 symposium on Software reusability: putting software reuse in context (2001)
17. Eskenazi, E., Fioukov, A., Hammer, D.: Performance prediction for component compositions. In: Crnković, I., Stafford, J.A., Schmidt, H.W., Wallnau, K. (eds.) CBSE 2004. LNCS, vol. 3054. Springer, Heidelberg (2004)
18. Hamlet, D., Mason, D., Woit, D.: Component-based software development: Case studies. Series on Component-Based Software Development, vol. 1, pp. 129–159. World Scientific Publishing Company, Singapore (2004)
19. Liu, Y., Fekete, A., Gorton, I.: Design-Level Performance Prediction of Component-Based Applications 31(11), 928–941 (2005)
20. Bondarev, E., de With, P., Chaudron, M., Musken, J.: Modelling of Input-Parameter Dependency for Performance Predictions of Component-Based Embedded Systems. In: Proceedings of the 31th EUROMICRO Conference (EUROMICRO 2005) (2005)

21. Bertolino, A., Mirandola, R.: CB-SPE Tool: Putting Component-Based Performance Engineering into Practice. In: Crnković, I., Stafford, J.A., Schmidt, H.W., Wallnau, K.C. (eds.) CBSE 2004. LNCS, vol. 3054, pp. 233–248. Springer, Heidelberg (2004)
22. Reussner, R., Becker, S., Koziolek, H., Happe, J., Kuperberg, M., Krogmann, K.: The palladio component model. Technical report, University of Karlsruhe (to be published, 2007)
23. IEEE P1471: IEEE Recommended practice for architectural description of software-intensive systems (2000)
24. (OMG), O.M.G.: The CORBA homepage, http://www.corba.org
25. Budinsky, F., Steinberg, D., Merks, E., Ellersick, R., Grose, T.J.: Eclipse Modeling Framework. Eclipse Series. Addison-Wesley, Reading (2004)
26. Object Management Group (OMG): Object constraint language, v2.0 (formal/06-05-01) (2006)
27. Becker, S., Koziolek, H., Reussner, R.: Model-based Performance Prediction with the Palladio Component Model. In: Workshop on Software and Performance (WOSP 2007). ACM Sigsoft, New York (2007)
28. Koziolek, H., Happe, J., Becker, S.: Parameter Dependent Performance Specification of Software Components. In: Hofmeister, C., Crnković, I., Reussner, R. (eds.) QoSA 2006. LNCS, vol. 4214. Springer, Heidelberg (2006)
29. Becker, S., Happe, J., Koziolek, H.: Putting Components into Context: Supporting QoS-Predictions with an explicit Context Model. In: Reussner, R., Szyperski, C., Weck, W. (eds.) Proceedings of the 11th International Workshop on Component Oriented Programming (WCOP 2006), Nantes, France (2006)
30. Sun Microsystems Corp.: The Enterprise Java Beans homepage, http://java.sun.com/products/ejb/
31. Völter, M., Stahl, T.: Model-Driven Software Development. Wiley, Chichester (2006)
32. Koziolek, H., Firus, V., Becker, S., Reussner, R.: Bewertungstechniken fr die performanz. In: Hasselbring, W., Reussner, R. (eds.) Handbuch der Software-Architektur, pp. 311–326. dpunkt-Verlag (2006)
33. Eclipse Foundation: Eclipse Rich Client Platform, http://www.eclipse.org/home/categories/rcp.php
34. Eclipse Foundation: Eclipse Modeling Framework (EMF), http://www.eclipse.org/modeling/emf/
35. Eclipse Foundation: Graphical Modeling Framework (GMF), http://www.eclipse.org/gmf
36. Kappler, T.: Code-Analysis Using Eclipse to Support Performance Prediction for Java Components. Master's thesis, Institute for Programmstructures and Data Organisation, University of Karlsruhe (TH) (2007)

13 KLAPER: An Intermediate Language for Model-Driven Predictive Analysis of Performance and Reliability

Vincenzo Grassi[1], Raffaela Mirandola[2], Enrico Randazzo[3], and Antonino Sabetta[4]

[1] Dipartimento di Informatica, Sistemi e Produzione Università di Roma "Tor Vergata", Italy
[2] Politecnico di Milano, Piazza Leonardo Da Vinci, 32, 20133 Milano, Italy
[3] Intecs S.p.A., Roma, Italy
[4] ISTI-CNR, Pisa, Italy

Abstract. Automatic prediction tools play a key role in enabling the application of non-functional analysis to the selection and the assembly of components for component-based systems, without requiring extensive knowledge of analysis methodologies to the application designer. A key idea to achieve this goal is to define a *model transformation* that takes as input some "design-oriented" model of the component assembly and produces as a result an "analysis-oriented" model that lends itself to the application of some analysis methodology. For this purpose, we define a model-driven transformation framework, centered around a kernel language whose aim is to capture the relevant information for the analysis of non-functional attributes of component-based systems, with a focus on performance and reliability. Using this kernel language as a bridge between design-oriented and analysis-oriented notations we reduce the burden of defining a variety of direct transformations from the former to the latter to the less complex problem of defining transformations to/from the kernel language. The proposed kernel language is defined within the MOF (Meta-Object Facility) framework, to allow the exploitation of existing model transformation facilities. In this chapter, we present the key concepts of our methodology and we show its application to the CoCoME case study.

13.1 Introduction

It has been widely argued that the analysis of non-functional attributes (e.g. performance or reliability) should be performed starting from the design phase of software systems, before their actual implementation, to reduce the costs of late problem fixing [1]. The goal of our approach is to support the early analysis of non-functional attributes for software systems built according to a component-based development (CBD) paradigm. According to CBD, a software system is an assembly of pre-existing, independently developed components, with the focus

A. Rausch et al. (Eds.): Common Component Modeling Example, LNCS 5153, pp. 327–356, 2008.

of system development shifting from custom design and implementation to the selection, composition and coordination of components [2,3]. Hence, the application of the above argument to CBD means that the analysis of non-functional attributes of a component assembly should be performed before actually assembling the components, to drive the selection of the components themselves and of the possible ways of composing and coordinating them, as also argued in [2] (chapters 8 and 9).

An obvious implication of the introduction of non-functional analysis from the design phase of software systems is that such analysis must be based on *predictive* methodologies applied to some suitable system model. In this respect one of the main problems to be faced is represented by the lack of sufficient expertise of the application designers in non-functional analysis methodologies. To overcome this problem, supporting tools have been recently proposed, whose key idea is to define automatic *model transformations* that take as input some "design-oriented" model of the software system (augmented with additional information related to the non-functional attributes of interest) and generates an "analysis-oriented" model, that lends itself to the application of some analysis methodology [4,5]. Most of these proposals assume a UML notation for the design-oriented model [6], and generate as output a variety of analysis-oriented models, spanning queueing networks, Petri nets, Markov processes, simulation models. The idea of looking at the construction of an analysis-oriented model as the result of a transformation from a design-oriented model, has the additional advantage that non-functional analysis can be better integrated within the recently emerged *model driven development* (MDD) [7] paradigm for software system, where a central role is played by models and model transformations. Indeed, the adoption of MDD methodologies and tools have been recently proposed to support the definition of model transformations from design-oriented models of the software system to analysis-oriented models [8,9].

However, defining such a "single step" transformation could be quite cumbersome, for several reasons: the large semantic gap between the source and target model of the transformation, the heterogeneous design notations that could be used by different component providers, and the different target analysis notations one could be interested in, to support different kinds of analysis (e.g. queueing networks for performance analysis, Markov processes for reliability analysis). To alleviate these problems, some intermediate modeling languages have been recently proposed, to capture and express the relevant information for the analysis of QoS attributes. Their goal is to help in distilling this information from complex design-oriented models, serving as a bridge between design-oriented and analysis-oriented notations [10,11,12]. In this way, the direct transformation from source to target models can be split into a two-step transformation from the source model to an intermediate model expressed using this intermediate language, and then from the intermediate model to the target model. Our work belongs to this group of approaches. The next subsections give an overview of our approach that is then detailed in the rest of the chapter.

13.1.1 Goals and Scope of the Model

Our approach is centered on the definition of a suitable intermediate language, called KLAPER (Kernel LAnguage for PErformance and Reliability analysis) [10], whose goal is to support the generation of stochastic models for the predictive analysis of performance and reliability, starting from the design-level model of a component-based (C-B) software system. This intermediate language, specified through a MOF metamodel, is based on an abstract notion of Resource, which can be used to model both application level components, platform level devices. Resources, which offer Services that may require in turn other services, are composed through a client/server-like composition with both synchronous and asynchronous interactions. A KLAPER model is derived from a design-level model (by means of transformation rules), to make performance or reliability predictions, independently of the availability of an implementation of the application itself (which anyway is be useful to parameterize the model). Since deployment information could not be known at early design stage, a KLAPER model can be built without using this information and can then be incrementally updated once this information is made available.

13.1.2 Modeled Cutout of CoCoME

As remarked above we model non-functional properties focusing on stochastic performance analysis. Even though KLAPER supports also reliability analysis, for the CoCoME example we do not analyze reliability. The verification of functional properties is out of the scope of our approach.

Specifically, for the CoCoME example, we modeled only use cases UC1 and UC3 (due to time limitations); they were modeled considering only their main flow, excluding alternative behaviors. For these use cases we evaluated performance measures such as server utilization, throughput, response time.

13.1.3 Benefit of the Modeling

One of main strengths of KLAPER is its independence of specific component models design notation. On the negative side, it should be noted that KLAPER is inherently based on a client-server architectural model. Other styles, e.g. event-based interactions, are not considered yet. Including support for them would require a modification, possibly minimal, of the metamodel of KLAPER.

Also, the usability of KLAPER is still quite low, mostly because of the incomplete implementation of supporting tools, such as automatic transformations and graphical editors (both are in the works, as of this writing).

13.1.4 Effort and Lessons Learned

The modeling and the analysis of CoCoME involved 2 person months (performing by hand most of the transformations). We estimate that this effort can become as low as a few days once the transformation tools are available. Moreover, we estimate that the complete modeling of CoCoME (i.e. taking into account alternative behaviours) would involve 5 more person months (given the the present state of the transformation framework).

By modelling the CoCoME example we gained considerable insights in the problems caused by lack of (or possible mismatch between) performance/reliability information expected as input by the KLAPER model, and the information that is actually available in the source design model (UML in the case of CoCoME).

The remainder of this chapter is organized as follows. Section 2 presents the main characteristics of the MDD-based approach we followed and of the KLAPER intermediate language. Section 3 shows the modelling of the CoCoMe example through KLAPER, and Section 4 presents both the derivation of a performance model for CoCoME and the analysis of the results obtained. Section 5 outlines the framework that supports the KLAPER application and section 6 concludes the paper.

13.2   The KLAPER Model: An Abstraction for Component Models

In this section we first present the key points of our MDD-based approach to the generation of a performance/reliability model for a C-B system (section 13.2.1). Then we present the metamodel of the intermediate language that we propose to support this approach (section 13.2.2).

13.2.1   The Basic Methodology

The central element of our approach is the definition of KLAPER [10]. As we mentioned in the introduction, the goal of an intermediate language is split the complex task of deriving an analysis model (e.g. a queueing network) from a high level design model (expressed using UML or other component-oriented notations) into two separate and presumably simpler tasks:

- extracting from the design model only the information that is relevant for the analysis of some QoS attribute and expressing it in terms of the key concepts provided by the intermediate language;
- generating an analysis model based on the information expressed in the intermediate language.

These two tasks may be solved independently of each other. Moreover, as a positive side effect of this two-step approach, we mitigate the "n-by-m" problem of translating n heterogeneous design notations (that could be used by different component providers) into m analysis notations (that support different kinds of analysis), reducing it to a less complex task of defining $n + m$ transformations: n from different design notations to the intermediate language, and m from it to different analysis notations (see Figure 1).

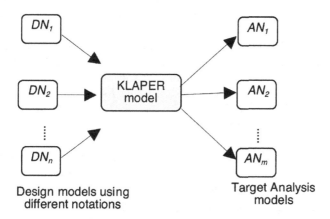

Fig. 1. Our contribution within a transformation path from design models of C-B applications (expressed using notations DN1, ..,DNn) to different types of performance/reliability models (expressed by notations AN1, .., ANm)

The KLAPER goal is to capture in a lightweight and compact model only the relevant information for the stochastic performance and reliability analysis of C-B systems, while abstracting away irrelevant details. In particular, we point out that KLAPER is neither a language to be used for the system design (notations like UML are better suited for this purpose), nor is it an analysis language (specific notations exist for this purpose, e.g. stochastic process algebras). KLAPER has been designed as an intermediate "distilled" language to help define transformations between design-oriented and analysis-oriented notations, by bridging the large semantic gap that usually separates them.

To integrate this kernel language into an MDD framework, leveraging the current state of the art in the field of model transformation methodologies, we have defined KLAPER as a Meta-Object Facility (MOF) metamodel [13]. MOF is the metamodeling framework proposed by the Object Management Group (OMG) for the management of models and their transformations within the OMG "implementation" of the MDD paradigm, known as Model Driven Architecture (MDA) [14]. According to MOF, a (meta)model is basically a constrained directed labeled graph, and a metamodel defines the syntactic and semantic rules to build legal models.

Hence, we can use the MDA-MOF facilities to devise transformations to/from KLAPER models, provided that a MOF metamodel exists for the corresponding source/target model. According to the MDD perspective, these transformations can be defined as a set of rules that map elements of the source metamodel onto elements of the target metamodel.

13.2.2   The KLAPER Metamodel

Fig. 2 shows the structure of the KLAPER MOF metamodel, while Fig. 3 summarizes the list of attributes and associations for the relevant KLAPER metaclasses.

We refer to [10] for the complete MOF specification and to [15] for an up-to-date view of its implementation status.

To support the distillation from the design models of a C-B system of the relevant information for stochastic performance/reliability analysis, KLAPER is built around an abstract representation of such a system, modeled (including the underlying platform) as an assembly of interacting *Resources*. Each Resource offers (and possibly requires) one or more *Services*. A KLAPER Resource is thus an abstract modeling concept that can be used to represent both software components and physical resources like processors and communication links.

A *scheduling policy* and a *multiplicity* (number of concurrent requests that can be served in parallel) can be associated with a resource to possibly model access control policies for the services offered by that resource. Each service offered by a resource is characterized by its *formal parameters* that can be instantiated with actual values by other resources requiring that service, We point out that both the formal parameters and their corresponding actual parameters are intended to represent a suitable abstraction (for the analysis purposes) of the real service parameters. For example, a real list parameter for some list processing software component could be abstractly represented as an integer valued random variable, where the integer value represents the list size, and its probability distribution provides information about the likelihood of different sizes in a given analysis scenario. We explicitly introduce service parameters to better support compositional and parametric analysis.

To bring performance/reliability related information within such an abstract model, each activity in the system is modeled as the execution of a *Step* that may take time to be completed, and/or may fail before its completion: the *internalExecTime*, *internalFailTime* and *internalFailProb* attributes of each step may be used to give a probabilistic characterization of this aspects of a step execution.

Steps are grouped in *Behaviors* (directed graphs of nodes) that may be associated either with the Services offered by Resources (reactive behavior), or with a *Workload* modeling the demand injected into the system by external entities like the system users (proactive behavior). *Control steps* can be used to regulate the flow of control from step to step, according to a probabilistic setting.

A *ServiceCall* step is a special kind of Step which models the relationship between required and offered services. Each ServiceCall specifies the name of the requested service and the type of resource that should provide it.

In the original metamodel presented in [10], ServiceCalls were directly associated with the actual service instances representing the required services. With respect to [10], in this chapter we present an slightly modified metamodel where the relationship between a ServiceCall and the actual recipient of the call is represented separately by means of instances of the *Binding* metaclass. This allows a clear separation between the models of the components (by means of Resources/Services) and the model of their composition. In fact a set of bindings can be regarded as a self-contained specification of an assembly. Similarly, since the service call concept is also used at the KLAPER level to model the access

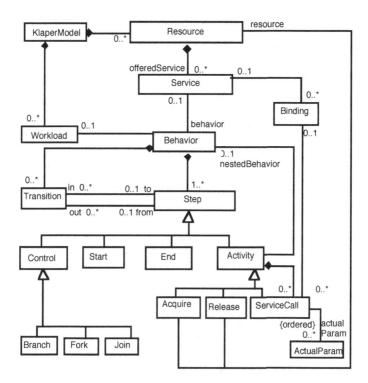

Fig. 2. The KLAPER MOF metamodel

of software components to platform level services, a suitable set of bindings can model as well the deployment of the application components on the underlying platform.

Finally, we point out that the performance/reliability attributes associated with a behavior step concern only the *internal* characteristics of the behavior; they do not take into account possible delays or failures caused by the use of other required services, that are needed to complete that step. In this respect, we remark that when we build a KLAPER model (first task outlined above) our goal is mainly "descriptive". The Bindings included in the model help to identify which external services may cause additional delays or failure possibilities. How to properly mix this "external" information with the internal information to get an overall picture of the service performance or reliability is out of the KLAPER scope. This problem must be solved during the generation and solution of an analysis model derived from a KLAPER model.

13.2.3 KLAPER-Based Model Generation

Figure 4 illustrates the main steps of our general KLAPER-based transformation framework.

> **Resource:** *attributes*: name, type, capacity, schedulingPolicy, description; *associations*: offeredService.
> **Service**: *attributes*:name, formalParams, speedAttr, failAttr, description; *associations*: behavior, resource.
> **Behavior** : *associations*: service, step, workload.
> **Step** : *attributes*: name; *associations*: in, out.
> **Activity** : *attributes*: name, repetition, /internalExecTime, /internalFailProb, /internalFailTime,completionModel; *associations*: nestedBehavior, serviceCall.
> **Branch** : *attributes*: branchProbs.
> **Acquire** : *attributes* : resourceUnits; *associations*: resource
> **Release** : *attributes*: resourceUnits; *associations*: resource
> **ServiceCall** : *attributes*: resourceType, serviceName, isSynch; *associations*: step, actualParam, calledService
> **Workload** : *attributes*: workloadType, arrivalProcess, population, initialResource; *associations*: behavior.
> **ActualParam** : *attributes*: value.
> **Transition** : *associations*: to, from.
> **Binding** : *associations* : serviceCall, service.

Fig. 3. Attributes and associations of the main KLAPER metaclasses

The input of our framework (Step 0) is represented by a design-level model of a C-B system, expressed by possibly heterogeneous notations (which may include UML and other suitable notations). In general, design models may lack performance and/or reliability information which is necessary to derive meaningful analysis models. Therefore (Step 1), design models must be annotated with missing information about non-functional attributes. In the case of UML design models, annotations can be added following the OMG standard SPT profile [16]. In this way we obtain what we call Performance/Reliability-aware models.

At Step 2 we generate KLAPER models from the design models with performance/reliability annotations. We distinguish a *pre-assembly time* case (Step 2.1) from an *assembly time* case (Step 2.2): in the former case information about how the selected resources and services are assembled and deployed on some platform is not yet available, while this information is available in the latter case. Hence at step 2.1 we can only map models of isolated elements of a C-B system onto corresponding KLAPER models, using suitable transformation rules (*transformation rules 1*).

The main missing elements in the resulting models of Step 2.1 are the *Binding* associations between ServiceCall steps and the corresponding services. These associations depend on how the single elements are assembled. When this information is available, we can specify all the needed *Binding* associations, so getting a complete assembly model (*transformation rules 2*). Finally, at Step 3, we can generate from this overall model a performance, reliability or performability model (*transformation rules 3*) expressed in some machine interpretable notation, and then we can solve it using suitable solution methodologies. The predictions obtained from the analysis of performance and/or reliability models obtained at Step 3 can be exploited to perform *what-if* experiments and to drive

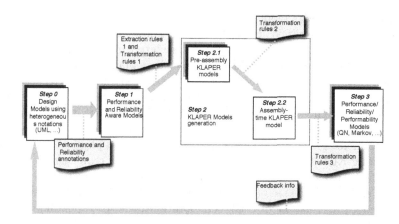

Fig. 4. KLAPER-based modeling framework

decisions about which components should be used and how they should be architected so as to meet the quality requirements imposed on the design (feedback info to Step 0).

13.3 Modelling the CoCoME: Generation of a **KLAPER** Model from a Design-Level Model

In this section, we first outline the main steps of the transformation process from design models to KLAPER models, assuming UML as design-level notation. Then we give examples of the KLAPER models we can obtain applying these rules to the CoCoME example. As already pointed out, we are currently working toward their actual definition as a set of QVT-based [17] transformation rules between elements of the corresponding metamodels.

13.3.1 Transformation from the UML to the **KLAPER** Metamodel (Pre-assembly)

We refer to UML models of (parts of) component-based systems where *components* are modeled according to the UML 2.0 specification [6]. Hence, we assume that each software component is modeled as a UML 2.0 component, with its associated set of *provided* and *required* interfaces. The internal behavior of a component is described by a UML *state machine* or *activity diagram*. The interactions among components occur according to "interaction protocols" modeled as UML *collaborations*. The physical devices of some supporting platform are modeled as UML *nodes*, and the mapping of components onto these nodes is modeled by *deployment diagrams*. Component use cases are modeled using UML *sequence* or *activity diagrams*.

Moreover, we assume that the UML model is enriched with performance/ reliability information expressed using the notation of the standard UML-SPT profile [16].

Mapping these UML model elements onto KLAPER elements is relatively straightforward, as outlined in the following. The basic idea is to map UML components, nodes and collaborations (with the latter modeling interaction protocols) onto KLAPER resources. Each of these three mappings is further refined as follows. In the case of UML components, the offered and required services of the corresponding KLAPER resource are derived from the provided and required interfaces of the component. For each KLAPER offered service its associated behavior is derived from the state machine or activity diagram of the corresponding UML component. In the case of UML nodes (which model physical devices), the corresponding KLAPER resource offers a simple (i.e. not requiring the services of other resources) service, whose behavior consists, besides the *Start* and *End* steps, of a single *Activity* step (modeling, for example, a processing activity for a cpu-type node). In the case of UML collaborations, the corresponding KLAPER resource offers an "interaction service" (and possibly requires other services, like processing or communication), whose associated behavior is derived from the UML diagram modeling the collaboration dynamics.

Then, we map the UML diagrams modeling component use cases onto suitable KLAPER workloads, with their associated behaviors derived from the UML diagrams (e.g. sequence diagrams) modeling the use case dynamics.

Finally, we give some additional information for the mapping from UML behavioral diagram (i.e. state machine, sequence and activity diagrams) onto KLAPER Behavior. The flow of control within these diagrams can be easily mapped onto suitable KLAPER control steps. Since KLAPER is based on a stochastic behavior model, this mapping could require a transformation from a deterministic to a corresponding stochastic setting. For example, two alternative control paths selected by means of some logical condition can be mapped to a KLAPER Branch control step with a pair of branching probabilities, whose values should represent the frequency of the cases where the condition holds true or false, respectively. This information should be expressed by a suitable UML-SPT annotation included in the UML model provided by the component provider. If this is not the case, the KLAPER branching probabilities are left unspecified, and must be specified to get a complete KLAPER model. Then, we map each *PAstep* labeled as *PAdemand* in the UML diagram onto a KLAPER *ServiceCall* step addressed to a cpu-type resource, and each *PAstep* labeled as a "network" *PAextop* to a KLAPER *ServiceCall* step addressed to a network-type resource. Moreover, we map each service request (e.g. a message in a UML sequence diagram) addressed to some component onto a *ServiceCall* step addressed to a resource of suitable type. For all the above outlined mappings, the attributes of KLAPER modeling elements are mainly derived from information expressed by the UML-SPT annotations included in the UML models.

13.3.2   Transformation from the UML to the KLAPER Metamodel (Post-assembly)

Using the transformations outlined above we can map models of isolated elements of a component-based system (and of the underlying platform) to corresponding

KLAPER models. The main missing information in the resulting models concerns the *Binding* associations between offered and required services, that depend on how the single elements are assembled together. Of course, without these associations, we cannot use the KLAPER model to carry out any analysis of the overall assembly. At assembly time this information becomes available. Hence we can specify all the needed *Bindings*, so getting a complete KLAPER assembly model. For this purpose, we can proceed by visiting the behavior associated with each service in the KLAPER resource models, searching for *ServiceCall* steps. For each such step, we distinguish two cases, that is whether it models a request addressed to a physical device (like a processor or a network link) or to a software component.

In the former case, we use deployment information provided by the source design model to create *Bindings* between the *ServiceCall* step and the offered service of the KLAPER resource modeling that physical device.

In the latter case, we know from the assembly model whether the request is mediated by some connector. If this is not the case, then we proceed similarly to requests addressed to physical devices. Otherwise, our goal is to make explicit in the KLAPER model the resource consumption due to the use of that connector. For this purpose, the general idea is to transform the service request to a software component into a service request addressed to the KLAPER resource modeling the connector, which in turn will "forward" it to the software component. How to actually implement this general idea depends on the type of connector used in the components assembly. Examples of KLAPER models of some connector types can be found in [10,18]. The following subsection includes an example of KLAPER modeling of a connection between two remote components.

13.3.3   Examples of KLAPER Modeling of CoCoME

Figures from 5 to 9 show some examples of the KLAPER models obtained applying the previous rules to the CoCoME description. For these examples we have selected the CoCoME use cases UC1 (which is the "main" use case) and UC3. Specifically we show the KLAPER models derived from the UC1 main operation (figure 5) and from the UC3 main operation (Figure 6), from the UC3 Store-Get-product operation when the deployment has not been specified yet (Figure 7) and the UC3 Store-Get-product operation when the deployment has been specified (Figure 8).

The KLAPER model of Figure 5 has been derived from the UML sequence diagram describing the UC1 main operation. This sequence diagram models the "service demand" addressed to the cash system by the arriving customers. Hence, it has been mapped to a KLAPER workload (whose arrivalProcess attribute is derived from the *arr-1* CoCoME specification). The first step of its behavior models the start of a new sale: it has an internalExecTime attribute whose value is derived from the *t12-1* CoCoME specification, and is used to model the "human time" to complete this operation. This step is modeled as a ServiceCall since it also involves an interaction with a CashBox resource: hence, the total time to complete the step will include the time for the completion of the called

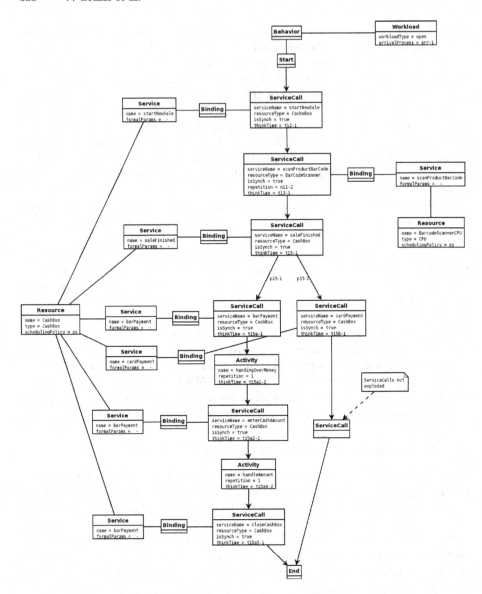

Fig. 5. A KLAPER Workload modeling the UC1 main operation

CashBox service. The next step in the KLAPER model models the sequence diagram loop for the processing of all the items to be payed: the number of loop iterations is modeled by the repetition attribute (whose value is derived from the *n11-2* CoCoME specification). Again, this step is a ServiceCall addressed to a BarCodeScanner resource, and the same considerations made before for the total completion time of this kind of step hold here. This step is followed by another step (modeling the sale completion) and then by the conditional choice between two steps corresponding to the two possible payment modes.

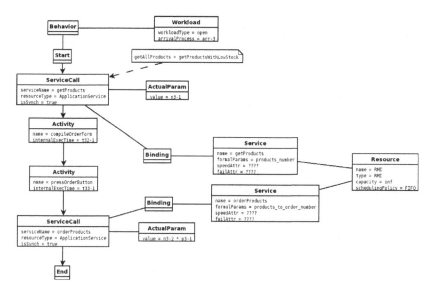

Fig. 6. A KLAPER Workload modeling the UC3 main operation

In the stochastic setting adopted by KLAPER, this conditional choice has been mapped to a probabilistic selection (with probabilities derived form the CoCoME specifications *p15-1* and *p15-2*). As a final remark for the model shown in Fig. 5, we point out that it is a "post-assembly" KLAPER model: indeed it includes the specification of the bindings of the ServiceCall steps with the services offered by suitable Resources (not completely shown in the figure for the sake of simplicity). We could obtain the corresponding "pre-assembly" model by simply dropping the shown bindings.

The KLAPER model in Figure 6 has been obtained from the CoCoME UC3 main operation model. Analogously to the previous case, the source model has been mapped to a KLAPER workload. A notable difference of this example with respect to the previous one is the presence of actual parameters in some ServiceCall steps of the workload behavior, thus showing the KLAPER flexibility in modeling the composition of services. For example, this is the case of the first step, whose actual parameter models the number of products for the getProducts operation. We point out that its value, derived from the *n3-1* CoCoME specification, should be intended in a probabilistic way (e.g. as an average value), according to the general KLAPER setting. This actual parameter matches with the formal parameter (*product-number*) of the service to which the service call is bound.

Figures 7 and 8 have been obtained from the specification of the CoCoME UC3 get-product operation, and are examples of the different kinds of KLAPER models that can be generated at different stages of the design process. Indeed, the model in Fig. 7 has been generated starting from a source design model where only the assembly of application level components is specified, while their deployment is not specified. On the contrary, the model in Fig. 8 has been generated

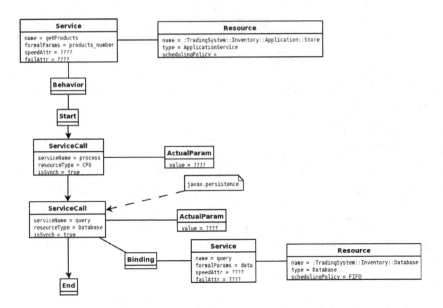

Fig. 7. KLAPER model of the UC3 Store get-product operation (pre-deployment)

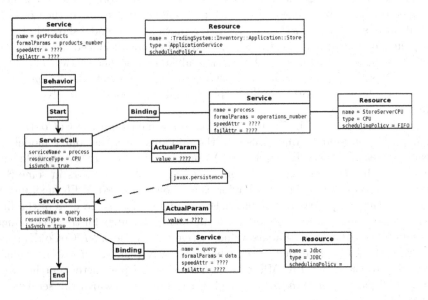

Fig. 8. KLAPER model of the UC3 Store get-product operation (post-deployment)

from a source design model where both the assembly of application components and their deployment are specified. In both figures the get-product operation is modeled as a Service offered by a Resource of type ApplicationService. Its associated Behavior starts with a ServiceCall step addressed to a CPU Resource, which

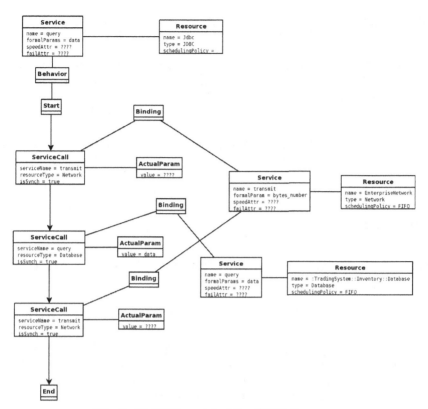

Fig. 9. KLAPER model of the JDBC Resource

models the execution of some internal operations. Then, it is followed by a ServiceCall step addressed to the "query" service offered by a Database Resource.
As a consequence of the lack of deployment information, the KLAPER model in
Fig. 7 only specifies the direct binding between the requested and offered query
service. No binding is specified for the processing service request, as we do not
know the identity of the node where the ApplicationService will be deployed.
Instead, this binding is specified in Fig. 8 (with a StoreServerCPU resource),
thanks to the information extracted from the source UML deployment diagram
(see Chapter 3, Figure 14).As another difference, it can be seen that in Fig. 8
the "query" service request is no longer directly bound to the corresponding
DataBase query service, but to an analogous service offered by a JDBC resource
(whose KLAPER model is shown in Fig. 9). Indeed, according to the deployment
diagram, the Application Store and the Inventory DataBase are deployed on
two different nodes (StoreServer and EnterpriseServer, respectively), with the
JDBC resource playing the role of connector between the two components. The
KLAPER model of Fig. 9 shows how, at the KLAPER level, we can model the
use of the platform resources for this remote connection. Indeed the behavior of
the service offered by the JDBC resource, besides forwarding the query request
to the remote DataBase (second ServiceCall step), also includes two ServiceCall

steps (first and third step), both bound to a Network resource. They model the use of some local network (EnterpriseNetwork) to transmit the query and to get the response. Their actual parameter (which matches the formal parameter of the Network resource) models the number of bytes to be transmitted.

The KLAPER model shown in Fig. 9 has been obtained as the result of a transformation rule from UML to KLAPER that only takes into account the utilization of a network resource for the remote connection. We point out that we could also use a different, more refined transformation rule, which also takes into account the utilization of a CPU-type resources at both ends of the connection (e.g. for the marshaling/unmarshaling of the transmitted message). In this case, the behavior shown in Fig. 9 would have included also ServiceCall steps addressed to suitable CPU-type resources.

A description of additional KLAPER models derived from the CoCoME specification can be found in [15].

13.4   Transformations from **KLAPER** Models to Analysis Models

In this section, we consider the second part of a KLAPER-based transformation process from a source design model to a target analysis model, that is the transformation from a KLAPER model to the target model. To give a concrete transformation example, we focus on performance analysis, and assume that the target notation to support this analysis is the *layered queueing network* (LQN) notation [19]. Hence, we first outline the characteristics of LQN and present a possible LQN MOF metamodel. Then we outline the main transformations rules from KLAPER models to LQNs. Finally, we give examples of the LQN models we can obtain applying these rules to the CoCoME example, and of the results we can get from the solution of these models.

13.4.1   The LQN Model

The LQN model was developed as an extension of the well-known Queueing Network model [20,19]. A LQN model is an acyclic graph, with nodes representing software entities and hardware devices, and arcs denoting service requests. The software entities, also known as *tasks*, are drawn as parallelograms, while the hardware devices are drawn as circles. Each kind of service offered by a LQN task is modeled as a so-called *entry*, drawn as a smaller parallelogram. The behavior of an entry can be described in two alternative ways, using either *activities* or *phases*. Activities allow to describe more complex behaviors, e.g. with control structures such as forks and joins and loops. Phases are used for notational convenience to specify activities that are sequences of one to three steps. During the first phase, the client is blocked waiting for the server reply, which is sent at the end of the phase. The client then continues its execution, and the server completes its 2nd and 3rd phases (if any) in parallel with the

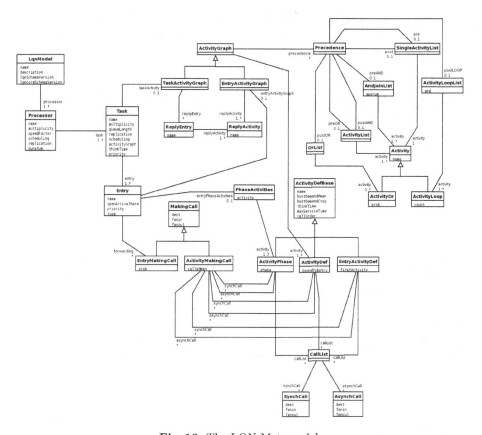

Fig. 10. The LQN Metamodel

client. Each phase has its own execution time demands and requests for other services, represented as arcs to other entries. LQN has more features that are not described here for the sake of simplicity.

The tools developed at Carleton University allow to express LQN models in different formats, such as a textual syntax, specified by a BNF grammar, and an XML-based language for which an XML-Schema has been defined [12]. Since the key point of the framework proposed in this paper is to leverage model-driven techniques, and especially automated model transformation, we defined a MOF metamodel for LQN and we implemented it as an Ecore metamodel [21]. This metamodel was derived from the XML-Schema and its concepts map one-to-one to the concepts defined in the schema [22]. Having a MOF metamodel for LQN (depicted in Fig. 10) allows us to use LQN as a target notation of MOF-based model transformations that take a KLAPER model as input. For a detailed description of the elements of the metamodel, we refer to the documentation about the corresponding XML element [23].

13.4.2   Transformation Rules from KLAPER to LQN

The transformation from a KLAPER model to a performance model based on LQN consists of several steps. At first, each KLAPER workload is mapped onto a LQN task with an Entry where the kind of workload, open or closed, is specified. Each KLAPER Resource is mapped onto a LQN task. Furthermore, each KLAPER Resource that models a hardware device originates a LQN processor.

Each KLAPER service becomes an LQN Entry of a suitable LQN Task, and each ServiceCall of a KLAPER service is mapped onto an activity of an LQN Entry, synchronous or asynchronous according to the attribute of the ServiceCall, and with service time equal to the corresponding service time in KLAPER. The KLAPER activities are mapped onto LQN activities annotated with the service time present in KLAPER. To compute the average number of entry calls in the LQN model we distinguish two cases: if the caller Activity calls an Entry that in turn calls other Entries, then the average calls number of the Entry is set equal to the Repetition attribute of the corresponding ServiceCall in KLAPER, which models the number of invocations of the called Service (typically 1); if the caller Activity calls an Entry that does not call other Entries (i.e., it corresponds to an Entry modelling an hardware resource), then the average number of calls is set equal to the Repetition attribute of the corresponding ServiceCall in KLAPER multiplied by the value of its ActualParam attribute. The multiplication is due to the assumption we make that in a KLAPER model the ActualParam value of a ServiceCall addressed to a Resource modeling a hardware device (e.g. a CPU or a communication link) represents the whole amount of operations requested to that device (i.e. number of CPU cycles or bytes to be transmitted). Correspondingly, the Service time of a LQN Entry modelling a hardware device should have a value corresponding to the time necessary to elaborate a single operation (as specified in the KLAPER Resource which models that hardware device). The conditions OR, AND and LOOP in KLAPER are directly mapped onto the corresponding LQN conditions.

13.4.3   Examples of Target LQN Models of CoCoME

As an example, we show in Figures 11 and 12 the LQNs we obtained starting for the CoCoME use cases UC1 and UC3, respectively. From a structural point of view both figures 11 and 12 show the typical aspect of an LQN network characterized by its subsequent layers. Each layer in the graph typically corresponds to a layer in the model; this is a natural and logical representation but however this is not a rule (for example in figure 11 CashBoxController requires some services of the CashDeskApplication that is in the same graphical layer but the two are not at the same model layer). While in figure 12 (that is the translation of use case UC3) we have only synchronous calls represented by filled arrows, in figure 11 (that is the translation of use case UC1) we can see also some asynchronous calls represented by non filled arrows. Another interesting aspect is that in both figures it is very easy to distinguish tasks that represent hardware resources from tasks that represent software resources; the former use Phases while the latter are based on Activity graphs.

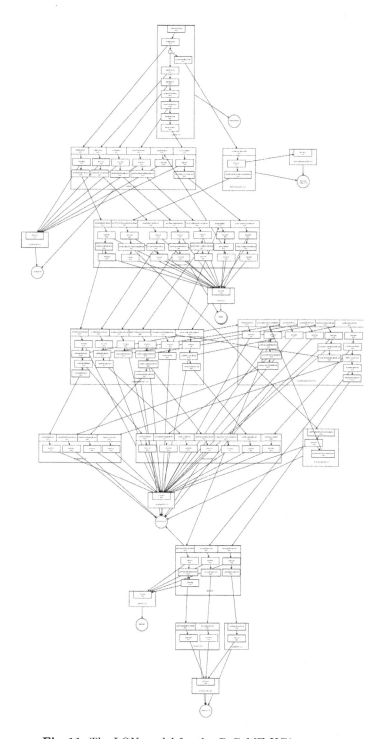

Fig. 11. The LQN model for the CoCoME UC1 use case

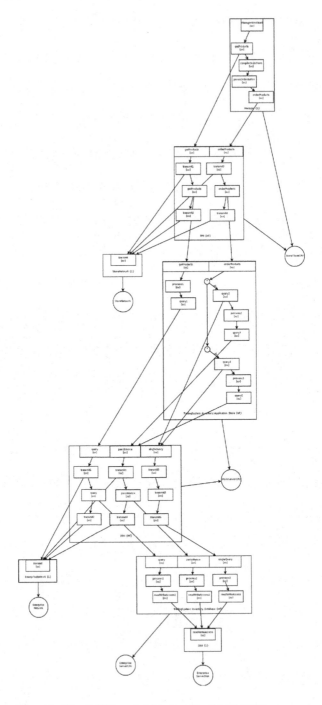

Fig. 12. The LQN model for the CoCoME UC3 use case

13.5   Analysis

The LQN models have been solved using the analytic solver LQNS [23]. The input parameters were derived from several sources: the CoCoME usage profile (e.g. from parameter $n32$ modeling the distribution of the number of items running out of stock, we have derived an average of about 300 items), experimental data (e.g., the time necessary to transfer a byte in a Ethernet LAN with a speed of 100 Mbps and the data reading rate in hard disks), and educated guesses (e.g., the processing time needed for data visualization). As for the characteristics of the processors in the LQN model we have made the following assumptions: the processor that models the disk has a First-In-First-Out (FIFO) scheduling discipline, while all the other processors have a Processor Sharing (PS) scheduling discipline with a quantum time of 1ms.

The following figures give examples of the kind of analysis results that can be derived applying the LQN solver to the obtained LQN models. In these experiments, we have analyzed four different configurations of the platform underlying the CoCoME application, named base,cpu_2x, internet, slow_disk, characterized as follows.

The basic configuration (base) is characterized by:

- processors Pentium III with 500 MHz and 1354 MIPS
- networks resources with 100 Mbps
- database disk with a rate of 300 MBps

The cpu_2x configuration has the same parameters as base except for the processors, whose frequency is doubled.

The internet configuration has the same parameters of base except for the network, which has a smaller bandwidth of 4 Mbps.

Finally, the slow_disk configuration has the same parameters of base except for the the database disk which has a lower rate of 100 MBps.

For all the configurations, we assumed that the application is used by a single store with 8 checkouts.

Figures 13 through 18 show the analysis results we have obtained for the UC3 use case, considering the four different system configurations. For example, figure 13 illustrates the different UC3 tasks utilizations by varying the system configuration.

By comparing the results obtained for the base and the cpu_2x configurations, we can make the following considerations. Firstly, tasks that do not directly depend on the network or on disks have a lower utilization in the latter configuration. The same is true, of course, for all CPUs. The throughput of tasks does not change significantly, as the arrival rate is kept constant. Having faster CPUs is beneficial to satisfy Requirement $t34$-1, especially on the server and on the database, where a large amount of data can be processed more quickly. This causes a noticeable decrease of service time. Analogously, faster CPUs reduce the execution time of the queries involved in UC3.

When switching from the base configuration to the internet configuration, the network bandwidth is reduced and, as a consequence, network utilization

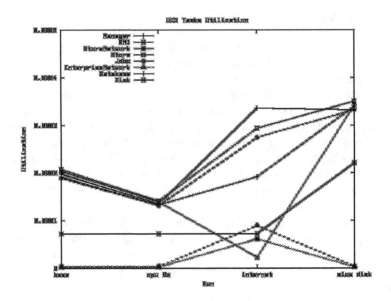

Fig. 13. CoCoME UC3 tasks utilizations

increases. Most activities of the Task Manager use directly or indirectly network resources, so their utilization increases too. In this case though, it is worth remarking that disk utilization is not affected by the network slowdown, and is the same as in the base case. Furthermore, the utilization of the RMI task decreases, possibly because the execution time of services in the lower layers

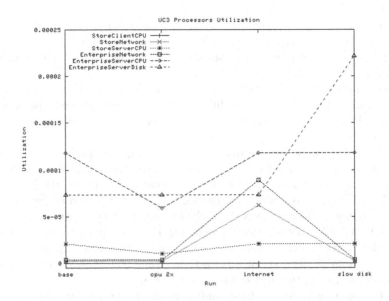

Fig. 14. CoCoME UC3 processors utilizations

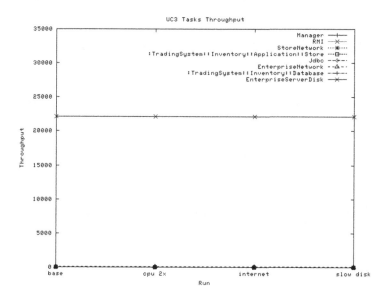

Fig. 15. CoCoME UC3 tasks Throughput

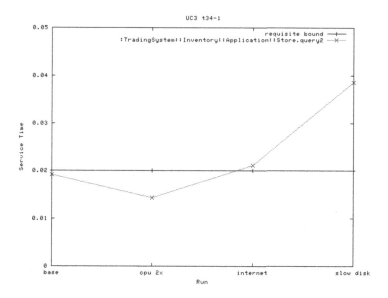

Fig. 16. CoCoME UC3: service time for requirement *t34-1*

are higher on average. The system is far from saturation, and the throughput is unchanged. The increase of the average service time of network resources may affect significantly Requirements *t34-1, t34-2 e t34-3*.

Finally, we compare the base configuration with the slow_disk configuration. When the data transfer rate is reduced, we observe a general system slow-down,

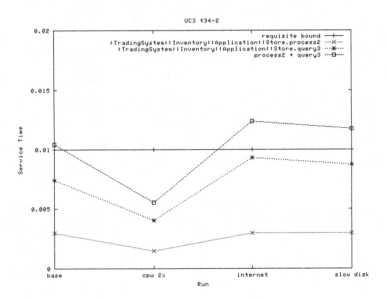

Fig. 17. CoCoME UC3: service time for requirement *t34-2*

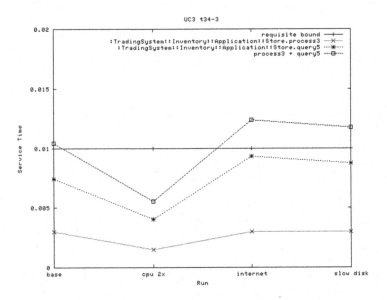

Fig. 18. CoCoME UC3: service time for requirement *t34-3*

which is explained by the fact that all services involved in UC3 use the disk of the database every time they make a query. As a consequence, the utilization of all tasks (except those belonging to network resources) increases. Conversely, network resources experience a lighter load for the exact same reason: the other tasks are busier, so they transmit data over the network with a reduced rate. This

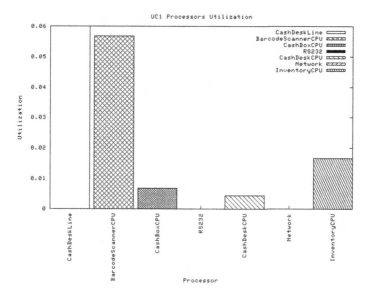

Fig. 19. CoCoME UC1 processors utilizations

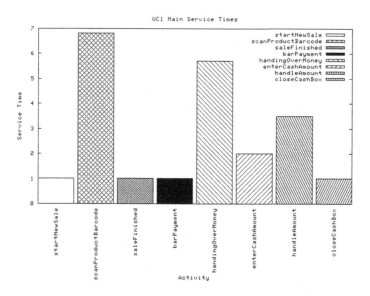

Fig. 20. CoCoME UC1 main service time

phenomenon is evident also by looking at the utilization of processors, which is higher for disks, unchanged for CPUs, and lower for networks. Also in this case the throughput of the system does not change significantly due to the fact that the overall system is far from saturation. The critical role played by the disk resource in the overall system performance is evident if we consider the values observed for the metrics involved in Requirements *t34-1, t34-2 e t34-3*. The increase of average service time is caused by the longer service time required for each disk access; this higher latency in turn impacts most services in the upper layers, which are kept waiting for disk operations to complete.

Figure 15 depicts the values of the throughput for UC3 tasks. In this case the "EnterpriseServerDisk" task has a throughput equal to 2.2e+04, while the throughput computed for the others tasks is less than one and therefore all the lines related to these tasks appear to coincide with the x-axis.

Considering use case UC1 the kind of analysis results we show is a little bit different, due to the different nature of the two use cases considered. Indeed, as far as UC1 is concerned, the operations executed by the system are very "light", often based on simple event notifications, whose service time is orders of magnitude smaller than the times of the activities of human actors. Consequently, analyzing system performance under different platform configurations for this use case would not give any really meaningful insights, as the differences would be negligible compared to the impact of human activities. Therefore, Figures 19 and 20 just illustrate the processors utilizations and the average service times for the different activities of the UC1, respectively.

13.6   Tools

The modeling framework we propose includes the KLAPER language, a set of supporting tools (e.g. model editors, transformations), and the general methodology, described in section 2.3.

The architecture of the tool is illustrated in Fig. 21. The blocks represent the constituent modules of the tool, while the "rounded rectangles" exemplify the XMI information exchanged among them. Our approach is to re-use as much as possible of existing free tools. To this end, we exploit the Eclipse environment [24] and the Omondo plug-in for UML editing [25]. Omondo was specifically augmented to process also the performance annotations, and it generates XML/XMI files that constitute the input to the other modules of the tooling framework. The first block of the framework is the KLAPER Model Generator. According to the rules defined in section 3, this component generates the pre-assembly and the post-assembly KLAPER models, depending on how much information is specified in the source design model. The KLAPER Editor can be used to inspect and modify the models produced by the the Model Generator. As of this writing, the Model Generator is still under development, so the use of the KLAPER editor is necessary to complete the partial model obtained from the Model Generator. Figure 23 shows a screenshot of the KLAPER editor.

The KLAPER models are then given as input to the Performance Model Generator, which is used in this paper to derive an LQN model. The Performance Model Generator, which is under development, will support the generation of several performance models, according to different analysis formalisms. Figures 23 and 22 show two screenshots of the LQN editor that we defined to support this step.

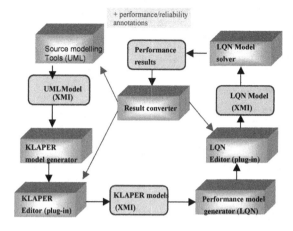

Fig. 21. The KLAPER environment

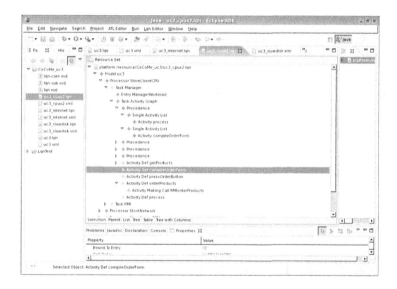

Fig. 22. The Eclipse editor for LQN models

The product of the Performance Model Generator must be fed into a suitable analyzer. As the target analysis formalism used in this work is LQN, we use the LQNS tool ad the analyzer.

LQNS [23] was developed at Carleton University and is able to solve LQN models, using both simulation and analytic techniques. Finally, the module called Result Converter, also under development, is used to perform *what-if* experiments and to feed the results of the analysis back to the designer.

The described architecture refers to a model transformation scenario where the source design model is expressed using UML (as in CoCoME), and the target

Fig. 23. Using the LQN editor to output an XML LQN model

model is a LQN model. Other source/target notations can be (and partly already are) supported by the same architecture. For example, modules dealing with a different source notation could substitute the UML-specific modules shown in Figure 21, leaving the remaining modules untouched. In this way, we would generate a LQN model starting from a different source notation. Similarly, by replacing the LQN-specific modules with corresponding modules for another target notation (e.g. Markov models) we would generate a different kind of analysis model from the same UML source model. As of this writing, early prototypes of modules to generate Markov models and simulation models from a KLAPER model are already available or in the works [15].

13.7   Summary

The definition of automatic tools for the transformation from design models of component-based application to analysis models is a crucial issue for the effective introduction of early non-functional analysis in CBD. We have addressed this problem defining a modeling framework centered around a kernel language called KLAPER, which is specified as a MOF metamodel and can thus be used in combination with OMG-MDA tools. The purpose of KLAPER is to capture the information which is relevant for the analysis of non-functional characteristics of component-based systems (especially performance and reliability). Using KLAPER as a bridge between design-oriented and analysis-oriented notations we reduce the burden of defining a variety of direct transformations from the former to the latter to the less complex problem of defining transformations to/from the kernel language.

In particular, in this chapter, we have used **KLAPER** to derive performance models, expressed as a Layered Queueing Network, starting from UML models annotated in accordance to the SPT profile. We have described the mapping of **KLAPER** concepts onto corresponding concepts of the LQN. The original XML-based language used to specify LQNs have been reverse-engineered and an Ecore metamodel has been defined for it. We also implemented an Eclipse editor plug-in for Ecore LQN models. This plug-in is capable of generating models that are readily analyzable by existing LQN tools.

We have used this infrastructure in combination with pre-existing **KLAPER** and LQN tools (**KLAPER** metamodel and editor, LQN analytic solver and simulator) to apply the proposed methodology to the CoCoMe case-study. Performance indices, such as utilization, service time, and throughput have been estimated for the CoCoME application deployed on platforms with different characteristics, and the alternative configurations have been compared on a quantitative basis.

The long-term goal of our research is to enhance the implementation of this framework, to provide system designers with a richer toolkit that allows to generate automatically different performance and reliability models starting from design models, possibly expressed using different notations. In particular, future work will address the implementation of automatic model transformations using QVT-based languages.

References

1. Smith, C.U., Williams, L.G.: Performance and Scalability of Distributed Software Architectures: an SPE Approach. Addison-Wesley, Reading (2002)
2. Crnkovic, I.: Building Reliable Component-Based Software Systems. Artech House, Inc., Norwood (2002)
3. Szyperski, C.: Component Software: Beyond Object-Oriented Programming. Addison-Wesley Longman Publishing Co., Inc., Boston (2002)
4. Balsamo, S., DiMarco, A., Inverardi, P., Simeoni, M.: Model-based performance prediction in software development: A survey. IEEE Transactions on Software Engineering 30(5), 295–310 (2004)
5. Hissam, S.A., Moreno, G.A., Stafford, J.A., Wallnau, K.C.: Packaging predictable assembly. In: Bishop, J.M. (ed.) CD 2002. LNCS, vol. 2370, pp. 108–124. Springer, Heidelberg (2002)
6. Object Management Group: UML 2.0 superstructure specification (2002)
7. Atkinson, C., Kühne, T.: Model-driven development: A metamodeling foundation. IEEE Softw. 20(5), 36–41 (2003)
8. Cortellessa, V., Marco, A.D., Inverardi, P.: Software performance model-driven architecture. In: SAC, pp. 1218–1223 (2006)
9. Solberg, A., Oldevik, J., Aagedal, J.Ø.: A framework for qos-aware model transformation, using a pattern-based approach. In: Meersman, R., Tari, Z. (eds.) OTM 2004. LNCS, vol. 3291, pp. 1190–1207. Springer, Heidelberg (2004)
10. Grassi, V., Mirandola, R., Sabetta, A.: Filling the gap between design and performance/reliability models of component-based systems: A model-driven approach. J. Syst. Softw. 80(4), 528–558 (2007)

11. Gu, G.P., Petriu, D.C.: From uml to lqn by xml algebra-based model transformations. In: WOSP 2005: Proceedings of the 5th international workshop on Software and performance, pp. 99–110. ACM Press, New York (2005)
12. Woodside, M., Petriu, D.C., Petriu, D.B., Shen, H., Israr, T., Merseguer, J.: Performance by unified model analysis (puma). In: WOSP 2005: Proceedings of the 5th international workshop on Software and performance, pp. 1–12. ACM Press, New York (2005)
13. Object Management Group: MOF version 2.0, ptc/04-10-15 (2004)
14. Object Management Group: OMG model driven architecture (2006), http://www.omg.org/mda/
15. Project website, K., http://klaper.sf.net
16. Object Management Group: UML profile for schedulability, performance, and time specification (2002)
17. QVT Partners: Revised submission for MOF 2.0 Query / Views /Transformations RFP (2003)
18. Grassi, V., Mirandola, R., Sabetta, A.: A model transformation approach for the early performance and reliability analysis of component-based systems. In: Gorton, I., Heineman, G.T., Crnković, I., Schmidt, H.W., Stafford, J.A., Szyperski, C.A., Wallnau, K. (eds.) CBSE 2006. LNCS, vol. 4063, pp. 270–284. Springer, Heidelberg (2006)
19. Woodside, M., Neilson, J., Petriu, D., Majumdar, S.: The stochastic rendezvous network model for performance of synchronous client-server-like distributed software. IEEE Transactions on Computers 44(1), 20–34 (1995)
20. Rolia, J.A., Sevcik, K.C.: The method of layers. IEEE Transactions on Software Engineering 21(8), 689–700 (1995)
21. (Eclipse emf project homepage), http://www.eclipse.org/modeling/emf/
22. Franks, G., Maly, P., Woodside, M., Petriu, D.C., Hubbard, A.: Layered queueing network solver and simulator user manual, lqn software documentation (2006)
23. LQN, http://www.sce.carleton.ca/rads/lqn/lqn-documentation/
24. (Eclipse homepage), http://www.eclipse.org
25. (Omondo webpage), http://www.omondo.com

14   CoCoME in Fractal*

Lubomír Bulej[1,2], Tomáš Bureš[1,2], Thierry Coupaye[3], Martin Děcký[1],
Pavel Ježek[1], Pavel Parízek[1], František Plášil[1,2], Tomáš Poch[1],
Nicolas Rivierre[3], Ondřej Šerý[1], and Petr Tůma[1]

[1] Department of Software Engineering
Faculty of Mathematics and Physics, Charles University
Malostranské náměstí 25, Prague 1, 11800, Czech Republic
{lubomir.bulej,tomas.bures,martin.decky,pavel.jezek,
pavel.parizek,frantisek.plasil,tomas.poch,ondrej.sery,
petr.tuma}@dsrg.mff.cuni.cz
[2] Institute of Computer Science, Academy of Sciences of the Czech Republic
Pod Vodárenskou věží, Prague 8, 18000, CzechRepublic
{bulej,bures,plasil}@cs.cas.cz
[3] France Telecom R&D
Issy les Moulineaux, France
{thierry.coupaye,nicolas.rivierre}@orange-ftgroup.com

This chapter presents our solution to the CoCoME assignment that is based on
the Fractal component model. The solution involves (i) modeling architecture in
Fractal ADL, (ii) specification of component behavior via behavior protocols,
(iii) checking compatibility of components, (iv) verification of correspondence
between component code and behavior specification, and (v) run-time monitoring of non-functional properties. Among the issues we have faced was the need
to modify the architecture - the component hierarchy was reorganized in order
to improve clarity of the design and the hierarchical bus was split into two independent buses. These were modeled by primitive components, since Fractal
does not support message bus as a first-class entity. Since the CoCoME assignment does not include a complete UML behavior specification (e.g. via activity
diagrams and state charts), behavior protocols for all the components are based
on the provided plain-English use cases, the UML sequence diagrams, and the
reference Java implementation.

14.1   Introduction

14.1.1   Goals and Scope of the Component Model

Fractal [4] is a classical component model with concepts stemming from Darwin [19]. It supports components as first-class concepts and allows their hierarchical
nesting. Since first published in 2002, Fractal has gained attention of the professional
community and become quite popular; it is one of the key projects hosted by

---

* This work was partially supported by the Czech Academy of Sciences project 1ET400300504
and its results will be used in the ITEA/EUREKA project OSIRIS Σ!2023.

A. Rausch et al. (Eds.): Common Component Modeling Example, LNCS 5153, pp. 357–387, 2008.

the OW2 Consortium[1] and it has been often used as the core platform for other OW2 projects. Annual Fractal workshops take place collocated with international conferences.

Fractal aims at providing support for modeling at different levels of abstraction. It focuses not only on the design of an application, but it also provides tools and environment for development, deployment, and runtime. Fractal also tries to address the limitations in extensibility and adaptation, which are often found in other run-time supporting component systems (e.g., EJB [30], CCM [23], or .Net [22]). By providing an open set of control capabilities, Fractal allows customizing the component model with regard to the target platform (e.g. to lower memory footprint of an embedded mobile application by excluding reflection capabilities and lifecycle management).

In Fractal, a component is both design and runtime entity with explicit provided and required interfaces. Each component consists of two parts: a *content* that is responsible for application functionality (i.e. implements the component's frame), and a *membrane*, which contains a set of controllers that implement non-functional aspects. For the purpose of composition, all components are defined by their *frame* and *architecture*. A frame is formed by external interfaces of a component, while an architecture defines the internal structure of the component, i.e. its subcomponents and their composition (via binding of interfaces). Semantics of the composition is defined via behavior protocols (a specific process algebra); Fractal also supports divide and conquer via interface specification.

Component behavior is specified using behavior protocols (BP) that allow to model and verify the behavior compliance. The verification tools can verify (i) the composition correctness (both horizontal and vertical) with respect to behavior specification (in BP) independently of the implementation, and (ii) the relation between the model (in BP) and implementation (in Java).

Deployment description is not a part of the architecture and behavior specification.

14.1.2 Modeled Cutout of CoCoME

We model all aspects of the CoCoME example with the exception of extra-functional properties, which were not modeled but were monitored at runtime. In the process of modeling the example in Fractal, we modified the original architecture in order to improve clarity of the design and to cope with limitations of Fractal. In particular, the hierarchical bus was split into two independent buses that were modeled via components, since Fractal does not support message buses. We verify correctness of composition (i.e. behavior compliance) with respect to behavior for all components, and correspondence of code to behavior specification for primitive components (our approach allows modeling only such behavior that fits a regular language); the verification tools are based on the BP checker and Java PathFinder. Performance of components was monitored via a custom controller.

14.1.3 Benefit of the Modeling

The two major benefits of our approach to modeling are: (i) verification of composition correctness with respect to behavior specification, and (ii) verification of

---

[1] OW2 Consortium is an international community of open source middleware developers.

correspondence between code and behavior specification. Other benefits include generation of code skeletons from the model and runtime monitoring.

Usage of Fractal with behavior protocols and verification tools is quite easy; learning curves of both Fractal and behavior protocols are short and both can be used in a matter of days.

14.1.4 Effort and Lessons Learned

We have needed approximately 10 person-months to model the CoCoME example in its entirety (we treat nearly all aspects of the example). As detailed further in the text, the lessons learned include detailed understanding of the limits that our architecture model and behavior specification has, especially where support for legacy technologies that do not fit the model framework is concerned.

14.1.5 Structure of the Chapter

The rest of this paper is organized as follows. Sect. 2 introduces the Fractal component model and its behavior protocol extension. Sect. 3 presents our solution for the CoCoME assignment using Fractal. Sect. 4 presents automated transformation from FractalADL to code skeletons, which significantly helps during the implementation process. In Sect. 5, the analytic techniques for verification of behavior compliance of components are presented. In Sect. 6, the available tools supporting the verification are then summarized and accompanied with results of our experiments.

14.2 Component Model

Fractal is specified as a platform independent component model. The specification (now in version 2.0) [5] defines the key concepts of Fractal and their relations. It also defines controlling (management) functionality of components to be implemented by component controllers (Sect. 2.1). Controllers serve, e.g., for creating components, their reconfiguration, lifecycle management; the interfaces of controllers are defined in pseudo IDL with mapping to Java, C and CORBA IDL.

The platform independent specification of Fractal has been reified by a number of implementations. To the most important ones belong Julia [4] (a Java implementation with support for mobile devices), AOKell [28] (a Java implementation employing aspect oriented programming), and FractNet [7] (a .NET implementation). Moreover, there are Fractal implementations aiming at specific application domains. To these belong Plasma [17] (C++ multimedia applications), ProActive [3] (Java grid computing), and Think [31] (operating system kernel C development).

There are also a number of tools, extensions and libraries for Fractal ranging from graphical development of applications to a Swing and JMX support. For the purpose of this paper, to the most notable tools and extensions belong the FractalRMI [11] (seamless distribution using RMI), FractalADL [9] (XML-based ADL language for defining architectures of Fractal components), and FractalBPC [10] (Fractal Behavior Protocol Checker), which is an extension allowing specification of component behavior and verification of component communication compliance.

14.2.1 Static View (Metamodel)

The Fractal component model relies on components as basic building blocks. Since Fractal is a hierarchical model, components may be either composite or primitive. In the case of a composite component, the component contains a number of sub-components. An application in Fractal is represented by a single (typically composite) top-level component.

A component may have a number of interfaces ("ports" in other component systems such as Darwin) which are the points of access to the component. Each interface is an instance of its type, which states the signature of the interface, its kind, contingency and cardinality. The interface kind is either *server* or *client*, which corresponds to provided and required interfaces in Darwin.

The contingency specifies whether an interface is *mandatory* or *optional*. In the case of client interfaces, contingency is useful to express what of the component requirements are vital to its functionality, and which do not have to be addressed while still guaranteeing a consistent component behavior. In the case of server interfaces, contingency is used to express e.g. the fact that a server interface of a composite component does not have to be bound to a sub-component (effectively leaving such functionality unimplemented). The cardinality is either *singleton* or *collection*, permitting either a single or multiple interface instance(s).

An interesting concept of Fractal is *shared component*. This concept allows an instance of a component to be a part of several (non-nested) parent components. It is especially useful when modeling shared resources.

Internally, a Fractal component is formed by a *membrane* and *content*. The membrane encapsulates the component's functional "business" interfaces and also the controllers with their "management" interfaces. The content consists of several sub-components (in the case of a composite component) or implementation code, encapsulation of legacy components, etc. (in the case of a primitive component). Each of the controllers is responsible for particular management functionality. Predefined controllers include the lifecycle controller for managing the lifecycle, binding controller for binding client interfaces, content controller for introspecting and managing sub-components, etc. As mentioned in Sect. 1, Fractal is an open model, thus the set of controllers is customizable and extensible. The actual way controllers are implemented depends on a particular Fractal implementation. In Julia, a dedicated technique of combining *mixins* using the ASM tool [2] for byte-code manipulation is employed, while AOKell relies on aspect oriented programming using either AspectJ or Spoon.

Instantiation of Fractal components is performed using an API defined by Fractal specification. It defines a bootstrap component factory that serves for creating component instances. The created instances are nested and connected according to the application architecture using controller interfaces. This way of instantiation implies that an application requires a main class that instantiates and starts particular components using the API.

Besides creating such a main class manually, specifically for each application, there is also an option of using FractalADL. This tool allows defining architecture of components using an ADL. It parses the ADL description and builds the application accordingly using Fractal API.

FractalADL is in fact a declarative description of how to instantiate components. This, however, implies that FractalADL operates with component instances as opposed to components (such as found in UML 2) and that it is not possible to specify component cardinality.

More information on the development process in Fractal may be found in [21][18].

14.2.2 Behavioral View

The applications behavior is specified via behavior protocols originally employed in the SOFA component model [27]. In the Fractal platform this formalism is used by FractalBPC which is a Fractal extension allowing specification of component behavior and verification of component communication compliance.

The behavior is not captured as a whole (by a single behavior protocol). Instead, each of the application's components has one behavior protocol associated with it (*frame protocol*) that describes the component's behavior as it is observable by the environment of the component, i.e. the component's code is abstracted in terms of capturing the traces of events related to method calls crossing the component boundary. Assuming component A requires an interface I that is provided by component B and assuming the interfaces A.I and B.I are bound together, these events are: (i) issuing a method request M on component A's required interface I: $!I.M\uparrow$, (ii) accepting a method request M on component B's provided interface I: $?I.M\uparrow$, (iii) sending a response to method request on component B's provided interface I: $!I.M\downarrow$, (iv) accepting a response to method request issued on component A's required interface I: $?I.M\downarrow$. Component's behavior is then described by an expression (component's frame protocol), where these events can be connected together using several operators (; for sequence, + for alternative, * for repetition and | for parallel execution). To simplify expressing method calls, the following abbreviations are introduced: ?I.M (stands for $?I.M\uparrow$; $!I.M\downarrow$), ?I.M{P} (stands for $?I.M\uparrow$; P; $!I.M\downarrow$), where {P} specifies a reaction to accepting the method call (P is a protocol here). The abbreviations !I.M, and !I.M{P} have a similar meaning.

Having a set of components with formal specification of their behavior via their frame protocols, the components can be connected together and compatibility of their behavior can be verified [1] (components horizontal compliance – meaning compliance at a particular level of nesting).

Every composite component also has a hand-written frame protocol that specifies its behavior. During the development of process of a composite component, its frame protocol can be verified against the behavior of its internals [1] (the vertical compliance – meaning compliance of components on adjacent levels of nesting) – the internal behavior of a composite component is described by an *architecture protocol* of its subcomponents (this behavior protocol is however not hand-written, but it is, in a way, automatically generated from frame protocols of the components that are part of the composite component's architecture).

The verification process of the horizontal and vertical compliance assures that the application's architecture is composed correctly. In addition to it, the verification of primitive components' frame protocols against their code can be done (code model checking) [1], which guarantees that the behavior described by the top-level architecture protocol corresponds to the true behavior of the application. However, model checking of a single component faces a significant problem, as most of today's model checkers require a complete program to verify – a so-called missing environment problem [25]. This problem can be solved by generating an artificial environment and combining it with the code of the component, forming a complete program – such a program can then be passed to a modified JPF model checker [32] and its compliance to the component's frame protocol can be verified [26].

14.2.3 Deployment View

The Fractal specification does not address issues related to deployment. As a result, each implementation of Fractal deals with deployment in a specific way. For instance, Julia, the most widely used Fractal implementation in Java, is local (i.e., it provides no support for distribution). A Fractal application in Julia is executed by a dedicated Java class that instantiates and starts the components of the application. Besides having such a class specifically created for each application, it is possible to use a generic launcher that is part of FractalADL.

Although Julia does not support distribution by itself, it is possible to use extending libraries which add this feature. This is the case of FractalRMI library, which provides distribution using RMI. FractalRMI, however, is not tied only to Julia, it introduces distribution to other Java-based implementations of Fractal (e.g. AOKell).

FractalRMI is integrated with FractalADL. Thus, it is possible to specify a target deployment node for each component in FractalADL and subsequently use the FractalADL launcher to instantiate a distributed application.

Apart from local implementations of Fractal there also exist special purpose implementations which bring the support for distribution already in their core and do not need any extensions. This is for example the case of ProActive, which aims at grid computing.

Another important issue of deployment related to the CoCoME example is the support for different communication styles (e.g., method invocation, asynchronous message delivery, etc.), which are reified by different middleware (e.g., RMI, JMS, etc). Fractal does not provide any direct support for modeling different communication styles. It addresses this issue only partially by defining so called *composite bindings*, which are in fact regular components that encapsulate the use of middleware. Such binding components can be built using the Dream framework [7] which provides Fractal components for construction of middleware.

14.3 Modeling the CoCoME

Employing Fractal in the CoCoME assignment revealed several issues that required modifications of the architecture. These modifications are presented and justified in Sect. 3.1 (Static view). Since behavior specification using Behavior Protocols is supported by Fractal, each of the components of the Trading System was annotated with its frame protocol. As CoCoME assignment does not include complete behavior specification, these protocols are created based on the CoCoME UML specification and the reference implementation and further described in Sect. 3.2 (Behavioral view). Sect. 3.3 (Deployment view) presents deployment and distribution using

Fractal-specific means (FractalRMI and FractalADL). In Sect. 3.4 (Implementation view), we describe beside the basic Fractal implementation strategy also the details related to performance evaluation and estimation. Additionally, Sect. 3.5 presents behavior specification of two components featuring non-trivial behavior (Cash-DeskApplication and CeshDeskBus) in more detail. Behavior specification of the rest of the components can be found in Appendix and on the Fractal-CoCoME web page [33].

14.3.1 Static View

As the architecture of the Trading System used in Fractal differs slightly from the Co-CoME assignment, this section presents the modified architecture and justifies the modifications made. In general, there are two sorts of modifications: (i) Modifications which are not directly related to Fractal and do not influence complexity of the solution, but rather contribute to the clarity of the design and the other views (in Sect. 3.2 – 3.4). (ii) Modifications directly forced by specific properties of Fractal. These modifications reveal strengths and limitations of Fractal and therefore should be taken into account in the comparison between different modeling approaches.

The (i) modifications include reorganization of the component hierarchy and explicit partitioning of EventBus into two independent buses. All primitive components are left unchanged, but the composed components GUI and Application located in the Inventory component are substituted by components StoreApplication, ReportingApplication (compare Fig. 1 and Fig. 3). The new components more clearly encapsulate the logical units featuring orthogonal functionality, whereas the old ones merely present a general three tier architecture. The StoreApplication component encapsulates the store functionality as required by the CashDeskLine component in UC1 (use case #1 in CoCoME assignment), whereas ReportingApplication encapsulates functionality for

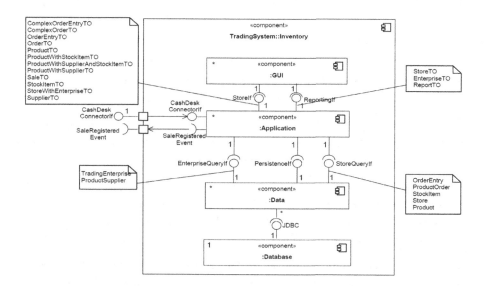

Fig. 1. The original design of the Inventory component in CoCoME

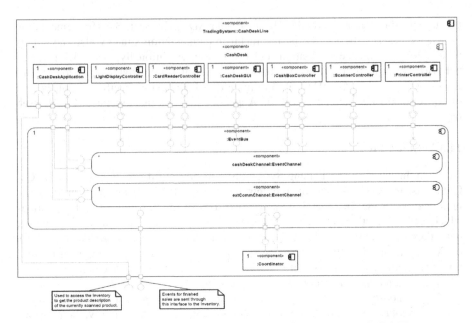

Fig. 2. The original design of the CashDeskLine component in CoCoME

managing goods as used in UC3 – UC7. The Data component is left unchanged. Second modification of the component hierarchy relates to UC8, as neither the architecture in CoCoME assignment, nor its reference implementation provides a full UC8 functionality. Specifically, UC8 expects communication among EnterpriseServer and StoreServers; however no interface for the communication is present. Moreover, the reference implementation includes UC8 functionality as a part of UC1, which, however, should be independent. The reference implementation deeply exploits the fact that it is not distributed and accesses the shared database, which would not be the case in a real-life implementation. Therefore, the new architecture is enriched by explicitly distinguishing the EnterpriseServer component and the ProductDispatcherIf and MoveGoodsIf interfaces that encapsulate UC 8 functionality (Fig. 3).

EventBus from the CoCoME assignment (Fig. 2) represents a composite of buses eventChannel and extCommChannel. As there is no apparent benefit of having the eventChannel outside the CashDesk component, EventBus is split into two independent buses CashDeskLineBus and CashDeskBus, which correspond to extCommChannel and eventChannel, respectively. Moreover, CashDeskBus is moved inside the CashDesk component where it more naturally belongs, since it mediates mostly the communication among the components and devices internal to CashDesk.

As to the (ii) modifications, Fractal does not support message bus as a first-class entity. Therefore, the CashDeskLineBus and CashDeskBus buses are modeled as primitive components, multiplexing the published messages to each of the subscribers (compare Fig. 2 and Fig. 3).

Despite the modifications made, many parts of the original design and prototype implementation are adopted even when "unrealistic", such as the CardReader component communicating with Bank through CashDeskApplication instead of directly, which presents a security threat with PIN code interception possibility. In order to share as much of the CoCoME assignment as possible, other parts of the design such as the data model and the transfer objects are left unmodified. The Fractal implementation is designed to use Hibernate and Derby database for persistency as is the case with the prototype implementation.

14.3.2 Behavioral View

The behavior protocols describing application's behavior are meant to be part of the specification of the application. Created at the application design stage, they allow developers to verify that the implementation is compliant with the design, or, in other words, that it really implements the specification. However, as the behavior protocols were not part of the specification of the CoCoME assignment, they had to be recreated from the description provided in it.

The provided specification contains only sequence diagrams and use-cases, which do not provide as precise and unambiguous specification of the application's behavior as it is required to formally verify the resulting implementation correctness (in order to be sufficient, the specification would have to include more complete UML description, like collaboration and activity diagrams or state machines). For this reason, we had to use the reference implementation provided also as a part of the specification and use both the UML descriptions and the reference implementation to create the behavior protocols for the application. A problem has however arisen during the behavior protocol development process – we found that the reference implementation is not fully compliant with the CoCoME UML specification as provided – there are two major differences between the reference implementation and the specification: (i) missing continuation of the payment process after erroneous credit card payment – UC1, (ii) missing implementation of UC8. We solved this problem by creating two alternatives of the protocols – the first specifying the behavior imposed by the CoCoME UML specification, and the second specifying the behavior observable in the reference implementation. As our component-based implementation of the application is based on the reference implementation (we have reused as much of the reference implementation code as possible), we show later in the text that our implementation (and the reference implementation) is not exactly following the requirements imposed by the CoCoME UML specification (by formally refuting it).

Regarding the behavior specification, it is also worth noting that we do not model the behavior of the actors (e.g. customer, cashier) specified by the UML model as we model only the software components that are part of the application's architecture. However, as the behavior of agents is observable via interfaces provided for the GUI part of the application, the behavior protocols describing the behavior of application's components also transitively impose restrictions on behavior of agents, though the actual formal verification is done against the GUI components.

We show that creating behavior protocols as part of the application specification allows precisely defining the required application's behavior early in the development process (in the application design stage). Such specification then provides not only the global view that is required to correctly create the application's architecture, but also a per component behavioral view that can serve as a precise guide for developers of

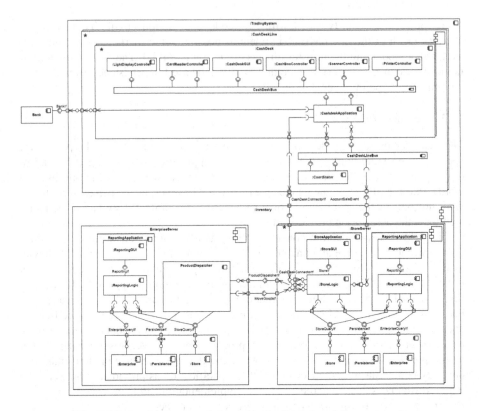

Fig. 3. Final architecture, as it is used in the Fractal modeling approach

specific component implementations. Furthermore, the specification can be used to formally verify that the implementation really complies with the specification requirements and that all the application components (although each might be implemented by a different developer) are compatible and together provide the functionality (exposed by their behavior) required by the specification.

14.3.3 Deployment View

From the deployment point of view, we introduced a few changes mainly to the middleware used in the reference architecture. These changes were motivated by the way Fractal can be distributed and by the libraries available for the distribution.

We have used FractalRMI instead of Sun RMI. FractalRMI is a library for Fractal that allows transparent distribution. The components are not aware of the fact that they communicate remotely.

In a similar fashion, we have eliminated the use of JMS, which has been used in the reference architecture for implementing buses. We have replaced each of the both busses by a component that is responsible for routing the messages. Remote communication in this case may be again transparently realized using FractalRMI.

The Fractal specification also lays out another way of solving distribution and various communication styles. It defines so called composite bindings. Each composite binding consists of a number of binding components. These components are classical components from the Fractal point of view, their responsibilities are to encapsulate or implement middleware. A significant help in implementing the composite bindings is provided by the Dream framework, which implements Fractal components that support construction of communication middleware with various communication styles, including JMS.

Our choice of FractalRMI is transparent and requires no additional implementation effort. We did not use the composite bindings and Dream also because Dream is still under development; additionally, our solution brings no restrictions to the modeled CoCoME example.

Another important aspect of deployment is the way deployment is planned and performed. In our approach, we have put the information about deployment into FractalADL. Each specified component is annotated with an element virtual-node which states the deployment node to which the component is to be deployed. The actual distribution is then realized via FractalRMI.

14.3.4 Implementation View

The Fractal implementation is based both on the Fractal architecture model of the application and the provided reference implementation. We have created a FractalADL model of the application architecture using the FractalGUI modeling tool [11], taking into account the changes mentioned in Sect. 2.3 and Sect. 3.3. The resulting model was then extended by hand to accommodate behavior protocol specification, because it is not supported by the modeling tool.

To speed up and simplify the development, we have used a tool to create component skeletons from the architecture model. More detailed description of the transformation can be found in Sect. 4. The functional part of the application was then adapted from the CoCoME reference implementation and integrated into the generated component skeletons.

14.3.4.1 Testing the Implementation against Use-Case Scenarios

To enable the testing of functional properties specified by behavior protocols, FractalBPC allows monitoring communication on the interfaces of a component C when the application is running. The runtime checker integrated in FractalBPC automatically tests whether C communicates with other components in a way that is allowed by C's frame protocol. Any violation of the frame protocol by C or one of the components communicating with C is reported.

In addition, the reference implementation of the trading system contains a small test suite for testing the behavior of the implementation against the use case scenarios described in the CoCoME assignment. The test suite, based on the jUnit [16] framework, contains a number of tests which exercise operations prescribed by the respective use cases and verify that the system responds accordingly.

As it is, however, the test suite from the reference implementation is unsuitable for testing. The key issues are testing of crosscutting concerns, test design, and insufficient automation.

The tests attempt to verify not only that the implementation functions correctly, but also impose timing constraints on the executed operations. This makes the tests unreliable, because two orthogonal aspects are tested at the same time. Combined with rather immodest resource requirements of the application arising from the use of "heavy-duty" middleware packages for database functionality, persistence, and message-based communication, the application often fails to meet the test deadlines on common desktop hardware, even though it functions correctly.

Moreover, the tests always expect to find the trading system in a specific state, which is a very strong requirement. To accommodate it, all the applications comprising the trading system are restarted and the database is reinitialized after each test run, which adds extreme overhead to the testing process.

This is further exacerbated by insufficient automation of the testing infrastructure. The trading system consists of a number of components, such as the enterprise server and clients, store server and clients, database server, etc. Starting the trading system is a long and complicated process, which can take several minutes in the best case, and fail due to insufficient synchronization between parts of the system in the worst case. Manual starting of the trading system, combined with the need for restarting the system after each test run, makes the test suite in its present form unusable.

To enable testing in a reasonably small environment, we take the following steps to eliminate or mitigate the key issues, leading to a considerable increase in the reliability of the tests as well as reduced testing time:

- We simplify the implementation of the trading system by eliminating the GUI components, leaving just the business functionality, which allows the trading system to be operated in headless mode.
- We eliminate the validation of extra-functional properties from testing; timing properties of the trading system are gathered at runtime by a monitoring infrastructure described in Sect. 3.4.2. Validation of extra-functional system properties is independent from functional testing and is based on the data obtained during monitoring.
- We improve the testing infrastructure by automating the start of the trading system. This required identifying essential and unnecessary code paths and fixing synchronization issues between various parts of the system.

14.3.4.2 Runtime Monitoring of Extra-Functional Properties

The extra-functional properties articulated in the CoCoME assignment enhance the functional specification with information related to timing, reliability, and usage profile. The specification provides two kinds of properties: assumed and required. Assumed properties reflect domain knowledge and describe the environment in which the system will be expected to operate. The required properties reflect the requirements on performance of the system within the environment.

These parameters can be used in performance analysis of the system architecture preceding the implementation of the system to verify that the proposed architecture has the potential to satisfy performance requirements. However, pure model-based performance analysis is typically used to determine principal performance behavior, such trends in response to requests, not the actual performance of a real system in a real environment.

Deciding whether a particular instance of a system satisfies the performance requirements dictated by the specification requires analyzing performance data from a real system. Runtime monitoring requires the analysis of performance data to be performed isochronously with system execution. This limits the level of detail compared to offline analysis, but provides immediate information on high-level performance attributes. On the other hand, the data from performance measurements intended for offline analysis can be used to correct the assumptions and to calibrate a generic performance model to reflect the environment and properties of a particular instance of the system.

High-level performance data suitable for monitoring are typically exported by applications using technologies such as JMX [14] and SNMP [29], for which generic monitoring tools are available. However, exporting performance data is the final step. The data has to be first obtained using either an application-specific or a generic approach.

Application-specific approach requires that an application collects performance data internally, using its own measurement infrastructure. This allows obtaining certain application and domain specific performance metrics that cannot be obtained using a generic approach, but it also requires including support for performance measurements in various places directly in the implementation of application components, which in turn requires mixing functional and non-functional aspects of implementation. This can be alleviated using aspect-oriented programming which allow separating the implementation of functional and non-functional aspects of a system.

A generic approach based on architectural aspects exploits the description of application architecture as well as the capabilities of the runtime to obtain performance data. Architectural aspects are used to instrument an application with performance data collection capabilities, but their application is less intrusive than in the case of classical aspect oriented programming, because it is performed only at the design-level boundaries exposed by the application architecture. As a result, the instrumentation is completely transparent to the developer and does not require modifications in the implementation of an application, which in turn allows the work on performance monitoring to be done in parallel with development. Another advantage of using architectural aspects is that the application source code does not have to be available, but that was not an issue in this particular case.

Selecting performance properties for monitoring
To demonstrate the concept of using architectural aspects for performance monitoring, we have identified the following extra-functional properties from the CoCoME assignment that would be suitable for monitoring:

- t13-3: Time for signaling an error and rejecting an ID
- t15b2-2: Time waiting for validation
- t14-1: Time for showing the product description, price, and running total
- t34-1: Time for querying the inventory data store

We have taken into account the importance of the properties with respect to the performance of the system, therefore the preference was mostly on required properties associated with internal actions of the system (e.g. time to execute a database query) and not external actors and hardware (e.g. time to switch a light display). We have also taken into account assumed properties that have the potential to be covered by a Service Level Agreement (i.e. guaranteed by an external service provider, such as a bank in case of credit card validation), where monitoring can be used to ensure that an external contractor fulfills its obligations.

Performance related extra-functional properties typically specify acceptable ranges for various performance metrics. An important aspect considered during selection of properties for monitoring was also the observability of the required performance metrics on the design level of abstraction, i.e. at component boundaries represented by component interfaces. Performance metrics that could not be calculated from data collected at component boundaries would have to be explicitly supported by the implementation.

Technical implementation

To obtain performance data from a system implemented using the Fractal component model, we have taken advantage of the mixin-based construction of controllers within a component membrane (see Sect. 2.1) supported by the Julia implementation of Fractal.

We have extended the membrane to include a performance monitoring controller and an interceptor on component business interfaces. The interceptor provides events related to business method invocations to the controller, which stores these events and calculates simple statistics and durations of method invocations. When an application stops, it writes the collected data to disk. For runtime performance monitoring, the controller provides a simple JMX based interface which allows configuring what methods and events should be observed and also allows accessing the simple summary statistics.

This approach is similar to that of FractalJMX [12], which is a Fractal extension that allows exposing the functional and control interfaces of Fractal components in a JMX agent and collecting simple statistics related to method invocations We have however implemented a custom interceptor which provides low-level data to the performance monitoring controller. The data can be used both for offline analysis and performance monitoring. JMX interface is used for management of monitoring controllers and for exposing simple statistics calculated from the low-level data.

Measurement results

Of the above extra-functional properties, we have decided to focus on t15b2-2, which is the assumed time of credit card validation. Using a simple simulator of the UC1 scenario, we have collected performance data related to invocations of the validateCard() method on the BankIf interface of the Bank component. The simulation was configured for 50 cash desks, started in 1 second intervals, and each processing 50 sales. The validateCard() method in the Bank component was implemented to wait a random time according to the histogram specification associated with the t15b2-2 property.

The distribution of validateCard() invocation times calculated from the measured data is identical to the specified distribution, which served as a basic validation of the approach. Using the measured data, we have performed an analysis with the goal to determine the average load on the Bank component, expressed as the number of validateCard() method invocations during a 60-second interval. This load may be covered

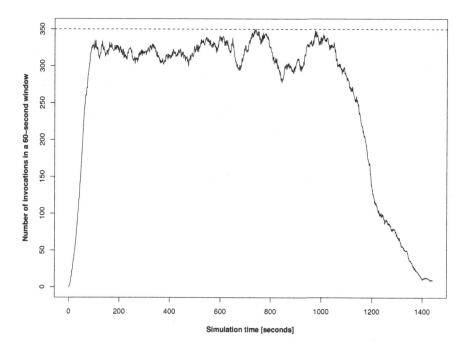

Fig. 4. The load on the card validation service of the Bank component

by a Service Level Agreement with a bank, which may only guarantee specific performance of its card validation service in response to a specific load.

The results of the analysis are shown in Fig. 4, with the dashed line denoting the maximal load on the Bank component given the above simulation parameters. The rising edge of the curve starting at time 0 corresponds to the delayed startup of individual cash desks, while the falling edge starting approx at time 1100 corresponds to closing of cash desks after they have processed 50 sales.

We would like to emphasize that the above analysis has been performed on data collected without actually modifying a single line of application code. Information about the distribution of durations of validateCard() invocations could be used to monitor the performance of the card validation service provided by a bank. On the other hand, runtime analysis (and throttling) of validateCard() invocation rate can be used to ensure that a store does not violate a Service Level Agreement.

The overhead of the measurement was 40 microseconds per method invocation, in 99% of cases, without any attempt at performance optimization. The duration of validateCard() invocation was between 4 and 5 seconds in 90% of cases. The difference between the times is 5 orders of magnitude, which in this particular case makes the overhead of the measurement insignificant. Due space constraints, we have only included the above analysis. The Distributed System Research Group project page on CoCoME in Fractal [33] provides additional measurement results.

14.3.5 Specification of Selected Components

This section is mostly focused on behavioral view of CoCoMe components. More specifically, it assumes that the specification of component structure, interfaces, and overall architecture is taken over from the CoCoMe assignment with the few modification mentioned in Sect. 3.1. As emphasized in Sect. 3.2, the behavior specification provided here is done in behavior protocols and stems from the CoCoMe use cases and the component behavior encoded in the Java implementation provided in the CoCoMe assignment. Since the behavior specification of the whole application is too large to fit into space reserved for this chapter, two "interesting" components (Cash-DeskApplication and CashDeskBus) were chosen to demonstrate the capabilities of behavior protocols. Interested reader may find the specification of other "interesting" components in the appendix and full specification at [33].

Demonstrating the ordinary usage of this formalism, the behavior protocol of CashDeskApplication describes the actual behavior of a cash desk. In principle, it captures the state machine corresponding to the sale process. In contrast, the behavior protocol of CashDeskBus illustrates the specific way of expressing mutual exclusion.

Since both these protocols are non-trivial, their "uninteresting" fragments are omitted in this section.

14.3.5.1 CashDeskApplication

The CashDeskApplication has application specific behavior – its frame protocol reflects the state of the current sale. It indicates what actions a cash desk allows the cashier to perform in a specific current sale state. The "interesting" parts of the protocol take the following form.

```
(
  # INITIALISED
  (
    ?CashDeskApplicationHandler.onSaleStarted
  );

  # SALE_STARTED
  (
    ?CashDeskApplicationHandler.onProductBarcodeScanned{
        !CashDeskConnector.getProductWithStockItem;
        !CashDeskApplicationDispatcher.sendProductBarcodeNotValid+
        !CashDeskApplicationDispatcher.sendRunningTotalChanged
    }
  )*; # <--- LOOP

  ?CashDeskApplicationHandler.onSaleFinished;

  # SALE_FINISHED
  (
    ?CashDeskApplicationHandler.onPaymentMode
  );

  # PAYING_BY_CASH
  (
    (
      (
        ?CashDeskApplicationHandler.onCashAmountEntered
      )*;
```

```
# On Enter
?CashDeskApplicationHandler.onCashAmountCompleted{
  !CashDeskApplicationDispatcher.sendChangeAmountCalculated
};

?CashDeskApplicationHandler.onCashBoxClosed{
  !CashDeskApplicationDispatcher.sendSaleSuccess;
  !CDLEventDispatcher.sendAccountSale;
  !CDLEventDispatcher.sendSaleRegistered
}
)
)
)* | (
# Enable Express Mode
?CDLEventHandler.onExpressModeEnabled{
  !CashDeskApplicationDispatcher.sendExpressModeEnabled
}
)* | (
# Disable Express Mode
?CashDeskApplicationHandler.onExpressModeDisabled
)*
```

To communicate with each of the buses CashDeskBus and CashDeskLineBus, the component features a pair of interfaces (CashDeskApplicationHandler, CashDeskApplicationDispatcher and CDLEventHandler, CDLEventDispatcher). The interfaces contain a specific method for each event type that can occur on a bus. In addition, the interface, CashDeskInterface serves to get the data from Inventory.

The protocol specifies three parallel activities. The first one is the sale process itself, while the other two deal with cash desk mode switching. In the initial state, the sale process activity is waiting for SaleStartedEvent on the CashDeskBus (?Cash-DeskApplicationHandler.onSaleStarted). It denotes beginning of a new sale. Then (; operator) BarcodeScannedEvent is accepted (?CashDeskApplication-Handler.onProductBarcodeScanned) for each sale item. Repetition operator (*) ensures that arbitrary finite number of events can be accepted. In reaction (the expression enclosed in {}) to each BarcodeScannedEvent, the price is obtained from Inventory. (!CashDeskConnector.getProductWithStockItem) . Depending on the result, the rest of the CashDesk is informed about the change of total sale price (!Cash-DeskApplicationDispatcher.sendRunningTotalChanged) or, alternatively (+ operator), ProductBarcodeNotValidEvent is issued (!CashDeskApplication-Dispatcher.sendProductBarcodeNotValid). When SaleFinishedEvent is accepted (?CashDeskApplicationHandler.onSaleFinished), the sale process reaches the payment phase which is specified in similar manner. When one sale is finished, the sale process activity returns to the initial state to accept another sale (repetition operator *). In parallel operators (|), the cash desk performs two other activities to process cash desk mode switching events coming from either of the buses.

This simplified version of the frame protocol does not capture paying by credit card and does not cope with events not allowed in a particular sale process state.

14.3.5.2 CashDeskBus

The particular bus behavior comprises of two different aspects – events serialization and multiplexing. While the former aspect takes part in modeling "many to one" messages, the latter aspect is related to "one to many" messages. The event passing is synchronous, meaning that if an event is emitted by a publisher component, the component is blocked until all subscribers process the event. If there is another component wanting to emit a message when the bus is processing another message, the component is also blocked. Such behavior corresponds to the implementation using FractalRMI. This behavior might be prone to deadlocks, but fortunately, absence of deadlocks is one of properties we can verify using the behavior protocols.

As discussed in Sect. 3.1, the bus is implemented as a component. For every publisher and subscriber, it has an interface containing a method for every event type. As the bus component does not contain any application logic, its protocol can be generated using the information from the architecture – which components are involved in subscriber role, which components are involved in publisher role and what event types do they accept, resp. emit. This situation is not typical for behavior protocols.

The method used to model the serialization in behavior protocols follows the typical model of mutual exclusion in Petri nets – borrowing a token. The protocol representing the bus is accepting events from event producers in parallel, but it does not propagate them to the subscribers immediately. Instead of it, the bus protocol is waiting for the token event which is emitted by helper protocol. As the helper protocol does not produce another event until it receives response from the previous one, the bus event propagation parts are mutually excluded. Finally, the bus protocol must have empty parallel branch accepting the spare token events. Although the helper protocol in the model produces many spare token events which are just accepted by the empty parallel branch with no other use, this is not a performance issue in the implementation. In the implementation, standard Java synchronization with passive waiting is used to achieve the mutual exclusion – important is observable behavior, the means can differ in the implementation and model.

The multiplexing is straightforward – when the bus accepts an event from a producer and the token, the event is propagated to all subscribers.

The following protocol is a fragment of the CashDeskBus protocol $P_{CashDeskBus}$.

```
(?CashBoxControllerDispatcher.sendExpressModeDisabled{
    ?Helper.token{
        !CashDeskGUIHandler.onExpressModeDisabled|
        !LightDisplayControllerHandler.onExpressModeDisabled|
        !CardReaderControllerHandler.onExpressModeDisabled|
        !CashDeskApplicationHandler.onExpressModeDisabled
        }
    }
)*
|
(?CashDeskApplicationDispatcher.sendExpressModeEnabled{
    ?Helper.token{
        !CashDeskGUIHandler.onExpressModeEnabled|
        !LightDisplayHandler.onExpressModeEnabled|
        !CardReaderControllerHandler.onExpressModeEnabled
        }
    }
)*
|?Helper.token*
```

The fragment captures the synchronous delivering of ExpressModeEnabled and ExpressModeDisabled events. When the CashBoxController component emits the ExpressModeDisabled event, it is accepted by the bus (?CashBoxController-Dispatcher.sendExpressModeDisabled). Then, after accepting the token event, the

ExpressModeDisabled event is delivered in parallel to all subscribers (CashDeskGUI, LightDisplayController and CardReaderController). As the method calls are synchronous in behavior protocols, the bus waits until all subscribers acknowledge the event delivery. Then, the token is returned (the first closing curly brace) and finally, the CashBoxController is notified about successful delivery to all subscribers (the second closing curly brace). In the similar manner, the ExpressModeEnabled event is processed.

While the events from producers are accepted in parallel, which ensures that no producer can issue an event in a wrong moment, waiting for the equal token within the processing of distinct events ensures the mutual exclusion of the event deliveries, so the subscribers need not to care about parallelism. The final part of the fragment (?Helper.token*) accepts the unnecessary token events.

As there must be a token event source, the specification must be enriched by a helper protocol P_{Helper}: !Helper.token*. The complete frame protocol of the Cash-DeskBus component featuring mutual exclusion is then obtained by composing the protocols $P_{CashDeskBus}$ and P_{Helper} by the consent operator - $P_{CashDeskBus} \nabla_{\{Helper.Token\}} P_{Helper}$. It synchronizes the opposite actions (!Helper.token and ?Helper.token) and replaces them by single internal action.

14.4 Transformations

In the process of implementing CoCoME components in Fractal, we have used a tool allowing for automated transformation of FractalADL specification to component code fragments. The tool runs as a backend to FractalADL and operates on the abstract syntax tree of a parsed ADL description. The implementation artifacts it can produce comprise code skeletons of component interfaces and code skeletons for primitive components.

A fragment of a code skeleton generated by the tool is provided below, showing the Coordinator component from the CoCoME example.

```
public class CoordinatorImpl implements
    BindingController, CoordinatorEventHandlerIf {

  // -------------------------------------------------------
  // Required interface CoordinatorEventDispatcherIf
  // -------------------------------------------------------
  protected                              CoordinatorEventDispatcherIf
    CoordinatorEventDispatcherIf;

  // -------------------------------------------------------
  //        Provided      interface      CoordinatorEventHandlerIf
  // -------------------------------------------------------
  public void onSaleRegisteredEvent(
      org...cashdeskline.SaleRegisteredEvent arg0) {
    // TODO: Generated method
  }

  // -------------------------------------------------------
  // Implementation of the BindingController interface
  // -------------------------------------------------------
```

```
public Object lookupFc(String clientItfName) ... {
    if (clientItfName.equals("CoordinatorEventDispatcherIf")) {
      return CoordinatorEventDispatcherIf;
    }
    ...
  }

  public void bindFc(String cltItfName, Object serverItf) ... {
    if (cltItfName.equals("CoordinatorEventDispatcherIf")) {
      CoordinatorEventDispatcherIf =
        (CoordinatorEventDispatcherIf) serverItf;
      return;
    }
    ...
  }
  ...
}
```

The generated code contains implementation of the binding controller, which is vital for binding required (client) interfaces. The required interfaces are reflected in the code by protected instance variables containing references to the bound provided interfaces of other components. The provided interfaces offered by the component are reflected in the *implements* clause of the generated class. The tool also generates a skeleton for each method of the provided interfaces.

14.5 Analysis

As a behavior protocol specifies behavior via allowable sequences of method calls on component's interfaces, the property to be analyzed is compliance of the behavior of components as correctness of communication on component's interfaces. In general, by correctness of communication, we mean absence of communication errors, i.e. a situation in which two or more components do not meet expectations of the others. Three types of communication errors are identified: *bad activity* – the issued event cannot be accepted, *no activity* (deadlock) – all of the ready events' tokens are prefixed by "?", and *infinite activity* (divergence) – the composed protocols "cannot reach their final events at the same time", so that the composed behavior would contain an infinite trace (only finite traces are allowed).

The compliance of behavior is of two kinds: *horizontal compliance* and *vertical compliance*. Horizontal compliance refers to correctness of communication among components on the same level of component hierarchy, whereas *vertical compliance* refers to correctness of communication on adjacent levels of component hierarchy, i.e. whether a composed component is correctly implemented by its subcomponents. The vertical compliance is therefore a kind of behavioral subtyping.

Checking of horizontal and vertical compliance makes sense only if behavior of each primitive component corresponds to its frame protocol, i.e. if each primitive component can accept and emit method calls on its external interfaces only in sequences that are determined by its frame protocol. This correspondence can be checked in two ways: (i) code model checking with the modified Java PathFinder [15] (JPF) and (ii) run-time checking.

Code model checking of primitive components with JPF allows exhaustive verification whether the implementation of each primitive component corresponds to its frame protocol. Since each primitive component is checked in isolation, the problem of missing environment has to be faced (Java PathFinder checks only complete programs) via constructing an artificial environment for a component and checking the complete program composed of the component and environment. The behavior of an environment is specified by the component's inverted frame protocol, which is derived from the frame protocol by replacing all the accept events with emit events and vice versa.

Although the well-know problem of state explosion is partially mitigated by application of code model checking to isolated primitive components (a single component has a smaller state space than the whole application), still the checking has very high time and space complexity; for highly parallel components, it may even not be feasible. We address this by optional heuristic transformations of environment's behavior specification that help reduce the complexity of a component environment, while making the checking not exhaustive (not all thread interleavings are checked if the heuristic transformations are used). Alternatively, it is also possible to use run-time checking in such a case.

The basic idea of run-time checking is to monitor method call-related events on the component's external interfaces at run-time and check whether the trace composed from the events is specified by the component's frame protocol. Since only a single run of an application is checked in this way (run-time checking is inherently not exhaustive), a violation of a frame protocol may not be detected for many runs of the application that involves the erroneous component; in this respect, the technique of run-time checking is similar to testing.

14.6 Tools and Results

Verification of an application consists of two steps. First step is checking the protocols compliance. Protocols of all components used to implement a composite component are checked against the frame protocol of the composite component. Second step is checking whether the implementation of the primitive components correspond to their protocols.

Compliance of the whole Trading System was checked using the dChecker [6] tool with positive result. The dChecker tool is based on translation of the protocols into minimized finite state machines. Then, composite state space is generated on the fly to discover a potential bad activity error or deadlock. Moreover, in order to fight the state explosion problem, dChecker supports both parallel and distributed verification, so that the full computational power of multiprocessor and multicomputer systems is exploited. For illustration, correctness of the whole architecture takes 192 seconds to be verified on a 2xDualCore at 2.3GHz with 4GB RAM PC. Specifically, the protocol of CashDeskApplication is translated into finite state machine consisting of 944 states. The composite state space of CashDesk features 398029 states and it takes 8 seconds to be verified (on the same PC).

Correspondence of the implementation of primitive components to their frame protocols is verified by the Java PathFinder (JPF) model checker. Since JPF, by default, checks only low level properties like deadlocks and uncaught exceptions, we use JPF in combination with the behavior protocol checker (BPC) [26]. Component environment is represented by a set of Java classes that are constructed in a semi-automated way: (i) The EnvGen tool (Environment Generator for JPF) is used to generate the classes according to the behavior specification of the environment via the component's inverted frame protocol, and (ii) the generated classes are manually modified if the environment has to respect data-flow and the component's state in order to behave correctly (original behavior protocols do not model data and component's state explicitly).

By code checking implementation of the CashDeskApplication against the frame protocol created according to the reference specification of UC1, we were able to detect the inconsistency between the reference implementation and specification of UC1 that is first mentioned in Sect 3.2. Detection of this inconsistency took 2 seconds on a 2xDualCore at 2.3GHz with 4 GB RAM PC. Code checking of the implementation of CashDeskApplication against the frame protocol created according to the reference implementation has not reported any error and took 14 seconds. Nevertheless, switching between the express and normal mode is not checked, since the environment is not able to find whether the application is in the express mode or not, and thus it does not know whether it can trigger payment by credit card (forbidden in the express mode). Moreover, we also had to introduce the CashAmountCompleted event into the frame protocol and implementation of CashDeskApplication. This change was motivated by the need to explicitly denote the moment when the cash amount is completely specified (originally, the CashAmountEntered event with a specific value of its argument was used for this purpose). Were the CashAmountCompleted event not added, the environment for CashDeskApplication would exercise the component in such a way that a spurious violation of its frame protocol would be reported by JPF.

As for run-time checking, the special version of BPC is used again. The difference is that notification is not performed by JPF, but by runtime interceptors of method calls on component's external interfaces; moreover, no backtracking in BPC is needed since only a single run of the application is checked.

When using the tools, however, the state explosion problem became an issue. Some of the behavior protocols (namely CashDeskBus and Data) originally featured prohibitively large state space. Thus, in order to fight the state explosion problem, heuristics were employed. First, CashDeskBus protocol is separated into multiple protocols (as if for multiple components), so that it can be represented by multiple smaller finite state machines in contrast to a single unfeasibly large state machine. Second, method calls inside behavior protocol of the Data component are explicitly annotated by the thread number. This is again in order to the fight state explosion as this makes the protocol more deterministic while preserving the same level of parallelism. For these reasons, protocols on the CoCoME Fractal web page differ from the protocols described in Sect. 3.5 and Appendix, as they include also the heuristics.

14.7 Summary

In this chapter, we presented our solution to the CoCoME assignment that is based on the Fractal component model extended with support for component behavior specification.

Several issues in the UML specification and reference implementation were discovered and solved during implementation of the CoCoME assignment in the Fractal component model. Most notably, the component hierarchy was reorganized in order to improve clarity of the design and the hierarchical bus was split into two independent buses. These were modeled by primitive components, since Fractal does not support message bus as a first-class entity.

Behavior of all components of the Trading System is specified via behavior protocols. Since the CoCoME assignment does not include a complete UML behavior specification (e.g. via activity diagrams and state charts), behavior protocols for all the components are based on the provided plain-English use cases, the UML sequence diagrams, and the reference Java implementation. By application of code model checking to our implementation (based on the reference implementation), we were able to detect inconsistency between the specification and reference implementation of UC1 (details in Sect. 3.2. and Sect. 5). Consequently, we have created two versions of behavior protocols for several components – one version corresponds to the UML specification and the second to the reference implementation.

For deployment and distribution, we have used Fractal-specific means (FractalRMI and FractalADL). Since the buses are represented by primitive components that route the message, use of JMS was eliminated.

One limitation of our approach is only partial support for extra-functional properties via monitoring (no static analysis is employed). In particular, performance is monitored by custom component controllers for the Julia implementation of Fractal.

Very useful is support for verification of primitive component's code against the behavior specification (behavior protocols). Using that, it was possible to check whether the implementation corresponds to the behavior specification created at design time.

Acknowledgements

The authors would like to thank Marc Leger (France Telecom R&D) for providing the transformation tool that generates primitive component skeletons from FractalADL.

References

1. Adamek, J., Bures, T., Jezek, P., Kofron, J., Mencl, V., Parizek, P., Plasil, F.: Component Reliability Extensions for Fractal Component Model (2006),
   http://kraken.cs.cas.cz/ft/public/public_index.phtml
2. ASM, http://asm.objectweb.org/
3. Baude, F., Baduel, L., Caromel, D., Contes, A., Huet, F., Morel, M., Quilici, R.: Programming, Composing, Deploying for the Grid. In: Cunha, J.C., Rana, O.F. (eds.) GRID COMPUTING: Software Environments and Tools. Springer, Heidelberg (January 2006)
4. Bruneton, E., Coupaye, T., Leclercq, M., Quema, V., Stefani, J.B.: The FRACTAL component model and its support in Java. Softw., Pract. Exper. 36(11-12) (2006)
5. Bruneton, E., Coupaye, T., Stefani, J.B.: Fractal Component Model, version 2.0-3 (February 2004)
6. dChecker, http://dsrg.mff.cuni.cz/projects.phtml?p=dchecker

7. Dream, http://dream.objectweb.org/
8. FRACTNET, http://www-adele.imag.fr/fractnet/
9. Fractal ADL, http://fractal.objectweb.org/fractaladl/index.html
10. Fractal BPC, http://fractal.objectweb.org/fractalbpc/index.html
11. Fractal GUI, http://fractal.objectweb.org/fractalgui/
12. Fractal JMX, http://fractal.objectweb.org/fractaljmx/
13. Fractal RMI, http://fractal.objectweb.org/fractalrmi/index.html
14. Java Management Extensions (JMX) Specification, version 2.0, JSR 255, http://jcp.org/en/jsr/detail?id=255
15. Java PathFinder, http://javapathfinder.sourceforge.net/
16. JUnit, http://www.junit.org/
17. Layaida, O., Hagimont, D.: PLASMA: A Component-based Framework for Building Self-Adaptive Applications. In: Proceedings of SPIE/IS&T Symposium On Electronic Imaging, Conference on Embedded Multimedia Processing and Communications, San Jose, CA, USA (January 2004)
18. Loiret, F., Servat, D., Seinturier, L.: A First Experimentation on High-Level Tooling Support upon Fractal. In: Proceedings of the 5th International ECOOP Workshop on Fractal Component Model (Fractal 2006), Nantes, France (July 2006)
19. Magee, J., Dulay, N., Eisenbach, S., Kramer, J.: Specifying Distributed Software Architecture, Proceeding of the 5th European Software Engineering Conference (ESE'C 1995). In: Botella, P., Schäfer, W. (eds.) ESEC 1995. LNCS, vol. 989, pp. 137–153. Springer, Heidelberg (1995)
20. Mencl, V., Bures, T.: Microcomponent-Based Component Controllers: A Foundation for Component Aspects. In: Proceedings of APSEC 2005, Taipei, Taiwan, December 2005, IEEE CS, Los Alamitos (2005)
21. Mencl, V., Polak, M.: UML 2.0 Components and Fractal: An Analysis. In: Proceedings of the 5th International ECOOP Workshop on Fractal Component Model (Fractal 2006), Nantes, France (July 2006)
22. Microsoft .NET Framework, http://www.microsoft.com/net/
23. Object Management Group, Corba Components, version 3.0 (June 2002), http://www.omg.org/docs/formal/02-06-65.pdf
24. OMG, Object Management Group: UML Profile for Schedulability, Performance and Time (2005), http://www.omg.org/cgi-bin/doc?formal/2005-01-02
25. Parízek, P., Plášil, F.: Modeling Environment for Compoment Model Checking from Hierarchical Architecture. In: Proceedings of Formal Aspects of Component Software (FACS 2006), Prague, Czech Republic (September 2006)
26. Parízek, P., Plášil, F., Kofroň, J.: Model checking of Software Components: Combining Java PathFinder and Behavior Protocol Model Checker. In: Proceedings of 30th IEEE/NASA Sofrware Engineering Workshop (SEW-30), January 2007, pp. 133–141. IEEE Computer Society, Los Alamitos (2007)
27. Plášil, F., Višňovský, S.: Behavior Protocols for Software Components. IEEE Transactions on Software Engineering 28(11) (November 2002)
28. Seinturier, L., Pessemier, N., Duchien, L., Coupaye, T.: A Component Model Engineered with Components and Aspects. In: Gorton, I., Heineman, G.T., Crnković, I., Schmidt, H.W., Stafford, J.A., Szyperski, C.A., Wallnau, K. (eds.) CBSE 2006. LNCS, vol. 4063. Springer, Heidelberg (2006)
29. Simple Network Management Protocol (SNMP), RFC (1157), http://www.faqs.org/rfcs/rfc1157.html
30. Sun Microsystems, JSR 220: Enterprise JavaBeansTM, Version 3.0

31. THINK, `http://think.objectweb.org`
32. Visser, W., Havelund, K., Brat., G., Park, S., Lerda, F.: Model Checking Programs. Automated Software Engineering Journal 10(2) (April 2003)
33. Fractal CoCoME, `http://dsrg.mff.cuni.cz/cocome/fractal`

Appendix

This section contains the full behavior specification of the CashDeskApplication and CashDeskBus components discussed in the Sect. 3.5, the CashDeskBox component, and the StoreApplication component. In comparison to the protocols published on the project site [33], the interface names are slightly abbreviated for brevity. In a similar vein, the CashDeskBus protocol is presented for simplicity in a form of a single protocol containing a number of parallel activities - as mentioned in Sect. 6, the CashDeskBus protocol used for compliance checking was split into smaller parts to overcome technical difficulties with state explosion.

TradingSystem::CashDeskLine::CashDesk::CashDeskApplication

```
(
# INITIALISED
(
 ( #Accept and throw away events that are not expected in this phase
  ?CashDeskApplicationHandler.onSaleFinishedEvent+
  ?CashDeskApplicationHandler.onPaymentModeEvent+
  ?CashDeskApplicationHandler.onCashAmountEnteredEvent+
  ?CashDeskApplicationHandler.onCashBoxClosedEvent+
  ?CashDeskApplicationHandler.onProductBarcodeScannedEvent+
  ?CashDeskApplicationHandler.onCreditCardScannedEvent+
  ?CashDeskApplicationHandler.onPINEnteredEvent
 )*;
 ### The important part:
 ?CashDeskApplicationHandler.onSaleStartedEvent
);


# SALE_STARTED
(
 ### The important part:
 ?CashDeskApplicationHandler.onProductBarcodeScannedEvent {
  # ExpressMode & products.size == 8
  NULL
  +
  (
   !CashDeskConnectorIf.getProductWithStockItem;

   !CashDeskApplicationDispatcher.sendProductBarcodeNotValidEvent
   +
   !CashDeskApplicationDispatcher.sendRunningTotalChangedEvent
  )
 ###
 } +
 ?CashDeskApplicationHandler.onSaleStartedEvent+
 ?CashDeskApplicationHandler.onPaymentModeEvent+
 ?CashDeskApplicationHandler.onCashAmountEnteredEvent+
 ?CashDeskApplicationHandler.onCashBoxClosedEvent+
 ?CashDeskApplicationHandler.onCreditCardScannedEvent+
 ?CashDeskApplicationHandler.onPINEnteredEvent
)*;  # <--- LOOP
```

```
(
 ### The important part:
 ?CashDeskApplicationHandler.onSaleFinishedEvent;
 (
  ?CashDeskApplicationHandler.onSaleStartedEvent+
  ?CashDeskApplicationHandler.onSaleFinishedEvent+
  ?CashDeskApplicationHandler.onCashAmountEnteredEvent+
  ?CashDeskApplicationHandler.onCashBoxClosedEvent+
  ?CashDeskApplicationHandler.onCreditCardScannedEvent+
  ?CashDeskApplicationHandler.onPINEnteredEvent+
  ?CashDeskApplicationHandler.onProductBarcodeScannedEvent
 ) *
);

# SALE_FINISHED
(
 ### The important part:
 ?CashDeskApplicationHandler.onPaymentModeEvent;
 ###
 (
  ?CashDeskApplicationHandler.onSaleStartedEvent+
  ?CashDeskApplicationHandler.onSaleFinishedEvent+
  ?CashDeskApplicationHandler.onCashBoxClosedEvent+
  ?CashDeskApplicationHandler.onPaymentModeEvent+
  ?CashDeskApplicationHandler.onProductBarcodeScannedEvent+
  ?CashDeskApplicationHandler.onPINEnteredEvent
 ) *
);

# PAYING_BY_CASH
(
 (
  (
   ?CashDeskApplicationHandler.onSaleStartedEvent+
   ?CashDeskApplicationHandler.onSaleFinishedEvent+
   ?CashDeskApplicationHandler.onCashBoxClosedEvent+
   ?CashDeskApplicationHandler.onPaymentModeEvent+
   ?CashDeskApplicationHandler.onProductBarcodeScannedEvent+
   ?CashDeskApplicationHandler.onPINEnteredEvent+
   ?CashDeskApplicationHandler.onCreditCardScannedEvent+
   ### The important part:
   ?CashDeskApplicationHandler.onCashAmountEnteredEvent
  ) *;

  # On Enter
  ### The important part:
  ?CashDeskApplicationHandler.onCashAmountEnteredEvent {
   !CashDeskApplicationDispatcher.sendChangeAmountCalculatedEvent
  };

  (
   ?CashDeskApplicationHandler.onSaleStartedEvent+
   ?CashDeskApplicationHandler.onSaleFinishedEvent+
   ?CashDeskApplicationHandler.onPaymentModeEvent+
   ?CashDeskApplicationHandler.onCashAmountEnteredEvent+
   ?CashDeskApplicationHandler.onProductBarcodeScannedEvent+
   ?CashDeskApplicationHandler.onPINEnteredEvent+
   ?CashDeskApplicationHandler.onCreditCardScannedEvent
  ) *;
  ### The important part:
  ?CashDeskApplicationHandler.onCashBoxClosedEvent {
   !CashDeskApplicationDispatcher.sendSaleSuccessEvent;
   !CashDeskDispatcher.sendAccountSaleEvent;
   !CashDeskDispatcher.sendSaleRegisteredEvent
  }
 )
```

```
+

# PAYING_BY_CREDITCARD
(
 (
   ?CashDeskApplicationHandler.onCreditCardScannedEvent;

   # CREDITCARD_SCANNED
   (
    ?CashDeskApplicationHandler.onPINEnteredEvent {
      !BankLock.lock;
      !BankIf.validateCard;
      (
       !CashDeskApplicationDispatcher.sendInvalidCreditCardEvent
       +
       (
         !BankIf.debitCard;
         !CashDeskApplicationDispatcher.sendInvalidCreditCardEvent
       )
      );
      !BankLock.unlock
    }
    +
    ?CashDeskApplicationHandler.onSaleStartedEvent+
    ?CashDeskApplicationHandler.onSaleFinishedEvent+
    ?CashDeskApplicationHandler.onPaymentModeEvent+
    ?CashDeskApplicationHandler.onCashAmountEnteredEvent+
    ?CashDeskApplicationHandler.onProductBarcodeScannedEvent+
    ?CashDeskApplicationHandler.onCreditCardScannedEvent+
    ?CashDeskApplicationHandler.onCashBoxClosedEvent
   )*;
   ?CashDeskApplicationHandler.onPINEnteredEvent {
     !BankLock.lock;
     !BankIf.validateCard;
     !BankIf.debitCard;
     !CashDeskApplicationDispatcher.sendInvalidCreditCardEvent;
     !BankLock.unlock
   }
 )*;


 ?CashDeskApplicationHandler.onCreditCardScannedEvent;

 # CREDITCARD_SCANNED
 (
   ?CashDeskApplicationHandler.onSaleStartedEvent+
   ?CashDeskApplicationHandler.onSaleFinishedEvent+
   ?CashDeskApplicationHandler.onPaymentModeEvent+
   ?CashDeskApplicationHandler.onCashAmountEnteredEvent+
   ?CashDeskApplicationHandler.onProductBarcodeScannedEvent+
   ?CashDeskApplicationHandler.onCreditCardScannedEvent+
   ?CashDeskApplicationHandler.onCashBoxClosedEvent
 )*;

 ### The important part:
 ?CashDeskApplicationHandler.onPINEnteredEvent {
   !BankLock.lock;
   !BankIf.validateCard;
   !BankIf.debitCard;
   !BankLock.unlock;
   !CashDeskApplicationDispatcher.sendSaleSuccessEvent;
   !CashDeskDispatcher.sendAccountSaleEvent;
   !CashDeskDispatcher.sendSaleRegisteredEvent
 }
)

)
```

```
)* |   (
  # Enable Express Mode
  ?CashDeskHandler.onExpressModeEnabledEvent {
    !CashDeskApplicationDispatcher.sendExpressModeEnabledEvent
  }

)* |   (
  # Disable Express Mode
  ?CashDeskApplicationHandler.onExpressModeDisabledEvent
)*
```

TradingSystem::CashDeskLine::CashDesk::CashDeskBus

```
(!Helper.token)*

sync{Helper.token}

(?CashBoxControllerDispatcher.sendCashAmountEnteredEvent{
  ?Helper.token{
    !CashDeskApplicationHandler.onCashAmountEnteredEvent|
    !PrinterControllerHandler.onCashAmountEnteredEvent|
    !CashDeskGUIHandler.onCashAmountEnteredEvent
  }
})*
|
(?CashBoxControllerDispatcher.sendCashBoxClosedEvent{
  ?Helper.token{
    !CashDeskApplicationHandler.onCashBoxClosedEvent|
    !PrinterControllerHandler.onCashBoxClosedEvent
  }
})*
|
(?CardReaderControllerDispatcher.sendCreditCardScannedEvent{
  ?Helper.token{
    !CashDeskApplicationHandler.onCreditCardScannedEvent
  }
})*
|
(?CashBoxControllerDispatcher.sendExpressModeDisabledEvent{
  ?Helper.token{
    !CashDeskGUIHandler.onExpressModeDisabledEvent|
    !LightDisplayControllerHandler.onExpressModeDisabledEvent|
    !CardReaderController.onExpressModeDisabledEvent|
    !CashDeskApplicationHandler.onExpressModeDisabledEvent
  }
})*
|
(?CashDeskApplicationDispatcher.sendExpressModeEnabledEvent{
  ?Helper.token{
    !CashDeskGUIHandler.onExpressModeEnabledEvent|
    !LightDisplayControllerHandler.onExpressModeEnabledEvent|
    !CardReaderController.onExpressModeEnabledEvent
  }
})*
|
(?CashDeskApplicationDispatcher.sendChangeAmountCalculatedEvent{
    !CashDeskGUIHandler.onChangeAmountCalculatedEvent|
    !PrinterControllerHandler.onChangeAmountCalculatedEvent|
    !CashBoxController.onChangeAmountCalculatedEvent
  }
)*
|
(?CashDeskApplicationDispatcher.sendInvalidCreditCardEvent{
    !CashDeskGUIHandler.onInvalidCreditCardEvent
  }
)*
```

```
|
(?CashBoxControllerDispatcher.sendPaymentModeEvent{
 ?Helper.token{
  !CashDeskApplicationHandler.onPaymentModeEvent
  }
 })*
|
(?CardReaderControllerDispatcher.sendPINEnteredEvent{
 ?Helper.token{
  !CashDeskApplicationHandler.onPINEnteredEvent
  }
 })*
|
(?CashDeskApplicationDispatcher.sendProductBarcodeNotValidEvent{
  !CashDeskGUIHandler.onProductBarcodeNotValidEvent
  }
)*
|
(?ScannerControllerDispatcher.sendProductBarcodeScannedEvent{
 ?Helper.token{
  !CashDeskApplicationHandler.onProductBarcodeScannedEvent
  }
 })*
|
(?CashDeskApplicationDispatcher.sendRunningTotalChangedEvent{
  !CashDeskGUIHandler.onRunningTotalChangedEvent|
  !PrinterControllerHandler.onRunningTotalChangedEvent
  }
)*
|
(?CashBoxControllerDispatcher.sendSaleFinishedEvent{
 ?Helper.token{
  !CashDeskApplicationHandler.onSaleFinishedEvent|
  !PrinterControllerHandler.onSaleFinishedEvent
  }
 })*
|
(?CashBoxControllerDispatcher.sendSaleStartedEvent{
 ?Helper.token{
  !PrinterControllerHandler.onSaleStartedEvent |
  !CashDeskApplicationHandler.onSaleStartedEvent|
  !CashDeskGUIHandler.onSaleStartedEvent
  }
 })*
|
(?CashDeskApplicationDispatcher.sendSaleSuccessEvent{
  !PrinterControllerHandler.onSaleSuccessEvent|
  !CashDeskGUIHandler.onSaleSuccessEvent
  }
)*
|
# accept spare tokens
?Helper.token*
```

TradingSystem::CashDeskLine::CashDesk::CashBox protocol

This component is an example of simple bus event producer and subscriber containing no internal state information. In response to the cashier actions, which are not modeled, it is sending events and in parallel it is able to receive the ChangeAmount-Calculated event.

```
(
 !CashBoxControllerDispatcherIf.sendCashAmountEnteredEvent
 +
```

```
!CashBoxControllerDispatcherIf.sendCashBoxClosedEvent
+
!CashBoxControllerDispatcherIf.sendExpressModeDisabledEvent
+
!CashBoxControllerDispatcherIf.sendPaymentModeEvent
+
!CashBoxControllerDispatcherIf.sendSaleFinishedEvent
+
!CashBoxControllerDispatcherIf.sendSaleStartedEvent
)* |
?CashBoxController.onChangeAmountCalculatedEvent*
```

TradingSystem::Inventory::StoreApplication protocol

This component is an example of a component from the Inventory part of the application which does not directly communicate with a bus.

```
(
 (
  ?CashDeskConnectorIf.getProductWithStockItem  {
   !PersistenceQueryIf_1.getPersistenceContext_1;
   !StoreQueryIf_1.queryStockItem_1
  }
 )
 +
 (
  ?AccountSaleEvent.bookSale {
   !PersistenceQueryIf_1.getPersistenceContext_1;
   !StoreQueryIf_1.queryStockItemById_1*;

   !PersistenceQueryIf_1.getPersistenceContext_1;
   !StoreQueryIf_1.queryLowStockItems_1;
   !StoreQueryIf_1.queryStoreById_1;
   !ProductDispatcherIf.orderProductsAvailableAtOtherStores;
   (!StoreQueryIf_1.orderProductsAvailableAtOtherStores_1 + NULL)
  }
 )
)*
|
(
 !PersistenceQueryIf_1.getPersistenceContext_2;
 (
  (
   !StoreQueryIf_1.queryProductById_2*;
   !StoreQueryIf_1.queryStoreById_2*
  )
  +
  (# Fig. 20
   !StoreQueryIf_1.queryOrderById_2;
   !StoreQueryIf_1.queryStockItem_2*
  )
  +
  ( # Fig. 21
   !StoreQueryIf_1.queryStoreById_2;
   !StoreQueryIf_1.queryAllStockItems_2
  )
  +
  ( # Fig. 23
   !StoreQueryIf_1.queryStockItemById_2
  )
  +
  (
   !StoreQueryIf_1.queryLowStockItems_2
  )
  +
  (
```

```
   !StoreQueryIf_1.queryProducts_2
  )
 )
) *
|
(
 ?MoveGoodsIf.queryGoodAmount{
  !PersistenceQueryIf_1.getPersistenceContext_3;
  !StoreQueryIf_1.queryProductById_3*
 }
 +
 ?MoveGoodsIf.sendToOtherStore{
  !PersistenceQueryIf_1.getPersistenceContext_3;
  !StoreQueryIf_1.queryStockItem_3*
 }
) *
|
?MoveGoodsIf.acceptFromOtherStore{
 !PersistenceQueryIf_1.getPersistenceContext_4;
 !StoreQueryIf_1.queryProductById_4*
} *
```

15   CoCoME in SOFA*

Tomáš Bureš[1,2], Martin Děcký[1], Petr Hnětynka[1], Jan Kofroň[1,2], Pavel Parízek[1],
František Plášil[1,2], Tomáš Poch[1], Ondřej Šerý[1], and Petr Tůma[1]

[1] Department of Software Engineering
Faculty of Mathematics and Physics, Charles University
Malostranské náměstí 25, Prague 1, 11800, Czech Republic
{tomas.bures,martin.decky,petr.hnetynka,jan.kofron,
pavel.parizek,frantisek.plasil,tomas.poch,
ondrej.sery,petr.tuma}@dsrg.mff.cuni.cz
[2] Institute of Computer Science, Academy of Sciences of the Czech Republic
Pod Vodárenskou věží, Prague 8, 18000, Czech Republic
{bures,kofron,plasil}@cs.cas.cz

Abstract. This chapter presents our solution to the CoCoME assignment that is
based on the SOFA 2.0 (SOFtware Appliances) hierarchical component model.
The solution involves (i) modeling architecture in SOFA meta-model, (ii) specification of component behavior via extended behavior protocols, (iii) checking
behavior compliance of components, (iv) verification of correspondence between selected component Java code and behavior specification, (v) deployment to SOFA run-time environment (using connectors that support RMI and
JMS), and (vi) modeling of performance and resource usage via layered queueing networks. We faced several issues during implementation of the CoCoME
assignment in SOFA 2.0. Most notably, the architecture was modified in order
to improve clarity of the design – in particular, the hierarchical bus was replaced by two separate buses and the Inventory component was restructured.
Extended behavior protocols for all the components are based on the provided
plain-English use cases, the UML sequence diagrams, and the reference Java
implementation (the assignment does not include a complete UML behavior
specification e.g. via activity diagrams and state charts).

15.1   Introduction

15.1.1   Goals and Scope of the Component Model

SOFA 2.0 [9] is a component model employing hierarchically composed components.
It is a direct successor of the SOFA component model [24], which has provided the
following features: ADL-based design, behavior specification using behavior protocols [25], automatically generated connectors supporting seamless and transparent
distribution of applications, and distributed runtime environment with dynamic update
of components.

---

* This work was partially supported by the Grant Agency of the Czech Republic project
201/06/0770, the results will be used in the ITEA/EUREKA project OSIRIS Σ!2023.

A. Rausch et al. (Eds.): Common Component Modeling Example, LNCS 5153, pp. 388–417, 2008.

From its predecessor, SOFA 2.0 has inherited the core component model, which is enhanced in the following way: (i) the component model is defined by means of its meta-model; (ii) it allows for dynamic reconfiguration of component architecture and for accessing components under the SOA concepts; (iii) via connectors, it supports not only plain method invocation, but in fact any communication style [8]; (iv) it clearly separates and makes extensible the control (extra-functional) part of component implementations. Similar to its predecessor, SOFA 2.0 is not only a tool for modeling, but it provides a complete framework [28] supporting all the stages of an application lifecycle from development to execution.

In SOFA 2.0, a component is primarily treated as a black-box with well-defined interfaces and exists at design time, deployment time, and run time. Components are defined using their *frame* and *architecture*. A frame provides a black-box view of a component via defining component's interfaces. An architecture implements at least one frame and defines internal structure of the component, i.e. subcomponents and their composition. Semantics of the composition is defined via Extended Behavior Protocols; SOFA 2.0 also supports divide and conquer via interface specification.

The component specification is separated from the implementation and is defined using models (based on the SOFA 2.0 meta-model). Extra functional properties (EFP) are specified by separate annotations and resource model.

Component behavior is specified using Extended Behavior Protocols (EPB). EBPs allow to model and verify the behavior compliance and LTL_{-X} properties. The verification tools can verify the component architecture independently from the implementation, and the relation of the model and implementation.

Deployment-related features are specified separately from the architecture specification in a deployment plan.

15.1.2 Modeled Cutout of CoCoME

We model (and verify) nearly all aspects of the CoCoME example; regarding EFPs, however, we do not model other properties than resource and performance related.

To allow modeling of the example in SOFA 2.0, we have introduced minor changes to the original architecture. In particular, these include replacement of buses, introducing Enterprise server, and restructuring StoreServer. We verify behavior compliance of all components of the example and the results of performance prediction are compared with benchmarks of the reference implementation. For fully automatic behavior verification, we use a tool chain consisting of EBP to Promela translator and the Spin model checker; for performance prediction we use the Carleton LQN solver.

15.1.3 Benefit of the Modeling

The biggest advantages of our approach are namely (i) behavior verification, (ii) performance and resource usage performance prediction at design time, and (iii) the potential of checking whether a given use case is really implemented.

On the other hand, our approach cannot treat behavior that cannot be modeled by a regular language (e.g. recursion). Together with the manual preparation of the resource usage model, this remains the weakest part of our approach for now.

Usage of SOFA 2.0 and the verification and prediction tools and approaches is quite easy; an average computer science student takes approximately five days to learn about SOFA 2.0 itself and another five days to write behavior specification of simple components.

15.1.4 Effort and Lessons Learned

We have spent approximately 10 person-months to model the CoCoME example (we treat nearly all its aspects). Besides the modeling itself, this includes also modifications of the prototype implementation and collection of performance data on the prototype, required for comparison with the performance modeling results.

Major lessons learned from the modeling effort include the number of details that need to be covered to model a project in its entirety, as opposed to modeling only selected aspects. Having the fully modeled CoCoME example at hand is also extremely useful for further research into what other properties can be modeled and checked.

The chapter continues as follows. Section 2 provides an in-depth description of SOFA 2.0, as well as a brief comparison of SOFA 2.0 and other contemporary component models. In Section 3, we present our modeling of the CoCoME example in SOFA 2.0 and Section 4 provides short note about used transformation. In Section 5, we analyze modeling results while Section 6 presents used tools and achieved results. Section 7 concludes the paper.

15.2 Component Model

15.2.1 Static View

SOFA 2.0 uses a hierarchical component model with connectors, which are also first-class entities like components. The component model is defined using a meta-model [22]. In comparison to an ADL-based component model definition (like in the previous SOFA version), or even just plain language description, such an approach has many advantages like support of MDD, the possibility of automated generation of meta-data repositories with a standard interface, a standard format for data exchange among repositories, support for automated generation of model editors, etc. As the particular technology for defining the meta-model and generating a meta-data repository, we have been using EMF [10]. The meta-model is depicted in Appendix A; a brief description of main entities of the meta-model follows (a more complete description is available in [9]).

The *NamedEntity* and *VersionedEntity* classes[1] are reused multiple times in the meta-model. All other classes featuring a name inherit from *NamedEntity*. The *VersionedEntity* class further extends *NamedEntity* by adding a version (the versioning model used in SOFA is described in [9]).

A black-box view of a component is defined by the *Frame* class (it inherits from the *VersionedEntity*). The provided, resp, required, interfaces of a frame are modeled

---

[1] Like other elements in the meta-model, they are meta-classes but for better readability we omit the meta- prefix of meta-classes, meta-associations, etc. in the rest of the paper.

by the *provideInterface,* resp. *requiredInterface,* association with the *Interface* class, which is further associated with the *InterfaceType* class defining the real type of the interface. Also, *Frame* is associated with the *Property* class, which defines the name-value properties used to parameterize components (these values are specified at the deployment time).

A gray-box view of a component is defined by the *Architecture* class. The component's architecture implements at least one frame captured by the association between the *Frame* and *Architecture* classes (the option of multiple frames for an architecture allow for taking different views on the component behavior) and contains subcomponents and connections among them. If the architecture is empty, then the component is *primitive* and is directly implemented. Architectures can also add other properties (again captured via the association with the *Property* class), and/or can expose subcomponents' properties as their own (captured by the association with the *MappedProperty* class).

Connections among subcomponents are realized via connectors. At the meta-model level, connectors are just links among components' interfaces and they are captured by the *Connection* and *Endpoint* classes. The communication style of a connector and its non-functional features, which it has to provide at runtime (like secure connection, etc.) are defined by the *Feature* class, which is associated with *Interface*.

The dynamic reconfigurations [15] are allowed through well-defined reconfiguration patterns. Currently, SOFA 2.0 supports three patterns: factory pattern, removal pattern, and utility interface pattern. The factory pattern allows adding new components to the architecture at runtime; the removal pattern is complementary to the former and allows removing components at runtime. In the meta-model, the *Factory* class (which inherits from *Annotation*) can be used to mark an interface that it can create new component instances. The last pattern on the list introduces the concept of *utility* interfaces (in the meta-model the *connectionType* attribute of the *Interface*), which stems from SOA and allows accessing interfaces across the component boundaries (orthogonally to component hierarchy). In more detail, a provided utility interface can be accessed by any component at any level of nesting or from a completely different application (even non-component based), and the reference to such an interface can be freely passed among components. Thus, it serves as a generally accessible service. In a similar vein, a required utility interface can be connected across the application hierarchy. The concept of utility interfaces combines the advantages of component-based design and SOA.

15.2.2 Behavior View

For modeling behavior of SOFA 2.0 components, *Extended Behavior Protocols (EBP)* [16] are used; they have been derived from the original behavior protocols [2] by addition of enumeration data types and synchronization of multiple events [16].

Behavior protocols describe the behavior of software components as a set of traces of events appearing on component interfaces (method calls requests and returns from the calls (responses)). A behavior protocol is an expression built up from event tokens combined by classical regular (';', '+', '*') and the operator expressing parallel composition by event interleaving ('|'). For parallel composition, there is also another operator ∇ (*consent*), which allows to detect communication errors as explained further in this section. As an example, consider the following protocol:

(?i.open ; (?i.read + ?i.write)* ; ?i.close) | ?ctrl.status*

This behavior protocol generates the set of those traces starting with the *open* method and ending with the *close* method on the *i* interface with an arbitrary sequence of repeating the *read* and *write* methods on the same interface between them. The traces may be interleaved with an arbitrary number of the *status* method calls on the *ctrl* interface. As an aside, syntactically, this protocol is composed by means of the abbreviations 8-10 mentioned below.

The Extended Behavior Protocols (EBP) are able to describe the derived behavior more precisely than BP, since method parameters and local variables (e.g. for capturing component modes [12]) become a part of the specification.

A *frame protocol* is associated with each component frame; it describes the behavior of the component as the sequence of events appearing on the component frame. Furthermore, the *architecture protocol* is a parallel composition of frame protocols of the first-level-of-nesting subcomponents of a composite component.

As an example frame protocol, consider the following specification of the Light-Display component. In the example, the behavior specification of the component is divided into three parts: (1) type definitions (**types**), (2) local variable definitions (**vars**), and (3) behavior definition (**behavior**) containing an extended behavior protocol (the entities introduced in (1) and (2) are employed here).

```
component LightDisplay {

  types {
    states = {LIGHT_ENABLED, LIGHT_DISABLED}
  }

  vars {
    states state = LIGHT_ENABLED
  }

  behavior {
    ?LDispCtrlEventHandlerIf.onEvent(EVENT ExpModeEnabledEvent){
      state <- LIGHT_ENABLED
    }*
    |
    ?LDispCtrlEventHandlerIf.onEvent(EVENT ExpModeDisableEvent){
      state <- LIGHT_DISABLED
    }*
  }
}
```

Extended behavior protocol is an expression defining the set of allowed sequences of events (method call requests and responses) appearing on the frame of a component. It is formed using event tokens, operators, and control statements. Event tokens are of seven forms:

1. ?interface.method(type1 arg1, type2 arg2, ...)↑
2. ?interface.method(val1, val2, ...)↑

3. ?interface.method↓
4. !interface.method(val1, val2, ...) ↑
5. !interface.method↓
6. @multisynchronization_event
7. local_var <- symbolic_value

Furthermore, the following abbreviations are defined:

8. ?interface.method(...)   for ?interface.method(...)↑ ; !interface.method↓
9. !interface.method(...)   for !interface.method(...)↑ ; ?interface.method↓
10. ?interface.method(...) {expr} for
                              ?interface.method(...)↑ ; expr; !interface.method↓

The event tokens (1) – (10) represent primitive terms, which can be combined into expressions via the operators: ';' (sequencing), '+' (alternative), '*' (repetition), and '|' (parallel composition) as in the example above.

Each of the event tokens (1) – (7) represents an atomically occurring event (events do not overlap). The event token (1) stands for accepting a method call request (↑) and assigning the values provided by the caller to variables arg1 of type1, arg2 of type2, etc. The event token (2) is similar to (1), but it represents acceptance of a method call request only if it has been emitted with parameter the values val1, val2, etc. The event token (3) denotes an event representing acceptance of a response (↓) from a method call. The event token (4) stands for emitting a method call request providing val1, val2, ... as the parameters – the type of each parameter must correspond to the values declared at the callee (server) side. The event token (5) denotes emitting of a method call response event. The multisynchronization event (6), e.g. @x, is a blocking event taking place only if the all protocols in a parallel composition which contain @x are able to execute it at once. Then, it is executed as a single event atomically and simultaneously by all the protocols. The event token (7) denotes the event of assignment of a value to the local variable. The last two event tokens are not associated with a method call events.

Additionally, the behavior of a component may depend on the value of a local variable or a parameter via using the *switch* statement. The semantics of the *switch* statement is the same as in common programming languages. As an example, consider the following specification fragment:

```
switch (local_var) {
  value1: { protocol1 }
  value2: { protocol2 }
}
```

Finally, a *while* loop can be used for modeling finite repetitions that are done while a condition holds. The syntax of a *while* cycle follows:

```
while (local_var == value) {
  repeated-part
}
```

Another protocol operator ∇ (*consent*) is a specific parallel composition which, in addition to classical event interleavings and joining two complementary events (?x and !x) into a single internal τ-event (visible but no more composable with another event), detects the following communication errors:

(i) *bad activity* – the inability of components to accept an emit event at the time the event is emitted;

(ii) *no activity* – deadlock.

The *divergence* composition error, detected in the original behavior protocols, is omitted here because of two reasons. (i) Its implementation is of a very high complexity, and (ii) our experience shows that it occurs very rarely.

Having all components of an application specified using extended behavior protocols, two types of component compliance relations can be verified:

1) Horizontal compliance captures the correctness of communication among protocols of first-level-of-nesting subcomponents of a composite component, i.e., the absence of errors inside of an architecture protocol.

2) Vertical compliance captures the compliance of a composite component and its subcomponents, i.e., verifies the component frame against architecture protocols.

15.2.3 Deployment View

The *SOFAnode* is a distributed runtime environment, which consist of a single *repository* and set of *deployment docks*. The repository serves as storage for both component meta-data and code and is generated from the meta-model. The deployment dock is a container inside which the components are instantiated and running.

From the implementation view, components have two parts – *functional* and *control*. While the functional part provides the business functionality of a component and is directly implemented or in the case of a composite component composed of subcomponents, the control part controls the non-functional features (like managing lifecycle and bindings, intercepting calls, etc.) of a component and is composed of so called *micro-components* [19]. Micro-components allow for a modular fully extensible way to build the control part of a component; individual extensions are applied as aspects (using AOP techniques). Also, micro-components can expose themselves via *control interfaces*.

A SOFA application has the following lifecycle. First, a developer creates new components and uploads them to the repository and/or reuses already existing components from the repository. The next stage is assembly, where subcomponents defined using frames are "refined" by corresponding architectures. The assembly process starts with the top-level component (which represents the whole application) and recursively continues till primitive architectures. Finally, the assembled application can be deployed and launched. A deployer (i.e. a person responsible for deploying) chooses and assigns components of the application to particular deployment docks in the SOFAnode and sets values for components' properties. Also at this stage, the deployer can choose which control aspects have to be applied in the application. As a next part of the deployment process, connectors are generated. The connector generator [8] takes as an input the "development-time" connectors (edges with non-functional properties and communication style assigned – see 2.1) and current assignment of components to docks and automatically generates the code of these connectors, which transparently connects the components and have all required properties.

All the deployment information (i.e. assignment of components to particular docks, connectors and other information mentioned in the paragraph above together with a reference to the application architecture) is stored in a *deployment plan*, which serves as a recipe for launching the application. Note that besides driving the application launch process, the deployment plan is also used for performance modeling.

At runtime, code of the components is automatically obtained by deployment docks from the repository. SOFA also supports versioning of components; every component can exist in multiple versions and these can be simultaneously used (if desired) even in a single application and/or deployed in a single dock.

15.2.4 Performance View

Previously described views can be used individually or in combination with other views to reason about properties such as security, quality of service, etc. Some models can be derived directly from the behavior model, but to describe quality of service needed e.g. for service level agreements, a separate performance model is needed. The reasoning about service times and related properties cannot be based simply on the output of the behavior model (such as the number of method invocations) – it has to take into account the real execution time.

In general, the performance modeling process deals with predicting common performance attributes, such as roundtrip and throughput. Here, however, we consider precise prediction of individual performance attributes to be a secondary goal. Our primary goal is using the performance modeling process to predict how the performance attributes change when the scale of the application changes. This choice of priorities is motivated by perceived practical relevance of the results – when building an application, if it turns out that its real throughput differs from the predicted one by a constant, it is often possible to adjust the real throughput simply by installing more powerful hardware – but when the difference impacts scalability, no such adjustment is possible.

Typical approaches to performance modeling of component systems [32, 33] start with the behavior model of the system. This model is transformed into one of the well known formal performance models such as Layered Queueing Networks (LQN) [31] or Stochastic Petri Nets (SPN) [13]. The performance model is then populated by the performance attributes of the primitive components and solved to predict the performance.

A problem of this approach is that the performance attributes of the primitive components may change when the primitive components are composed, simply because the composed components share resource such as processor cores or memory caches. The typical approaches tackle this problem by including the resources in the performance model, which requires detailed knowledge of shared resources and in the end leads to excessively complex models [12].

To keep the performance model simple while taking into account the effect of shared resources, we have adopted an iterative approach, in which the usage of shared resources forms a basis for calculating the performance attributes of the primitive components. The performance attributes are fed to the performance model, which predicts the performance but also provides feedback to adjust resource usage. The entire cycle is repeated until stable resource usage and performance results are obtained.

When building the resource usage model, we have to take into account that even though it is the primitive components that consume resources, the fact that resources are consumed in the first place is not caused by the individual primitive components, but by the interaction of multiple primitive components.

Most primitive components are passive and consume resources only when some of their methods are invoked and only as much as those invocations dictate. In the resource usage model, we capture this behavior by annotating invocations with *resource demand hints*, which carry information related to resource usage, and by annotating components with *resource usage rules*, which describe how to calculate resource usage from resource demand hints. The choice of the annotations depends on the resources whose usage impacts performance, and can be determined by prior experience or by benchmarking experiments with primitive components.

The allocation of resources in a specific usage scenario whose performance is to be modeled is described by the deployment model, which assigns the components to the deployment docks and connects the components using the connectors, all at the level of individual instances. In the scenario, the interaction of primitive components can be captured by event traces generated from EBP. These event traces are used to direct the propagation of resource demand hints to components whose resource usage rules should apply.

To summarize, our performance view models the performance aspects of both component interaction and resource usage. As the output of the performance modeling process, we not only predict the common performance attributes such as roundtrip and throughput, but especially predict the trends of how these attributes change when the scale of the application changes.

15.2.5 Comparison with Other Component Models

Darwin [18] is a classical component model based on an architecture description language. It has influenced almost all of other component models. It employs hierarchical components without connectors and allows for describing dynamic architectures, but in a quite limited way and without any possibility to control the dynamic reconfiguration. Also, it is mainly just a specification language (ADL), not providing any runtime environment; at the same time, it includes the option to specify behavior of primitive components by means of finite state processes (FSP) [17]. Behavior specification of composite component is constructed as a parallel composition of the behaviors of subcomponents.

Another classical ADL is Wright [4]. It also uses hierarchical component but with connectors. Even more, it allows describing behavior of components and connectors formally using a CSP-like notation. But like Darwin, it is just a specification language without any runtime support.

The contemporary industry-supported component models like EJB [30] and CORBA Component Model [21], are just flat component models (no hierarchical component composition) and focus mainly on providing a stable and mature runtime environment. An exception is Koala [23] developed by Philips – it uses a hierarchical component model also significantly inspired by Darwin. It aims at being a development platform for embedded software for TVs, set-top-boxes, etc. Koala strongly focuses on component design and optimizations of an architecture; the Koala compiler (a tool which from ADL generates skeletons of implementations) allows for removing unused components and further architectural optimization. But the runtime options are quite limited, since the model is targeted to an embedded environment.

Fractal [7] is a component model very close to SOFA 2.0; it defines a number of abstractions and their interfaces in support of their existence at run-time (there are several Fractal implementations). Fractal defines a hierarchical component model without connectors (if the connectors are required, the Fractal specification instructs to simulate them using components which, however, leads to rather unclean architectures, mixing different levels of abstractions). Like SOFA, Fractal also separates functional and control parts of components. In addition, it supports shared components, i.e. a single component is subcomponent of several composite components. Such an approach allows for easy managing of dynamic reconfigurations but it breaks component encapsulation. An integral part of Fractal is Fractal ADL, which is an XML-based language for designing components and architectures; its usage is optional though since components can be built at runtime using Fractal API. Even though Fractal does not provide any formal behavioral descriptions of components, there are two projects adding it [1].

Like SOFA, the Fractal implementations (e.g., Julia, AOkell [26]) also provide complete environments for not only designing and modeling components, but also executing applications composed of them.

Both SOFA 2.0 and most of the Fractal implementations are built over the Java platform, being conceptually just code libraries. A different approach is taken by the ArchJava [3] and Java/A [5] component models, which modify the Java language by introducing new constructs for creating components. According to their authors, this approach prevents uncontrolled architecture modifications at runtime ("architecture erosion"). Nevertheless, the SOFA runtime (and also the Fractal implementations) prevents this completely.

15.3 Modeling the CoCoME

15.3.1 Static View

The architecture applied to the SOFA component model is based on the original architecture as defined in the CoCoME assignment. The modifications include (i) replacement of the hierarchical bus by two separated buses, (ii) interfaces and bindings necessary for the UC8 implementation, and (iii) restructuring of the Inventory component. All these modifications are justified and explained below.

As to (i), the hierarchical bus in the CashDesk was replaced by buses CashDeskLine and CashDeskBus, since this modification better reflects the orthogonal activities of CashDeskApplication and Coordinator with respect to other components in the CashDesk devices (Figure 1). This also elegantly reflects the fact that the number of instances of CashDesk and cashDeskChannel has to be the same, which is impossible to capture by the UML diagram from the CoCoME assignment (Figure 12, in the assignment). The direction of communication with buses is determined by their push semantics.

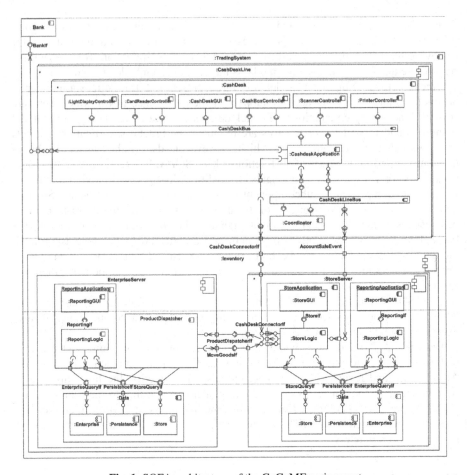

Fig. 1. SOFA architecture of the CoCoME assignment

As for (ii), this change relates to the Inventory component. The most visible modification here is the introduction of enterprise server and store server as explicit entities in support of UC8 implementation (EnterpriseServer and StoreServer components were brought up). According to the deployment diagram in the CoCoME assignment, the enterprise server is just a simplification of the store server, but UC8 requires additional functionality to capture transportation among different stores. This functionality is implemented by the EnterpriseServer component, in particular by its internal component ProductDispatcher. The rest of EnterpriseServer uses the same components as StoreServer which corresponds to the original idea of component reuse.

Finally, the modification (iii) comprises the replacement of two composite components TradingSystem::Inventory::Application and TradingSystem::Inventory::GUI by two other composite components – StoreApplication and ReportingApplication. The new componens group the primitive components in orthogonal way. The modification was motivated by the fact that Store and Reporting, the two internal components of the GUI (resp. Application) component are independent and communicate only with the corresponding component from the Application (resp. GUI) component over the binding from the higher level of the hierarchy (Figure 2 – there is no binding among the primitive components Store and Reporting). The fact that the behavior of Store and Reporting is orthogonal is much better captured by the modification shown in Figure 1. Here, the design functionality is covered by the components StoreApplication and ReportingApplication, each of them composed of two communicating subcomponents – one reflecting GUI and the second the business logic. This way, the communication between StoreGUI and StoreLogic is hidden within the StoreApplication component. Similar argument holds for ReportingApplication. Since the Data component provides interfaces needed by both StoreApplication and ReportingApplication, it is on the same level of nesting. Finally, the Database component from the CoCoME assignment is not in the diagram, as it is accessed via JDBC, not the SOFA framework. Since this is another level of abstraction it is not modeled in the diagram.

15.3.2 Behavioral View

Although the design of SOFA 2.0 supports different behavior specification backends, the default specification language is EBP (Extended Behavior Protocols) already described in Sect. 2.2. When specifying Trading System using EBP, the basic decision is whether to base the specification on the CoCoME assignment UML specification or rather on the reference implementation. On one hand, the CoCoME assignment UML specification does not constitute an unambiguous complete specification. The sequence diagrams specify only individual runs of the application, in contrast to the overall behavioral interplay of components. Unfortunately, other UML means for behavior specification (collaboration diagrams, activity diagrams, state charts) are not used. Moreover, when it comes to UC8, the CoCoME assignment UML specification is ambiguous, as the component diagrams lack interfaces for EnterpriseServer to StoreServer communication specified in UC8. Therefore, an analysis of the reference implementation provides additional behavioral information. On the other hand, the reference implementation conflicts with UC1 and UC8, introducing additional ambiguities. In UC1, the reference implementation differs during CreditCard payment and does not allow manual BarCode entry. UC8 is implemented as a part of UC1 exploiting direct access to the shared database).

Finally, the EBP specification is based partly on the provided use cases and sequence diagrams (UC3 – UC8) and partly on the reference implementation (UC1, UC2). Additionally, the EBP specification related to UC8 is also influenced by the architectural modifications mentioned in Sect. 3.1.

The actual EBP behavior specification is created per component at a particular level of nesting, i.e. both primitive and composed components are annotated by their frame protocol. This way, the EBP specification provides a better picture than the sequence diagrams, which follow the calls ignoring the component hierarchy (i.e. orthogonal to the hierarchy). Moreover, an EBP protocol describes the overall interaction, in contrast to a single application run.

The actors (Customer, Cashier, StockManager, and Manager) were not directly modeled; however, their behavior is modeled as an autonomous activity of the UI components (CashDeskGUI, CashBoxController, CardReaderController, ScannerController, StoreGUI, and ReportingGUI).

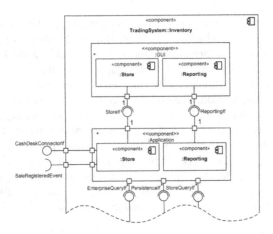

Fig. 2. Fragment of the original architecture

15.3.3 Deployment View

From the deployment point of view, the most important aspects of the CoCoME example have been the way deployment is described and managed, and the way distribution is addressed.

With regard to the description of deployment and its management, we have benefited from the full fledged deployment and runtime environment of SOFA 2.0. We have specified the implementation artifacts and the actual placement of components in a deployment plan. Subsequently, we used the SOFA 2.0 tools to launch deployment docks and start the application according to the deployment plan.

The actual distribution of the application in SOFA 2.0 has been performed via connectors. They encapsulate middleware and realize the distribution transparently to component. Since they support different communication style, we were able to model method invocations (realized by RMI in the reference architecture) as well as busses (realized by JMS in the reference architecture).

The connectors in SOFA 2.0 are automatically generated, thus a component developer is not forced to prescribe a particular middleware during design. The choice of middleware is performed at deployment time and it is done automatically by the connector generator (by constraint programming techniques). The generator also automatically creates an implementation of connectors to be used at runtime to actually address the distribution.

15.3.4 Implementation View

The implementation in fact completely follows the original reference implementation; several changes of the application architecture are described in Sect. 3.1. Connections among components are implemented via connectors (Sect. 3.3).

In SOFA 2.0, an application is represented by its model. Technically, the model is expressed a set of files containing architecture specification in SOFA 2.0 ADL. All the ADL files related to the CoCoME in SOFA application in are available on [27].

Further, the ADL files are processed by the *Cushion* development tool (Sect. 6.3), which validates them for syntactical correctness and semantical compliance and enters the model determined by them into the SOFA repository. Moreover, Cushion also controls verification of the component behavior specification.

15.3.5 Performance View

For our chosen approach, which iterates between modeling resource usage and modeling performance, it is necessary that the resource usage model provides performance attributes of primitive components to the performance model, and that the performance model provides feedback on resource usage to the resource usage model.

In CoCoME, we have decided to adopt LQN as the performance model – the feedback from LQN takes the form of queue length and processor utilization values. Another choice would be adopting SPN as the performance model – the feedback from SPN would take the form of numbers of tokens in selected places. Both LQN and SPN were reported to achieve good results when modeling enterprise information systems [5].

Our resource usage model in CoCoME is a hybrid model that uses benchmarking of primitive components under varying resource usage conditions to provide basic understanding of how resource usage influences the performance attributes. Additional benchmarking under specific resource usage conditions is coupled with modeling of resource usage through resource demand hints and resource usage rules to provide input to the performance model.

Because of the presence of the resource usage model, building the performance model does not need to go beyond the level of detail captured in the deployment plan and the behavior model. As described below, we have built the LQN model mechanically and in fact even introduced additional simplifications. We hope to eventually generate the performance model from the deployment plan and the behavior model, potentially simplifying it manually afterwards.

The first layer of LQN contains tasks generating the external requests on the system. These are the customers present at each store and coming to a cash desk at a given average rate, store managers accessing store clients for ordering stock items and enterprise managers accessing enterprise clients for generating reports.

The requests of the customers for processing their sale are handled by the cash desks. The multiplicity represents the number of cash desks in a store and the internal description of the cash desk activity (a complex probabilistic behavior description) represents the properties of a typical sale (the figures were taken from the extrafunctional properties of CoCoME). The load generated by the cash desks corresponds to UC1.

Each store also has a store client and a store server, and the system also includes an enterprise client and an enterprise server. All these tasks serve the purpose of generating disruptions of the standard load by the other use cases.

The database task represents the server part of the architecture which is actually performing the data lookups and is the place where resources are shared. The utilization of the processor running the database task represents the amount of concurrency.

The most challenging issue with using LQN was the representation of multiple stores. A trivial approach – using just the multiplicity of tasks – might not be appropriate because the multiplicity does not model the queueing in a realistic way, but it has the semantics of choosing any of the available cash desk by any customer regardless of the store he or she is in.

Our choice was to create all the separate instances of stores and cash desks inside them individually. Moreover, the LQN model is created by a generator script which can be thus seen as a meta-model. One instance of the model is shown on Figure 3.

Our benchmarking of primitive components under varying resource usage conditions has suggested that the resource whose sharing affects the performance attributes most significantly is – perhaps not surprisingly – memory of the StoreApplication and Data components. For sake of brevity, we limit ourselves to these components, which are in fact pivotal to the usage scenario most relevant to customers (UC 1).

The implementation of StoreApplication uses Hibernate, which caches data separately for each transaction. The memory usage of StoreApplication therefore grows linearly (i) with the number of transactions executing simultaneously and (ii) with the size of the data fetched in each transaction. Neither the number of simultaneous transactions nor the size of fetched data is limited - the former depends on the number of invocations coming to StoreApplication over RMI, which uses a thread pool of unlimited size, while the latter depends on the number of items in queries executed by StoreApplication, which can span all application data.

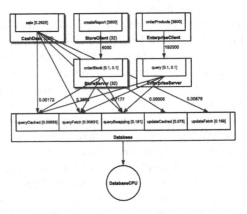

Fig. 3. Simplified LQN model for UC1

The implementation of Data uses Derby, which keeps separate context for each connection and caches pages for all transactions together. The memory usage of Data therefore grows linearly (i) with the number of connections opened simultaneously and (ii) with the size of the data cached for all transactions. The number of connections opened simultaneously is limited, as each instance of StoreApplication uses Hibernate, which has a connection pool of limited size. Similarly, the size of the data cached for all transactions is limited, as Derby uses a page cache of limited size.

The above description forms the basis for the resource usage rules of the StoreApplication and Data components. We get the complete resource usage rules by adding the information on static memory consumption, collected through benchmarking, and the information on the number of concurrent invocations, collected from the performance model in the iteration loop:

$mem_{\text{StoreApplication}} = base\_usage + sum\_per\_invocation\_type$ (aver-age_number_of_concurrent_invocations_of_this_type * query_size_per_invocation * memory_usage_per_unit_query_size)

$mem_{\text{data}} = base\_usage + \min(average\_number\_of\_connections_{\text{StoreApplication}},$ connec-tion_pool_limit) * #StoreApplications * memory_usage_per_connection + $\min(page\_cache\_size\_limit, database\_size\_in\_items *$ page_cache_occupation_per_item)

The resource demand hints used along the event trace, supply us with the query size per invocation, which is one for getProductWithStockItem queries and average shopping cart size for bookSale updates. The resource demand hints can be deduced from the complete event trace of UC1, which was generated from the behavior protocols. The key resource demand hints are the query and update sizes per invocations – one item for getProductWithStockItem queries and average shopping cart size for bookSale updates. The resource demand hints are associated individually with all relevant invocations along the event trace.

We have also determined the effect of memory usage on performance attributes by benchmarking, which shows that there are two milestones in memory usage that impact the roundtrip time as the performance attribute of choice. First, the duration of queries depends on whether the queries are satisfied from the page cache. We approximate this behavior by adjusting the mean roundtrip time of queries with the probability that a query is satisfied from the page cache:

$P(query\_cached) = \min(1, max\_cache\_size / data\_size)$
$T_{\text{query}} = T_{\text{query\_cached}} * P(query\_cached) + T_{\text{query\_from\_disk}} * (1 - P(query\_cached))$

Second, the duration of all operations depends on whether the memory used by the operations has been paged out and therefore needs paging in. To approximate this behavior, we would need to know (among other things) the memory access patterns of individual operations, which would make the model too complex. We therefore simplify the model by taking the sizes of the individual components to be correlated with the sizes of their memory access patterns (we can afford to do this especially because with any but insignificant amount of swapping, the system becomes overloaded – the estimate of the very onset of swapping, rather than exact performance under swapping, is therefore of interest):

$P(swapping\_needed) = occupied\_physical\_memory / occupied\_virtual\_memory$
$T_{\text{operation}} = T_{\text{operation\_without\_swapping}} + T_{\text{swapping\_overhead}} * operation\_component\_size *$
$P(swapping\_needed)$

Other milestones in memory usage that could potentially impact the roundtrip time are situations when the processor cache becomes exhausted and situations when the file cache becomes exhausted. On contemporary processors, the size of the processor cache is way below the memory usage of CoCoME, diminishing the importance of the first milestone. Similarly, as the memory usage increases, the size of the file cache decreases way below the size of the page cache, diminishing the importance of the second milestone.

15.3.6 Specification of CashDeskApplication

To give a rough idea about the resulting behavior specification, frame protocols of
CashDeskApplication and CashDeskBus in EBP formalism (Sect. 3.7) – being probably the two most interesting components from the behavioral point of view – are presented below (the rest of EBPs can be found in the appendix and on [27]).

As the state transitions of the CashDeskApplication component can be easily expressed as a state chart (states representing different phases during a single sale), it is
very important that the behavior specification were as easy to comprehend as the state
chart, while containing additional information on the method calls interplay. In this
respect, the frame protocol of CashDeskApplication shown bellow satisfies this requirement and shows how EBP can cope with specifying this kind of behavior.

Since EBP can explicitly model component's internal state (via local state variables), expressing CashDeskApplication's behavior is straightforward, as can be seen
on the CashDeskApplication frame protocol; here, the interface and method names
are shorten for the sake of brevity. In our view, having the states explicitly expressed
in the behavior specification of a component and revealing it to the outer world contributes to the clarity of the EBP specification.

```
component CashDeskApplication {
  types {
    states = { INITIALIZED, SALE_STARTED, SALE_FINISHED,
      PAYING_BY_CREDITCARD, CREDIT_CARD_SCANNED,
      PAYING_BY_CASH, PAID }
  }
  vars { states state = INITIALIZED }

  behavior {
    (
        ?CDAppEvHandler.onEvent(SaleStarted) {
          switch (state) {
            INITIALIZED:
              { state <- SALE_STARTED }
            default:
              { NULL }
          }
        } +
        ?CDAppEvHandler.onEvent(ProductBarcodeScanned) {
          switch (state) {
            SALE_STARTED: {
              !CDConnector.getProductWithStockItem;
              (
                !CDAppEvDisp.send(ProductBarcodeNotValid) +
                !CDAppEvDisp.send(RunningTotalChanged)
              )}
            default:
              { NULL }
          }
        } +
```

```
?CDAppEvHandler.onEvent(SaleFinished) {
  switch (state) {
    SALE_STARTED:
      { state <- SALE_FINISHED }
    default:
      { NULL }
  }
} +
?CDAppEvHandler.onEvent(CashAmountEntered) {
  switch (state) {
    PAYING_BY_CASH: {
      NULL + (
        !CDAppEvDisp.send(ChangeAmountCalculated);
        state <- PAID
      ) }
    default:
      { NULL }
  }
} +
?CDAppEvHandlerIf.onEvent(CashBoxClosed) {
  switch (state) {
    PAID: {
      !CDAppEvDisp.send(SaleSuccess);
      !CashDeskEventDisp.send(AccountSale);
      !CashDeskEventDisp.send(SaleRegistered);
      state <- INITIALIZED }
    default:
      { NULL }
  }
} +
?CDAppEvHandlerIf.onEvent(CreditCardScanned) {
  switch (state) {
    PAYING_BY_CREDITCARD:
      { state <- CREDIT_CARD_SCANNED }
    CREDIT_CARD_SCANNED:
      { state <- CREDIT_CARD_SCANNED }
    default:
      { NULL }
  }
} +
?CDAppEvHandlerIf.onEvent(PINEntered) {
  switch (state) {
    CREDIT_CARD_SCANNED: {
      !BankIf.validateCard; (
      !CDAppEvDisp.send(InvalidCreditCard) +
      (
        !BankIf.debitCard; (
          !CDAppEvDisp.send(InvalidCreditCard); (
            NULL +
            state <- PAYING_BY_CREDITCARD) + (
              !CDAppEvDisp.send(SaleSuccess);
              !CDEvDisp.send(AccountSale);
```

```
                    !CDEvDisp.send(SaleRegistered);
                    state <- INITIALIZED
                )
            )
          )
        ) }
      default:
        { NULL }
      }
    }
  )* | (
    ?CDEvHandler.onEvent(ExpressModeEnabled) {
      !CDAppEvDisp.send(ExpressModeEnabled)
    }
  )* | (
    ?CDAppEvHandler.onEvent(ExpressModeDisabled)
  )*
  }
}
}
```

The EBP specification above consists of (1) definition of types via enumerating their values, (2) definition of component's local variables, the `state` variable representing state of a single sale, and (3) the actual behavior. The CashDeskApplication accepts and publishes events from/through two buses, CashDeskBus and CashDeskLineBus, via its interfaces `CDAppEvDisp`, `CDAppEvHandler`, `CDEvDisp`, and `CDEvHandler`. Behavior of CashDeskApplication during a single sale (state transtion) is specified in the first and longest one of three parallel subprotocols, separated by the parallel operator "|". The other two subprotocols specify switching on and off the express mode as a reaction on the ExpressModeEnable and ExpressModeDisable events.

In more detail, the first subprotocol specifies different reactions, note the alternative operator "+", on sale-related events depending on the actual event received from the CashDeskBus (e.g. `SaleStarted` as a parameter of the `onEvent` method). The reaction then typically depends on the current state, stored in the `state` local variable (the `switch` statement), and consists of communication over the buses and/or switching transition to another state using the assignment statement "<-".

15.3.7 Specification of Component CashDeskBus

The second EBP snippet is protocol of the CashDeskBus component. The component implements a classical publisher-subscriber pattern, i.e. the message publishing method `send()` blocks until all subscribers receive the published message via the `onEvent()` method.

The key feature of the CashDeskBus component is that it synchronizes delivery of notification messages with next event acceptance, i.e. a notification message is delivered to all subscribers before another event message is accepted. To model this behavior, a technique which resembles the way a mutual exclusion is expressed in Petri nets. There is an auxiliary component Token which repeatedly (and sequentially) produces tokens via the `Helper.token` method. The CashDeskBus accepts the token and, while still "holding it" (until return from the `Helper.token` method), CashDeskBus distributes the corresponding notification message to all subscribers. This way, processing of other messages is blocked until the token is released. As a technicality, the CashDeskBus protocol can always accept the token when there are no event messages to accept.

```
component Token {
  behavior {
    !Helper.token*
  }
}

component CashDeskBus {
  behavior {
    ?CashBoxControllerEvDisp.send(CashAmountEntered) {
      ?Helper.token {
        !CDAppEvHandler.onEvent(CashAmountEntered) |
        !PrinterControllerEvHandler.onEvent(CashAmountEntered) |
        !CDGUIEvHandler.onEvent(CashAmountEntered)
      }
    }*
    |
    ?CashBoxControllerEvDisp.send(CashBoxClosed) {
      ?Helper.token {
        !CDAppEvHandler.onEvent(CashBoxClosed) |
        !PrinterControllerEvHandler.onEvent(CashBoxClosed)
      }
    }*
    |
    ?CardReaderControllerEvDispatcher.send(CreditCardScanned) {
      ?Helper.token {
        !CDAppEvHandler.onEvent(CreditCardScanned)
      }
    }*
    |
    . . .
    |
    ?Helper.token*
  }
}
```

It is fair to say that the presented technique takes advantage of the fact that notification messages are handled synchronously with event acceptance. In contrast, if the handling was asynchronous (i.e. message buffering was necessary), the modeling would be much harder (and obviously impossible for unbounded buffer).

15.4 Transformations

The modeling process of SOFA can be viewed as a series of transformations. The most notable transformations include the deployment process, which represents a transformation from the component model into the deployment plan, and the performance modeling process, which represents a transformation from the deployment plan and the behavior model into the resource usage model, and a transformation from the component model and the behavior model into the performance model.

The transformation from the component model into the deployment plan is mostly done manually, with some parts which can be automated. The decisions are particularly based on information like geographical properties of the deployment instance, hardware configuration, which is available, etc. Partial automation can be achieved by defining well-known deployment patterns in the component model (e.g. if some components are connected with a connector representing a bus, they should be deployed in the same deployment dock). This transformation is one-way.

The creation of the performance and resource models starts with a decision what use cases of the modeled system are actually interesting. This heavily depends on the SLA and QoS expectations of the real implementation (e.g. the real time duration of some use cases might be of very low importance for the service customers). Also some components from the component model can be manually eliminated or merged for the purpose of performance and resource modeling, when it is clear that their performance impact is either negligible (which is assumed) or fatal (which would make the performance model instantly useless).

After this selection and elimination, the performance model is derived automatically from the component model (components becoming tasks of the performance model) and behavior model (the behavior describes both the methods of the tasks and the kind and probability of their interaction). The decisions and transformation can be done iteratively when the performance model is too complex (difficult to solve) or oversimplified (captures only trivial interaction).

After the manual decisions on the importance have been made, the transformation from the deployment plan and behavior model into resource usage model can be also automatic. Basically the assignment of the tasks to processing units directly reflects the assignment of components to deployment docks. The behavior description is used to distinguish different types of processing units – tasks which act as pure clients (generating load) use unlimited processing units (with unbounded parallelism), whilst other tasks use processing units with a given multiplicity (which is derived from the number of instances of the given component in the deployment plan). This transformation is usually one-way.

15.5 Analysis

15.5.1 Compliance Both Vertical and Horizontal

Both the vertical and the horizontal compliance verification is done using a tool chain. The parts of the chain are EBP2PR (Extended Behavior Protocols to Promela Translator) and Spin [29] (described in detail in Sect. 6). Basically, the EBP2PR tool translates the specification in EBP into the Promela language. After that, this output is verified by the Spin model checker. Here, each EBP is modeled as a Promela process and the absence of communication errors is transformed (by a technical trick) into absence of deadlocks.

The tool chain was applied to the frame protocols associated with all of the components in the CoCoME application (Figure 1). The data on the time the tool chain spent on verification in this process is available at the project web site [27]. For illustration, Tab.1 below provides data on the time spent on the verification of the horizontal compliance of the CashDeskApplication and CashDeskBus frame protocols. In the first column, the size of the state space generated by the frame protocols' composition is shown. The other columns show the time spent in particular parts of the verification process – *EBP2PR* is the time required for transformation of the specification in EBP into Promela, *Verification* represents the time Spin spent on the verification process. As the composition of the CashDeskApplication and CashDeskBus frame protocols generates the most demanding state space in the context of the CoCoME application, the total time spent on behavior verification of the other parts of the application was shorter.

This particular horizontal compliance verification was performed on the following hardware and software configuration: PC 2x Intel Core2 Duo (dual core) processor with 4 MiB L2 cache and 4 GiB operational memory running the Linux (kernel version 2.6.19), and Spin version 4.2.9.

Table 1. The result of vertical compliance verification of the CashDesk component

# of states	EBP2PR [s]	Verification [s]	Total time [s]
3 335 950	41.5	46.1	95,6

Vertical compliance evaluation starts with inversion of the frame protocol of the composite component (the emitting and accepting events are swapped, e.g. !i.a↑ is replaced by ?i.a↑ and vice versa). Via the consent operator, the actual vertical compliance is verified by composing the inverted frame protocol with the architecture protocol capturing the composed behavior of the subcomponents; as an aside, this way vertical compliance is converted into horizontal compliance [2]. The complete data on verification are listed on [27].

15.5.2 Verification of Code against Frame Protocols

Checking of horizontal and vertical compliance makes sense only if implementation of each primitive component in a particular architecture obeys (is compliant with) the component's frame protocol. In order to check this property, we apply the technique of code model checking to individual primitive components. However, an isolated primitive component cannot be checked by a typical code model checker (like Java PathFinder), since such a component does not form a complete Java program required by a model checker – an environment that forms a complete program together with the component is needed. The environment is constructed from its behavior specification (component's inverted frame protocol) in such a way that forces the model checker to verify all reasonable control-flow paths in the component's implementation.

Although the well-known problem of state explosion is partially mitigated by application of model checking to a single component (having a smaller state space than the whole application), still the technique has very high time and space complexity since it exhaustively verifies all possible runs of the code; for highly parallel components, model checking may even be infeasible. In such a case, we recommend to use run-time checking to check the property of obeying a frame protocol at least partially (i.e. not exhaustively).

15.5.3 Run Time Checking against Code

The basic idea of run-time checking is to monitor method call-related events on the component's external interfaces at run-time and check whether the trace composed from the events is specified by the component's frame protocol. Since run-time checking can verify only a single trace recorded during a single run of an application and is therefore not exhaustive, an error (violation of a frame protocol) may not be detected for many runs of the application; in this respect, the technique of run-time checking is similar to testing.

15.5.4 Performance Analysis

The basis for our performance analysis is the CoCoME reference implementation, which was benchmarked to provide input for the resource usage and performance models. We have run several types of benchmarks on the implementation to identify those parts of code that have significant performance impact and resource consumption. Our further reasoning about scalability was based on these benchmarks (for detailed benchmark results, see [27]).

We have focused our analysis on a simple but practical configuration for both benchmarking and modeling performance, which is a repeated execution of Use Case 1. While quite simple, it represents a typical load on the system generated in a production environment. Other use cases serve the purpose of generating disruptions (the Reporting components in both Enterprise and Store can submit queries that can trash the database cache occasionally, but it would not make sense to consider a continuous reporting use case).

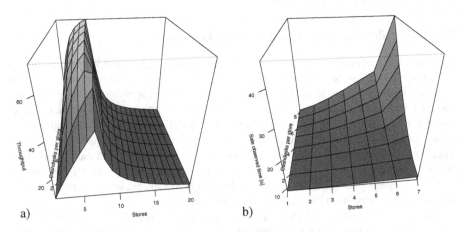

Fig. 4. Calculated a) throughput and b) average service time of Use Case 1

It is our assumption that a cash desk by itself cannot be overloaded (the throughput is strictly limited by the cashier interacting with the cash desk – the rate of his or her requests is significantly below any reasonable value which might be considered a high load) and its resource consumption is constant. We can therefore focus on the performance of the inventory components under the aggregated load by requests generated by several cash desks in several stores.

The results of our modeling are on Figure 4a, which shows the dependency of the overall enterprise throughput in terms of item queries processed per second on the number of stores in the enterprise, and on Figure 4b, which shows the dependency of the time to perform a single sale on the number of stores in the enterprise. We see that when the infrastructure is saturated or overloaded by requests from the cash desks, insufficient performance is noticeable even on the cash desk side, since the cash desks are unable to get answers to item queries within a reasonable time (however, the operations performed in the cash desks still take the same constant time, independent on the state of other components).

To evaluate the results of our modeling, we have measured the performance of the modeled scenario on the prototype implementation. The benchmark, as well as the benchmark experiments used to obtain the average durations of the atomic actions, have used an Intel Pentium 4 Xeon 2.2 GHz machine with 512 MB RAM running Fedora Core 6 and the database cache of 10000 pages for the server machine, and a dual Intel Core 2 Quad Xeon 1.8 GHz machine with 8 GB RAM running Fedora Core 6 for the client machine. The relatively low amount of memory on the server machine was used deliberately to allow the manifestation of swapping with a reasonably small number of cash desks and stores.

The results on Figure 5 suggest that our approach is reasonably precise in predicting the item query throughput and single sale roundtrip values. We have also predicted getting within 10% of the maximum throughput around 2 stores, when the measurement shows this happening around 3 stores, and the degradation in performance due to swapping around 8 stores, when the measurement shows this happening

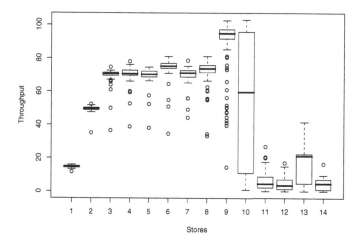

Fig. 5. Benchmarked throughput of Use Case 1

around 10 stores. Some difference in these results can be explained by our inability to determine the precise memory requirements of the individual components, something that is difficult to do with current tools.

15.6   Tools and Results

15.6.1   BP Checker

The EBP2PR tool is used to transform the specification in EBP into Promela (input language of the Spin model checker). On its input, this tool accepts the frame protocol of a composite component and the architecture protocol capturing behavior of its subcomponents. The output is a corresponding Promela model. This section describes the transformation process in detail.

As the semantics of the Promela language and EBP differ in many aspects (e.g. in handling nondeterminism), a straightforward translation of EBP into Promela is not possible. Therefore, the following sequence of transformations is applied: Each EBP on its input is first transformed into a corresponding nondeterministic finite automaton (NFA) (local variables and method parameters are not considered). This NFA is transformed into an equivalent deterministic finite automaton (DFA) that is minimized. Finally, Promela code modeling the minimal DFA is generated and the local variables and method parameters (ignored in the preceding steps) are added as variables of a Promela enumeration type.

As to communication errors (bad activity and no activity), bad activity is modeled as Promela deadlock in the following way: Each time a Promela process (recall that each EBP is modeled as a Promela process) emits an event e, it first acquires a lock (shared variable) and then emits e. If no other process is ready to accept e, a deadlock occurs since, due to the lock, no other event may be either accepted or emitted before accepting e. Technically, an event is represented by a dedicated shared variable. No activity is modeled naturally as a deadlock when the lock is not acquired.

If a communication error is discovered during the verification process, the verification is stopped, and the Promela error trace is used to guide the Spin simulation (i.e., only the error trace is executed) to generate the corresponding error trace in the EBP.

15.6.2   Modified JPF and BP Checker

As indicated in Sect. 5.2, we use the technique of code model checking to verify that a primitive component obeys its frame protocol. Since the SOFA component model is strictly Java-based, we use the Java PathFinder (JPF) tool, which is a highly extensible model checker for Java byte code, in combination with the old version of behavior protocol checker (BPC) that supports only old behavior protocols – there is no Java-based checker for new behavior protocols.

Technically, JPF and BPC cooperate while traversing their own state spaces and since both checkers work at different levels of abstraction, we defined a mapping from the JPF state space into the state space of BPC to make such cooperation possible. The mapping is implemented via a JPF plug-in that traces traversal of JPF state space and drives BPC in traversal of its own state space; for each executed byte code instruction related to method calls on the component's external interfaces, JPF plug-in tells BPC what transition it has to take in its state space. If such a transition does not exist in the BPC state space, a violation of a frame protocol is detected and reported. Environment for a primitive component is constructed in a semi-automated way: (i) the EnvGen tool generates stub implementations of component's required interfaces and skeleton of a driver program, and (ii) the driver program is manually modified so that the environment behaves correctly (with respect to data-flow and component's state).. Translation of EBP into the old behavior protocols (BP) is performed in an automated way. EBP-specific features are translated into constructs supported by the old BP with the possible loss of information (some behaviors may be added).

Run-time checker is also based on the old Java-based version of BPC. However, in this case, the state space traversal in BPC is driven by run-time notification performed by micro-components that intercept method calls on the component's external interfaces; moreover, no coordination of backtracking is needed since only a single run of the application is checked.

By application of our tool to the implementation of CashDeskApplication and its frame protocol created according to the reference specification of UC1, we were able to detect the inconsistency between the reference implementation and specification of UC1 that is first mentioned in Sect 3.2. Detection of this inconsistency took 2 seconds on a 2xDualCore at 2.3GHz with 4 GB RAM PC. Code checking of CashDeskApplication against the frame protocol based on the reference implementation (i.e. with no UC1-related inconsistency) has not reported any error and took 14 seconds.

Nevertheless, correctness of switching between the express and normal mode is not checked, since the environment is not able to find whether the application is in the express mode or not, and thus does not know whether it can trigger payment by credit card (which is being forbidden in the express mode). Moreover, we added the CashAmountCompleted event into the frame protocol and implementation of Cash-DeskApplication in order to explicitly denote the moment when the cash amount is completely specified (originally, the CashAmountEntered event with a specific value of its argument was used for this purpose). Were the CashAmountCompleted event not added, the environment for CashDeskApplication would exercise the component in such a way that a spurious violation of its frame protocol would be reported by JPF.

15.6.3 Cushion Development Support Tool

As mentioned in Sect. 3.4, Cushion (available as a part of the SOFA 2.0 implementation [28]) is a tool supporting development of SOFA 2.0 applications. It allows adding new ADL specification of interfaces, frames, and architectures to the repository, retrieving already existing specifications from the repository for further development (multiple versions are supported), etc. Also, it controls behavior validation of components. Further, Cushion serves as a build tool; it supports compilation of the code of primitive components, preparation of deployment plan, etc.

By its design, Cushion is fully extensible. In fact, by itself, Cushion provides just a core; all the above described functionality is implemented as extensions.

In addition to Cushion (command-line tool by nature), SOFA 2.0 application can be developed in a graphical development environment (designed as an Eclipse IDE plugin); unfortunately is has been still under the development at the time of writing, not being ready for a no-trivial use such as CoCoME.

15.7 Summary

In this paper, we presented our experience and results of using the SOFA 2.0 component model for specification and implementation of components of the CoCoME application. The architecture was modified in order to improve clarity of the design – in particular, the hierarchical bus was replaced by two separated buses and the Inventory component was restructured. All these modification, as well as the motivation for them, were described in Sect. 3.1. To demonstrate the modeling power of SOFA 2.0 in terms of behavior specification at the ADL level, Extended Behavior Protocols described in Sect. 2.2 were used. They further extend the expressive power of Behavior protocols via introducing local variables of enumeration type, method parameters of these types, and add simple control structures (loop, switch, if). By taking advantage of the EBP specification, the behavior compliance of communicating components was verified (Sect. 5.1). Furthermore, compliance of a part of the implementation (the CashDeskApplication component) against its EBP specification was also verified. This illustrated that the question whether the implementation fulfills the specification in EBP can be answered in an automated way at an early stage of the application development.

The deployment of the CoCoME application was done by the runtime and deployment environment of SOFA 2.0. Thanks to the presence of connectors in SOFA 2.0, RMI for remote method invocation and JMS for modeling buses could be used for implementation of the communication among components. For modeling the performance and resource usage, Layered Queueing Networks coupled with an extra resource usage model were used. Specifically, the performance of a particular enterprise under a varying spectrum of load conditions was modeled. By comparing the results with measurements on the prototype implementation, our model was shown to successfully predict changes in performance due to resource sharing and resource exhaustion.

As a future work, we plan to integrate the verification tool chain into the SOFA 2.0 framework and to predict performance of a component application by using a combination of formal methods and benchmarking.

References

1. Adamek, J., Bures, T., Jezek, P., Kofron, J., Mencl, V., Parizek, P., Plasil, F.: Component Reliability Extensions for Fractal Component Model (2006),
   http://kraken.cs.cas.cz/ft/public/public_index.phtml
2. Adamek, J., Plasil, F.: Component Composition Errors and Update Atomicity: Static Analysis. Journal of Software Maintenance and Evolution: Research and Practice 17(5) (September 2005)
3. Aldrich, J., Chambers, C., Notkin, D.: ArchJava: Connecting Software Architecture to Implementation. In: Proc. of ICSE 2002, Orlando, USA (May 2002)
4. Allen, R.J.: A Formal Approach to Software Architecture, Ph.D. Thesis, School of Computer Science, Carnegie Mellon University (May 1997)
5. Balsamo, S., DiMarco, A., Inverardi, P., Simeoni, M.: Model-based Performance Prediction in Software Development. IEEE Transactions on Software Engineering 30(5) (May 2004)

6. Baumeister, H., Hacklinger, F., Hennicker, R., Knapp, A., Wirsing, M.: A Component Model for Architectural Programming. In: ENTCS, Vol. 160 (August 2006)
7. Bruneton, E., Coupaye, T., Leclercq, M., Quema, V., Stefani, J.-B.: The Fractal Component Model and Its Support in Java. Software Practice and Experience, Special issue on Experiences with Auto-adaptive and Reconfigurable Systems 36(11-12) (2006)
8. Bures, T.: Generating Connectors for Homogeneous and Heterogeneous Deployment, Ph.D. Thesis, Dep. of SW Engineering, Charles University, Prague (September 2006)
9. Bures, T., Hnetynka, P., Plasil, F.: SOFA 2.0: Balancing Advanced Features in a Hierarchical Component Model. In: Proc. of SERA 2006, Seattle, USA, August 2006, IEEE CS, Los Alamitos (2006)
10. Eclipse Modeling Framework, http://www.eclipse.org/emf/
11. Enterprise Java Beans specification, version 2.1, Sun Microsystems (November 2003)
12. Ghosh, A., Givargis, T.: Cache optimization for embedded processor cores: An analytical approach. ACM Transactions on Design Automation of Electronic Systems (TODAES), 9(4) (October 2004)
13. Haas, P.J.: Stochastic Petri Nets: Modelling. Springer, New York (2002)
14. Hirsch, D., Kramer, J., Magee, J., Uchitel, S.: Modes for Software Architectures. In: Gruhn, V., Oquendo, F. (eds.) EWSA 2006. LNCS, vol. 4344. Springer, Heidelberg (2006)
15. Hnetynka, P., Plasil, F.: Dynamic Reconfiguration and Access to Services in Hierarchical Component Models. In: Gorton, I., Heineman, G.T., Crnković, I., Schmidt, H.W., Stafford, J.A., Szyperski, C.A., Wallnau, K. (eds.) CBSE 2006. LNCS, vol. 4063. Springer, Heidelberg (2006)
16. Kofron, J.: Extending Behavior Protocols With Data and Multisynchronization, Tech. Report No. 2006/10, Dep. of SW Engineering, Charles University in Prague (October 2006)
17. Magee, J., Kramer, J.: Concurrency State Models & Java Programs. Wiley, Chichester (1999)
18. Magee, J., Kramer, J.: Dynamic structure in software architectures. In: Proc. of FSE 2004, San Francisco, USA (October 1996)
19. Mencl, V., Bures, T.: Microcomponent-Based Component Controllers: A Foundation for Component Aspects. In: Proc. of APSEC 2005, Taipei, Taiwan, December 2005, IEEE CS, Los Alamitos (2005)
20. OMG: UML Profile for Schedulability, Performance and Time, OMG document formal/2005-01-02 (January 2005)
21. OMG: CORBA Components, v 3.0, OMG document formal/02-06-65 (June 2002)
22. OMG: MDA Guide, v. 1.0.1, OMG document omg/03-06-01 (Jun 2003)
23. van Ommering, R., van der Linden, F., Kramer, J., Magee, J.: The Koala Component Model for Consumer Electronics Software. IEEE Computer 33(3) (March 2000)
24. Plasil, F., Balek, D., Janecek, R.: SOFA/DCUP: Architecture for Component Trading and Dynamic Updating. In: Proc. of ICCDS 1998, Annapolis, USA. IEEE CS Press, Los Alamitos (May 1998)
25. Plasil, F., Visnovsky, S.: Behavior Protocols for Software Components. IEEE Transactions on Software Engineering 28(11) (November 2002)
26. Seinturier, L., Pessemier, N., Duchien, L., Coupaye, T.: A Component Model Engineered with Components and Aspects. In: Gorton, I., Heineman, G.T., Crnković, I., Schmidt, H.W., Stafford, J.A., Szyperski, C.A., Wallnau, K. (eds.) CBSE 2006. LNCS, vol. 4063. Springer, Heidelberg (2006)
27. SOFA CoCoME (2007), http://dsrg.mff.cuni.cz/cocome/sofa
28. SOFA 2.0 implementation, http://sofa.objectweb.org/
29. Spin, http://www.spinroot.com/

30. Sun Microsystems, JSR 220: Enterprise JavaBeansTM, Version 3.0
31. Woodside, C.M., Neron, E., Ho, E.D.S., Mondoux, B.: An Active-Server Model for the Performance of Parallel Programs Written Using Rendezvous. Journal of Systems and Software (1986)
32. Xu, J., Oufimtsev, A., Woddside, C.M., Murphy, L.: Performance Modeling and Prediction of Enterprise JavaBeans with Layered Queueing Network Templates. ACM SIGSOFT Software Engineering Notes 31(2) (March 2006)
33. Wu, X.P., Woodside, C.M.: Performance Modeling from Software Components. In: Proc. of WOSP 2004, Redwood Shores, USA (January 2004)

Appendix A: SOFA 2.0 Meta-model

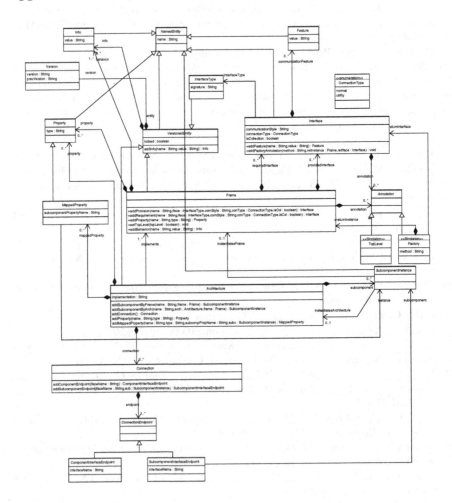

Appendix B: Specification of Selected Components

The full version of CoCoME EBP specification is available at the SOFA CoCoME project web site [27]. As the space allotted for this chapter is limited, this appendix contains EBP specification only of selected, "representative" components CashDesk-Line and CardReader – those which are discussed elsewhere in the text.

```
component CashDeskLine {
  behavior {
    (
      !CDConnector1.getProductWithStockItem*;
      ( !BankIf1.validateCard*;
        !BankIf1.debitCard
      )*;
      !CDLineEvDisp1.send(AccountSale);
      !CDLineEvDisp2.send(SaleRegistered)
    )*
    |
    (
      !CDConnector2.getProductWithStockItem*;
      (
        !BankIf2.validateCard*;
        !BankIf2.debitCard
      )*;
      !CDLineEvDisp2.send(AccountSale);
      !CDLineEvDisp2.send(SaleRegistered)
    )
  }
}

component CardReader {
  types {
    states = {CARD_READER_ENABLED, CARD_READER_DISABLED}
  }
  vars {
    states state = CARD_READER_ENABLED
  }
  behavior {
    (
      !CardReaderControllerEvDispatcher.send(PINEntered) +
      !CardReaderControllerEvDispatcher.send(CreditCardScanned)
    )*
    |
    ?CardReaderController.onEvent(ExpressModeDisabled){
      state <- CARD_READER_DISABLED
    }*
    |
    ?CardReaderController.onEvent(ExpressModeEnabled) {
      state <- CARD_READER_ENABLED
    }*
  }
}
```

16 A Specification Language for Distributed Components Implemented in GCM/ProActive

Antonio Cansado, Denis Caromel, Ludovic Henrio, Eric Madelaine,
Marcela Rivera, and Emil Salageanu

INRIA Sophia-Antipolis, Université de Nice Sophia-Antipolis, CNRS, France
{first.last}@sophia.inria.fr

16.1 Introduction

16.1.1 Goals and Scope of the Component Model

This chapter is based on a component model for distributed components called
GCM for *Grid Component Model*. We present here this component model, its
reference implementation based on the Java middleware ProActive, our specification language, *JDC*, adapted to distributed software components, and the
associated specification platform: *Vercors*. From the specification of components
and their behaviour, our aim is to both verify properties of this behaviour and
generate code for real GCM components.

The OASIS team works in the area of distributed systems, with a stress on
programming methodology and tools for computational grids. We base our programming model on active objects: each active object has its own (and unique)
thread, processing asynchronous method calls on the object.

Analysing the behaviour of distributed systems always has been more difficult
than for traditional systems, because of the complexity of temporal interactions
between remote parts of the application. However, the programming model proposed by our team (featured by the ProActive library [1] implementing the ASP
calculus[2]) intends to ease the analysis of concurrency by clearly identifying
entry points for communications and limiting the concurrency aspects to several remote method calls on the same object. Moreover, structuring distributed
systems using components is somewhat better, because it requires interaction
points (service points, but also required interfaces) to be well defined. Additionally, these well-defined boundaries reduce the amount of information that one
component needs to have about its environment.

Unfortunately, developers still have to face non-trivial runtime incompatibil-
ities when assembling off-the-shelf components. These arise due to the lack of
a precise dynamic specification of the component behaviour (the protocols for
inter-component communication). In fact, state-of-the-art implementations of
component models such as Fractal [3] and the CORBA Component Model [4]
only consider type-compatibility for binding interfaces.

Nonetheless, a much more precise, sound static compatibility check of bound
interfaces can be achieved if behavioural information is added to the components.
In such effort, we proposed in [5] to attach behaviour as part of the architecture

A. Rausch et al. (Eds.): Common Component Modeling Example, LNCS 5153, pp. 418–448, 2008.
© Springer-Verlag Berlin Heidelberg 2008

specification, defined in terms of parameterized networks of transition systems. The compatibility between these behaviours can be checked using model-checkers as we did in [6]. In the same spirit, "behavior protocols" [7] and "component-interaction automata" [8] are ongoing research projects with similar goals. They both adopt a simpler model than ours, for example the "behavior protocols" framework uses a regular-language to describe traces of the component behaviour (without data), while we are able to take into account an abstraction of the data-flow which fulfils value-passing and routing.

One question that may rise is why to create a new specification language. Some of them, like the ISO language LOTOS, are very expressive both on the side of describing parallelism and synchronisation and on the side of data types. We argue that none of them fits well when it comes to distributed components (DCs), like the ones used in Grid computing to aid software design. In Grid computing, latency plays a major role, so asynchrony is a must for optimum resource usage. Additionally, designs usually exploit physical symmetries but are often obstructed by specification languages expressiveness. For example, in Fractal's standard Architecture Description Language (ADL), it is not possible to define *multiple components* (i.e., sets of identical components) and bindings between them in a natural way. Moreover, as DCs may be deployed over thousands of machines, collective interfaces have been defined as an extension of "classical" component models to address scalability of both designs and implementations. Last, most existing models focus only on the functional (business) behaviour, whereas we are interested in the non-functional behaviour as well. In Fractal and GCM vocabulary, non-functional behaviour includes mainly deployment, life-cycle and reconfiguration aspects such as replacing components and dynamically creating components. Within our models we are able to prove correctness of deployment and basic reconfiguration [9, 10].

In addition to the GCM component model and its implementation in ProActive, we propose here a new specification language called JDC (for Java Distributed Component) for answering requirements of DC applications, with stress on Grid programming. Part of this language may also be specified as UML 2 component diagrams and state-machines; we have developed a tool named CTTool for editing those diagrams and interfacing with verification tools. Being verifiable, the JDC specification can guarantee various safety properties in the derived implementation.

16.1.2   Contribution

In this chapter, we shall:

- introduce the Grid Component Model (GCM) and its reference implementation with the ProActive middleware (16.2.1 and 16.2.2), the JDC specification language (16.2.4), and the CTTool diagram editor (16.2.5);
- present each JDC feature with examples using small pieces of CoCoME;
- give an integrated example of one of the CoCoME components;
- present and comment the implementation of the CoCoME we realised with GCM/ProActive;

– explain how CoCoME requirements can be checked from the JDC specification, using our verification platform (16.5).

In addition, the case-study is available at our website[1], including the JDC specification, the CTTool diagrams, and a GCM/ProActive implementation.

16.1.3   Part of CoCoME Modelled

We did not model the complete CoCoME but focus on the CashDeskLine component, of which we gave a full and detailed specification. For the rest of the system (the inventory and the bank) we only provided simple components with a minimal behaviour, enough to act as an environment to the CashDeskLine. Throughout our approach we tried to stick with the original architecture as much as possible. This includes modelling the routing capabilities of the EventBus, and multiplicity of CashDesks.

The CoCoME as given does not represent a usual GCM design, and therefore does not profit from most of its features. For example, in Fractal and GCM there are no such thing as *Channel* components. They were modelled as a "normal" GCM component which is costly in performance and in the number of communications: the EventBus works as an intermediate component which replicates the calls as a router. More specifically for the ProActive/GCM implementation, in the CoCoME most of the calls are void which do not take advantage of the future mechanism, but only of the asynchronous calls featured by our programming model. We could have restructured the system with the GCM in mind, but it would have been a different design, unmatched with the rest of the book.

16.1.4   Benefits

Our methodology is based on a rich specification of hierarchical and distributed components. In fact, data is considered explicitly inside the behavioural model. This allows us to reason about value-passing properties as well as data used in routing within parameterized components.

These specifications can be verified against functional properties, as well as non-functional properties, expressed as branching-time temporal properties. We support the modelling with either the JDC language, or its graphical subset in UML, and the generation of behavioural models based on the specification.

The JDC developer starts by specifying the system behaviour and architecture, then checks properties and verifies coherence of his components, and finally generates code-skeletons with the control code of his application. Then, this generated code must be completed with the detailed business code, that should be written by the programmer, with the constraint that it does not affect the behaviour. We expect this technique to be applicable by non-experts on formal methods, specially when using our UML 2 graphical modelling tools.

---

[1] http://www-sop.inria.fr/oasis/Vercors/Cocome/

16.1.5 Lessons Learned

Our objective when modelling the CoCoME was to show the effectiveness of our approach for modelling and verifying the behaviour of a medium-scale example, not particularly fitted to the GCM (as explained in Section 16.1.3 above).

The modelling allowed us to stress our tools with a medium-scale case-study, and we were able to generate the full state-space for a synchronous version of CoCoME. An asynchronous model would generate a much bigger state-space; however for a large class of temporal formulas (typically reachability, but not absence of deadlocks) we are able to use on-the-fly techniques which do not require brute-force generation of the state-space. The conclusion of this chapter details the current limitations of our tool platform.

16.2 Component Model

This section first presents the GCM and its ProActive implementation. Then we give a short description of our low-level semantic model, called pNets [11]. Then we describe the JDC specification language, giving its syntax and an informal semantics, and finally present the CTTool diagram editor.

16.2.1 The Grid Component Model (GCM)

The Grid Component Model (GCM) [12] is a novel component model being defined by the european Network of Excellence CoreGrid and implemented by the EU project GridCOMP. The GCM is based on the Fractal Component Model [3], and extends it to address Grid concerns.

Fractal is a hierarchical component model, meaning that every component is either a composite, i.e. it is composed of other components (and thus its content is known), or primitive if its content cannot be decomposed. Fractal components interact through interfaces which correspond to object interfaces, so interactions between components are method calls. *Server interfaces* receive invocations, whereas *client interfaces* send invocations. A general view of a composite component is seen in Figure 1. Interfaces on the left side are *server interfaces*, on the right side *client interfaces*, and on top *non-functional server interfaces*.

From Fractal, GCM inherits a hierarchical structure with strong separation of concerns between functional and non-functional behaviours. For example, it defines non-functional interfaces managing the application life-cycle and deployment. GCM also inherits from Fractal introspection of components and reconfiguration capabilities, mainly consisting in the possibility to change the content of a composite component and the bindings between components. Grids consider thousands of computers all over the world, for that, GCM extends Fractal using asynchronous method calls for dealing with latency. Grid applications usually have numerous similar components, so the GCM defines collective interfaces which ease design and implementation as they provide some synchronisation and distribution capacities. There are mainly two kinds of collective interfaces in the GCM: multicast interfaces that distribute one message with its parameters to a

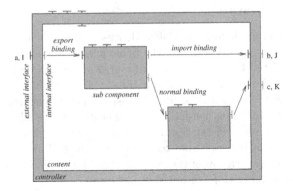

Fig. 1. A composite component as defined in Fractal Specification

set of destinations; and gathercast interfaces that synchronise and gather a set of messages with their parameters. A client interface may be a multicast interface, meaning that a call toward this interface can be distributed to many server interfaces depending on the distribution used. Similarly, a server interface may be a gathercast interface, meaning that multiple client calls will be synchronised and a single call will be performed towards the service component.

For adaptivity purposes, the GCM first extends the reconfiguration capabilities of Fractal to the non-functional aspects: the control of a component can be reconfigured dynamically, moreover, the GCM specifies interfaces for the autonomic management and adaptation of components.

The Architecture Description Language (ADL) of both Fractal and the GCM is an XML-based format, that contains both the structural definition of the system components (subcomponents, interfaces and bindings), and also the definition of so-called *virtual nodes* (VN) that are an abstraction of the physical infrastructure on which the application will be deployed: the ADL only refers to an abstract architecture, and the mapping between the abstract architecture and a real one is given separately as a deployment descriptor.

16.2.2   A GCM Reference Implementation: GCM/ProActive

A GCM reference implementation is based on ProActive [1], an Open Source middleware. In this implementation, an active object is used to implement each primitive component and each composite membrane. Although composite components do not have functional code themselves, they have a membrane that encapsulates controllers, and dispatches functional calls to inner subcomponents. As a consequence, this implementation also inherits some constraints and properties w.r.t. the programming model:

- components communicate through asynchronous method calls with transparent futures. These futures are first order objects: they can be forwarded to any component in a non-blocking manner;
- there is no shared memory between components;

— a single control thread is available for each component, either primitive or composite.

To ensure causal ordering of requests, method calls use a rendez-vous protocol: the caller is momentarily blocked while requests are en-queued in the callee (server) side, and a future is created as a placeholder for the returned result. Then, the caller's execution may freely continue up to a point where the concrete value of the result is needed. At this moment it is blocked until the concrete value is available in a mechanism called *wait-by-necessity*. Therefore, there is an implicit data-flow synchronisation generated by the flow of futures. A precise operational semantics of ProActive is given by the ASP-calculus [2, 13]; it allows the proof of generic and important properties of ProActive's constructs on top of which we base our specification language.

Each primitive component is associated to an active object that should be written by the programmer (or generated by a JDC specification, as we will see in the following), whereas the active object managing a composite is generic and provided by the GCM/ProActive platform. Like in Fractal, GCM/ProActive component interfaces are realised by object interfaces. The particularity of GCM/ProActive is that those method calls are necessarily asynchronous, a method call on a server interface adds a request to its *request queue*. If this component is a composite, then it should simply forward the request to the contained component that is connected to this server interface. If the component is a primitive, then the required functionality should be addressed by the active object encapsulated in the primitive, so the request will be treated locally. Most of the time, requests are served in a FIFO order but any *service policy* can be specified when programming active objects (that is for primitive components), by writing a specific method called runActivity(). Note that futures create some kinds of implicit return channels, which are only used to return one value to a component that might need it. One particularity of this approach is that it unifies the concept of component with the unit of distribution and parallelism.

Indeed, one essential property of ProActive, inherited from the ASP calculus, is that the global behaviour of a ProActive application is totally independent of the physical localisation of active objects and components on a distributed architecture. This allows us to totally separate the deployment file from the system specification: the deployment is one part of the implementation, and is isolated in a specific file so that the application need not be changed when run on different infrastructures (even going from a single JVM on one machine to a full multi-site heterogeneous grid of hundreds of machines).

16.2.3 pNets and Behavioural Models

In a previous work [11] we introduced "Parameterized Networks of Transition Systems" (pNets), as a powerful model and a generic low-level formalism, able to express communicating processes with value passing and parameterized topologies of processes. Parameterized synchronisation vectors allow to encode many different synchronisation and communication mechanisms amongst asynchronous processes.

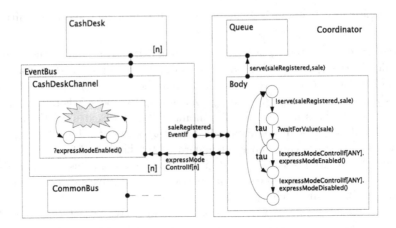

Fig. 2. A partial pNets model of CoCoME

We have shown how to describe the behaviour of ProActive's active objects with pNets. Then, in [9, 10] we synthesised a behavioural model for GCM/ProActive components, including their functional and non-functional behaviour. In Figure 2, we provide a partial model of CoCoME in pNets. Components are represented as parameterized processes, n being a parameterization over the number of CashDesks and of CashDeskChannels for representing multiple components. Note that this parameter is also used to provide multiple ports (collection interfaces in GCM language). Transitions encode communication with value passing, and internal actions (tau) provide both the hiding mechanisms necessary for component visibility rules, and the non-determinism required by specification-level abstractions. Other processes appear as additional transition systems, for example the *Queue* which encodes part of the ProActive's behaviour. Then, the automaton representing the Coordinator component is explicitly given: first it synchronises with the Queue for serving requests; then synchronises with the argument sent; finally it may non-deterministically restart its functional behaviour, enable a Cashdesk, or disable a CashDesk. For that, it synchronises with an arbitrary port within `expressModeControlIf` with the *ANY* keyword. Note that this port is parameterized and the index is used to address a specific CashDeskChannel. We do not go deeper into the pNets model in here, however the interested reader may refer to [11].

In each of these applications, the models express potentially infinite automata. In theory this allows us to apply many different proof methods, including inductive theorem proving techniques, state-of-the-art engines implementing decision procedures for decidable fragments of predicate logics or for regular structures. In practice, the current version of our verification platform only uses explicit-state model-checkers. For those, we first transform the pNet model into a network of finite Labelled Transition Systems (LTSs), using abstractions based on finite partitions of the parameter domains.

The pNet formalism is too low-level to be used directly as a specification language, and lacks the high-level concepts particular to the different context in which we want to use it. But in [10] we have shown that it plays an important role as an intermediate format between the platform tools; it can be viewed as the low-level semantic notation expressing both behaviour, structure and synchronisation of our components. This pNet model is the main intermediate format used by our tools to interface with the verification tools (see Section 16.4.1).

16.2.4 The Java Distributed Component Specification Language (JDC)

In order to bridge the gap between an architecture specification and a Java implementation, we have defined JDC for specifying distributed components. The JDC is meant to be used by developers at the early stages of conception of a component or of an application. A JDC specification will be used:

- on one hand to check the correctness of the component structure: model-checking against user requirements or scenarios, and against the global black-box specification of composite components, correct assembly of components,
- on the other hand to generate ADL definitions for the composite components and Java skeleton code for each of the primitive component, in which the developer will only need to fill-in the body of service methods.

In the remaining of this section we describe the syntax of JDC, introducing one by one its main concepts (but without going too deep in the details of the grammar). For each construct we refer to lines of code within the following sections in which an example can be found.

Components: JDC's main construct reflects the structure of a component: a component declaration comprises a part defining its external view, that is the definition of its interfaces and the specification of the black-box behaviour (interaction between services). For composite components, the declaration also comprises the definition of its architecture, that is the declaration of subcomponents and of their bindings. See an example in lines 60-66, page 433.

In addition, standard Java files are used to define the component interfaces signatures (as Java interfaces), and user-defined data-types (as Java classes).

In the following abstract syntax, the interface section is mandatory, the services section is mandatory for primitives and optional for composites, the architecture section is mandatory for composites. Remark that a component can be seen as a primitive in a JDC specification, and later be implemented by a composite. In that case the behavioural specification of this component will allow for a formal check of compatibility (or substitutability in the vocabulary of [8]).

```
1 component <NAME> (<Params>) {
    interfaces
3       <interface> *
    services
5       <service> *
    architecture
```

```
 7     contents
           <component> *
 9     bindings
           <binding> *
11  endComponent}
```

Interfaces: Interface definitions come in two parts: the first is a declaration within the JDC component structure, specifying each server (provided) and client (required) interface of the component, together with its type, its name, and optionally its parameter list. See lines 62-64.

```
12  <interface> := (server|client) interface <InterfaceType> <InterfaceName>[<Params>]
```

The second part is a standard Java Interface that defines the interface type, including the list of methods with their signature. This corresponds more generally to the Interface Definition Languages (IDLs) of some other component frameworks. See lines 67-78.

Services and policies: This section of the component specification defines the behaviour acceptable at the interfaces of the component. That is to say, how the component provides services when viewed as a black-box. This includes the required protocols, expressed as temporal ordering of the interactions (method calls) on the interfaces, but also the dataflow induced by the parameters of those methods, and that can be relevant to the behaviour logics. See lines 79-114.

```
       <service> =
14         service "{"
               <Local Variable Declaration> *
16             policy "{" <RegularExpression> "}" *
               <Service Method Declaration> *
18             <Local Method Declaration> *
               "}"
```

The protocols themselves are (non-deterministic) state-machines, expressed using regular expressions. Their events are either service instructions, or direct local method calls. The service instructions allow the user to specify, depending on the internal state of the protocol, which kind of methods to select, and in which order to pick them from the queue. See lines 81-85 and 201-209.

```
20  <regularExpression> =
        <serveMode> "(" <filter> * ")"
22      | <Method Call>
        | <regularExpression> ";" <regularExpression>
24      | <regularExpression> "|" <regularExpression>
        | <regularExpression> "*"
26
        <filter> = <InterfaceName>
28            | <InterfaceName> "." <MethodName>
```

Then for each method in each server interface, we need a method declaration, that will capture at least the relevant dataflow between input parameters and results of the method. The method body contains Java code, with eventual calls to client interface methods, and possibly a special "oracle" function called __ANY(..) that non-deterministically returns an arbitrary value of a given class. Service methods and local methods are not authorised to access the request queue. Their bodies consist of standard Java syntax (we do not provide a grammar for them). See e.g. lines 209-223.

Subcomponents and bindings: In this part of the specification, we specify the subcomponents of a composite component, as instances of components (types) that may be defined separately (see lines 120-126), and bindings (lines 127-158) connecting subcomponent's interfaces with internal interfaces of the composite (import and export bindings in Figure 1), and connecting subcomponents together (normal bindings in Figure 1).

For grid structures, it is important to be able to have indexed sets of subcomponents within a composite, and to have syntax to specify their bindings in terms depending on their indexes. For that, parameters may be defined within the **for** statement (as **Params**), and used within the **bind** statement as a subset of these parameters in the **ActualParams**. See lines 134-136.

```
     <component> =
30   <ComponentType> "(" <Params> ")" <ComponentName>

32   <binding> =
        bind "(" <ComponentName>"."<InterfaceName>, <ComponentName>"."<InterfaceName> ")"
34   | for "(" <Params> ")" "{"
          bind "(" (<ComponentName> | <ComponentName> "[" <ActualParam> "]" ) "."
36                 (<InterfaceName> | <InterfaceName> "[" <ActualParam> "]" ) ","
                   (<ComponentName> | <ComponentName> "[" <ActualParam> "]" ) "."
38                 (<InterfaceName> | <InterfaceName> "[" <ActualParam> "]" ) ")"
        "}"
```

Exceptions: For dealing with latency, GCM provides asynchronous communications and exception handling. Exceptions typically influence the control flow of the application, and therefore are important to consider within a JDC specification. JDC allows for asynchronous method calls with exceptions, but with some restrictions: the control flow may not leave the **try** block where the exception should be thrown. For that, before leaving a **try**, all pending exceptions act as a barrier until its safe execution path is known. Additionally, a future which result comes from a method with exceptions cannot be sent as argument to another component, i.e., it is implicitly blocked before calling the method until the return value is known. Below, we show the abstract syntax of both method with exception definition and a control block. The reader should find it familiar to Java. See lines 102-112.

```
40   <ReturnType> <MethodName>(<Params>) throws "(" <ExceptionType> ")" *

42   try "{"
          <UserCode> *
44   "}"
        catch "(" <ExceptionType> <ExceptionName> ")" "{"
46        <UserCode> *
        "}"
```

Parameters and collective interfaces: Another feature dealing with GCM is collective interfaces. There are multicast and gathercast interfaces for providing distribution and synchronisation of data. In JDC, these can be defined both at a black-box level or at an architecture level. Moreover, the designer also defines the parameter distribution that applies. For example, a multicast interface may broadcast a same method call to multiple components. The abstract syntax is as follows:

```
48    multicast "(" <ComponentName>"."<InterfaceName>"," <DistributionType> ")" "{"
         bind "(" <ComponentName>"."<InterfaceName>"," <ComponentName>"."<InterfaceName> "
            )" *
50    "}"
```

Data abstraction: Apart from the specific component structure constructs, the JDC syntax is intentionally very close to the Java language. This is mainly because all code within the JDC specification uses real Java datatypes to keep compatibility with Java. However, if one wants to verify the specification (using model-checking or equivalence-checking), it is mandatory to provide a data abstraction of every user-class used in the specification into (first order) Simple Types. This is particularly important to avoid usual state-explosion during the model-checking of the system, and to allow exhaustive search of execution paths. Moreover, Simple Types are the only datatypes accepted by pNets, for more fundamental reasons: this is the basis for the preservation of safety properties by finite abstraction in our verification method. So every class in the JDC specification must be mapped towards Simple Types, and this mapping must be an abstract interpretation. See an example in lines 224-240.

These are given in Java classes and may be used within a JDC specification. Concretely, they are:

- integers, enumerated types, strings, booleans;
- intervals of integers;
- records of simple types;
- arrays of simple types.

```
      class <ClassName> "{"
52        (public | private | protected)":" *
          <ClassType> <FieldName>";" *
54        <ClassType> <FieldName> abstracted as <SimpleType>";" *
          <ReturnType> <MethodName> "(" <Params> ")" <Exception>";" *
56        <ReturnType> <MethodName> "(" <Params> ")" <Exception> abstracted as "{"
             <UserCode> *
58        "}" *
      "}"
```

In the abstract syntax above, data abstraction is done over all methods and attributes used within the JDC specification. For these, the keyword **abstracted as** is used to map whatever method or attribute into Simple Types. In the method body, usual JDC code can be used as far as the final result is a Simple Type, and all data used is mapped to Simple Types as well. Other methods and attributes not used within the specification can be left unspecified as they are not considered by neither code generation nor model generation.

16.2.5   UML Component Diagrams, and the CTTool Editor

The JDC is a textual language, certainly adequate for trained developers, and for specifying big and/or complex systems. However, for casual users, or for fast

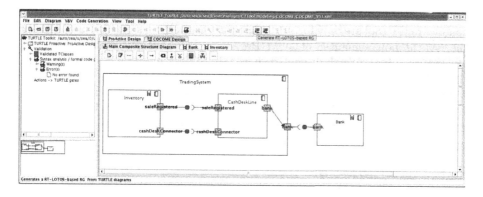

Fig. 3. The *CTTool* UML2.0 modelling software

design in the first steps of the development cycle, one may prefer a graphical language. With this goal, we have built a UML editor, called CTTool (Figure 3), dedicated to component specification, and providing an integrated interface with a model generator and a model checker.

The main constructs can be found in Figure 4.

Component Diagram	
	Producer
Component	
IN port	
OUT port	
Connector	
Delegate connector	
Interface signature	Contingency : OPTIONAL

State Machine Diagram	
(named) State	ready
Start/Stop points	
Submachine	
Receive/Send message	
Action	stock = stock+1
Choice	[stock = 0] [stock > 0]
Non-determinism	

Fig. 4. Component and State Machine Diagram Constructs

CTTool was developed starting from a similar software named TTool, developed by a research team at ENST-Paris [14]. TTool is more specifically dedicated to the design and verification of embedded systems, or systems on chips. Compared with TTool, CTTool features UML2.0 diagrams (component and statemachines) with hierarchical designs (Fig. 4); it inherits from the connection of TTool with the CADP verification tools [15], through generation of LOTOS code.

The current version of CTTool is an intermediate step, in the sense that it has no primitive for specifying distributed features of our components, and consequently no Grid specific primitive. Moreover the generated code has the same synchronous semantics than the original TTool, so the proofs that one can conduct in CTTool are only for synchronous components systems, rather than for the asynchronous semantics of GCM/ProActive including asynchronous requests and future values. We shall explain how this has influenced the verification of the CoCoME scenarios in section 16.5.1

Still we found usefull to provide CTTool drawings, together with the corresponding JDC code in the following pages. In future versions, CTTool will have specific high-level constructs for distributed Grid applications (service policies, multicast and gathercast communications, etc). It will certainly be re-engineered to produce JDC code, or at least generate the proper asynchronous semantics in the constructed models.

16.3   Modelling the CoCoME

Including in this chapter the specification of the full CoCoME case-study would not be possible. We have chosen to include only the specification of two components, with the required views of each, with the JDC text, and some of the CTTool diagrams as illustrations. The first one is the (composite) CashDesk component (Chapter 3, Figure 13), for which we include and explain:

- its black-box view with the definition of external interfaces, and the specification of its visible behaviour;
- its architectural view with its subcomponents and bindings;
- its GCM view, with excerpts of the generated ADL code.

The second one is the (primitive) CashBoxController component, with:

- its black-box view with its interfaces and behaviour, with much more details on the definition of its service methods;
- no architecture as it is primitive;
- an abstraction specification of a user-defined datatype;
- pieces of generated Java/ProActive code;
- a fragment of its deployment specification.

Before starting with those examples of component specifications, let us define what are the different views that we use.

16.3.1   Black-Box View

We call black-box view of a component its externally visible architecture and behaviour. Therefore it includes the common part of both primitive and composite component: list of its interfaces (defining which are client and server interfaces), and definition of these interfaces (the Java methods and their signatures). The black-box view allows to use the component without knowing anything of its internals. This is usual in many programming languages when thinking simply of (static) typing of the interfaces; but here we aim at dynamic compatibility of components, so we need a precise enough specification of the protocol of its interactions with other components, namely the temporal ordering of activation of service methods, and of calls to external (client) methods. In such a protocol we include the synchronisation, control flow and data flow of the system, as observed during communications between components.

In [10] we have shown how to specify both the functional and the non-functional behaviour of GCM/ProActive components; however for the time being we focus only on the functional (also known as business) behaviour, leaving the non-functional parts (life-cycle, bindings, reconfiguration management) to further developments of the JDC.

16.3.2   Architectural View

The architectural view gives a one-level refinement of a component as a composition of subcomponents. For each one of these subcomponents, the designer must provide its black-box view. Note that, when an architecture is provided for a component, the **policy** section in the black-box definition is optional as it is implicitly defined by the architecture.

From the user point of view, the architecture specification is a functional delegation to subcomponents, similar to what the GCM ADL stands for. In it, subcomponents and internally visible bindings of a component are defined (see Figure 1); bindings can be either between the parent component and one of its subcomponent (export binding), between a subcomponent and the parent (import binding), or bindings between subcomponents (normal binding).

We did not use the GCM ADL for defining the architecture because we want to provide more expressive power than usually expressed within an ADL. Typically, one may want to define dynamic architectures, i.e., systems with dynamic instantiation of components. These kind of architectural specifications are not meant to be captured by the GCM ADL, though they might be possible by extending the language.

For the CoCoME model, we have specified the architecture, whenever given in the CoCoME reference, of every component except for the Inventory. The latter was given only a black-box specification to simplify the model. Within this section we show the architecture of the CashDesk component.

16.3.3   GCM View

Our objective is to generate GCM components from the JDC specification. JDC is rich enough to be able to generate automatically both the ADL describing the structure of the application, and the skeleton of the primitive components in ProActive.

For the composite components, the ADL can be automatically inferred from the architectural view presented above. For the primitive components, the ADL mainly consists in the definition of interfaces and can be generated automatically. The skeleton of the Java class implementing the primitive can be generated from the JDC black-box specifying the behaviour of the component. The user then only has to write the business code, resolving all the abstractions and non-determinism present in the black-box definition.

Concerning non-functional aspects, they are not specified for now in the JDC. Thus it is also the role of the programmer to provide and compose these aspects. In general, most of those aspects are provided by the component middleware, e.g. Fractal requires basic management controllers to be implemented by each component. In most cases, dealing with non-functional aspects consists in invoking operations on these controllers. For the moment, those invocations have to be performed manually by the programmer; but on the long term basis we would like to include them in the JDC so that it is possible to study and verify the interaction between functional and non-functional concerns.

The generation of code from the JDC specification is not working yet; thus based on the JDC specification we wrote the GCM/ProActive code for the Co-CoME example. This code consists of a set of composite components defined in the ADL, and a set of primitive components written in Java and using ProActive. Recall that, at deployment, a thread is created for each primitive and each composite component, and those components communicate by asynchronous method calls with transparent futures, leading to a parallel and distributed implementation of the application.

16.3.4   Deployment View

The deployment view of an application is out-of-scope for the JDC specification as we leave it as a middleware concern. However, since the modelling of distributed aspects is an important part of a specification, this section outlines the ProActive deployment scheme, and shows how the distribution nature of GCM components can be captured. Further, using the CoCoME architecture as an example, it is shown how to map the components to the physical infrastructure.

ProActive and GCM comprehensive deployment framework is based on the concept of *Virtual Node* (VN). A VN is above all an *application abstraction* that, at modelling or programming time, captures the distributed nature of a system. Typically, a given application is specified to deploy on several VNs (e.g. each component on a separate VN), each capturing a specific entity or related set of entities of the application. At deployment, each VN is mapped to one or several machines on the network, using appropriate protocols.

The number and characteristics of VNs are chosen by the application designer, providing both guidance and constraints to be used and enforced at deployment time. Both parallelism and de facto distribution can be captured by VNs. Moreover, the designer can also specify multi-threaded constraints by using a single VN for several components, capturing a forced co-allocation. When building composite components, one has the possibility to merge some inner VNs into a single one, specifying co-allocation of the corresponding inner components. One also has the possibility to maintain at the level of the composite some of the inner VNs, specifying an independent mapping of the corresponding inner components to the physical infrastructure.

A VN has several characteristics. The most important is its *cardinality*, which can be *single* or *multiple*. The former captures the fact that a single node of the infrastructure has to be used to execute the corresponding component, the later gives the possibility at deployment to map the component on several machines. This powerful possibility is to be related to multicast and gathercast interfaces: a collective interface often corresponds to a Multiple VN with the same cardinality.

At deployment time, all the VNs of the CoCoME specification will be mapped to one or several machines of the physical infrastructure using an XML file. The ProActive implementation makes it possible to choose from many protocols to select and access the actual nodes (rsh, ssh, LSF, PBS, Globus, etc.), and to control the number of components per machine, and per process (JVM).

16.3.5   Specification of the CashDesk Component

In this subsection, we specify the CashDesk component. We give its black-box specification together with a matching architecture specification. Finally, we outline its implementation within the GCM/ProActive.

Black-Box View of the CashDesk. The black-box of the CashDesk starts by defining its server and client interfaces. In there, we see that the bankIf is a collection interface as it addresses multiple banks, but method calls are routed to one bank at a time. Note that CTTool's diagrams do not have the definitive method signatures as type-checking is still limited within the tool.

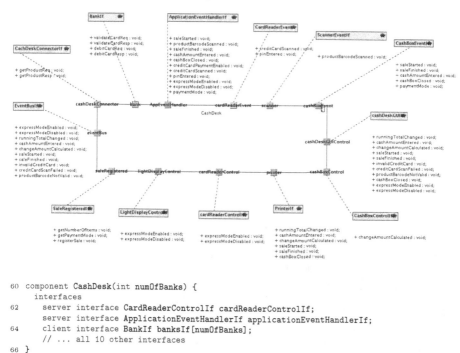

```
60  component CashDesk(int numOfBanks) {
       interfaces
62       server interface CardReaderControlIf cardReaderControlIf;
         server interface ApplicationEventHandlerIf applicationEventHandlerIf;
64       client interface BankIf banksIf [numOfBanks];
         // ... all 10 other interfaces
66  }
```

These interfaces must be properly defined. For example, in the code below we see the definition of the `ApplicationEventHandlerIf` interface, which exposes the full method signature using user-classes.

```
     public interface ApplicationEventHandlerIf {
68       void saleStarted() throws NotIdleException;
         void saleFinished() throws SaleNotFinishedException;
70       void cashAmountEntered(CashAmount moneyAmountEntered) throws NotPayingException,
             WrongPaymentModeException;
         void cashBoxClosed() throws NotPayingException, WrongPaymentModeException;
72       void creditCardScanned(CreditCardScanned creditCardScanned) throws
             NotAcceptingCreditCardException, WrongPaymentModeException;
         void pinEntered(PIN pin);
74       void paymentMode(PaymentMode paymentMode) throws WrongPaymentModeException;
         void expressModeDisabled();
76       void expressModeEnabled();
         void productBarcodeScanned(ProductBarcode barcode) throws ExceededNumberOfProducts;
78   }
```

No matter how the component is to be implemented (either by a primitive or a composite component), in JDC it is mandatory to provide a behavioural specification, either in the form of a black-box definition, or in the form of its architectural implementation, or both. For this component, we provide a black-box specification; this starts with the service policy defined with a regular expression. In the case of the CashDesk, there are multiple services denoting that there are multiple processes visible from the outside. This stands for a compact representation of the interleavings admitted by the component.

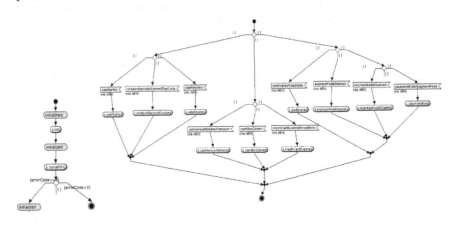

```
     services
80       service { // CardReaderController
             policy {
82               ((emit() | serveOldest(cardReaderControlIf.expressModeDisabled))*;
                 serveOldest(cardReaderControlIf.expressModeEnabled);
84               serveOldest(cardReaderControlIf.expressModeDisabled))*
             }
86           void emit() {
                 if (__ANY(bool)) // non-deterministic choice
88                   cardReaderEventIf.creditCardScanned(__ANY(CreditCard));
             }
90           // ... cardReaderControlIf.expressModeEnabled
             // ... cardReaderControlIf.expressModeDisabled
92       }
         service { // CashDeskApplication
94           locals {
                 CashState cashState;
96               // ... other local variables
             }
```

```
 98        policy {
               init(); expressModeDisabled();
100            serveOldest(applicationEventHandlerIf) *
           }
102        void applicationEventHandlerIf.saleStarted() throws NotIdleException {
               switch (cashState.getState()) {
104                case cashState.IDLE:
                       cashState = cashState.STARTED;
106                    break;
                   case cashState.STARTED:
108                case cashState.PAYING:
                       throw new NotIdleException();
110                    break;
               }
112        }
           // ... other methods
114    }
     }
```

Note that each service defines its own service methods and possibly its own local variables.

In Section 16.3.6 we illustrate different aspects of the behavioural specification. Then in Section 16.4.2 we give example of code generated from the CashDesk service definition.

Architectural View of the CashDesk. As the black-box specification only defines the externally visible behaviour and not how it is implemented, there are, of course, several architecture definitions that match the same component's black-box specification. A possible architecture implementing the CashDesk is shown in the following. Note that we added a logger just to trap and print exceptions but it does not influence the component behaviour.

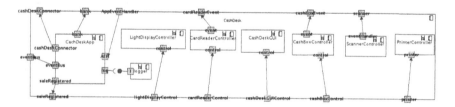

The first part of the architecture defines the subcomponents which compose the component. When applies, they are provided with parameters for their correct deployment as with the CashDeskApplication.

```
118 architecture CashDesk(int numOfBanks) {
        contents
120         component CashDeskApplication(numOfBanks) application;
            component CashReaderController cashReader;
122         component CashDeskGUI cashDeskGUI;
            component cashBoxController cashBoxController;
124         component LightDisplayController lightDisplayController;
            component PrinterController printerController;
126         component ScannerController scannerController;
```

Then, we define the bindings section exposing how the functional delegation takes place, and synchronisations between components. Note that it is possible to address either a specific component or a specific collection interface.

```
      bindings
128       // application
          bind(this.applicationEventHandlerIf, application.applicationEventHandlerIf);
130       bind(application.cashDeskConnectorIf, this.cashDeskConnectorIf);
          bind(application.eventBusIf, this.eventBusIf);
132       bind(application.saleRegisteredIf, this.saleRegisteredIf);

134       // bind all bank interfaces
          for (int i: numOfBanks) {
136           bind(application.banksIf[i], this.banksIf[i]);
          }
138
          // cashReader
140       bind(this.cashReaderControlIf, cashReader.controlIf);
          bind(cashReader.eventIf, this.eventIf);
142
          // cashDeskGUI
144       bind(this.cashDeskGUIControlIf, cashDeskGUI.controlIf);

146       // cashBoxController
          bind(this.cashBoxControllerControlIf, cashBoxController.controlIf);
148       bind(cashBoxController.eventIf, this.cashBoxControllerEventIf);

150       // lightDisplayController
          bind(this.lightDisplayControllerControlIf, lightDisplayController.controlIf);
152
          // printerController
154       bind(this.printerIf, printerController.printerIf);

156       // scannerController
          bind(scannerController.scannerIf, this.scannerIf);
158 }
```

The corresponding ADL file, in XML format, will be generated from this part of the specification. It will then be used both to generate the synchronisation structures for the model-checker, and as an input to the component factory of ProActive at deployment time, but all this is left as future work for the moment.

GCM View of the CashDesk. Now, we present a simplified ADL description of the CashDesk component. It focuses on the CashDeskApplication subcomponent, the other subcomponents being similar. The ADL description starts with the definition of the external interfaces of the CashDesk component, together with their roles (client or server).

```
      <component name="CashDesk">
160     <interface signature="CashDeskLine.if.LightDisplayControlIf" role="server" name="
            lightDisplayControlIf"/>
        <interface signature="CashDeskLine.if.CardReaderControlIf" role="server" name="
            cardReaderControlIf"/>
162     <interface signature="CashDeskLine.if.CashDeskGUIIf" role="server" name="
            cashDeskGUIIf"/>
        <interface signature="CashDeskLine.if.CashBoxControlIf" role="server" name="
            cashBoxControlIf"/>
164     <interface signature="CashDeskLine.if.PrinterIf" role="server" name="printerIf"/>
        <interface signature="CashDeskLine.if.ApplicationEventHandlerIf" role="server" name="
            applicationEventHandlerIf"/>
166     <interface signature="if.CashDeskConnectorIf" role="client" name="cashDeskConnectorIf
            "/>
        <interface signature="if.SaleRegisteredIf" role="client" name="saleRegisteredIf"/>
168     <interface signature="CashDeskLine.if.CardReaderEventIf" role="client" name="
            cardReaderEventIf"/>
        <interface signature="CashDeskLine.if.CashBoxEventIf" role="client" name="
            cashBoxEventIf"/>
```

```
170    <interface signature="CashDeskLine.if.ScannerEventIf" role="client" name="
          scannerEventIf"/>
       <interface signature="if.BankIf" role="client" name="bankIf"/>
172    <interface signature="CashDeskLine.if.EventBusIf" role="client" name="eventBusIf"/>
```

Then the subcomponent CashDeskApplication is described by its external interfaces, this component is a primitive one (line 180), so the path of its implementation is given (line 179).

```
       <component name="CashDeskApplication">
174      <interface signature="CashDeskLine.if.ApplicationEventHandlerIf" role="server" name
            ="applicationEventHandlerIf"/>
         <interface signature="if.CashDeskConnectorIf" role="client" name="
            cashDeskConnectorIf"/>
176      <interface signature="if.SaleRegisteredIf" role="client" name="saleRegisteredIf"/>
         <interface signature="CashDeskLine.if.EventBusIf" role="client" name="eventBusIf"/>
178      <interface signature="if.BankIf" role="client" name="bankIf"/>
         <content class="CashDeskLine.CashDesk.CashDeskApplication"/>
180      <controller desc="primitive"/>
       </component>
182    <component name="CardReaderController"> ...          </component>
       <component name="LightDisplayController"> ...        </component>
184    <component name="ScannerController">        ...       </component>
       <component name="PrinterController">       ...        </component>
186    <component name="CashBoxController">       ...        </component>
       <component name="CaskDeskGUI">            ...         </component>
```

Finally, the bindings of the CashDeskApplication are described, in this example only two kinds of bindings are shown: import bindings like the first one, and export bindings like the others.

```
188    <binding client="this.applicationEventHandlerIf" server="CashDeskApplication.
          applicationEventHandlerIf"/>
       <binding client="CashDeskApplication.cashDeskConnectorIf" server="this.
          cashDeskConnectorIf"/>
190    <binding client="CashDeskApplication.saleRegisteredIf" server="this.saleRegisteredIf"
          />
       <binding client="CashDeskApplication.eventBusIf" server="this.eventBusIf"/>
192    <binding client="CashDeskApplication.bankIf" server="this.bankIf"/>
       ...
194    <controller desc="composite"/>
       </component>
```

Deployment View of the CashDesk. When defining the CashDeskLine composite, a VN `CashDeskLineVN`, cardinality Multiple is specified as the composition of all the `CashDeskVN`. The effective cardinality of this VN is attached to the number of cashDesks (`numOfCashDesks` in the specification).

16.3.6   Specification of the CashBoxController Component

In this section, we specify the CashBoxController component. We give its blackbox view, but the architectural view does not apply because we do not decompose the behaviour of the CashBoxController into subcomponents.

Black-Box View of the CashBoxController. The component has a client and a server interface, and defines a non-trivial service policy. The controller can be seen as an active component in the sense that it triggers events regarding the cashbox, so it is not awaiting for any signal to be received.

```
196 component CashBoxController {
        interfaces
198         server interface CashBoxControlIf controlIf;
            client interface CashBoxEventIf eventIf;
200
        services
202         service {
                policy {
204                 ( eventIf.saleStarted(); eventIf.saleFinished();
                        ( cashMode(); cashAmount(); serveOldest(controlIf.changeAmountCalculated
                            ); eventIf.cashBoxClosed() )
206                     |
                        ( creditCardMode() )
208                 )*
                }
```

There are no state variables (variables defined within the "locals" block),
nevertheless the component is not stateless; the service policy implicitly defines
that the component cycles through some states, each one defining which are the
actions that the CashBoxController may do. For example, the component only
serves requests from the queue when a client is paying with cash; otherwise, the
component is seen as a machine sending events regardless of the environment
(as the environment does not take the hardware interaction into account).

The component defines local methods and service methods; the latter have
their method names prefixed by the interface they belong. For the method
changeAmountCalculated(..), and from the behavioural point of view, we are
only interested in the access to the variable sent as argument, but not what we
actually do with it; so the behavioural model can block the execution until the
concrete value of the variable is known.

```
            // local methods
210             void cashMode() {
                    eventIf.paymentMode(new PaymentMode(CASH));
212             }
                void creditCardMode() {
214                 eventIf.paymentMode(new PaymentMode(CREDIT));
                }
216             void cashAmount() {
                    eventIf.cashAmount(__ANY(CashAmount));
218             }
            // service methods
220             void controlIf.changeAmountCalculated(CashAmount changeAmount) {
                    changeAmount.waitForValue();
222         }}
        } // end of CashBoxController black-box definition
```

There are some non-deterministic choices, both in the events that may be
sent, and in the data sent. For example, we do not know exactly which amount
the user paid, so we use the "oracle" function __ANY(CashAmount) to choose any
value within the variable domain. It will be up to the data abstraction to define
this domain, or in the case of the implementation, to the programmer to define
its real value. A mapping of this class into Simple Types is given as:

```
224 public class CashAmount {
        private double amount abstracted as enum {"ZERO", "NOT_ZERO" };
226
        public __ANY() {
228         return new enum {"ZERO", "NOT_ZERO" };
        }
230     public double getAmount() abstracted as {
```

```
          return amount;
232    }
       public void add(CashAmount purchasePrice) abstracted as {
234       if (this.amount == "ZERO" && purchasePrice.getAmount() == "ZERO")
             amount = "ZERO";
236       else
             // non-determinism within the data abstraction as a negative
238          // value could leave the amount in zero
             amount = __ANY(CashAmount);
240 }}
```

GCM View of the CashBoxController. Next, we give the implementation
of the CashBoxController primitive component. This Java code is to be instantiated as an active object (in Java implementing the RunActive interface). The
active object implements the CashBoxControlIf server interface and contains
a field named cashBoxEventIf implementing the client interface of the component. Finally, it also implements Fractal's BindingController interface to allow
dynamic binding of its interfaces.

```
       public class CashBoxController implements CashBoxControlIf, BindingController,
          RunActive {
242    public final static String CASHBOXEVENTIF_BINDING = "cashBoxEventIf";
       private CashBoxEventIf cashBoxEventIf;
244
       public CashBoxController () { } // empty constructor required by ProActive
```

Note that necessary hooks for Fractal controllers are implemented on the form
of the four first methods of the object. These are generated automatically.

```
246    // Implementation of the Controller interfaces
       public String[] listFc () {return new String[] { CASHBOXEVENTIF_BINDING };}
248
       public Object lookupFc (final String clientItfName) {
250       if (CASHBOXEVENTIF_BINDING.equals(clientItfName))
             return cashBoxEventIf;
252       return null;
       }
254    public void bindFc (final String clientItfName,final Object serverItf){
          if (CASHBOXEVENTIF_BINDING.equals(clientItfName))
256          cashBoxEventIf = (CashBoxEventIf)serverItf;
       }
258    public void unbindFc (final String clientItfName){
          if (CASHBOXEVENTIF_BINDING.equals(clientItfName))
260          cashBoxEventIf = null;
       }
```

Recall that changeAmountCalculated is the only method of the server interface, requests addressed to this component will be asynchronous calls to this
method. It corresponds to the same method as in the black-box view above.

```
262    // Implementation of the functional interfaces
       public void changeAmountCalculated(CashAmount changeAmount) {
264       System.out.println(changeAmount.getAmount()); // the amount to be returned as
          change
       }
```

Then, the service method in ProActive (runActivity) implements the service
policy. It is the kernel of a ProActive component as it exposes the component's
behaviour, and is called by the middleware when the component is started. It
consists of a set of invocations on the client interface (cashBoxEventIf), together
with a blocking service on the changeAmountCalculated method. This method

is a direct translation of the policy section of the black-box presented above and should not be modified by the ProActive programmer.

```
266    public void runActivity(Body body) {
           Service service = new Service(body);
268        while (body.isActive()) {
               cashBoxEventIf.saleStarted();
270            cashBoxEventIf.saleFinished();
               if ((new AnyBool()).prob(50)) {
272                cashMode();
                   cashAmount();
274                service.blockingServeOldest("changeAmountCalculated");
                   cashBoxEventIf.cashBoxClosed();
276            } else
                   creditCardMode();
278    }}
```

By contrast the service method and the local (private) methods that are declared in the JDC (CashBoxController service declaration will contain the true functional code of the component, and are directly modifiable.

```
       private void cashMode() {
280        cashBoxEventIf.paymentMode(new PaymentModeImpl(PaymentModeImpl.CASH));
       }
282    private void creditCardMode() {
           cashBoxEventIf.paymentMode(new PaymentModeImpl(PaymentModeImpl.CREDIT));
284    }
       private void cashAmount() {
286        cashBoxEventIf.cashAmountEntered(new CashAmountImpl(1000)); // the client paid
               1000
       }
288 } // end of CashBoxController implementation
```

Deployment View of the CashBoxController. If we want to model a system where a cashBoxController can be instantiated on its own processing element, then a VN, for instance named cashBoxControllerVN, cardinality single has to be specified and exported at the level of the CashDesk. At the next level, when building the CashDeskLine component, the middleware will be able to take care of transforming this VN into an appropriate VN at the composite level.

```
       <exportedVirtualNodes>
290        <exportedVirtualNode name="cashBoxControllerVN">
               <composedFrom>
292                <composingVirtualNode component="this" name="cashBoxControllerVN"/>
               </composedFrom>
294        </exportedVirtualNode>
       </exportedVirtualNodes>
296    <content class="CashDeskLine.CashDesk.CashBoxController"/>
       <virtual-node name="cashBoxControllerVN" cardinality="single"/>
```

16.4   Transformations

In this section we first describe the software tools that we are building for editing and analysing JDC specifications and CTTool diagrams, and generating ProActive code skeletons. Then we explain on an example how we intend to generate "safe by construction" code.

16.4.1 Tools Overview

In Figure 5 we sketch the general architecture overview of the specification and analysis platform that we are building, so-called Vercors. This figure does not show the architecture of the current version of CTTool, that contains its own model generation engine, and its own bridges [14] with the CADP provers through intermediate LOTOS code.

A JDC specification can be edited directly in a text editor, or generated from the diagrams of CTTool; but we also plan to develop an Eclipse plug-in that will ease the JDC development, and give an integrated interface to the various analysis and generation functions of the platform. For the moment, JDC has been conceptually defined, but does not have any tool support yet, so the description in this chapter is mostly left as mid-term future work. However, the synchronous version of CTTool is operational and available at our website.

The first part of the platform deals with data abstraction: data types in a JDC specification are standard, user-defined Java classes, but those must be mapped to Simple Types before generating the behavioural models and running the verification tools. The abstraction is part of the JDC syntax, but the tool will offer guidance to help define correct mappings that are correct abstract interpretations. This phase ends-up with a "JDC Abstracted Specification" in which all data are Simple Types, that are provided as a predefined library.

Such an Abstract Specification is then given as input to our model generator ADL2N [6], that implements the behavioural semantics of the language, and builds a model in terms of pNets, including all necessary controllers for non-functional and asynchronous capabilities of the components. Note that the current version of ADL2N works on ADL and LOTOS files rather than JDC. Additionally ADL2N implements a second step of abstraction, that uses finite partitions of the Simple Types to build finite models for classical (explicit-state) model-checkers. Potentially this step could be automatically derived from the syntax of a formula. In any case the pNets objects are hierarchical and very

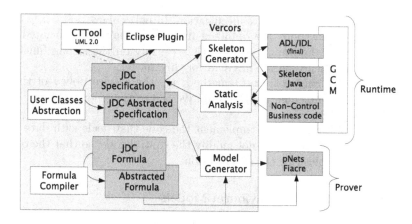

Fig. 5. The Vercors platform

compact as in pNets datatypes are kept parameterized – not instantiated – as well as families of processes (for multiple components).

Just like CTTool, our Vercors platform is using the CADP toolset [15] for state-space generation, hierarchical minimisation, (on-the-fly) model-checking, and equivalence checking (strong/weak bisimulation). The JDC property specifications will also be subject to the same abstractions, and will be translated into regular μ-calculus formula to be fed into the model-checker. In the future, we plan to use other state-of-the-art provers, and in particular apply so-called "infinite system" provers to deal directly with certain types of parameterized systems.

The upper right part of the figure is dedicated to code generation, that will be detailed in Section 16.4.2. The ADL files in XML syntax, the Java interface declarations, and all the Java code that constitute the control part of a component (the implementation of the service policies) will be generated. The method declarations for the service methods are created too, they can be then filled-in by the developper. This constitutes a runnable ProActive component or full application.

16.4.2   Generation of Safe GCM/ProActive Code

Although the code generation is not implemented yet, we give in here its main constructs. As an alternative to static analysis methods for proving that a user-implemented component conforms to its JDC specification, we rely on the generation of an ADL model plus GCM/ProActive code-skeletons from the specification. Then, we set rules stating what the user can do in the remaining code in such a way that the generated code will be guaranteed to be correct. We base our method on the following steps:

- the GCM ADL definition is automatically generated from JDC as it includes the architecture, interface signatures and component cardinality;
- the skeleton for the primitive, mainly consisting of its control flow, is given by the JDC's black-box specification: every possible method call and data-usage must appear in the black-box specification. In particular:
  - the service methods are obtained from the behaviour associated with the same method name in the JDC. We rely on the strong functional behaviour encapsulation of GCM for this matter;
  - ProActive's runActivity() method, i.e. the service policy of the active object implementing the primitive is directly generated from JDC's serving policy;
- then, the programmer must implement the code that deals with data management details, but should not modify the control code, so that the code is certified to comply with the specification.

16.4.3   Generation of Behavioural Models

Again, the generation of behavioural models from JDC specifications is not implemented yet, but we state that JDC specfications are suitable for such. The checking tools used in our verification platform [6] are based mainly on explicit-state models, so we need to build models that abstract the concrete behaviour of our components in a way that preserves our specifications. We plan to do this in three steps. First, we shall transform the original JDC specification using the mapping to simple types. Then we shall build pNets models as described in previous work [9, 10]. Finally, for each formula to be checked, we will use finite partitions as a domain abstraction for each parameter in the model, that will give a finite model usable in a model-checker. In [6], we described a tool called ADL2N for quasi-automatic behavioural model generation. In JDC a similar technique applies, but with a better expressivity as JDC includes information about control and data flow.

We only comment here the pNets construction. It involves two aspects: mapping (abstracting) user data types, i.e., mapping arbitrary Java classes into Simple Types that are the only parameter domains allowed in pNets as described in Section 16.2.3; and building synchronisation objects corresponding to the various architecture and communication primitives of JDC.

Building the behaviour model for a JDC component requires to: (1) turn the pseudo code in each JDC method (the service policy and service methods) into a pLTS (parameterized Labelled Transition System) (2) generate pLTSs for specific primitives or library element of JDC, e.g. request queues, NF controllers, etc; (3) generate synchronisation structures (pNets) for relating these pLTS, depending on the types of bindings and interfaces used.

16.5 Analysis

The models obtained in the previous section allow us to generate both parameterized and finite abstractions of the system behaviour, either for a single component, or for an arbitrary assembly. In principle, this allows for checking:

- simple "press-button" properties, like the absence of deadlocks, or the absence of certain types of events (predefined error events),
- more complex temporal properties expressed as temporal logic formulas, or in a formalism that can be translated into the temporal logic language understood by the model-checker,
- conformance between the implementation of a component (computed from the behaviour of its architecture) and its black-box specification, expressed as an equivalence or a preorder relation (as in [8]).

In this chapter we only consider verification performed on the finite abstraction of the model, and the verification is done by the Evaluator model-checker (from the CADP toolset). Both the parameterized case (using "infinite-state" engines), and the conformance checking are left for further work.

In the following pages, we give examples of verification of the CoCoME requirement scenarios, that we have performed with the current version of CTTool, and explain a number of results of this analysis.

16.5.1 System Verification

The JDC tool support itself being not yet available, we have conducted the analysis activities in this section using directly the capabilities of CTTool: it works by generating LOTOS code that implements a (synchronous) semantics of UML component diagrams and state-machines (including data-types), and passing this LOTOS code to the CADP verification toolset. CTTool itself includes a user interface that hides most of the verification engine complexity, and provides a number of menus for controlling the CADP functions.

There are many ways of encoding formulas. Some of them are very powerful as μ-calculus, but at the same time hardly usable by non-experts. So, having software engineer's expertise and JDC in mind, we propose to write formulas using automata. Transitions contain predicates with logic quantifiers and states can be marked as either acceptance or rejection. The automata may change to any state whose transition predicates are satisfied. If a final state is unreachable, the formula is false. Moreover, there are special predicates:

- ANY meaning that any label satisfies the predicate;
- NOT(i), (i AND j), (i OR j) meaning that any label but i given satisfies the expression, both i and j must satisfy the expression and either i or j may satisfy the expression respectively;
- and ANYOTHER meaning that all labels not satisfying other transitions from the state satisfies the predicate.

Then, formulas are readable and easy to write, and have language constructs compatible with both CTTool's state-machines and JDC's regular expressions.

Absence of Deadlocks. There are basic formulas that can be proved, the most common being the absence of deadlocks. In the case of our CTTool specification, this ends-up being trivially false because of two reasons:

- the specification of exceptions: in our specification, any time an exception is raised, we just block the system. So we may want to search for deadlocks that are not following an exception;
- the synchronous semantics of CTTool components: in CTTool, components are mono-threaded, and communications are synchronous. As a result, the system deadlocks due to race conditions over the EventBus. Concretely, events are not atomic within the EventBus, so a controller may trigger an event (and therefore block the EventBus) while the Application is running an ongoing sale. At this moment, if-ever the Application needs to access any of its controllers (through the EventBus), the system deadlocks.

To show this, we write a formula expressing that all deadlocks are the consequence of an exception, and to model-check this formula. More precisely we write the negation, i.e. that any transition is followed by some other transition as long as an exception has not been raised.

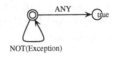

The answer we get when we evaluate the former formula is "false" (the formula does not stand). As a diagnostic we receive a trace in which the Scanner-Controller triggers a ProductBarCodeScanEvent, blocking the EventBus. Meanwhile, the application is trying to synchronise with the EventBus for querying the price of the previously scanned product.

Note that these kind of scenarios would not be present in a real ProActive application because of the asynchronous method calls which buffers requests in the queues: we have more deadlocks in a synchronous implementation of the system than those we would have with ProActive. Nevertheless, using the CTTool specification we were able to prove some interesting scenarios, and to find some errors (or underspecifications) within the reference CoCoME specification.

Main Sale Process. This scenario relates to "Use Case 1" (Chapter 3, Figures 15 and Figure 16) To illustrate the capabilities of our approach to verify more specific properties, we have checked (still in the synchronous model) some of the usage scenarios listed in the CoCoME specification. Our first scenario is defined in CoCoME's requirements as a trace in UML sequence diagram. We successfully verified that this trace is feasible in the state-space generated by CADP. An even more interesting scenario can be encoded as a negation of the following: a sale starts; before it finishes, valid products are scanned; the client pays with enough cash; the sale is not registered and a new sale starts. CADP's diagnostic strikes out that it is not possible to start a new sale before booking the former one.

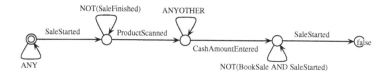

Booking an Empty Sale. This scenario relates to "Use Case 1" (Chapter 3, Figure 16)Although it may not be an error, it is strange that a system allows an empty sale to be booked. This trace was found when searching for the shortest path (by using Breadth-First Search algorithm) that books a sale. Alternatively, a software engineer may want to explicitly verify if this scenario is feasible with the automaton below. A sale is started; no products are scanned; the sale is booked.

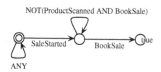

Successful Sale with Insufficient Money. This scenario relates to "Use Case 1" (Chapter 3, Figures 15 and Figure 16) We found that it was possible to book a sale even if the client pays with insufficient money. The problem is reflected by the fact that there is no way of aborting a sale when paying with cash, and there is no verification whether the money fulfils expenses. Note that this issue was verified running the CoCoME reference implementation – which allowed to pay $0 – and going through the UML specification – which has nothing relative to it. In fact, the insufficient funds exception was only foreseen within a credit card payment. Nonetheless, in general, once a sale is started, it is not possible to abort, so the system must book the sale before proceding.

Note that for this scenario, the data abstraction plays an important role as it plays a role in the control-flow of the application. The amount that the client pays then is abstracted with two values: one with insufficient money and the other with sufficient money.

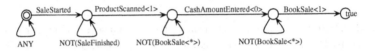

Safety of the Express Mode. This scenario relates to "Use Case 2" (Chapter 3, Figure 18). A non-precised scenario was found. There is nothing within the CoCoME reference specification that states when a CashDesk may switch from/to an express mode. In fact, the system ends-up in an inconsistent state if an express mode signal is triggered during an ongoing sale. This scenario can be found using the following property:

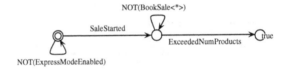

16.6   Summary

In this chapter we presented the Grid Component Model (GCM) and the Java Distributed Component specification language (JDC) as a means to address robust distributed component system design. Our approach aims at integrating at the level of the specification language the architecture specification and its implementation together with the black-box behaviour of the components in order to generate safe code by construction.

We started by presenting the GCM and its reference implementation using the ProActive library. Then, we have defined the JDC specification language as the kernel of our framework. Then, we gave the JDC specification of two of the CoCoME components, the full specification being available in an extended version of this chapter.[2] In addition we gave an alternative method for building JDC specifications, using UML 2 diagrams available in our CTTool software. From these specifications, we created by hand a GCM/ProActive implementation showing how the control code can be automatically generated from the JDC

---

[2] http://www-sop.inria.fr/oasis/Vercors/Cocome/

specification. From the same specification, completed by abstraction functions, we have shown how to generate models suitable for verification, in the form of parameterized networks of synchronised transition systems.

Finally, the CTTool specification was used to check for safety properties of the reference CoCoME specification scenarios. Because of our synchronous encoding, the EventBus component ended-up being a source of deadlocks. As a result of this verification activity, we found a number of interesting features, that we interpreted as bugs or under-specifications in the CoCoME official definition.

Limitations. There are number of features that are not considered in this approach: we do not consider any "performance" aspect of the specification (response time or other quality of service measures); neither do we try to fully specify the functional part of the code (data computation), as could be done in some proof-assistant based approaches.

Other limitations come from the early state of some of our software platform: our model generator is currently limited to the synchronous interpretation of the component systems (only the synchronous controllers are generated), so the features relying on asynchronous communication, and in particular the existence of functional deadlocks in Grid-based systems cannot be analysed. These developments are planned for the next version of the tool. Currently we have no direct support for the JDC language itself, so we rely on the existing CTTool platform to provide an alternative tool suite. We are working on an analysis platform with direct support for JDC, in which the CTTool diagrams will only be an alternative syntax for the specification. The JDC development platform will include an Eclipse plug-in, a Java code generation tool, a model generation tool, and a JDC formula compiler. With them, we hope to answer the software engineer's needs when developping distributed components.

References

1. Caromel, D., Delbé, C., di Costanzo, A., Leyton, M.: ProActive: an integrated platform for programming and running applications on grids and P2P systems. Computational Methods in Science and Technology 12(1), 69–77 (2006)
2. Caromel, D., Henrio, L.: A Theory of Distributed Object. Springer, Heidelberg (2005)
3. Bruneton, E., Coupaye, T., Leclercp, M., Quema, V., Stefani, J.: An open component model and its support in java. In: Crnković, I., Stafford, J.A., Schmidt, H.W., Wallnau, K. (eds.) CBSE 2004. LNCS, vol. 3054. Springer, Heidelberg (2004)
4. OMG: Corba components, version 3. Document formal/02-06-65 (2002)
5. Cansado, A., Henrio, L., Madelaine, E.: Towards real case component model-checking. In: 5th Fractal Workshop, Nantes, France (July 2006)
6. Barros, T., Cansado, A., Madelaine, E., Rivera, M.: Model checking distributed components: The Vercors platform. In: 3rd workshop on Formal Aspects of Component Systems. ENTCS, Prague, Czech Republic (2006)
7. Jezek, P., Kofron, J., Plasil, F.: Model checking of component behavior specification: A real life experience. In: International Workshop on Formal Aspects of Component Software (FACS 2005). Electronic Notes in Theoretical Computer Science (ENTCS), Macao (2005)

8. Černá, I., Vařeková, P., Zimmerova, B.: Component substitutability via equivalencies of component-interaction automata. In: Proceedings of the Workshop on Formal Aspects of Component Software (FACS 2006). ENTCS, Prague, Czech Republic (to appear, 2006)

9. Barros, T., Henrio, L., Madelaine, E.: Behavioural models for hierarchical components. In: Godefroid, P. (ed.) SPIN 2005. LNCS, vol. 3639. Springer, Heidelberg (2005)

10. Barros, T., Henrio, L., Madelaine, E.: Verification of distributed hierarchical components. In: International Workshop on Formal Aspects of Component Software (FACS 2005). ENTCS, Macao (2005)

11. Barros, T., Boulifa, R., Madelaine, E.: Parameterized models for distributed java objects. In: de Frutos-Escrig, D., Núñez, M. (eds.) FORTE 2004. LNCS, vol. 3235. Springer, Heidelberg (2004)

12. CoreGRID, Programming Model Institute: Basic features of the grid component model (assessed), Deliverable D.PM.04 (2006),
http://www.coregrid.net/mambo/images/stories/Deliverables/d.pm.04.pdf

13. Caromel, D., Henrio, L., Serpette, B.: Asynchronous and deterministic objects. In: Proceedings of the 31st ACM SIGPLAN-SIGACT symposium on Principles of programming languages, Venice, Italy, pp. 123–134. ACM Press, New York (2004)

14. Apvrille, L.: Turtle documentation (2005),
http://labsoc.comelec.enst.fr/turtle/help/

15. Garavel, H., Lang, F., Mateescu, R.: An overview of CADP 2001. European Association for Software Science and Technology (EASST) Newsletter 4, 13–24 (2002)

17 CoCoME Jury Evaluation and Conclusion

Manfred Broy[1], Johannes Siedersleben[2], and Clemens Szyperski[3]

[1] Technische Universität München, Germany
[2] T-Systems International, Germany
[3] Microsoft, USA

Abstract. The CoCoME Jury attended the two-day seminar with presentations from all participating teams. The jury provided individual feedback to each of the teams. This chapter is an attempt at both organizing the contributions into groups of related themes and summarizing some of the more salient feedback. The jury concludes with a few observations about the CoCoME contest as such and its overall outcome.

17.1 Introduction and Overview

As already described in Chapter 2, the main goal of the CoCoME contest is to evaluate and compare the practical appliance of the existing component models and the corresponding specification techniques. Based on a UML-based description of CoCoME, a provided sample implementation, and test cases, the participating teams elaborated their own modeling of CoCoME, applying their own component model and description techniques. After an internal peer review each team presented their results in a joint GI-Dagstuhl Research Seminar, where an international jury–the authors of this chapter–was present.

The jury's task was to evaluate and compare the different modeling approaches based on the respective team's presentation at the seminar as well as the team chapter, which was provided to the jury ahead of the seminar. It became clear that it is not possible to come up with a unified ranking of the presented approaches, based on how well each modeled CoCoME. This is because the approaches varied widely with respect to each approach's target objectives, used component model, applied description technique, modeled part of CoCoME, and the resulting benefits and outcomes of the modeling effort.

Rather, it turned out that each approach has its individual strengths and drawbacks. For that reason, the jury and the organizers decided during the GI-Dagstuhl Research Seminar not to come up with a ranking, but instead to provide for each approach an individual non-comparing evaluation and assessment that could be one starting point to further improve the specific approach.

In the following sections these individual jury evaluations will be presented. To enable some comparative reading, the jury organized the various approaches into a number of groups. The first group covers *semi-formal modeling approaches*. Instead of an own underlying formal semantic model, these approaches are UML-extensions and use the semi-formal model and informal and more or less intuitive semantics of UML.

A. Rausch et al. (Eds.): Common Component Modeling Example, LNCS 5153, pp. 449–458, 2008.

The next group, also the largest, comprises *formal models focused on functional correctness*. This group can be subdivided into three subgroups with respect to the underlying formal semantics: The first subgroup has *formal state semantics*, the second has *formal algebraic semantics*, and the third subgroup has an *formal object semantics*. All approaches in this subgroup share the same overall goal: The resulting models are used to verify and validate the functional correctness of the resulting models. Therefore, these approaches provide to varying extend forms of consistency checking, refinement calculus, simulation support, and code generation.

The third group is about *formal models focused on behavior and quality properties*. The main goal of these models is to enable the modeler to analyze, simulate, and predict the capabilities of the modeled solution with respect to specific behavior or quality properties, such as performance or reliability.

The last group contains *models tailored for a specific application domain*, such as grid computing. Hence, the used component model and the applied description techniques are domain specific and not general purpose. The main goal of these approaches is it to come up with a more specific and restricted model and description technique with respect to the target domain and thus provide results on higher semantic level, such as functional correctness or prediction of quality properties.

17.2   Semi-formal Modeling

KobrA. KobrA is a UML-based method for describing components and component-based systems. The acronym (derived from German) stands for "Component-based Application Development". The approach makes use of UML as a specification and realization language, but other languages can be used. The basic goal of KobrA is to allow the design of a complex system to be split into separate parts (i.e., components), which can be tackled separately. KobrA focuses on describing the architecture of components and component-based systems at the design level. Therefore, the benefits of applying KobrA include the ability to experiment with potential designs before committing to concrete implementations, the availability of easy-to-read descriptions (e.g. system specification) that can be understood by (and discussed with) customers and users, and the creation of a platform-independent record of the system structure and project design decisions.

The recognized biggest obstacle to practical adoption of KobrA at the present time is the lack of a dedicated tool that understands KobrA and is able to ensure that UML is applied in a KobrA-compliant way. Other aspects to be considered/improved are: the specification of the non-functional properties of components and the provision of clear guidelines on how to use KobrA in a more formal style. The jury was quite perplexed about the actual usefulness of KobrA because of its strong resemblance to standard UML.

Rich Services. Rich Services is an approach leveraging the SOA (Service-Oriented Architectures) principles. It models an application as a set of services communicating via a bus. Services may be hierarchically decomposed–a service is recursively modeled as a set of services connected to a bus. In addition to functional decomposition, Rich Services allows for capturing cross-cutting concerns (security, policies, failure management, QoS, etc.) using dedicated services that intercept and route messages flowing through a bus. From the deployment point of view, Rich Services may be mapped to the existing ESB middleware (e.g. Mule).

Rich Services utilizes Message Sequence Charts (MSCs) to define interactions (including temporal properties). The existing tool support is then able to synthesize executable code from MSCs. Verification is possible by translating MSCs to Promela.

Another important aspect of Rich Services is that they come with a service-oriented development process, which clearly separates a system's logical model from its implementation. This allows, for example, to introduce performance optimizations at deployment time by flattening the system's architecture.

In modeling CoCoME, the authors followed the Rich Services development process from requirements to actual deployment. It has to be noted, that this resulted in an architecture quite different from the original CoCoME architecture to be modeled. Where the other approaches tried to model the orginal architecture as intended, the Rich Services approach is hard to compare to the other approaches, as it remains unclear which benefits the other approaches would have had, if they had also changed the architecture of CoCoME to optimize for their methods. However, the Rich Services approach proved to be usable in capturing service contracts and different cross-cutting concerns.

17.3 Formal Modeling, Focused on Functional Correctness

Formal State Models

rCOS. rCOS is a relational calculus for object and component systems based on Hoares and Hes Unifying Theories of Programming (UTP) for object-oriented and component-based programming. It allows to model the system at different level of abstraction. Between these levels a clear refinement relation is provided. At each level, the model can be described by a set of different views–the static structural view, the interaction view, the dynamic view– as well as their timing apspects.

Thereby the rCOS approach claims to support a formal development process starting out with analysis and in an stepwise refinement approach finally ending up with a component model ready for an object-oriented implementation. The main promised benefits are: consistency rules between the various views in a modeling step, guided refinement rules from one modeling step to the next one, and finally a formally founded specification technique to support verification and analysis on the model level.

The rCOS team has modeled two use cases on the analysis model level. This cutout has been refined to an object-oriented model. Finally, the object-oriented model has been encapsulated in a set of components.

The main strength of the rCOS approach lies in its clear and straight-forward object-oriented analysis model. The relationship to the component model should be further improved as it is not clear at all how the component model will be derived from the object-oriented analysis model and what the relationship between these two models formally is. Finally, the authors could not show which properties were actually proved resp. proveable by their model. Hence it is not determinable whether one main goal of rCOS–to verfiy and analyze properties of the system–can be reached or not.

CoIn. The CoIn approach to modeling the CoCoME application is based on the concept of component-interaction automata, which are used to capture the behavior of components in the system using a labeled transition system. For each primitive component, a distinct automaton is created that models the component behavior. In the case of composite components, the automaton is obtained through composition of automata associated with primitive components. The composition operator is parametrized, which allows different kinds of composition to be performed in different scenarios. Through composition, this approach allows for the constructing of complex, whole-picture models, based on much simpler behavioral models of primitive components. Using the model of an entire system, various properties specified in linear temporal logic, modified for the use with component-interaction automata (CI-LTL), can be verified.

The main strength of the presented approach lies in its expressive power and flexibility. The authors of the CoIn approach chose to create a model of the Co-CoME application based mainly on its prototype implementation as the most precise specification, using the UML models mainly to extract structural information concerning system architecture. By using different kinds of composition (cube-like, star-like, and handshake-like) depending on the context of composition of primitive components, they were able to create a very detailed model of the whole system. Using the UML use cases and test scenarios for the prototype implementation, they were able to formulate a set for properties, the validity of which has been verified using the DiVinE model checker.

The level of detail, completeness of the model, and the model checking tool support are noteworthy and it is evident that the CoIn approach is very suitable, thanks to its powerful composition operator, for construction of models in a bottom-up manner. Alternatively, the CoIn approach could be used to model the CoCoME application in a top-down manner, which is often more suitable in the initial phases of system design. However, in top-down approach to construction of a system model, the power of the composition operator would play a minor role, leaving the designers alone with the task of creating the model. It can be argued though, that a model created in a top-down manner would not need to be nearly as complex as the one obtained in bottom-up manner. The authors did not model/verify any extra-functional properties because the CoIn approach does not support that. However, this cannot be considered a serious drawback, mainly because the CI automata were designed for the different goal of the verification of functional properties.

Formal Algebraic Models

Focus/AutoFocus. The Focus/AutoFocus approach provides a top-down development process based upon the formally founded mathematical model Focus (timed infinite streams) as the semantic model for component behaviour. The development process (and the formal model) is designed for distributed reactive systems and starts out with informal requirements and ends up–over various refinement steps–with an implementation model.

The main goal of the approach is to provide a development processes that guides the software engineer from given informal requirements via well defined refinement steps to an implementation model, which can be used to simulate the system and finally generate an implementation of the system. As the model is based on a formally founded mathematical system model, the varification of the correctness of the refinement steps from one abstraction level to the the next more detailed level is guaranteed. Moreover analysis, simulation, verification and code generation can be supported by additional tool support or external tool integration.

The modeling of the Focus/AutoFocus team focused on the cash desk part of CoCoME. As Focus/AutoFocus is an approach tailored for reactive systems, the information system part of CoCoME was not modeled by the team. Moreover, the non-functional and extra quality properties of CoCoME were also not modeled by the Focus/AutoFocus approach.

Hence, as Focus/AutoFocus claim to have a rigid and formally founded development process supporting correct refinement steps from requirements to an implementaion model, the results of applying Focus/AutoFocus are mainly focused on the cash-desk part of CoCoME. Therefore, the Focus/AutoFocus team showed a convincing approach following a clear and rigid development process. Moreover, the underlying formal system model enabled the team to generate an executing system out of their model, showing an online simulation of the system. The main deficit of the approach is that Focus/AutoFocus is not being able to model instantiation and thus the dynamic structure of a system–the running system is modeled as having fixed structure. Especially, when modeling the information-system part of CoCoME such a capability to model at instance level would be required. Moreover, the concept of blocking method calls as a basic communication primitive would also be required. Nevertheless, for the reactive part of the system, the Focus/AutoFocus approach is a well tailored and formalized approach providing convincing results to its users.

Java/A. Java/A is a component model based mostly on several concepts of UML 2.0 which it extends by analysis and verification techniques. Development of applications using the Java/A component model is encouraged through its support of a Java-like programming language, which allows embedding structural and behavioral information concerning application architecture directly in the application source code. This tight coupling of architectural description and implementation allows programmers and maintainers of Java/A applications to avoid architectural erosion, which typically plagues approaches where architectural and behavioral description is kept separately and sometimes without direct association with implementation. This level of integration in Java/A allows for more natural and direct mapping of UML 2.0 component concepts into program code.

Behavioral description of Java/A components is split between a component and its ports containing pairs of required/provided interfaces. The description comes in the form of UML state machines, which are then translated into I/O transition system, on which formal verification is performed.

Concerning modeling the CoCoME application, the authors of the Java/A approach used mainly the UML use-case descriptions and sequence diagrams to create the model of the system. The resulting model captures the architecture of the whole system, but since the authors focused mainly on the embedded part of CoCoME, behavioral model and analysis have only been done for the CashDeskLine component.

The main strength of the Java/A functional analysis lies in the ability to support modular analysis and verification techniques through derivation of global properties (composite components) from local ones (primitive components). The functional analysis supports checking for correctness of primitive components with respect to their port protocol and checking for deadlock-freedom of a composite. However, the notion of observational equivalence, required to support the analysis, may be considered too strong.

The authors have also performed quantitative analysis of the system, using the specification of extra-functional properties. They had explicitly modeled Use Case 1, using a stochastic process algebra (PEPA), and have shown that the benefit of the express-checkout cash desk does not really match intuitive expectation. Since neither the Java/A component model nor the programming language supports capturing quantitative aspects of an architecture, it may be beneficial to consider integrating description of quantitative aspects into Java/A, similar to integration of the structural and behavioral aspects.

Formal Object Models

Cowch. The Cowch approach is based on a hierarchical component model for object-oriented programming, called the Box Model. A box is a runtime entity with state and a semantics-based encapsulation boundary. The implementation of a box consists of a number of classes and interfaces of the underlying programming language. To structure communication between boxes directed ports and channels are used. Ports are named interfaces and can be incoming or outgoing. All box boundary crossing references must be modeled by using ports. A graphical UML-like description technique is provided for the Cowch approach.

The main goal of the Cowch approach is to fill the gap between high-level description techniques and architecture modeling on the level of component-based architectures and object-oriented programming languages. Thus the functional and strcutural features of the designed component architecture can be enforced on the object level by verification as well as static and dynamic analysis.

The Cowch team has completely modeled the functional and structural properties of CoCoME, where the main focus was on the runtime structure. The functional and behavioural part was not modeled; instead, relying on the Java code for this purpose. The non-functional and qualitiy properties have not been modeled.

The main strength of the approach is the clear semantic foundation on top of an object-oriented programming language. Thus the Cowch team was able to model the complete CoCoME. However, this benefit is also the main drawback of the approach. Cowch cannot provide a high level of abstraction - all is more or less treated at code level. And, as the approach is still under development, the tool support and thereby the achievable verification and analysis support and results are currently not clear at all.

DisCComp. DisCComp (<u>Dis</u>tributed <u>C</u>oncurrent <u>C</u>omponents) is a formal model based on set-theoretic formalizations of distributed concurrent systems. It allows modeling of dynamically changing structures, a shared global state and asynchronous message communication, as well as synchronous and concurrent message calls. DisCComp provides a sound semantic model for concurrently executed components that is realistic enough to serve as a formal foundation for component technologies currently in use. The approach is supported by tools for code generation as well as simulation and execution of such specifications for testing purposes. At present, the specification technique is adequate for functional properties, while it is not able to deal with non-functional properties. The jury was quite unclear on the actual CoCoME coverage achieved, since the presentation was mainly focused on the formal model.

17.4   Formal Models, Focusing on Behavior and Quality Properties

Palladio. Palladio is a complete component modeling approach including both modeling and performance analysis facilities in an integrated and automated framework. To this end, the Palladio approach includes a meta-model for structural views, component behavior specifications, resource environment, and the modeling of system usage; and multiple analysis techniques ranging from process algebra analysis to discrete event simulation.

Palladio supports hierarchical composite components and is able to model the usage profile of a system, the component behavior, the composition/assembly structure, the deployment context, and the resource environment. For each of these models, the performance relevant aspects (delays, data abstractions, etc) are modeled and analyzed. All analyses can be performed without an implementation, supporting early design time predictions. This way, Palladio enables software architects to analyze different architectural design alternatives supporting their design decisions with quantitative performance predictions. The CoCoME modeling and analysis has been focused on the most complex use case number 8, providing a nice exposure of the Palladio potential. The good discussion of the approach and the extensive performance analysis carried out on the case study have positively impressed the jury.

KLAPER. KLAPER plays a specific role in this context. It does not provide a model to design component-based systems, but it acts as an intermediate language between design meta models and analysis meta models. While design models support the design of a software systems in a notation and terminology familiar with a software designer, analysis models enable the application of specific analysis techniques. As from both kinds of models (design and analysis) several kinds with specific benefits and drawbacks exist, there are good reasons to support the translation of each design meta model to as many as possible analysis meta models. However, the definition and implementation of $m \times n$ transformations (given m design meta models and n analysis meta models) is not realistic. The solution to such a problem is known from compiler construction: an intermediate language defines a common format where the m design meta models define transformations to, as well as transformations are defined from the intermediate language to the n analysis models. By this, only $m + n$ transformations are required.

From a modeling perspective, KLAPER is defined by a MOF meta-model which includes ways to specify components and software architectures as well as resources. When modeling CoCoME with KLAPER, one started to translate an UML model into KLAPER and than transformed an KLAPER model into a layered queuing network (LQN). The prediction results on resource utilization and response time were impressive, although no direct comparison to the implementation was made, as the implementation deviates from the specification in performance-relevant aspects. The jury was impressed by the elegance of the modeling and the ability to perform analyses on response time and utilization. Areas for future work include improvements of scalability as well as a systematic way to feed back the analysis results into the original design model.

Fractal. Fractal is a hierarchical component model which provides means to describe architectures by the definition of component bindings and resources. Specifically, components have membranes (encapsulation of the inner), content (either wired sub-components or an implementation) and controllers with specific control interfaces. The behavioral view can be specified by traces in the FractalBPC language (which originates from the SOFA component model). Modeling the deployment view is not specified in Fractal, but implementation specific. Noteworthy are the various formal consistency checks, such as component interaction, compliance of inner components with outer component specification and consistency between implementation and interfaces. In particular, it also supports the description of dynamically changing architectures. It was initiated by researchers of the France Telekom where also larger case studies were modeled in Fractal. By this, Fractal forms one of the stronger validated models of the CoCoME contest.

CoCoME was modeled well in Fractal, however, the communication bus was modeled as a separate component which was not present in the original specification. This was motivated by the need to explicitly introduce interfaces which were not present in the original CoCoME. Except for that, using Fractal for modeling the CoCoME proved easy and beneficial due to the extensive compliance checks. Modeling extra-functional properties is not yet possible in Fractal, although in the specific model of the CoCoME also performance data was collected by monitoring.

SOFA. SoFA (Software For Appliances) is a component model which allows to define the structural view of software architectures as well as behavioral specifications of basic and composed components. Specific to it is the frame protocol which specifies the behavior of a composed component and which can be checked against the composition of inner component protocols. Protocols are modeled by regular expressions. However, since sending and receiving a call as well as call and return of an invocation are modeled explicitly, asynchronous behavior can be specified also. Compliance checking (interoperability, substitutability, compliancy between frame-protocol and inner protocols) is realized by a connection to Promela which allows to use the SPIN model checker.

There is also the deployment view where the distribution of compoennts–their mapping to computing resources–can be specified. Finally, SoFA includes a performance view which is linked to the deployment and behavioural view. Interesting is the comparison to the conceptually related Fractal model: while SoFA allows similar checks also in comparable time, its specification is considerably more compact (1500 LOC vs. 2700 LOC), which makes SoFA a well applicable language with good verification possibilities.

17.5   Models Tailored for a Specific Application Domain

GCM/ProActive. GCM is a component model based on Fractal. It uses the Fractal concept of hierarchical components with provided and required interfaces and explicit treatment of control interfaces. GCM focuses on grid computing, thus in addition to standard Fractal features, it adds the possibility of asynchronous method calls using *futures* and defines collective interfaces (multicast and gathercast) to ease synchronization and work distribution. As an ADL, GCM uses FractalADL enhanced by the concept of a *virtual node*–an abstraction of the physical infrastructure to which an application is deployed.

From the behavior point of view, GCM uses a low-level model called pNets. It is basically a network of parameterized LTSs tailored to suit the needs of grid computing. GCM also offers a high-level language called JDC (Java Distributed Component Specification Language). It combines ADL specification with a behavior specification written in a notation similar to Java. The aim of JDC is providing a modeling language from which the pNets behavior models and skeletons of implementation artifacts could be generated. In addition to textual specification, graphical design is also supported via a UML editor called CTTool.

Modeling of CoCoME was possible in GCM. Especially the distribution was rather seamless thanks to the *virtual node* abstraction. The actual behavior specification and analysis was done by employing the CTTool and eventually verified by LOTOS/CADP as the whole toolchain spanning from JDC to pNets has not been completely implemented yet.

17.6   Conclusions

Each of the modeling approaches, when applied to CoCoME, exhibited an interesting set of strengths and weaknesses. While, pointwise, there is much to be learned from each of the approaches, the jury concludes with a mixed message. CoCoME's top-level challenge was and is about all-of-system modeling and none of the approaches enabled comprehensive modeling at that level. To be fair, the approaches at hand are the results of ongoing research and it isn't the purpose of research efforts to deliver fully rounded "complete" solutions. However, the gap between practical applicability and demonstrated modeling capability remains significant, leaving much room for further work.

Author Index

Lecture Notes in Computer Science

Sublibrary 2: Programming and Software Engineering

For information about Vols. 1– 4552
please contact your bookseller or Springer

Vol. 4902: P. Hudak, D.S. Warren (Eds.), Practical Aspects of Declarative Languages. X, 333 pages. 2007.

Vol. 4899: K. Yorav (Ed.), Hardware and Software: Verification and Testing. XII, 267 pages. 2008.

Vol. 4888: F. Kordon, O. Sokolsky (Eds.), Composition of Embedded Systems. XII, 221 pages. 2007.

Vol. 4880: S. Overhage, C.A. Szyperski, R. Reussner, J.A. Stafford (Eds.), Software Architectures, Components, and Applications. X, 249 pages. 2008.

Vol. 4849: M. Winckler, H. Johnson, P. Palanque (Eds.), Task Models and Diagrams for User Interface Design. XIII, 299 pages. 2007.

Vol. 4839: O. Sokolsky, S. Taşıran (Eds.), Runtime Verification. VI, 215 pages. 2007.

Vol. 4834: R. Cerqueira, R.H. Campbell (Eds.), Middleware 2007. XIII, 451 pages. 2007.

Vol. 4829: M. Lumpe, W. Vanderperren (Eds.), Software Composition. VIII, 281 pages. 2007.

Vol. 4824: A. Paschke, Y. Biletskiy (Eds.), Advances in Rule Interchange and Applications. XIII, 243 pages. 2007.

Vol. 4821: J. Bennedsen, M.E. Caspersen, M. Kölling (Eds.), Reflections on the Teaching of Programming. X, 261 pages. 2008.

Vol. 4807: Z. Shao (Ed.), Programming Languages and Systems. XI, 431 pages. 2007.

Vol. 4799: A. Holzinger (Ed.), HCI and Usability for Medicine and Health Care. XVI, 458 pages. 2007.

Vol. 4789: M. Butler, M.G. Hinchey, M.M. Larrondo-Petrie (Eds.), Formal Methods and Software Engineering. VIII, 387 pages. 2007.

Vol. 4767: F. Arbab, M. Sirjani (Eds.), International Symposium on Fundamentals of Software Engineering. XIII, 450 pages. 2007.

Vol. 4765: A. Moreira, J. Grundy (Eds.), Early Aspects: Current Challenges and Future Directions. X, 199 pages. 2007.

Vol. 4764: P. Abrahamsson, N. Baddoo, T. Margaria, R. Messnarz (Eds.), Software Process Improvement. XI, 225 pages. 2007.

Vol. 4762: K.S. Namjoshi, T. Yoneda, T. Higashino, Y. Okamura (Eds.), Automated Technology for Verification and Analysis. XIV, 566 pages. 2007.

Vol. 4758: F. Oquendo (Ed.), Software Architecture. XVI, 340 pages. 2007.

Vol. 4757: F. Cappello, T. Herault, J. Dongarra (Eds.), Recent Advances in Parallel Virtual Machine and Message Passing Interface. XVI, 396 pages. 2007.

Vol. 4753: E. Duval, R. Klamma, M. Wolpers (Eds.), Creating New Learning Experiences on a Global Scale. XII, 518 pages. 2007.

Vol. 4749: B.J. Krämer, K.-J. Lin, P. Narasimhan (Eds.), Service-Oriented Computing – ICSOC 2007. XIX, 629 pages. 2007.

Vol. 4748: K. Wolter (Ed.), Formal Methods and Stochastic Models for Performance Evaluation. X, 301 pages. 2007.

Vol. 4741: C. Bessière (Ed.), Principles and Practice of Constraint Programming – CP 2007. XV, 890 pages. 2007.

Vol. 4735: G. Engels, B. Opdyke, D.C. Schmidt, F. Weil (Eds.), Model Driven Engineering Languages and Systems. XV, 698 pages. 2007.

Vol. 4716: B. Meyer, M. Joseph (Eds.), Software Engineering Approaches for Offshore and Outsourced Development. X, 201 pages. 2007.

Vol. 4709: F.S. de Boer, M.M. Bonsangue, S. Graf, W.-P. de Roever (Eds.), Formal Methods for Components and Objects. VIII, 297 pages. 2007.

Vol. 4680: F. Saglietti, N. Oster (Eds.), Computer Safety, Reliability, and Security. XV, 548 pages. 2007.

Vol. 4670: V. Dahl, I. Niemelä (Eds.), Logic Programming. XII, 470 pages. 2007.

Vol. 4652: D. Georgakopoulos, N. Ritter, B. Benatallah, C. Zirpins, G. Feuerlicht, M. Schoenherr, H.R. Motahari-Nezhad (Eds.), Service-Oriented Computing ICSOC 2006. XVI, 201 pages. 2007.

Vol. 4640: A. Rashid, M. Aksit (Eds.), Transactions on Aspect-Oriented Software Development IV. IX, 191 pages. 2007.

Vol. 4634: H. Riis Nielson, G. Filé (Eds.), Static Analysis. XI, 469 pages. 2007.

Vol. 4620: A. Rashid, M. Aksit (Eds.), Transactions on Aspect-Oriented Software Development III. IX, 201 pages. 2007.

Vol. 4615: R. de Lemos, C. Gacek, A. Romanovsky (Eds.), Architecting Dependable Systems IV. XIV, 435 pages. 2007.

Vol. 4610: B. Xiao, L.T. Yang, J. Ma, C. Muller-Schloer, Y. Hua (Eds.), Autonomic and Trusted Computing. XVIII, 571 pages. 2007.

Vol. 4609: E. Ernst (Ed.), ECOOP 2007 – Object-Oriented Programming. XIII, 625 pages. 2007.

Vol. 4608: H.W. Schmidt, I. Crnković, G.T. Heineman, J.A. Stafford (Eds.), Component-Based Software Engineering. XII, 283 pages. 2007.

Vol. 4591: J. Davies, J. Gibbons (Eds.), Integrated Formal Methods. IX, 660 pages. 2007.

Vol. 4589: J. Münch, P. Abrahamsson (Eds.), Product-Focused Software Process Improvement. XII, 414 pages. 2007.

Vol. 4574: J. Derrick, J. Vain (Eds.), Formal Techniques for Networked and Distributed Systems – FORTE 2007. XI, 375 pages. 2007.

Vol. 4556: C. Stephanidis (Ed.), Universal Access in Human-Computer Interaction, Part III. XXII, 1020 pages. 2007.

Vol. 4555: C. Stephanidis (Ed.), Universal Access in Human-Computer Interaction, Part II. XXII, 1066 pages. 2007.

Vol. 4554: C. Stephanidis (Ed.), Universal Acess in Human Computer Interaction, Part I. XXII, 1054 pages. 2007.

Vol. 4553: J.A. Jacko (Ed.), Human-Computer Interaction, Part IV. XXIV, 1225 pages. 2007.